adolescence

a
sociological
analysis

Sociology Series
John F. Cuber, *Editor*
Alfred C. Clarke, *Associate Editor*

adolescence
a
sociological
analysis

HANS SEBALD
ARIZONA STATE UNIVERSITY

New York

APPLETON-CENTURY-CROFTS
EDUCATIONAL DIVISION
MEREDITH CORPORATION

To

my parents

PREFACE

Rarely in the history of man has the process of entering adult status become as difficult and uncertain as it is today. The life of the American teen-ager is characterized by the confusion and uncertainty of not knowing exactly what his role expectations are during the period of transition from childhood to adulthood. It is this vague no-man's land that is defined as "adolescence."

The difficulties, frustrations, and anxieties which accompany the transition from the child to the adult status express themselves in various ways. Many of the expressions, dysfunctional to society, are variously called juvenile, teen-age, or adolescent "problems." Symptoms of this type are responsible for the popular attention that is lavished on adolescence. Unfortunately, popular analysis and explanation often fall short of precision and objectivity. Indeed, most popular attempts should not even be called "analyses" because they fail to understand and formulate the antecedents of the problem. These ubiquitous popular statements are primarily value judgments or, at best, disgruntled descriptions of existing or even imagined youth problems.

An assessment of adolescence should be both *analytical* and *comprehensive*—analytical in the sense of showing the causes and the consequences of adolescence, and comprehensive in the sense of describing the broader social context in which adolescence occurs. This book attempts to present a systematic synthesis of these two qualities by using the structural-functional approach. In less technical language one might call this approach the antecedent-consequent framework—the framework that actually *is* sociology, according to the prevailing opinion of sociologists. The basic principle of the structural-functional question is relatively simple: Given a certain structure, what are its consequences (functions)? In the course of this book, a number of conditions and their effects on adolescence are examined. The inquiry focuses primarily on sociological and social psychological variables.

A meaningful portrayal of adolescence requires the coordination of interdisciplinary aspects. A number of these aspects have traditionally been regarded as the "property" of sociology of the family, sociology of education, social psychology, psychology, anthropology, the study of mass communication, the study of collective behavior, the study of social problems, etc. Such an arbitrary division of labor has disadvantages and tends to violate the correct representation of reality. Reality itself is obviously not subdivided into academic fields, but rather consists of an unified entity with intricately inter-related features. It is the scientist who cuts reality into more or less arbitrary disciplines. To alleviate such artificial categorization, a number of otherwise separate disciplines—such as anthropology, education, psychology, and soci-ology—are being "trespassed."

This study of adolescence is divided into five parts: (1) *definition and introduction*; (2) *antecedent conditions*, involving conditions of social struc-ture, cultural values and norms, psychological problems of identity, and bio-logical maturation; (3) *consequences*, including the formation of teen-age subcultures; (4) *diversity of the adolescent experience*, considering specific socioeconomic or racial groupings such as Negro, American Indian, lower class, etc.; and (5) *specific problems*, including discussions on delinquency, drinking and drug addiction, the school drop-out, sexual behavior. Part six is devoted to conclusions and summary.

No attempt is made to impress the reader by theoretical essays written by professors of sociology for professors of sociology or by academic inbreed-ing that excludes sources not found in the traditional and prestigious academic journals. Rather, the style of presenting the material in this book aspires to create a healthy balance between learned, analytical, and technical theories, on the one hand, and descriptive accounts illustrating actual teen-age behavior on the other. Just as there is no hesitation to present usable theories, there is no hesitation to draw from popular and non-professional sources of information.

Motivation to pursue this particular inquiry was initially inspired by two professors at The Ohio State University, Professors A. R. Mangus and Henry Quarantelli. In the more immediate context of research and writing, the book has benefited from repeated discussions with Dr. John H. Kunkel, critical comment on early draft material by Professor Thomas F. Hoult, helpful advice on demographic data by Professor Fred B. Lindstrom, and advice on the chapter on juvenile delinquency by Dr. Peter G. Garabedian; all at the Arizona State University. For patient research assistance and clerical work, thanks go to Michael A. Garrick, Carol L. Huffine, Virginia M. Fischer, William C. Fay, Barbara A. Stearman, and Coleen Brewer.

H. S.

TABLE OF CONTENTS

part

I

introduction

1

adolescence—definitions and introduction

Today's urban-industrial societies are confronted with the unprecedented recession of its young from the adult world and the resultant formation of an adolescent subculture virtually separate from that of the adult. The furor caused by these young people through their values, appearances, and practices has been echoed not only in the United States, but in many other countries and indicates the need to investigate the state of adolescence in greater detail than previously has been done.

Comparison of various countries reveals several features in common concerning the causes as well as the symptoms of adolescence. (By features in common we mean a number of social structural dimensions and cultural tendencies which are characteristic of most highly urbanized and industrialized societies.) Adolescence may be considered a nearly universal product of technologically advanced societies. These urban-industrial conditions, as they impinge upon adolescence, are examined in subsequent chapters.

The diversity of adolescent experiences is also examined. Bearing in mind that a heterogeneous population like that of the United States produces diverse environments with distinctly different life conditions which have corresponding impact on the adolescents' lives, there is not just one style of adolescent expression, but a number of different styles. In general, however, this analysis places more emphasis on adolescence as it emerges in the general American middle class (rather than in lower or upper socioeconomic strata) or in various racial and ethnic minority groups. Two reasons for this emphasis concern themselves with the numerical strength as well as the social influence of the American middle class. Thus, it is not until Part IV that the variegated forms of adolescence receive specific attention. Similarly, the broad and general introductory treatment of adolescence should not obscure the fact that a number of highly significant problems related to the adolescent period are discussed extensively in later chapters.

The assumption that there is in fact a teen-age subculture has not gone unchallenged in this text. The reader should not assume that, because no initial treatment of this controversy is offered, this question has therefore been ignored. Although the first chapters reflect the tacit assumption that an adolescent subculture *does* exist, a detailed discussion of this question is considered in Chapter eight.

To set the stage for the discussion of adolescence, the strikingly similar characteristics of adolescence in a number of different countries are sampled and briefly described. These symptoms manifest themselves in terms of subcultural behavior, i.e., the teen-agers' own fads, fashions, music, argot, etc., and in terms, often, of delinquent behavior.

Cross-Cultural Appearance of Adolescence

England produced Rockers and Mods, feuding camps within the adolescent world. The Rockers derived their name from rock 'n' roll, which the Mods abandoned for what they judged to be "finer styles." Mod signifies "modish" and "modernist." Rockers dress in black leather-jackets and ride heavy motorcycles. Mods prefer stylish clothes, long hair, high-heeled shoes (boys also), and motor scooters. Each group defines the other as the out-group and each is visibly identifiable, forming a ready target for the other. The hostility between the two subcultures is combined with a vehement commitment of these adolescents to their in-groups. In the fall of 1964, rivalry and hostility reached dimensions of street fighting and vandalism, necessitating the airlifting of riot police into Hastings, a famous seaside resort town. By the time the police checked the vandalism and subdued the fighting youths, the incident had evoked international comment. It must be noted that these two factions of English youth culture are generally not considered delinquent, but tolerated as slightly deviant and eccentric subcultures.

In addition to the activities of generally nondelinquent youth subcultures, juvenile delinquency rates have sharply increased in England. This upward trend has been typical of most European countries during the 1960's. Juvenile crimes in England have more than doubled during the last 15 years. So-called "hooliganism" spread through the entire country, the most extreme expressions reported from London, where organized groups and gangs engage in affrays, especially at dance halls, where the revelers make it clear that their violent behavior is non-utilitarian and purely a function of in-group reinforcement.[1]

Significant of English teen-agers is their remarkable affluence and in-group identification by means of expensive material implementations. Mods and Rockers, for example, utilize their finances to acquire their subculture's material identifications in terms of "in" clothes, scooters, motorcycles, etc. Observers agree that such material implementation serves the function of reinforcing the feeling of belonging to one's group and of achieving prestige among one's peers. In short, certain clothes and gadgets serve as membership identification for one's particular subculture.

The rise of adolescent subcultures can be observed in other European countries. Even Russia has not been spared social problems arising from the formation of uniquely adolescent styles and activities. Increasingly over the past decade, news has reached the Western world about the activities of the *stilyagi*. These adolescents were originally not thought of as delinquents, but rather as "style chasers," often imitating Western youth fashions and setting trends and teen-age styles in Russia. Thus their social impact was more comparable to that of English Mods or Rockers or the American "drug-store" cowboy than to that of purely delinquent youth. Part of *stilyagi* jargon was the use of American nicknames, a practice supported and implemented by the use of black-marketed American rock 'n' roll and jazz records. Other characteristics included imitation of American haircuts, bright American-style shirts, tight trousers or tight skirts. However, over the years, *stilyagi* came to be a catch-all label for almost any teen-ager displaying delinquent or antisocial conduct, including young hooligans who were reported to stage drunken brawls, youthful black marketeers, the "center-boys" who trade counterfeit ikons for foreign tourist clothes, and the "gilded youth" who use their parents' influence to evade social duties and responsibilities.[2]

The surest indication, probably, of the existence of a teen-age subculture is the development of teen-age slang, a lingo apart from the language of the adults. Such special teen-age argot has been spreading among Soviet youth, with the press labeling it "*stilyagi-ism* of speech." Some observers think there is a tendency for this lingo to spread gradually from teen-agers and students to workers. The Soviets' attempts to stamp out what is officially referred to as "linguistic nihilism" range from

---

[1] John B. Mays, "Teenage Culture in Contemporary Britain and Europe," *Annals of the American Academy of Political and Social Sciences,* Vol. 338 (November, 1961), p. 27.

[2] George Sherman, "Soviet Youth: Myth and Reality," *Daedalus,* Vol. 91 (Winter, 1962), pp. 216–37.

press campaigns to "Comrade Courts" in factories and offices to life-sized posters ridiculing young culprits apprehended by the People's Militia.[3]

Besides such expressions, which in the rest of the Western world would largely be defined as nondelinquent teen-age subcultural styles, Soviet Russia has been troubled by serious juvenile delinquency. Occasionally, news reaching the outside world indicates the existence of adolescent drinking parties, occasional orgies, assaults, and various other delinquent patterns among Soviet youth in the larger cities. Reports from Moscow in 1965 told of gangs of teen-agers who killed two men, tried to hang a small boy, and robbed stores. Public opinion in the Soviet Union tended to accuse police, prosecutors, and the courts of sluggishness in dealing with the problem. As a result of increasing delinquency, the city government of Moscow imposed a curfew on youth under the age of 16. According to this new rule, which became effective December 28, 1965, minors are barred from the streets, theaters, or other public places after 9:00 P.M., unless accompanied by an adult. During school vacation this curfew is extended to 10:00 P.M. The offical reason for this new regulation was that teen-agers spend too much time out in the street in the evening and sometimes "misbehave and hinder traffic."[4]

Poland is another country behind the Iron Curtain that is known to have problems similar to Russia's. Reports from Warsaw complain that teen-agers have made it dangerous to be out after dark and that they have on occasion assaulted and injured innocent pedestrians.

West Germany's adolescent subculture is represented by the *Halbstarken*, teen-agers with juvenile and sometimes hippie-like types of behavior. Germans also refer to their adolescents as *Teen-agers*, using the actual English word. The term is used in more or less the same manner and with the same meaning as in American culture, and has, from the point of view of the adult world, a slightly derogatory connotation. It also implies a subculture that is a world apart from the adult world. The term *Teen-ager* has become an addition to the German vocabulary and has been accepted as if it were a word of perfect Teutonic origin. Most German teen-agers would probably never suspect that it is an innovation from the American culture. The word has been incorporated into regional dialects and, for example, it is often used in Bavaria with an added "l" to produce *Teen-agerl*, a noun suggesting the diminutive, a "softer," and more favorable version of teen-ager. However, the generally unfavorable image of the teen-ager is still prevalent and is frequently reinforced by the antisocial or destructive conduct of German adolescents. Such destructive conduct is not necessarily the outcrop of

---

[3] Reference 2,
[4] UPI Report (Moscow, April 3, 1966).

delinquent gangs, but rather the side-product of general, and usually non-delinquent teen-age fads and subcultural standards.

The general prominence and unacceptability of the teen-age sub-culture in Germany was demonstrated in the fall of 1965 when a per-formance by Britain's Rolling Stones resulted in property damage of approximately $150,000, caused by their teen-age fans. Almost $50,000 damage was inflicted on the Communist-run elevated railway alone. (Under a post-war agreement, East Germany runs the elevated railway in both East and West Berlin.) When the East German Transport Min-ister demanded compensation from the West Berlin government, he received an official apology and a promise that the guilty would be punished, but West Berlin refused to accept responsibility for the actions of hoodlums.[5] It is a remarkable teen-age achievement indeed to stir up such political negotiation and polemic.

France's adolescent problems are expressed in terms of the *blousons noirs* and *teen-agers*. The latter term—again a direct and untranslated innovation from the American culture—is frequently branded by patri-otic Frenchmen as an undesirable example of "Franglais," the intrusion of English linguistic elements into the French language. The opponents of such cross-cultural innovations base their objection on the assumption that with the introduction of Anglo-Saxon words the "l'American way of life" is also introduced, since new concepts can serve as models of new patterns of behavior. Their analysis is relatively correct: the typical teen-ager as we know him in the United States has become a mode of life in France.

In Sweden, there is concern about the *raggare*. The Japanese public is worried about what their *thunder boys* will do next. Austrians watch with mixed feelings as Buben and Mädel abandon yodeling and dirndls and turn to rock 'n' roll and hippie-style clothing. In Australia, adults are confronted with a growing number of *bodgies*, adolescents who tend to form gangs and who are continually becoming a more distinct collective power vis-a-vis the adult society. The list of countries confronted by the collective phenomenon of adolescence could be expanded to include most, if not all, urban-industrial nations, and serves to suggest the range of this modern problem of youth versus adults.

The country that is internationally viewed as the prototype of an adolescence-troubled nation is the United States. Many observers go as far as to assert that the American teen-age subculture serves as a model for youngsters in other countries and gives impetus to the development of various vernacular versions. It is undoubtedly true that the American teen-ager has had "form-inspiring" influence upon youngsters in a num-

---

[5] UPI Report (Berlin, Sept. 17, 1965).

ber of other societies through the mass media, which, effectively, have permeated international boundaries. However, it is questionable whether the American influence is entirely responsible for the teen-age movements which are springing up everywhere in the world. It is probably more accurate to say that similar social and cultural conditions have arisen in these societies and that these conditions are responsible for the development of adolescence. The expressions of Teen-land U.S.A. may only have suggested directions to already existing tendencies. It is probably more correct to say that the emergence of adolescent subcultures is caused by basic characteristics in the social structure and cultural ethos of a nation rather than by the imitation of youth of another country. The development of adolescence is basically due (1) to a finely-divided division of labor, which produces a very technical and complex social structure; and (2) to the failure of a culture to provide its members with a convincing and compelling ideation, which would result in a strong identity and a feeling of purpose. The combination of these two variables, one having to do with the nature of the social structure and the other with the salience of the culture, form the requisite and sustaining conditions for adolescence.

Both the social structure and culture of American society are probably more adolescence-inducing than those of most other societies. The social structure in the United States contains a disturbing discontinuity between the status of the child and of the adult. Also, cultural guidance is relatively weak and nonspecific. A social structure which produces discontinuity between the status of the child and of the adult may cause only minor forms of adolescent expression *if* the culture is able to compensate for the structural vagueness, i.e., if the culture is able to infuse a sense of identity and meaning into the interim between the two statuses. The assumption here is that in a typical urban-industrial environment, the interim between-child-and-adult status is usually unstructured and consequently void of the type of meaning and identity that evolves from a definite career or from a goal-oriented apprenticeship. The burden of providing meaning during these interim years falls therefore on the over-all ethos of the culture. If the culture fails to compensate for the social-structural no-man's land, adolescence is bound to express itself with all its confused force and compensating substitutes. This appears to be the situation in the United States.

Symptoms of adolescence can be observed in the higher as well as in the lower socioeconomic classes in America. Nationwide publicity was given to the vandalism committed a few years ago, by the teen-age sons and daughters of the upper social class at Southampton, Long Island, who ended a prestigious debutante party by destroying a luxurious home. More often, however, publicity is given to lower-class adolescents who commit delinquent acts in the big cities. New York City serves as a typical example. Acts of willful destruction and personal violence by individual adolescents or gangs had become sufficiently prevalent in 1964 and 1965 to prompt city administrators to place police as protection on every subway train operating in the city. Gang activities, then as now, included almost all conceivable crimes, from molesting to stealing, from spontaneous street fighting to premeditated murder.

The less violent activities of the American teen-age subculture include fads, styles in clothes, in-group music, and distinctive lingo. These suggest how much a teen world exists apart from the adult world. Never before has there been such an intense youth-focused effort by the mass media as in American society. Adolescents have their own magazines, TV shows, and radio programs to such extent that some social scientists maintain that the teen-age society is only tenuously related to the adult society—somewhat like two different countries maintaining diplomatic relations with each other.[6]

Definitions: Juvenile, Youth, Teen-ager, and Adolescent

One function of this introduction is to clarify the concept of adolescence. What precisely is the basic process that underlies the various adolescent expressions previously described? This question tries to explore the nomothetic elements of the subject matter, attempting to determine the common causative conditions in the social structure and the cultural ethos of the various societies and to recognize the identical processes underlying varying adolescent manifestations.

The endeavor to clearly determine the basic adolescent process is complicated at its outset by the usage of confusing pseudosynonyms, such as *juvenile, youth,* and *teen-ager.* Some of these terms succeeed in capturing certain aspects of what should be included in the concept of adolescence, but more often they leave out important qualities. Thus, the terms should not be used interchangeably, but with much more discrimination. A typical example of equating terms and thereby blurring valuable distinctions was presented in a recent publication where the terms "juvenile" and "adolescent" were used as if they apply to the same phenomenon. According to Eric Hoffer, a juvenile *or* adolescent is a person, young or old, who is confused by change—*any* type of change.

---

[6] James S. Coleman, *The Adolescent Society* (New York, Free Press, 1963), pp. 3 *ff.*

It is useless, he feels, to explain the behavior of adolescents by attempting to find differences in the brain structure and nervous system between the adolescent and the adult. On the other hand, he asserts, we should assume that the adolescent's behavior is largely a function of his environmental situation. It follows from his line of reasoning that adults would exhibit similar behavior patterns when placed in similar circumstances.

Hoffer contends that the primary characteristic of the "adolescent" situation is its "inbetweenness"; i.e., it is a transitional period between statuses or affiliation and which is characterized by rootlessness and a high rate of change. This drastic change renders most of one's past experience useless and produces a state of anxiety in any person who is confronted with a completely novel situation in which he has few norms to guide his behavior. When the "adolescent" is placed in such a situation the inevitable result is "some degree of primitive behavior."[7]

It is true that adolescence in the sociological sense refers to individuals in the process of change, but it is not correct to apply indiscriminately the concept to every person who undergoes some drastic change. The concept should be reserved for one specific change: the change from child to adult. Hoffer does not limit the use of the concept to this particular change, feeling free, for example, to refer to the 55-year-old Pope Julius II, to President Sukarno, to DeGaulle, and to the Ku Klux Klan members as adolescents or juveniles.[8] According to his theory, a society could exist that has adolescents but no youths. It is unlikely that we would ever find an empirical counterpart for this hypothetical situation, since it describes a population lacking a younger generation and having adults profoundly disturbed and confused by some radical change.

Societies in which youth and adolescence are merged are much more commonly found. This type of adolescence-troubled society is the main focus of subsequent discussions. There are also some contemporary societies which have only youth and no adolescents. These are usually agricultural or small tribal societies with a social structure and a cultural credo that *allow definite and smooth transition from child to adult status.*

Another clarification concerning the concept of *juvenile* should be mentioned. The established definition of juvenile refers to law violation and law provisions, as used in terms such as juvenile delinquency, juvenile courts, juvenile detention homes, etc. It seems advisable to concur with this usage and to limit the application of the concept of juvenile to the legal context.

---

[7] Eric Hoffer, "An Age for Juveniles," *Harper's* (June, 1965), pp. 18, 21.
[8] Hoffer, *op. cit.*, pp. 16, 18.

The term *youth* generally refers to some relatively young age bracket. The exact age delimitation is not rigidly established; youth is often equated with the "younger generation," with teen-age members of the society, with young adults. The concept is practically universally applicable, since all societies normally have a younger generation. Since adolescence is not necessarily a universal phenomenon and certain societies, as has been mentioned above, may have youth but no adolescents, the two terms are therefore not interchangeable.

The term *teen-ager* is probably the most widely used word referring to young people in current American society. However, does the concept exclusively denote the particular age-bracket that it implies by the combination of "teen" and "age"? It would appear that it is not strictly limited to the age denotation, but includes also important additional connotations of behavior. This behavior has been stereotyped "teen-age behavior"—a behavior that rarely finds the whole-hearted approval of the adult world. When adults talk about "teen-age behavior," there is often a trace of derogation and a tendency to label it "immature" or "improper." There is also the connotation of collectivity which suggests that teen-agers exist in terms of groups rather than in terms of distinct individuals. It is this latter connotation that is of great sociological significance because it purports to explain teen-age behavior in terms of the norms and values of the peer group.

The meanings ascribed to "adolescent" and to "teen-ager" are obviously closely related. Referring to a person as an "adolescent" means that we emphasize the peculiar interim existence between the status of child and of adult; referring to a person as a "teen-ager" means that we call attention to his age and to the tendency to group together with peers and engage in subcultural activities. Adolescence may actually lead to the type of behavior that is typical for the teen-ager, because he tries to compensate for the uncertain and vague position in which he finds himself. Thus, although not exactly identical, the two concepts are closely related and suggest different aspects of the same process.

It is necessary to examine more closely the reasons why the concept of adolescence is so important to social scientists. In terms of etymology, "adolescence" comes from the Latin word *adolescere* which means "to grow up" or "to grow into maturity." The reference to growth is nonspecific and could conceivably apply to physiological, psychological, or social growth. It is necessary therefore to agree upon a relatively arbitrary definition. Adolescence in the social-psychological sense refers to the experience of passing through *the unstructured and ill-defined phase that lies between childhood and adulthood.* In short, adolescence is characterized by the crisis of *discontinuity* of statuses which creates a poorly structured no man's-land. The vast majority of our modern youth seems to experience this uncertain phase during their teen years.

It is difficult to determine the exact age at which a young person enters adolescence. It corresponds roughly with the onset of pubescence. This would set the modal entrance age at any time between 11 to 14 years for girls and 13 to 16 for boys. It is even more difficult to determine the termination of adolescence:

> The upper age limit of adolescence is even less clearly marked than the onset of pubescence, since there are no objective physiological phenomena that can be used to define the termination. Observable social phenomena such as financial independence, successful employment, and marriage are useful. But, in the first place, they do not necessarily indicate psychological independence and maturity; secondly, no agreement has been reached as to their relative importance. Finally, the psychological and even the sociological meaning of such phenomena differ according to the sociocultural environment; how to determine when adulthood, maturity, self-determination, and independence have been reached depends on the definition that these terms have in a given social setting.

> In primitive society, the period of adolescence may be very brief and may be terminated by initiation rituals after which the individual obtains adult status. In contrast to this example of a short period of adolescence, the psychologist, G. Stanley Hall, wrote in 1904 that adolescence in the United States lasts until the twenty-fourth or twenty-fifth year. To speak of the termination of adolescence in age terms is possible only if the sociocultural environment is specified.

> In most of the states of the United States the twenty-one-year-old acquires the right to vote. Other aspects of being a minor, such as restrictions on buying liquor, driving a car, marriage, employment, etc., are removed at an earlier age, with variations from state to state. In a legal sense twenty-one is the termination of adolescence, since at that age the law removes the last legal protective aspects of "immaturity" and gives a person his full rights, legal independence, and responsibility.

> However, as Kuhlen points out, adolescence is the period of sexual, social, ideological, and vocational adjustment, and of striving for independence from parents. Therefore, from a psychological standpoint, the criterion for termination of adolescence is not so much a certain chronological age as it is the degree to which those adjustments are made. A person who marries after graduation from high school and becomes successfully employed and financially self-sufficient is more likely to have attained maturity than his friend

who goes on to college supported by his family. Furthermore, a person can be old in a chronological sense and still show the behavioral and social characteristics of adolescence.[9]

From Rolf E. Muuss's discussion we gather that adolescence normally terminates with the completion of at least two interrelated processes. It terminates *psychologically* with the establishment of realistic and relatively consistent patterns of dealing with internal conflicts and the demands of the social and physical environment. It terminates *socially* at the time when the sociocultural environment yields sufficient consensus to declare the individual an adult. The progress of the two processes does not necessarily run in a one-to-one relationship, since one may proceed ahead of the other. It is possible, for example, that a person has established realistic and well-integrated modes of problem-solving and is socially still not defined as an adult; and vice versa, an individual may have entered adult status according to the general sociocultural definition and may still be lacking in realistic and effective patterns of problem-solving. However, if the degree of inability to cope with the environment exceeds a certain limit, society can withdraw the status of adulthood from the individual regardless of his chronological age and declare him mentally incapable of handling life on his own. Usually, such a person is placed under the supervision and responsibility of special institutions, such as mental hospitals. Normally, however, psychological and social development are expected to coincide and produce a normally functioning young adult by the late teens.

The process of physiological development is a natural part of adolescence. Also, as stated above, the onset of pubescence usually heralds the onset of adolescence—at least in American society. But the fact that a person has achieved a mature body structure and mature glandular functioning, especially in those aspects directly related to the reproductive system, does not automatically signify the termination of adolescence. While a young individual may have achieved *biological* adulthood in terms of physical strength and reproductive ability, *socioculturally* he is not yet considered an adult. The vast majority of American adolescents experiences this awkward situation.

It can hardly be overemphasized that adolescence as the intermediate state between childhood and adulthood is chronologically *not* a sharply defined time span. Rather, adolescence includes a time span, the beginning and the end of which are greatly blurred. This means that the transition from child to adolescent and the transition from adolescent to adult are of a gradual and uncertain nature. It must be understood,

---

[9] Rolf E. Muuss, *Theories of Adolescence* (New York, Random House, 1962), pp. 9–10.

moreover, that natural growth processes do not occur in distinct and discrete stages. Man shows considerable arbitrariness in defining life stages. He seems to be compelled to establish this type of structural order to facilitate social predictability and communication. In reality, it is obvious that life is a continuous process and that adulthood is the result of an irregular and variable maturation that began with the fusion of the ovum and the sperm. It is, therefore, a more or less arbitrary and heuristic practice to subdivide the period of adolescence into pre-adolescence, early adolescence, and late adolescence.[10] It is doubtful whether these divisions contribute to the overall understanding of the adolescent phenomenon. However, it is possible that such divisions are of clinical value for purposes of counseling young teen-agers at specific phases of their development.

It has been said that an adolescent is one who, if not treated as an adult, acts like an infant. There is a social-psychological truism in this aphorism: if role expectations are poorly defined—as they are during adolescence—the resulting confusion and bewilderment may induce a youngster to resort to one of the adjacent roles—either as adult or as child. Either alternative—as unfitting to the situation as it may appear to the observer—constitutes a solution for the young individual and provides him with a clear form of reaction. This, of course, is usually a merely situational solution. In general, decision-making during the time of adolescence is a most difficult, often painful process because the child's familiar and habitual forms of responding to a situation are no longer encouraged and judged to be adequate, and new response patterns have not yet been developed.

Urban-Industrial Conditions

Status discontinuity, as defined by the concept of adolescence, does not necessarily represent an entirely new social phenomenon in the history of civilization. Many adults who are persistently alarmed by the current "adolescent problem" seem to be unaware that it has been with us, at least to some degree, for a long time. The specific expressions and symptoms may have changed, but the underlying problem has remained the same. With few exceptions, all highly urbanized societies experience adolescent problems to some extent simply because they contain a number of adolescence-generating conditions. The list of the main factors responsible for the evolvement of adolescence in such societies includes

---

[10] E. B. Hurlock, *Adolescent Development* (New York, McGraw-Hill, 1949).

the separation of the location of work from the domicile, the highly specialized division of labor, the necessity of a long period of education and training in preparation for a position within the complex urban-industrial structure, the availability to the young of a considerable share of the economic affluence, and the relatively high social and geographic mobility so characteristic of urban-industrial life. (Later discussion elaborates upon these conditions.) These variables have a significant influence on the nature of status transition and tend to create an unstructured interim between the status of the child and the status of the adult. This no-man's land, whose boundaries are unknown and blurred, is characterized by a confusing lack of role prescriptions for the young individual.

One should not confuse the basic causal influence of urban-industrial conditions on adolescence with the mere catalytic function of American models of adolescence in such countries as have been mentioned earlier. It is difficult to determine the extent to which the adolescent cultures of contemporary Europe have been derived from American models or the extent to which they are the products of indigenous processes within the respective countries themselves. It is probably true that American teen-age expressions have *influenced* European developments, because they presented ready and visible models which could be imitated and emulated. Whatever outside influence there was fell on prepared and fertile ground. The urban-industrial conditions of the various European countries were well along in the process of generating their *own* brand of adolescence. Perhaps the American model added a peculiarly American color to it, but it would be an overstatement to call it a causal influence. In many modern countries structural and cultural forces are at work which have a *similar* conditioning effect. It is these forces to which young people in Germany, France, England, the U.S.A., the Soviet Union, Japan, etc., are similarly exposed. Social and cultural similarities permeate work, schooling, leisure, and family patterns in all these different countries which, in turn, produce similarities in the expressions of the youth. In all these countries the life conditions produce a discontinuity between child and adult status. Given certain emotional predispositions of young people, a cue or a model, however distant, is of sufficient catalytic force to produce a distinct crystallization of emotions into what is known as typical adolescent behavior patterns.

It is interesting to observe the progress that many of the so-called underdeveloped nations have made toward a more urban-industrial life and the *concomitant* development of juvenile and adolescent problems. Normally, adolescence is a symptom of a well developed and relatively affluent society. If this is true, then many of the rural and semi-urban societies may anticipate a development of the phenomenon of adolescence along with technological maturation.

Historical Aspects

Prior to the industrial revolution, the role of youth as a collective entity
was of little or no significance to the larger society. Indeed, the concept
of the "younger generation" as we emphasize it today, was hardly established. Until well into the 17th century, children in Europe were both
indulged and ignored. Medieval artists appeared ignorant of what children looked like and habitually portraited them as small adults. For
example, a 12th-century painting illustrating Jesus' injunction to "suffer
the little children to come unto me" shows Christ surrounded by a dozen
undersized men. Throughout the Middle Ages, a child passed directly
into the adult world between the ages of five and seven. Schooling was
of minimal importance and rarely extended into the teens. Work, in a
strictly adult environment, came early and with little confusion or uncertainty. This rapid transition resembles the custom of primitive societies
where children become full-fledged members of the tribe in one painful
and often hazardous initiation, which compresses—or even abolishes—
the confusion and terror of entering adult life.[11]

In that time, when the life span as well as the period of education
was far shorter than today, the young were incorporated into adult life
at an early age and sometimes made history at an age when the modern
young are still going to high school: Edward the Black Prince was 16
when he triumphed at the battle of Crécy; Joan of Arc was 17 when she
took Orléans from the English; and Ivan the Terrible was the same age
when he commenced to make his name as the "Terrible" and had himself crowned Czar of Russia.

Beginning in the 17th century, increasing urbanization and industrialization brought about many important social changes. For ordinary
people, life became a slower progression toward experience and eventual
adult status. Most youngsters who lived in the towns and cities went
through an apprenticeship, which prepared them for a trade and a profession as a journeyman in the guild system. Gradually, with greater
concern for youth and more schooling and vocational training, a novel
stage of life emerged between childhood and adulthood: adolescence,
a new combination of weal and woe that profoundly altered social institutions and attitudes.

The Industrial Revolution accentuated and disseminated the adolescent problem more than any other social development in the history
of man. For increasing numbers of young people, the rural setting and

---

[11] See for comprehensive treatment: Philippe Ariès, *Centuries of Childhood*
(New York, Alfred A. Knopf, 1962).

the simple observable work arrangements were gone forever. The complex division of labor that gradually emerged, divorced the place of work from the place of residence and made them two entirely different settings; the adult at work became progressively less visible to the young. Formal education and training for future jobs developed as new institutions. Concomitantly, ambiguity developed in respect to the nature of the status of the individual who found himself in this interim period of training and education. This was the beginning of the *era of adolescence.*

There are numerous documentary descriptions of this early stage. The English historian Lord Thomas B. Macaulay wrote about the London of 1685:

> When the evening closed in, the difficulty and danger of walking about London became serious indeed. . . . Thieves and robbers plied their trade with impunity: yet they were hardly as terrible to peaceable citizens as another class of ruffians. It was a favorite amusement of dissolute young gentlemen to swagger by night about the town, breaking windows, upsetting sedans, beating quiet men, and offering rude caresses to pretty women. Several dynasties of these tyrants had, since the Restoration, domineered over the streets. The Muns and Tityre Tus had given place to the Hectors, and the Hectors had been recently succeeded by the Scourers. At a later period arose the Nicker, the Hawcubite, and the yet more dreaded name of Mohawk.[12]

The reader of diaries such as Macaulay's is easily convinced that there was much adolescent villainy and violence in earlier times. There is a striking similarity between adolescent gang activities in large modern cities such as New York, Chicago, Los Angeles, etc., and the actions of adolescent gangs in London almost 300 years ago. This casts considerable doubt on the justifiability of the perennial complaint of many adults who negatively compare the youth of our day with the youth of previous generations. These complaints frequently conclude that youth has never been more degenerate than at present. Such reminiscing is more sentimental than factual. Socrates, more than 2200 years ago, talked in a fashion that one finds repeated ever since—and one that possibly antedated him. He referred to the children of his time as being infatuated with luxury, behaving with bad manners and with disrespect for authority, and—reminiscent of certain descriptions of present-day American middle-class families—as being tyrants of their households.

An examination of the American society of roughly 100 years ago shows that there was no lack of adolescent and delinquent problems.

---

[12]Thomas B. Macauley, *History of England,* Vol. 2 (Boston, Houghton Mifflin Company, 1899), p. 81.

Newspaper reports concerning adolescent gang violence during the middle of the last century have such striking resemblance to today's headlines that the main difference seems to lie only in the names of the gangs. In 1857, the *New York Times* printed articles concerning the deplorable activities of New York City gangs with such names as the "Dead Rabbits" and the "Bowery Boys." It was even necessary to call out the state militia in 1857 to squelch the street fighting between rival gangs and reestablish peace and order.[13] New Orleans also reported youthful violence. Newspapers described the activities of teen-agers who roamed the streets beating, stabbing, and robbing innocent citizens.[14]

The tremendous influx of immigrants into the United States during the early 1900's did nothing to improve the adolescent problem. *Anomie* and marginality tinged the life and the status struggle of the immigrants' first-generation-American children. While the immigrant parents continued to draw identity and response patterns from their Old World background, their children were faced with the problem of choosing between the values of their Old-World-oriented parents and the demands of the American society. Presumably, the ultimate choice was made in favor of the New World. But the process of choosing and adjusting was not easy for the youngsters of various ethnic minorities. Ernest W. Burgess and Harvey J. Locke offer a case study which illustrates the youth problem of immigrant families. Here is the example of an Italian family:

> . . . The third son is in Leavenworth: He is an original "42" [a notorious criminal gang which was located on the West Side of Chicago]. He finished two years of high school. At this point his family moved only about three blocks but into the midst of the "42" gang. Here the boy picked up delinquent cronies, cultivated new pleasures and habits, became delinquent and ended up as a big-time robber, the accomplice in professional stick-ups, the pal of notorious, big gangsters. There was nothing the family could do to save the boy. The family affections were always too strong to throw him out or disown him. Repeatedly, the family made big sacrifices for bonds and lawyers and "fixers" only to find themselves in the same situation soon again. Finally nothing could save him from a prison sentence.[15]

Another social movement that aggravated the problem of adolescence in the United States was rural-urban migration. In the early decades of this century, there were conspicuous indications that the

---

[13] Reported in David Gottlieb and Charles Ramsey, *The American Adolescent* (Homewood, Ill., The Dorsey Press, 1964), p. 4.

[14] Gottlieb and Ramsey, pp. 4–5.

[15] Ernest W. Burgess and Harvey J. Locke, *The Family: From Institution To Companionship* (New York, The American Book Co., 1945), p. 124.

uprooted rural youth had to make difficult adjustments to city life. One such adjustment was to an unaccustomed freedom from direct parental supervision and family obligations. As a result, the ex-farm youth found himself financially as well as morally independent. This mode of living represented a sudden change from previous life conditions that had included living as a closely integrated member of a common family enterprise. Many observers—then as well as today—judged the rural-urban migration of farm youth as an extremely dangerous and undesirable trend. Statements illustrating this anti-city philosophy reflect more moralism than objective assessment. Big-city life was viewed as incompatible with "wholesome" living for youth. It was thought that the youngster would be tempted by the "bright lights" and the "evil influences" of the city. Here is an example reflecting this type of concern:

> One has only to compare the broken, bent, and depraved youth of the city with the honest and firm farm child to see what evil the city offers. On the farm the young person learns to respect work and to disregard evil influences. The air about him is fresh and he does not breath the stench of the factory or narcotics. He can take pride in the accomplishments of his work and the pleasures of his family. In the city, youth are always subject to the wicked and have little opportunity for wholesome outdoor play.[16]

The adjustment problems arising from ex-rural youth living in urban centers are not necessarily problems of the past, but are relatively timeless and still exist in the United States today. The youth with farm or rural-slum backgrounds who have migrated from Appalachia to the big cities of the Midwest are current examples. The following statement, made in 1910, could be easily applied today and would describe the contemporary situation in such cities as Columbus, Cleveland, Philadelphia, and Indianapolis, which all receive a heavy influx of youth from the hills of Kentucky, West Virginia, and Tennessee.

> Never before in civilization have such numbers of young girls been suddenly released from the protection of the home and permitted to walk unattended upon city streets and to work under alien roofs; for the first time they are being prized more for their labor power than for their innocence, their tender beauty, their ephemeral gaiety. . . .
>
> Never before have such numbers of young boys earned money independently of the family life, and felt themselves free to spend it as they choose in the midst of vice deliberately disguised as pleasure.[17]

---

[16] Annual Report of the Ohio State Board of Agriculture; *Agricultural Record, 1912,* p. 476.

[17] Jane Addams, *The Spirit of Youth and the City Streets* (New York, The Macmillan Co., 1910), pp. 5–6.

Again, the value judgment and the journalistic style of this statement obscure the more technical aspects of the sociological problem. But the report does succeed in conveying a general picture of the situation.

This chronological sketch showing that the adolescent problem is not a newcomer to the space age could be continued in more detail, but the above examples must suffice to illustrate the fact that adolescence has been with us uninterruptedly as America has changed from pastoral simplicity to urban complexity, from the plough to the assembly line, from apple cider to Coca Cola.

The Question of Universality of Adolescence

It is true that there is a high correlation between urban-industrial conditions and the adolescent problem. But the correlation is not absolute and exceptions can be found. These exceptions can only be explained by understanding the difference between *social-structural conditions* and *cultural forces*. The former variable deals with the network of positions— sometimes referred to as the division of labor—that a given society has developed. In order to have adolescence, the division of labor must be complex enough to require a long transition from the child to the adult status, a transitional period that presumably prepares the young individual for adult life and during which he is considered neither child nor adult. The social-structural circumstances can therefore be called the *necessary* cause for adolescence. This is comparable to the situation in which the necessary cause for the virus disease X is the presence of the X virus. But the presence of the necessary cause alone does not mean that the disease results automatically. If the attacked organism provides enough resistance, the virus may be powerless and the organism will not exhibit the symptoms of disease X. But if the organism cannot rally sufficient resistance and strength, it falls victim to the virus. The analogy is applicable to the question of adolescence and may be helpful in clarifying the causal process. If the cultural "resistance" is strong enough and can provide the adequate "antibiotics," adolescence may not express itself. On the other hand, if the cultural ideation and identity-forces are too weak and nondescript, adolescence will appear. The cultural circumstances can therefore be called the source of the *sufficient* cause of adolescence. Cultural forces are thus able to prevent adolescence in the face of social-structural conditions that invite the adolescent problem. Adolescence can be curbed, or possibly altogether precluded, if a society provides a compelling and convincing ideology or religion for its members and succeeds in indoctrinating the young with it. The most reliable and lasting social control mechanism is the internalized fervor and conviction that becomes part of the "conscience" of the people themselves. Little or no outside enforcement is needed to obtain firm adherence to the cultural norms and values once people have made them part of their outlook on life. If a society succeeds in implanting such supra-social-structural identity and a feeling of meaningful belonging, symptoms of adolescence will be minimal. This minimization is especially noticeable in cases where a specific youth program is designed to infuse ideological directives in the young people. As a result, the void created by the structural discontinuity between child and adult status is filled with meaning and purpose. The combination of the feeling of belonging to the general culture and the exposure to specific youth programs creates an identity in the young that does not depend on a specific position in the division of labor. In a sense, the young individual has the *status* of a meaningful and vital member of the society and cannot be classified as an adolescent.

There are some examples in recent history that illustrate this ideological compensation for adolescence-inducing urban-industrial structures. The *Hitler-Jugend* in Nazi Germany, the *Pioneers* and the *Komsomol* in the Soviet Union, and the *Red Guard* movement in China were or, perhaps still, are instances where the urban-industrial conditions failed to produce adolescence. Strong ideological indoctrination must be held responsible for this failure. (The example of the Soviet Union needs considerable modification. As has been noted previously, adolescence and delinquent activities have been increasing in the Soviet Union during the past two decades. As urban-industrial conditions progress and affluence spreads to the young members of the Soviet society, the ideological commitment of Russian youth seems to decrease. Thus, the era when strong ideation compensated for urban and adolescence-inducing conditions is gradually becoming history.) In the case of these three societies, the political philosophy of the state extended an identity to the young people that neutralized the social-structural features containing the status-discontinuing elements. A new and socially recognized and approved position was established: an official and well-organized position for the "youth of the nation." Labels, symbols, uniforms, and youth programs were important instruments and were employed to give and maintain an identity for the teen-agers. Being Hitler-Youth, for example, implied clear standards, predictable behavior patterns, well-defined rights and obligations that were known and respected by the majority, or at least the power elite, of the nation. This public status for youth resulted in alleviation, if not elimination, of the crisis of discontinuity between the status of the child and the adult. A new status was interjected. As a result, there was an absence of the adolescent symptoms and expressions that are typical in the more democratic societies which do not extend a compelling ideology and, thereby, fail to infuse a powerful identity into the young.

Because of modern urban-industrial youth's intense need for clear identity, they can easily fall prey to demagogues' promises, charismatic leaders' call to action, and the various appeals of a "True Belief." The development of many totalitarian regimes was only possible because of a leader's or a power elite's success in winning the enthusiasm and loyalty of the nation's adolescents. Psychiatrist Maurice N. Walsh feels that the rise of Nazi Germany was possible partially because of the National Socialists' success in indoctrinating the nation's adolescents and thereby influencing the destiny of a whole nation—and indeed of the whole world.

> It is a mistake to assume that the Nazis gained control in Germany solely by means of brutality and terror. No one who knows Germany can believe such a myth. Control was gained by seduction, and seduction of adolescents was a powerful tool in preparing the young Germans, through the Hitler-Jugend, for their sacrifice in the coming war. Seduction of many of their parents was also carried out, but the older generation is never so easily seduced as is the younger. The reasons reside in the emotional instability of the adolescent, who is passing through a critical period in his emotional life and development.[18]

The reference to these historical events is obviously not to be interpreted as an endorsement of totalitarian systems that show the ability to change adolescence to active, cooperating, and goal-oriented members of the society. The above account is not to be understood as a suggestion to trade adolescence for compelling ideological indoctrination. The purpose of presenting these historical situations is to elucidate the structural-functional principle that assumes that if certain cultural dimensions prevail, certain behavioral consequences follow. The German, Russian, and Chinese examples indicate modifications of the generalization that adolescence is a universal trait of modern urban-industrial societies.

Pitirim Sorokin's classification of types of societies, or the specific phases through which most societies pass, may be helpful in the context of this discussion.[19] A society characterized by a monolithic ideation may find it relatively easy to extend a consistent and logically integrated identity to every member of the social system, even though the immediate social-structural position may lack structural specificity. But this lack

---

[18] Maurice N. Walsh, M.D., "The Case of Rudolf Hess: A Specimen Study of a Narcissistic Leader," *Humanist*, Vol. 27 (March/April, 1967), p. 51.

[19] Pitirim A. Sorokin, *The Crisis of Our Age: The Social and Cultural Outlook* (New York, E. P. Dutton, 1941).

of structural specificity may not even be noticed or found disturbing, since the over-all cultural identity and the feeling of belonging to a meaningful culture is ample compensation. Indeed, the mere fact of belonging to an important cultural movement may be perceived as a position in its own right—the position of being a member of the totalitarian society. This membership enables the young to answer satisfactorily the question "Who am I?" The situation in the Middle Ages exemplified this state of affairs. Millions of devoted people would have answered the basic question of identity by saying: "I am a member of the Church," or more basically: "I am a child of God." The "True Believer," who feels that he is a child and envisages a powerful "Father" who knows him personally, is characterized by a mental structure that provides him with an identity that is as strong as or even stronger than any specific social position that he could ever occupy. In effect, then, the tenets of the religio-cultural ethos were sufficiently meaningful to involve the believing member of the society. The sociological significance of the answerability of the basic question of identity by means of the general cultural ethos lies in its supra-positional quality. This means that the members of the society, young or old, were able to derive an identity from the larger cultural context with relative independence from social differentiation, such as age-specific categories, positions in the division of labor, or socioeconomic class status. This undifferentiating quality is one of the functions of an ideational society. The central belief system offers identity and belonging at any phase in the life cycle of the individual, regardless of social differentiation.

But societies change and do not remain forever in the ideational phase. The theory holds that the subsequent stage is usually the *idealistic* period. This implies that the previously monolithic creed has loosened up and changed into a multitude of different factions. The religious and primarily theological character of the preceding ideation proliferates into philosophies more this-worldly than other-worldly. The age of the Renaissance is thought of as marking the idealistic phase of Western civilization and the beginning of serious weakening of the ideational forces that could have functioned as a check on the development of adolescence. The cultural forces that had extended basic identity diminished in strength and lost their monopolizing persuasion. The idealistic period is followed by the *sensate* period which, according to the theory, includes our present age. The unified cultural credo has declined, if not disappeared altogether. Rather than being concerned with ideational precepts from which he deduces directives for daily living, modern man is intent on satisfying immediate sensate needs and cravings. Values and ideas in general are valued according to their practical, material, and pleasurable—in short, sensate—results. There is no longer a convincing ideational system that extends basic identity to its members. The cultural norms and values have become nonspecific and allow a comparatively liberal degree of individual freedom. This individual freedom has been held responsible for modern man's anxiety about, and confused searching for, identity. *The most striking sociological effect of this loss of basic cultural identity is the burdening of the social structure with the demand for an identity that is no longer available anywhere else.* An interesting shift in identity-genesis has occurred: what the general culture can no longer provide is now expected from specific social positions. This means that the members of contemporary society depend—more strongly than ever before in Western civilization—on a social position for identity. The specific role of a given social position, be it that of an auto mechanic or a physician, has become the core of modern man's identity. Cut off from such social-structural anchors, modern man tends to suffer problems of identity. Such distress symptoms can be observed among adolescents who have not yet entered an occupational career and among retired persons who are no longer actively involved in their identity-reinforcing occupation but who, however, unlike adolescents, can at least draw identity, retrospectively.

Summary

Adolescence refers to the *crisis of status discontinuity* and has become part of the public life in many contemporary societies. It is a period in the life of the young individual when the status of the child has vanished and the status of the adult is not yet fully available. This situation of discontinuity includes social-structural, cultural, psychological, and physiological aspects. Discontinuity may approach such degrees of disruption of familiar life conditions for the young person that the designation of *crisis* is justified. This crisis, since experienced by many same-aged youngsters, has evolved into collective compensations, i.e., into teen-age subcultures. While the definition of *adolescent* is based on the experience of an unstructured interim between status of child and status of adult, the term *juvenile* is used in connection with legal implications. The term *teen-ager* is more than just a denotation of age; it connotes immaturity and a collective phenomenon. *Youth* is a term used broadly to refer to the "younger generation" or to young adults. Adolescence as a collective phenomenon is nearly universal today. Some countries exhibit a greater degree of it than others, usually depending on the degree of urban-industrial development. There seems to be a direct correlation between the degree of urban-industrial advancement and the extent of adolescence. Adolescence should therefore not be described—let alone explained—as an exclusively American characteristic that has spread to other countries, but rather as an outgrowth of certain social and cultural conditions that can be found in many societies today. The causal conditions include social-structural discontinuity as the necessary cause and the cultural idiom as the sufficient cause of adolescence. Only when the two conditions coincide in yielding adolescence-inducing circumstances can adolescence develop. Historically speaking, adolescence is not entirely new. Recorders in all ages have collected comments that seem to indicate the existence of a certain amount of adolescent problems. However, it was not until the onset of the Industrial Revolution that the social structure showed those peculiar features that made for discontinuity between the statuses. Likewise, it was not until the Renaissance that the compelling ideational forces of Medieval Christendom weakened to the degree that they lost their identity-providing function. As a result, it is now the social structure that is a more effective source for identity than the general culture. In the few cases where totalitarian states succeeded in indoctrinating their youth with compelling convictions, the social-structural void between the statuses was filled with definite meaning and purpose—and adolescence was prevented. However, in most contemporary urban societies teen-agers find themselves in an unstructured and ill-defined interim phase, suffering from the modern dilemma of adolescence.

antecedent conditions of adolescence

the structure of the
modern family

The causes of adolescence form a complex and interrelated constellation. It is almost impossible to examine all of them in one book and a decision must be made to select only the most relevant and important. These antecedent conditions can be divided roughly into the social-structural, cultural, and psychological aspects. It goes without mention that these aspects are overlapping and interdependent, and that they are treated separately for the purpose of clear communication, only.

Among the social-structural conditions that are of great importance in the formation of adolescence are the youth's group affiliations. Within these various group affiliations, the experience of being a member of the family group probably has the most profound influence on the process of forming an identity and acquiring adult status. Since the quality of human interaction within the family group and the possibility of producing adolescence are significantly affected by the family structure, the first part of the discussion is devoted to an examination of the structure of the modern family.

It is obvious that there is not just *one* American family, but many different types, depending on such background features as ethnicity, race, socioeconomic status, religion, etc. The adolescent experience varies accordingly, and distinctions should be drawn among the diverse adolescent processes that can be found in the lives of Negro, Jewish, American Indian, rural, urban, lower-class, or upper-class youth. A number of these diverse processes are discussed in Part IV, where an attempt is made to recognize the different modes of adolescence and to find the factors that explain differences and similarities. This chapter, on the other hand, deals primarily with historical trends and changes that have affected most types of American families and have patterned them into smaller and more urban-industrial family groups. The concern, therefore, of this initial discussion is to point out *common* features rather than to detect differing traits among American families. The main point is to recognize new structural conditions that have combined to give rise to the modern adolescent phenomenon.

In order to view the present adolescence-inducing family structure in its proper perspective, it is necessary to begin with a description of the changes that have taken place over the past generations.

The typical traditional family in America was the rural family. In 1800, more than 90 per cent of the population of the United States was classified as rural. This proportion consistently declined to 85 per cent in 1850 and 60 per cent in 1900.[1] In 1920, the United States Census introduced a more sensitive inquiry, distinguishing between rural population in general (including rural-nonfarm) and farm population in specific. It was found that only 30 per cent of the population of the United States was farm population. This proportion decreased rapidly to 25 per cent in 1930, 23 per cent in 1940, 15 per cent in 1950, 9 per cent in 1960, and 6 per cent in 1965.[2]

The traditional rural family was not limited to the members of the nuclear family, consisting of parents and their offspring only, but often included such close relatives as grandparents, uncles, aunts, and cousins. In this extended or consanguine family group, the child grew up in close association with a number of blood relatives that included adults as well as other children. In addition to relatives, the traditional family occasionally took in nonrelatives who became permanent members of the household and, in a sense, were looked upon as members of the family.[3] The majority of such nonrelatives were maids and farm hands. This situation exists to some extent today in some rural areas, but it is rapidly declining. While in 1910 almost every fourth American family included a nonrelative member, in 1961 only every twentieth family included such a person. (See Table 2-1.) Statistics show that due to such additional related and nonrelated members of the household (justifying therefore the definition of "extended" family) plus on the average a larger number of children, the typical household of the 19th century was more than two persons larger than that of today. (See Table 2-2.)

In today's more urban-industrial setting, it is customary to establish new households at the time of marriage. In the traditional family this was not necessary and many married children remained with their fami-

---

[1] *Historical Statistics of the United States, Colonial Times to 1957* (Washington, D.C., Bureau of the Census with the Cooperation of the Social Science Research Council, 1960), p. 14.

[2] *Statistical Abstract of the United States: 1966* (Washington, D.C., Bureau of the Census, 1966), p. 616.

[3] The Bureau of the Census counted these *non*relatives as regular members of the household: *Historical Statistics, op. cit.,* p. 16.

TABLE 2–1. Average Number of Relatives (to Head of Household) and
Nonrelatives (to Head of Household) per Household, 1910–
1961, On a Nationwide Basis.

Year	Number of Relatives per Household	Number of Nonrelatives per Household
1910[a]	2.46	.22
1930[a]	2.07	.18
1940[a]	1.81	.16
1950[a]	1.55	.10
1960[b]	1.54	.06
1961[b]	1.52	.05

[a] Adapted from *Historical Statistics of the United States, Colonial Times to 1957*
(Washington, D. C., Bureau of the Census, 1960), p. 16.

[b] Adapted from *Historical Statistics of the United States, Continuation to 1962
and Revisions* (Washington, D.C., Bureau of the Census, 1965), p. 4.

TABLE 2–2. Average Number of Persons per Family Household, 1790–1962.

Year	Persons per Household
1790[a]	5.8
1850[a]	5.6
1900[a]	4.8
1910[a]	4.5
1920[a]	4.3
1930[a]	4.1
1940[a]	3.8
1950[a]	3.5
1960[b]	3.4
1962[b]	3.3

[a] Adapted from *Historical Statistics of the United States, Colonial Times to 1957*
(Washington, D. C., Bureau of the Census, 1960), p. 16.

[b] Adapted from *Historical Statistics of the United States, Continuation to 1962
and Revisions* (Washington, D. C., Bureau of the Census, 1965), p. 4.

lies in the household of their family of orientation. This trend has been
borne out by historical statistics, which show that, in 1910, 7.7% of
married couples did not live in an independent household, while by 1962
this proportion had steadily decreased to 2.1%. (See Table 2-3.)

Another way of recognizing this trend is by looking at the percentage
distribution of different family sizes. Statistics indicate a drastic decline

TABLE 2–3.   Proportion of U.S. Married Couples Setting Up Dependent Households, 1947–1962.

Year	Total	Per Cent of Dependent Households
1947[a]	33,543	8.7%
1948[a]	34,364	7.2%
1949[a]	35,425	6.1%
1950[a]	36,091	5.5%
1951[a]	36,136	4.9%
1952[a]	36,696	4.2%
1953[a]	37,106	4.2%
1954[a]	37,346	3.5%
1955[a]	37,570	3.5%
1956[a]	38,306	3.3%
1957[a]	38,940	3.2%
1958[b]	39,182	3.1%
1959[b]	39,529	2.8%
1960[b]	40,205	2.4%
1961[b]	40,524	2.4%
1962[b]	41,218	2.1%

[a] Adapted from *Historical Statistics of the United States, Colonial Times to 1957* (Washington, D. C., Bureau of the Census, 1960), p. 16.

[b] Adapted from *Historical Statistics of the United States, Continuation to 1962 and Revision* (Washington, D. C., Bureau of the Census, 1965), p. 4.

in the proportion of families with six or more members. In 1790, slightly more than half of all American families were large households that included six or more members. At the turn of the century, only about one-third of the families were that large. Today, only about 14% of all families have six or more members. On the other hand, the small 2- or 3-person family has become markedly more frequent and has increased from 20% in 1870 to 34% in 1900 and to more than 50% today. (See Table 2-4 for details.) This trend should be qualified by pointing out that there has been a slight increase in the percentage of larger families since about the mid-1950's.

This change in the structure of the family has had a definite influence on the development of adolescence in American society. Generally speaking, it has had the effect of intensifying the discontinuity between the status of the child and of the adult. This is more clearly demonstrated in the discussions following where a number of specific consequences of this structural change are mentioned.

TABLE 2–4.   Per Cent of U. S. Families with Specified Number of Persons, 1790–1964.

Number of Persons	1790[a]	1900[a]	1930[a]	1940[a]	1950[a]	1953[a]	1956[a]	1960[b]	1964[c]
2	8.1	15.8	26.1	28.6	32.8	33.5	32.5	32.7	32.2
3	12.1	18.5	22.5	24.4	25.2	24.2	22.8	21.6	20.7
4	14.3	17.8	18.8	19.5	19.8	20.3	20.9	19.9	19.9
5	14.4	15.0	12.8	11.8	11.1	11.4	12.3	12.8	13.2
6 or more	50.8	32.8	19.7	15.7	11.0	10.6	11.6	13.0	14.0

[a] Adapted from: William F. Kenkel, *The Family in Perspective*, 2nd Ed. (New York, Appleton-Century-Crofts, 1966), p. 201.

[b] Adapted from *U.S. Census of Population 1960, U.S. Summary*, PC(1) 1D U.S., Table 187, p. 1, 465.

[c] Adapted from *Statistical Abstracts of U.S. 1965* (Washington, D. C., Bureau of the Census, 1965), Table 40, p. 39.

Limited Adult Models

The extended family was able to provide a number of adults who could serve as "significant others," i.e., as models whose attitudes and behavior could be emulated by the younger members of the family system. The young boy or girl had the opportunity to choose models from among a number of visible adult relatives and could derive an image of what he or she wanted to be. This process, although rarely on the conscious level, helped the young to learn patterns of problem-solving and patterns of value orientation by observing the expressions and behavior styles of significant adult figures. In the isolated nuclear family, by contrast, learning from actually observable and imitable persons is extremely limited. Normally, there is only one adult member of each sex represented, and if this parent is not readily observable, the youngster is deprived of his needed model. A current concern of many social scientists is the position of the middle-class boy, which exemplifies the situation in which the sex-role model is largely absent. Identity problems can frequently be observed that seem to have been brought on by excessive absence of the father from the home. (See Chapters 4 and 7.)

Even if the child has the opportunity to associate with his father and observe his actions, one must take into account the possibility that this model is not *acceptable* to him. Since the father is usually the only adult male in the nuclear family, the son may lack alternative adult male models. The rejection of the father could lead to a complicated situation in which the father changes from a model to an object of rebellion. A frequent theme underlying many cases of father rejections is the youth's refusal to accept as a model a person whose only qualification may be the occupancy of the *position* of father. The regard for institutions and formal positions has changed from the "sacred" to the "secular."[4] Rather than considering the established and traditional position as the absolute norm for carrying out certain functions and regarding them as the unchangeable pattern to which man must adjust, modern secular man tends to view himself and his needs as the supreme objective and expects that his needs will be fulfilled—if necessary, untraditionally. Accordingly, it is the occupant of a position and not the position itself that draws the reaction, and the reaction can be positive or negative. It may be respect and emulation or it may be rejection. Modern youth prefer to respond to specific persons and not to abstract positions, and they may resent the pressure of the adult society to render reverence and obedience to a person occupying a superior position if they feel that he is not qualified for the position.

Trying to uphold the decree of reverence and obedience for a given position when it is occupied by an unqualified person may result in serious dysfunctions. These disturbances are likely to affect the larger social system, because no position or set of positional interactions stands isolated from other sets of social interactions. According to some social scientists, the structure of the nuclear family has definite dysfunctional aspects in relation to the socialization of the young. Barrington Moore, a well-known advocate of this view, has expressed one of the most poignant opinions on this matter. He believes that the family as we know it today is dysfunctional, anachronistic—in short, obsolete. In his controversial "Thoughts on the Future of the Family," he accused the modern nuclear family of being beset with "obsolete and barbaric features." Moore referred especially to the cultural expectation according to which the youngster has "the obligation to give affection as a duty to a particular set of persons because of the accident of birth." Moore also called attention to "the exploitation of socially sanctioned demands for gratitude, when the existing social situation no longer generates any genuine feeling of warmth."[5] This family critic concluded that someday "human society may realize that the part-time family, already a prominent part

[4] Howard S. Becker, "Interpreting Family Life in Context," in Howard S. Becker and Reuben Hill (eds.), *Family, Marriage and Parenthood* (Boston; D. C. Heath & Co., 1955), pp. 19–40.

[5] Barrington Moore, "Thoughts on the Future of the Family," in Maurice R. Stein, Arthur J. Vidich, and Daniel M. White (eds.), *Identity and Anxiety* (Glencoe, Ill., The Free Press, 1960), pp. 393–94.

Barrington Moore

of our social landscape, has undergone a qualitative transformation into a system of mechanized and bureaucratized child rearing," since "an institutional environment can be . . . warmer than a family torn by obligations its members resent."[6] Moore considers the problems of adolescents to be the specific outgrowth of the modern family's incapability of stabilizing the human personality, and he regards adolescence primarily as the result of the dysfunctional and obsolete modern family system. He suggests that we give serious thought to the development of more adequate functional equivalents for the family as it is known today.

While the unconventional ideas of sociologist Moore may have validity, they are only partial explanations and are hardly exhaustive of the multiple variables affecting modern adolescence. Nevertheless, the core idea appears to be sociologically acceptable: a serious deprivation of role models may develop in those situations where the offspring refuses to acknowledge the authority of his parents—notwithstanding the traditional demand to obey them because of their parental positions. When frequent father-absenteeism is added to this secular and rebellious situation as another critical condition of the modern nuclear family, it is not surpising to observe that the process of sex-role identification suffers from defects and incompleteness. In the final analysis, a family characterized by some combination of these dysfunctional conditions is prone to contribute to the complexity of the adolescent process. The chances that these dysfunctional conditions would arise in the extended family system were less than in the modern nuclear—and especially middle-class—family. The extended family usually provided more than one "significant other" of the same sex and therefore offered a greater flexibility in choosing a model. In sum, then, a consequence of the structural peculiarity of the nuclear family is its difficulty in providing more than one adult model for a given boy or girl, thereby complicating and often delaying the transition from childhood to adulthood.

Nonfamilial Peers

In the extended family the child usually grew up with peers who were blood-related members of his family group. They functioned as playmates for each other and thereby eliminated the necessity of stepping outside of the family to find playmates. Besides having their playmates right at home, the children of the extended family system also had playmates with whom they shared the same or similar sentiments and activi-

---

[6] Moore, *op. cit.*, p. 401.

ties. Charles H. Cooley's concept of the primary group found a near-perfect empirical referent in this arrangement.[7] The interaction was intimate, face-to-face, and self-perception proceeded in terms of "we" instead of in terms of "I and they."

In contrast, most nuclear families are isolated from their kin and cannot provide playmates who are blood relatives. A modern youngster may grow up seeing few, if any, of his relatives. In some cases this may be due to great distances separating kinsfolk, and in other cases it may be due to the desire for freedom from familistic obligations. Another reason why a sizable proportion of American youth may not be exposed to their kinsfolk is due to family disruptions, manifested by the high rate of divorce and separation. Many children live and grow up with only one parent, customarily the mother. As a result, the child tends to be alienated from half of his relatives, in most cases his paternal relatives.

As a consequence, children of nuclear families seek their playmates outside of the kin group and commonly transform the school environment into a primary source of peer friends. Unlike cousins and siblings who have grown up in the same household, non-familial peers frequently lack commonality of attitudes and interests and, most significantly, do not share a common loyalty and feeling of belonging to one family. They are therefore prone to form a peer group that is independent of family life. The peer group, once the members reach their teens, becomes part of the adolescent subculture, which provides an improvised and ambiguous "bridge" existence between the status of the child and of the adult. Thus, the teen-ager achieves, in a sense, a marginal status with respect to both the family of orientation and the family of procreation. He is no longer integrated in the former and has not yet attained the status of the latter. In other words, he is no longer an intrinsic part of the parental home and has not yet formed his own family where he will be spouse and parent. He is suspended between two membership groups and compensates for this dilemma by temporarily belonging to a subculture, trying in this way to meet a basic personality need, i.e., the need to feel accepted and to belong. Although he may achieve status *within* the adolescent subculture, from the vantage point of the adult culture he has a poorly defined status and his subcultural activities are not always approved.

In previously existing folk societies, and also in some contemporary ones, the extended family blended primary and secondary socialization into a single process. Marginality, in the sense that is described above, was prevented because the integration into the consanguine family sys-

---

[7] Charles H. Cooley, *Social Organization* (New York, Scribner's, 1909), p. 23.

tem was a lifelong proposition. When the young married, chances were that they would settle in the neighborhood, in the same community, or even in the same large household as the family of orientation.

The main conclusion to be drawn from this discussion is that the previously smooth transition from child to adult status has been replaced by a more tenuous transition via the adolescent subculture. The modern nuclear family does not provide consanguine peers, so that outside peer friendships tend to develop into subcultural group life, competing with the family for loyalty and a sense of belonging. Generally, such divergent reference groups do not contribute to the stabilization of the personality of the young, but rather generate conflicting loyalties, clashing value orientations, overlapping time commitments, and other opposing factors.

Invisibility of Adult Work

If the modern youth were able to see clearly the composition of adult responsibilities, he could make the transition to the adult status much more easily. In the extended rural family, the youngster first observed, then participated as if he were a full-time apprentice, and finally assumed adult responsibilities which always had been familiar to him. The agricultural chores did not come as a sudden surprise, since the adult tasks did not have to be learned apart from the natural setting of the home life. Family life and occupational responsibilities were closely related—in fact, were the same. On the other hand, a youngster in the nuclear family setting may grow into his teens and never observe his father at his vocational work. This may be the reason why relatively few teen-agers follow in the occupational footsteps of their fathers. A survey revealed that 23% of the boys in small towns and only 9.8% of the high-school boys in city and suburban schools planned to enter their fathers' occuptions.[8] (There are significant differences between the identification processes of the boy and the girl. Detailed discussions of these differences are offered later in the book, particularly in chapters 5 and 7.) Indeed, the modern youngster may never have seen *anybody* doing the type of work he plans to assume after finishing his education. He may have heard or read about the particular job he has in mind, but may never have observed a specific adult whom he could use for imitation and emulation. This lack of visibility concerning future responsibil-

---

[8] James S. Coleman, *The Adolescent Society* (New York, The Free Press, 1963), p. 7.

ities necessitates formal and prolonged education and training. There is no such thing as *growing into* adult responsibilities; rather, the growth into the adult role by means of direct association with adults is replaced by years of formal education and training away from home. What is the youth's status during these years of preparation for some more or less obscure occupation? Is he still a child? Is he already an adult? The answer is not clear. The status during these interim years is poorly defined and is beset with a number of corollary problems. One of these problems is the issue of *in loco parentis*.

The Question of "in loco parentis"

The necessity of training and education away from home raises the question of authority over the youngsters while they are away from home. The concept of *in loco parentis* has become important in this context. Literally translated, *in loco parentis* means "in lieu of the parents." The question of guardianship over the youngsters is primarily a legal issue that attempts to determine who has immediate authority over the young persons during their institutional affiliation. Since their education and training are no longer associated with their home life—either psychologically or physically—it is deemed appropriate that not the parents but rather the administrators of the various institutions deal out rewards and punishments. In addition, far-reaching decisions *about* and *for* the young person are made by the administrators. It is quite common that formal institutions, such as high schools and colleges, with their offices of guidance, testing, and counseling, offer specific occupational suggestions to the young individual. The suggestion is usually supplemented with detailed directives prescribing how to prepare for the occupation. Ready-made programs of preparatory work and study are assigned to the candidate, while his parents may not even be informed of such plans and arrangements. Even if they should be notified, they might not quite understand the implications, because the lingo of academe has become esoteric. Administrators and testing centers speak authoritatively about aptitude tests, proficiency tests, and various coefficients and correlates to such an extent that most parents are sufficiently impressed or dumbfounded that they may decide to let the "experts" make the decisions.

The frequent incidence of institutional authority competing with or overriding parental authority has become the focus of lively discussions at many institutions of higher learning. For example, there are a number of critics who oppose the institution's habit of assuming *in loco parentis* authority over the students. These critics are usually not trying to return the authority to the parents, but argue that the young men and the coeds should be allowed to make more independent decisions of their own. These proponents of greater independence and more "self-rule" of the young people believe that if meaningful and important decision-making is taken away from youngsters, they are forced into "perpetual adolescence." From numerous educational institutions across the nation come reports about the on-going disputes concerning institutional authority. At Arizona State University, a rule that no coed under the age of 23 could reside off campus in private housing was finally rescinded in 1967 when the age limit was lowered to 21. Another typical controversy about *in loco parentis* took place at Ohio State University:

> Professor Douglas Crown of the psychology department said last night at a meeting of the subcommittee of the Student Affairs Commission on *in loco parentis* that the "notion of *in loco parentis* is an inappropriate one."
>
> The subcommittee is studying the effects of *in loco parentis* on the development of responsibility in students. According to Jeffrey Schwartz, subcommittee chairman, under the *in loco parentis* program, responsibility is taken from the student and is assumed by the University. This is done through the enforcement of rules set up by the University for students.
>
> Professor Crown said that the effect of the *in loco parentis* program is to cast the student into a "perpetual adolescence. This isn't the way one learns to experience maturity."
>
> He said that to deny to the student that he is capable of responsibility "tends to create a system the student tries to beat. It tends to foster a rebellious attitude where the objective is to get away with something. The lack of academic seriousness is attributed to student alienation."
>
> Although Crown said he did not advocate the complete absence of rules, he did say, "I really don't know what concern it is of the University. It isn't the function of the University to legislate moralities." [9]

The controversy at Ohio State University is a typical illustration of the fact that the modern socialization process has shifted away from the family to a noticeable degree. The shift of the socialization function—besides the shift of several other functions away from the family—has caused considerable concern and extensive discussion among social scientists. The focus of concern centers around the question: is the family becoming obsolete? This question leads to the following inquiry.

---

[9] *The Ohio State Lantern* (November 9, 1962).

The Question of the "Personality" Function of the Modern Family

The question of whether the modern family can meet basic personality needs, in particular such needs as the feeling of belonging and security, deals with important elements in the socialization process. The affirmation of the question is important for the youth's physical as well as mental health. It is especially important for the development of a stable personality. The experience of structural discontinuity between the status of the child and of the adult is difficult and confusing under normal and secure circumstances. If, in addition, a sufficient degree of psychological security is lacking, the youth may be entering an extremely difficult phase in his life.

Many sociologists have attempted to answer the question of whether the modern family is able to offer this vital security. In the process of trying to offer an answer, two main theories have been established. Roughly speaking, the interpretations of the changes in family life have led one group to answer "no" and another to answer "yes" to the question of the family's psychological functionality. For example, Barrington Moore would be classified as a proponent of the "no" answer. But the best-known spokesman of this category is Carl C. Zimmerman, who wrote *Family and Civilization.*[10] This work offers an extensive historical study, draws conclusions from previous societal situations, applies them to the contemporary scene, and predicts the doom of the modern family. The hypothesis is supported by an impressive amount of historical data that lead to the conclusion that the modern family has lost too many functions to be of any more importance to contemporary man.

An opposing view disagrees with this theory of the decline of the modern family. A prominent speaker for this theory is Talcott Parsons, who, in his book with Robert F. Bales, *Family, Socialization and Interaction Process*, presents a more optimistic point of view.[11] The changes that have occurred are interpreted as processes reforming the family into a more specialized agency. It is true, proponents of this theory would concede, that various traditional functions have shifted away from the family to become functions of other institutions. Conspicuous examples of such shifts would include the economic and religious functions. It is thought that even the traditional socialization function has shifted, at

---

[10] Carl C. Zimmerman, *Family and Civilization* (New York, Harper and Brothers, 1947).

[11] Talcott Parsons and Robert F. Bales, *Family, Socialization and Interaction Process* (Chicago, The Free Press of Glencoe, 1955).

least to some degree, from the family to schools, kindergartens, churches, and other so-called "secondary" institutions. However, many sociologists feel that a new function has evolved that preserves the family as an important institution, preventing its disintegration and disappearance. Although not completely new, this function seems to become the most vital feature of modern marriage and the family. It is commonly called the "personality function" and seems to indicate that contemporary Americans try to derive from the family a psychological security and a feeling of belonging to a degree heretofore unknown. These acute psychological needs appear to be symptomatic of the problem of identity which can be considered the typical and most prominent mental problem of the modern era. It is within the confines of the family that modern man hopes to find the answer to the basic question, who am I? This burdens the family institution with an immense responsibility. If people fail to find the coveted identity and feeling of security in a particular marriage or family, they are apt to terminate membership to it and try anew with different partners and in a different setting. According to Parsons, this insistence upon "self-fulfillment" explains the high divorce rate in modern America. This rate, as alarming as it may seem to most observers, does not necessarily indicate the doom of the present family institution, but rather reflects the needs of contemporary man and his desire to succeed in gratifying these needs, regardless of circumstances and initial failures. If the need is not met in one particular setting, the setting is changed. However, the same conventional institution, marriage and the family, is used, reused, and upheld.[12]

In essence, it cannot be denied that the structure and the functions of the family have changed. Yet, how these changes are to be interpreted and whether, eventually, they will bring about the downfall of the family system as we know it today is a speculation that probably cannot adequately be put to an empirical test at this time. In any case, the functional changes of the modern family can be summed up in three main points: (1) A number of traditional family functions have been transferred to other institutions. (2) The modern family has become a specialized agency. (3) People turn to the family to derive a sense of belonging and psychological security.

---

[12] There is a significant difference between a particular family group and the institution of the family. The two should never be confused. The former refers to a specific group of people, in this case a primary group within which the members engage in an intimate face-to-face interaction. On the other hand, the concept of institution is much more abstract. It does not refer to specific people or groups of people; rather, it refers to the norms, values, customs, and laws which society maintains to regulate family life.

Without necessarily endorsing an outlook that is as extremely negative as the one offered by Zimmerman, there still remains sufficient evidence to support the notion that the modern family is falling short of fulfilling crucial psychological needs for modern man. Symptoms of marital and familial discontent include the high rates of divorce and desertion, frequently observed personality conflicts, and ubiquitous complaints about marital difficulties. As family sociologist Charles W. Hobert put it:

> Americans are getting married with greater frequency than ever before, a reflection, perhaps, of the increasing significance of companionship and emotional security within the family for people today. But if they marry for companionship and security, the high level of divorce rate suggests that Americans seek divorce when they fail to attain these goals.[13]

A large proportion of married Americans evidently fail to attain this emotional security. If the current divorce rate is an indication of failure to satisfy basic emotional needs, then nongratification in modern family life is widespread and intense. This is reflected in the consistent rise of the divorce rate over the past decades, amounting to roughly one divorce out of four marriages. (See Table 2-5.)

Another type of marital disintegration is separation. The Census Bureau revealed that in 1960, for example, 903,000 married men and 1,304,000 married women were reported separated.[14] (The figures for the sexes do not match because the data were gathered by questionnaire, and responses depended on the subjective interpretation of the individual.) The addition of other types of marital disintegration, such as desertions (which are not recorded anywhere), would result in further shrinkage of the proportion of stable and successful marriages.

The nuclear family apparently includes characteristics that reduce family stability in general and personality stabilization in particular. Among the dysfunctional features is the modern family's high degree of geographic mobility, often held responsible for impairing the development of stability and identity formation in the young. The mobility factor plays a particularly important roles in the lives of businessmen, white collar workers, and young executives who are constantly on relocation call for the corporation and have been called "corporate nomads." The price of promotion and social mobility includes a willingness to be geographically mobile. A typical example is the mobility record of a

---

[13] Charles W. Hobart, "Commitment, Value Conflict and the Future of the American Family," *Marriage and Family Living*, Vol. 25 (November, 1963), p. 406.

[14] U. S. Bureau of the Census, "Marital Status and Family Status: March 1960," *Current Population Reports*, Series P–20, No. 105 (Nov. 2, 1960), p. 8.

TABLE 2–5.   Divorces and Divorce Rates in the United States, 1870–1965.

Year	Divorces Per 1,000 Population	Divorces per 100 Marriages Performed in Year
1870[a]	.3	3.1
1880[a]	.4	4.3
1890[a]	.5	5.9
1900[a]	.7	7.9
1910[a]	.9	8.8
1920[a]	1.6	13.4
1930[a]	1.6	17.4
1940[a]	2.0	16.5
1950[a]	2.6	23.0
1960[b]	2.2	26.3
1965[c]	2.5	26.9

[a] Adapted from *Vital Statistics, Special Reports,* Vol. 36, No. 2 (Washington, D. C., U.S. Dept. of Health, Education, and Welfare, June 5, 1951), p. 25.

[b] Adapted from *Statistical Abstracts of the United States, 1965* (Washington, D. C., Bureau of the Census, 1965), p. 47.

[c] Adapted from *Monthly Vital Statistics Reports, Annual Summary for the United States, 1965,* pp. 1, 6.

newly promoted assistant secretary to Humble Oil and Refining Co. who at the age of 33 had moved six times in eleven years. His nine-year-old son had never finished a single grade in the same school.[15] Within ten months, a young aspiring executive of Johnson Wax was moved from Wisconsin to New York and then to Chicago to become regional office manager, with his son going through kindergarten in three different schools as a consequence.[16] In 1966, Union Carbide moved 1,200 of its executives, doubling their mobility rate over the preceding five years.[17]

Youth need consistency in life patterns, including physical as well as social arrangements, to achieve adequate transition to the adult status. It is especially in the realm of *social* relationships that consistency plays an important role. There are informal associations such as the peer group, neighborhood, friendships, etc., and formal associations such as school, church, clubs, etc. These associations in effect constitute social control mechanisms and youth's exposure to and integration into them can often be of major stabilizing influence—provided that this exposure is consistent and continues over a long period of time. It appears how-

[15] "The Job: Corporate Nomads," *Time* (September 29, 1967), p. 56.
[16] *Ibid.*
[17] *Ibid.*

ever, that modern family living does not allow for much consistency and repose, and the high rate of geographic mobility often tends to tear apart human relationships.

The rate of spatial mobility of Americans today is remarkable: In the last decade one half of all families in the States have moved every five years. Some consequences of this unprecedented movement have been (1) increase in the number and variety of readjustments which a family must make; (2) radical loss of support of the family by neighborhood, friendship, and kinship primary groups; and (3) weakened discouragement of separation and divorce by these groups. Thus increased mobility may be seen as (1) precipitating more crises and adjustment difficulties within the family, (2) stripping the family of external supports at the very time of heightened stress, and (3) weakening the opposition to traditionally disapproved means of resolving difficulties, such as divorce.[18]

In a sense, quality has been replaced by quantity; i.e., the youngster may now meet more people than the youngster of previous generations, but the quality of the relationships tends to be ephemeral and superficial. Mobility does not allow sufficient time for people to cultivate human relationships and to actually get to *know* other people.

> . . . given extensive and rapid spatial and vertical mobility, almost all relationships tend to be shifting sand, lacking in dependability and security, providing no basis on which to build a life. The very impermanence of these manifold relationships heightens the need for *some* relationships which are dependable; which can be invariably counted on; which will not be weakened or destroyed by the incessant moving about of people. Such secure relationships can only be found, given the structural peculiarities for our society today, within the family.[19]

The implications of this high rate of mobility are serious. First, it involves physical removal from established patterns of interaction and may often involve the loss of "significant others," such as friends and adult models. Second, combined with the loss of affiliations is the loss of the informal control which these groups or persons exert over the young individual. It has been found that the absence of such control factors frequently results in delinquent behavior. Children of families subject to occasional or frequent moving experience as a consequence a superficiality in social relationships outside of their immediate family, and it is only natural that they should try to fall back on their own family group for companionship, security, and belonging. *But*, as has been emphasized earlier, the nuclear family has its own disturbing short-

---

[18] Hobart, *op. cit.*, p. 406.
[19] Hobart, *op. cit.*, p. 407.

comings, its structural features limiting the degree of security and companionship that can be given to the young. As a consequence, the youngster faces a serious dilemma: he oscillates between two equally frustrating systems, the ineffective family and the confusing outside world, failing to derive the necessary security from either.

Change from Status Ascription to Status Achievement

Another type of mobility that should be examined in this context is social mobility, sometimes also referred to as "vertical" mobility. An individual growing up in the traditional family rarely had to concern himself with the question of social mobility, since he "inherited" the status of his family. A teen-ager at the turn of the century was exposed to considerably less intergenerational mobility than his peer of the mid-20th century. It was neither a time of "status seeking" nor a time of confusion and identity problems for the young. Familistic norms and values mitigated to a large extent the problem of adolescent discontinuity and, at least, prevented it from becoming a collective power in its own right. A teen-ager knew his "place" in his family as well as in the larger society, the family serving as an undisputed placement agency. The placement function of the family precluded the young individual's effort to achieve a different status from that of his family. The confusion and anxiety that accompany contemporary youth's task of determining their own "place" and subsequent prestige in the social structure was thereby avoided. The ensuing clarity of status in the traditional setting provided a sound basis for personal identity. Today, the dynamics of social life have become accelerated, and intergenerational mobility is more common than at any other time in American history. The process of "finding one's place" is considerably less familistic and much more individualistic. Although there is no doubt that family background, especially if the family belongs to either extreme of the socioeconomic spectrum, is still an important influence on status achievement in the life of modern man, this influence has diminished, and status differences between parents and offsprings are more common than ever before. In many instances, it is difficult to speak of the modern family as a *status unit.* Many modern families consist of members whose social prestige differs from one to another, primarily because the members have different occupations and careers. In short, the criterion for social status in modern society is based more on occupational achievement than on family reputation.

In many modern urban families, individualism in norm and practice has increased to the point where active family membership has become optional. This is exemplified by the absence of any official deterrents imposed on those who prefer solitary and family-alienated existence. Gone are the days of the Puritans when in New England a special tax was levied on unmarried males. In contrast to this emphasis on familism, mid-20th-century society puts a premium on individual achievement. Some family sociologists go so far as to conclude that family obligations in a modern urban-industrial society tend to distract and detract from single-minded pursuit of highly prized personal success, be the goal scholarly, commercial, or professional.

A trend in American society which appears to have a powerful potential for further weakening the family is suggested by the phrase "proliferation of associations," "personality market," "individuation." These suggest a growing contrast with the recent past when most close relationships of people were traditionally defined ascribed relationships with mate and children, with other kin, with fellow parishioners. Today, more and more relationships are achieved. They are "cultivated" in school, at work, in voluntary associations; they are promoted through friends and professional or business contacts.

The significant point is that rather than being ascribed, and thus traditionally defined and delimited, relationships are now more often achieved and thus more idiosyncratic and potentially boundless. Herein lies their threat to the family, for they, like many other aspects of contemporary life, may readily infringe upon family claims, may alienate members from the family.[20]

The modern family's loss of the "placement function" and, thus, its abdication of the status ascription function, has direct pertinence to the problem of adolescence: the teen-ager cannot expect too much help from his home during the process of working out a status for and by himself. His parents' status has little finality in determining his status. While the family background is of minimal ascriptive effect, the achievement syndrome is of maximal importance. The absence of status certainty and the prospects of an uncharted journey toward some yet undefined and obscure adult status may create feelings that are aptly described by contemporary teen-agers when they say that they feel "confused" or "lost."

---

[20] Hobart, *op. cit.*, pp. 405–06.

Changes in Primary-Group Quality

The family is the primary group that is normally held responsible for passing on to the young the most basic human characteristics. In fact, so profound is the socialization experience in the family group that what can be conceptualized as "human nature" must be traced back to this early primary group association. Early socialization practices are not only profoundly impressive, but also evoke extremely sensitive reactions to the slightest variation in the style of socialization. Some modes of early socialization are more conducive to intensifying or complicating the adolescent experience than others. It is hypothesized that a child growing up in a family group that fulfills the criteria of a true primary group is going to be better equipped to deal with the problems of adolescent discontinuity than a child whose early experience has a more secondary group quality. Before pursuing this argument further, the question of what a primary group is must be clarified. The original and most authoritative definition of primary group includes the following:

> By primary groups I mean those characterized by intimate face-to-face association and co-operation. They are primary in several senses, but chiefly in that they are fundamental in forming the social nature and ideals of the individual. The result of intimate association, psychologically, is a certain fusion of individualities in a common whole, so that one's very self, for many purposes at least, is the common life and purpose of the group. Perhaps the simplest way of describing this wholeness is by saying that it is a "we"; it involves the sort of sympathy and mutual identification for which "we" is the natural expression. One lives in the feeling of the whole and finds the chief aim of his will in that feeling.

> It is not to be supposed that the unity of the primary group is one of mere harmony and love. It is always a differentiated and usually a competitive unity, admitting of self-assertion and various appropriative passions; but these passions are socialized by sympathy, and come, or tend to come, under the discipline of a common spirit. The individual will be ambitious, but the chief object of his ambition will be some desired place in the thought of the others, and he will feel allegiance to common standards of service and fair play. So the boy will dispute with his fellows a place on the team, but above such disputes will place the common glory of his class and school.

> The most important spheres of this intimate association and co-operation—though by no means the only ones—are the family, the play-group of children, and the neighborhood or community group

of elders. These are practically universal, belonging to all times and all stages of development; and are accordingly a chief basis of what is universal in human nature and human ideals.[21]

The definition of secondary groups would consist of elements in sharp contrast to the primary group—impermanence, casualness of contact, fewer ties of deep sentiment among the members, and a lesser degree of derivation of basic values from the group's norms, standards, and goals. It must be remembered that in reality groups do not come neatly divided into either primary or secondary types.[22] Actually, social reality presents us with a continuum, the poles of which we define as primariness and secondariness of group quality. Groups differ from one another not categorically, but in the *degree* to which the interacting behavior of the participants reflects primariness.

Has the American family shifted along the continuum of primary–secondary group relations? In other words, is the nuclear family less primary than the traditional family? To accurately answer this question, it is helpful to examine specific elements of the criteria of primariness. Examination of the value orientation of contemporary youth seems to reveal that values, often basic ones, are sometimes derived from nonfamily sources as often as from the family group. Modern socialization patterns appear to facilitate this trend:

> Children have more and more been turned over to schools, and, in some instances, nursery schools and Sunday schools, for a major portion of their socialization, as parents occupy themselves with other activities. More important than the time turned over to such institutional socialization of children is the responsibility that parents more than willingly relinquish or do not recognize as theirs. There appears to be little concern in America today that the shaping of a human life, a human personality, a future of happiness or hell, which is best accomplished in the primary group, is turned over even earlier and for longer periods to secondary, impersonal, social agencies. In these agencies children can only be "handled" and manipulated in groups, rather than cared for as individuals.

> Leisure time is used by some to cultivate companionship with wife and children. But for many it appears that what time is spent together is seldom spent primarily in *being* together, but rather in *doing* simultaneously: watching TV, going someplace, being entertained.[23]

[21] Charles H. Cooley, *op. cit.*, pp. 23–24.

[22] Definitions such as "primary" or "secondary" are ideal-type definitions, i.e., they are useful—yet arbitrary—typologies. They are useful for tracing trends, comparing different systems, and in facilitating communication. Ideal-type concepts are instrumental in many social analyses and can be called *heuristic* in nature.

[23] Hobart, *op. cit.*, p. 408.

It is interesting to note that teen-agers themselves complain that their parents fail to give them guidance and direction and that their parents are too permissive. It seems that they themselves recognize their need for more authoritative guidance by their elders. A national probability sample found that teen-agers ascribe primary responsibility for excessive teen-age drinking, the use of "goofballs," "dope," etc., to their parents' failure to wield enough authority.[24] This attitude seems to illustrate the teen-agers' dissatisfaction with modern home *anomie*—normlessness—which allows them a high degree of individual freedom but also creates excessive uncertainty and confusion. *Anomie* and confusion of standards are not characteristic of a primary-group setting. A group that is truly "primary" offers firm rules and values that are of insuperable aid in the process of stabilizing the personality of its members.

Another tenet from Cooley's definition is: ". . . they [primary groups] are fundamental in forming the social nature and ideals of the individual."[25] Does the modern family influence the development of the "social nature" as much as the traditional family did? Probably not, because the influence of several other institutions, notably the school, has taken over part—in many instances the major part—of the task of socializing the young. In addition, the mass media have penetrated into every home, and TV, radio, and the press are in serious competition with parental influence. As a rule, the parents surrender willingly and let other agencies take over the job of socializing the young. Nurseries, kindergartens, schools, churches, and the various media of entertainment encounter little resistance on the part of the parents. The parents willingly surrender a territory that means fatiguing work, time consumption, and often frustration for them. TV in particular has become a convenient baby-sitting device, and it has been said that the TV set has changed the family circle to a semicircle, the truncating line being the attention-holding screen.

Cooley's definition also includes the tenet that "a certain fusion of individualities in a common whole exists, so that one's very self, for many purposes at least, is the common life and purpose of the group."[26] Again, it appears that common goals have given way to individual goals. The modern youngster lives in a secular age that no longer respects the family as being "sacred" *per se*. The individual is no longer willing to subordinate his goals and aspirations. The family has become a *means* for the individual, rather than an end in itself.

---

[24] Leonard Gross, "America's Mood Today," *Look* (June 29, 1965), p. 21.
[25] Cooley, *op. cit.*, p. 23.
[26] *Ibid.*

This definitely does not mean that the average family of today is of secondary-group quality. All that can be said is that there has been a *shift on the continuum* toward more secondariness of group qualities. As a consequence, the family plays a modified role in the process of extending identity and belonging to the young members. The proliferation of secondary-group affiliations and the impact of the mass media are to some extent replacing a major traditional function of the family, the socialization function. It seems that both the family as well as the secondary influences are rendering a service that does not quite meet modern needs. As was mentioned, the result is an ambivalent situation: the youngster turns constantly to the family for identity and warmth, but is confronted with the modern family's ineffectiveness in stabilizing personality and is thus driven back to the associational proliferation with its conflicting and piecemeal socialization. It seems that the youth of today are helplessly suspended between familial ineffectualness and a confusing proliferation of secondary associations.

Summary

The structural changes of the family have resulted in a rearrangement of the patterns of interaction and reaction. The new patterns promote discontinuity between child and adult status. A number of adolescence-generating difficulties, innate in the nuclear structure, were discussed: (1) The number of potential adult models is severely limited. (2) Playmates and peer friends, extraneous to the family system, tend to form adolescent subcultures. (3) Adult work and responsibilities are largely invisible to youth. (4) Guidance and authority increasingly are transferred from the family to impersonal secondary institutions. (5) The modern family is limited in meeting basic personality needs of belonging and security. (6) Ascription of status to the young by the family as a unit has declined, and status has to be achieved by the individual in a more or less solitary fashion. (7) Various tenets of primary-group quality have declined, particularly the "we" feeling among the members of the nuclear family and the profound value indoctrination by the family as a unit.

A final word. The above discussion should not be interpreted as a nostalgic view of a bygone familistic era. The purpose of this chapter is not to convey sentiments of regret that the extended family has been replaced by the nuclear family. This would be fruitless and unduly subjective. Changes are continual in the nature of things, and every change has many repercussions. Some aspects of the multiple consequences of a change may be socially acceptable and appear constructive, others may be unacceptable and appear destructive. To evaluate a structural change on the basis of a few arbitrarily selected consequences would result in an incomplete, biased, and unrealistic picture. It is true that in the above discussion of the nuclear family, *aspects were selected that appear to promote adolescence,* and that, viewed from most angles, prove to be dysfunctional for literally everyone involved. But these adolescence-generating consequences do not exhaust all the consequences which have emanated from the structural change of the family, i.e., the change from the traditional to the nuclear family. One could, for example, point to many liberating effects which this change has brought about. It has liberated creative activities from the bondage of familistic servitude and opened up the personality market for freer unfolding of talent, aptitude, and individualistic choice. In short, one must not lose sight of the general principle that any change brings about a host of reactions. Some may be judged functional and some dysfunctional.

effects of rapid social change: intergenerational conflict

Conflicting Norms Between Generations

Conflict between the older and the younger generations may be counted as a perennial force in the history of man. The social dynamics of every society undergoing cultural and social change exhibit some degree of tension between the generations. In a rapidly changing society, the established and respected norm of one generation may be obsolete and unacceptable to the next. The older generation may greet innovations with various opinions and emotions ranging from caution and reservation to objection and hostility. Nostalgia and praise concerning the "good old days" can be discovered universally as the reactions of elders to changing and unfamiliar behavior patterns. The older generation's lack of familiarity with and acceptance of new styles and expressions are frequently reflected in the tendency to label innovations as "weird," "immoral," "unnatural," "subversive," etc. These epithets, describing and reprimanding the younger generation, can be found in the diaries of virtually all eras. Exceptions to this rule would probably be limited to a few simple-structured tribal societies in an isolated environment where social change is paced almost imperceptibly. In most other societies sociocultural change is a perceptible and continuous process.

The tempo of sociocultural change varies thus from society to society and can be measured on a continuum ranging from near-stagnancy and slow social dynamics to revolutionary reorganization of the social structure and cultural values. One way of classifying societies by their internal dynamics is in terms of the folk-urban continuum, referring to slow-changing and usually rural folk societies at one end and to dynamic urban-industrial societies at the other end.[1]

Tempo of change is directly correlated with imbalance of attitudes, perceptions, and behavior patterns between the generations. This means that the faster a society changes, the wider the psychological distance between the older and the younger generations. In a nearly unchanging society, as, for example, in some of the recently discovered tribes on New Guinea, it was observed that the young behave completely in accordance with the norms and the goals of the older generation and that the sociocultural fabric of the tribal society does not change from one generation to the next. In contrast, in a dynamic society undergoing rapid social change one would find the young clashing with the older generation, whose norms and goals have become unacceptable and/or obsolete.

Modern American society is a prime example of such a rapidly changing social system, exhibiting a comparatively fast pace of sociocultural change and a noticeable degree of conflict between the generations. The turnover of technological and social innovations is rapid enough to create a milieu for each new generation that is notably different from that of the preceding generation, thus inviting adults to perceive youth as "rebellious" and youth to perceive adults as "old-fashioned." American life shows frequent instances of friction and misunderstanding between the generations that are intense enough to resemble the encounter and the clash between different cultures.

The explanation for the unusual amount of parent–youth conflict in modern Western society can be summed up by a number of specific and interrelated propositions:

(1) Each generation learns the culture early, and as age progresses there is greater difficulty in changing views of right and wrong.

(2) The cultural content in American society is changing rapidly.

(3) The culture learned by the parental generation was much different than that learned by the offspring, insofar as the adolescent learns from peers and from adults who are more current in their thinking.

(4) Therefore there is a culture conflict experienced by parents and their offspring.[2]

---

[1] Robert Redfield, "The Folk Society," *American Journal of Sociology*, Vol. 52 (May, 1947), pp. 293–309.

[2] Kingsley Davis, "The Sociology of Parent-Youth Conflict," *American Sociological Review*, Vol. 5 (August, 1940), pp. 523–536.

Competing Authorities: Parents vs. Experts

The third proposition in the above outline emphasizes that ". . . the adolescent learns from . . . adults who are more current in their thinking," suggesting that they are more current *than parents*. This is a circumstance growing out of the dynamics of the urban-industrial society, which creates an awkward and conflict-producing situation: on one hand, parents are endowed with the privilege and the obligation of introducing children to society, of proceeding with the necessary training, of exerting the necessary control to make the child conform to the demands of the culture. On the other hand, however, parents suffer from cultural lag that leaves them constantly a few paces behind in knowledge and insight concerning many vital areas of modern life. Modern science has changed, modified, and added a multitude of insights in all branches of scientific knowledge, be this chemistry, biology, or the social sciences. The future in a modern urban-industrial society calls for constant reorientation that parents would find difficult to introduce. The vastly changed nature of life in the future includes necessities for which preparation can be made only by experts, scientifically trained personnel, and not by the cultural-lag-afflicted parents. Psychologist Gordon W. Allport called attention to a number of future necessities that largely escape the awareness of contemporary parents. These imperatives for which parents are not prepared and do not prepare include: (1) An increasing domination of life by science, technology, and automation. (2) The impossibility of living any longer in the state of condescension toward colored peoples in the world and the necessity of radical revision of centuries of discrimination and segregation. (3) The immense problems that the current population explosion is bringing about—the magnitude of which can hardly be exaggerated. (4) A profoundly revised view of international relations that must include an understanding of cultural relativism and allow for the acceptance of some form of global confederation to forestall the threat of thermonuclear war. (5) A planetary, maybe even interplanetary, world view.[3]

Even the tools of science, mathematics, for example, have undergone significant alterations. Children are now in a position to explain to their parents the meaning of "new math." In some instances official effort has been made to assist parents in keeping up, or catching, up, with their better-informed offspring. For example, in Phoenix, Arizona, school officials called the parents' attention to a program available under the title "Facts and Fiction About Modern Math—Something Parents Should

---

[3] Gordon W. Allport, "Values and Our Youth," *Teachers College Record*, Vol. 63 (December, 1961), pp. 211–219.

Know." The timely need for the program was explained by the State Board of Education on the basis of the imminent adoption of new mathematics textbooks in the elementary school.

In spite of such examples of parental effort, it is not probable that parents will be able to keep up with their children in all areas of learning. Our modern era is accumulating knowledge at too fast a rate and is preventing parents from carrying out a significant portion of their traditional function of instructing and informing the offspring. Just as in any other sector of the urban-industrial society, the process of teaching and training has become a specialization that is no longer the prerogative of the parents but has been divided up within the complex division of labor and become the responsibility of "experts."

> . . . the world in which we live and the probable world of tomorrow are so different and likely to be so different that the problems and challenges facing the present generation of teen-agers are unique in many respects.
>
> Today's younger generation has grown up in the midst of the greatest scientific breakthrough in history, one which simultaneously shrank and extended the ordinary man's world almost beyond recognition. When we consider that some 90% of the research scientists who have ever lived are still alive today, and that about half the research and development money spent in all the history of the United States was spent in the last eight years, we can be sure that this technological acceleration is by no means at an end. These expenditures are going to continue going up, with increasing effects on our daily lives. The great question is: What kind of effects?[4]

The transferral of the information function has rendered parents relatively helpless and increasingly poorly informed. It is normally impossible for parents to be specialists in more than one or a few fields of knowledge and skill. Children and teen-agers must therefore seek instruction and advice from specialists and experts outside of their families. Through schooling, modern youth has access to sources of the most recent discoveries in nearly all branches of science and can acquire insights and up-to-date information that ordinarily never reach the parents. The layman parent is preoccupied with making a living and affording his children an education. Consequently, he learns about the latest developments and discoveries—often inadequately and incompletely— only via secondary channels, such as popular magazines, newspapers, radio, and TV. As a novelty in human history, he is now also instructed by his children.

---

[4] Blaine R. Porter, "American Teen-Agers of the 1960's—Our Despair Or Hope?," *Journal of Marriage and the Family,* Vol. 27 (May, 1965), p. 139.

The socialization functions of the parents are of course not limited to mere factual instruction and scientific information, but include such aspects as ethical guidance, religious indoctrination, and practical advice in everyday activities. Yet the failure and the often conspicuous inability of parents to offer the latest scientific knowledge and understanding tend to have a generalizing effect on the child, inducing him to disregard other aspects of parental authority and competence. Evidence of incompetence in one area tempts children to suspect incompetence in other areas also and often makes them doubt the ability of parents to introduce them to the adult world in general. This reluctance on the part of the children to accept the traditional socialization authority of the parents has resulted in a conflict situation in which parents hold legal authority over the young but often exhibit insufficient ability to carry out the necessary socialization responsibility. It is the extra-familial "experts" who are doing a substantial part of the rearing and instructing. The modern controversy of *in loco parentis* testifies to the fact of increasing transfer of the socialization function and the accompanying authority to other institutions. In a sense, the modern teacher with his expanded socialization functions that include counseling and advising (in matters of personal problems, sex, vocational plans, etc.) has unintentionally promoted parental obsolescence by placing parents in the role of laymen, in which they can afford little assistance to and authority over the young.

Modern adolescents show intense resentment when put in a situation where parents attempt to wield authority over them when they feel that parents are not qualified to do so. Teen-agers insist on being independent decision-makers in areas which previously were under parental sovereignty. For example, the decision concerning the choice of occupational career of the youngster was traditionally up to the parents or to the family as a unit. The mid-20th-century mood of the American teen-ager was revealed by a nationwide survey that indicated that about 60% of contemporary teen-agers think that parents seldom have the right to make this decision for the youngster.[5]

Parenthood: The Last Stand of the Amateur

The type of teen-age assessment of parental authority as illustrated above is in support of some sociologists' contention that the conventional family customs have to a significant degree become "dysfunctional" in

[5] H. H. Remmers and D. H. Radler, *The American Teenager* (New York, The Bobbs-Merrill Co., 1957), p. 89.

the modern urban-industrial environment.[6] Controversial sociological criticism has declared as dysfunctional the arrangement whereby young people owe subordination and emotional servitude to a set of adults with whom they may have nothing in common except the accident of biological relatedness. According to sociologists, the type of authority that is exerted merely on grounds of biological progenitorship or social position can be defined as irrational, while authority based on ability and not merely on position can be defined as rational. There are enough indications to show that the younger generation is in favor of rational authority when parents are concerned. Insistence on irrational authority elicits youth's resentment, which is often reflected in adolescent behavior patterns.

Another argument that will probably increasingly affect the traditional privilege of uncontrolled reproduction by married couples deals with the threatening expansion of the world population. A number of social scientists believe that the time has come when society should reconsider the privilege of uncontrolled reproduction and put into effect regulations with the purpose of achieving a more narrow definition for the marital reproduction privilege. Such regulations are considered necessary because otherwise the continuation of the current population increase will in the long run literally over-crowd the earth. Sociologist Kingsley Davis, director of international population and urban research at the University of California, points to a number of possible checks on parenthood by economic sanctions and encouragement of older age at marriage. Among specific measures in the future: Charging high fees for marriage licenses; levying a "child tax"; ceasing higher taxation of single persons over married persons; abolishing tax exemptions for children; legalizing sterilization and abortion.[7] Sociologists have been joined on this issue by scientists of other disciplines. Among them is H. Bentley Glass, vice president and professor of biology at the State University of New York, who believes—and more or less recommends—that in the

---

[6] See a representative statement of this type by family sociologist Barrington Moore, "Thoughts on the Future of the Family," in Maurice R. Stein, Arthur J. Vidich, and Daniel M. White (eds.), *Identity and Anxiety* (Glencoe, Ill., The Free Press, 1960).

[7] Kingsley Davis, "Population Policy: Will Current Programs Succeed?" *Science*, Vol. 158 (November 10, 1967), p. 738. A number of other sociologists have made statements that are basically in agreement with Kingsley Davis' concern and have expressed their opinion at the conference on Behavioral Sciences and Family Planning, held in June 1967 at Bethesda, Maryland. Among those making public statements were: Michael Young, Ronald Freeman, Bernard Berelson, Philip Hauser, Orville Brim, Jr., Brewster Smith, Reuben Hill, George M. Foster, Everett Rogers, Nicholas Demerath, and others. See: "Meetings: Behavioral Sciences and Family Planning," *Science*, Vol. 158 (November 3, 1967), pp. 677–82.

future parenthood will be allowed only after a married couple obtains a specific "child license."[8] The argument that is advanced warns that further unchecked population increase will reduce living standard and life chances for everyone. Glass and a number of demographers hold that the conventional view of parenthood as an *asset* to society needs drastic reorientation. According to these experts in biology and demography, parenthood has become a *liability* to society and is endangering societal survival. Regardless of the different premises, both these social and biological scientists agree that parenthood as it has been practiced traditionally is obsolete and dysfunctional.

The proposition of controlled parenthood embodies two conflicting considerations. On one side, there is the desire to preserve individual freedom and privacy in a most vital and private sector of human behavior. On the other side, the American public is daily confronted with the ill effect of unqualified and truly "amateur" parenthood. Some of these negative effects have been serious enough to cause concern among high federal officials who see a need for more adequate socialization of America's children.

> A federal official thinks the time may have come for society to provide "institutional substitutes for parents" who can't, or won't, provide an adequate family life for youngsters.
>
> The suggestion comes from James W. Symington, executive director of the President's Committee on Juvenile Delinquency and son of the veteran senator from Missouri.
>
> He said in an interview that crumbling family ties play an important role in creating youthful crime, not only in slums but in the affluent neighborhoods of suburbia as well.
>
> Symington proposes that society, through the combined efforts of public and private agencies, set out to provide youngsters with the leadership, challenges, understanding and recognition that may be lacking at home.
>
> The idea is new, so Symington has no detailed plan on how this would be done.
>
> Programs such as the Neighborhood Youth Corps can help accomplish the purpose among the poor, he said, but children of the middle and upper class present "a more difficult challenge." He believes that school is the logical place to reach them.
>
> "It is a vexing challenge for a hands-off democratic society to have to produce institutional substitutes for parents," Symington said.

---

[8] Los Angeles Times Service (June 24, 1964); AP Report (Atlantic City, N.J., Feb. 13, 1967).

"But, when parents fail to give the child everything he needs psychologically as well as materially for balance and direction, then he must get it somewhere else."[9]

A brief discussion should be added concerning the idea of alternative structures for conventional child-rearing in the family. Raising children in institutional family substitutes has been a long-standing research topic of sociologists and psychologists. It has been repeatedly suggested that institutional raising is likely to have detrimental effects on children's personalities. Research has shown that among young children, the deprivation of maternal care has nearly always resulted in the retardation of physical, mental, and social growth.[10] Occasionally, the retardation has been found to be irremedial. Recent observations in a large family-substitute institution seem to support the hypothesis that such institutions fall short of giving children the type of security and maturity that they would acquire through the socialization process in the normal family settings. The institutional environment usually fails to meet certain basic needs of the children, such as the need for personal attention, physical contact, touch, and caress. Most institutions are understaffed and cannot give sufficient individual attention to each child. Also, the institutional routine consists of work shifts for the personnel, and it is customary that the child's social contact with adults is divided into eight-hour shifts, thereby breaking continuity and consistency with adult models. One counselor wakes the child in the morning, another puts him to bed at night, a third appears if he wakes up during the night, and the following morning he may see a fourth face because it is the first counselor's day off.

At Junior Village, Washington, D. C., a home for children without a parental home, there is only one adult for as many as 28 children in a cottage.[11] Observers have noticed that some children actually regress in their achievements while living in the Village. For example, in one case a small boy was beginning to walk when he entered, but ceased walking after his admission, while in another case, a little girl was beginning

---

[9] UPI Report (Washington, D.C., Oct. 19, 1965).

[10] Among numerous pertinent studies and research findings supporting this assumption see: Lauretta Bender, "There Is No Substitute For Family Life," *Child Study*, Vol. 23, (Winter, 1945–1946), pp. 74–78; Lauretta Bender and H. Yarnell, "An Observation Nursery," *American Journal of Psychiatry*, Vol. 97 (March, 1941), pp. 1158–1174; William Goldfarb, "The Effects of Early Institutional Care on Adolescent Personality," *The Journal of Experimental Education*, Vol. 12 (December, 1943), pp. 106–129; Arnold Gesell and Catherine Amatruda, *Developmental Diagnosis* (New York, Hoeber, 1947); John Bowlby, *Maternal Care and Mental Health* (Geneva, World Health Organization, 1951).

[11] J. W. Anderson, "A Special Hell For Children In Washington," *Harper's* (November, 1965), pp. 51–56.

to talk in sentences, but soon reduced her linguistic activities to only single words. This type of regression was brought on by the children's isolation, which tends to be greater in the institution than in the most disorganized family, and occurs in spite of the physical crowdedness of the Village. If a child passes his early years without having experienced affection, he may become impervious to it later. Simultaneously, he becomes impervious to guilt as well. Large institutions for children with an anonymous atmosphere are a frequent source of the sociopathic personality.

Charles H. Cooley attempted to understand the nature of the elements that add up to create what is commonly called "human nature" and found that they consist of a synthesis of two major processes: (1) the individual's innate needs and drives, and (2) the primary group experience.[12] From this synthesis spring the universal traits and values which are considered as typically human. This explanation does not ignore the fact that cultural relativism does exist, but ranks it secondary in influence on the formation of human nature. Culturally relative forces enter later in the life experiences of the child, after the primary-group experience has laid the basis for "humanness." It follows logically that as a consequence of the similar family-group experience, man everywhere exhibits some common traits. The primary-group quality of the family inculcates a sense of cooperation with others, a sense of loyalty to other humans, an understanding of affection and kindness. No human could be raised and could survive without experiencing some expressions of such qualities. This experience creates the basic ability for future understanding and cooperation with fellow men in general. In short, life in the primary-group setting of the family gives rise to social ideals and sentiments that are universal and a basic part of human nature.

Under ideal conditions, it is possible to raise healthy personalities in institutional homes. These conditions should include, first of all, more adequate staffing, allowing one adult for every four to six children. Second, the substitute mothers and/or fathers should be with the children 24 hours, or, at least, from morning to bedtime to provide continuity of care and intimacy. However, such conditions have seldom been met in institutional settings.

In conclusion, it is doubtful that the traditional family will be replaced on a large scale by new institutional child-rearing or that the concept of traditional parenthood will be changed in the near future. This means that parenthood continues to be considered the "natural right" of married couples and that regulations, censorship, or sanction systems that would aim at abrogating this "right" are doomed to fail in

---

[12] Charles H. Cooley, *Social Organization* (New York, Scribner's, 1915), pp. 23*ff*.

the face of the traditional American ethos. The continuance of this "natural right" in the near future will probably remain relatively unaffected by the voices of concerned social and biological scientists who are recommending that qualifications and limitations be placed on parenthood. While the biologists' argument deals primarily with the presumably imminent demographic complications, such as the consequences of the population "explosion," the sociologists' argument focuses on problems of interpersonal relationships caused by amateur and unqualified parents. It has been hypothesized that it is precisely this sociological argument that connects the problem of unqualified parenthood with the problem of adolescence. The majority of parents are, in a sense, unlicensed laymen and amateurs, subject to cultural lag, thus limited in the quantity and quality of information they can pass on to their children. On the other side, however, they are still entrusted with official authority over the young and by tradition expect their children to show affection and subservience. Yet, because of rapid social and technological change, the younger generation's life experiences call for reactions and adjustments that are significantly different from those of their elders, thus challenging the traditional parental functions of authoritative counseling, advising, and decision-making. Teen-agers may find it disappointing to turn to their parents for advice concerning educational problems and occupational plans, because parents may be lacking in proper information. Yet, this intellectual shortcoming does not necessarily exhaust the entire functionality in respect to the personality development of the children. But children and teen-agers often find it difficult to make the distinction between emotional maturity and intellectual acuity—a distinction that must often be drawn between parents on one side and "experts" on the other. Children are prone to generalize their parents' lack of knowledge in intellectual matters to emotional and decision-making matters. As a result, a conflict situation may arise: if parents, in spite of their cultural lag, *insist* on continuance of their traditional role and on exertion of their authority—authority that has by definition become "irrational"—a number of dysfunctional consequences will develop. Among the consequences are intergenerational friction and intensification of adolescent rebellion and confusion.

Parental Reaction I: Permissiveness and Acquiescence

Many parents have become aware of their cultural-lag position and are willing to remedy this condition. An expression of their concern and willingness to keep communicating with their teen-age children is evidenced by the wave of self-effacing literature that can be described as a "how-to-deal-with-parents" or "parents-are-problems" campaign. Personally and through the mass media, some parents have shown their eagerness to learn from, adjust to, and listen to teen-agers. This desire is manifested in a new style of intrafamilial interaction where the flow of information and instruction is reversed to a surprising degree and where teen-agers are in a position to instruct parents about the latest scientific discoveries and happenings. To some degree, the status of parent has unabashedly become a social problem, and parents are often apologetic about being parents. Examples of the "educational" literature of teen-agers concerning the "up-bringing" of their parents can be found in volumes or articles with such titles as, "Why Parents Act the Way they Do"[13] or *How to Deal with Parents and Other Problems.*[14] The helplessness and cultural-lag condition of the parents have also been appraised in popular teen-age songs, advising more seriously than facetiously that teen-agers should try to understand parents in spite of all the "foolish things they are doing," since they are at a difficult stage in life and need youth's understanding and forgiveness. Another source of indications that the socialization process has undergone considerable reversal are personal interviews with teen-agers. Typical opinions of teen-agers concerning the communication gap between parents and youth include the statement of a 17-year-old girl who thought that "parents have to want to listen before the teen-agers can tell them anything. There must be cooperation before there can be communication. Life is very different for a teen-ager now than it was for them. Parents must bridge the gap by thinking as a teen-ager, making themselves available and understanding."[15] Such literary, popular, and personal expressions reflect the fact that the direction of understanding and instruction has been reversed to a notable degree and that it now proceeds *from adolescent to adult*.

This modification of the traditional socialization process could evolve only because the American ethos includes emphasis on fairness and equality regardless of social status—or age level. Lack of *a priori* respect or exaltation of old age is characteristic of American life and allows for a situation where parents are willing to learn from their children and even try to adjust to them. It is primarily this basic attitude that underlies the attempt of many American parents to reduce intergenerational conflict and misunderstandings. They seem to be sincerely willing to prepare themselves for the critical time when their offspring

---

[13] Maxine Davis, *Sex And The Adolescent* (New York, Permabook, 1958).

[14] Ernest G. Osborne, *How To Deal With Parents and Other Problems* (New York, Grosset and Dunlap, 1962).

[15] UPI Report (New York, November 3, 1965).

will enter adolescence. Innumerable articles, books, conferences, and PTA meetings have been vying with one another for the attention of the parents, trying to educate them for their children and teen-agers. Some representative examples illustrating parental self-scrutiny include such works as "Parents Grow Too."[16] "The Dilemma of Parents"[17] and "Widening Horizons in Parent Education,"[18] etc.

Other indications of the parental effort to establish *rapprochement* with teen-agers include a number of adaptations of customs, fashions, and modes of behavior to suit teen-age styles. The tastes of American teen-agers have influenced the styles of clothes, automobiles, recreation, plus a vast range of other public features. In various institutions, adults have been promoting teen styles to win and retain the adolescents' loyalty. Teen innovations can even be observed in religious institutions. In some instances, services have been patterned according to teen-age tastes, employing the type of music, the style of prayer, and even the kind of dance that is preferred by teen-agers. Folk singers have been used in worship services, a jazz Mass was performed in Los Angeles, a church in Boston initiated dancing in the aisles as a combo accompanied a litany that went "Praise His name with rock 'n' roll. . . . " In 1967, even the Roman Catholic Church modernized its rules concerning liturgy and religious music. Pope Paul VI issued a document that marked a revolution in the Church's 2,000-year-old sacred music tradition, opening the way for possible use of blues, "beat" rhythms, spirituals, and jazz in religious services.[19] The teen-age invasion of liturgy is surprising, since churches have usually been the strongholds of convention and tradition. In addition, secular institutions, more than religious institutions, have exhibited acculturation to teen-age tastes and styles.

The philosophical basis on which adults attempt *rapprochement* with the youth culture consists of at least three principles: *democracy, communication,* and *information*. Most adult-initiated programs purporting to bring about understanding between the generations are based, explicitly or implicitly, on these three key concepts. The concept of democracy is applied to remind parents to consider teen-agers as equals. The emphasis on communication is meant to encourage parents to keep in touch with the teen-agers and to diligently work out misunderstandings. The emphasis on information refers to the need of parents to remedy their knowledge gap and to acquire up-to-date information in as

---

[16] Ernest G. Osborne, "Parents Grow Too," *Parents' Magazine*, Vol. 20 (June, 1945), pp. 31*ff.*

[17] Remmers and Radler, *op. cit.*, Chapter IV.

[18] Ernest G. Osborne, "Widening Horizons In Parent Education," *Teachers College Record*, Vol. 41 (October, 1939), pp. 25–33.

[19] AP Report (Vatican City, March 8, 1967).

many vital areas of life as possible. As an adjunct to the concept of information, it is suggested that parents become familiar with basic principles of child and adolescent psychology and sociology in order to be better prepared to deal with intergenerational conflict.

Parental Reaction II: Reassertion of Traditional Authority

The permissive response of parents, and adults in general, to the teenagers' invasion of public life and important social institutions is not unanimous. A number of influential writers and public figures have expressed their concern about and frank opposition to the spreading influence of adolescent tastes and behavior patterns.[20] Although it is too early to make a conclusive statement, it seems that there is some evidence that the general public is aware of these reasserting voices and is gradually modifying its permissive attitude toward teen-agers and children.

Besides whatever influence individual spokesmen may contribute to the change toward stricter child-rearing practices, there is the parents' negative reaction to their failure to achieve recognizable success in their pursuit of *democratic, communicative,* and *informative* ideals with

---

[20] The development of stricter discipline in child-rearing practices has been forecast by such popular writers as Grace and Fred M. Hechinger, *Teen-Age Tyranny* (New York, William Morrow & Co., 1963); and by psychiatrist Graham B. Blaine, Jr., *Youth and the Hazards of Affluence* (New York, Harper and Row, 1965), see especially p. 24.

A comprehensive and involved sociological investigation into the fluctuating child-rearing practices in the United States has been completed by Urie Bronfenbrenner, "Socialization and Social Class Through Time and Space," in Eleanor E. Maccoby *et. al.* (eds.), *Readings in Social Psychology* (New York, Holt, Rinehart, and Winston, 1958). It was found that child-rearing practices vary among social classes and are likely to change most quickly in those segments of society which have closest access and are most receptive to the agencies of change, e.g., mass media, clinics, physicians, counselors, books, etc. According to this finding, the middle-class parents are leading the fluctuating modes and standards of child rearing, while lower-class and rural families lag behind. Evaluation of various sociological researches led Bronfenbrenner to conclude that before World War II, working-class mothers were markedly more permissive than those of the middle class. After World War II, middle-class mothers developed more permissive, acceptant, and equalitarian attitudes, while working-class mothers gradually assumed a stricter and more disciplinary child-rearing role.

If this fluctuating rhythm continues, and there is recent evidence that it will, it can be expected that another reversal of attitudes is imminent, and that middle-class parents will revert to stricter and more demanding attitudes.

which they hoped to bridge the gap between the older and the younger generations. This failure has resulted in disappointment and some degree of confusion among adults. It is therefore not surprising to observe a changing mood among American parents, a tendency to recall the "traditional rights," and a parental demand for new respect from adolescents. Perhaps parents have come to recognize or to feel that the notion of *equality* between parents and children is unrealistic and merely an ideological Utopia not applicable in daily life.

By necessity, parents and adults have always been and probably always will remain the general *socializers*, with the children as the *socializees*. This universal practice is necessitated by the fact that children are born unsocialized and culturally "unprogramed," thus requiring socialization through adult members of the social system. It would be totally unrealistic to believe that the young in the society always submit willingly and in appropriate manner to the manifold enculturation pressures exerted by their elders. The adult society determines the standards of "right" and "wrong" conduct, and it is virtually impossible to discuss and explain the societal codes to the young in every situation of intergenerational controversy. Rather, it is frequently necessary to over- and out-rule the offspring without giving them an "equal" opportunity. For example, children are not given a choice when a decision is made about going to school or not going to school, or about playing with toys or with fire, etc. If necessary, adults will *coerce* children to comply with the standards and regulations of the society. Thus, by definition the socialization process implies inequality.

Parents may also have come to feel that a similarly unrealistic attitude underlies the assumption that *communication* is a solution to the intergenerational conflicts and differences. It has been found that the time required to resolve basic conflicts and differences between the generations exceeds the time resource of most parents. Moreover, it is doubtful whether intellectual communication can resolve basic *emotional* differences and preferences. It may be possible to establish an intellectual understanding of certain differences in tastes or convictions and still not arrive at any degree of *rapprochement* between the parties.

Finally, the vast majority of parents may have found it impossible to keep abreast of their children's advanced scientific knowledge and information. To keep up with well-informed pupils would require that parents literally go to school with their offspring, listen to the same lectures, study the same lessons, and read the same up-to-date books and research reports. Few parents can afford such synchronization of their offspring's educational process with their own academic efforts.

It seems that as a reaction to the failure of the parental campaign to "promote equality," to "communicate," and to "be informed," parents are gradually expressing a more militant mood and renewed insistence on their authority. ". . . the parent will not 'catch up' with the child's point of view because he is supposed to dominate rather than follow."[21] There are already a few indications in the current literature suggesting the advent of new qualities in the parent-youth confrontation. Teen-agers are increasingly viewed as "tyrants" who have forced immaturity on public life, and realignment of the socialization patterns to traditional norms is advocated. Some of the most outspoken advocates of this new trend are Fred M. and Grace Hechinger, the authors of *Teen-Age Tyranny*.[22] Fred M. Hechinger, education editor for the *New York Times*, and his wife commence with the firm assumption that mid-20th-century American society is dominated by teen-agers and their tastes, fads, and immaturity. The authors believe further that "the world can belong to adults again" if adults firmly decide to wrest it from the control of teen-agers—who have won it by default. The treatise holds out hope of "emancipation" for adults if only they practice more decisiveness and fortitude. The authors emphatically do not believe that adolescents know best or should be left in charge of their own lives, much less in control of the lives of any adults they can persuade or intimidate. It has been observed that American civilization tends to overrate and over-respect its teen-agers because of its deep-seated adoration of youth. It is feared by a number of critics that, as a result, teen-age influence has permeated the daily and public life of adults, imposing teen-age standards of thought, culture, and goals. It is this adolescence-expanding process that has caused great concern among critical observers and has led them to call "corruption of adulthood" a "creeping disease." This "disease" is symptomized by the fashioning of immature goals in music, art, and literature, the replacement of adult English with the limited vocabulary of the teen culture, the teen invasion of newspapers, TV, and movies, and the commercial exploitation of these trends. Many commercial pursuits are noteworthy because they set off chain reactions that continuously reinforce patterns of teen-age tastes and styles.

The teen-age influence, or dominance, in many sectors of adult life is more a function of the omission of certain responsibilities by adults than the commission and initiation of certain acts by adolescents. It appears that American parents increasingly perceive the spread of teen-age culture as being primarily a function of their failure to exert their traditional authority. As a consequence, a philosophy of child-rearing and an interpretation of the adolescent phenomenon are gradually emerging that seem to herald stricter socialization practices.

---

[21] Kingsley Davis, *op. cit.*, p. 529.
[22] Hechinger and Hechinger, *op. cit.*

It should be added that in American society, socialization philosophies fluctuate over time, and that the current trend will probably not be of permanent duration. This presents vexing problems to American adolescents who, unlike youth in simpler folk societies, are not able to predict significant changes of modal attitudes and practices of the adult society toward the young. Such impermanence, relativity, and transience of socialization practices are a perpetual source of confusion and readjustment, thereby intensifying and complicating the period of adolescence.

The "Clash of Inferiority Complexes"

The American culture is responsible for the evolvement of two consequential complexes that have become integral elements in the current intergenerational conflict. They are the inferiority complex of teen-agers and the inferiority complex of the parents. These emotional dispositions have a reinforcing effect on each other and frequently lead to considerable tension and misunderstanding between the generations. Sociologist Clifford Kirkpatrick conceptualized this aspect of intergenerational interaction as the "clash of inferiority complexes."

> The phrase "clash of inferiority complexes" may be used to describe subtle aspects of the process by which parents are dethroned by their youthful offspring. Youth feels inferior because it is untried and lacking in experience or poise. There may be over-compensation for the inferiority of youth in an adult world by aggressiveness, brashness, grandiose expectations and pseudosophistication. On the other hand, parents may feel inferior because of lack of youthful attractiveness, declining sex powers, awareness of modest achievement, and the prospect of decreasing importance in the general scheme of things. . . . Given such disparate attitudes it is easy to see how the process of cumulative-circular-social-response may come into play, for cockiness begets renewed insistence by parents that their authoritarian role must be respected. Thus alienation between parents and children may result, sometimes superficial and temporary but occasionally of tragic duration.[23]

Kirkpatrick's theory implies that parents feel inferior because of one set of conditions and that teen-agers feel inferior because of another, and that many symptoms of the respective inferiority complexes add to the tension between the generations. Tensions resulting from the collision of the inferiority complexes *reinforce* the inferiority feelings of the

---

[23] Clifford Kirkpatrick, *The Family As Process and Institution* (New York, The Ronald Press, 1955), pp. 266–67.

two parties and, consequently, generate *more* conflict and tension. Thus, in a sense, this process tends to perpetuate the parent-youth conflict. The cyclic nature of this process has been referred to as the "cumulative-circular-social response."

An element of the American ethos that directly relates to the inferiority complex of the parents, especially older parents, is the "cult of youth." The American culture ascribes value to youth *in abstracto* and minimizes the role of the aged as a source of wisdom and a center of authority. Americans value and admire the activism of youth and tend to assume that middle or old age precludes persons from being active and inventive. Old age has the connotation of passive contemplativeness that is perceived as the nemesis of youthful activism. Trial-and-error procedure is closer to the heart of the American than armchair philosophizing and theorizing. The "doers" are thought of as young people who have the physical vigor and stamina to experiment and to create. For example, at 45 years of age, a highly trained and experienced pilot is grounded because "he is too old for flying." This practice of "defunctioning" the middle- and old-aged citizen may actually result in "resigned" and "no-longer-needed" attitudes. The aged are "cared for" and are kindly entertained—but safely away from the mainstream of life, in physical and mental isolation.

The "youth cult" focuses on the active young, allowing them to set the pace, themes, goals, and tastes. Older people can frequently be observed imitating the practices and the crazes of the young generation. It is an almost entirely new historical occurrence that dancing styles and music forms are passed from the teen-agers to the adults. For example, the rock 'n' roll style and the "twist" were teen-age crazes, but ultimately were taken up by the general adult population. The Beatles, youthful heroes of the rock 'n' rollers, were given awards by the Queen of England, personally, and were officially elevated to the rank of Members of the British Empire. In the fall of 1965, "their Beatleships" were invited to Buckingham Palace to receive the medals from the hand of the Queen. In protest, a number of adult holders of this title returned their awards to the Queen, refusing to be put on a par with adolescents.

It is virtually impossible to determine the causal direction between the cult of youth and the parental inferiority complex. In other words, has the youth cult created parental inferiority feelings, or are the parents trying to compensate for bygone youthful attractiveness by adoration and imitation of the ways of youth? The question of the causal direction can probably never be answered in any definite manner. Although it may be suspected that the adults' inferiority complex had considerable influence on the formation of the youth cult, it is more important at this time to study the mutually reinforcing relationship between the two phenomena.

The display of the parents' youth cult is not necessarily well received by the teen-agers. They do not care to be imitated by adults. In order to understand this negative reaction, it must be remembered that the teen-agers feel inferior about themselves and about many of their activities. According to Kirkpatrick's theory, adolescents feel inferior because they are "untried and lacking in experience or poise." It should be added that the adolescent's inferiority complex is intensified by his experience of actual inferior status in respect to legal, political, and occupational opportunities, rights, and decision-making. There appears to exist the tendency that persons who perceive themselves as inferior and then observe actions of others that reflect behavior patterns of their own, are prone to judge these actions as being just as inferior as they feel their own actions are. A college freshman was quoted complaining that his parents were trying to behave like teen-agers: "When you see yourself reflected in your folks, it's just awful."[24] Teen-agers have apparently become aware that they live in a youth-obsessed society and that they hold immense influence and power, but they find it uncomfortable when roles are reversed and adults assume teen-age behavior. Adolescents, by definition insecure and uncertain, find their lives directionless in a social environment that decides to rely on their judgments and tastes. Adolescents are in need of parents who are adult models and not "buddies," "friends," imitators of their styles. The teenage peer group already provides for companionship among like-minded, trial-and-error-oriented friends. Adults trying to join their ranks are perceived as unwelcome renegades from the ranks of potentially helpful adult models, through their desertion depriving youngsters of important models and "significant others." What adolescents basically seek from adults is not comradeship but direction.

Summary

Intergenerational conflict and tension are unavoidable in a rapidly changing society. The changing aspects in America include economic practices, technological innovations, and modifications of sociocultural elements. Such changes affect relations between the generations and, in effect, create a different social climate for each generation. The consequences of

---

[24] Grace Hechinger and Fred M. Hechinger, "In The Time It Takes You To Read These Lines, The American Teenager Will Have Spent $2,378.22," *Esquire* (July, 1965), p. 114.

this dynamic urban-industrial setting, pertinent to the understanding of the adolescent phenomenon, include the following points: (1) The cultural environment is not exactly the same for each generation, confronting adults and youth with conflicting norms, goals, and behavioral procedures. (2) Parents suffer from perennial "cultural lag"—a situation that renders them helpless, relatively poorly informed, and places them against "experts" who have taken over a sizeable proportion of the socialization process. Children and teen-agers show a tendency to generalize the inefficiency of parents as instructors and have started to question their reliability as *educators in general*. (3) Parenthood as a traditional "natural right" has become the last stand of the amateur in American society. The traditionally unquestioned *a priori* authority of the parents over their children—authority based primarily on progenitorship and thus definable as "irrational"—has finally been questioned by biological and social scientists who believe that certain educational and legal reforms are called for to check unqualified parenthood. Unqualified parenthood has been proposed as being responsible for intensifying the adolescent problem. (4) The democratic ethos of the American culture has stimulated a parental reaction to the rise of the teen-age subculture that can be defined as acquiescence and retreat from the traditional authority of parents and adults in general. Teen-agers have invaded adult institutions with the cooperation of adults and are adding their peculiar style to activities and functions that previously were strictly adult. (5) Failure to establish a *rapprochement* between the older and the younger generations, in spite of sincere efforts to make use of equalitarian, communicative, and informative principles, has been disillusioning to parents and adults. A more militant mood is gradually developing, and parents seem to begin to reassert their traditional authority roles. (6) To fully understand the persistence and severity of the intergenerational friction, certain emotional dispositions of adults and of youth must be understood. While the "youth cult" of the American culture constantly reminds parents of their declining youthfulness, youths are reminded of their lack of life experiences, inferior legal, political, and occupational qualifications, and their uncertain status in society. Social interaction motivated by these emotional propensities marshals the older and the younger generations against each other in what has been called the "clash of inferiority complexes."

In the final analysis, the main consequences of rapid social change in modern American society that are of pertinence to the discussion of adolescence include: (1) the adolescent's reluctance to accept parents as fully valid authority figures; (2) the adolescent's subsequent lack of sufficient adult models that could be functional for the development of a stable identity; (3) the widening gap between the generations; and (4) the prolonging of the poorly defined interim stage between child and adult status.

momism

The Nature and Rise of Momism

Philip Wylie, in his controversial book of 1942, *Generation of Vipers*, was one of the first to publicly insist that American motherhood had become a social problem.[1] Hitherto, the American mother had been so busy raising a large family and keeping house, that "she was rarely a problem to her family or to her equally busy friends, and never one to herself."[2] Wylie's exposition was more a polemic than a scientific treatment of the topic. Yet, in as far as his writings stimulated more precise and objective inquiry into the subject matter, he may be considered a pioneer of the conceptualization of the problem of modern Mom. Since then, more objective and scientific analyses have been offered by such qualified observers of American society as psychiatrists Edward A. Strecker,[3] David M. Levy,[4] and Erik H. Erikson,[5] social critic Martha W. Lear,[6] anthropologist Margaret Mead,[7] sociologist Arnold W. Green,[8] and a number of critics and journalists who have occasionally noted their observations in magazine articles or professional reports.

---

[1] Philip Wylie, *Generation of Vipers* (New York, Rinehart and Co., 1942).

[2] *Ibid.*, p. 186.

[3] Edward A. Strecker, *Their Mothers' Sons, The Psychiatrist Examines an American Problem* (New York, Lippincott Co., 1946).

[4] David M. Levy, *Maternal Overprotection* (New York, Columbia University Press, 1943).

[5] Erik H. Erikson, *Childhood and Society* (New York, W. W. Norton, Inc., 1963).

[6] Martha W. Lear, *The Child-Worshipers* (New York, Crown Publishers, 1963).

[7] Margaret Mead, "What is Happening to the American Family?" *Journal of Social Casework*, Vol. 28 (November, 1947), pp. 323–30. Also: "The Contemporary American Family as an Anthropologist Sees It," in Jerome M. Seidman (ed.), *The Adolescent* (New York, Holt, Rinehart and Winston, 1960), pp. 362–72.

[8] Arnold W. Green, "The Middle-Class Male Child and Neurosis," *American Sociological Review*, Vol. 11 (February, 1946), pp. 31–41.

The new Mom arose primarily in the middle class, where the feminist "emancipation" achieved its crescendo and its largest following. In previous generations, the wife-mother role was the only role available to the female. As a result, there was limited freedom, but also limited anxiety. However, this conventional wife-mother role became only *one* among the newly available multiple roles. This proliferation of role possibilities has added considerable freedom to the life of the American female. The price that has to be paid for this novel freedom expresses itself in feelings of insecurity and the anguish of endless pondering whether or not she has made the right role decision. If she has chosen, as most have, the wife–mother role, she may wonder if she *really* has made the proper decision. Research by a team of psychiatrists has indicated that in the vast majority of Momistically disturbed boys, the mother had serious conflicts about her role as a woman and in her attitudes toward men in general.[9] Many relatively well-educated females who have chosen this traditional wife–mother role try to compensate for their role conflicts, frustrations, and anxieties by "absorbing" the personality of the child.

However, as Erik H. Erikson, one of the best known analysts of the phenomenon of Momism, contends, Mom does not derive happiness from her Momistic success; in fact, she herself is a troubled victim of her own emotional dispositions and obsessions.

> . . . "Mom" is a woman in whose life cycle remnants of infantility join advanced senility to crowd out the middle range of mature womanhood, which thus becomes self-absorbed and stagnant. In fact, she mistrusts her own feelings as a woman and mother. Even her overconcern does not provide trust, but lasting mistrust. But let it be said that this "Mom"—or better: any woman who reminds herself and others of the stereotype Mom—is not happy; she does not like herself; she is ridden by the anxiety that her life was a waste. She knows that her children do not genuinely love her, despite Mother's Day offerings. Mom is a victim, not a victor.[10]

Although generalizations concerning the *differential* incidence rate of Momism in the social structure are limited and should be approached with caution, it appears that a number of conditions prevalent in the American middle class invite a greater occurrence of Momism than can be found in any other segment of the population. Among the conditions of the middle class that tend to induce Momistic relationships can be found the following aspects: (1) The home is characterized by frequent

---

[9] Howard E. Wylie and Ralph A. Degado, "A Pattern of Mother-Son Relationship Involving the Absence of the Father," *American Journal of Orthopsychiatry*, Vol. 29 (July, 1959), pp. 644–49.

[10] Erikson, *op. cit.*, p. 291.

father-absence. (2) The mother is relatively well-educated. (3) The mother experiences conflicts between career possibilities outside of the home and her wife–mother role in the home. (4) The mother tries to resolve her conflict by focusing on her child, determined to be a successful "career mother." (5) The mother is the constant supervisor and companion of the child, often employng the so-called "scientific" child-rearing principles.

These conditions can create a situation where the combination of the failure to provide a consistent adult male model in the home and the peculiar emotional disposition of the mother result in serious emotional harm to the male child. It must be emphasized that Momism usually refers to the mother–child relationship where the child involved is a *boy*. The reason for this is the relative ease with which a girl, even if dominated by the mother, can adopt her manners, imitate her, and take on her role. In this way, the girl may be able to avoid serious personality problems—especially those connected with problems of identity, since the girl can look to her mother as a model, even if she is a Mom-type. The girl can pattern her opinions, attitudes, and behavior after the example of the mother, since the model and imitator are both of the same sex. As a result, the young girl has a much easier task of establishing an identity than the young boy. She can use the available and visible model, while the boy cannot. A number of researches have found that, accordingly, the girl tends to resemble her mother in personality, attitudes, and behavior patterns much more than the boy resembles his father.[11] In fact, the perpetuation of Moms proceeds usually by the daughter's imitation of her mother's possessive ways. On the other side, the young boy must reject his mother as a model, since he is supposed to take on the male role and is constantly told to be "manly." In other words, a girl may take her Momistic mother as a *role model*, while a boy in contemporary American society, which strongly emphasizes that the role of the male is opposite that of the female, cannot identify himself with his mother without serious emotional consequences.

In the middle-class setting, the father's white-collar occupation and the accompanying social obligations of parties, golf, trips, and dinners often take him away from the home, and thus he is not readily available

---

[11] Reliable examples of such studies include: Ruth E. Hartley, "Children's Concepts of Male and Female Roles," *Merill-Palmer Quarterly*, Vol. 6 (January, 1960), pp. 83–91; Susan W. Gray, "Masculinity and Femininity in Relation to Anxiety and Social Acceptance," *Child Development*, Vol. 28 (1957), pp. 203–14. Lionel M. Lasowick, "On the Nature of Identification," *Journal of Abnormal and Social Psychology*, Vol. 51 (September, 1955), pp. 175–83. David B. Lynn, "The Process of Learning Parental and Sex-Role Identification," *Journal of Marriage and the Family*, Vol. 28 (November, 1966), pp. 466–70.

to act as a model for his son. The boy is then left almost exclusively under the care and sway of females—his mother; Sunday school, nursery, kindergarten supervisors; and grammar school teachers. Taken together —the initial possessiveness of the mother, the absence of the father, the lack of other male models, and societal emphasis on sex-role differentiation—and the conditions may be prime for the son involved to suffer the consequences of Momism.

It must be noted that father-absence by itself does not inevitably result in Momism. A matricentric family style sometimes occurs, mainly in lower-class homes, where the father is absent and the mother heads the household in his place. She may be a strong authority figure who provides the income, makes decisions, and delegates duties, but yet she does not absorb or manipulate the personality of the child, as would a Momistic woman.

Recent research in Mexico has yielded interesting support for the hypothesis that it is really the typical middle-class conditions that are at the root of Momism and not matricentrism as such. The slowly evolving middle-class segment of the Mexican population has shown evidence that Momistic problems are concomitantly increasing because of the relatively emancipated wives who undergo a frustration "shock" after marriage. The style of life of the middle-class female before marriage has progressively become freer and more equalitarian in respect to men. But after marriage, this achieved equalitarianism is suddenly replaced by the traditional and restrictive life opportunities of the Mexican wife– mother role. Sociological research has found that as a result many frustrated middle-class Mexican mothers attempt to compensate for their restriction and unfulfilled needs by, first, having children to thereby reestablish themselves as important persons and, second, by "possessing" the children so that they can completely control them, limit both their behavior and thinking, and make certain that they are faithful. These mothers employ affection as the principal means of control, since this provides them with an outlet for all the "love" they cannot share with their husbands. A survey has revealed that Momistic "smothering" and the tendency to manipulate the child by "conditional love" are directly correlated with denied needs, conflicts, and frustrations, of the middle-class mother who feels relatively deprived of other life goals. It was concluded that, not unlike the American middle-class Mom, the Mexican counterpart aspires to "successful" motherhood since successful careers outside of the home are denied her.[12]

---

[12] Noel F. McGinn, "Marriage and Family in Middle-Class Mexico," *Journal of Marriage and the Family,* Vol. 28 (August, 1966), pp. 305–13.

A Model Study of Middle-Class Boys and Momism

Two different types of family settings have been compared to determine the circumstances under which Momism will or will not occur. The comparison demonstrated how the conditions mentioned in the preceding section—middle-class home, frequent father-absence, and immature needs of the mother—work together to produce Momism. A study focusing on these conditions was presented by sociologist Arnold W. Green in his research, "The Middle-Class Male Child and Neurosis."[13] It was found that certain variables were directly correlated with Momistic consequences. The group of families characterized by the Momistic features can be referred to as the experimental group, while the families free of such conditions may be called the control group.

The control group was composed of families in an urban Polish-American community, who were characterized by several common features which can be enumerated by the following points: (1) The parents had a peasant system of values alien to both the American culture and to their own children. (2) Usually, both parents worked in factories and thus were often away from home. (3) The parents frequently wielded excessive authoritarianism over their children, often resulting in corporal punishment. (4) Apparently as a partial result of the above factors, a notable degree of hostility existed between the parents and their children.

In this group, it was observed that the children were not neurotic and did not suffer from the typical "blanketing-out" of the personality. Observations suggested the following reasons why this crippling outcome was avoided. (1) The children had direct contact with many adults in their larger family or neighborhood who could serve as potential models, so that their identification process was not limited to the parents only. (2) There was no constant supervision of the children's activities. Rather, a relaxed home atmosphere prevailed without frequent admonitions about such things as protecting furniture, observing cleanliness, and watching manners. (3) The children were free to roam around the neighborhood at will. (4) The children did not have to repress or sublimate hostilities toward their parents, but could express them openly. They did not feel *obligated* to show love toward their parents, nor was there any urging, demanding, or trading for affection. (5) The children had developed techniques of parent-avoidance whereby they could stay out of the parents' way when parental criticism or punishment might be pending.

---

[13] Green, *op. cit.*

The experimental group was made up primarily of native white Protestant middle class families, who were college-educated also lived in urban areas. Several prevalent features were noted in this group: (1) The fathers had typical middle-class occupations in which there was pressure to succeed and in which business and related social activities took them away from the home to a considerable extent. They were to a large degree the "property" of the corporation and had to conform to time-demanding occupational obligations if they wanted to make progress toward success. Often, the father's social activities, largely integral parts of his occuptional career and including such activities as parties, golf, and travel, took him away from home life. (2) The mothers were characterized by feelings of conflict between the role of a housewife and the role of a professional career woman. Having decided on the role of wife-mother, they experienced feelings of dissatisfaction at being limited to that one role and exhibited definite signs of regret and and neurotic discontent. Many of them had come to believe that their dedication to child rearing was a poor substitute for the success they could have achieved in a career for which they felt they had the necessary talent, skill, and proficiency. But full and open admission of these negative feelings would have been tantamount to admitting defeat and would only have deepened the feelings of frustration. Since the wife–mother role was a *fait accompli* from which there was no actual escape, many of these mothers, motivated by their basic frustration, resolved to turn parenthood into a career and to become "career mothers." The mark of a successful "career mother" was thought to be seen in the "good" behavior of the child. Thus, her child became her success symbol and had to prove to the world that she was successful. In the final analysis, the mother wanted to live through her child. (3) One way of measuring the success of the child, and thus the mother, was by continually comparing him with other boys and urging him to compete with his peers. (4) Mother was the constant and almost sole companion of the preschool boy 24 hours a day. (5) "Scientific child care" was applied, involving constant supervision and correction of the child. (6) The mother manipulated the child's behavior by extending or withdrawing her love, or by promising to do so.

It is precisely this use of powerful "love-oriented" sanctions which, according to Green and other social scientists, is the basis for many modern neuroses. In this type of situation, the child is constantly reminded that he should be grateful for his mother's "loving care," and that in return he must "stay out of trouble" and do what pleases her— or risk losing her all-important love. As a result, he lives with constant anxiety about losing affection and acceptance and knows these qualities only as something *conditional*—contingent on how he behaves and not as something he deserves because of his own innate qualities or worth. Once the child has been conditioned in this fashion for a good part of his childhood, the slightest controversy, argument, or failure may cause him to doubt his personal worth and acceptability and would ultimately generate acute feelings of fear, shame, and inferiority. Such inferiority feelings beget agonizing feelings of insecurity. In order to obtain security, the child will conform, obey, remain a child, and, above all, desperately try to avoid being alone. The anxious conformance to social expectations, often so conspicuously concomitant with the search for security, cancels the development of unique personality expression and shape the child's personality into slavish dependence on his mother or, later, on mother substitutes.

An important element of this conditioning process is the boy's belief that he *needs* that love. He comes to depend upon it. "Not the need for parental love, but the constant threat of its withdrawal *after the child has been conditioned to the need,* lies at the root of the most characteristic modern neurosis."[14] The threat of withdrawal is an all-powerful tool to make the child do whatever mother wants him to do. There is empirical evidence suggesting that maternal achievement pressures are more effective than paternal pressures because of mother's use of the powerful "love-oriented" sanctions.[15]

With this process in mind, it can be concluded from Green's study that *lack of parental love, the exertion of irrational authority, and the use of corporal punishment may leave a personality relatively unharmed —if there is freedom in choosing models elsewhere and if love is not used as a tool of conditioning.*

Types and Techniques of the Moms

The mother turned Mom does not constitute a uniform type, but can be classified according to the causes of her Momistic attitudes or according to the Momistic techniques she uses.

The causative factors accountable for the rise of a particular Mom can be one or several of a great variety of causes, including compensation for career uncertainty, resolution of role conflict, the desire for an exclusive "possession," the need to live through her child, etc. One of the most frequent background features of Moms is, as was already men-

---

[14] Green, op. cit., p. 39, italics added.

[15] R. R. Sears, E. E. Maccoby, and H. Levin, *Patterns of Child-Rearing* (Evanston, Ill., Row & Peterson, 1957).

tioned, the middle-class setting where the college-educated mother has doubts whether the simple home-maker role is commensurate with her educational achievements, talents, and aptitudes, and where she compensates for anxieties by becoming a "career mother."

It would be extremely difficult to reliably trace the causative circumstances that made a Mom and properly apply the derived information for classificatory purposes, since much of the needed information would deal with past processes that could be obtained only through recall or inference. On the other side, a typology based on the techniques used by the Momistic mothers would deal with current behavior and thus present us with more reliable and verifiable data. For this reason, it appears that a typology based on Momistic techniques is more meaningful and preferable.

As different as the various techniques may appear, the major end product is identical or at least extremely similar: in every instance of Momism, Mom molds her son into an emotional parasite in order to satisfy her own conscious or unconscious needs. It must also be remembered that some Moms use more than one distinct technique and achieve the Momistic effect through some combination of methods. Yet, for easier discussion and for clear characterization of the *main* types, the following typology is suggested.

The overindulgent Mom. One of the ways a Mom can establish the Momistic and neurotic dependency in her child is by furnishing the child with everything he desires, so that, in a sense, he becomes "addicted" to her. In the process, the narcissistic and naturally egocentric tendencies of the child go relatively unchecked and are not subject to learning the give-and-take attitudes which are normal and imperative for mature adult life. His mother's style of conditioning deprives him of learning how to share or to cooperate and will render him greatly handicapped when the time comes for him to enter adult life.

The overprotective Mom. This type of Mom uses her overprotective "love" as a weapon to enforce the boy's dependency on her. Psychiatrist David M. Levy, in his classic study *Maternal Overprotection*,[16] pointed to at least four manifestations of overprotection as revealed by maternal activities that prevent the boy from developing independent and responsible attitudes and behavior patterns: (1) *Infantilization*. Early child-care practices are prolonged beyond the time when such practices are actually needed and culturally recommended. Methods of handling the growing child as an infant may include breast-feeding, toilet-training, inappropriate style of punishing or rewarding, and helping the boy in such tasks as tying shoelaces, dressing,

---

[16] Levy, *op. cit.*

and washing. A typical example would be a mother helping a 13-year-old son dress or punishing him by putting him to bed in the afternoon. Another example would be a mother breast-feeding her child through his third year. Called upon to explain her behavior, a mother exhibiting such behavior replied: "You know he was all I had," and "I hated to start weaning."[17] (2) *Prevention of social maturity.* Basically, this type of maternal manifestation prevents the son from growing in the direction of self-reliance and general independent behavior. The mother preserves the child's egocentric attitudes by reinforcing and lauding his selfish acts exhibited in interaction with other persons. She shields her child from all harm and woe and does not let him confront any of the inevitable everyday conflicts that might cause pain or frustration. Serious problems are never discussed and are pushed out of the conscious realm of things. She might defend her behavior as a necessary protection for the child who "will learn the cruel facts of life soon enough anyway." In the course of this conditioning process, mother succeeds in tying the child to her, so that the child comes to need her to avert problems. It is the mother figure that ultimately means security and total warmth, since she emanates a problemless atmosphere. This habitual ignoring of reality becomes a self-perpetuating mechanism—the older the child grows the more difficult he finds it to face responsibilities and problems, since they increase in importance and complexity. In the end result, he is unable to function as an autonomous individual without her protection and security. (3) *Excessive contact.* A mother may bind the child to herself by excessive fondling or by sleeping with the young child long past infancy. This Mom fails to wean the child from her constant physical presence and contact, insisting on continuous companionship. (4) *Maternal anxiety about the welfare of the child.* This attitude already permeates, of course, the above-mentioned criteria, but becomes particularly explicit in mother's refusal to take risks for the child. Specific manifestations of this anxiety are excessive nursing and oversolicitude during the time of real or imagined illness of the boy and preoccupation with possible future problems that might befall the offspring.

The permissive Mom. This mother observes a complete lack of parental control. She is subservient to the demands and whims of the son and overindulges him, trying to meet his every wish. She may or may not be overprotective, but always is permissive and uncritical of his actions. She sometimes uses the martyr-to-motherhood technique, ostentatiously sacrificing herself in order to take on all responsibilities and duties for the child, to "make life easier for him," so that "he'll never have to suffer like I did." The case study of a young man, the victim of

---

[17] Levy, *op. cit.*, p. 57.

permissive and overprotective Momism, revealed that the young man died at age 25 under conditions that justified surmise of suicide. The young man had displayed an extremely unstable career, irresponsible and self-indulgent behavior, and truancy from school and later from jobs. He married at age 19, had one child, and never supported his family. In a constant show of financial irresponsibility, he would charge anything he wanted and respond to his wife as if she were an overindulgent mother, always assuming that some "help would come." Throughout all the years, his mother remained an uncritical defender of his actions—in spite of the glaring maladjustments of the son.[18]

It is interesting to note that most victims of permissive Momism do not reveal their deviation from normal behavior until the adolescent years, or even later, because of the cultural permissiveness that allows egocentric expression of children and more or less takes it for granted. However, at the moment when serious responsibilities are expected, the victim of the permissive and overprotective Mom shows his emotional shortcomings and sociopathic condition.

The domineering Mom. This mother does not tolerate self-expression on the part of the offspring. Her method of preventing personality expression of the child is to use stern discipline combined with such ego-destroying techniques as public ridicule and/or disclosure of his failures and mistakes to other persons. In addition, the boy has no recourse to parent-avoiding techniques and is under constant supervision. The domineering mother often tends to belittle even the abilities and the worth of the father, trying to impress the offspring with how much she is doing for him and how little other people care about him. She jealously guards her exclusive command over the son, trying to retain an uncontested monopoly over him. Instead of guiding him to make independent decisions, she commands the decisions or ridicules the decision that he has tried to make.

The "child worshiper." Along with such middle-class values as success and education, the American woman is also impressed by another middle-class value—the praise of motherhood. This value gives one type of Mom, whom Martha Lear aptly called the "child worshiper,"[19] the advantage of being able to practice her unwittingly harmful technique with the appearance of "doing what's best for the child," and be applauded for it all the while. Such a mother may be raising her family

---

[18] Levy, op. cit., p. 222.
[19] Lear, *op. cit.*

with the simple goal of "being a good mother to her children," but may actually pursue this goal with such determination and industry that "being a good mother" comes to be an end in itself, "a status symbol that eventually makes parenthood a competitive sport." In striving to make her child the model of the community, she ceases to be concerned about or to provide for the child's personalized nurture and, instead, uses him to prove that she herself is an outstanding mother. By manipulating and using him as an ornament to gain status, she thereby denies him individuality and blights his own character growth.

An important aspect of this success syndrome is the craving on the part of the mother to see the child become popular. (It is via the child's popularity that many parents try to relive their own, sometimes unpopular, youth.) Martha Lear cited several examples of this type of procedure. She reported a mother who expressed great relief over the fact that her 11-year-old son had finally succeeded in getting his first date, since she had been worried that he would be shunned socially because he was so small. Several other examples of the "child worshiper" are the Moms who prepare lavish birthday parties for two-year-olds, provide 9-year-old girls with training bras, arrange pseudo-cocktail parties for elementary school pupils, and teach 8-year-olds how to accessorize their wardrobes and style their hair.

The typical child-worshiping Mom basically makes these efforts not for the sake of the child, but for the satisfaction of her own needs, thereby using and manipulating the child as a status symbol and severely hampering the unfolding of the child's personality.

The "star" Mom. A mother can also exert personality-absorbing dominance over the child by appearing as the "star" or "great beauty," using her physical attractiveness and popularity in an effort to charm her friends, associates, and children into admiring submission to her wishes. Her son may be impressed by the admiration which friends and family members lavish on her and may come to perceive her as a famous beauty. Her physical attractiveness augmented by skillful use of make-up and effective choice of clothing, plus the worshipful behavior of others toward her, cause the child to grow afraid to rebel against the glamorous mother. As a result, the intimidated child can be manipulated easily— frequently far beyond the age at which such manipulation is necessary or conducive to the development of an independent and healthy personality.

The "absolute authority." This mother is an assertive pseudo intellectual who proceeds by expressing information and opinion about almost any subject, freely criticizing the ideas and actions of others, and

so intimidating her offspring and inculcating him with the belief in her infallibility that he accepts and respects her seemingly all-pervasive knowledge. The youth grows afraid to argue with mother or express his own opinion, since she defeats him each time. In the end, the boy may acquire a passive attitude and start to depend largely on his mother's reasoning and information. Again, responsible occupancy of the adult status can be seriously delayed.

The "ailing" Mom. Occasionally, a mother with extremely immature needs and Momistic tendencies may exhibit some kind of ailment to attract the son, appeal to his compassion and sense of filial duty, and thereby keep him close to her. In such situations, a Mom has free rein to capitalize on the early-instilled guilt-readiness of the child. She succeeds in generating a sense of guilt and a state of anxiety in her off-spring whenever he tries to disobey her or embark on independent thought or action. Her technique is the powerful "love-oriented" sanction that would cause the child to experience acute anxiety if he was made to feel "ungrateful" or "undeserving of love." Through this type of child manipulation, a control mechanism evoles in the child that represents an extreme version of what has been called "adaptive" or "socialized" anxiety by Allison Davis.[20] The nature of this anxiety makes it easy for mother to control the son, since this anxiety can be allayed only by avoidance of disapproved behavior and by constant compliance with the wishes of others.

The ailment of the mother may be an act of conscious pretense or may be psychosomatic, and thus real in the mother's perception. In either case, consciously or unconsciously, the ailment is used to engender feelings of pity and guilt and bring the son back to her side. Her almost custodial care and his "socialized" anxiety about ingratitude will combine to the extent of making it impossible for the boy to extricate himself from mother's influence. A striking illustration of the power of the "ailing" Mom was discovered by a team of New York welfare work-ers who found that the prevention and cure of drug addiction was thwarted by possessive mothers. In one case, they found that the reason why an addict did not abandon heroin was his mother complained of an ear infection whenever the son planned to hospitalize himself and in-sisted that he stay at her side and nurse her.[21]

[20] Allison Davis, "Socialization and Adolescent Personality," in Guy E. Swanson, Theodore M. Newcomb, and Eugene L. Hartley (eds.), *Readings in Social Psychology* (New York, Henry Holt and Co., 1952), pp. 520–31.
[21] "Mom Is The Villain," *Time* (May 21, 1965), p. 83.

Consequences of Momism: A Variety from "True Believer" to Suicide

As different as the above-described techniques seem, when appearing in the Momistic situation they have a number of common elements. First, in order to be effective, the technique must be applied constantly. Second, the mother must be the preponderant supervisor of the child, excluding the influence of "significant others" from the socialization process. If these two conditions exist to a sufficient degree of consistency and intensity, the Momistic outcome is almost predictable. The common elements of the Momistically crippled sons, regardless of the specific technique applied, include: (1) inability to make own decisions, (2) feelings of inferiority, (3) a particular brand of "socialized" anxiety, (4) patterns of irresponsible action, and (5) general emotional parasitism, i.e., insufficiently controlled narcissism and egocentrism that may be permissible for infants but not for adults.

Many valid illustrations of such consequences of Momism can be gathered from the mass media. Some reports illustrating consequences of Momism are quite explicit and readily identify the Momistic nature of the incident,—as, for example, in the case of the Momistic interference with preventive and curative measures aimed at drug addicts in New York City. A team of social workers and ministers trying to discover why they were unsuccessful in helping young addicts quit the habit found that the mothers of the young men engaged in various Momistic techniques to actually keep the son addicted and thereby maintain a dependency relationship. In one case, as mentioned above, a Mom employed the "ailing" technique; in another case they found that a mother:

> . . . bailed her boy out of jail while he was waiting to enter a hospital for addicts because she could not bear to have him wash his own underwear. Some mothers even encouraged their sons' habits by giving them $5 for a $1.50 haircut, or $15 for a $5 shirt, knowing that the money would go for a fix. . . .

> What motivated the women to be so destructive? Most of them, said Social Worker Barish, fitted a neurotic pattern. They were "suffering, protective and interfering." Usually their husbands had left them, and so great was their need for their sons' love that they managed to ignore the boys' addiction to heroin. "The mother," explained Clergyman Brown, "has a vested interest in perpetuating the addiction, as it gratifies her need for a dependent son."

. . . Now he is campaigning to have the sons leave home, but he finds Mom just as tough a campaigner. A few weeks ago, one mother searched through more than 50 rooming houses on Manhattan's 14th Street until she turned up her addict-son and talked him into coming home with her.[22]

That drug addiction is frequently associated with the lack of a significant male figure for the young male addict has been verified by several studies. Stanley Einstein, for example, reported that in more than 50 per cent of a sample of youthful addicts, there was a lack of an effective father figure during childhood.[23] David Laskowitz reported that the mother's behavior is a crucial determinent of addiction, and that it is especially the mother's indulgent attitudes that are highly correlated with addiction.[24]

The effects of Momism are not always conspicuous or easily identifiable. The behavior of victims of Momism is frequently so passive, inconspicuous, and law-abiding that it escapes the attention of most people. Unless a conscious effort is made to detect these elements of passivity in situations where a young individual fails to make his own decision or to express his own opinion, the fact that he suffers from Momism may go undetected. A report describing the opinionless behavior of a 19-year-old draftee is an example of this type of inconspicuous personality absorption by Mom. A most vital decision in the life of the young man was passively left to his mother's discretion. He had neither a word of consent nor dissent.

A mother who believes in segregation with religious fervor has sworn to petition President Johnson in her battle to have her son guaranteed "all white" military duty.

Mrs. Gaillot stormed out of a draft board hearing Friday and said her son Kenneth, 19, will appear to take his physical as ordered next Tuesday—but will do it under protest if Negroes are present.

"If Kenneth is forced to integrate against his religious convictions, that means the first amendment is void," she said.

"I am going to send a wire to the president and ask him if he knows if the amendment is void."

"This is not Nazi Germany or a Communist country, but America, and my son Kenneth must obey me under God and law."

Mrs. Gaillot said she told the draft board's legal adviser, Lt. Col. Douglas Pritchard, that "Anyone who forces my son to disobey

---

[22] "Mom Is The Villian," p. 83.

[23] Stanley Einstein, "The Future Time Perspective of the Adolescent Narcotic Addict," in Ernest Harms (ed.), *Drug Addiction in Youth* (New York, Pergamon Press, 1965), p. 96.

[24] David Laskowitz, "The Adolescent Drug Addict: An Adlerian View," *Journal of Individual Psychology*, Vol. 17 (May, 1961), pp. 68–79.

God, it is better for them to commit suicide rather than cause one to sin."

"That comes from Matthew 18:6," she said, "and that's the penalty on their heads."

The verse says:

"But whoever shall offend one of these little ones which believe in Me, it were better for him that a millstone were hanged around his neck, and that he were drowned in the depth of the sea."

Kenneth declined comment on the hassle.

"I'll let my mother do the talking."[25]

It is interesting to note that the mother in the above illustration selected a Scriptural passage that referred to the "little ones"—as if applicable to her 19-year-old son.

Another case, made public a few years ago, concerned a 37-year-old Wisconsin man whose mother took him everywhere in a wheel cart, allegedly because he was suffering from paralysis inflicted by a childhood bout with polio. Welfare officials finally prevailed on the mother to have her son examined by physicians, who pronounced him healthy and capable of walking. Further study revealed that in reality it was his *mother*, not polio, that had disabled him. Under psychiatric investigation, it was found that when the son was temporarily removed from the mother at age 15 to attend school, he curled up in a fetal position and remained in this position for 22 years, spoon-fed, diapered, and wheeled around by his mother who insisted that "I like him just the way he is."[26] The mother reinforced her son's reaction, did not even allow attempts at walking and, in fact, convinced him that he could not walk at all.

One of the most common and often undetected outcomes of Momism is that an individual who has always relied on his mother for guidance and decision-making may seek a substitute decision-making figure when faced with a situation requiring independent action. He may possibly, become as was mentioned earlier, a "True Believer," who exhibits a fanatic adherence and loyalty to some supposedly universal, infallible, and omnipotent ideology or charismatic leader.[27] He submits, and in effect hands himself over, to an outside directing authority, usually in the form of an organization, religion, or movement. It is from ranks of this temper that idealistic movements recruit some of their most passionate campaigners and that charismatic leaders draw their most devoted supporters. From a psychological point of view, it

[25] AP Report (New Orleans, Sept. 4, 1965).

[26] "Rehabilitation: Return From the Womb," *Time* (May 17, 1963), p. 93.

[27] Eric Hoffer, *The True Believer* (New York, Mentor Books, 1951).

does not seem to matter what the True Belief is, for what it essentially amounts to is a substitute Mom-in-disguise who again pulls all the strings for him and operates his marionette personality. Suitable media for Mom substitution may include fanatical adherence to a religion, ideology, any of a variety of save-our-country movements, or any other crusading movement. According to Hoffer, the emotional satisfaction that the True Belief gives may be derived from the Christian credo just as well as from the Communist ideology.[28] Religion is mentioned here because it may not only serve as an escape from reality, it may also provide for submittal of all problems to a higher power. The Christian religion allows an individual to submit his problems, anxieties, and grievances to an always kind and forgiving power. Decisions can be based on "what the Lord wants me to do," rather than on one's own deliberations and efforts to understand a situation and come to grips with it. Similarly, Communism is in a position to offer a higher cause for a victim of Momism. The party and the ideological dicta make the decisions for him. He "belongs" again, and responsibility for his actions rests with the authority that tells him what to do.

This is not to say that all True Believers are victims of Momism or to throw doubt on the maturity, normalcy, or sincerity of many followers of various movements. The purpose here is merely to point out *potential* avenues of substitution open to victims of Momism.

Without doubt, a True Belief, the conviction of having found the only eternal, absolute, and universal Truth, holds a strong attraction for an individual who is craving for authority and decision-making outside himself. He tends to welcome a powerful agent who makes infallible decisions for him. "Faith in a holy cause is to a considerable extent a substitute for the lost faith in ourselves."[29] Actually, it would be more correct to say that victims of Momism have *not lost* faith in themselves, they *never had* faith in themselves. They depended on Mom; they had faith in Mom. Later, when removed from Mom, something else has to be substituted. A True Belief, in conjunction with the group of fellow True Believers, can serve as one of the most powerful substitutes.

Some of the difficulties that a victim of Momism can experience, when forced to meet alone an important situation demanding a major decision can evolve into some of mankind's greatest tragedies. The shock and anxiety of the experience may cause him to turn away from reality. Escapist reactions may take on the form of alcoholism, drug addiction, mental illness, homosexuality, or suicide—all of which allow

---

[28] Hoffer, *op. cit.*, pp. 25–29.
[29] Hoffer, *op. cit.*, p. 22.

him either to evade or to withdraw from reality in order to circumvent responsibilities and to rid himself of pain, guilt, and insecurity.

In the process of treating a vast number of psychoneurotic patients who were "rejects" from the United States armed forces, psychiatrist Edward A. Strecker discovered that many of them suffered from one of the most severe consequences of Momism, from schizophrenia functioning as a "Mom surrogate."[30] This form of escape takes place because the "immaturity is so great and complex that the only path open for the child is the retreat into the fantasy—of schizophrenia—to remain there forever enwombed."[31] Psychiatric literature increasingly deals with the problem of the "schizophrenogenic" mother who would not let her child go, dominated him, and expressed hostility under the protective cover of mother love.[32] A particular type of schizophrenia, occasionally observed among victims of Momism, is the absolute rejection of *all* reality, including such symptoms as maintenance of a rigid, curled body position, no reaction to pain, and refusal to eat. This catatonic form is an extreme outcome and, of course, comparatively rare. On the other hand, one of the most common means of shutting out reality is through alcoholism or drug addiction. Both drugs and alcohol give the user an opportunity to escape into fantasy or oblivion. Homosexuality is another possible result of Momism, where the son may compare all feminine contacts with his mother. This comparison is likely to generate sexual aversion, preventing him from developing a normal interest in the opposite sex. If this is combined with a Mom's inculcation of poor sexual attitudes, telling her son that sex is impure, evil, and a sign of weakness, a strong aversion toward heterosexual activities may be established. Certain Moms, in interacting with their sons, tend to degrade girls because they represent a threat to their monopoly over the son. The internalization of antiheterosexual attitudes may mean that any sexual desires must be met some way other than through the normal man-woman relations, and homosexuality may possibly be the outcome.

Sometimes the product of Momism is not just one clear-cut symptom, but a conglomeration of various neurotic complexes, including at one and the same time such features as antisocial behavior, sexual inhibitions, sadistic practices, and extreme mother-dependency. One of

---

[30] Strecker, *op. cit.*

[31] *Ibid.*, pp. 111–12.

[32] See three pertinent examples: Elliot G. Mishler and Nancy E. Waxler, "Family Processes and Schizophrenia," *Psychiatry and Social Science Bookshelf*, Vol. 1 (Sept. 15, 1966), p. 9. David Marcus, M.D., *et al.*, "A Clinical Approach to the Understanding of Normal and Pathologic Adolescence," *Archives of General Psychiatry*, Vol. 15 (December, 1966), pp. 569–76. James C. Coleman, *Abnormal Behavior and Modern Life* (Chicago, Scott, Foresman & Co., 1964), pp. 255, 293, 296, 367.

the most striking examples in recent history of this mixture of emotionally deviant behavior because of Momistic conditioning occurred in
France in 1965:

Matronly Yvonne Vasseur, 69, has had but one consuming passion in her life: her son Jacques, now 45. When he was a child, she
gave him dolls to play with and kept him away from other little
boys and girls. When the Nazis invaded France, she begged her son
to do anything that they asked in order to stay near her, rather than
be shipped off to a forced-labor camp in Germany. When he returned, a hunted, hated collaborator, to her after the war, she hid
him in the empty garret above her second-story apartment in a
grim, red-brick building in a working-class suburb of Lille.

There he stayed for 17 years. Police kept him on their "wanted"
list, but cunningly, Yvonne Vasseur shopped for two on her tiny
widow's pension by dividing her purchases among several shops.
She knit him special slippers with felt soles, so that the neighbors
would not hear him. In his garret Vasseur learned seven languages
to add to his French and German; she learned Latin to help him
along, brought him down to watch TV on quiet nights. In 1962,
police discovered him accidentally. Paying a routine call on Mme.
Vasseur, they rang the neighbor's doorbell down stairs by mistake,
then knocked on Mme. Vasseur's door—and found her son hiding
behind a curtain. He could, of course, have easily escaped from
France any time before then, but as he explained, "I was in perfect
joy to stay with *Maman.*"

All through his trial this month, Mme. Vasseur devoured her
son with her eyes. A five-man court for State Security in Paris
heard him accused of responsibility for 430 arrests, 310 deporta-
tions, and the deaths of 230 of his countrymen while employed at
Gestapo headquarters in the city of Angers. Some 200 witnesses
recounted the now almost forgotten horrors: how Vasseur, known
as "Vasseur the Terror," beat them, tortured them, and condemned
their fathers, brothers, and sweethearts to death.

One man recalled having been bull-whipped for ten hours
by Vasseur, who looked "mighty pleased with himself." A woman
told how he burned her breasts with a cigarette. Vasseur listened
impassively, commenting, "It's possible" or "It's plausible." His
mother blamed herself. Taking the stand, she cried: "I had a very
strict mother. I wanted to spare my son. I sinned in the other direction. It is not he who ought to be on trial. It's me. It is my fault.
Punish me, but let him go."

The defense produced a psychiatrist who, in a certain sense
agreed with Mme. Vasseur. He testified that Vasseur was "emotionally castrated" by her as a child, and embraced his grisly
Gestapo duties because they gave him a chance to express his
virility. "To this day," observed the psychiatrist, "he always refers

to her as *Maman* (Mummy), and suffered most in jail from seeing *Maman* only once a week." The court listened impassively, then sentenced him to be shot unless—as seems unlikely—Charles de Gaulle grants him a pardon. To the end he maintained that, although guilty of many crimes, "I swear on my mother's head that I never killed anybody."[33]

Another, and probably the most extreme outcome of Momistic conditioning, is occasionally indicated by suicide. In a study conducted in Scandinavian countries, Dr. Herbert Hendin, a Columbia University psychiatric instructor, reported correlations between the suicide rate and the style of child-rearing practiced.[34] Denmark, which has one of the world's highest suicide rates (20.3 per 100,000 population) is characterized by a particular child-rearing style that, according to Hendin, predisposes children to suicide by creating highly guilt-conscious, aggression-inhibited, and dependent personalities. Norway, with one of the Western hemisphere's lowest suicide rates (7.8 per 100,000 population), is much like Denmark in most variables, *except* that it employs different procedures in bringing up children. Manipulating the feeling of guilt in the child is a principal disciplinary tool in Denmark. When a child disobeys, the mother tells him that "you are hurting mama—you are making her unhappy." This technique of conditioning is coupled with the curbing of aggression.

Hendin's study continued to compare also the child-rearing patterns in Denmark and Sweden. Sweden is another country with an unusually high suicide rate, 17.4 per 100,000 population. The findings revealed that Swedish child-rearing practices were akin to the Danish mode. In Sweden the young are discouraged from expressing emotion and are taught to be "reasonable," regardless of how disturbing a situation might be. In respect to performance, the child is encouraged to excel and may consider himself unlovable unless he scores high in achievement. Also, young boys are emphatically discouraged from crying. In Norway, on the other hand, Dr. Hendin found a greater permissiveness for emotions. Aggression is permitted and hostility may be shown openly. The child is far less supervised and much less emotionally mother-tied than his Danish cousin. He is allowed to direct his aggression outward to the environment. He need not be first or best and can console himself with success in fantasy, unlike his Swedish and Danish counterpart.

---

[33] "Maman's Boy," *Time* (Nov. 19, 1965), pp. 46–47. (Reprinted by permission from *Time,* The Weekly Newsmagazine; Copyright *Time* Inc. 1966.)

[34] Herbert Hendin, *Suicide and Scandinavia* (New York, Grune and Stratton, Inc., 1964).

Children in Denmark and Sweden appear, as a consequence, much "better behaved" than most of their Norwegian or American peers, and they exhibit more passive and dependent manners. These techniques of conditioning and manipulating youngsters are closely akin to Momistic style. It is therefore suggested that the child-rearing variable can be held accountable for the differential suicide rate—an argument that is further strengthened because *no other* social scientific theory to explain Denmark's high suicide rate has been advanced with such credibility. Unfortunately, no statistical data are available in the United States to show the differential suicide rates for those who have been brought up in a Momistic relationship and those who have not. But with Dr. Hendin's study in mind, suggesting that Denmark's and Sweden's high suicide rates may be explained by a peculiar type of child-rearing which includes some crucial elements of a typical Momistic relationship, it may, nevertheless, be hypothesized that in the United States *also,* (with a suicide rate of 10.8 per 100,000 population) some cases of suicide are again a tragic outcome of Momism.

This array of personality consequences of Momism should be understood with the following *points of caution* in mind: (1) The various effects rarely appear isolated from each other; rather, they overlap, form combinations, and symptomize themselves in a number of permutations. (2) A multitude of specific effects of mother-influence is, of course, to be expected in the life of entirely normal males, and no pathological connotations should be attached to such symptoms. The fact that the mother is the earliest and primary socializer leaves indelible female-created orientations and impressions in the personality of the male. To worry about such normal personality residues, to develop a "hypochondria" about mother-influence is unnecessary and would ultimately be a vain endeavor, since such female-induced features are both deep-seated and pervasive. (3) Momism should therefore be understood as a result of Momistic conditioning that *exceeds normal mother influence* —to the point of emotionally crippling the male child. (4) The duration of the symptoms of Momistic impairment differs from victim to victim. In some cases the impairment may last a lifetime, in other cases it may disappear soon after the son leaves home. In a situation of simple over-dependency where the influence has not been too constant or deep, the proverbial apron string can sometimes be broken. The Army often has this effect. Because of the duration of separation and the distance involved, the son is forced to act and make decisions by himself. In addition, the influence of the men he meets in the service may help break the tie. However, there are exceptions, and it has been observed that mother-dependency does not necessarily stop when the Mom is physically absent. Soldiers have been known to go A.W.O.L., break down, and show emotional disturbance when receiving letters from their mothers, criticizing them for leaving or begging them to come home.[35] Even with her death, dependency on a Mom may not stop. Some men in their fifties have become completely lost upon the death of their mother and have never regained normal contact with society. (5) It should be obvious that the disturbance of only a certain *proportion* of those males suffering from such problems as drug addiction, homosexuality, suicidal tendencies, etc., can be traced to a Momistic experience. The problems of the rest of these males have different etiologies. (6) Finally, it should be remembered that the diagnosis of a personality disturbance as an outcome of Momistic child-rearing is often extremely difficult and should be attempted only after careful, professionally competent scrutiny of the life history of a given problem person.

The Minimized Role of the Father

The National Association for Mental Health has shown concern for the detrimental aspects of child-rearing practices in America. Among other efforts, it has published folders and pamphlets and distributed them widely, usually free of charge, with the hope of reaching parents and future parents. Under the motto "What every child needs for good mental health," emphasis is put on the principles of basic acceptance of the child and his preparation for independence. This nationwide campaign is based upon the assumption that it is the education of parents and future parents that is the most effective means of curbing the production of emotionally disturbed males in American homes. However, it is interesting to note that these folders and pamphlets (see, for example, pamphlet #525, The National Association for Mental Health, Inc.), presumably addressed to *parents*, are in actuality, as demonstrated through the pictures and the drawings accompanying the text, almost exclusively oriented toward the mother-child relationship. The role of the father goes virtually unmentioned.

Behavioral scientists hold that if the NAMH is to successfully promote more balanced child-rearing patterns, it would have to include clarification and encouragement of the child-rearing functions of the father. His role is a crucial element in the normal socialization process of the child—especially of the male child.

---

[35] Strecker, *op. cit.*, pp. 33–34.

Summary

The concept of Momism developed from an early formulation that was mainly social comment and caustic polemic to a more scientific application that attempted to analyze and explain a presumably spreading problem of American family life. The definition of the concept as currently used refers to a *mother-son relationship where the child is forced into virtually complete emotional dependency on a mother who is prompted by deep-seated psychological needs for such a dominance-submission reationship.* In most of the incidents it can be assumed that the child's personality is overpowered by his mother and that, as a result, he tends to display lack of initiative, inability to make decisions, and impairment of his potential to be creative.

Momism seems to be concentrated in the American middle class, where researchers have found a number of Momism-inducing conditions: (1) frequent father-absence; (2) a relatively well-educated mother; (3) the mother suffering from role conflict, trying to find an identity as a woman; (4) the mother attempting to resolve the role conflict by becoming a "career mother" and thereby compensating for the perceived loss of other successful careers; (5) the mother being the constant supervisor of the child and tending to employ principles of so-called scientific child rearing.

The impact of these conditions was studied and compared between two sets of urban families. It was found that Momistic neurosis in the male child does *not* stem from a lack of "love" or affection, from corporal punishment, open expression of hostility, or from authoritarian treatment of the child, but rather from conditioning the child into emotional dependency on mother through the powerful "conditional love" technique.

The types of Moms, classified by the principal dependency-establishing technique employed, include: (1) the over-indulgent Mom; (2) the over-protective Mom; (3) the permissive Mom; (4) the domineering Mom; (5) the "child worshiping" Mom; (6) the "star" Mom; (7) the "absolute authority" Mom; and (8) the "ailing" Mom.

The various effects of Momism on the child may range from infantile dependency to, in extreme cases, suicide. Normally functioning individuals must of necessity develop into viable personalities who are able to make their own decisions and arrange and carry out their own life style. The victims of Momism, however, are subject to a form of neurosis that impairs their ability to adequately make the transition from child to adult status—that retards them emotionally and that often condemns them to permanent adolescence.

Finally, any attempt to correct Momistic child-rearing patterns must necessarily start with clarifying and encouraging the child-rearing functions of the father, as Momism can only flourish in a situation of weak or absent adult male models.

conditions of
urban-industrial life

As mentioned earlier, if the nature of the social structure causes discontinuity between the status of the child and of the adult, the primary condition for adolescence is established—a condition that prevails in most urban-industrial societies. If, in addition, the "sufficient cause" exists, a nonspecific and noncompelling ideation, the society in question is bound to show the symptoms of adolescence. This chapter deals with a number of conditions of the social structure that create such discontinuity.

Multi-Specificity of the Division of Labor

Probably the most striking feature of an urban-industrial society is its complex network of positions. The division of labor, the way society splits up and distributes the various responsibilities and functions necessary for its maintenance, includes such fine subdivisions that most members of urban-industrial settings would be unable to identify most of them. An example would be the military establishment. Rarely does a layman know all the aspects of its structure. There are so many branches, offices, ranks, responsibilities, and controls that it would take the knowledge of an expert or extensive study by a layman to understand their multiple purposes and interrelationships. Another example would be the whole apparatus that regulates the use of the automobile in America. There are multitudinous offices that cooperate in carrying out this gigantic function: the operator licensing office, the auto licensing office, laws, courts, law enforcement agencies, the Departments of Roads and Highways, driver's education classes, insurance companies, etc. The prototype of the modern division of labor, on a miniature scale, is the assembly line. Every worker completes a highly specialized task, breaking up the process of manufacture into endless fragmentary jobs. The individual worker may lose sight of the complete process, as he makes only a tiny contribution to the overall manufacture.

There is a highly sensitive interrelationship among the various positions, one depending upon the other. If one position were eliminated and not immediately replaced by a substitute or alternative position, the whole structure would be apt to collapse.

American working conditions rarely give the individual a chance to do a "whole" job. In an age of assembly-line production, it is common practice that a man does only one specific detail in a longer process—be it within the military establishment, the motor vehicle bureau, the industrial plant, or the educational system. This industrial condition entails sharp discontinuity between the life of the child and the life of the working adult. The life of the child is more holistic, in that his early education and training usually take in the broadest range of different curricula and activities. In late adolescence, when the youth enters a job, this broad range narrows abruptly, and the young individual has to focus on one particular activity for which he probably was not specifically prepared and which may require entirely new training and education. His job may be so specialized that, as a child or teenager, he may not have been provided with a model or role definition to understand his new situation. As a result, thousands of teen-agers who try to enter the labor force immediately after, or even before high school graduation, are unable to decide which vocation will provide them with lasting satisfaction and personal fulfillment. Their reactions often take the form of discontent, frequent changes of jobs, and even delinquency.

Since there are relatively few instances in American society where the institution of apprenticeship is part of the process of learning a trade, the newness of the work situation and the abrupt onset of adult responsibilities is likely to create some degree of anxiety and confusion in the young individual. Apprenticeship basically was an Old World institution whereby the young members of the society were gradually introduced into a trade and, thereby, into the adult position. The status of apprentice was well defined, and the rights and obligations clearly spelled out, often laid out in the form of legal contracts. At the end of the apprenticeship period, which varied anywhere from three to six years depending on the particular trade, the youth was formally initiated (rite of passage) into the ranks of the full-fledged journeymen and was henceforth regarded as an adult. Such facilitation is seldom available to the contemporary American teen-ager as he bridges the gap between the "generalist" status of the child and the specialist status of the adult.

To set the discussion on the multispecific nature of modern social structure in the right perspective, it is necessary to elaborate on two complexly interrelated phenomena. One is the nature of the general culture and the other is the process of achieving personal identity. As was already mentioned in the introductory chapter, there seems to be a gradual shift of identity genesis from the general culture as a basic orienting force to one's specific social position as an identity-forming experience. This trend was probably brought about by the diminishing persuasiveness of the culture and, at the same time, by an increasing social-structural specialization. The multispecific social system makes interpretation of its variegated life experiences into generally understandable terms increasingly difficult. One of the few social scientists who has been successful in clearly recognizing and conceptualizing this new development in Western civilization is sociologist Daniel Bell:

> . . . the growth of technical specialization creates a strain on the cultural level of society, the term is used here not in its anthropological sense but in the sense that culture is the symbolic expression of what is occurring in society. People try to symbolize their experiences in order to make them intelligible to each other. This is the way nineteenth-century culture developed, a culture that arose out of an awareness of social mobility. The novels of the time represented the way in which the awareness of the new experiences of society found symbolic expression. It will become more and more difficult to find common symbolic expressions of the forms of specialization that are now developing. As a consequence an increasing disjunction between the culture and the society may arise. This is not just a problem of the political alienation of the intelligentsia but a much more pervasive problem of the inability of the society to find cultural terms for expressing what is occurring in the realm of science and in life itself. This is not just the "two cultures" problem presented by Snow because it is not just a matter of the education of people. It is, rather, the problem of the inability to find symbolic expressions for the kinds of experiences that take place in the work life created by the new forms of intellectual technology.[1]

In the long run, the situation so perceptively described by Bell is apt to result in human isolation, even social alienation. Young people would be affected by this urban and super-industrialized life style in a particularly acute manner. They would experience extra strain, be-

---

[1] Daniel Bell, "The Post-Industrial Society," in Eli Ginzberg (ed.), *Technology and Social Change* (New York, Columbia University Press, 1964), pp. 50–51.

cause they grow up as generalists and confront a system of isolated and discrete positions that require them to learn or relearn specific tasks for which they may have been insufficiently prepared. However, the main point here is that the general culture, which should include the symbolic expressions of common life experiences of the members of the society, is finding it increasingly difficult to incorporate and reflect these multifarious experiences. People involved in a societal situation of this nature gradually become dependent on the discrete and specific social position and come to partially ignore a culture that is necessarily vague and is too general to meaningfully reflect the multitude of diverse life experiences. In such a situation, culture actually *cannot* afford to be specific since it would run the danger of violating, contradicting, or discriminating against life experiences of many members because of the near-impossibility of presenting all points of view.

This situation touches on identity problems for youth. While still a generalist, dependent on a vague and nonspecific cultural "blueprint," youth can easily suffer from an *anomic* condition that creates difficulty in answering the question "Who am I?" unless parental guidance and value indoctrination compensate for general cultural nonspecificity. It is not until the youth recognizes, enters, and feels at home in a specific position of the division of labor that a sense of trustworthy identity and security develops. This, then, is the dilemma of the modern adolescent. Cast between the generalist status of the child and the relatively unknown specialized status of the adult he suffers from uncertainty about a future and vaguely known specialization.

The Separation of Home and Work

In industrialized societies, the setting for raising children and the setting for employment have usually become separate realms. It seems that the practice of commuting from the home to the place of employment is directly correlated with the degree of industrial development of a country. For example, in the 1950's, West Germany had roughly 3 million people commuting to jobs in communities outside their own. In 1965, with progressing technology, industrialization, and affluence the count of such commuters was 6.3 million.[2]

Most families in the urban setting no longer practice the tradition whereby the son takes on the occupation of his father and the daughter

---

[2] *The Bulletin*, Official Publication of the Federal Republic of Germany (Nov. 9, 1965), p. 6.

that of her mother. (However, it seems that most girls still learn the wife-mother role through the mother.) James S. Coleman found that in the city and the suburbs, less than one out of ten boys intended to pursue the same occupation as his father.[3] In most cases, the children are not familiar with the specific type of work their fathers do, and, when they assume their own vocational activities, they are received into a completely new surrounding. The abrupt change from the primary socialization of the nuclear family to the secondary socialization in the job can create considerable confusion. Unfamiliarity with the new social environment invites role and status uncertainty. By contrast, in a folk society where the children grow up in the consanguine family, the young have opportunity to observe a number of adult relatives at work, since the place of residence and the place of work are usually combined. Primary and secondary socialization are thus blended into one process. This makes for transition into the larger society that is gradual and without anxiety and uncertainty. The concept of "marginality" can be applied to the situation of teen-agers who grow up in strictly nuclear families. They occupy an intermediary or marginal status with respect to their family of orientation and their family of procreation, i.e., they are no longer integrated in their parental family as children, and they have not yet married and established their own procreative family.

The conditions of the modern industrial society have gradually changed the family from a production unit to a consumption unit. Each member is *individually* engaged in the production process. This is strikingly different from the tribal or folk societies where the family is a production unit as well as a consumption unit, and where only the most elementary division of labor exists. The network of positions may comprise merely a few simple status definitions, such as hunters, warriors, chiefs, home-keepers, etc. This type of social structure prevents the development of discontinuity between the position of the child and of the adult, since the children experience an early involvement in the visible and imitable work and responsibilities of the adults.

In contrast, in a rapidly changing and highly rationalized society, education is not limited to the "natural processes" within the family system as is the case in the folk societies, but has been replaced by more formalized institutions that are set apart from the family and that cover an ever longer span of the time of youth. It is interesting to note that the institutionalization of nonfamilial education and training has resulted in an unintentional by-product, sociologically defined as a "latent function": the evolvement of distinct *social systems* that resemble subcultures with norms and values of their own and often appear to oppose and reject

---

[3] James S. Coleman, *The Adolescent Society* (New York, Free Press, 1963), p. 7.

adult demands. As a result, not only have education and job training been removed from parental supervision and the family setting, but, in a sense, so has the youth himself. He now belongs to a society of peers, a society whose natural habitat is the halls and classrooms of the high school, the teen-age canteens, the corner drugstore, the automobile, and other typical gathering places. The population of this teen-age habitat has risen sharply over the last decades. Many contemporary Americans tend to perceive high schools as institutions that have always existed. Although this may be true to some degree, they have not existed to the *extent* and number that they do today. In 1900, only 11 per cent of America's high-school-aged youth were *in* high school; in 1930, the proportion was 51 per cent; today it is estimated to be approximately 90 per cent.[4] The emphasis on formal education is directly correlated with industrial development. This principle can be observed in other countries. For example, a parallel trend, delayed by about one to two decades, can be seen in Soviet Russia where 50 to 60 years ago, in a more primitive stage of industrialization, comparatively few persons needed the lengthy training that is offered by the modern high school.

Longer and Nonfamilial Period of Education

The complexity of the social structure and the specialization that accompanies most positions require extensive education and training. This training and education is extended over a progressively longer period of time and usually takes place away from the family setting.

This feature of the urban-industrial society is illustrated by the almost perennial conflicts with the law on the part of the Amish, a small Protestant sect living a simple-structured rural life, who have attempted to maintain their small society as an enclave within the larger society. Their views on and their needs for education differ considerably from the requirements set up by the laws of most states. In opposition to the "wordly" laws, Amish elders maintain that, "Worldly wisdom taught in public schools conflicts with our way of life. Our religion is built around simplicity."[5] Conflicts have been reported from several midwestern states. One of the more recent clashes between the Amish and the state education laws occurred in November, 1965, in Iowa:

> Hazleton, Iowa. Hymn-chanting Amish children and their sobbing parents yesterday won a "moratorium" on efforts to root

---

[4] James S. Coleman, *Adolescents and the Schools* (New York, Basic Books, 1965), p. 7.

[5] "Ironed All Day," *Newsweek* (Jan. 26, 1959), p. 64.

them out of their sect's private schools and haul them off to public school.

The Amish children, screaming and chanting the Sunday school hymn "Jesus Loves Me," repulsed a public school truant officer, county officials and sheriff's deputies who sought to bus them to public school. . . .

The Amish parents have contended, during a three-year running battle with local school officials, that their children do not need a high school education and can get all the schooling they need from Amish teachers who have only an eighth-grade education.

The Amish, who still travel by horse-drawn vehicles in the jet age and wear simple, homespun clothing similar to that of pioneer days, contend public schools are "too worldly." The Amish have not paid the fines levied against them and the county has placed liens against their property.[6]

The resistance of the Amish has at least two reasons: besides the objection to the undesirable "wisdom of the world," by which outside education would imperil the religious credo of their community, there is the simple reason that their rural way of life requires only a minimum of education.

By contrast, the dynamic patterns of the urban-industrial setting create unusually complex educational and vocational needs. These needs are due to at least three major conditions. First, there is rapid social change. American parents cannot mold their children in their own image, since they suffer from chronic cultural lag which may render a portion of their skills, knowledge, and attitudes obsolete or unusable. The second factor deals with the strong emphasis on individualism that prevents parents from determining the occupation of the young by familial traditions and consensus and puts a premium on individual choice and initiative. Rather than relying on familial norms and models for deciding on their future occupation, the young may prefer nonfamilial formal training and education. This preference is related to the third condition, the high degree of specialization characteristic of modern occupational careers, which usually calls for vocational preparation outside of the family system. The urban-industrial social structure contains more positions than most parents could give adequate advice, counseling, and preparation for.

The effect of these three conditions has been to shift the responsibility of preparing offspring for their future "specialities" from the family to specialized institutions of education and training, and to ensconce the young more and more in nonfamilial institutions, from nursery school through college.

---

[6] UPI Report (Hazelton, Iowa, Nov. 23, 1965).

The development of nonfamilial institutions of socialization, result-ing in considerable age segregation, represents only one of the functions of this era of specialization. Another function is that youth's training period grows longer. Increasingly, the occupations in modern society require more specialized and longer periods of training. With industrial progress, the functionality of unskilled or semiskilled workers is con-stantly declining, while the functionality of technical and managerial per-sonnel is rising in significance. Thus, modern society not only relegates education and training to institutions other than the family, but also keeps the youth there longer, until he is deemed properly "processed" and fit to take his place in a specialized position.

During such long socialization periods, the youth is no longer thought of as occupying the status of child, yet neither is he regarded as an adult. He passes through a marginal situation, and the longer the training period lasts, the longer marginality has to be endured.

As a concomitant feature, as we have seen, the question of *in loco parentis* is gaining prominence, adding to the confusion about the status of youth and intensifying the crisis of adolescence.

Mobility and Generational Discontinuity

The concept of mobility has several meanings. One meaning refers to movement within the social structure either *vertically*, up or down in socioeconomic status, or *horizontally*, from one position to another within the same socioeconomic class.[7] Changing from the occupation of student to that of doctor would be an example of vertical mobility, while chang-ing from factory worker to construction worker would be an example of horizontal mobility. The other meaning given to mobility refers to geo-graphic movement from one locale to another and could be illustrated by rural-urban migration. Both types of mobility, social and geographic, are prevalent in American life, and both can, to some degree, be held respon-sible for adding to the problem of adolescence.

An earlier discussion noted that the geographic mobility of Ameri-cans is remarkable. For example, between March, 1960, and March, 1961, approximately 35.5 million people, about a fifth of the whole United States population, moved from one house or apartment to another.[8] As a result, disruption of life patterns cannot be prevented, often thereby

---

[7] Leonard Broom and Philip Selznick, *Sociology*, 3rd ed. (New York, Harper and Row, 1963), p. 204.

[8] United States Department of Labor, *Economic Forces in the United States*, 7th ed., Bulletin # 1384 (Washington, D. C., Government Printing Office, 1963).

prolonging the period of adolescence and aggravating the typical confusion and anxiety. The present discussion, however, is more concerned
with how vertical mobility affects the young.

Vertical mobility can be defined by comparing members of one
generation with the next, called *generational* mobility, or by comparing
different stages in the life of a member of one generation, called *career*
mobility.[9] The focus of this discussion is generational mobility and discontinuity of social prestige level as they affect adolescence.

A full understanding of the background of the mobility syndrome
would require an investigation of historical and cultural data that would
exceed this frame. A summary statement must therefore be sufficient.
Probably the most formative influence on the mobility syndrome can be
traced to early religiocultural values related to the Protestant Reformation
and the rise of capitalism in Europe. The concept of mobility ethic
evolved from the ideational involvement that urged man to improve his
position in life.[10] Another influential force encouraging mobility is American materialism, stimulated by economic opportunities, free land, natural
resources, and rapidly expanding business. These two themes, the ideational and the economic, established the basic attitudes for mobility. A
number of characteristics in the organization of American life facilitated
the materialization of these attitudes. Among the promoting circumstances
were these: (1) The millions of immigrants, most of whom had to start
at the bottom of the socioeconomic hierarchy, facilitated upward mobility
for earlier settlers. (2) Mechanization and industrialization reduced the
proportion of positions for which unskilled labor was suitable and
effected an upward trend in occupations from one generation to the
next. (3) Differential fertility between the socioeconomic classes—with
the reproduction rate of the lower income brackets being more than 50
per cent higher than that of the top brackets—effected upward mobility
of the lower-class "surplus" population into middle-class occupations and
professions.

It is against this background of religiocultural, materialistic, and
social-organizational forces that the adolescent's problem of status and
identity must be viewed. The young American is confronted with a dynamic society in which the status he may occupy as an adult is not necessarily conterminal with the status of his family of orientaion. In addition
to the social structure allowing status striving, the cultural dicta even encourage and urge seeking an "improved" status. This, then, is the social
scene which the adolescent enters.

---

[9] Broom and Selznick, *op. cit.*, p. 205.

[10] For detail see: Max Weber, *The Protestant Ethic and the Spirit of Capitalism*
(New York, Charles Scribner's Sons, 1930).

In most industrial societies, the placement function of the family has greatly declined. While it is true that initially the child identifies and is identified with the general status and prestige of his family, as a teen-ager and young adult he becomes relatively detached from his family's influence, and his social standing depends increasingly on his personal achievements in school and in the labor force. The status he eventually achieves may be on a different level from that of his parents'. In the modern urban-industrial society, family origin affects the social status of the individual only indirectly, by influencing opportunities for educational and occupational achievements. Most research in generational mobility has indicated that approximately two-thirds of the sons have been vertically mobile, either upward or downward, taking the father's socioeconomic class stratum as the point of departure. Generational mobility, then, is twice as frequent as generational continuity.[11] Most of the mobility mentioned in the research reports involves shifts limited to occupational levels immediately adjacent to those of the fathers'. Professors North and Hatt have conducted a survey that illustrates the son's deviation from the father's occupation.[12] (See Table 5–1.) Since the time this research was conducted, in 1947, it may be assumed that generational mobility has developed to an even greater extent. The researchers' data reveal that, with the sole exception of farming, no occupational category achieved more than one-third generational continuity. In addition, it should be realized that the information presented in Table 5–1 deals with relatively broad categories and that all those who classified their occupation in the same general class as their fathers' do not occupy the same *specific* occupation as the father, implying that a great deal of horizontal mobility exists *within* the broad occupational classes.

Some of the consequences of generational mobility are relevant to the discussion of the adolescent problem. For those adolescents who fail in the process of status striving, as some must, in a society that encourages all to strive and that promises success to those who are capable, failure is considered evidence of personal inadequacy. For those who achieve upward mobility, difficult adjustments are required. This problem is frequently evident in both the research literature and the popular "success" story, describing the situation of the rich and successful, but unhappy and maladjusted, man.

Widespread lack of family continuity and tradition may present teenagers with an obscure future for which they have no clear and visible

---

[11] Richard Centers, "Occupational Mobility of Urban Occupational Strata," *American Sociological Review*, Vol. 13 (April, 1948), pp. 197–203.

[12] Cecil C. North and Paul K. Hatt, "Jobs and Occupations: A Popular Evaluation," *Opinion News*, Vol. 9 (September, 1947), pp. 9–12.

TABLE 5–1. Generational Mobility in a Representative Sample of the American Population.

	Occupational Categories of Father								
	Pro-fes-sional	Busi-ness	White Collar	Skill-ed	Semi-Skill-ed	Serv-ice	Farm	Non Farm Labor	Don't Know
Occupation of Sons:									
Professional	23	24	10	13	5	5	17	2	1
Business	4	31	9	18	8	3	25	2	*
White-collar work	9	23	15	21	10	3	16	3	*
Skilled work	3	7	4	30	14	5	29	7	1
Semiskilled work	2	11	6	19	19	3	32	7	1
Domestic and personal service work	4	6	3	20	12	8	28	12	7
Farming	2	2	2	3	4	*	84	3	..
Nonfarm labor	3	12	..	9	17	1	32	19	7

* Less than .5%.

Source: Cecil C. North and Paul K. Hatt, "Jobs and Occupations: A Popular Evaluation," *Opinion News*, Vol. 9, National Opinion Research Center, (September, 1947), pp. 3–13; (Reprinted with the permission of the publisher.)

models. They are called upon to define their own occupational prefer-ences and to make one of the most vital decisions in life—choosing a career. The mobility ethic, expecting the teen-ager to go beyond his family's level of achievement and improve his level of social prestige, contributes additional pressures. By largely ruling out parents as occupa-tional models, a whole *Gestalt* of points of references, a social milieu, and a familiar sociocultural orientation is rendered irrelevant for the youth. Most teen-agers who assume an occupation or vocational training that differs significantly from that of their parents experience a shift and change in life orientation that can often be compared to a type of "culture shock." Symptoms of this shock and the pressure of the mobility ethic show themselves in the form of feelings of anxiety, guilt, and/or inferiority.

The Home Away from Home

A proportion of American children are raised, partially or wholly, away from the parental home. One such type of child is entrusted to the care of a *partial* home while the mother—frequently because of the absence of a father—is employed full-time outside of the home. Another type of relocated child, the victim of disabled, amateurish, or even delinquent parents, grows up in an institution that can be classified as a welfare institution, as illustrated in the case of the earlier-mentioned Junior Village in Washington, D.C.[13] Still another type of child is the delinquent youth who serves time in an industrial school, detention home, or other type of penal, corrective, or rehabilitative institution. (Problems related to delinquent circumstances are touched upon in a later chapter, "The Delinquent Adolescent.")

The present discussion deals briefly with the first two types of child: those part-time in day-care centers and those full-time in welfare institutions.

The vast majority of children spending time in partial homes come from approximately 10 million full-time working mothers, a 1965 figure that had doubled since 1950. It was found that one out of every three mothers with children under 18 was gainfully employed outside of the home, and that one out of every four mothers with children under six years of age was employed, the latter category amounting to 3.6 million in 1965, which, again, was double the figure of 1950.[14] The extent to which the children were expected to care for themselves while their mothers were at work seemed to be greater among the lower-income families. For example, 10 percent of the children in families with incomes under $3000, as compared to 7 percent in families with incomes exceeding $6000 were left to look after themselves. It is noteworthy, however, that day-care arrangements (family day care or group care) were *not* correlated with family income and were observed occurring in comparable proportions at all levels of family income.[15]

These statistics lead to an increasingly acute question: what happens to the child while the mother is at work? According to 1958 statistics of the U. S. Children's Bureau, this question involved more than five million children under the age of 12.[16] One attempted solution to the problem was the the "latchkey child"—the child who is entrusted with a house key to be used when the parents are away from the home. The U. S. Children's Bureau estimated that there were close to one-half million such children under the age of 12 in the United States.[17]

---

[13] J. W. Anderson, "A Special Hell for Children in Washington," *Harper's* (November, 1965), pp. 51–56.

[14] *Child Care Arrangements of the Nation's Working Mothers, A Preliminary Report* (Washington, D.C., U. S. Children's Bureau, 1965), p. 1.

[15] *Child Care Arrangements of the Nation's Working Mothers, A Preliminary Report*.

[16] Henry C. Lajewski, *Child Care Arrangements of Full-time Working Mothers* (Washington, D.C., U. S. Childrens' Bureau, Publication No. 378, 1959), p. 15.

[17] *Ibid.*

Among other "solutions" was entrusting the care of 558,000 children under the age of 12 to their brothers and sisters under 18 years of age.[18] The older children were thus, in some cases, kept from attending school. Other arrangements included using older relatives, father, neighbors, friends as baby sitters or caretakers of the children and the home while mother was working. A more formal arrangement involved approximately 120,000 children under 12 who were cared for away from their homes, placed in day nurseries, daycare centers; settlement houses, after-school centers, nursery schools, etc.[19] In other words, these children received *group* care while their mothers worked. It is especially this group of children, who experience a "home away from home," or in a sense, a *dual* home situation, that has attracted the attention of behavioral scientists.

The effects of maternal employment on the children's personalities have been the object of study of a large number of investigations. A careful examination of the research literature by Lois M. Stolz revealed an array of different, sometimes opposing, and mostly inconclusive findings in this area.[20] The researcher discovered that the professional literature reflects an abundance of findings and conclusions regarding the linkage between employment of the mother and such manifestations in the children as delinquency, type of school and personal adjustment, and academic achievement. One obtains the impression that a good deal of this confusion resulted from researchers' failure to carefully control or match important variables, such as socioeconomic status, family integration, size of family, type of maternal employment, mother's attitude, ethnic background, etc. One researcher illustrated this need for a more sensitive investigation by noticing that mother's attitude toward her work made a significant difference in the children's adjustment to partial absence of the mother.[21] Lois W. Hoffman found that the mother who liked working had a more positive emotional relationship with her children, used milder discipline, refrained from burdening the children with an excess of household tasks. On the other side, the mother who disliked her outside job exhibited a higher degree of alienation from her children and tended to make considerable demands on them to help with household chores. While the children of both types of mother manifested maladjustments, they showed different syndromes. Children of the first type of mother tended to be nonassertive and dependent, whereas

[18] Reference 16.

[19] *Ibid.*

[20] Lois M. Stolz, "Effects of Maternal Employment on Children: Evidence from Report.

[21] Lois W. Hoffman, "Effects of Maternal Employment on the Child," *Child Development,* Vol. 32 (March, 1961), pp. 187–197.

children of the second type tended to be assertive and hostile. In general, however, studies of the effects of maternal employment are relatively non-generalizable and, at this time, are not yet very reliable.

On the other side, information that has been derived from studying children experiencing full-time substitutes for the parental home is markedly more definite and conclusive and enjoys greater consensus among experts. Clinicians and social psychologists have long agreed that maternal deprivation has severely detrimental effects on children.[22] Dr. Lauretta Bender, observing approximately 6,000 children in New York's Bellevue Hospital over more than a decade, noted that children who had been maternally deprived for one or more years were not able to adjust in foster homes. "They all appear retarded, untrained, impulsive, unpatterned in their behavior. As they grow older and the demands of society on them increase, their behavior becomes progressively more asocial. Even their motor habits are retarded—as in their ability to walk and to use their arms and legs and body in the kind of play that we expect of the nursery school child."[23]

One of the most crucial shortcomings of such substitute homes is the number of youths per adult supervisor or nurse. The Child Welfare League of America has recommended that there should be no more than approximately six children per adult.[24] In most institutional settings, this suggestion has not been materialized and remains a Utopia. The consequences of serious understaffing and maternal deprivation can be summed up in the following points: (1) With understaffing, a certain degree of anonymity is unavoidable. The child with his needs, opinions, and dreams does not receive sufficient attention *to feel known.* In fact, it is usually necessary for the nurse or supervisor to avoid emotional involvement with individual children. To carry the emotional burden of each child would be beyond the staff member's endurance. Certainly, a sympathetic approach is needed, but it can rarely reach depths capable of replacing the parental function of assuring the child continued attention and understanding. (2) The child may recognize and be disturbed about the perfunctory atmosphere of the institution and wonder whether he is really wanted. The feeling of *full acceptance* is immensely significant to the child, and its absence can result in feelings of personal worth-

---

[22] See examples: Arnold Gesell and Catherine Amatruda, *Developmental Diagnosis* (New York, Hoeber, 1947); William Goldfarb, "Infant Rearing and Problem Behavior," *American Journal of Orthopsychiatry,* Vol. 13 (April, 1943), pp. 249–65; John Bowlby, *Maternal Care and Mental Health* (Geneva, World Health Organization, 1951); Lauretta Bender, "There is no Substitute for Family Life." *Child Study,* Vol. 23 (Winter, 1945–1946), pp. 74–78.

[23] Bender, *op. cit.,* p. 75.

[24] Anderson, *op. cit.,* p. 53.

lessness and depression. (3) The experience of *physical affection* is of utmost significance in the development of a healthy personality. The favorable effect of physical closeness and caressing touch has been demonstrated experimentally with laboratory animals. In demonstrations with two sets of rats all variables were kept strictly constant, except that in the experimental group physical caresses were administered daily. It was soon observed that the fondled rats gained weight faster, matured earlier, appeared healthier, and, generally speaking, expressed more exuberance and greater vitality than the rats in the control group.[25] It is assumed that the basic condition underlying this finding can be extrapolated to humans. The significance of this finding applies to the institutional setting in that it rarely affords conditions where the child can find as much affection and physical intimacy as he normally would in the parental home. (4) A child has an interminable need for *question–answer* interaction. His constant "why," "how," and "what-is-this" can hardly draw adequate responses in an institutional environment with a number of children assigned to the care of one adult. His curiosity must go unsatisfied. Ultimately this may generate indifference, dullness, in extreme cases even retardation.

Certain consequences, having bearing on adolescence, evolve from these dysfunctional conditions of institutional child-rearing: (1) There are a number of human qualities that appear to be the unique product of the primary family group—a sense of loyalty, cooperation, affection, and consideration. As Cooley pointed out, these qualities are universal because of the universal primary-group experience and constitute essential elements of what is loosely called "human nature."[26] The question that arises in conjunction with the substitution of institutional homes for the primary familial home is: what modifications, if any, does the institutional substitute have on the "human nature" of the child? Will the child's sense of kindness, sympathy, and affection be reduced? Will he develop characteristics of the sociopathic personality, showing little regard and sympathy for the suffering of others? A vast amount of research findings, a few of them mentioned above, indicate that these questions unfortunately can often be answered by pointing to example after example of antisocial and even sociopathic products of institutional child-rearing. (2) Institutional upbringing may add complications to the process of transition from child to adult status. A common criticism of the practice of subjecting the child to all-day adult supervision is that it may

[25] Victor H. Denenberg, "Animal Studies On Developmental Determinants of Behavioral Adaptability," in O. J. Harvey (ed.), *Experience, Structure and Adaptability* (New York, Springer Publishing Co., 1966), pp. 123–47.

[26] Charles H. Cooley, *Social Organization* (New York, Scribner's, 1915), pp. 23–24.

prolong dependency more than would ordinarily be necessary. The child may be deprived of so many opportunities for making independent decisions that, eventually, he becomes unable to make any decisions of his own when called upon. He lacks opportunities to roam about, to avoid adult supervision and sanctions—conditions that, according to an earlier-mentioned study by Arnold W. Green,[27] are crucial in preserving independent personality expression of the youth. Under constant supervision, the child may become passive and may prefer to let others take the initiative. Obviously, such attitude patterns will cause serious problems when the individual tries to assume adult responsibilities. (3) In some instances, another complication may appear in the form of pseudo-retardation, brought on by the imposed anonymity and the lack of attention during childhood, which gradually disappears during the teens when the adolescent experiences more opportunities for inquiry and expression. However, during this "catching-up" period, the youth may attempt to answer too many questions in too short a time, thereby failing and inviting feelings of inferiority and anxiety. (4) Another consequence of institutional upbringing is the child's tendency to shift loyalty and value-orientation from the parental home to the institutional peer group. Observers of the adolescent subculture hold that its origin is partially due to the fact that children and teen-agers are isolated in a sort of youth "ghetto"—from kindergarten through high school and even college, where they learn norms and values significantly different from those of the home and the adult world. This process often has its roots in the child's experience of spending more of his time with peers in the day-care center than with parents. For many children this experience is a forerunner of the adolescent subculture.

The Adolescents' Share of Affluence

While the unprecedented affluence of mid-century America does not cause adolescence *per se*, it definitely has promoted its spread and survival as a *collective* expression, perceptible in the form of teen-age sub-cultures. This subcultural or collective identity of American adolescents, as it is facilitated and maintained by affluence, is examined in this section.

The underlying premise of this discussion is that access to the affluence of the nation both promotes and reinforces the "typical" (note the collective connotation) teen-age behavior. The reinforcement of teen-

---

[27] Arnold W. Green, "The Middle-Class Male Child and Neurosis," *American Sociological Review*, Vol. 11 (February, 1946), pp. 31–41.

age behavior is primarily a result of the rewards obtained through adhering and conforming to peer norms and behavior patterns. These rewards come in the form of acceptance by and popularity in the peer
group. Adherence and conformity to peer patterns often necessitate some
material implementation. This may mean a car, new clothes, sports
equipment. In order to keep implementing the latest fad and fashion of
the subculture, a teen-ager must have financial means. Statistics indicate
that such means are available and that modern teen-agers control a surprisingly large share of society's affluence.

In 1965, the nation's teen-agers (between 13 and 19 years of age)
numbered nearly 25 million and were growing as an age bracket three
times faster than the total population.[28] Merchants, admen, and market
researchers have begun to understand the enormous potential available
for exploitation. It was estimated that teen-agers have approximately
$12 billion a year in freely disposable cash—cash not required for the
teen-agers' own maintenance, such as room, board, basic clothing, transportation, and schooling.[29] The annual rate of increase in teen-age financial power has been about $3 billion within the past few years and is
expected to total well above $20 billion by 1970.

In the fall of 1965, at the National Convention of Economists in
Philadelphia, this teen-age spending power was credited as the major
reason for the steady growth of the United States economy. It was also
predicted that the economic power of the 12- to 19-year-old group will
increase in the future. The reason for the increasing economic power of
teen-agers lies not only in the increase of actual financial means but
primarily in the peculiar market orientation that has developed in the
United States. Fashions, styles, appliances, cars, songs, movies, and TV
programs, etc., are significantly influenced—if not determined—by the
fads and tastes of the teen-age world. "The teen-ager," reports U.C.L.A.
Market Researcher Charles R. Campbell, "originates most mass buying
trends that reach the adult market. Youth is the carrier of news to the
family circle."[30]

In order to fully understand the teen-age influence on the United
States market, it is necessary to refer to the country's population statistics.
By the end of 1965, more than half of the American population was under
25 years of age. Between 1960 and 1965, while the total United States
population increased by 8%, the teen-age population from the ages of
13 to 19 increased by approximately 30%. In 1965, this segment made up
12% of the United States population and because of high post-war birth

---

[28] "Teen-Age Consumers—Dynamic Force in the United States Economy," *Senior
Scholastic,* Vol.. 86 (Feb. 25, 1965), p. 5.

[29] *Ibid.*

[30] "The Teen-Age Tide," *Time* (Oct. 9, 1964), p. 98.

rates, will swell to 20% by 1970.[31] David L. Yunich, president of Macy's in New York, is credited with foresight into the problem: "The teen-ager is here to stay and probably in increasing numbers, since children become teen-agers earlier every year. They date earlier, drive earlier, drink earlier, rebel earlier. And since so many of them continue from school to college to graduate school, they seem to stay teen-agers psychologically longer, as well."[32]

The affluent behavior patterns of American teen-agers have indeed become conspicuous and been examined by various researchers. *Time* investigated this subject matter and disclosed the following data.[33] Teen-agers spend more than $1.5 billion a year for entertainment. The "youth-market" orientation of the movie industry caters to an audience that is more than half teen-agers. More than 40% of all records and cameras are purchased by teen-agers. Teen-agers give the record industry about $700 million a year. (Estimates for boys are about $380 million, $320 million for girls.) In 1964, over half a million guitars were bought by teen-agers. Another area of teen-age spending involves cosmetics. Although they comprise only 11% of the total female population, teen-age girls buy 23% of all cosmetic and toilet goods (amounting to $450 million each year), and take home 20% of all women's clothes sold (amounting to $3.6 billion in 1963). Teen-age boys spend $120 million a year on such items as hair cream, mouth wash, and deodorants. Teen-age spending power has come to include even stock. Between 1960 and 1965, the number of teen-age stockholders tripled to 500,000; fully 10% of the stock of the new Communications Satellite Corporation is in the hands of minors. Teen-agers also participate in the credit system with long-term installment payments and credit cards. It has been estimated that one 17-year-old girl in five and two boys in five have their own charge accounts.[33]

Another source of information concerning the teen-agers' wealth and possessions is *Senior Scholastic*, which reported survey findings showing that of the teen-agers interviewed, 78% own watches, 27% own type-writers, 49% own record players, 81% own radios, 6% own cars, and 30% had bought records within the last 30 days.[34] It was also found that teen-age purchases account for 55% of soft drink sales, 53% of movie

---

[31] "Teen-Age Consumers—Dynamic Force in the United States Economy," *op. cit.*

[32] Quoted Grace Hechinger and Fred M. Hechinger, "In the Time it Takes You to Read These Lines, the American Teenager will have Spent $2,378.22," *Esquire* (July, 1965), pp. 65–68.

[33] "The Teen-Age Tide," *op. cit.*, pp. 96–98.

[34] "Teen-Age Consumers—Dynamic Force in the United States Economy," *op. cit.*, pp. 5–7.

ticket sales, 44% of camera sales, 43% of record sales, 30% of watch sales, and 26% of cosmetic sales.[35]

Fred M. Hechinger, education editor for the *New York Times,* and his wife Grace have also studied the financial power and the related buying patterns of American teen-agers and have published data on this subject matter over the past several years. According to their findings, approximately 20% of all cars (used or new) sold in the U.S. are owned by teen-agers. They also found that in 1965 about 60% of all first-time brides were teen-agers and that their homemaking enthusiasm—frequently backed up by parental support—afforded a boost to the real estate, home appliances, and furtniture market; moreover, their fertility spurred the manufacture of baby supplies.[36]

The business world has obviously been eager to exploit the purchasing power of teen-agers and has devised a number of different techniques to capture youthful attention and establish "brand loyalties." "Tell Mummie to buy . . ." or words to this effect can be heard in increasing numbers of commercials beamed at the teen-agers and at their infant brothers and sisters. An advertiser who succeeds in capturing the interest of youth can generally count on a market with the parents. This enormous emphasis on the youth market in the long run results in a total shift of preference and taste. Through the daily exposure to the youth slant in goods and services, adults come to accept the youth style without being aware of it, thus encouraging the formation of a so-called "youth cult."

Another technique applied by many big stores consists of arranging special sections for young shoppers. For example, Macy's in New York opened twelve new "Young American" rooms in 1965 especially for customers ranging from ages six to twenty-five. However, the experience of many store managers is that such "youth" sections attract a surprising number of adults. Many women prefer to shop in a store that "looks young and thinks young."

Some of the big stores have equipped themselves with safeguards against miscalculating fads and trends and risking financial loss through an overstock of unsellable items. They consult teen-agers directly and have established teen-age advisory boards. A teen coordinator is the liaison betwen the teen-age advisors and the store management. From her observations and from the direct suggestions of the teen-age board members, she derives current information on what teen-agers are likely to purchase.

---

[35] "Teen-Age Consumers—Dynamic Force in the United States Economy," p. 6.
[36] Hechinger and Hechinger, *op. cit.*

Another sales technique is the mailing list. Teen-agers are asked to submit their names and addresses in order to be added to a mailing list. Macy's department store has used a device called *The Pacesetters' Notebook,* a monthly newsletter that supplies young customers with news about styles and activities. Once the store has caught the teen-agers' interest, fads and fashions become the product of mutual influence. The store is now able to manipulate the taste of the teen-agers.

To forego loss, influential teen-agers—such as popular high school students or winners of beauty contests—are used as stabilizers. A most successful "stabilizer" was used by Catalina swimwear a few years ago. The winner of a Miss Universe Contest traveled across the United States from big store to big store and presented the latest Catalina swimwear, convincing American teen-agers that Catalina swimwear was desirable. Another example of business success was a Cutex advertisement campaign that promised to make teen-agers more kissable if they used grape-flavored or cola-tasting lipstick. Expanding the range of available flavors from caramel to peppermint, they succeeded in selling eight million such items.[37]

An example of systematically exploring the mood of teen-agers was the method used by Kayser-Roth, a manufacturer of lingerie. This firm arranged to have a sample of a new shift-type nightshirt, along with a questionnaire, sent to teen-age representatives in strategic locales across the nation. These representatives submitted the product as well as questions to a number of other teen-agers. Kayser-Roth evaluated the resultant information and made a number of profitable changes before mass-producing the new garment.[38]

Another tool for maintaining and expanding the teen-age market is direct-mail advertising sent to selected youths. Mailbag International was introduced in the United States in 1963 with the purpose of contacting the more popular and well-known teen-agers by using a list that included 2 million high school boys and girls, plus about 800,000 college coeds.[39] The majority of the addresses were high-school seniors, since it was believed that their patterns of fashion and preference would be more stable and influential. The selected youth received regular advertisements and free samples of the merchandise, usually cosmetics such as skin lotions, hair sprays, or lipsticks. The initiators of this program believed that teen-agers would regard this form of personal address as a recognition of their maturity and importance. Mailbag International may have made the correct assessment, since it received approximately 800 to 1,000

---

[37] Hechinger and Hechinger, op. cit., p. 113.
[38] *Ibid.*
[39] *Ibid.*

letters a month from its youthful clients. Retail agents reported a direct correlation between gift-advertisements and sales of the product.

One of the latest techniques for obtaining entrance into the teen-age market was devised by Remington Rand Co., which introduced the electric shaver to teen-agers with the suggestion that they ask mother or father to purchase them one for Christmas. The advertisement concluded with the promise that the teen-ager would receive a special "refund certificate" worth $5.00 after he obtained the article.[40]

Among the manufacturers conscious of teen-age style-setting power are the makers of automobiles. Some models, such as Ford's Mustang, General Motor's Monza, Chrysler's Barracuda, and American Motor's Marlin, are known as teenagers' specials and are often sold to youth-cultist adults on the strength of that recommendation. Several of the main manufacturers lend new cars to editors of some college newspapers, and approximately 10,000 new cars are currently at the disposal of high-school driver-education classes.[41] The Mailbag International for girls recently included an invitation from Ford to help design the "Ford of the Future." Ford wanted the girls' opinions regarding color, styling, and fabric to guide the experts in "building for you the Mustangs and Thunderbirds of tomorrow." It assured the girls that they did not have to be licensed drivers to be eligible for the Ford Advisory Council. Their eligibility was established by the fact that they were, as Ford put it, young and had a fresh, new, and imaginative viewpoint. Ford promised to send, from time to time, "Fun to Fill In" forms concerning the latest models. The approach to the boys was similar, except for more technical and mechanical details. The same privilege was offered in return for their "advice and counsel"—eligibility for the Ford Advisory Council.

Another area in which teen-age affluence is reflected and in which business interest is increasingly focusing on youth is travel. Travel agents and educational-tour leaders agree that a youth travel boom has developed over the last decade. The high-school-age group has come to almost match the extent of traveling done by the college-age group. In fact, overseas travel has taken on dimensions causing concern to the federal government, which considers it a major cause of tourist-dollar imbalance. While it is difficult to obtain accurate statistics on overseas travel involving nonstudent youth or students going independently, there are figures available concerning the student tour market. A survey published in the official trade magazine of the travel industry, *Travel Weekly*, revealed that summer (including June, July, and August) overseas travel of U.S. students in tour arrangements has consistently increased during past

[40] Hechinger and Hechinger, *op. cit.*
[41] *Ibid.*

years. Most of these tours went to Europe, although trips to the Orient and around the world are becoming increasingly popular. The number of students involved was 130,000 in 1963; 150,000 in 1964; 172,000 in 1965; 208,000 in 1966; and was forecast to be close to 250,000 in 1967.[42] These consistent increases can be attributed to the steady reduction of transportation costs, the growing desire on the part of young Americans to broaden their cultural background through foreign study and travel (40% of the tour programs combine recreation and studies with academic credit hours), the larger segment of the U.S. population in the 13 to 18 age group, and the increasing affluence of the young, which enables 90% of the participants to stay abroad for more than 40 days.

A number of conclusions can be derived from the preceding examples: (1) American teen-agers have control over suprisingly powerful financial resources. (2) American business has recognized the affluence of the teen-agers and is trying to profit from their financial power. (3) Business not only caters to fads and fashions, but actively accentuates, prolongs, and even initiates them. (4) The combination of the teen-agers' financial power and the business world's cultivation of fads and fashions has resulted in facilitating various forms of collective identification, implying that the formation and spread of teen-age subcultures are thereby considerably encouraged. (A more detailed discussion of the collective expression of teen-age style is reserved for chapters 8 and, especially, 9).

Before leaving the topic of adolescent affluence, one more question is asked: how do teen-agers acquire their financial resources?

One of the most common sources is the allowance. Some parents extend progressively large allowances, which have been estimated to average $6 a week for boys and $4 for girls.[43] But the allowance is not the only source of income for teen-agers. The majority of youths supplement their allowance by gainful work, be it occasional baby-sitting or regular employment in a factory. A survey of nearly 1500 high-school students showed that 68% of the boys and over 40% of the girls 15 to 18 years old joined the labor force temporarily and were gainfully employed during the summer of 1964—a practice that increases every summer.[44] The composite result of the allowance, income from jobs outside of the home, and income from jobs in the home was an average weekly income of between $9 to $10 for the 15-year- to 18-year-old

---

[42] Jon McInerney, "Anticipating Boom in Student Tours as Advanced Sales Increase 13%," *Travel Weekly*, Vol. 26 (April 18, 1967), pp. 1, 69A, 94.

[43] "The Teen-Age Tide," *op. cit.*, p. 96.

[44] *1965 Youth Market Consumer Survey* (New York, Scholastic Research Center and Institute of Student Opinion, 1965), p. 5.

high-school students.[45] This amounted to an annual income of roughly $500 per capita for the 15 to 18 age bracket. More specifically, the survey found that boys between 15 and 18 averaged $11.50 per week and boys between 12 and 14 averaged $5.00 per week. Girls between 15 and 18 averaged $6.88 per week and girls between 12 and 14 averaged $4.35 per week.[46]

Concerning summer employment, teen-agers have definite ideas about the nature and rewards of work. Low-paying outdoor jobs and jobs that provide social contacts are prized, while factory work is generally shunned. If teen-agers work for their parents in the family business, the job is expected to pay more than one away from home, either in cash or learning. The type of summer employment most valued is that of the resort lifeguard, who earns more than $60 a week, gets free room and board, and enjoys a wide variety of social contacts. Other favorites are construction work, camp supervision, truck driving, and selling. Girls favor sales jobs, especially those in the garment category. Bagging in supermarkets is considered a rather unprestigious job. The lowest evaluation is reserved for busing and washing dishes in restaurant.

In addition to summer work, many teen-agers hold year-round part-time jobs while going to school. Beyond that, concerning primarily out-of-school youth, nationwide statistics show that 43.8% or 4½ million boys of 14 to 19 years of age and 28.9% or nearly 3 million girls of 14 to 19 years of age were employed full-time in 1965.[47]

Labor Secretary W. Willard Wirtz pointed out the innovation of a number of income possibilities for needy youth.[48] A source of income for underprivileged youth opened up with the Neighborhood Youth Corps program of the Office of Economic Opportunity. At the end of 1965, the federal government had provided approximately 150,000 jobs as gardeners, maintenance men, playground supervisors, traffic controllers, office help, etc., for youths from low-income groups. Another 17,000 youths were involved in residential work-training programs of the Job Corps. An additional 100,000 college students benefited from the work-study program, providing them with income that enabled many of them to stay in school.

---

[45] *1965 Youth Market Consumer Survey.*

[46] *Ibid.*

[47] U. S. Department of Commerce, Bureau of the Census, *Statistical Abstract of the United States, 1965,* 86th Edition, (Washington, D. C., Government Printing Office, 1965), p. 219.

[48] W. Willard Wirtz, "Foreword," in Eli E. Cohen and Louise Kapp (Eds.), *Manpower Policies for Youth* (New York, Columbia University Press, 1966), p. vii.

With increasing financial means, the proportion that teen-agers spend for necessities decrease and the proportion spent for luxuries increases. Thus, when a boy spends $300 on customizing his car, he is buying luxury and attention and no longer just a _car_. When he buys a stylish corduroy suit, he is not only buying garments to keep warm, he is acquiring style and prestige.

However, such expenses are not made in a random fashion, but rather selectively invested in goods and services that enhance prestige and add to popularity among peers. The selections are frequently in accordance with short-lived, well-defined fashions and values of the teen-age subculture and create in the teen-ager a feeling of belonging to the peer group. This means that material implementation furthers identification with subcultural standards and in this way promotes the evolvement and survival of the subculture. Also, material implementation facilitates communication within the subculture—communication that does not have to be verbal, but can speak through the visible common style and fashion. It is only natural that members, or those aspiring to membership, strive to display these identifying signs. The rewards obtained for displaying them are popularity, acceptance by the peers, and a feeling of belonging to the group. Ultimately, these rewards and the resultant conformity strengthen the collective identity of the adolescent population.

It is exactly through this reinforcement process that the uncertain no-man's-land of adolescence has been modified, has obtained some degree of structure and internal status, and has become a way of life. However, this way of life is not wholly acceptable to the adult world and is viewed with ambivalence and uncertainty. In the final analysis, then, it seems that the paradox of adolescent "status" can be viewed as relatively structured from the _inside_ of the subculture, but also as both unstructured _from_ the adult viewpoint as well as uncertain _within_ the adult world. (See elaboration and further explanation of this question of differential analysis in Chapter 8.)

Earlier and Superior Biological Maturation

The most significant biological process during the period of adolescence is pubescence. (The words "puberty" and "pubescence" are derived from the Latin _pubertas,_ "the age of manhood," and _pubescere,_ "to grow hairy" or "to reach puberty.") While adolescence refers to the period of social maturation, the time of transition from dependent child to self-sufficient adult, pubescence refers to the time span of physiological development during which the reproductive system matures. This process includes the development of the secondary sex characteristics as well as the physiological maturation of the genital organs. Pubescence normally corresponds with the early stage of adolescence and ends with the appearances of all secondary sex characteristics and the achievement of reproductive ability. These changes usually take place over approximately two years. The exact age at which reproductive maturity is achieved varies widely and is influenced by many factors.

Of these factors, sex difference plays a major role: girls mature about two years earlier than boys. Climate, on the other hand, seems to make little difference. It was once thought that girls who grew up in a hot climate developed earlier than those who grew up in a cold one. Actually, researchers found a slight tendency toward earlier maturation in the *temperate* zone rather than in either the tropical or arctic regions.[49] In general, however, scientists tend to reject assumptions of climatic determination.[50] The factor of race seems to have even less effect than climate. In two studies, the age at menarche (first menstruation) for Negro girls did not vary significantly from that of white girls who lived in the same places and had the same or similar socioeconomic backgrounds.[51]

The most influential factors seem to be nutritional, medical, and technological practices. A social environment that makes use of the latest scientific insights in these areas usually has the effect of lowering the age of pubescence. Among the various aspects of scientific progress, knowledge and practice of better nutritional habits is probably the most significant single factor. Modern scientific standards concerning nutrition, sanitation, hygiene, and medication are more common in urban-industrial societies than in tribal or agricultural societies, and more common in the middle and upper socioeconomic classes than in the lower classes. This is the reason why a consistent difference of menarcheal age exists between the higher and lower socioeconomic classes. This difference has been found in a number of international studies.

The menarcheal difference between higher and lower classes was found to be two months in Copenhagen, Denmark; three months in Bristol, England; eight months among Negroes in New York; six months

[49] David P. Ausubel. *The Theory and Problem of Adolescent Development* (New York, Grune and Stratton, 1954).

[50] Luella Cole and Irma Nelson Hall, *Psychology of Adolescence*, 6th ed., (New York, Holt, Rinehart and Winston, 1965), p. 19.

[51] Comradge L. Henton, "A Comparative Study of the Onset of Menarche among Negro and White Children," *Journal of Psychology*, Vol. 46 (July, 1958), pp. 65–73; N. Michelson, "Studies in Physical Development of Negroes, IV. Onset of Puberty," *American Journal of Physical Anthropology*, N. S. Vol. 2 (June 1944), pp. 151–66.

among Hindus; ten months in Durham, South Africa; and five months among South African Bantu.[52] The most important factor that was found to explain these differences was varying nutrition. Since better nutrition is correlated with social class, a more rapid growth rate can be observed among girls from upper-class homes. One study demonstrates particularly clearly the influence of nutritional standards. Japanese girls born in Japan but reared in California almost from birth were one and a half years ahead of Japanese girls born in California but reared in Japan. The racial factor was constant between the two groups, and the groups were large enough to include comparable cross sections from the total range of the social stratification. The researcher concluded, therefore, that the relatively large difference is explicable by the better diet and more adequate care given to the girls who grew up in California.[53]

The factor of family heredity also contributes to the determination of the exact time at which a girl will experience menarche. Daughters of early-pubescent mothers tend to reach menarche earlier than those of late-pubescent mothers.[54]

It should be understood that the effects of the various factors sometimes reinforce each other and at other times neutralize each other. This means, for example, that if a German girl whose mother matured at eleven is brought up during the war and experiences nutritional deficiencies, she may start menstruation at a later age. On the other hand, the daughter of a late-maturing mother who came from a poor family may reach menarche earlier than her mother, because the family has moved up the socioeconomic ladder and can provide her with a better diet. A double effect is obtained in the case of the daughter of a late-maturing mother who has been deserted by the husband and lives under depressed economic standards. The girl is prone to reach menarche at even a later age than her mother did.

---

[52] K. W. Boylen, G. Rasch, and M. Weis-Bentzon, "The Age Incidence of Menarche in Copenhagen," *Acta Obstetrica et Gynecologia Scandinavica*, Vol. 33 (1954), pp. 405–33; R. C. Wofenden and A. L. Smallwood, "Annual Report of the Principal Medical Officer to City and County of Bristol Education Committee," (1958); E. Kark, "Puberty of South African Girls, III, Social Class in Relation to the Menarche," *South African Journal of Laboratory and Clinical Medicine*, Vol. 2 (1956), pp. 84–88; A. G. Oettlé and J. Higginson, "Age at Menarche in South African Bantu Girls," *Human Biology*, Vol. 33 (May, 1961), pp. 181–90.

[53] Paul K. Ito, "Comparative Biometrical Study of Physiques of Japanese Women Born and Reared under Different Environments," *Human Biology*, Vol. 14 (September, 1942), pp. 279–351.

[54] Harley N. Gould and Mary R. Gould, "Age of First Menstruation in Mothers and Daughters," *Journal of the American Medical Association*, Vol. 98 (April, 1932), pp. 1349–52.

In terms of statistical averages, intergenerational comparisons of the ages at menarche reveal an ever-decreasing menarcheal age in most societies. This holds especially true for societies that have undergone marked change toward more urban-industrial conditions, where modern standards of nutrition and sanitation are the natural conseqences of technological and medical progress. In such advanced countries, proper nutrition and modern medicine result in earlier maturation. Several European countries have records that reach back for 100 years or more and show the age at which the women of the population first menstruated. One of the most complete sets of records is available in Norway, covering the period from 1840 to 1950. The average menarcheal age in 1840 was 17 years, 1 month. This age decreased consistently, until in 1950 it had arrived at 13 years, 3 months—a decrease of almost four years.[55] Similar changes have been found in Sweden, Germany, Denmark, England, Finland, Japan, and the United States.

In the United States, a study published in 1932 comparing the menarcheal ages of 357 mothers and their 680 daughters found for the relatively short period of one generation a menarcheal age difference of .38 years. The average menarcheal age for the mothers was 13.99 years, for the daughters 13.61 years.[56] Another study found that in the United States for a sample of college women who were born around 1920, the age at first menstruation was about one-half year lower than for a sample born around 1900.[57]

The reason why reference is almost exclusively confined to the pubescent process of girls is that there is no clearly defined method for determining the onset of pubescence among boys. There is no equivalent symptom that is as definite and unmistakable as menstruation. The major physiological symptoms associated with male pubescence are the appearance of pubic hair, voice change, and nocturnal emission. However, research indicates that not all of these pubescent characteristics appear in a boy at the same time, several of the symptoms may go unnoticed for a relatively long period.

The modern conditions of the urban-industrial society have influenced not only the timing of maturation, but also its quality. In 1961, two researchers compared measurements of 9-, 11-, and 13-year-old white Iowa public school girls with those of same-aged girls taken in

---

[55] V. Kiil, "Menarche-alderen hos skolepeker i Oslo og sammenhengen mellom menarche-older og fysiskutwicklung Statistiche," *Kvartalashelft*, Vol. 43 (Oslo, 1954), pp. 84–88.

[56] Gould and Gould, *op. cit.*

[57] Clarence A. Mills, "Further Evidence on the Reversal Human-Growth Tide," *Human Biology*, Vol. 13 (September, 1941), p. 365.

the years of 1880, 1899, 1916–19, and 1937–39.[58] (Fortunately for poster-
ity Iowa City school administrators had compiled records of such measurements.) The measurements concerned stature, body weight, stem
length, leg girth, and head and face width. The comparison shows a
progressive increase in all of these physical aspects, except head width.
The researchers point out that comparison of means at age 13 of United
States white girls, representing the years 1880 and 1960, shows that the
girls of 1960 are: (1) taller by approximately 10 cm.; (2) heavier by
more than 10 kg.; (3) larger in stem length by at least 4 cm.; (4) larger
in leg girth by no less than 3½ cm.; (5) larger in face width by approximately 0.4 cm.; and (6) *not* different in head width. Translating
items (1) and (2) into English units, today's 13-year-old school girls
are shown to be larger by 4 inches in mean stature and heavier by 22
pounds in mean weight than their counterparts of 80 years ago.

Similar comparisons were made between boys of today and of 1880.
It was found that the average 14-year-old is 5 inches taller and 24
pounds heavier than his counterpart in 1880. Even in the past 20 to 30
years there has been an increase of 3 inches in height and a gain of 15
pounds for the average 12-year-old boy.[59]

Other studies indicate that the average GI in the United States
Army during World War II was three-fifths of an inch taller, almost 10
pounds heavier, and better nourished than the average World War I
soldier.[60] Also, college students today are taller, heavier, and in a more
adequate state of nutrition than their counterparts of only 25 years ago.
Sports records also show that today's athletes far outstrip yesterday's
stars in nearly every discipline. In the middle of the 18th century, the
King of Prussia, Frederick the Great, had to search all over *Europe* to
find enough men six feet tall to serve as his special guard. Today, he
could find that many in almost every large high school in California.
Visitors to European museums are frequently astounded by the un-
believably small size of armor and other garments that were worn by
Medieval knights and mercenaries. They give the impression that 12- to
14-year-old children went on the Crusades. Actually, armor was worn
by adults whose average size was several inches shorter than that of
today's adult. The measurements of recruits in countries that have had
universal military draft for decades show consistent increases in both

---

[58] Howard V. Meredith and Virginia B. Knott, "Descriptive and Comparative
Study of Body Size on United States School Girls," *Growth*, Vol. 26 (December,
1962), pp. 283–95.

[59] Luella Cole and Irma N. Hall, *op cit.*, p. 23.

[60] *Ibid.*

height and weight from the earliest to the most recent generations in the same population.[61]

One could continue and expand the list of statistical references demonstrating that there is a general world trend toward an increase in stature and that this trend can be traced over the last two or three centuries. The above examples suffice to support the assumption that these increases are due to the greater availability of food, a more balanced diet even among the poor, a more equitable distribution of the countries' wealth, improved medical care and the resulting decrease in illness and epidemics, and the virtual elimination of child labor.

Virtually all pertinent research reports singled out nutrition as the most crucial variable. A number of "natural experiments" tested the role of nutrition and revealed that there is a direct correlation between the quality of nutrition and physical development. The adverse effect of inadequate nutrition upon growth has been observed during the first half of the 20 century when three serious socioeconomic upheavals occurred: World War I, the Great Depression of the 1930's, and World War II. All three catastrophes had direct impact upon the growth of children and teen-agers. During World War I, there was a slowing-down of growth among the children of the nations that were most intensely involved in the war action. However, few precise measurements have been preserved. During and right after World War II, more reliable data were recorded, and retardation of growth was studied with special care in Germany, England, Belgium, France, and Japan.

One of the most reliably documented illustrations of the correlation between nutrition and physical measurements comes from the city of Stuttgart, West Germany.[62] In Stuttgart, all public school children were measured twice every year since 1910, with complete records available for both the Volksschule (elementary school) and the Oberschule (secondary school). For pupils of both school systems, the records show marked reductions in weight and height during times of national crisis. For example, around 1925, the average weight for all age levels declined sharply. These were years of severe inflation, comparable to the Great Depression in the United States. Concomitantly with recovery from the national economic disaster, there was an upswing in physical measurements. From roughly 1930 to 1938, there was a plateau of relatively high physical measurements, due to peaceful prosperity. During the first two years (1938–1940) of World War II, there was an increase in weight, probably because Germany acquired sufficient food supplies through military con-

---

[61] Reference 59.

[62] Paul E. Howe and Maria Schiller, "Growth Responses of the School Child to Change in the Diet and Environmental Factors," *Journal of Applied Physiology,* Vol. 5 (August, 1952), pp. 51–61.

quests. Over the subsequent four years, however, the average weight declined rapidly and remained low for two or three years after the end of the war (1945), with a gradual return to prewar averages around 1950.

Besides the longitudinal fluctuations of measurements, as determined by national crises, a consistent difference between the two types of schools was observable. Since the German school system allows youths of the same age to attend either the Volksschule or the Oberschule, comparison between same-aged pupils in the Volksschule and the Oberschule was made possible. The Oberschule, which is mandatory for university entrance but not for the general education requirement of German youth, draws its enrollment primarily from the upper socioeconomic classes. And, as is universally true, children with upper-class backgrounds are usually better fed and receive better medical care. Although the impact of the national crises affected the pupils of both school systems, decreasing the measurements of pupils in the Oberschule just as noticeably as those of the pupils in the Volksschule, the average measurements of the Oberschule pupils *always* remained above those of the Volksschule pupils.[63]

Another instance showing the reflection of a national crisis in the growth pattern of children occurred in the United States during the Great Depression. The most noticeable impact was felt among the children of middle-class parents, who tried to meet the crisis by reducing the quality and quantity of food rather than by relying on charity or public relief. Interestingly enough, the children of the lowest income groups actually gained weight during those years, presumably because the food given to them in public kitchens, or by charities was more nourishing than the diet their parents were able to provide for them.[64]

Most researchers who have examined the rate and quality of growth have found that they correlate positively with socioeconomic status. Usually, the differences are small but exceedingly consistent from one study to another. The children of professional men or of business executives are on the average slightly taller and heavier than those from middle-class homes, who, in turn, exceed in all aspects of growth the children from the lowest socioeconomic class.

The American society is characterized by all these factors favoring earlier maturation and superior quality of physiological characteristics: (1) There is no national crisis that would diminish an adequate supply of food. (2) The urban-industrial environment within which most American teen-agers are reared offers a number of technological features that

---

[63] Reference 62.

[64] C. E. Palmer, "Height and Weight of the Depression Poor," *United States Public Health Reports*, Vol. 50 (1935), pp. 1106–13.

are highly improved over previous generations, including better hygiene, sanitation, and medical care. (3) American children and teen-agers are protected by laws that shield them from labor exploitation, rough treatment, neglect, and harsh attitudes in general. As a consequence, both the onset of maturation as well as its quality are highly influenced.

Earlier as well as superior maturation have an intensifying effect on adolescence: earlier maturation has had the effect of creating a longer period of adolescence, and superior maturation has produced a youth with capabilities and the physical appearance of an adult, while he is actually prohibited from acting as an adult.

Extrapolating the current trends, it can be assumed that the future will see a teen-age subculture that includes 10–19-year-old youths, rather than 13–19-year-old youths. Entrance into the teen-age world and commencement of corollary social activities, sexual behavior, the increased use of cosmetics, fads, and fashions, the observance as well as the experience of being neither child nor adult can be expected to continue occurring at an ever-earlier age.

The Shifting Sex Ratio

The sex ratio indicates how many males there are in relation to females in a given population. This ratio can be applied to the entire population of a country or to the population of a specific age bracket, as, for example, to the newly born or to people in the age bracket of 60 to 75. It can be applied even to the ratio at conception. Generally, however, the concept deals with the postnatal ratio of males to females.

For some not yet entirely understood reason, nature does not present us with a matching ratio, which could be stated in terms of an even 100 to 100. Rather, markedly uneven sex ratios can be observed for many age brackets, including even the conception ratio. It has been estimated that at the time of conception, the ratio is approximately 120 to 150 males for each 100 females. This ratio changes to about 105 males for each 100 females at birth [65] because the male fetus, like the postnatal male, is evidently less fit for survival. Infant mortality (deaths under one year) again reflects the unequal survival fitness of the sexes, with 1965 national rates of 27.7 deaths per 1000 male infants and 21.5 deaths per 1000 female infants.[66] By around the age of 30, the sex ratio usually

---

[65] U. S. Department of Health Education, and Welfare, *Monthly Vital Statistics Report,* Vol. 15 (Feb. 10, 1967), p. 2.

[66] U. S. Department of Health, Education, and Welfare, *Monthly Vital Statistics Report,* Vol. 16 (April 14, 1967), p. 2.

reaches an even 100 to 100, because of greater male mortality. After age 30, the ratio changes rapidly in favor of the females, and by old age there are considerably more females than males.

Medical research has indicated that the female organism is endowed with a more effective endocrine system, lending superior resistance and endurance. This fact can be observed almost universally. With few exceptions (most notably India, where cultural conditions create an atypical ratio), females have a higher life expectancy than males all over the world. (See Table 5-2.)

Significant differences between the sexes can be observed in the reactions of children, teen-agers, and adults to malnutrition, illness, and various types of environmental stress. Girls, on the average, react with a lesser degree of retardation in growth pattern when exposed to poor nutrition or diseases and seem to be able to make up deficiencies in height and weight faster than boys after adequate diet is resumed. For example, girls in a Belgian orphanage at the end of World War II met standards of normal growth and development much more closely than boys, although both sexes received the same food and care. Also, again under matched conditions, when the diet was improved, the girls recov-

TABLE 5-2.   Life Expectancy at Birth for Selected Countries, at Various Dates.

| Country | Expectation of Life at Birth | | |
	Male	Female	Year
Argentina	56.9	61.4	1947
Australia	67.14	72.75	1953–55
Belgium	62.04	67.26	1946–49
Canada	68.35	74.17	1960–62
Costa Rica	54.65	57.05	1949–51
Denmark	70.38	73.76	1956–60
Egypt*	35.65	41.48	1936–38
England and Wales	68.0	73.9	1961–63
France	67.2	74.1	1963
India	41.89	40.55	1951–60
Israel (Jewish population only)	70.88	73.01	1963
Japan	67.21	72.34	1963
Switzerland	69.5	74.8	1959–61
United States	66.6	73.4	1963

Adapted from Office of the United Nations, *Demographic Yearbook, 1964* (New York, United Nations Service, 1965), Table 3, pp. 112–19; Table 23, pp. 620–24.
    * *Demographic Yearbook, 1957*, Table 8, pp. 186–99; Table 24, pp. 558–73.

ered six months earlier than the boys.[67] Examination of children who survived the Hiroshima and Nagasaki atomic bombings again showed the girls recovering more quickly and more permanently.[68] After children of Guam had suffered several years of dietary deficiencies, the girls showed less retardation in height, weight, and skeletal growth than the boys.[69]

As a consequence of differential resistance and life expectancy, there have always been more females in the older age brackets. However, this ratio may undergo drastic change in the future. Modern medicine and sanitation continue to improve life conditions and are constantly reducing infant mortality. Reduction of infant mortality would disproportionately increase the number of males, since there are more males than females that can be saved. If, in addition, modern medicine finds ways to further reduce *prenatal* mortality, there may be nearly 50 per cent more boys than girls *at birth*. This would mean that in higher age brackets there could be as many as 150 males per 100 females.

This change in the population composition would have a number of sociological consequences. Virtually all social institutions would be affected, among them the institutions of dating, courtship, marriage, and the family—all institutions which deeply influence adolescents. If medical progress continues, the imbalance of the sex ratio will become more pronounced for each new generation, calling for continuous adjustment and reorientation in social interaction. This means that the degree of adjustment made by one generation will no longer be sufficient for the next, and few parents will be able to fully understand and adequately advise their children in social relationships. This "cultural-lag" affliction of the parents plus the ambiguity of the general culture concerning directives for the new demographic circumstances would subject youth to frustrating *anomic* experiences.

Summary

Urban-industrial life is characterized by a number of circumstances that permit the development and spread of adolescent problems.

---

[67] E. M. Widdowson and R. A. McCance, "Studies on the Nutritive Value of Bread and the Effect of Variation in Extraction Rate on the Growth of Undernourished Children," *Medical Research Council Special Report*, No. 287 (1954).

[68] William W. Greulich, C. S. Crissman, and M. L. Turner, "The Physical Growth and Development of Children Who Survived the Atomic Bombing of Hiroshima or Nagasaki" *Journal of Pediatrics*, Vol. 43 (August, 1953), pp. 121–45.

[69] William W. Greulich, "The Growth and Developmental Status of Guamanian School Children in 1947," *American Journal of Physical Anthropology*, N. S. Vol. 9 (March, 1951), pp. 55–70.

Probably the most influential factor is found in the complex and finely divided network of positions that makes continuity from child status to adult status difficult. The division of labor in modern society requires specialists to occupy the vast range of highly specific positions. Since children are not reared as specialists, but as "generalists," when they enter into the adolescent years this generalist social standing becomes dysfunctional, and they are faced with the decision of choosing a specialized position. The process of entering the specialized division of labor is rarely facilitated by parents, whose work and vocational responsibilities are usually separate from home life and therefore invisible to the young. Many teen-agers know very little about their parents' occupational responsibilities and skills, and only a small proportion of sons follow the occupation of their fathers. This situation calls for nonfamilial preparation for the adult position. Institutions of learning and training have replaced traditional preparation within the family setting and, at the same time, have assumed *in loco parentis* authority over the adolescents. Since technological progress is continuously eliminating unskilled manual labor and creating new technical and managerial positions, their training and education have become more complex and time-consuming. Often, this time factor adds additional years of poorly defined status to the adolescent experience.

In addition to uprooting geographic mobility, extensive generational mobility increases uncertainty and anxiety and marks the period of adolescence by inducing—even urging—the teen-ager to improve, strive, and enter a career with higher social prestige than that of his father.

Another characteristic of American life is the increasing socialization of the young by nonfamilial institutions. Clinicians and social psychologists have repeatedly found that maternal deprivation has disabling effects on the young, including defects in achievement, identity, assumption of adult responsibilities, and acquisition of normal and healthy emotions. Psychological impairment of this sort often intensifies and prolongs adolescence.

Probably the most conspicuous aspect of modern adolescents is their affluence, which allows them to materially implement peer standards. By signifying membership in teen-age gangs or subcultures, material implementation reinforces the collective identity and maintains and extends the subcultural expression.

Modern medicine and technology are constantly lowering the age of onset of puberty. This means that entry into the adolescent period occurs progressively earlier. At the same time, however, the upper limit of adolescence is not lowered, thus including increasing proportions of America's youth in the adolescent period. Also the quality of biological maturation has been improved, and modern adolescents are healthier and stronger than their counterparts of previous generations.

Finally, the shifting sex ratio may affect a number of institutions in which adolescents are deeply involved. This demographic change will call for adjustments and reorientations that probably cannot be adequately initiated by parents and thus will leave the adolescent in frustrating *anomic* situations.

american culture influences

Culture: A Sociological Emphasis

As a preliminary step to the following discussion, it is necessary to clarify the concept of culture, since it tends to vary with the frame of reference. For example, the colloquial connotation of the term usually deals with the so-called "finer things" in life, such as art, music, theater, dance, literature, etc. When anthropologists use the term, they may refer to either physical or nonphysical culture or to both combined—including *all* creations of man. Physical aspects of culture refer to the products of man's technology, inclusive of all manmade objects from simple pottery to complex computers. Nonphysical aspects of culture refer to man's ideas and bodies of knowledge. It is this latter connotation that is of primary importance to a sociological discussion, emphasizing particularly those ideas of man that spell out the *rules, expectations, and values of society*. These norms and values can be called the "blueprint" for behavior which society imposes upon its members. This blueprint, consisting of the conglomerate of cultural dicta, is *enforced by social sanctions*, by *punishment* for deviation, and by *reward* for conformity. The cultural "blueprint" is a powerful force, capable of evoking compelling reactions in the members of the society, such as guilt and shame in case of violation and pride and self-esteem in case of adherence.

The following discussion uses the term culture primarily in the sense of a blueprint for behavior imposed by society on its members and maintained by formal as well as informal sanction systems.

Pubescence and Cultural Norms

The preceding chapter dealt with a number of urban-industrial features causing earlier onset of pubescence and extending the period of adolescence into younger age groups. This implies that maturation and its concomitant sexual needs occur at a progressively younger age. In this section, the role of cultural norms and values is to be examined, which either ignore or prohibit adolescent expression of sexual tensions and needs.

The youngster's awareness of his physiological changes—even if there were no particular cultural interpretations of them—would be enough to cause him alarm. Fright and confusion frequently accompany the process of maturation because the bodily changes take place so rapidly that the youngster does not have enough time for gradual adjustment to his new physical properties. Although physiological change takes place at all age levels, the rate of change during the period of pubescence is considerably greater than in the years that precede or follow it.

When a negative cultural interpretation of sexual expression is added to the experience of rapid physiological change, a convergent condition evolves that exerts powerful and far-reaching influence on the personality development of the young individual. It seems, thus, that pubescence in conjunction with certain tenets of the American culture reinforce adolescence in several ways.

Generally, American culture presents either a negative view or no view at all regarding the meaning of pubescence, since the topic falls into the general taboo area. Symptoms of sexual maturity are not openly discussed, and the first menstruation of a girl is often cloaked in secrecy. Many girls feel ashamed, embarrassed, and frightened at that time, since they are frequently poorly prepared to understand and to accept these overt symptoms of pubescence. In contrast, in a number of other societies, notably in many of the so-called primitive tribal societies, the first menstruation is considered a joyful and festive occasion, an event of which the girl can be proud and which is publicly celebrated. For example, the Apache Indian girl's first menstruation was considered a potent supernatural blessing, and the priest knelt before her to obtain the blessing of her touch.[1] The American culture, on the other hand, presents a view of pubescence that turns it into an adolescence-reinforcing event by making the youngster feel that she is going through an "unmentionable," "impure," and unacceptable stage in life. Both the girl and the boy are therefore afflicted with ambiguous perceptions of the bodily changes, and their reactions often generate feelings of anxiety and nonacceptance of themselves.

---

[1] Ruth Benedict, *Patterns of Culture* (New York, The New American Library, 1950), p. 28.

The Nature–Nurture Controversy

Although social scientists observing the American scene agree that teen-agers are characterized by restless and confused behavior, the explanation for this behavior of "storm and stress" sometimes lacks consensus and can be divided into two camps. Sociologists and social psychologists tend to argue for an environmental, primarily cultural, explanation, while some psychologists, relatively few, argue for a biogenetic origin of typical adolescent behavior. The question of whether *nature* (biological conditions) or *nurture* (social environment) is responsible for a given behavior pattern is of course on old one and has often been asked in relation to various stages in the life cycle of man, including the teen-age period. The assumption that a causal relationship exists between the physiological, especially endocrinological, changes during pubescence and the behavioral and social phenomena of adolescence has been largely discarded in favor of the cultural explanation.

It is therefore more or less of historical interest that reference is made to the psychologist G. Stanley Hall, frequently called the father of the psychology of adolescence, who promoted a biogenetic theory of adolescence that became well known in the 1910's and 1920's and was the credo of a large number of educators and psychologists at that time.[2] His psychology of adolescence assumed a specific causal relationship between puberal changes and the social-psychological adjustment problems of adolescents. Hall translated Darwin's concept of biological evolution of the species into a psychological theory of individual recapitulation, asserting that the experiential history of the human species had become part of the genetic structure of each individual. This law of recapitulation maintained that the individual organism, during its development, passes through phases that correspond to phases of the history of mankind. The individual, according to the theory, reexperiences the developmental stages of the human race from early animal-like primitiveness, through an era of savagery, to the more recent, allegedly more civilized, ways of life which characterize maturity.

Hall's first major developmental phase is during infancy, including the first four years of life, when the child is still crawling. Presumably this corresponds to the animal stage of the human race when the species was still using four legs. The period of childhood, ranging from about

---

[2] G. Stanley Hall, *Adolescence*, Vols. I and II (New York, Appleton-Century-Crofts, 1916).

four to eight, <u>corresponds to the epoch when hunting and fishing</u> were man's main activities. This ancient primitive way of living is reflected in the children's play preferences, such as playing cowboy and Indian, using toy weapons, building caves, shacks, and other hiding places. The latter activities putatively parallel the cave-dwelling culture of early history. <u>Youth</u>, from eight to twelve, <u>recapitulates the life of savagery</u> of several thousand years ago. Hall considered this stage as very favorable for learning skills and a certain degree of discipline. <u>Adolescence ranges from puberty to attainment of full adult status</u>, which, according to Hall, occurs between 22 and 25 years of age. Hall ascribed the idiom *Sturm und Drang*[3] (storm and stress) to this developmental stage and likened it to the time when the human race was in a turbulent, transitional stage. <u>In late adolescence, the individual recapitulates the initial phase of modern civilization and enters the end phase of the developmental process: he attains maturity</u>.

These developmental stages are presumably brought about by biologically innate forces which control growth and behavior. Human behavior manifests itself therefore in inevitable and unchangeable behavior patterns which are universal, regardless of the cultural environment. Cultural anthropologists and sociologists challenged this assertion and showed that Hall's theory was untenable in the light of cross-cultural observations. They were able to point to a number of societies where the phenomenon of adolescence did not exist, thereby rendering invalid Hall's claim that the adolescents' behavioral predispositions are direct expressions of universal physiological drives.

In the meantime, however, Hall and his followers continued to insist that socially unacceptable behavior, the type held analogous to earlier historical phases of man, must be tolerated by parents and educators since it is part of the necessary and unavoidable stages in the social development of the individual. These psychologists of adolescence reassured parents and teachers that this objectionable behavior would vanish of its own accord in subsequent stages of development, and that corrective or disciplinary measures are neither necessary nor advisable. Remnants of this theory still occupy a prominent place in American educational philosophy embedded in such ideas as Gesell's concept of

---

[3] Hall was strongly influenced by a movement in German literature which included especially the works of Schiller and Goethe. This was a literary trend full of idealism, search for goals, revolution against the old, expression of personal feelings, passion, and suffering. Hall recognized an analogy between the objectives of this group of youthful writers at the turn of the 18th century and the psychological characteristics of adolescence.

maturation.[4] As a matter of fact, Hall's formerly influential theory may have played a role in the formation of the educational philosophy of leniency and permissiveness in child-rearing practices—a style that has become widespread in America. Like Rousseau, whose educational philosophy is illustrated in *Emile*, Hall believed that the adult should not interfere with the natural course of development, which is determined and controlled by directional forces innate to man.

A realistic assessment of the nature-nurture question will probably result in neither an extreme environmental nor an extreme biogenetic statement, but rather in a balanced view that takes both factors into consideration. Without doubt, the physiological upheavals during early adolescence are capable of profoundly influencing the psychological processes and the social behavior of the young individual. However, the vast majority of modern behavioral scientists ascribe greater influencing power to the sociocultural environment that offers *interpretations* of this physiological turbulence than to the physiological processes *per se*. Sociocultural interpretations, as maintained by the majority of the people in a society, establish the meaning of an event, thing, or physiological process. Man, the symbolic creature, does not react to things and happenings as such, but mainly to the *meanings attached* to them. From a cross-cultural point of view, it is possible to observe a near-endless *differential interpretation of neural impulses*; i.e., one and the same physiological process can be perceived in totally different ways from one culture to the next. It is thus the meaning ascribed to the physiological processes at adolescence that determines the American teen-ager's reaction to them.

The Disparity Between Biological Adulthood and Social Adulthood

The discussion concerning the interplay between biological and sociocultural forces during adolescence should include still another adolescence-deepening problem. This problem is a result of the cultural interpretation of sexual maturation during the teen years. The American

---

[4] Arnold Gesell maintained that maturation and growth is a process that cannot be facilitated and that should not be interfered with. He assumed that time alone will solve most of the normal problems of the child and that difficulties and deviations will be outgrown. This permissive attitude advocates that the infant is left to self-regulation of sleep and demand for food. Rather than disciplining the child, Gesell recommends that mothers should make the baby "with all its inborn wisdom a working partner." See: Arnold Gesell and Frances L. Ilg, *Infant and Child in the Culture of Today* (New York, Harper & Bros., 1943), p. 57.

culture imposes sexual impotency and "neuterness" at a time when the young have just achieved sexual potency and are characterized by intense sexual tensions. From a biological point of view, the vast majority of adolescents are just as capable of the reproductive act and are just as much in need of release from erotic tensions as the adult. This implies that while he is sexually "adult," *socially* he is not yet considered adult. This cultural norm appears in legal context in most states restricting independent decision-making in regard to marriage for the young man under 21 years of age and for the young woman under 18 years. Parents, being social adults in charge of their "minor" offspring, have the authority to either give or withhold permission for marriage under these age requirements.

The social immaturity ascribed to teen-agers has serious implications for their sex life. The publicly proclaimed American folkways and mores do not allow a young adolescent to express his sexual urges and cravings, and for all practical purposes, in the eyes of the public he is still "sexless." Any sexual expression, be it heterosexual, homosexual, or autoerotic, is looked upon with strong disapproval. Consequently, the young individual faces almost total prohibition of sexual expression. On the cultural-ideal level, spontaneous nocturnal emission is the only permissable release of sexual tension. Although within the realm of the permitted, since uncontrollable, the nocturnal emission nevertheless falls under the taboo topics and is considered an embarrassing issue that is outside "respectable" conversation. However, the large majority of young adolescents have been exposed to enough inciting suggestions by the mass media and are sufficiently under the influence of their "knowledgeable" peers that sexual release usually does not remain limited to nocturnal emission. Several researchers [5] have found evidence that nocturnal emission is gradually supplemented and replaced by such means as masturbation, sex play, intercourse, and even bestiality. Ramsey found in his survey that masturbation may begin in infancy and is practiced by a fourth of the boys by the time they are eight years old. By age 12, over 75 per cent of the boys engaged in masturbation, and virtually all of them practiced it by the age of 16. Kinsey accumulated similar evidence and found that boys' indulgence in sex play, including auto-, hetero-, and homosexual activities, had virtually reached 100 per cent by the age of 14.[6] Hollingshead's findings, stemming from his study of *Elmtown,* a Midwestern community, corroborated these findings and indicated a relatively high

---

[5] Glenn V. Ramsey, "The Sex Development of Boys," *American Journal of Psychology,* Vol. 56 (April, 1943), pp. 217–33; A. C. Kinsey, *Sexual Behavior in the Human Female* (Philadelphia, W. B. Saunders Co., 1953); August B. Hollingshead, *Elmtown's Youth* (New York, John Wiley & Sons, 1949).

[6] Kinsey, *op. cit.,* p. 175.

rate of socially unacceptable sexual activities among the local high-school-age youth, including, in addition to other more common sex practices, visits to prostitutes and even acts of bestiality on the part of a number of farm youth.[7]

Since the various types of sexual behavior are in violation of particularly sensitive and stringent cultural norms, feelings of guilt and shame are probable for many teen-agers in American society. Knowing that they have violated standards which the adult world imposes upon them, they develop a strong sense of alienation. Young people cannot help but gather from the forbidding and secretive atmosphere surrounding sexual questions that violation of the sexual codes will brand them as unacceptable to most adults.

Intense feelings of shame and guilt are surprisingly effective in ultimately generating feelings of rejection and hatred against those causing these unpleasant emotions. It seems to be a principle of human interaction that persons who feel rejected eventually generate feelings of rejection toward the original source. Ultimately, a reinforcing vicious cycle forms between the rejector and the rejectee. This holds especially true when the parties involved are collectivities, since feelings of rejection toward outsiders thrive best and most vigorously if an in-group supports and rewards such resentful and hostile attitudes.

The feelings of rejection which teen-agers perceive because of their sexual attitudes and activities are in this way transformed into feelings of belonging to their peer group, which accepts them as they are. In essence, then, adolescents do not feel accepted in the adult world and therefore tend to set up their own world wherein they can act more comfortably, according to their biological maturity. They establish, thereby, an environment that gives them license for enactment of biological adulthood in spite of the denial of social adulthood.

The Lack of Rite of Passage

The life of an individual in any society consists of a series of passages from one age group to another, from one occupation to another, from one institutional membership to the next—in other words, from one status to another. In many parts of the world, the progression from one social position to the next is accompanied by special acts or ceremonies that publicly proclaim the entry into a new status. Sometimes these ceremonies are of sacred nature, suggesting divine sanction of the new role

---

[7] Hollingshead, *op. cit.*, p. 416.

and assuring the individual of rights and obligations that are not man-made. In all cases, however, these rites are never private acts but rather public rituals, manifesting the consensual quality of the transition.

Certain transitions are universal. Birth, puberty, assumption of adult responsibility, marriage, parenthood, death are examples of universal experiences. These and other crises in man's life are usually accompanied by culturally determined ceremonies, called *rites of passage,* which are designed to carry the individual from one phase of human experience to another. Although the ritual celebrations may differ in detail and manner from one culture to another, wherever they are present they serve essentially the same purpose: guiding the individual from one social position to another.

Owing to the universality of these transitions, a general similarity can be observed among ceremonies marking birth, childhood, puberty, betrothal, marriage, pregnancy, fatherhood, initiation into religious organizations, and funerals. In a sense, this regularity of transitions in man's life resembles nature, from which neither the individual nor the society stands independent. The universe itself seems to be governed by a periodicity which has repercussions on human life, influencing man's orientation in respect to the space and time dimensions. One could therefore include among rites of passage those ceremonies and festivals occasioned by celestial changes, such as the changeover from month to month (ceremonies of the full moon), from season to season (festivals including solstices and equinoxes), and from year to year (New Year's Day).

The rite of passage of particular concern in the context of adolescence is the transition from the status of the child to the status of the adult. It is popularly held that this transition is indicated, if at all, by the puberty rite. However, this assumption is an oversimplification, and it is necessary to distinguish between the rite of passage concerning physiological puberty and "social puberty." They are two essentially different and only occasionally converging phenomena.

The physical puberty of females is marked by swelling of the breasts, broadening of the pelvis, appearance of pubic hair, and, above all, the first menstrual flow. Therefore, it would seem plausible to determine the transition from childhood to adulthod by the first appearance of these signs. However, from the point of view of the social definition that is not the case, and it is rare that the young individual is ascribed the privileges and duties of adulthood at this time. The primary and often sole meaning of the onset of pubescence is that the female can now conceive and the male produce sperm.

The question of physical puberty is even more complicated for the boy than for the girl because the variability is increased by the fact that the first emission of sperm may be preceded by emission of mucus that is often unnoticed. Also, in the case of most boys, first emission occurs only as a catalytic shock whose time of occurrence depends on circum-stances usually impossible to foresee or direct. As a consequence, a boy's puberty is usually established in the opinion of the public by an increase in stature, the growth of facial and bodily hair, and change of voice. But in this respect, too, ethnic and individual variations must be considered.

Many aspects, such as sexual fulfillment, marriageability, and adult responsibilities, do not depend on puberty, but may be experienced earlier or later, depending on the individual and his social environment. The nonsynchronization of physiological puberty and social puberty can be illustrated by many examples, such as the fact that in Rome girls are legally marriageable at the age of 12, an age at which only about 8 per cent of Roman girls have started menstruating, while the majority reach puberty between 14 and 15. In Paris it is legal to get married at 16½ years of age, but the average age at puberty is again between 14 and 15 years.[8] Thus, in Italy social puberty precedes physiological puberty while in Paris it follows.

The distinction between physiological puberty and social puberty is most strikingly visible in certain ceremonies performed by the Todas in India. These people are polyandrous and are betrothed from the age of three. Their cultural norms dictate that sometime before physiological puberty a man, who belongs to a clan different from the girl's, comes to her village during the day, lies down beside her and stretches out his coat so that it covers both of them. After they stay that way for a few minutes, the man leaves. Two weeks later, a strong and well-built man belonging to any section or clan comes to spend the night with the young girl and deflowers her. It is important to the Todas that this happens *before* menarche, since if this ceremony should be delayed till after puberty, it is considered such a disgrace that men might even refuse to marry the young girl.[9]

Among the Lekugnen, a Salish tribe of British Columbia, member-ship in one of the endogamous adult classes proceeds by a name-giving ceremony, which always comes later than the ceremony of puberty. The father prepares an elaborate feast and invites a great many relatives. When all have gathered, the father leads his son, together with sponsors, onto the roof of the house (whose interior is hollowed out of the ground) and begins a prescribed dance and song. This is followed by a distribu-tion of gifts in the name of the ancestors. Then the father asks forty nobles to act as witnesses, while two elder chiefs step forward with

---

[8] Arnold van Gennep, *The Rites of Passage* (Chicago, The University of Chicago Press 1960), p. 66.

[9] W. H. R. Rivers, *The Todas* (London, The Macmillan Co., 1906), p. 503.

the young man between them and announce in loud voices the name and the titles of that ancestor after whom the father wishes the son to be named. In most cases it is usually the grandfather. The consent of the gathered crowd is expressed through hand-clapping and shouts. Once more, gifts are distributed, a meal follows, and afterward the young man is known only by the name and title received at the ceremony.[10]

This custom is really not as unique as it may seem *prima facie*. Very similar ceremonies have been in use elsewhere—for example, in Japan and in Europe of the Middle Ages. The coat of arms corresponds to the representation of the totem and to such signs as sacrifications and tatoos for age groups and secret societies. The affixing of the coat of arms, like that of the totemic emblem, is a rite of incorporation or passage into an adult group.[11]

Among the Masai, a proud Negro people in Kenya, circumcision as a ritual of social puberty occurs as soon as the boys are considered strong enough to undergo the elaborate rite of passage, which is usually between the age of 12 and 16. The date depends sometimes on the economic ability of the boy's family: social puberty may be performed earlier if the parents are rich, but if the parents are poor, the ceremony is delayed until they can pay the cost. The ritual of circumcision takes place every four to six years and all those who are circumcised at the same time belong to an age group bearing a special name chosen by the chief. Simultaneously with or prior to the rite of passage for the boy the father must undergo the rite of passage called "passing the fence," signifying his acceptance of the status of an "old man," after which he is called "father-of—(name of his offspring)."[12]

Another study reports about the initiation rituals of Australian aborigines at the turning point between childhood and adulthood. Bronislaw Malinowski found that the rite of passage clarified in particular two aspects of the new role. First, it declared the young individuals marriageable, and, second, it freed the young men from parental authority and allowed them to move from their home of orientation.[13]

Another interesting example of the independence of the initiation rite from actual puberty is the Bar Mitzvah of the Jews. It takes place when the boy has completed his thirteenth year and presumably enters the age of responsibility and religious duty, thereby acquiring adult status. It is interesting to note that Bar Mitzvah has been effectively reduced within

---

[10] Gennep, *op. cit.*, p. 101.

[11] Gennep, *op. cit.*, pp. 101–02.

[12] M. Merker, *Die Massai, Ethnographische Monographie Eines Ostafrikanischen Semiten-Volkes* (Berlin, Reimer, 1904), p. 55.

[13] Bronislaw Malinowski, *The Family Among the Australian Aborigines* (London, University Press, 1913).

the American Jewish subculture to a mere religious ceremony with little or no bearing upon the public and secular life of the young boy. For example, in previous ages Bar Mitzvah signified that the boy was ready to get married and assume adult membership in the community. At present, obviously, a thirteen-year-old boy is not eligible for marriage according to the laws of American society. Likewise, a boy cannot be held responsible when entering into any form of legal contract before the age of 21. Furthermore, the urban-industrial conditions of American life rarely allow a boy of such age to earn economic independence from his parents. The declining significance of Bar Mitzvah among American Jews seems to be due to the fact that many of the privileges that the status presumably entails are in conflict with the laws of American society, that the economic dependence upon parents impairs adult functions, and that there are no exclusive Jewish communities to which a young Jew of 13 years may be presented as an adult.

The list of esoteric initiation rites, as apart from or coinciding with physiological puberty, could be extended, and many more striking practices could be cited from ethnological research. However, the above-mentioned examples have to suffice at this time.

Because of the discrepancy between physiological maturation and the ascription of adult status, it is preferable not to refer to *initiation rites,* the ritual of entry into the adult status, as puberty rites. In virtually all societies the age at which young men and women are allowed to marry does not coincide with the moment of their physiological puberty, and if one day these two moments, one social and the other physiological, come to coincide, they will do so only as a result of scientific progress and deliberate planning.

In American society, social puberty lags behind physiological puberty by several years, with most state laws setting the independent marriageable age at 18 for the female and at 21 for the male. (See Table 6-1.)

Transition from child to adult in American society is beset by more conflict than merely a discrepancy between physiological and social maturation. The real problem stems from the fact that the American culture lacks *both* puberty and initiation rites. Puberty, as concluded earlier, is a taboo issue and relatively meaningless in respect to marking an orientation point in an individual's life. The symptoms of physiological maturation are not accompanied by a public ritual with status-clarifying effect. Likewise, there is no definitive rite of initiation into the adult world, although it is true that a certain legal age is set for marriageability and right of franchise. However, prior to these particular privileges and obligations of adulthood, there is a partial assumption of other adult responsibilities and privileges, such as military service, entering an occupational position, driving an automobile, etc.—all activities that are obviously of adult nature. Therefore, one cannot speak of a certain age at which the young members of our society make the transition from one to the other status. There is no *one* definite rite of passage, and the adolescent cannot enjoy the certainty of occupying a status that is clearly defined and characterized by consensual validation. The young teen-ager, going through puberty, is deprived of a consistent assessment of this particular span of life and is confused as to how to cope with his new appearance and new feelings. On the one hand, he knows that he has changed and no longer is a child, but on the other hand, he can tell that he is not yet considered an adult as he experiences dependency upon parental authority and is subject to legal limitations. Therefore, the important questions for him is: "*When* will I be an adult?" A serious dilemma of the American culture is that the youngster cannot find a clear answer. In fact, given the current cultural patterns, no one can give him a definite answer. The American society simply is too complex to be able to offer a rite of passage in the sense of initiation into the adult world. The urban-industrial conditions impose a long-drawn-out process that extends between child and adult status without clearly marking the transitions at the beginning or at the end of the process.

It seems that clarity of one's social position and of one's integration into the social system is a recognizable need of man. In order to meet this need, a number of prerequisites must be completed, one being a clear introduction into one's status. The introduction should occur by way of a definite rite of passage. The absence of such rites may greatly reduce the awareness and clarity of one's status, and certain behavior patterns are likely to ensue that are conventionally designated as symptoms of maladjustment. Many of the typically adolescent behavior styles can be defined as manifestations of their maladjustment to a world that is poorly defined for them.

An understanding of the reasons that underly these symptoms of maladjustment can be furthered by applying social-analytic propositions, such as those suggested by Leonard S. Cottrell:

(1) The degree of adjustment to roles which a society assigns to its age-sex categories varies directly with the clarity with which such roles are defined.

(2) Clarity of definition of role is reduced by inconsistency in the response and in the expectations exhibited to the individual by members of his social world.

(3) The degree of adjustment to a future role varies directly with the degree of importance attached to it and the definiteness of the transitional procedures used by the society in designating the change of role.

TABLE 6–1. Minimum Age for Marriage With and Without Parental Consent for Males and Females by States.

| States | Minimum Age | | | |
| | With Parental Consent | | Without Parental Consent | |
	Male	Female	Male	Female
Alabama	17	14	21	18
Alaska	18	16	21	18
Arizona	18	16	21	18
Arkansas	18	16	21	18
California	18	16	21	18
Colorado	16	16	21	18
Connecticut	16	16	21	21
Delaware	18	16	21	18
District of Columbia	18	16	21	18
Florida	18	16	21	21
Georgia	17	14	21	18
Hawaii	18	16	20	20
Idaho	15	15	18	18
Illinois	18	16	21	18
Indiana	18	16	21	18
Iowa	18	16	21	18
Kansas	18	16	21	18
Kentucky	18	16	21	21
Louisiana	18	16	21	18
Maine	16	16	21	18
Maryland	18	16	21	18
Massachusetts	14	12	21	18
Michigan	18	16	18	18
Minnesota	18	16	21	18
Mississippi	[a]	[a]	21	18
Missouri	15	15	21	18
Montana	18	16	21	18
Nebraska	18	16	21	21
Nevada	18	16	21	18
New Hampshire	14	13	20	18

TABLE 6–1. (continued)

States	With Parental Consent		Without Parental Consent	
	Male	Female	Male	Female
New Jersey	18	16	21	18
New Mexico	18	16	21	18
New York	16	14	21	18
North Carolina	16	15	18	18
North Dakota	18	16	21	18
Ohio	18	16	21	21
Oklahoma	18	15	21	18
Oregon	18	15	21	18
Pennsylvania	16	16	21	21
Rhode Island	18	16	21	21
South Carolina	16	14	18	18
South Dakota	18	16	21	21
Tennessee	16	16	21	21
Texas	16	14	21	18
Utah	16	14	21	18
Vermont	18	16	21	18
Virginia	18	16	21	21
Washington	b	15	21	18
West Virginia	18	16	21	21
Wisconsin	18	16	21	21
Wyoming	18	16	21	21

[a] No minimum specified.

[b] Male under 21 may marry with parental consent but no minimum age specified.

Adapted from Henry A. Bowman, *Marriage for Moderns*, (New York, McGraw-Hill Book Co., 1965), p. 682.

(4) The degree of adjustment to a future role varies directly with the completeness of the shift in the responses and expectations exhibited by the society to the individual in his new role.[14]

---

[14] Leonard S. Cottrell, Jr., "The Adjustment of the Individual to his Age and Sex Roles," *American Sociological Review*, Vol. 7 (October, 1942), pp. 618–19

In the opinion of Cottrell, the application of these and other propositions in the form of questions would yield answers that indicate the degree of adjustment which individuals are likely to make to their roles. The answers would also reveal the main sources of the maladjustment. In addition, if the questions were applied to a series of social roles comprising a given social system, the answers would indicate the points in the social structure with the greatest dangers to social adjustment and the probable sources of such dangers.

If the above propositions are applied to the situation of the American teen-ager, an evaluation clearly indicates an extremely low degree of role clarity, a very inconsistent response pattern on the part of the larger society toward the young individual, a lack of definite transitional procedure, and a confusing incompleteness of expectations which fit neither child nor adult.

Among these various interrelated reasons for the adolescents' maladjustment, attention is focused on the significance of the rite of passage for the American teen-ager. In conclusion, it can be said that he is deprived of a definite transitional ritual and that its absence has a considerably aggravating effect on the crisis of adolescence.

The All-American Dichotomies of Cultural Values

It has been said that whatever one may consider a truly American trait can be shown to have its equally characteristic opposite. Although dualism in value patterns can be observed in most present-day larger societies, American society appears to subject its members to more extreme contrasts than is normally the case. Americans are faced during their lifetimes with alternatives which frequently represent such polarities as harsh competition and kind cooperation, a virtual fanaticism for hard work and a craving for leisure time, a pious-religious orientation and generous free thinking. These dynamic polarities complicate role definitions, make the smooth flow of a uniformly patterned life cycle impossible, and disturb the individual with a number of value discontinuities.

It would require an involved historical treatment to explore the roots of these dualisms in the American ethos and to arrive at a valid explanation for their development. Such elaboration is obviously not possible here, and brief reference to a number of historical antecedents must be sufficient. First, the Judeo–Christian heritage, so abundant in basic dualisms, has exerted one of the strongest influences. Second, some schisms and inconsistencies in American culture can be explained by the heterogeneous background of the United States' population. Unlike the cultural development of other countries, the American ethos did not evolve from one homogeneous group but from a conglomerate of ethnic and racial groups, each with its own convictions and mode of life. Third, a number of value dichotomies have evolved out of a unique interplay of social forces, including the American experience of opening up the New World and the adherence to certain moral and humanitarian principles. The challenge of the new and vast continent and the tasks of mastering it called for a sense of pragmatism, efficiency, and prompt style of problem-solving that often violated equally accepted moral and humanitarian principles such as cooperation, kindness, honesty, and respect for individuality. As a result of these divergent cultural themes, there is frequent value conflict or evasive compartmentalization of incompatible attitudes.

Among the manifold value schisms, some deserve specific mention because they cause confusion and uncertainty for Americans in general and for youth in specific. One must not lose sight of the fact that for a young individual who is in the process of forming his identity, there are not many conditions as exasperating and vexing as conflicting norms and values. Conflicting norms and values on the societal level normally have their lasting counterparts on the personal level. The following are examples of the prevalent polarities in American culture.

Competition vs. Cooperation. One of the central themes among American values is the stress on personal achievement, especially in respect to occupational achievement. The "success story" outlook and the esteem accorded to the "self-made man" are distinctly American traits. The American society maintains the value of fierce competition and glorifies "winners"—whether this be the queen of a beauty contest or the farmer raising the finest cattle. Perhaps what has been said about American life is true, namely, that the values of the businessman dominate and permeate national life. Economic success has been so heavily stressed as to impose a widespread and persistent strain upon institutional regulation of permissible means for the attainment of this goal. In some extreme instances, only questions of technical effectiveness have entered into the choice of means for the success goal, and slogans such as "business is business" have been the apology of the "Robber Barons," much of organized crime, vice, and racketeering.

On the other hand, the proverbial generosity of the American people toward individuals, collectivities, and other countries facing catastrophes such as earthquakes, floods, famine, and epidemics is sincere and almost exaggerated. It is a real index of the religious or philosophical theme of the brotherhood of man. There exists an enormous range of effective voluntary humanitarian activities in America, such as the Community

Chest, various "service club" projects, public welfare agencies, numerous private philanthropies, the domestic peace corps, and the overseas Peace Corps. In all, it has been estimated that some 30 million Americans give unpaid help to various religious, social, political, civic, and service organizations.[15] A report about such voluntary aid and cooperation comes from the Southwest:

> Phoenix, Arizona. A total of 3,638 migrant farm worker families received surplus food and other supplies during a rain-caused emergency in December and early January, relief agencies disclosed yesterday.
>
> The aid went to 19,361 individuals. It was coordinated by Salvation Army workers. The cost from State Welfare Department funds amounted to $68,672.
>
> The relief operation started because prolonged rains kept farm laborers out of the fields. . . .
>
> . . . 44 tons of food were distributed to 6,239 persons in the last two weeks of December. . . . Another 11 tons of food went to 1,300 jobless farm workers during the same period in the Eloy-Stanfield area.
>
> And $1,700 in private donations was collected. . . . Some of that money was used to pay for the gasoline farm laborers used in driving to emergency distribution centers. . . . The Migrant and Indian Ministry also gave out 2½ tons of canned goods and 200 pounds of clothing.[16]

This polarity of competition and cooperation can be found to be a part of many specific situations in American life, including recurrent situations that involve young people. For example, in American schools, which are largely coeducational, boys and girls become aware very early that they are competing with one another, presumably for academic achievement, although it is probably more often for social prestige. The typical American grading system, the "on-the-curve" method, automatically converts boys and girls into competitors. Yet, on the other hand, they are expected to show mutual cooperation and helpfulness when it comes to other aspects of interaction, such as dating, courting, and marriage. The necessity of frequent abrupt switches from one style of interpersonal relation to another and the unclarity of when and how to do so introduce a high degree of stress and confusion into the boy–girl, and later the man–woman, relationship.

Work vs. Leisure. The Puritan tradition gave secular occupational activities religious sanction and viewed successful work as a sign of divine grace. This metaphysical compulsion to work was especially prevalent in

---

[15] *Survey Graphics* (March, 1949), p. 137.
[16] *Arizona Republic* (Feb. 4, 1966), p. 19.

the older rural culture of America and still is explicit in rural areas and certain subcultures that have not yet fully assimilated the more recent culture of leisure and conspicuous consumption. This, however, is not to say that work as a value in itself has vanished from the American scene; it merely has been diminished and now runs parallel with the new values of leisure and consumption. Thus, another typical Americanism can be observed: the seeming paradox of people engaging in hard work all year, only to spend their earnings in one or two grandiose gestures.

Piety vs. Freethinking. Public opinion polls have shown that freedom in general, or in specific application, such as freedom of the press or of worship, repeatedly is mentioned as one of the most cherished advantages of the American form of government. Most Americans are proud to member freethinkers, such as Walt Whitman, Emerson, Thoreau, and others, and endorse the principles of freethinking—however, usually only *in abstracto.* When it comes to concrete instances, "free thought" rapidly declines in stature and favorable appraisal. It is often said that America is a land of freedom *of* religion, but hardly *from* religion. For example, one who admits being an atheist generally meets with suspicion, rejection, and often active intolerance. This conflict between "free thought" and Christian piety has been visible in the long-drawn-out battles and polemics concerning prayer in public schools. Many parents are afraid that their children will suffer confusion at the hand of this open conflict. As one indignant mother put it:

> What sort of country is this becoming! My son asked me the other day: "Mother, why can't we pray in school anymore?" I didn't know what to tell him. This nation has a great Christian heritage and should insist upon teaching and showing it in the class room. How can I make my child understand that he is living in a God-fearing country, if at the same time he is not allowed to pray in class rooms?

Individualism vs. Conformity. Americans are eager to report that their country was settled, cultivated, and advanced by "rugged individuals." The "individual," in the American conception, is an independent and inventive agent, relatively autonomous and morally responsible to himself. A proliferation of specific propositions concerning "human nature" was derived from this ethnocentric premise. For example, a man was ideally allowed to voice his disagreement with the decisions and practices of the authorities, he was expected to choose the occupation of his preference and be self-supporting, and he was encouraged to follow his own convictions and beliefs. While these cultural propositions are still maintained, at least on the ideal level, in reality a considerable degree of dependency and conformity has developed. A number of regulations have been introduced, presumably guaranteeing security and consistency of economic well-being for all Americans; these include, for example, such institutions as Social Security, Medicare, obligatory retirement funds, and other similar measures. Critics call these measures "welfare state" practices and claim that freedom is no longer clearly tied to a social system of private property and passive government. In the opinion of many Americans, this trend threatens standards of individualism by unduly restricting personal determination, decisions, and choices.

In the industrial realm, modern technology and its efficiency have resulted in establishing norms and standards for production *as well as consumption.* The American emphasis on efficiency and expediency has always been of fascination to outside observers. The Germans coined the term *Fordismus* to describe the standardization, mass production, and "streamlined" efficiency of the American industry and business world, assuming that Ford represented the protoype of American productivity. In the course of this growing industrial efficiency and expediency, individualistic and creative participation in the production process has become greatly reduced for the vast majority of employees. There is even a question whether the product itself meets standards of individuality and uniqueness, since it has been mass-produced and is designed to suit the tastes of thousands of people.

American youth, on one hand, are brought up in the knowledge of American history, which includes many well-known and glorified examples of "rugged individualism," and are encouraged to emulate this "truly American" trait. On the other hand, however, American youth are constantly challenged to conform to national and patriotic standards requiring high degrees of conformity to majority opinion. Although these conflicting values have of course been a natural part of any era, they appear to have been unusually intense during the late 1960's when dissent and counterdissent concerning the war in South Vietnam ran high. Some of the basic questions that emerged for the sociological observer concerned the surprisingly widespread public opinion which perceived dissent not as an expression of independent individual thinking and believing but as subversive and "un-American" conduct. If one studies, in addition, reliable national survey data that captures the mood of contemporary American teen-agers, one is inclined to conclude that the original "rugged individualism" is now juxtaposed with a strong emphasis on conformity. This emphasis stood out in survey data published by the Purdue University opinion research center, showing that "more than 50 per cent [of the teen-agers] think the large mass of us in the United States simply aren't capable of deciding for ourselves what's right and what's wrong."[17]

---

[17] H. H. Remmers and D. H. Radler, *The American Teenager* (New York, The Bobbs-Merrill Co., 1957), p. 16.

It appears then that there is a serious discrepancy between the American ideal of "rugged individualism" and its actual implementation. A teen-ager has to learn carefully that this blueprint for American individualism is not generalizable and that there are definite areas of limitations and prohibitions. The fact of non-generalizability destroys the simplicity and predictability of always responding to the same cue in identical or similar ways, thereby complicating the learning process and rendering the behavioral blueprint ambiguous and situational.

Sex vs. Chastity. One of the most notorious confusions within the blueprint of the American society concerns sex. Attitudes on sex oscillate from the romantic-holy to the prosaic-evil. On the one side, sex and "love" are eulogized *in abstracto* and, on the other side, there ensues a furtive, shameful, and guilt-ridden apprehension when questions are raised concerning the facts and specific activities of sex.

Sex education is an embarrassing task that usually is evaded or passed from one institution to the other, and it is rare that any of them accomplish adequate instruction. There still is considerable unclarity and disagreement about whether it is the family, the school, the medical doctor, the minister, or the mass media that should render the service of instructing and enlightening the young.

All the while during this pedagogic impasse, movies and literature continue to invite the teen-agers to participate in a type of "love" that magnifies sensuous and exploitative perspectives. Sex and "love" have, to a large degree, become part of the overall American "fun" concept, although contemporary law, religious tradition, and public opinion still prescribe a way of life for unmarried persons—thus for most teen-agers— that upholds premarital chastity. Political pronouncements, educational advisements, and religious dogma emphasize "moral and spiritual values," condemning premarital sex as dangerous, lurid, and evil. Such verbal advocation has proven to be ineffectual and relatively hypocritical, since the ubiquitous fact is that the adult world's preoccupation with sex has saturated the adolescent's environment with inescapable images and incited him to partake of sexual activities and experimentation.

A striking manifestation of this schizoid combination of opposing cultural orientations occurred in Phoenix, Arizona, in 1966, when a number of city police officers were suspended from the force after it was learned that they had attended "unbecoming" parties where obscene films had been shown. In fact, the shows were at private, primarily all-police officers' parties. While on one side, the public officer of the law is a guardian of morality and is expected to enforce the so-called "immoral-ity ordinance" of the city, on the other side, he exhibits conformity to popular "fun-and-sex" values.[18]

It appears, then, that the American culture is beset with a set of schizoid values concerning sexual matters. These inconsistent polar concepts by necessity cause confusion and anxiety among adolescents, who are in the process of trying to arrive at a consistent blueprint for sexual behavior.

One could extend this list of polar blueprints and point out time and again the confusing effect they have, especially on young individuals trying to acquire a *Weltanschauung* and integrate their various life experiences. If the theory is accepted that a healthy personality requires an integrated *Gestalt* of views and attitudes, then it must be conceded that many of the clashing pairs of views that are part of the American culture will have disintegrating and confounding effects that are not conducive to successful personality development. The adolescent, in addition to many other problems, is faced with the puzzle of opposing sets of blueprints that diminish predictability in interactional situations and create uncertainty and confusion as to when one or the other should be applied.

The Child—Adult Dichotomies of Cultural Values

Besides the dichotomies of opposite value patterns that cut through the whole American culture, there is a division of values that distinguishes between those applicable to the child and those applicable to the adult. The American culture upholds this age-determined double standard more emphatically than most other societies and submits relatively well-defined expectations to each age group. However, the more discrete and isolated the status of child is from the status of adult, the more ambiguous and difficult is the transition from one to the other. In other words, the more distinct the dichotomous pattern, the more intense the status discontinuity experienced by the adolescent. Anthropologist Ruth Benedict is known for exploring the cultural qualities separating these two statuses, and the following discussion relies heavily on her work.[19]

No culture in the world can ascribe the same blueprint to all participants. Humans at different chronological stages have different needs and capabilities; nowhere is a child required to act like an adult, and

---

[18] "Policeman Appeals," *Arizona Republic* (Feb. 22, 1966), p. 27.

[19] Ruth Benedict, "Continuities and Discontinuities in Cultural Conditioning," *Psychiatry*, Vol. 1 (May, 1938), pp. 161–67.

neither is a mature and healthy adult allowed to act like a child for any length of time. The differences which various cultures have in respect to time of role transition and to degree of role distinction vary greatly. In some societies, mostly the small and so-called primitive societies, children assume adult roles at an early age, while in the large and modern societies, as in the American, children grow into adulthood via a nondescript phase that separates adulthood from childhood by as many as 6 to 10 years. In respect to the degree of role differentiation, the American culture goes to great lengths in emphasizing contrasts between the role of the child and the role of the adult, prescribing for each entirely distinct sets of expectations in a number of life sectors. This principle can be exemplified by a number of specific opposite role expectations.

Responsibility vs. Nonresponsibility. As an illustration of more relaxed role differentiation, the Canadian Ojibwa allow their children to engage in adult activities as soon as they are physically capable. The Indians of this tribe gain their livelihood by trapping animals, and the nuclear family lives the winter months alone on their extensive frozen hunting grounds. The boy accompanies the father on hunting trips and brings in his catch to his sister as his father does to his mother. It is the girl's responsibility to prepare the meat and skins for her brother just as the mother does for her husband. By the time the boy reaches 12 years, he usually operates his line of traps on a hunting territory of his own and returns to his parents' house only occasionally to bring the meat and skins to his sister. A child of this tribe is consistently taught at an early age to rely upon himself and to see the world of the adult as not much different from the world of the young.[20]

The child-rearing practices of the American culture handle this matter differently. The inside worlds of industry, business, professions, and labor are relatively inaccessible and largely unknown to the child. He does not make any contribution to the divsion of labor until he is in his late teens or early twenties. And then he assumes adult responsibilities in an abrupt fashion and not as a natural and gradual expansion of previous activities that were similar or identical. There is no such early partaking of adult functions as, for example, among the Cheyenne Indians who made a feast of the little boy's first snowbird catch. The Cheyenne boy was presented with a toy bow at birth and all through his childhood used serviceable bows which were made for him by the man of the family. He was taught in a graded series how to hunt animals and birds, beginning with those most easily taken. As he brought in the first of each species, his family made a feast of it and accepted his contributions

---

[20] Benedict, *op. cit.*, p. 163.

as gravely as they did the buffalo his father brought home. When the boy finally killed his first buffalo, it represented the terminal phase of his childhood conditioning rather than the abrupt assumption of an adult role from which his childhood experience had been discrepant.[21]

In many of these tribal societies, the child-rearing techniques achieve a continuity of activities that is not limited to certain daily nurturing patterns but is extended to include responsibilities that, in our society, are reserved to adults. For example, in the white United States population a child is conditioned to eat three meals a day. The child comes to consider this a normal and natural routine and carry it over to adult life without much thought or difficulty. However, in other areas of life, Americans do not engage in such uniform and consistent conditioning. A child is declared nonresponsible in respect to serious adult work and, as a matter of fact, is even prevented from playfully imitating most adult responsibilities, since they are invisible to him. Americans tend to consider it a universal rule that the child wants to play and that the adult has to work, forgetting that in many societies the mothers take their babies along to their daily work, carrying them in shawls or baskets close to the body. With the mother doing her work in this fashion in garden or field, the child has an opportunity to observe adult work. As soon as the child is old enough to run about, he takes on tasks that are important and yet suited to his strength—thereby precluding the formation of a dichotomy of work and play. Adult tasks are gradually introduced to the child while elders give patient advice, yet do not offer to do the task in the child's place. An observer tells of sitting amidst a group of Papago elders in Arizona when the man of the house turned to his little 3-year-old granddaughter and asked her to close the door.

> The door was heavy and hard to shut. The child tried but it did not move. Several times the grandfather repeated: Yes, close the door." No one jumped to the child's assistance. No one took the responsibility away from her. On the other hand there was no impatience, for after all the child was small. They sat gravely waiting till the child succeeded and her grandfather gravely thanked her. It was assumed that the task would not be asked of her unless she could perform it, and, having been asked, the responsibility was hers alone just as if she were a grown woman.[22]

The effect of such child training is that the child is consistently encouraged in responsible social participation early in life, while at the same time the tasks that are expected of him are commensurate with his capacity.

---

[21] Reference 20.
[22] *Ibid.*

The American society proceeds differently. Even the law reflects these differences and provides that a child cannot be accused of a crime but only of "delinquency." Then, the legal and moral burden is still the parents' because the child presumably has not yet reached the "age of legal responsibility." The question of *when* the social and legal reaction to a child's "delinquency," either in terms of penalty or correction, is commensurate with the child's understanding of his delinquent act raises a most difficult issue. There has been suspicion lately that permissive and "understanding" attitudes toward juvenile delinquents may be inappropriate and may defeat the purpose of prevention as well as "rehabilitation," since permissive counseling will only reinforce and reward the delinquent pattern. What is needed, according to some psychiatric experts, is a new approach, a "Reality Therapy" [23] that readjusts social reactions to make them more commensurate with the understanding that the juvenile may actually have of his acts. Readjustment of the law machinery in this direction would mean that in the future the juvenile would be held responsible for his deeds to a greater extent than is currently customary.

The questioning of the legal appropriateness of methods of dealing with juveniles has come about partly because of recent suspicion that children are greatly underestimated in their ability to comprehend their actions and to accomplish intellectual and manual tasks. Jerome S. Bruner, professor of psychology and head of the center for cognitive studies at Harvard, thinks that we grossly underestimate the perceptual and comprehensive capability of our children. Bruner holds that children can learn any subject at any stage of their development and advocates that they be required to perform far more complicated tasks than they do today. By not expecting much from children, we in fact condition them not to give much, thereby creating and perpetuating the typical American myth that nonresponsibility for children is necessary, normal, and natural.[24]

Sex vs. Sexless. The area of sexual attitudes and activities represents the most complicated and controversial problem of continuity in cultural learning, not only for the American society but for almost all societies. There is virtually no society where the norms concerning sexual conduct are identical for children and adults. Sameness of sex standards is rarely found, since in virtually all societies the child must seriously modify his behavior at puberty or at marriage—these two occasions representing universal discontinuities in both sexual capability and sexual standards.

---

[23] William Glasser, *Reality Therapy* (New York, Harper & Row, 1965).

[24] Jerome S. Bruner, *The Process of Education* (Cambridge, Mass., Harvard University Press, 1963), p. 33*ff*.

At such times in the life cycle of an individual, the cultural prescriptions concerning sex may, for example, change preadolescent sexual license to marital fidelity or, as in a few societies, premarital virginity in either male or female to marital status with considerable extramarital sexual license.

Although one must consider the physiological occasions of puberty and marriage as rites of passage inevitably connected with some degree of discontinuity in sexual behavior and therefore as universal conditions, there still remains the possibility of continuity in a major aspect of sex. In the context of this discussion, _continuity in sexual expression means that the child is taught nothing he must unlearn later_. Therefore, in spite of the universal conditions of puberty and marriage one can classify some societies as facilitating continuity and others as imposing discontinuity. The adults among the Dakota Indians, for example, observe great privacy in sex acts and in no way stimulate or encourage children's sexual activities.[25] Yet one cannot speak of any discontinuity since the child is not indoctrinated in ways he has to unlearn later. In a culture with this type of sex pattern, adults view children's sexual experimentation as in no way wicked or dangerous, but rather as innocuous play which has no serious consequences. But the same _laissez-faire_ attitude may be taken by adults in societies where such play is encouraged and forms a major activity among young children. This is true of a number of the Melanesian cultures, especially those of Bali and the Marquesan Islands. Among these Melanesians, an overall cultural emphasis on sexual pleasures prevails, and the adults exhibit a great degree of permissiveness and even good-natured encouragement in regard to sexual expressions. Children undergo consistent conditioning and feel free to indulge in pleasurable sex play, including autoerotic, homosexual, and heterosexual practices. Although modified by marital regulation, the same open and hedonistic style of behavior is carried over into the adult status and no serious strain of discontinuity is experienced.[26] If a society's emphasis is on reproduction, as for instance among the Zuñi Indians of New Mexico, sexual expressions among children are not encouraged since they do not represent the primary use for which sex is intended. Zuñi practices display, however, an important difference from the Anglo-American child-rearing practices. Although the Zuñi child is impressed with the wickedness of premature sex experimentation, this wickedness is not generalized and associated, as in the American culture, with sex itself but only with sex at his specific age, thereby limiting discontinuity to an age factor and avoiding a basic moral issue.[27] In the Anglo-American culture, the adult often fails to unlearn the general connotation of evilness and dangerous-

---

[25] Benedict, _op. cit._, pp. 164–65.
[26] _Ibid._
[27] _Ibid._

ness of sex—a cultural tenet strongly impressed on him during his most formative years.

The American society is conspicuous for its drastic differentiation of sexual roles. The child is viewed as a virtually sexless and sterile creature who should not witness, let alone partake of, adult sexual activities. This cultural dictum is manifested by a number of prohibitions, such as age restrictions for certain movies, where the sign "Adults Only" tries to keep sex information and stimulation from the young—thereby, however, only inviting greater curiosity among teen-agers and children.

Dominance vs. Submission. In the American society, as in most societies, the child is under the authority of his parents by informal custom and by formal law. The cultural mores are reinforced by no lesser sanctions than the religious norms of the Judeo–Christian heritage, threatening whoever disobeys parental dictates with damnation. The problem of this arrangement, which has significant implications for the process of adolescence, lies in the fact that the individual, conditioned to one kind of behavior in childhood, must shift to the opposite as an adult. This, obviously, raises the question of the time and manner of transition from one to the other—a question that remains largely unanswered in the American society.

As would be a natural inclination in probably every culture, Americans tend to accept as universal the custom of viewing the adult-child, or specifically the parent-child, relationship in the light of a dominance-submission arrangement. The ethnocentrism of this assumption is illustrated by anthropological data pointing out that other cultures have employed different patterns of intergenerational relations. As a typical example, a Crow Indian father was reported to express his pride over his son's independent and, from our cultural point of view, almost insolent, behavior in spite of the fact that his own wishes were frustrated by the son's intractability.[28] The child-training practices among the Mohave Indians are also strikingly nonauthoritarian, and an anthropologist has reported the following episode:

> The child's mother was white and protested to its father (a Mohave Indian) that he must take action when the child disobeyed and struck him. "But why?" the father said, "he is little. He cannot possibly injure me." He did not know of any dichotomy according to which an adult expects obedience and a child must accord it. If his child had been docile he would simply have judged that it would become a docile adult—an eventuality of which he would not have approved.[29]

---

[28] Reference 25.
[29] *Ibid.*

It appears, thus, that a number of cultures are strikingly free of patterns of authoritarianism and observe a symmetrical relationship that precludes the "freezing" of the child-adult relationship into a dominance-submission relationship. In some of the so-called primitive cultures, the very terminology of address between father and son reflects this reciprocal relationship. The two individuals essentially are equals whose terms of relationship never change through their lifetime, similar to the reciprocal privileges and obligations which in our society exist only between age mates. When the son becomes a parent, he will establish the same reciprocal relationship with his child. Usually, in societies with this type of equalitarian father-son relationship, the actual paternal figure with disciplining function is a close male relative, such as the mother's brother among the Trobriand Islanders. The father–son relationship is, therefore, a continuous unchanging relationship which is enjoyed throughout life. For the purpose of this discussion, the significance of such kinship conventions lies in the fact that the child is allowed to practice from infancy on the same form of behavior upon which he may rely as an adult. Child-rearing practices of this nature make it unnecessary for behavior to be polarized into first submission and then dominance.

In conclusion, the American culture contains a number of important child–adult dichotomies which exert considerable strain on both the interpersonal process and the personality system. The main impact of this situation is felt by the young individual at the time when he finds himself between the two relatively well-defined roles, since the cultural blueprint lacks clear directives as to the exact time of termination of one role and the assumption of the next. The American adolescent is thrown in between the cultural dichotomies and is not clear in which situations and to what degree the nonresponsibility of the child and the complete responsibility of the adult apply to him. Likewise, he experiences feelings of frustration or guilt concerning his sexual needs and activities since the culture has not yet accorded him adult status, which presumably coincides with sexual maturity. Finally, he faces the serious problem of readjustment to a new position in the authority pattern of the society. During the time of transition, he experiences ambiguity in respect to freedom of activities, responsibilities, and allocation of power.

The Factor of Anomie

The preceding examinations of the American blueprint have revealed a number of dysfunctional consequences stemming from a negative interpretation of pubescence, a schizoid polarization of all-American values, and the schism of child–adult values. In these three discussions, the misleading impression may innocuously have been created that the societal blueprint, though polarized and at times considerably negative, nevertheless is clear and unambiguous.

A realistic appraisal of the cultural conditions must take into consideration a degree of vagueness or even the absence of cultural norms. Possibly the strongest dysfunctional effect consists not of the earlier-mentioned negative and conflicting interpretations, but of the partial or total failure to extend *any* cultural dictum for behavior in certain situations. The lack of behavioral directives may be of more serious and destructive consequence to both the personality system and to the social system than the existence of inappropriate and overly stringent norms. Even widespread deviation from obsolete norms seems to be less detrimental than the lack of any norms, since deviation implies a stable factor as the point of departure and thus represents at least a potential for orientation and direction. It seems that man needs a structure to go by, a *Gestalt* that conveys a sense of direction, orientation, and stability. Such guides are intimately dependent on comprehension of norms and expectations. A person not realizing any norms and expectations would be shiftless and unstable and would only vaguely resemble a normal personality. Emile Durkheim recognized the significance of this principle when he explored the reasons behind suicide at the turn of the century.[30] In his famous work, *Suicide,* he conceptualized one type (among several) of suicide as *anomic* suicide, suggesting that the absence of clear norms can be fatal to the human mind. If the blueprint is blurred and unrecognizable, the individual personality needing to operate according to a structure suffers confusion and disorientation, often leading to the point of self-destruction.

To avoid confusion concerning the meaning of *anomie,* it must be emphasized that it has little or nothing to do with deviation from norms, because deviation obviously implies a known standard from which deviation can be measured. *Anomie,* derived from the Greek *anomia,* originally meant "lack of order" and was used by Durkheim to describe a social milieu in which communal control over the members of the social system has broken down. This breakdown liberates the individual from the moral authority of the community, but at the same time results in a personal disequilibrium manifesting itself in a variety of antisocial behavior patterns that may include suicide, delinquency, the formation of subcultures, etc. This type of societal *anomie* applies, to some degree,

[30] Emile Durkheim, *Suicide: A Study in Sociology* (Glencoe, Ill., The Free Press, 1951). Translated by J. A. Spaulding and G. Simpson; (originally published in Paris: F. Alcan, 1897).

to most Americans, exempting, however, those who find a remedy through subcultural belonging and in this way internalize directives not available in the larger society.

Both individual and collective conduct can be organized and predicted only if there is some minimal clarity of norms. To the degree that this clarity and the corresponding regularity of behavior disappear, the individual is in a normless situation. If such dissolution of social regularity involves values central to the person's identity, a serious disintegration of the personality may follow. If this process were to become general throughout a given population, common orientation would vanish—and with it, society. Applied to the experience of specific segments of the population, consequences of low predictability can be observed among so-called "marginal" persons, adolescents, divorced persons, expatriates, displaced persons, organizational staffs undergoing drastic changes in structure, and uprooted and socially mobile populations. Changes in the social organization toward which an individual is oriented and in which his role perception is anchored, typically result in erratic behavior and often acute personality disturbance.

The American culture includes noticeable elements of *anomie*. At least three major conditions can be held responsible for the origin of this factor. (1) The stage for *anomie* was set by the heterogeneity of the United States population, involving a multiplicity of ethnic, racial, and religious backgrounds. Although they seem to be tied together by some common all-American values and goals, some of them originally differed enough from each other to necessitate an extremely nonspecific overall ethos so that they would feel sufficiently free and unhindered in the pursuit of their own subcultural goals and values. Over time, the subcultural distinctions and uniqueness wore off to some extent, while the salience of the overall American ethos hardly increased. The outcome of these cultural processes was some degree of societal *anomie*. (2) The democratic values, as a significant part of the American ethos, place considerable trust in the individual and his capability of working out problems by himself. This emphasis on individualism and "freedom" does not encourage the development of narrow and specific norms and values that would threaten to restrict personal choice and determination. (3) The American culture suggests grandiose values and ambitious goals often without clarifying the means of attaining them. This "big-style" American dream was probably shaped by the American experience of taking over a huge continent pregnant with "unlimited opportunities." Over time, however, discrepancy and unclarity evolved between the values and promises and the norms concerning their attainment. The distance between the abstract values and the corresponding norms and rules is directly correlated with the degree of *anomie* in a given society.

Values, usually tied up with general cultural goals suggesting *what* is to be valued and achieved, and norms, more specific rules of conduct spelling out *how* to go about achieving the values and goals, can be considered two independent cultural phenomena. The interrelationship between them varies and can be measured and classified in a number of ways. Robert Merton developed a useful typology and showed the emergence of *anomie* as a result of preoccupation with cultural goals in the absence of clear institutionalized norms and means. In other words, the American culture holds out goals and values but fails to indicate feasible ways of achieving them. As a general example, the American culture stresses monetary success, but fails to extend "a corresponding emphasis upon the legitimate avenues on which to march toward this goal."[31]

Related to this type of *anomie* is the problem of cultural apathy, manifesting itself in the rejection of goals and norms altogether. A prominent type of apathy is the loss of involvement in a cultural goal, after such goal is not attained in spite of intense and continued striving. The reaction to the failure may be a profound frustration expressed in the form of basic cynicism, moral fatigue, and indifference. If the loss includes central life goals, the individual may be left in a social vacuum, without focal direction or meaning.

The significance of *anomie* for the analysis of adolescence lies in the fact that anomie strikes hardest at the time when social-structural security is not yet obtained, when the young individual is still a "generalist" trying to orient himself in the *general* culture. The modifier "general" is emphasized because the youth lacks specific norms and directives, such as role expectations, which come along with adult positions. He has not yet entered such defined positions, and his search for values and norms consequently takes place within the suprapositional realm of the culture and not in the network of specific positions. It is thus in the general culture that *anomie* operates, and the teen-ager is bound to suffer frustrations when attempting to derive clear normative directions from it.

Adults are, of course, faced with the same *anomic* conditions when trying to orient themselves by abstract cultural features. However, adults have established directional clarity by means of their concrete living patterns—patterns that are facilitated and guided by defined positions in the social structure. Since the young are largely excluded from the division of labor of the adult world, they tend to group together and attempt to compensate for the cultural vacuum by forming a culture of their own. The *anomic* condition is thus instrumental in driving the teen-agers into subcultural environments where they find norms and values

---

[31] Robert K. Merton, "Social Structure and Anomie: Revisions and Extensions," in *Social Theory and Social Structure* (Glencoe, Ill., The Free Press, 1949), p. 133.

that add up to an integrated and meaningful *Gestalt*. This temporary *Gestalt* is helpful in the process of bridging the gap between childhood and the entry into adult positions.

Summary

In spite of incompleteness and certain elements of vagueness, enough cultural salience exists in the American society to exert a powerful influence over the behavior and perceptions of its members. The influence of a number of cultural forces appears to add complexity and anguish to the crisis of adolescence.

(1) The cultural interpretation of pubescence and its accompanying symptoms is more instrumental in patterning teen-age reactions than the physiological process itself. Earlier theories of tracing adolescent "storm and stress" to physiological maturation have largely been replaced by anthropological principles emphasizing the role of cultural relativity in perceiving such organic changes. In the American society, the prevalent interpretation of the pubescent process—in as far as explicit comment exists about this taboo subject—usually falls short of being reassuring and accepting. While the rapid physiological changes create adjustment problems for the young teen-ager, the American culture tends to ignore or evade giving adequate explanations for these changes, thus leaving the youth unaided in his attempt to cope with the new growth pattern.

(2) As in virtually all urban-industrial societies, social adulthood is not synchronized with the attainment of biological maturation, but lags behind by several years. During this time, when the teen-ager is sexually mature but socially underprivileged, cultural interpretations cause him to feel ashamed or guilty about sexual needs and expressions. The teen-agers' reactions to the source of such prohibitive interpretations and unpleasant emotions are rejection, hostility, and withdrawal. These reactions partially explain the development of subcultures wherein teen-agers can feel free from adult criticism.

(3) The American culture lacks rites of passage that would clarify the definite transition from one status to another and enable youngsters to view their new appearance and sensations in the light of a well-defined status. As Cottrell emphasized, there is a positive correlation between transitional unclarity and expressions of maladjustment.

(4) Americans are subject to a number of value dichotomies that are intrinsic to their national ethos. These inconsistent and clashing polar values place equal emphasis on such divergent themes as competition and cooperation, religiosity and free thinking, sex and chastity, work and

leisure, individualism and conformity. It is difficult for adults to decide which value theme applies in certain situations, and even more difficult for teen-agers still in the process of arriving at a basic cultural orientation.

(5) Another schism of values breaks the continuity between child and adult role expectations. Children are exempt or kept from most of those opportunities and responsibilities that would allow continuous involvement and decision-making. They have to relearn or unlearn many modes of thinking and of behaving when they enter adult positions. The problem for the adolescent consists of a nonspecific and confusing interim during which he encounters many instances when he does not know whether to choose child or adult standards.

(6) The American culture is afflicted with elements of *anomie*—normlessness—that have a disorienting and confusing effect on the nation's youth. Adolescents are more vulnerable to the effects of *anomie* than adults, because they do not yet have recourse to specific positions in the division of labor that would help them to derive a strong personal identity, and stability and predictability in behavior patterns.

In the final analysis, the reactions of teen-agers to certain characteristics of the American culture develop into those behavior patterns that are defined as *typically* adolescent. These emotional reactions include the following: (1) *Embarrassment* and *anxiety* due to the pubescent changes that occur either unaided and unguided or are negatively evaluated. (2) *Resentment* and *withdrawal* as a consequence of the disparity between sexual maturity and social maturity. (3) *Uncertainty* because there is no rite of passage that would signify the entry into the adult status. (4) *Confusion* as a result of the schismatic all-American value patterns. (5) *Ambiguity* as the result of the child-adult discontinuity in cultural values, making it often difficult for the teen-ager to decide which type of role is relevant in a given situation. (6) *Disorientation* as a consequence of *anomie*.

7

social–psychological conditions of personality development

The Concept of Personality

As with the concept of culture, personality connotes a multitude of different meanings, some referring to technical definitions and others to broad popular conceptions. The latter type of reference is frequently exemplified by the unintentionally hilarious phrase "he's got personality," or "he hasn't got any personality." The use of the term in this way is of course more name-calling than analytic since every person has a personality, indeed, must have a personality to be definable as a normal person.

The technical references to personality include a multitude of divergent formulations, including a range that extends from the biological to the sociocultural. In fact, the grossly oversimplified popular view of personality probably stems from the behavioral scientists' inability to propose a unified and consensual definition. Gordon W. Allport surveyed the professional literature and extracted 50 different definitions of personality.[1] The definitions can be grouped into several categories, such as sociological, biological, psychological, juridical, and cultural. A few examples may illustrate the diversity. E. Faris proposed a sociocultural definition by calling personality "the subjective aspect of culture." Ernest W. Burgess held that "personality is the integration of all the traits which determine the role and status of the person in society. Personality might therefore be defined as social effectiveness." C. H. Prince thought of personality as "the sum-total of all biological innate dispositions, impulses, tendencies, appetites, and instincts of the individual, and

---

[1] Gordon W. Allport, *Personality, A Psychological Interpretation* (New York, Holt, 1937)

the acquired dispositions and tendencies—acquired by experience." Arnold Gesell's definition stressed that personality is "the pervasive super-pattern which expresses the integrity and the characteristic behavioral individuality of the organism." Gordon W. Allport, the surveyer himself, added a psychologist's view, stressing adjustment, suggesting that "personality is the dynamic organization within the individual of those psychological systems that determine his unique adjustment to his environment."[2]

These illustrations show that the concept of personality has been used variously to emphasize such aspects as "appearance," "traits determining status," "individual uniqueness," sum totals of "innate" or "acquired" traits, impulses, dispositions, "styles of life," "adjustment to environment," "subjective aspect of culture," etc. Since the concept can refer to literally any type of man's behavior and is a concern of behavioral scientists of different disciplines, diversity is inevitable. It is hardly possible to synthesize all definitions. Rather than ask *what is* personality, it might be more fruitful to first determine *which aspect* of personality is to be discussed.

The problem of this chapter is to examine a number of specific aspects of personality and to understand how they manifest themselves in the adolescent. Of primary interest is the process frequently conceptualized as "identity" or "self-perception."

Basic Assumptions of Personality Theory

In spite of the wide terrain that is covered by the concept of personality, there are several basic assumptions that are generally accepted by social psychologists:

The social nature of personality. The aspects of personality in which a social psychologist is primarily interested are those that are socially learned. The very etymology of the term "personality" suggests learned behavior, the term being derived from the Latin *persona* which referred to the theatrical mask used by Roman actors in Greek dramas. This allusion to an "actor" or a "character" has a public connotation, implying that personality is a product of the social setting, of the social "stage," and not of some private biogenetic process.

The processual nature of personality. Personality is continuously affected by new social situations and experiences so that it is more

---

[2] Allport, *op. cit.*, pp. 25–54.

realistic to think of personality in terms of a process rather than in terms
of a completed entity at any one time.

The Gestalt nature of personality. Students of human behavior tend
to agree that normal behavior does not consist of unrelated fragments
and discrete processes. Separate acts are parts of a response *system* integrated in a manner lending continuity and meaning to behavior.
Gestalt emphasizes the meaningful and holistic integration of behavioral
elements, using the concept of *Prägnanz* to denote major structural features that offer direction and orientation.

Physiological prerequisites. The development of personality cannot
proceed, or at least is severely impeded, if an individual's brain functions are damaged, disoriented, or retarded. Such considerations can be
defined as retardation, feeble-mindedness, or mental illness. Also
young infants have not yet fully developed the physiological as well as
mental abilities that are needed to integrate the various fragments of
their behavior into a meaningful *Gestalt.* It is a long and complex
process, needing constant assistance, explanation, and direction on the
part of socializing agents, to gradually convert a young human animal
into a socialized being. No degree of effort, however, can convert a
mentally deficient infant into a mature and responsible personality. For
a normal unfolding of the personality, a certain degree of physiological
and mental health is prerequisite.

The human group environment. The type of social interaction in
which the young individual is enmeshed is of greatest significance to
his personality formation. If, for example, the primary family environment is disturbed, or partially or totally absent, virtually indelible marks
will be impressed on the personality. Kingsley Davis reported on the
case of Isabelle, an illegitimate child, who had lived secludedly with
her deaf-mute mother until she was nearly seven years old. When she
was discovered, her behavior was comparable to that of an unsocialized
animal, manifesting considerable fear and hostility. She had not learned
language and could make only inarticulate and croaking sounds. At first,
there was suspicion that she might be feeble-minded and that education and further development would be severely limited. However, after
careful and systematic training, Isabelle was able to progress, join the
public school system, and behave like a normal child.[3]

Such extreme cases are, of course, rare, and the case of Isabelle is
selected merely to make a basic point. There are less extreme instances
in evidence every day. For example, subtle personality deficiencies can
often develop in the thousands of orphans and parent-neglected children

---

[3] Kingsley Davis, "Final Note On A Case of Extreme Isolation," *American
Journal of Sociology,* Vol. 52 (March, 1947), pp. 432–37.

who grow up in institutional homes resembling more a secondary than a primary group environment. As mentioned earlier (in Chapter 5), observations in the large Junior Village at Washington, D.C. revealed that institutional youths suffer frequently from anonymity and fears of abandonment. Educators and linguists believe that adult-child verbal exchanges are needed at an early age if the children are to learn the fundamentals of language. However, because the institution was not only crowded but also segregated by age and sex, the two-year-olds could only speak with other two-year-olds. These conditions caused regressions in language skill and physical accomplishments.[4]

A New York study compared children in foster homes who had spent the first two to three years of their lives in an infant institution with children whose total experience had been in foster homes. The study found that the children placed in foster homes after a period of institutional rearing evidenced greater problem behavior than the children with complete foster home experience. The institutionally raised children demonstrated more anxiety, such as restlessness, hyperactivity, inability to concentrate, and expressions of aggression, such as temper displays, destructiveness, and cruelty without cause. In summary, institutional children were found to be less secure, less proficient in entering into meaningful human relationships, and emotionally retarded.[5]

Another New York study showed that institution children had great difficulty in adjusting to foster homes. Compared with children who were placed in foster homes immediately after birth, institutionally raised children were more frequently replaced because of problem behavior. "Deviant" and "strange" behavior were the most common reasons for the replacement of such children, while similar symptoms were extremely rare in the exclusively-foster-home group. The problems leading to the replacements in the institution group can be categorized into (1) aggressive, hyperactive behavior; (2) bizarre, disoriented, unreflective behavior; and (3) emotional unresponsiveness. In addition, the institution children displayed greater speech deficiencies, more serious school difficulties, and more frequent mental retardation. The basic conclusions from the research suggest that institutional children usually remain limited in their intellectual and emotional progress by a fixation on the more primitive levels of abstraction and conceptualization.[6]

---

[4] J. W. Anderson, "A Special Hell For Children In Washington," *Harper's* (November, 1965), pp. 51–6.

[5] William Goldfarb, "Infant Rearing and Problem Behavior," *American Journal Of Orthopsychiatry*, Vol. 13 (April, 1943), pp. 249–65.

[6] William Goldfarb, "The Effects Of Early Institutional Care On Adolescent Personality," *The Journal of Experimental Education*, Vol. 12 (December, 1943). pp. 106–29.

There are an impressive number of concurring studies that support the conclusions set forth in the preceding references, maintaining that the removal or the disturbance of the primary-group environment, as normally exemplified by the family, will tend to be detrimental to the personality of the young individual.[7] Because the group environment is so highly instrumental in forming the personality, the group's imprint on personality structure can be traced to even less extreme cases of deprivation than those indicated by the examples of institutional children. Research has shown the delinquency rate to be significantly higher for children whose family environment has been disturbed by separation or divorce of the parents.[8]

Reference Group

It is true that the young child depends heavily on an immediate, i.e., face-to-face, group environment for physical survival and for the formation of basic personality features. However, this does not imply that a young person, once he has learned how to relate to abstract ideas and images, must remain on the relatively primitive level of relating only to physically present persons, objects, and problems. Man's effort to understand himself and his universe is not limited, although it is highly influenced, by membership groups. No *direct* physical contact with other persons is necessary to absorb attitudes, ideas, philosophies, religions, etc. An example is that of a young man known to this author, of "pure" Anglo-Saxon background with no social connections to Greeks, Eastern European people, or corresponding ethnic subgroups in the United States, who decided to embrace Greek Orthodox Christianity as his religious conviction and to become a convert. His decision was based not on social interaction but entirely on abstract reading and reflecting.

This example illustrates the difference between the reference group and the membership group. Man's symbolic ability frees him from the

---

[7] See for example: R. A. Spitz, "Anaclitic Depression: An Inquiry Into The Genesis of Psychiatric Conditions In Early Childhood," *Psychoanalytic Study of The Child* (New York, International Universities Press, 1946), pp. 313–42; Lauretta Bender and H. Yarnell, "An Observational Nursery," *American Journal Of Psychiatry*, Vol. 97 (March, 1941), pp. 1158–74; D. Beres and S. J. Obers, "The Effects of Extreme Deprivation in Infancy on Psychic Structure: A Study in Ego Development," *Psychoanalytic Study of the Child* (New York, International Universities Press) 1950, pp. 212–35.

[8] William J. Goode, "Family Disorganization," in Robert K. Merton and Robert A. Nisbet (eds.), *Contemporary Social Problems* (New York, Harcourt, Brace & World, 1961), p. 549.

necessity of face-to-face interaction for obtaining information, deciding on a creed, acquiring values, etc. The concept of reference group was developed mainly to define the process whereby individuals can derive norms and values without necessarily being in physical contact with those persons holding the emulated view. Normally, however, most of a person's membership groups also function as reference groups for him. In the cases where the two groups do not coincide, serious conflicts may arise for the person who is involved in both. The concept is therefore most useful in that it calls attention to the fact that a group to which one does not belong can nevertheless serve as a reference group. A young Negro boy, for example, may attend a certain school with other boys and girls, many of them white. He goes to church, spends his leisure time with other Negro children in the neighborhood, and is active in an athletic club that is sponsored and supervised by the community. Which of these affiliations serves as an influential reference group for him? That of his white schoolmates? His Negro peers? His teachers? His parents? Those who discriminate against his race? The church officials? The staff of the athletic club? The fellow members on the athletic team? Or are his attitudes and aspirations influenced by more intangible visions, by groups and images which he has come to know through the printed page, the radio, the television, or the movie screen? All these possibilities must be considered if one wants to explain the boy's attitudes, aspirations, and behavior patterns, for each source represents a potential reference group with which he may identify and relate himself.

The relationship betwen adolescent behavior and reference groups is complex. The modern urban-industrial environment offers youth a heretofore unknown number of potential reference groups. Value references can be made in the context of scores of membership groups that are actually available to the teen-ager, ranging from religious affiliation to the neighborhood gang. Or, value derivations can proceed by more abstract processes, such as through the ubiquitous images and models presented in the mass media. As a result of the diversity and complexity of reference groups, the adolescent's personality development is beset with a numbr of complications.

Shifting reference groups. A significant aspect of the adolescent period is the gradual shift in orientation from teen-age standards to adult norms and values. Ultimately, the adolescent has no other choice but to accept adult cues for forming attitudes and behavior patterns. This is a universal process and requisite for entering adult positions. The process of assuming a new and responsible status is instrumental in breaking down adherence to the teen-age subculture.

Multiple reference groups. Often because of personal preference, but more often because of mandatory conditions, the adolescent is involved in a number of membership groups, which normally constitute reference groups at the same time. Some of the most common examples of such membership-reference group combinations for the adolescent are the family, school, church affiliation, and peer group.

Conflicting reference groups. The multiplicity of reference groups frequently leads to conflict and confusion. Most conflicts stem from the clash between the demands and standards of the peer group and those of the parents. Peers are known to represent a powerful reference group, and researchers have found that the clique's expectations often take precedence over norms and values held by family and adults. "The clique, then, acts as a protective structure which may oppose and evade adult authorities and sanctions." [9] James S. Coleman, in his study of high school youth, found that considerable conflict was generated in a situation where a teen-ager had to choose between the standards of the peers and the demands of the parents.[10] The researcher presented the subjects with a hypothetical situation, asking them what they would do if they were asked to join a particular club to which they had always wanted to belong, but at the same time faced the request of their parents not to join. It is interesting to note that the response pattern of the high school students depended on the type of community in which they lived and went to school. The responses, gathered from 10 different schools, ranged between 45–80% of the boys and 60–85% of the girls stating that they would probably or definitely not join the club against the parents' disapproval. The greatest regard for the parents' demands was shown in the smallest school, in "Farmdale," a rural community; and the least regard was apparent in "Executive Heights," a large suburban school. The four schools in which 70% or more of the boys preferred the parents' advice and the three schools in which 80% or more of the girls chose the parents as reference persons were located in smaller, nonurban communities. The schools in which girls and boys were least willing to conform to the parents' ideas were two suburban schools, "Newlawn," a working-class suburb, and "Executive Heights," an upper-middle-class suburb. These findings indicate that in "Farmdale" and "Marketville," the two smallest schools in a predominantly rural hinterland, the teen-agers enter adult responsibilities earlier and are more familistically oriented, while in "Executive Heights," adolescents assume adult responsibilities later and remain therefore more peer-oriented. These differences between a small farm community and an upper-middle-class suburb illus-

---

[9] Ernest A. Smith, *American Youth Culture* (Glencoe, Ill., The Free Press, 1962), p. 9.

[10] James S. Coleman, *The Adolescent Society* (New York, Free Press, 1963), pp. 138–40.

strate the differential influence of the adolescent reference group. "Executive Heights" reflects a style of life that is spreading in the United States. "Farmdale" and "Marketville" reflect a more familistic style that seems to be disappearing gradually.

Conflicting reference groups tend to interfere with the formation of a unified and unambiguous identity or self-conception. It is therefore unfortunate that during adolescence, when the quest for identity is most intense, the modern social system and culture offer many conflicting and incompatible reference groups. A coed, for example, upon being accepted into a sorority, may yield to informal pressure and develop modes of conduct such as smoking and social drinking that would cause her family's disapproval. Another example would be the conflict experienced by a teen-ager simultaneously involved in a delinquent gang and in a family of law-abiding parents and siblings, or the conflict caused by holding membership in a religious congregation and at the same time being a member of a delinquent neighborhood group.

Unclear reference groups. A majority of modern youths experience great difficulty in deciding between different, and often incompatible, reference groups, and are frequently torn between them, unable to clearly identify with any single one. This inability to identify completely with any reference group tends to thwart the formation of a clear and stable identity. Identity, related to a person's meaningful self-perception, is learned through and derived from a person's social involvements. In a sense, the social environment functions as a mirror showing the person an image of himself. The powerful influence of social repercussions on the person's identity or "self" has been widely accepted as a basic principle of social psychology.[11] If the mirror images are blurred, distorted, or markedly divergent, the personality residue most probably reflects these unclarities.

The Significant Other

One might insist that it is not groups and their standards but rather individuals and their attitudes that significantly influence attitudes— among them, self-attitudes. Social scientists, in an effort to capture the meaning of this important relationship, have suggested the concept of

---

[11] George H. Mead, *Mind, Self, and Society,* (Chicago, the University of Chicago Press, 1934), p. 164; Charles H. Cooley, *Human Nature and the Social Order* (New York, Scribner, 1902), p. 184; Alfred R. Lindesmith and Anselm L. Strauss, *Social Psychology* (New York, Holt-Dryden, 1956), pp. 413*ff.*

the "significant other." It was H. S. Sullivan[12] who first suggested this concept. He believed that significant persons have decisive and formative influence on the perception (including self-perception) of the socializee. (Robert K. Merton also tried to conceptualize this type of influence and suggested the term "reference person." [13] However, this term can be misunderstood and taken to imply volition, consciousness, and choice of reference on the part of the socializee—an assumption that would limit the application of the concept. The concept of significant other, on the other hand, does not convey such limitations, and thus allows for a greater variety of types of socializer-socializee relationships, rendering it more meaningful for the present discussion.)

The significant others who normally have the greatest formative impact on personality development are parents. Parental behavior, in so far as it is visible to children, constitutes a strong conditioning factor and a potential model for role learning. Since many roles can be learned only by observing others performing their roles, observability of role enactment becomes a critical issue. It is primarily through observation that the socializee is able to "take the role" of others. In the case of general roles, such as the feminine, masculine, marital, etc., role taking is largely an informal and unconscious process. On the other side, the more specific roles, such as professional responsibilities, are learned in a more formal and conscious manner. <u>Generally, the young acquire their role perceptions by informally and unconsciously imitating and internalizing norms and values as they are reflected by the behavior of their role models</u>. The importance of this basic social-psychological process can hardly be exaggerated, since acquired role perceptions form the core of one's identity. It is the internalized roles and their degrees of clarity and meaningfulness that make up one's identity. It follows logically that individuals who are expected to exemplify, teach, and transmit certain roles possess an immense influence and, to a large extent, bear the responsibility for role behavior of the next generation. This process of role learning and role transmitting may be influenced and disturbed by acts of commission and/or acts of omission. Acts of commission refer to any definite instances that exhibit role behavior, such as exerting parental authority, engaging in adult work, and carrying out adult responsibilities. Acts of omission, on the other hand, imply the absence

---

[12] As reported by Dorothy R. Blitsten, *The Social Theories of Harry S. Sullivan* (New York, The William-Frederick Press, 1953), pp. 74–75.

[13] Robert K. Merton, *Social Theory and Social Structure* (Glencoe, Ill., The Free Press, 1957), pp. 302–04.

of exemplification of role behavior, as for example, chronic father-absence affecting the male child. Failure to provide role models is of concern to many behavioral scientists, since in order to internalize role norms, the socializee depends on the visibility of the socializing agent's role performance. Problems of role confusion will inevitably arise when important norms are neither formally taught nor informally visible to the young. An extreme example would be the feminine self-perception and the resulting feminine behavior style of young boys whose mothers have served as the basic and near-exclusive role model.[14]

Children are highly dependent on their parents' example in the process of acquiring the sex role, the masculine or feminine way of behavior, and the marital role. These role concepts are part of the cultural heritage, i.e., they are *learned* ways of behaving and thinking. In many modern urban-industrial societies, the norms that distinguish between masculinity and femininity are no longer as distinct and discrete as they were during previous generations. They are now more similar and overlapping than ever before and have allowed a wide range of variations of sex role behavior. Of course, differentiating standards for the sexes still exist, and the changes that have occurred have diminished the social-psychological differences only in terms of degree. As Margaret Mead said fittingly a few years ago, men are behaving a little more like women and women are behaving a little more like men; in short, both are "behaving more like people." [15]

The combination of the relative vagueness in the general cultural blueprint concerning the sex-role definitions and the constantly decreasing visibility of the parental model have contributed to problems of identity. As discussed in Chapters 2 and 4 the young male in the American middle class seems to be particularly vulnerable to the effects of cultural *anomie* and father-absence. The traditional family—characterized by patriarchal authority, familistic attitudes, and domicile-work combination —has almost vanished in favor of the modern equalitarian family. In the contemporary family, particularly in the typical middle-class family, decision-making is an equalitarian process. Individualism instead of familism is practiced. Father-absence from the home has become frequent, and the young male has little or no opportunity to observe his father at work. Home life, *at least from the boy's perspective*, has become matriarchal.[16]

[14] Paul S. Ullman, "Parental Participation In Child Rearing As Evaluated By Social Deviates," *Pacific Sociological Review*, Vol. 3 (Fall, 1960), pp. 89–95.

[15] Margaret Mead, quoted in, "La Différence," *Time* (Sept. 28, 1959), p. 53.

[16] Talcott Parsons, "Age And Sex In The Social Structure Of The United States," *American Sociological Review*, Vol. 7 (October, 1942), pp. 604–16.

In recent years, social scientists have largely disputed the Freudian notion that distinguishes between love-object and identification-object.[17] The new approach suggests that the original relationship between infant and mother should be viewed as identification and not as love. Thus, the learning of the cultural norms of masculinity necessitates a shift from the original identification-object—mother—to a culturally more acceptable identification-object—to father or to some other adult male image. This, obviously, is not necessary for the girl. As several social scientists have pointed out, the young female has an initial advantage in progressing toward the appropriate sex-role identity.[18] The boy, on the other hand, faces a more precarious situation: if he does not make the shift of identification early enough during childhood, it may be difficult for him to achieve an adequate masculine identity. Father-absence complicates the shift in identification, and the boy finds himself learning the masculine role more by trial and error than by a consistent process of imitation. As a result, boys are more likely than girls to seek and obtain instruction outside of the family and tend to identify with a general cultural image, or with the male *position* in general, while girls identify with the mother as a *person* and not with an impersonal image or position.

A number of social scientists have studied the effects of this social situation and agree that the physical absence of the father, or the presence of a father who does not provide a sufficiently clear role model, impedes the development of such typically American male traits as independence and achievement orientation.[19] These authors conclude that boys lacking in adult role models develop more dependent and submissive personality features. In contrast, father-dominated socialization situations promote aggressive and assertive traits in the young.[20]

A word of caution should be added. There is reason to believe that these traditional assumptions and research findings should be carefully

---

[17] Orvall H. Mowrer, *Psychotherapy: Theory And Research* (New York, Ronald Press, 1953).

[18] Daniel G. Brown, "Inversion And Homosexuality," *American Journal Of Orthopsychiatry*, Vol. 28 (April, 1958), pp. 424–29. David B. Lynn, "Learning Masculine and Feminine Roles," *Marriage And Family Living*, Vol. 25 (February, 1963), pp. 103–05. David B. Lynn, "The Process of Learning Parental and Sex-Role Identification," *Journal of Marriage And The Family*, Vol. 28 (November, 1966), pp. 466–70.

[19] Talcott Parsons and Robert F. Bales, *Family, Socialization and Interaction Process* (Glencoe, Ill., The Free Press, 1955); Urie Bronfenbrenner, "Socialization and Social Class Through Time and Space," in Eleanor E. Maccoby, *et al.* (eds.), *Readings In Social Psychology* (New York, Holt, Rinehart, and Winston, 1958), pp. 400–25; Ullman, *op. cit.*

[20] Lois W. Hoffman, "The Father's Role In The Family And The Children's Peer Group Adjustment," *Merrill-Palmer Quarterly*, Vol. 7 (April, 1961), pp. 97–105.

reconsidered in the light of the increasing power and scope of the mass media. The constant exposure of youth to the characters and models of the mass media fare represents a change in socialization pattern that may call for modification of the conventional assumption that personal and physically present role models are irreplaceable. For example, a number of recent studies have found correlations and evidence that are too weak to support the notion that father-absent boys are more feminine, dependent, and less aggressive.[21] It is possible that the heroes of the mass media increasingly function as objects of identification. However, further research is needed to clarify the effects of this changing aspect of the socialization process.

The Role of the Mass Media

Reference groups as well as significant others serve as relatively continuous and consistent foci of emulation and value derivation. However, the increasing power of the various mass media represents another source of reference that supplements the reference group and the concrete "significant other." By means of the mass media, the actual live person or group can be by-passed, and personal interaction can be replaced by the spectator–mass-media relationship, allowing an almost unlimited range of vicarious experiences and identifications. As a result, the significance and the influence of actual persons and groups have been reduced.

However, one should not conclude that the personal significant other and the concrete group have been replaced entirely. Certain persons and group environments are as vital for the survival of the young today as they were generations ago. The feeling of security that a child derives from the association with accepting and caring parents is still of paramount importance for his personality development. But *needing* parents and *wanting to be like them* are two different processes. The first deals with the need for security and acceptance and the second with the absorption of ideas, impressions, and behavior styles. Parental care is a universal condition for survival that has rarely been successfully modified, while identification is a much more flexible process that allows alternative

---

[21] Hans Sebald, *Parent-Peer Control And Masculine-Marital Role Perceptions Of Adolescent Boys*, Unpublished Ph.D. Dissertation, The Ohio State University, 1963; Alan J. Crain and Caroline S. Stamm, "Intermittent Absence of Father and Children's Perception of Parents," *Journal of Marriage and the Family*, Vol. 27 (August, 1965), pp. 344–47; Joan McCord, William McCord, and Emily Thurber, "Some Effects of Paternal Absence on Male Children," *Journal Of Abnormal and Social Psychology*, Vol. 54 (May, 1962), pp. 361–69.

objects of identification. The mass media offer a vast number of such substitutes and alternatives. Modern children, although depending on their parents physically, are tempted to select ego images from the characters presented by the virtually ubiquitous mass media. By means of the screen, radio, and print, characters of many different types are presented to the youth, who cannot escape from the almost incessant flow of stimuli and who cannot avoid incorporating some aspects of what he perceives into his behavior patterns and into his more basic identity.

The types of effects which the mass media have on the personality of the young are not yet well known. It may safely be assumed, however, that the effects are not superficial, when one takes into consideration that over 90 per cent of all American homes (including Hawaii and Alaska) have one or more TV sets [22] and that in the 1960's children watched the screen an average of 20 to 24 hours per week, according to testimony before the United States Senate Subcommittee investigating the impact of motion pictures and TV.[23]

> In the decade of the 1950's, television came to dominate the non-sleep, nonschool time of the North American child. One-sixth of all the child's waking hours, from the age of three on, is now typically given over to the magic picture tube. During the first sixteen years of life, the typical child now spends, in total, at least as much time with television as in school. Television is probably the greatest source of common experience in the lives of children, and, along with the home and the school, it has come to play a major part in socializing the child.[24]

Since the impact of the mass media on personality formation can hardly be denied, a brief examination of its content should therefore be part of this chapter. It appears that a majority of programs directed toward children and teen-agers are colored by two main themes: *unrealism* and *violence*. Most of the fare consists of a combination of the two.

Unrealism penetrates many of the programs that are commonly thought of as humorous. Grossly unrealistic plots, achievements, and problem solutions were presented in such TV shows as *Batman,* which in 1966 become one of the great sudden successes in entertainment

---

[22] U.S. Bureau of the Census, *Statistical Abstracts of the U.S.; 1965,* 86th ed., (Washington, D.C., Government Printing Office, 1965), p. 523.

[23] U.S. Senate, Subcommittee to Investigate Juvenile Delinquency of the Committee on the Judiciary, "Summary Report On Findings And Recommendations Of The Conference On Impact Of Motion Pictures And Television On Youth," (Exhibit #7) S. Res. #48, 87th Congress, Investigation of Juvenile Delinquency in the U.S.; Part 9; March, 1961.

[24] Wilbur Schramm, Jack Lyle, and Edwin B. Parker, *Television In The Lives Of Our Children* (Stanford, Calif., Stanford University Press, 1961), p. 12.

history, and "The Addams Family" and "The Munsters," which in the mid-1960's were among the most popular shows for children and teen-agers. Unrealism was also reflected by the theater, which a few years ago presented *"It's a Bird . . . It's a Plane . . . It's Superman"* and *"The Mad Show,"* based on the theme of MAD Magazine.

Although the interest in unrealistic and lunatic characters is not new in history, the recent preoccupation with the unreal and the "mad" are of more than merely literary significance. For the first time in history, it is now possible to intensively and extensively expose children every day to such themes. Some interpretations of this preoccupation have de-scribed it as symptomatic of the present *anomic* age, as wishful thinking, as searching for solutions to current problems, as another version of man's belief in and longing for magic that can solve his apparently insurmountable problems, and, finally, as a temporary escape into fantasy from a world that often looms confused and perilous.

The other popular theme of the mass media, especially of TV and the movies, is violence. Gunslingers, psychopaths, and sadists have had leading roles in a significant portion of United States entertainment, and their behavior is shown to millions of households every day. Testimony in the United States Senate Subcommittee hearings in the early 1960's revealed that the amount of violence in TV programs has substantially increased.[25]

A content analysis of 100 television hours of the so-called children's hours, 4:00 to 9:00 P.M., Monday through Friday, produced an impressive list of nonhumorous (as distinct from "humorous" in cartoons and comedies) acts of violence. The sample of 100 hours included the following:

12 murders.
16 major gunfights.
21 persons shot (apparently not fatally).
21 other violent incidents with guns (ranging from shooting at the missing persons, to shooting up a town).
37 hand-to-hand fights (15 fist fights, 15 incidents in which one person slugged another, an attempted murder with a pitchfork, 2 stranglings, a fight in the water, a case in which a woman was gagged and tied to a bed, and so forth).
1 stabbing in the back with a butcher knife.
4 attempted suicides, three successful.
4 people falling or pushed over cliffs.
2 cars running over cliffs.
2 attempts made in automobiles to run over persons on the sidewalk.
A psychotic loose and raving, in a flying airliner.

25 U.S. Senate, *op. cit.*

2 mob scenes, in one of which the mob hangs the wrong man.

A horse grinding a man under its hooves.

A great deal of miscellaneous violence, including a plane fight, a hired killer stalking his prey, 2 robberies, a pickpocket working, a woman killed by falling from a train, a tidal wave, an earthquake, and a guillotining.[26]

It is of timely importance to examine the reactions of a child who watches aggressive personalities on television engage in extreme physical violence. What are the reactions in terms of value derivations, attitudes, and behavior patterns? Representatives of the broadcasting industry generally answer this question by claiming that television has no noticeable effects on the viewer. Mental health officials, social workers, teachers, and the general public are divided over the question, with some holding that exposure to violence breeds violence, and others assuming that exposure has a cathartic and pacifying effect, allowing children to identify with the aggressor and in this way rid themselves of pent-up hostile emotions. A statement representative of a sizable proportion of psychiatrists was made by Dr. Ralph Banay, who thinks that if "prison is college for crime, I believe for young disturbed adolescents, TV is a preparatory school for delinquency."[27]

Another expert opinion, substantiated by a series of experiments at the Stanford University psychological laboratories, provided a basis for evaluating the impact of televised aggression on preschool children. The experiments were designed to test the extent to which children will copy aggressive patterns of behavior when these patterns are demonstrated by models in three different situations: in real life, on film (TV), or as cartoon characters on film. The first step of the experiment consisted of dividing the children into four groups. While three groups witnessed violent behavior through the different media mentioned above, the fourth group (control group) was not shown any violence. After the children of the three groups had watched the acts of violence, they and the control-group children were individually placed in an observation room under conditions which mildly annoyed them. The observation room contained a variety of toys, including a three-foot Bobo doll which could be used as an object of aggression. Each child spent 20 minutes in the room, and his behavior was rated by psychologists observing him through a one-way mirror. The results left little doubt that exposure to violence stimulates aggressive tendencies. The children who had seen the aggres-

---

[26] Schramm *et al.*, *op. cit.*, pp. 139–40.

[27] Ralph S. Banay, "Testimony Before The Subcommittee To Investigate Juvenile Delinquency, Of The Committee On The Judiciary, U.S. Senate, 84th Congress," S. Res. #62, April 1955 (Washington, D.C., U.S. Government Printing Office, 1955), p. 83.

sive adult model showed approximately twice as much aggressiveness in the observation room as did those in the control group. The researchers reached three important conclusions about the effect of aggressive models on a child: (1) The exposure tends to reduce the child's inhibition to act in a violent and aggressive manner. (2) The exposure tends to shape the *form* of aggressive behavior. While most of the children from the first three groups sat on the Bobo doll and punched its nose, beat it on the head with a mallet, tossed it in the air, and kicked it around the room (the exact kinds of attack they had observed), the children of the control group rarely acted that way. (3) A display of violence on film is almost as influential as a display in real life. The child exhibits a high degree of imitation in both situations. On the other hand, the children were slow in imitating the cartoon character.[28]

The findings of the research suggest that televised models are important sources of social behavior and can no longer be ignored as influences on personality formation. However, one must distinguish between *learning* and *acting out*. Although children readily learn patterns of social behavior, including violent acts, from TV programs, their imitative behavior is limited by at least two factors: (1) Children ordinarily do not have access to the weapons necessary for duplicating what they have observed. If, however, they *had* switchblades, blackjacks, brass knuckles, and six-shooters, it is safe to predict that the incidence of harmful imitative aggression, patterned according to TV stories, would rise sharply. (2) Normally, parents quickly suppress any learning that conflicts with what they consider "right" conduct. Often such TV-produced conflicts are merely on the verbal level, and parents have no particular difficulty in correcting them. The influence of TV is ordinarily checked by the standards of parents and other adults, and the full impact of TV can be measured precisely only when parental supervision is removed and the children are given the instruments they need to reproduce the aggressive behavior.

It should be realized that these two conditions, the nonavailability of instruments and the supervision of parents, are often precariously weak and insufficient safeguards, and that many youths attempt or even successfully complete imitation of TV plots. Some striking illustrations of such imitations were reported.

> In a Boston suburb, a nine-year-old boy reluctantly showed his father a report card heavily decorated with red marks, then proposed one way of getting at the heart of the matter: they could give the teacher a box of poisoned chocolates for Christmas. "It's easy, Dad,

[28] Albert Bandura, Dorothea Ross, and Sheila A. Ross, "Imitation of Film-Mediated Aggressive Models," *Journal of Abnormal and Social Psychology*, Vol. 66, No. 1 (January, 1963), pp. 3–11.

they did it on television last week. A man wanted to kill his wife, so he gave her candy with poison in it and she didn't know who did it."

In Brooklyn, New York, a six-year-old son of a policeman asked his father for real bullets because his little sister "doesn't die for real when I shoot her like they do when Hopalong Cassidy kills 'em."

In Los Angeles, a housemaid caught a seven-year-old boy in the act of sprinkling ground glass into the family's lamb stew. There was no malice behind the act. It was purely experimental, having been inspired by curiosity to learn whether it would really work as well as it did on televsion.[29]

More recent examples of imitation of TV and movie violence include the incident in which a boy was seriously stabbed during a reenactment of a switchblade knife fight some boys had seen in a televised rerun of the James Dean movie, "Rebel Without a Cause."[30] Concomitant with the development of TV in other countries, imitations of televised behavior have been noted. For example, in June of 1966, a young Finn burned herself to death after watching a televised news program showing the self-immolation of a Buddhist nun in Vietnam.[31] From France came the report that three teen-age boys successfully duplicated two robberies that they had seen in the movies. Their mothers finally became aware of their imitative behavior and notified the police.[32]

It is often assumed that an ethical ending to a story, in which the villain is punished, will serve to extinguish what a child has learned from exposure to antisocial models and therefore keep him from imitating the violent behavior. Another experiment in the Stanford University laboratories tested this hypothesis.[33] A group of nursery-school children watched a TV movie in which Rocky, the villain, took all of Johnny's toys. Clearly, the story showed that aggression pays off. Another group of children saw the same program with a *different* ending; as Rocky tried to seize the toys, Johnny overpowered him and gave him a sound beating. The two groups of children were then tested. As might have been expected, children in the first group who witnessed that Rocky's aggression was rewarded readily imitated his physical violence and his hostile remarks, while children in the second group who saw him punished showed little imitative aggression. Further inquiry, however, presented the researchers with a surprise. It was discovered that *all* the children were

---

[29] *Saturday Review* (Dec. 24, 1949), p. 20.

[30] Bandura, Ross, and Ross, *op. cit.*, p. 3.

[31] AP Report (Helsinki, Finland, June 6, 1966).

[32] WNS Report (Fontenay, France, June 5, 1966).

[33] Albert Bandura, "Influence Of Models' Reinforcement Contingencies On The Acquisition Of Imitative Responses," *Journal Of Personality And Social Psychology*, Vol. 1 (June, 1965), pp. 589–95.

highly critical of the way Rocky behaved and called his action "mean," "harsh," etc., and that the children who imitated him did so because his aggression "paid off."

Another experiment testing this question found that when a fantasy sequence in a comicstrip pictured a villain as relatively successful, children were more likely to identify with him and want "to be like him," while they were reluctant to identify with or want to be like a weak hero, or "good guy." The children tended to admire and copy "what works" and preferred to be like the character who was *successful*, regardless of the specific method used in achieving the goal.[34]

These studies, in essence, suggest that when children see an individual punished, they are not likely to spontaneously imitate his behavior. However, they seem to retain information concerning the *method* of aggression, regardless of the punishment of the villain. There is no denying the possibility that they may put this knowledge into practice on future occasions if they are provoked, obtain access to the necessary weapons, and anticipate a sufficiently attractive reward. It appears, then, that the ethical ending of a story functions merely as a *suppressor* of violence, but not as an *extinguisher*.

It has often been surmised that a child who becomes addicted to the medium of TV is trying to substitute a different, maybe more interesting and pleasant, world for the real one. A child or teen-ager spending two to three hours a day watching TV has to do an extraordinary amount of switching back and forth between a world of fantasy and the real world. This oscillating existence may have various effects. Frequently, there is speculation that the effect is therapeutic, an outlet for frustration and a vicarious experience of success. At other times, the effect is feared to be detrimental, because fantasy leads away from reality and refuses to be bound by the rules of life. The handsome hero of fantasy is much more successful in getting the girl of his dreams than the average high school student. Superman or Batman may look like ordinary fellows in street clothes, but they can *fly*. Many of the TV crime-busters invite emulation, although public imitation of their techniques would be disastrous in real life. The world of fantasy has different rules and protects the foolhardy hero, picturing him wise and invincible.

Constant oscillation between fantasy and reality may create serious problems during the child's early learning processes. He may have initial difficulties in distinguishing between the make-believe and the real. This distinction is crucial and a vital aspect of maturity. If a child carries some of the rules of fantasy over into real life, if he acts as though he were

---

[34] Robert Zajonc, "Some Effects Of The 'Space' Serials," *Public Opinion Quarterly*, Vol. 18 (Nov. 4, 1954), pp. 367–74.

protected by the rules of fantasy, if he withdraws too often from the real world into the security and euphoria of make-believe, then he is bound for serious adjustment problems. He can hardly move in a fantasy world without simultaneously viewing *himself* in a fantasy light and acquiring a pseudoidentity. This identity would have to be qualified or entirely replaced in everyday life, thereby creating stress and often profound confusion.

However, it should be recalled that the process of fantasying and daydreaming can be defined differently, as, for example, in terms of "reasoning," which proves to be helpful for many people in the processes of problem-solving, insightful cognition, and creative intuition.[35] Research has found that exposure to TV—one of the most suggestive sources of fantasy—did not make much difference in the child's school performance. In fact, studies with two samples of children, one group with and the other without TV at home, indicated that the TV group entered school with larger vocabularies, although this effect was not of long duration. Also, it was found that there was little difference between the two groups in respect to interest in class work, completion of assignments, and test performance.[36] Another interpretation of exposure to fantasy and of fantasying itself is that it may serve to drain off some of the discontents resulting from the unavoidable frustrations of socialization.[37] Fantasying becomes dangerous only if it leads a child into prolonged withdrawal from reality, encourages confusion of real situations with fantasy situations, and thereby causes delay in learning the rules of the real world. Maybe the greatest danger is the possibility that the child may use certain mass media images and models to formulate an identity that becomes harmful not only to himself but to others as well.

It would be misleading to assume that the expression of unrealism and violence is restricted to the type of mass media fare that is *obviously* and *explicitly* fantasy. In fact, this type of entertainment may prove to be relatively ineffectual in respect to identification and personality formation because the youth *knows* that it is fantasy and entertainment and does not confuse it with real life. Such fare includes fairy tales, many cartoons and comicstrips, ghost stories, comedies, etc. Rather, it is the more subtle, pseudoreal programs that tempt youth to select identification objects. Movies are a frequent source of such identifiable images and models, including plots that range from "real-life" detective thrillers

---

[35] Lindesmith and Strauss, *op. cit.*, p. 208.

[36] Eleanor E. Maccoby, "The Effects Of TV On Children," in Wilbur Schramm (ed.), *The Science Of Human Communication* (New York, Basic Books, 1963), pp. 116–27.

[37] For more details on the function of fantasy see Eleanore E. Maccoby, "Why Do Children Watch TV?" *Public Opinion Quarterly*, Vol. 18 (Fall, 1954), pp. 239–44.

and Wild West epics to "wholesome" surfer stories. Books are another medium through which unrealism and/or violence is frequently conveyed. Interestingly enough, the invasion of the home by TV does not seem to have noteworthily reduced the amount of reading by children. In fact, research has found that TV stories often encourage children to read the book that was the basis for a given show.[38] Books therefore continue to be an important influence on the formation of attitudes and behavior patterns of the young. One of the most typical conveyors of hidden unrealism is the Gothic type of book, the novel that presents a plot where all the heroine need do is be beautiful, witty, and curious as she travels through mysterious adventures and ultimately finds fame, fortune, and the man of her dreams. These plots purport to depict real life, but actually are extremely selective of only certain aspects of life. They exaggerate to effect sensationalism, conveying situations, achievements, and human relationships that have little or no validity in the normal and real world of youth. The heroes—as well as villains—of these stories display superior strength, imagination, and achievements, making the parents seem pale and unimaginative and possibly causing parents to decline in efficacy as models and "significant others."

In sum, then, the main danger of presenting youth with excessive unrealism and violence consists in the possibility that fantasy or anti-social behavior will carry over into real life and cause emotional as well as cognitive disorientation. Overexposure to violence in the mass media is of particular significance, since it can lead to destructive behavior. It is suspected that (1) the young individual acquires an oversimplified conception of problem-solving because the characters depicted usually exhibit singularly effective master solutions; and that (2) he may be persuaded to adopt the style of problem solution. Whether he actually will carry out specific suggestions depends on the availability of the necessary instruments and the hope of being sufficiently rewarded for the effort. Research evidence indicates that children imitate violence if they are sufficiently annoyed, have the necessary instruments, and believe that they will not be punished. The necessity of eliminating unrealistic and/or destructive tendencies before maturing into adulthood may complicate and prolong the adolescent process.

It is interesting to note that almost all research on the influence of mass media deals with negative consequences. It should be allowed that the mass media, especially TV, have the potential of adding to the emotional as well as intellectual growth of children. Selective or, to some degree, even random exposure to TV, for example, can constitute a liberal education, with a sampling of history, music, the arts, political

---

[38] Maccoby, 1963, *op. cit.*

science, anthropology, the behavioral sciences, and the various physical and biological sciences. This encounter with the world of knowledge stimulates curiosity, interpersonal as well as intergroup communication, verbal skills, development of a larger vocabulary, etc. Probably the main reason why such positive effects have not been sufficiently researched is their nonproblematic nature. Positive effects are relatively inconspicuous because they are acceptable, do not arouse public concern, do not lead to social problems, and do not call for rectification. As an unfortunate result, this discussion can therefore not include concrete research findings illustrating the development of constructive and socially acceptable personality features and behavior patterns as primarily stimulated by the mass media.

Finally, it must be clearly understood that the influence of the mass media is limited, checked, and often counteracted by other agents of socialization. In many, if not most, spheres of life the mass media are not the major influence on youth's attitudes and value orientations. For example, when TV suggests values and models for behavior that are inconsistent with the principles parents have demonstrated to the children, there is no evidence that the influence of TV is paramount. One could generalize and say that when children have already internalized knowledge or values on a given subject and are not suffering from disturbing *anomic* blanks in their life view, TV models and values seem to have relatively little effect.[39] "It is in the area of the unfamiliar, where parents have not yet made clear their own point of view and where the child has little real-life experience to use as a guideline, that TV will influence beliefs and attitudes and establish stereotypes."[40]

Another student of mass communication, Irving L. Janis, adds to the list of conditions that significantly limit the persuasiveness of the mass media.[41] Janis studied high school and college students and found that reactions to persuasion attempts are determined by what is said, who says it, and the social and personal characteristics of the individual to whom it is said. Among the personal characteristics that seem to influence responsiveness to persuasion were the youth's (1) readiness to

---

[39] The relative ineffectualness of TV in trying to change a person's perception once definite images have been established was illustrated by a study with college students on the presidential election day in 1960. It was found that those students who had a definite image of and preference for a presidential candidate were hardly affected by the so-called Great Debate, the public TV confrontation of the candidates. See: Hans Sebald, "Limitations of Communication: Mechanisms of Image Maintenance in Form of Selective Perception, Selective Memory, and Selective Distortion," *Journal of Communication,* Vol. 12 (September 1962), pp. 347–51.

[40] Maccoby, 1963, *op. cit.,* p. 125.

[41] Irving L. Janis, "Personality As A Factor In Susceptibility To Persuasion," in Wilbur Schramm, 1963, *op. cit.*

accept a favorable or unfavorable position on the particular topic presented to him, (2) susceptibility to particular types of arguments and persuasive appeals, and (3) general level of susceptibility to any form of persuasion or social influence. The study concluded that youths tending to remain relatively uninfluenced by any form of persuasion can be categorized into two types. One type tends to display overt hostility toward people he encounters in his daily life. The other type shows definite symptoms of withdrawal from social involvement, stays aloof, maintains "weak and unreliable emotional attachments to love objects, marked preference for seclusive activities, and few affiliations with formal or informal groups within the community." On the other side, youths relatively responsive to persuasion attempts were found to be of the following types. One is the youth who is disposed to use rich imagery and exhibits strong emphatic responses to symbolic representations. The second type is the youth with low self-esteem, as manifested by feelings of personal inadequacy, social inhibitions, and habitual depressions. Another type of youth is the one who has an "other-directed" orientation, prefers group conformity, and enjoys multiple group affiliations.[42]

It appears, then, that generalization concerning the effects of the mass media on youth is extremely difficult. A range of important variables, among them differential personality tendencies, must be taken into consideration before an appreciable degree of predictability can be assumed.

Modern Social Interaction: Multiple "Personae" and Problems of Identity

Most characters of the mass media exert their influence on the development of personality traits and behavior patterns in an extremely situational fashion, i.e., they depict situations that are often unrealistically isolated from the overall life context of the person portrayed. This practice of limited character portrayal is responsible for a relatively novel type of learning process: instead of presenting a holistic "significant other," whose various actions follow logically from a certain premise of basic values and norms, enabling generalization and prediction about other possible actions, the mass media present characters who exhibit behavior forms applicable to only a specific situation. In effect, the model depicts only a *situation* and not a total person. A child continuously

---

[42] Janis, *op. cit.*, p. 60.

consulting the mass media for guidance tends to adopt such situational styles of problem-solving and as a result may come to exhibit incompatible behavior forms. In crisis situations the youth may recall a style of problem-solving that was shown to him by the hero or the successful villain of the mass media, and he may be induced to think and act accordingly. As a result, the manner of solving a problem in one moment may be logically and morally incongruent with the manner of solution in another moment, since the various manners of problem solution are not derived from a common premise. The overly influenced youth, who in addition to the continuous influence of the mass media has only minimal live models, tends to have no common premise, but instead only unrelated stereotypes by which to determine situational solutions.

In a sense, one could say that the youth behaves like a different person in each situation. Each situation brings out a different actor, and the question of who the "real" person is becomes hypothetical. The youth is equipped with a large number of different *personae*, which he can change from situation to situation with no one *persona* necessarily being more important or basic to him than any other.

Lest this type of individual be confused with an abnormal or mentally disturbed person, it should be emphasized that reference is being made to the so-called "normal" member of society, very much the same sort of person whom David Riesman described as the other-directed personality, who presumably is the prevailing personality type in modern American society.[43] Professor Riesman described this typical member of society as a gregarious creature, highly sensitive to the opinions and ideas of other people, constantly scanning the social horizon with a "radar screen" to pick up the "proper" and accepted modes of conduct. Ultimately, the pluralistic dependence on other-directedness creates a social atmosphere where actions are defined more by social sensitivity than by basic personality premises.

It would be misleading to suggest that other-directedness is the sole product of the mass media's characters and models. An equally prolific source of multiple *personae* is found in the division of labor. This is an age of multiple group membership and of multipositional responsibilities, implying that a person has to occupy a number of unrelated or even conflicting positions. A youth living in a modern urban-industrial environment is ensconced in a social structure that patterns life into discrete multipositional segments, thereby tending to produce a world view that reflects this confusion and conflict. For example, as a member of the family he is expected to respect parents and to conform to a way of life that is partially obsolete in the light of what he may

---

[43] David Riesman, *The Lonely Crowd* (New Haven, Yale University Press, 1950).

learn in school. In his religious congregation he is taught dogmas and assumptions that he may find difficult to reconcile with his scientific training and understanding. When he enters an occupational position, he is expected to interact differently with his superiors than he does with his colleagues. These behavior sets, in turn, may differ greatly from those expected by his family, peers, or religious fellowship. In sum, the different environments—family, job, school, church, peers, military, etc. —call for different manners, attitudes, and values. In a sense, these different environments call not only for different behavior, but virtually for different persons.

Erving Goffman in his book, *The Presentation of Self in Everyday Life*, applied the language of the theater to describe the multi-"stage" life of modern urban man.[44] Goffman agrees with Robert E. Park who feels that it is probably no coincidence that the term person meant mask, *persona*, in its original usage. It suggests that most social behavior consists of role playing and that "it is in these roles that we know each other; it is in these roles that we know ourselves."[45] Park and other earlier writers concerned with the relationship betwen social interaction and personality formation made an understandable assumption of their time, namely, that there exists uniformity and compatibility betwen the various roles a person carries out. James M. Baldwin,[46] Charles Cooley,[47] George H. Mead,[48] and others took as their point of departure the small community where a member was known in his entirety, as a total person whose actions exhibited logical and ethical coherence and continuity. These notions of personality growth presupposed the small-town environment characteristic of 19th-century America, where the primary group was the consistent and almost exclusive influence on the development of the social nature of the individual. These early social psychologists described the rise of the social "self" as the process of taking over consistent and integrated sets of attitudes by way of role playing, role taking, and internalization of the "generalized other." The product of this process was normally an integrated and consistent personality system.

Contemporary social psychologists do not usually disagree with the principle of this learning process, yet believe that since the social

[44] Erving Goffman, *The Presentation of Self In Everyday Life* (Garden City, N.Y., Doubleday and Co., 1959).

[45] Robert E. Park, *Race And Culture* (Glencoe, Ill., The Free Press, 1950), p. 249.

[46] James M. Baldwin, *Social And Ethical Interpretations In Mental Development* (New York, The Macmillan Co., 1897).

[47] Cooley, *op. cit.*

[48] George H. Mead, *op. cit.*

environment has undergone significant structural changes, the process and product of personality development have also changed. The typical socialization environment of the urban-industrial era is no longer the small intimate community where one basic set of values and norms was the orienting force underlying the different role performances of an individual; it is now the anonymous city, with compartmentalized positions and roles that are no longer uniformly coordinated by one and the same value premise. The typical member of modern society no longer develops a uniform and monistic outlook on life, but rather learns situational ways of solving problems. The absence of an over-all personality premise is related to what psychiatrists have come to define as "problems of identity." Since role performances normally have great formative impact on the development of a stable identity, the absence of coherence among the roles an individual enacts can result in lack of sufficient *Prägnanz* in a personality *Gestalt*. Uncertainty about one's place in life has a concomitant reflection in one's self-perception.

Max Lerner, in his book *America As A Civilization,* asserted that modern Americans are engaged in an intense search for models and called the symptoms of this groping the "neurosis of the ego."[49] Lerner's theory assumes that this type of mass neurosis is a relatively novel symptom of Western man and is quite different from previous mass problems. The theory holds that a previous widespread neurosis of Western civilization was the "neurosis of the id and the superego." This earlier problem arose primarily from the typical patriarchal family setting in Europe, with its strict values and discipline, which caused widespread repressions of personal needs and desires. In other words, while the causality of the modal European neurosis lay in patriarchal authoritarianism prompting various types of repressions, that of the more recent American problem lies in the lack of personal models and compelling convictions.

The reason for the lack of personal models can be traced to the nature of the modern social structure, containing discrete and almost mutually isolated sets of interaction. This "actor" existence of mid-20th-century man, who has to perform on various and often incompatible "stages" of social life, has been described in terms of "off-stage" and "on-stage," "team," "script," "front," "audience," "performance," etc. These terms of the theater can easily be translated into conventional social-structural concepts, such as positions, private and public, group, role, social behavior, the public, role enactment, etc.[50] The use of the dramaturgical imagery paints a vivid picture of modern man as multi-*personae*,

---

[49] Max Lerner, *America As A Civilization* (New York, Simon & Schuster, 1957), pp. 694–97.

[50] Goffman, *op. cit.*

as an opportunist, supersensitive to every ephemeral demand in the social environment. Life in society is described as analogous to an infinite array of different "stage plays" where every social situation calls for its own role (script) and character. The individual who is the character must keep one set of motives secret from the other. He compartment-alizes not only his conduct but also *his reasons for it.* There is always a different audience, there is always a different set of actors (team); and, finally, there are always different goals and different motivations. A performance has the purpose of influencing others and gaining success. This is usually done cooperatively by a team under the management of impressions for the audience. The vital techniques of the management of impressions are visible only back-stage, a part of the social interaction process that is closed to the audience. Whatever the participant conveys during the performance is expected to be aligned with his role and the character he is projecting. By means of impression management, a per-former learns those attributes needed for staging his character. Hence, according to a number of modern sociologists, in lieu of the concept of the self as an autonomous moral agent or as the humanistic man of taste, the self is now viewed as an opportunistic agent observing, at best, purely discretionary rules.[51] Recent literature concerning "self-improvement" is a striking indication that this new conceptualization has empirical referents. This literature is very similar to and reflects the language of merchandizing and is directed to people with "something to sell," suggesting ways of successful self-presentation and explaining techniques for "handling" people.[52]

In essence, then, personality development has come to be related to the activities of the marketplace, to the web of "strategy of success" within the manipulative process of interpersonal relations. Goals, norms, roles, and definitions fluctuate from one social situation to the other—and identity has lost its stable anchor. Modern man has become a *persona dramatis*—an actor of many scripts. The statement of actor Peter Sellers about his identity disposition may be a timely truism applicable to modern urban-industrial man in general: "I have no personality of my own. I only feel 'real' when I'm playing a part."[53]

The impact of situational character portrayal via the mass media and the diverse and discrete "stage" life of man enmeshed in modern social structure have aggravating effects on adolescent discontinuity. If adults suffer identity problems, how much more must adolescents, who

---

[51] Goffman, *op. cit.*; see also Don Martindale, *American Society* (New York, D. Van Nostrand Co., 1960), see especially chapter 3.

[52] A popular example of this self-sale pitch is Dale Carnegie, *How To Win Friends And Influence People* (New York, Simon & Schuster, 1936).

[53] Peter Sellers, quoted in *Life* (July 31, 1964), p. 28.

are intensely involved in the process of identity formation, suffer from such compartmentalized and ephemeralized social situations. If identification situations, positions, and roles are isolated from each other, situationally defined, and often incompatible, isomorphic reflections become noticeable in the personalities of the young. Situational definitions make learning difficult because the young individual can generalize only minimally and must learn the "proper" style for each separate situation. To accomplish such situational adroitness requires a longer period of time than the simple and old-fashioned specific-action-follows-general-premise style of learning. The adolescent is tied up with a multitude of situational learnings which were spared previous generations of adolescents. Adolescence can sometimes become a lifelong condition if a young individual is unable to find a common denominator, a basic premise for specific behavior, among or beyond the multiple personae which modern society demands from him. For most adolescents, performing multiple characters will remain a confusing and agonizing problem of identity.

Culture and Role Learning

Man is a role-learning animal. He has no innate knowledge or feeling as to what his roles are to be. It usually requires a long and effortful process of learning and imitating until he complies with and understands the specific cultural blueprints outlining his role. A role specifies how people are expected to act when they occupy a given position; i.e., it spells out the blueprint for behavior that goes along with a certain place in the social structure. This role behavior, noninherited and noninstinctive, is essential for the survival of the society, enabling it to be an on-going and viable process. The teaching of roles constitutes, therefore, an exceedingly important responsibility. As has been said: "In the behavioral world what we actually see is parents and other older and more experienced persons teaching younger and less experienced persons."[54]

There is almost no necessity for teaching role behavior in societies of animals such as bees and ants, because it is an unlearned, instinctive, and genetically inherited proficiency. Role behavior is reflexive for these insects; they are born "programed" to carry out complicated tasks and do not need to be instructed. For man to achieve role skills takes many

---

[54] Clyde Kluckhohn and O. H. Mowrer, "Culture And Personality; A Conceptual Scheme," *American Anthropologist*, Vol. 46 (January, 1944), p. 8.

years of intense effort, persuasion, and even coercion. Much of what is taught meets with initial resistance, for it thwarts some of the child's natural impulses and drives. Freud referred to a generally accepted social-psychological principle when he said "where id was, there shall superego be," meaning that the direct and unrefined hedonistic approach to gratification, a natural endowment and tendency of each child, must be replaced by culturally prescribed and socially acceptable modes of behavior.[55] The interval, during which this conversion to cultural standards takes place, is the most turbulent period in the socialization process, involving emotions of love and hate, conflict and anxiety, rejection and acceptance. The larger part of the youth's life is occupied with a complicated and symbolically mediated learning process that is of primary formative significance for the personality structure. The social behavior of the individual is not an autonomous *action* of the organism, as orthodox instinctivists would like to maintain, nor is it—like the behavior of the trained rat in a maze—solely *reaction* to external stimuli, as many behaviorists claim. Rather, human behavior is a product of *interaction*. The development of the human personality depends on interaction with other individuals. Interaction proceeds not in a random fashion, but usually according to specifications laid down as a result of collective consensus.

Man's obligation to learn positional blueprints applies even to his most basic roles, such as the sex roles. It would be a misconception to equate biological maleness and femaleness with learned, sociocultural masculinity and femininity. The cultural relativity of sex roles has been discovered by anthropological research in the cross-cultural as well as historical dimension. Cross-cultural studies reveal that the perception of masculinity and femininity depends upon cultural definitions and differs greatly from one culture to another. Each culture postulates values and norms, defining and clarifying actions and interactions of males and females, thus enabling social order and predictability. In a sense, role definitions are premises from which specific actions and reactions can be deduced, thus allowing prediction of behavior. Role premises and their application in everyday life therefore become integral parts of the social order—in fact, the *foundation* of social order. For the sake of social order, it does not matter greatly *how* the role premise is formulated, just as long as there is consensus and adherence to the given formulation. The variety of formulations and their successful functionality is exemplified by natives on some Polynesian islands who

[55] See Sigmund Freud's discussion of the repressive and often frustrating aspects of group life in his *Outline of Psychoanalysis* (New York, W. W. Norton, 1949), pp. 19, 121.

engage in sex-differentiated interaction that virtually reverses Western concepts of masculinity and femininity. Men tend the homes, the hearth, and the children, while females perform the more strenuous outdoor work, cutting wood or catching fish.

There are often noticeable modifications of definitions in the same society over a period of time. This, of course, is especially true in dynamic urban-industrial societies. One can safely assume, for example, that a few qualities looked upon as strictly masculine or feminine 50 years ago are not so considered today. Such changing cultural conceptions invalidate instruments of behavioral scientists that try to measure sex-differentiation criteria. Examination of one of the earliest (1936) and most widely accepted sex-differentiating instruments, a large battery of test items known as the M-F (masculinity-feminity) inventory,[56] shows that many items are no longer relevant in determining the degree of masculinity or femininity. Cultural conceptions have been modified—generally in the direction of more diffused standards between the sexes. One researcher has found that in order to devise a valid and reliable instrument applicable today, more than half of the test items of the original M-F inventory should be discarded, modified, or replaced.[57]

Learning to interact in terms of social roles is probably the most important function of the socialization process. To achieve adequate social participation, the young individual must internalize the role prescriptions as cognitive and affective predispositions, implying that he must look at the world in certain ways and experience certain socially defined emotions. A young boy may thus come to see manliness in terms of courage and physical prowess and experience profound emotional reactions should he be asked, for example, to wear girls' clothes. However, in order to perform any social role adequately, the boy must also be familiar with the other social roles in his environment. The understanding of this network of interacting roles has been conceptualized as the "generalized other."[58] Personality grows concomitantly with role understanding. In fact, internalization of roles is almost synonymous with growth of personality, and internalized roles with which one identifies form the core of one's personality, the "self."

To avoid the mistake of looking for identicalness of personality features where two individuals have internalized the same roles, it must be emphasized that a role, like any internalized "establishment" in the personality, is characterized by *personal* meaning. Its character is determined *in part* by the place it occupies in the particular personality

---

[56] Lewis M. Terman and Catherine C. Miles, *Sex And Personality* (New York, McGraw-Hill Book Co., 1936).

[57] Hans Sebald, *op. cit.*

[58] George H. Mead, *op. cit.*, p. 154.

—its place among the other internalized roles and attitudes. The motivation it commands in a particular personality will not be the same as in other personalities. Thus the uniform role requirements are modified by the psychological idiosyncracies of particular individuals. For example, the role of girl in a given society is part of the cultural blueprint of that society, but the role internalization of any particular girl is a specific variant of the cultural role and as such consists of more than just a mirror image of the blueprint.

Previous discussion mentioned that a major portion of role learning is transacted through "significant others" and various groups. Another way of looking at the process of role internalization is through a theory describing the relationship between the social structure and the personality system as a process of *isomorphic interpenetration*.[59] This theory assumes that cultural norms interpenetrate both the personality system and the social structure. In the personality system these norms manifest themselves as motivations, and in the social system they are known as role expectations attached to positions. In an "ideal-type" society, motivations and roles are isomorphic, i.e., both exhibit themselves in the same form.

However, such "ideal-type" societies seldom have empirical referents. In present-day American society there is considerable confusion and ambiguity concerning the specifics of the male and female role expectations. For example, the roles prescribed for college women in contemporary American society tend to be contradictory and sometimes mutually exclusive. One study, dealing with college coeds, found that some attitudes necessary for a woman to successfully play the "feminine" role tend to interfere with her performance of the role of the "modern" woman with its emphasis on efficiency, reliability, rationality, independence, and self-assertion.[60] At times it is the independent "modern" female with almost a touch of the traditional "masculine" role quality who will chafe under the pressure to conform to the "feminine" pattern, while at other times the family and the college will thrust the "modern" role on a reluctant girl. Generally speaking, the American culture confronts the young female with powerful challenges and pressures to excel in many competitive endeavors and to adopt techniques similar or even identical to those of the males. Later in life, however, the very success in meeting these challenges can cause frustration and anxiety. Psychiatric opinion holds that the early-learned habit of competing with the opposite sex can

---

[59] Talcott Parsons, "Psychology And Sociology," in John Gillin (ed.), *For A Science of Social Man* (New York, The Macmillan Co., 1954).

[60] Mirra Komarovsky, "Cultural Contradictions And Sex Roles," *American Journal Of Sociology*, Vol. 52 (November, 1946), pp. 184–89.

cause sexual and marital maladjustments, in many cases carrying the competitive attitudes into the realm of sexual relations.[61]

The American teen-ager's task of learning basic roles is complicated not only by the absence or the rejection of visible models as mentioned in earlier discussions, but also by a general vagueness of role definitions, which impairs the process of isomorphic interpenetration. This phenomenon of vague and diffused role concepts seems to be related to at least two conditions: (1) Parents suffer from "cultural lag" and have difficulty in conveying role definitions that fit the new technological, scientific, and social environments of their children. (2) The general culture is relatively nonspecific, emphasizing individuality and personal choice. In sum, then, the American ethos of individual freedom can act as an agent of uncertainty and anxiety, since it leaves the young without clearly differentiated sex-role definitions and requires extra time in search and confusion—time that may extend into what could be productive adult years.

Summary

Exploration of personality formation within the dynamic urban-industrial setting must contend with a number of difficulties and relatively novel conditions. First, there is considerable confusion about the definition of the concept of personality itself. There are, however, a number of consensual criteria of the definition, among them the social, processual, and *Gestalt* nature of personality; physiological prerequisites; and the dependence on the human group. Second, value derivation and behavioral orientation are not limited to membership groups, but can be a product of an individual's identification with reference groups that are abstract and not directly visible. Some of the problems that make understanding of the behavior of modern adolescents difficult are their exposure to multiple, shifting, conflicting, and sometimes unclear reference groups. This dynamic orientation accounts for a number of misunderstood and unexplained behavior patterns, including so-called deviations from adult norms, confused and situationally compartmentalized behavior, etc.

Third, "significant others" are personal models who are highly influential in the development of personality traits. Traditionally, parents served as these important figures, but it appears that a number of modern conditions have diminished the effectiveness and significance

---

[61] Bruno Bettelheim, "Growing Up Female," *Harper's* (October, 1962), pp. 120–28.

of personal models. Among these factors are the abundantly available reference groups, the relatively noncommittal nature of culture in defining sex roles, the relative invisibility or absence of personal models, and exposure to and dependence on characters portrayed in the mass media. This touches on a fourth condition, that the mass media have considerable power to influence the young. Television and other media have become powerful agents, apt to override the influence of previously prominent socializers, such as parents and teachers. While it is not suggested that the child's fascination with fictional characters necessarily results in sociopathological problems, the unrealism and/or violence observed on the screen may be carried over into real life to a degree sufficient for causing some confusion in the youth. The time that the child needs for learning the differences between the real and the make-believe could be used to acquire useful skills and applicable knowledge that would shorten the adolescent period and make it a smoother transition into the adult world.

A fifth condition deals with the circumstances surrounding the formation of the youth's identity. The characters of the mass media as well as the nature of the modern social structure with its multipositional life situations induce modern man to think and act in terms of isolated and situational sets of social interaction. The various "scripts" and ethics that are part of modern social existence tend to endow the individual actor with multiple *personae*. This has repercussions in the person's identity, since the basic question "Who am I?" can be answered only as part of a relatively ephemeral and situational social involvement.

Finally, a sixth condition deals with the lack of specific sex-role images and definitions in the American culture. Over the past few generations, the traditional sex-specific expectations have become somewhat diffused and the behavioral differentiation blurred. This nonspecificity has created a new freedom of choice in behavioral expression and career selection. However, the price for this freedom of individuality is considerable uncertainty and anxiety, especially noticeable during the teenage years.

Although several of the sociocultural factors discussed in this chapter have bearing on adults as well as young people, it appears that the adolescent is most crucially affected as he tries to make the transition to the adult status and a stable identity. If, to start with, the adult world is characterized by other-directedness, problems of identity and direction are thereby intensified for youth, who are normally dependent on adult norms and values. A recession of youth into their own subculture, with norms and values that lend temporary orientation, may be a compensating reaction to modern conditions of adolescence.

consequence of adolescence: the teen-age subculture

the etiology of subcultures

The focus of Part III shifts from the individual adolescent to the adolescent collectivity, thereby tending toward a sociological rather than social-psychological discussion. The purpose of this chapter is to explore the development of the teen-age subculture as a consequence of status discontinuity and social unstructuredness and to show how problems on the individual level can lead to solutions—achieved or attempted—on the collective level. This chapter presents a theoretical treatment of sub-cultural formation, introducing a number of etiological theories. The next chapter supplies the necessary illustrations and descriptions of sub-cultural behavior.

The Teen-Age Subculture: A Professional Controversy

The assumption that an adolescent subculture does in fact exist is not free of controversy. The professional views on this issue range from the affirmative to the negative, with such writers as James S. Coleman,[1] Albert K. Cohen,[2] Kingsley Davis,[3] Talcott Parsons,[4] Robin

---

[1] James S. Coleman, *The Adolescent Society* (New York, The Free Press, 1963).

[2] Albert K. Cohen, *Delinquent Boys: The Culture of the Gang* (Glencoe, Ill., The Free Press, 1955).

[3] Kingsley Davis, "Adolescence and the Social Structure," *The Annals of the American Academy of Political and Social Sciences,* Vol. 236 (November, 1944), pp. 8–16.

[4] Talcott Parsons, "Age and Sex in the Social Structure of the United States," *American Sociological Review,* Vol. 7 (October 1942), pp. 604–16.

M. Williams, Jr.[5] and Arnold W. Green[6] taking the affirmative stand, and Frederick Elkin and William A. Westley[7] proposing negative views.

The affirmative party in the controversy relies heavily on three major assumptions: (1) The typical adolescent is characterized by symptoms which can be described as socially-caused "storm and stress." These expressions stem primarily from the adolescents' uncertain position in the social structure. Some of the confusions and insecurities typical of the American adolescent arise from uncertainty of occupational choice, difficulties in identifying with adult models, inconsistencies in authority relationships, conflicts between generations, sexual frustrations because of conflict between physiological maturation and social prohibitions, and discontinuity in socialization patterns. A number of prominent sociologists have illustrated these various aspects of the adolescent dilemma:

> In our society . . . the adolescent finds an absence of definitely recognized, consistent patterns of authority. . . . [He] is subjected to a confusing array of competing authorities.[8]
> Adolescence is a period of crisis. Frequently, therefore, it is also a time of revolt. . . . The cultural patterns and sanctions of one generation rarely, in an era of accelerated change, obtain for another.[9]
> The relative lack of *rites de passage* for adolescence both reflects and contributes to the uncertainty and instability faced by the adolescent. . . . Boys and girls . . . often find it difficult when and how "adult" behavior is expected. . . .
> The adolescent reaches biological maturity considerably in advance of social maturity. The extended period of formal education and the compulsions to be economically self-supporting before marriage tend to defer marriage well beyond the age of full biological maturity. Yet the society emphasizes premarital chastity while at the same time it permits and encourages young people of opposite sexes to associate closely. The resulting strains and difficulties are themselves enhanced by an appreciable lack of clarity in *de facto* social codes.[10]

(2) The second assumption is that a teen-age subculture exists and is a widespread and powerful pattern among American adolescents. *The youth subculture is a social reaction to the young individual's un-*

---

[5] Robin M. Williams, Jr., *American Society: A Sociological Interpretation* (New York, Alfred Knopf, 1960).

[6] Arnold W. Green, *Sociology* (New York, McGraw-Hill Book Co., 1968).

[7] Frederick Elkin and William A. Westley, "The Myth of Adolescent Culture," *American Sociological Review*, Vol. 20 (December, 1955), pp. 680–84.

[8] Davis, *op. cit.*, p. 13.

[9] N. D. Humphrey, "Social Problems," in A. M. Lee (Ed.), *New Outline of the Principles of Sociology* (New York, Barnes and Noble, 1946), p. 24.

[10] Williams, *op. cit.*, p. 78.

certain status in the adult world and functions to ease "the transition from the security of childhood in the family of orientation to that of full adulthood in marriage and occupational status."[11] The teen-age subculture seems to be particularly dominant in metropolitan areas, exerting far-reaching demands on followers, creating a feeling of belonging among participants, and leading to a new status system within which behavior is judged by subcultural standards and not by the norms of the adult world. James S. Coleman, basing his statement on large-scale empirical research, pointed out that American children are becoming progressively more ensconced in secondary institutions, from nursery school through college:

> This setting-apart of our children in schools—which take on ever more functions, ever more "extra-curricular activities"—for an ever longer period of training has a singular impact on the child of high-school age. He is "cut-off" from the rest of society, forced inward toward his own age group, made to carry out his whole social life with others his own age. With his fellows, he comes to constitute a small society, one that has most of its important interactions *within* itself, and maintains only a few threads of connection with the outside adult society. In our modern world of mass communication and rapid diffusion of ideas and knowledge, it is hard to realize that subcultures can exist right under the very noses of adults— subcultures with languages all their own, with special symbols, and, most important, with value systems that may differ from adults.[12]

Further support for the contention that an adolescent subculture does in fact exist comes from Talcott Parsons, Robin M. Williams, Jr., and Arnold W. Green. Parsons thinks that the characteristics of the adolescent subculture include three main aspects: first, the rebelliousness of youth against adult expectations and authority; second, the tendency toward peer conformity, guarded by considerable in-group intolerance of differences; and third, a romantic adherence to emotionally significant objects.[13] Williams contends that the social distance between generations is sometimes so great that parents and children confront each other as members of vastly different subcultures.[14] Green also believes in the existence of a teen-age subculture and calls it a "world of irresponsibility, specialized lingo, dating, athleticism, and the like, which rather sharply cuts off adolescent experience from that of the child and from that of the adult."[15]

---

[11] Parsons, *op. cit.*, p. 614.

[12] Coleman, *op. cit.*, p. 3.

[13] Talcott Parsons, "Psychoanalysis and the Social Structure," *Psychoanalytic Quarterly*, Vol. 19 (July, 1950), pp. 378–79.

[14] Williams, *op. cit.*, p. 80.

[15] Green, *op. cit.*, p. 113.

(3) The third assumption suggests a causal relationship between the adolescent subculture and the "storm and stress" of the young individual, implying that the peer culture is a compensation providing a sense of security and belonging during the period of adolescent discontinuity. To understand the causal relationship between adolescent "storm and stress" and the subculture, one must interpret most teen-age behavior as efforts to solve problems arising from an interim position— the most basic problem consisting of the uncertainty concerning a structured place in society. A bilateral attempt to ameliorate the frustrating situation, including the teen-ager as an individual and the adult society as a whole, would only bring him defeat. On the other hand, a confrontation that includes him and his similarly troubled peers as one relatively united party and the adult world as another may prove to be more successful in providing him with a structured social environment and personal identity. This achievement of personal identity illustrates the social-psychological principle that identity is highly dependent on an identifiable and relatively stable position in the social order. The subcultural arrangement is ultimately reinforced and its survival guaranteed by the satisfaction the teen-agers derive from having found a clearer status among peers.

These three assumptions have not gone unchallenged, and a negative view of the subject matter insists that belief in the existence of an adolescent subculture may perpetuate an unjustified "myth." Elkin and Westley, the main advocates of this negating view, based their dissent on an early-1950's study of teen-agers in a Montreal suburb and concluded that teen-agers are more integrated in the adult society, its customs, norms, and values, than is generally thought.[16] The two researchers found that family ties were close, the degree of basic family consensus was high, and that in many areas of life there was joint participation by parents and children. The adolescents acknowledged their parents' rights to guide them and set rules concerning dating practices, discussed their choice of school courses and vacation plans with parents, and often engaged in joint parent-child activities, such as parties, dances, and community sport events. Elkin and Westley found that parents expressed few complaints about socialization problems or peer group activities of their teen-age children, and that the continuities of socialization were more striking than the discontinuities. In short, the patterns of the adolescent's social life were not significantly different from those of the older generation, and adolescents demonstrated "a high level of sophistication about their own activities, in many respects having internalized 'responsible' and 'adult' perspectives."[17]

---

[16] Elkin and Westley, *op. cit.*
[17] Elkin and Westley, *op. cit.*, p. 683.

There is reason to believe that the conclusions of the Canadian research are not generalizable and are based on weak data. The study included only "a sample of 20 adolescents and their parents (interviews), and 20 others through life history material."[18] This selection is by no means an adequate sample from which to safely draw conclusions and generalizations about the millions of American teen-agers—especially when the researchers themselves admitted that the sample may not have been completely representative of the community from which it was taken.[19] Also, allowances should be made for possible important differences between Canadian and American teen-agers. Montreal, definitely influenced by English and French traditions, may have a slightly different type of teen-ager than most United States cities. Moreover, the locale of the research was a well-to-do suburb, classified by the authors as upper-middle, where "typically, when a girl gives a party, she sends out formal invitations, and her guest list includes those she *should* invite as well as those she wants to invite. The girls take great pains to play their hostess roles properly, and the boys so strongly recognize their escort responsibilities. . . ."[20]

The formal and conventional manner of social interaction of youth in this suburb seems to be more typical of the United States upper class than of the broad middle class. Since the present focus is more on adolescents of the broad American middle class, Elkin and Westley's study has only minimal relevance to this discussion. In conclusion, therefore, the opinion of the authors espousing the affirmative view on the topic of adolescent subculture, i.e., asserting that the American teen-age subculture is an empirical reality, appears to represent the more credible interpretation of adolescent activities.

The Diversity of Teen-Age Subcultures

One of the more justified criticisms of the characterization of the adolescent subculture concerns not so much the basic question of whether a subculture does or does not exist, but rather the question of how it is diversified. This criticism calls attention to the fact that there is no one uniform subculture for all teen-agers, but a number of significantly different versions. Many sociologists deplore the blanket application of the concept "teen-age subculture" as if there were only one monolithic membership group for all teen-agers. Instead, they remind

---

[18] Elkin and Westley, *op. cit.*, p. 682.
[19] Elkin and Westley, *op. cit.*, p. 682n.
[20] Reference 18.

us of important differences in peer cultures based on such variables as socioeconomic class, age bracket, race, ethnicity, and rural or urban residence. Teen-agers exhibit different subcultural behavior patterns depending on whether they are characterized by one or more of such variables. A Negro teen-ager living in the slums of a metropolis will exhibit different values, have a different outlook on life, and belong to a radically different peer culture than a white middle-class teen-ager growing up in suburbia.

For the purpose of clear communication, this complication of sub-cultural diversity must be simplified by some arbitrary guidelines: when the unqualified term "adolescent subculture" or "teen-age peer culture" or a synonymous phrase appears, reference is made to the non-delinquent middle class, reaching over into the upper-lower socio-economic stratum. The teen-age groups, cliques, campus crowds, etc., of this socioeconomic range are characterized by their independence from and usually nonviolent rejection of many adult standards, their compulsive conformity to peer group patterns, their observance of teen-age fads and fashions, their romanticism, and their participation in "irresponsible" hedonistic activities. Specific expressions may include distinct ways of dressing, grooming, and talking. Their argot, "special language," is not shared with adults, representing a relatively exclusive communication system.

When the concept of subculture is applied to lower socioeconomic levels, it most often refers to delinquent behavior forms. Some segments of the upper-middle and upper socioeconomic classes of the American population can hardly be said to have an adolescent subculture. In these social strata one would most likely encounter the type of nonadolescent youth who is integrated in his family and community; as a result, he suffers little status uncertainty—often to the point where there is no need for a compensating and security-extending teen-age subculture. (A fuller treatment of the different versions of the adolescent problem and of diverse subcultural expressions as a result of the above-named variables is presented in later chapters.)

Adolescent Discontinuity and Teen-Age Role: A Paradox?

Classification of certain adolescent activities as subcultural behavior introduces another complex theoretical problem. How can the portrayal of the teen-ager as a confused and uncertain adolescent be reconciled with his protrayal as a member of the teen-age subculture, within which he presumably has found role security and certainty? This seeming paradox is not easily resolved, since the teen-ager is actually characterized by *both*. The decision as to which of the two characterizations is more applicable in a certain situation depends entirely on the *specific teen-ager–other* relationship that is to be analyzed. When examining the teen-ager's relationship with adults, a multitude of problems are detectable which in their sum total substantiate the claims of the existence of adolescent discontinuity and uncertainty. Problems intrinsic to this *teen-ager–adult* relationship include confused communication, unclear authority definitions, generalist-specialist discontinuity, incongruous standards, and many other problems that were discussed in previous chapters.

On the other hand, the *teen-ager–teen-ager* relationship is characterized by few, if any, such confusions and uncertainties. Teen-agers among themselves have created a relatively stable, though temporary, social structure. They know they belong together and observe norms and values not necessarily consistent with the adult world's folkways and mores. In other words, here is a subcultural arrangement that compensates for the experience of adolescence in those situations of interaction that include the adult world. In their peer culture they find status, and consequently, the *role of teen-ager*.

One can formulate still another relationship: the *teen-age-collectivity–adult* relationship. The definition of collectivity that is involved in this relationship is susceptible to subjective interpretation; it depends either on the adults' acknowledgment of teen-agers as a subculture with relatively "closed ranks," common problems, and common compensations, or on their perception of teen-agers as a mere accumulation of young individuals with more or less discrete problems and noncollective actions. Many adults, sociologically untrained as they may be, recognize that adolescents have found a way to collectively share the problems of their interim position and, *en masse*, compensate for them in a subcultural framework. If adults perceive and acknowledge that teen-agers occupy a position and perform a role within their peer culture, the characterization of adolescence as a subcultural phenomenon is largely endorsed.

In summary, then, the seeming paradox must be understood as a problem of differential analysis. Most modern teen-agers are *both* typically confused adolescents in the adult world and relatively self-assured and status-conscious members of their peer groups—depending on the set of interactions being analyzed.

A final word of modification should be added. Explicit allowance must be made for the fact that not *all* teen-agers are adolescents and members of teen-age subcultures. It is possible to be an adolescent and not a member of some discernible peer culture. This would be the case for a youth who is socially isolated from peers and suffers from adolescent discontinuity without recourse to an age-mate subculture. Such a youth might lack opportunity to communicate with his peers and become aware of the commonality of adolescent problems. However, such a socially isolated adolescent would be a rarity, because almost any degree of social interaction would provide him with enough opportunities to communicate, meet, and share problems with peers. In general, for American teen-agers the adolescent condition constitutes an ever-present latent force whose gravitational point is the formation of a compensating subculture.

It is also possible to be a member of the teen-age subculture and suffer minimally from adolescent tensions and confusions. This relatively conflict-free situation may be due to either one or both of two circumstances. First, the teen-ager may be so deeply involved in his peer subculture, may carry out peer commitments and follow peer standards to such a degree that he derives a feeling of total belonging to the subculture. Adult standards affect him only minimally, and he suffers little or no ambiguity and confusion as to where to place his loyalty. Second, a teen-ager may be a member of the peer culture not because of basic psychological needs and tensions but rather because of proximity and coincidental acquaintances, such as neighborhood friends and school environment. This nonadolescent teen-ager may be well integrated in his family, may have clear perceptions of his future occupation, may have satisfactory access to adult models which he accepts and emulates, and may freely adhere to the value orientations of the adults with which he has close contact. His participation in the teen-age subculture is therefore merely perfunctory and of superficial significance to his personality development. This type of youth is in the minority. It is safe to assume that the majority of American teen-agers are both adolescents and members of peer cultures.

Defining Subculture

The scientific approach demands that any specific event or phenomenon be explained by a general "lawful" principle that shows the recurrent and underlying features not only of this one event but of the total order of such events. This is the nomothetic nature of scientific inquiry. Even when we tell a child why the safety valve on a pressure cooker pops off when the interior of the cooker reaches a certain temperature, we first explain in general terms that there is a relationship between temperature and pressure (technically formulated in physics by Boyle's Law) and then we show him that the behavior of the valve is exactly what we should expect according to the scientific principle. We do the same when we explain the velocity of a falling object, the learning of a habit, the relationship between price fluctuations and conditions of the market— or the development of a subculture.

What, then, are the general, recurrent, and basic features of a subculture? Since for sociological purposes *culture* refers to a blueprint for behavior of a total society, the largest human grouping, *subculture* refers to the blueprint for behavior of a smaller group within the society. As Harry M. Johnson put it: "The culture of a subgroup is sometimes called a subculture. Just as 'groups' and 'subgroups' are relative to one another, so are culture and subculture."[21] In a sense, subculture is a subsidiary blueprint that frequently is formed without encouragement, acceptability, or full cognizance on the part of the "parent culture." It is a special blueprint that accommodates a number of people whose needs and desires are not provided for by the main and overall blueprint of the society. Thus, there are subcultures for narcotic addicts, longshore-men, inmates in prison, Texas oil men, those in the world of fashion, jazz musicians—and adolescents. Every society is internally differentiated into a multitude of subgroups, each with styles of thinking and acting that are in some respects singularly its own and that can usually be acquired only by participation in the subgroup. Differentiating factors may be region, ethnicity, race, socioeconomic class, occupation, age, and the specific problems of a status category. One can even speak of sub-cultures within subcultures. For example, there is the subculture of a university campus and the subcultural fraternity within the university; the subculture of a factory and a shop within the factory; the subculture of the military establishment and a specific post or rank within the establishment. Each of these groupings remains separate, at least to the degree of limiting its contacts with other groupings to impersonal, functionally-specific relations.

A frequent method used to define a subculture is through its *functions.* As noted earlier, the general function of the subculture is to compensate for the failure of the "parent culture" to provide a definite status, a feeling of acceptance, and need-satisfactions unique to a certain group of people. To accomplish this function and to make the subculture a viable process, a number of prerequisites must be met. The most im-

---

[21] Harry M. Johnson, *Sociology: A Systematic Introduction* (New York, Harcourt, Brace & Co., 1960), p. 11n.

portant are: (1) The establishment of common values and norms. (2) A specific lingo not shared with the larger culture expressing what is of particular significance to the participant. (3) A common style of behavior, including the observance of fads. (4) Standards specifying the right appearance in terms of dress, grooming, make-up, etc. (5) A feeling of belonging, thinking of one's peer group in terms of "we" instead of "they." (6) An understanding of status relations, i.e., the existence of a working order of social positions that, at the minimum, clarifies leader-follower relationships. (7) Gratification of specific needs for which the larger culture does not provide.

Checking these functions against the *teen-age subculture* shows that: (1) Adolescents derive from it a peculiar *set of values* that consists neither of adult nor of child standards. (2) They speak an *argot* that is often only partially understood and approved by adults. (3) Teen-agers cultivate relatively *independent vogues and fads,* for example, rock 'n' roll dancing, which they do not enjoy sharing with adults. In fact, they are prone to change to new styles once adults approve and adopt a teen-age fad. (4) They observe independent *standards of grooming and clothing.* Deviation from the accepted mode may be punished in various ways, ranging from sneering and name-calling to physical violence or ostracism. (5) They acquire a *primary-group* belonging in which they are accepted as total individuals. This primary-group involvement functions as a partial and progressively increasing substitute for the teen-ager's family of orientation, which he leaves gradually. In a sense, the adolescent peer group aids young individuals in their strides toward emancipation from parental control. (6) They derive *status relationships* that enable them to engage in predictable and consistent interaction with their peers and that ameliorate the disorientation and lack of social stability during the change from child to adult frame of reference. (7) Teen-agers find in the peer subculture an environment that facilitates *evasion of adult control* and, in a sense, forms a solid front in combating adult authority. The subculture allows the adolescent to immerse himself in a peer group that is psychologically as well as physically remote from adult overview. (8) Teen-agers are provided with opportunities for increasing *heterosexual contacts and adolescent sex behavior.* In other words, the typical teen-age dating syndrome, inclusive of sexual experimentation, is facilitated and promoted by the teen-age subculture.[22] (Specific details and illustrations of subcultural behavior are presented in the next chapter.)

_____

[22] These points are partially based on David P. Ausubel, *The Theory and Problem of Adolescent Development* (New York, Grune and Stratton, 1954).

The Question of Etiology of Subculture

What are the conditions and processes that make for the emergence of a subculture? It seems that the _necessary condition_ for the emergence of a subculture is the existence of a _number of persons_ in the society who seek a solution to common problems and who _effectively interact_ with one another. It might be added that every collective segment of society has its own problems. Certain social categories, determined, for example, by age, sex, race, ethnicity, occupation, etc., exhibit characteristic types of problems. "The structure of society generates, at each position within the system, characteristic combinations of personality and situation and therefore characteristic problems of adjustment."[23]

The early formative stage of a subculture, before the in-group structure and the norms and values become firmly established, includes a process of "exploratory gestures." This process consists of mutual explorations and joint elaborations of possible solutions, often accompanied by mass-communicative and/or physical (crowds, mobs) interchanges during which a set of common sentiments is specified and subsequently reinforced. This formative phase is of great interest to sociologists specializing in the study of collective behavior because it often includes such collective actions as crowd behavior and mob violence. Once a subculture is more firmly established, interaction moves in calmer and more routine channels.

The _sufficient conditions_ for the establishment of a subculture lies in the acceptance of common norms and values specifying the "proper" and "right" way of doing things. When a sufficiently elaborate corollary of symbols has become the unique property of the persons involved, a collective identity has been born. One can then speak of a subcultural or a new cultural form "because each actor's participation in this system is influenced by his perception of the same norms in fellow actors."[24]

Membership in such a group or category ordinarily functions not merely as a problem-solving device in a narrow and technical sense, but also as a source of values, which ultimately has formative influence on the individual's self-perception. In other words, the group is not only a membership group but becomes a reference group. The price for gaining a structured and clearly defined frame of reference is conformity to the norms of the group. In return, the member has access to ready-made conclusions, solutions, and peer-approved actions that help him to solve a number of conflicts and ambiguities. There are compelling incentives

[23] Cohen, _op. cit._, p. 55.
[24] Cohen, _op. cit._, p. 65.

not to deviate from the established ways of the group; fear of disapproval or even ostracism by the peers and fear of an inhospitable larger culture combine to keep the member within the confines of the subculture.

A collectivity of individuals becomes subcultural only when its system of norms and values is significantly different from the main culture. The solutions to the problems of the given collectivity are of a nature that is embodied in the larger society neither in terms of structural provision nor, frequently, in terms of normative acceptability. In other words, the subcultural collectivity has, by cognizant or crescive method, developed structural remedies as well as new norms and values to overcome the larger society's inability to provide effective solutions. The new solutions may conflict with the larger society's traditions and may result in the collectivity being labeled deviant, thereby generating antagonism and mistrust between the larger and the smaller cultural systems. From the subcultural point of view, the so-called deviant-solution approach may more effectively ameliorate needs and problems than any existing solution institutionalized in the larger society. In addition, the members of the subculture frequently do not feel that their activities and attitudes could harm individuals inside or outside of their group and thus see no reason to change their patterns. As a result, they tend to perceive their activities not only as effective but also as justified.

It seems to be the order rather than the exception that resistance to and suppression of subcultural ways result in strengthening them rather than in destroying them. History is replete with supporting examples. Probably the most outstanding instance in the history of Western civilization is the persecution of and the attempts to suppress the early Christians, who eventually were victorious and turned from being a rejected minority into a powerful majority that rose to dominate most of Western culture.

New solution approaches and signs symbolizing subcultural membership may, from the outsider's point of view, be perceived as relatively unstructured, haphazard, and undefined behavior. For the in-group members, however, it is structured and well defined. This misconception on the part of the outside observers arises because of a tendency to judge unfamiliar and strange behavior in terms of one's own norms and values, not realizing that the seemingly nonconformist behavior actually conforms to the expectations of the subculture.

One of the aspects most often ignored by outside observers is the subculture's different criteria for ascribing prestige. Frequently the members of the subculture, prior to their joining, have encountered serious obstacles in the path of achieving prestige and status in the larger society—a condition certainly true of adolescents. However, within the confines of the subculture there are new opportunities for acceptance and achievement of status and respect in the eyes of one's fellows. The solution for teen-agers who share this predicament of un-clear status and dubious respect in the adult world is, therefore, to gravitate toward one another and jointly establish new criteria of status which describe as meritorious those characteristics they *do* possess and the kinds of activities of which they *are* capable. This, quite obviously, is a group approach to a collective problem. If an individual adolescent tried to establish such criteria alone, he would probably not only fail to achieve status in the larger society, but also estrange himself from his peers. As Albert Cohen states:

> The continued serviceability and therefore the viability of a sub-cultural solution entails the emergence of a certain amount of group solidarity and heightened interaction among the participants in the subculture. . . . This accentuates still further the separateness of the group, the dependence of the members of the group and the rich-ness and the individuality of its subculture.

> Insofar as the new subsculture represents a new status system sanc-tioning behavior tabooed or frowned upon by the larger society, the acquisition of status within the new group is accompanied by a loss of status outside the group.[25]

Belonging to and depending on a subculture usually has far-reach-ing effects on the personality of its follower. The influence may be strong enough to provide the basic character of one's identity. Indeed, the de-cision to join a subculture is normally indicative of the person's desire and need for a clear identity. The subculture, then, comes to function as an important psychological refuge.

A chapter on the development of subcultures is not complete unless it describes, at least briefly, the pertinent etiological theories. Among the models purporting to explain the origin of subcultures are the psycho-genic, culture-transmission, and behavioristic. Familiarity with these theoretical frameworks aids in understanding specific elements in the complex process of subcultural development. Although they represent different ways of looking at the empirical phenomenon, they are not necessarily incompatible explanations but rather complementary views emphasizing different aspects of the process.

(1) *The Psychogenic Model.* The basic assumption of the psycho-genic theory holds that a subculture evolves from problems of adjust-ment that are common to a relatively large number of members of the society. Emphasis is put on the independence with which individuals contrive solutions. The individual is depicted as a creative innovator. Although the role of the social milieu as the genesis of the problem is

---

[25] Cohen, *op. cit.*, pp. 67–68.

recognized, its role in the determination of the solution is minimized. New cultural forms emerge as a *parallel* development of individual solutions which, more or less unaccountably, merge into a collective entity. The aspect of the subcultural development that is unaccounted for in this framework is the process of social interaction as a necessary condition during the incipient phase of a subculture.

The psychogenic approach views teen-age behavior as efforts to solve the problems characteristic of their frustrating and confusing so-journ in the no-man's-land of adolescence. Using the term "no-man's-land" in describing the adolescent phase points to an analytic truism: The adolescent, standing between child and adult status and being devoid of a clearly structured social position, may frequently ask himself the agonizing question of who he really is and come face to face with the issue of identity. With Erik H. Erikson,[26] Gordon W. Bronson,[27] Margaret Mead,[28] and other contemporary writers it can be maintained that the major task facing the adolescent is the search for meaningful identity. This task is obviously more difficult in the modern urban-industrial setting than in a smaller folk or tribal society. The activities and the value-orientations of the parents are not sufficiently visible to serve as models; even if they were visible, they may have become less effective when compared with the models provided by mass media. The adolescent, furthermore, is in the process of freeing himself from dependency on his parents and tends to be not only unresponsive but often antagonistic to adult standards. He prefers the standards of his peers to those of adults. The rapid pace of social change, exposure to a confusing variety of secular and religious value systems, and revolutionary technological innovations of the 20th century make the world appear too relativistic and unpredictable to provide the teen-ager with a stable frame of reference. Youth of previous generations experienced a more practical introduction to adult responsibilities, a sort of apprenticeship during which they could acquire an identity.

The modern teen-ager receives a much less practical and much more abstract introduction to life, which results in the perception of the world as utterly complex and ambiguous. He has great difficulties in seeing just where and how he fits in. For him it is a frightening confrontation with an impersonal and abstract world. His escape attempts lead him to other teen-agers. In concerted actions they establish a substitute for the identity that is denied them in the adult world and develop

---

[26] Erik H. Erikson, *Childhood and Society* (New York, W. W. Norton, 1963).

[27] Gordon W. Bronson, "Identity Diffusion in Late Adolescence," *Journal of Abnormal and Social Psychology*, Vol. 59 (November, 1959), pp. 414–17.

[28] Margaret Mead, "The Young Adult," in E. Ginzberg (ed.), *Values and Ideals of American Youth* (New York, Columbia University Press, 1961), pp. 37–51.

peer-group symbols to reinforce a subcultural identity. In the process of maintaining this identity, special clothes, special language, and special attitudes toward the world play an important role. In the past, this manner of symbolizing an identity was characteristic almost exclusively of deprived and/or delinquent groups who had no acknowledged or respected place in the society. Examples would be transvestites, members of delinquent gangs, beggars, narcotic addicts, etc. Today, a similar unacknowledged condition, though not necessarily arising from material deprivation or delinquency, is experienced by teen-agers *in general*— they are uncertain about their place in society and therefore set up their own structure. In short, the need for the peer culture with its peculiar symbolizations is psychogenic and basically symptomatic of the search for identity.

As far as the psychogenic model is applicable, it is useful and appears to accurately reflect empirical processes. However, it is considerably limited in its explanatory *range*, as it is unable to give an explanation of the exact nature of the *formative* process of the collectivity. One of the most difficult and unexplored areas in sociology remains the analysis of the bridging process that leads from discrete individual problems to the actual beginnings of a subculture.

(2) *The Culture-Transmission Model.* This theory is concerned with the perpetuation of an already established subculture by transmission of its norms, values, and unique patterns of behavior from one generation to the next or from one group to another. This approach is interested more in understanding the *learning process* whereby, for example, the younger teen-agers acquire their older peers' modes of thought and actions than in understanding the *prime* origin of these subcultural patterns. The limited scope of this approach often excludes from consideration those crucial problems that render the new subculture-bearers susceptible to the established subcultural form. At the most, this theory suggests a number of plausible mechanisms of subcultural transmission, such as the learning of a set of rules that lend orientation and direction to the life of the teen-ager and the role of the mass media in disseminating these rules and ideas.

Mass media are probably the most effective mechanisms for transmitting and perpetuating the teen-age subculture. Mass media offer ready-made solutions to teen-agers and promise to save them the effort of searching for new forms.

In a technologically advanced society there is no shortage of channels of communication. For example, the "Summary Report on Findings and Recommendation of the Conference on the Impact of Motion Pictures and Television on Youth," by the Subcommittee to Investigate Juvenile Delinquency of the Committee on the Judiciary, United States

Senate, included an estimate that American children on the average spend approximately 20 to 24 hours per week watching television.[29] It can be safely assumed that the various relatively unexplored effects of such extensive exposure include the tendency to imitate and conform to styles and manners depicted in the programs. The youthful audience is therefore encouraged to imitate common heroes, styles, and behavior patterns. In the process, children develop identical or similar preferences, tastes, and tendencies to think and act.

Besides TV, there are several influential teen-age magazines available at most newsstands and drugstores. In many instances, they try to attract the youth's attention by "teen"-connoting titles, such as *Teen World, Modern Teen, Teen Time, Teens Today, Teen Parade, Seventeen,* etc. Other magazines have taken their titles from slang vocabulary and have assumed that such terms as *Dig, Flip,* and *Hep Cats,* etc., would appeal to teen-agers. A survey in the early 1960's revealed that most of these teen magazines seem to have limited circulations. Typical examples are *Dig,* founded in 1955, with approximately 171,000, *Teen* with about 245,000, and *Modern Teen* with about 221,000 purchasers.[30] One reason for limited circulation is the fact that these magazines are aimed at specific readerships within the teen-age population. Teen-agers are discriminating and know that some of the magazines are for the younger teen-agers, some for girls only, some for the middle teen-agers, others for older teen-agers including college students. Still others have a certain socioeconomic slant, as for example *Seventeen,* which caters to upper-middle-class girls. One of the variables that distinguish one category from the other is the degree of sophistication, usually reflected in the style of humor. While publications for younger teen-agers appear intense and humorless, a more relaxed style emerges for older readers —to the degree of "making fun" of the teen-agers themselves. The factor that remains constant throughout all teen publications, and that is of foremost sociological importance, is the magazine's function of conveying a sense of unity and collective identity to its teen-age readership. This unity function can be illustrated particularly well by the large volume of "Letters to the Editor" in which teen-agers describe themselves, talk about their problems, give and ask advice, and state their

---

[29] U. S. Senate, Subcommittee to Investigate Juvenile Delinquency of the Committee on the Judiciary, "Summary Report on Findings and Recommendations of the Conference on Impact of Motion Pictures and Television on Youth," (Exhibit #7) S. Res. #48, 87th Congress, Investigation of Juvenile Delinquency in the United States, Part 9, March, 1961.

[30] Charles H. Brown, "Self-Portrait: The Teen-Type Magazine," *The Annals of the American Academy of Political and Social Sciences,* Vol. 338 (November, 1961), p. 20.

opinions. In addition, the magazines have fan club and pen pal departments. The close communication within the world of peers is strikingly
illustrated by the exchange of personal views and problems. The style
of sharing views is probably closer and more intimate than among
adults. An example from the column "Your Letters" of *Seventeen* illustrates this habit of sharing opinions, expressing a sense of adolescent
unity, and opposing the adult world:

> In my town those "beach-ski-surf-rock soap operas" are the
> hits. We love them and I think other average kids all over the
> country enjoy them too. We see them as the way we would like it
> to be for us—no homework, no curfews, no jobs or any of that
> other stuff.[31]

The tone of the letter reflects the belief in a peer group to which the
teen-ager belongs, "other *average* kids . . .," and the pronoun *"we"*
indicates the identification with this peer culture. This type of expression,
shared with other teen-agers, has the effect of mutually reinforcing the
typically adolescent manner of thinking and acting. The preference for
"no homework, no curfews, no jobs or any of that other stuff" illustrates
the withdrawal from the responsibilities and demands of the adult world
to more hedonistically palatable activities.

Another illustration of the function of teen-age magazines to facilitate communication and expression of in-group sentiments within the
subculture comes from *Teen* Magazine where a teen-ager voiced typical
concern over adult intrusion, manifested his awareness of teen-age
solidarity, and urged strict dissociation between the adult and the teen-
age cultures:

> Maybe the grown-ups don't realize what they're doing, but it's
> clear to me and some of my friends that the grown-ups are trying
> to act like teenagers. For instance, almost every dress in the teen
> fashion mags is copied for the older people. We can't even have our
> own style in dress without them taking over. Then, some of the
> grown-ups have to steal "our" music away—by that I mean rock 'n'
> roll. They try to talk the same way we do by using some of our neat
> words. If they have to have some sort of music, why don't they stick
> to the music made by people their own age, like Dean Martin, Perry
> Como, or Andy Williams? Why do they have to pretend to luv
> everything we adore? "Disgusted"[32]

Another characteristic of teen communication is its closed-circuit
nature. Information traveling within the teen world may not be accessible to outsiders, in this case, adults. An extreme example of closed-
circuit teen-age communication was discovered at the occasion of an

---

[31] *Seventeen* (May, 1966), p. 8.
[32] *Teen* (December, 1965), p. 10.

investigation of a multiple murder case in Tucson, Arizona, in 1965, when the murders of three teen-age girls were under investigation. The young man suspected of the murders was a well-known member of the teen set and had braggingly shared his macabre information with other teen-agers. However, it was not until one year after the disappearance of one of the girls and several months after the disappearance of the other two girls that investigators discovered that at least 30 teen-agers had known of their deaths at the hand of the young man and had kept this information within their closed-circuit communication system.

Almost as fantastic as the murders themselves was the disclosure that at least 30 teen-agers, all friends of Schmid's, had apparently heard him brag about the crimes—and said nothing. Confided one 16-year-old coed at Tucson's Palo Verde high school: "A lot of people knew, but it was already too late. Telling would just have made it tough on everyone."[33]

In summary, then, TV programs and movies beamed at the teen-agers, teen magazines with their "Letters" departments, and the physical proximity of teen-agers on school campuses and in gangs provide media for communication that spread and perpetuate subcultural thought and behavior. These media are not limited to one generation of teen-agers, but rather span generations of teen-agers, helping them to learn anew the ways of their older peers. Needless to say, these media are powerful conditioners, often commercially exploiting the need of teen-agers to communicate with other teen-agers and to derive a feeling of belonging to the culture of their peers.

(3) *The Behavioristic Model.* Although behaviorism, so far, has failed to successfully apply its framework to the question of subcultural formation and to formulate a precise etiological theory, it should at least be mentioned here as a promising possibility well capable of pointing out significant steps in the process of converting children into members of teen-age subcultures. It would be presumptuous to attempt to present a complete picture of the behavioristic approach in this limited context. A few passing remarks must suffice.

Application of behavioristic principles to explain the rise of subcultures has a definite resemblance to the psychogenic model. The point of departure again is the tensions and frustrations which youth experience during adolescence. If tensions, frustrations, and uncertainties are equated with painful experience, one finds that the American teen-agers are frequently exposed to pain when interacting with adults, technically called *aversive stimuli*. To carry the process to its logical conclusion, it follows that the teen-agers try to avoid this type of stimulus and tend

---

[33] "Crime," *Time* (Nov. 26, 1965), p. 27.

to withdraw from the adult world, which represents the source of pain. This type of behavior is defined as "escape behavior"[34] and is illustrated by escape attempts from the tensions of the youth-adult confrontation. This reaction is common to most adolescents since the same hedonistic principle applies to all. Graphically and simplistically speaking, on the escape route away from the adult world the adolescent meets other adolescents who have identical or very similar problems of tensions and frustrations. The result is a grouping-together that again can be explained by behavioristic principles. Through interaction among themselves, adolescents discover that they are freer of stringent adult expectations and rules that they have found difficult to meet and accept. As a result, they experience a lessening of tensions and frustrations. They experience their peer group as a more relaxed environment than the adult environment. As a consequence, interaction among peers can be described as experiencing a multitude of stimuli that are largely gratifying to participating teen-agers and that gradually form patterns of subcultural behavior. These stimuli can thus be called positive reinforcers. Positive reinforcers often are more powerful than negative reinforcers, because the natural enjoyment of the peer fellowing with its common activities and interests has a collectivizing tendency. Thus, independently from adolescent problems, normal gregarious activities help to form and sustain the peer culture.

In the final analysis, these two types of reinforcers, the negative (escape from pain) and the positive (finding security and the gratification of fellowship), effectively promote the establishment and perpetuation of the subcultural milieu.

There is still another aspect of the adolescent phenomenon that can effectively be explained by behavioristic principles. It deals with the differential consequences of consistent and inconsistent conditioning. Teen-agers are exposed to a variety of inconsistent stimuli. In one instance they are told to be responsible and independent, as are 18-year-old boys in the military, while in another instance they may be prevented from showing responsibility when refused a glass of beer because of their age. In many cases American coeds are expected to show responsibility and independence concerning vocational preparation, but must adhere to curfews that obviously manifest distrust of their maturity and their sense of responsibility. Such inconsistent stimuli are also definable as inconsistent and ambivalent role expectations, as mixing relatively indiscriminately a number of elements from the adult and the child roles. Incon-

---

[34] See for technical treatment and definition: Arthur W. and Carolyn K. Staats, *Complex Human Behavior—A Systematic Extension of Learning Principles* (New York: Holt, Rinehart, and Winston, 1964), p. 44.

sistent stimuli due to such inconsistent role expectations have a tendency to produce ambivalent behavior patterns—sometimes to the point of neurosis.[35] The initial reactions to such ambivalent conditioning include frustrations and tensions. Eventually, this frustration experience has the effect of making the adolescent choose the less frustrating conditioning system of the peer culture with its simpler, more uniform, and consistent adjustment processes.

Summary

Many prominent social scientists agree on the existence of the teen-age subculture as an empirical reality. Research and a multitude of daily manifestations seem to support their assumption. Care must be taken in defining subculture to specify *which* type of teen-age sub-culture is to be discussed. Generally speaking, the present discussion refers to the teen-age culture within the broad American middle class, taking in most of the upper-lower socioeconomic stratum. The seeming paradox that a teen-ager can be both an adolescent and at the same time a status-ascertained member of the peer culture can be resolved by resorting to *differential analysis*, by focusing, respectively, on the adolescent-adult or the adolescent-adolescent interaction. The functions of the teen-age subculture that are prerequisite for meeting the needs of the participants and enabling the subculture to become a continuous semi-institution include a number of "services": (1) Common norms and values. (2) A subcultural argot. (3) Fads and subcultural activities. (4) A unique appearance signifying belonging. (5) A feeling of solidarity among the members. (6) A status structure. (7) Behavior patterns avoiding dominance by the "parent culture." (8) Providing the setting for the dating syndrome.

It should be emphasized that motivation to join and maintain the normal nondelinquent teen-age subculture does not stem entirely from the need to alleviate adolescent frustration and confusion. Motivation also stems from gregarious propensities, the enjoyment of peer fellowship as may be observed in any age category. Teen-agers enjoy engaging in recreations and activities (for example, dating) and in sharing unique interests that are neither entirely child nor adult. This enjoyment of peer

---

[35] Behavioristically inclined psychologists have demonstrated the effect of ambivalent conditioning in lab situations using animals as their subjects. It has been found that inconsistent conditioning can result in neurotic disturbances, possibly to the extent of a so-called "nervous breakdown." See, for example, Jules H. Masserman, *Behavior and Neurosis* (Chicago, University of Chicago Press, 1943).

fellowship, then, functions to positively reinforce the formation and continuation of the teen-age subculture and operates in conjunction with the more negatively reinforcing influence of adolescent insecurity. In fact, for teen-agers relatively unaffected by adolescent disturbances, this positive reinforcer, the gregarious enjoyment, is of stronger motivating power for forming and joining the teen-age subculture than the negative reinforcer.

Three etiological theories appear to be relatively compatible and complementary in explaining the process of subcultural formation. Propositions within each theory elucidate a number of specific events and patterns of the subject matter. The psychogenic and behavioristic models focus on the prime origin of the subcultural evolvement and start with the problems characteristic of a number of persons. Behaviorism, with its premise of human nature as basically hedonistic, explains the gravitation of teen-agers toward their peer culture as an escape reaction to the painful confrontation with the adult culture and as a gravitation toward common activities and interests. The culture-transmission model deals with processes of learning and communicating. The various media of mass communication, such as TV, movies, radio, and magazines, play important roles in the process of perpetuating subcultural ways of thinking and acting. A shortcoming of all three models is the failure to precisely pinpoint the turning moment where individuals with common and parallel problems initiate concerted action and engage in collective behavior.

Nevertheless, the different emphases of the theoretical models add up to a helpful degree of complementarity. An eclectic approach utilizing the most workable precepts of each conveys a relatively complete picture of the emergence and persistence of teen-age subculture.

life in the subculture

While the preceding chapter was heavily theory-oriented, this chapter is a more descriptive treatment and as such draws more heavily from popular rather than professional sources. The reliance on popular sources helps to add a descriptive element to the sociological interpretation and to present illustrations that show the teen-agers' subcultural involvement.

The teen-age subculture differs from the adult world in a number of ways. Teen-agers tend to maintain their own styles in such areas as music, dancing, clothing, lingo, and grooming. These differences in behavior and appearance function as a means to overtly identify with and maintain an ethos different from the established parent culture. Only through constant behavioral commitments in the form of a distinct appearance, clearly distinguishable from the main society, can a subculture rally its members and pit them against the "outside." As a qualified observer remarked about the modern teen-ager: "With his fellows, he comes to constitute a small society, one that has most of its important interaction *within* itself, and maintains only a few threads of connection with the outside adult society."[1] James S. Coleman continued to describe the teen-age phenomenon as "subcultures with languages all their own, with special symbols, and, most importantly, with value systems that may differ from adults."[2] Values and folkways of the teen-age world exert pressures to conform on the individual youth as strongly as those of the adult world exert pressures to conform on the individual adult. The subculture is built on the insecurity arising from discontinuity between child and adult status, and therefore displays an excessive concern for safety. It seems that an environment that provides maximum security is one in which a member does not stand out in any way, but rather is inconspicuously submerged in vogues of "sameness." If every-

---

[1] James S. Coleman, *The Adolescent Society* (New York, Free Press, 1963), p. 3.
[2] *Ibid.*

body looks alike and acts alike, members of the subculture gain the impression of being indistinguishable from the rest of their peers and are therefore protected against being identified and lifted out from a safe and relaxed environment.

It is against this social-psychological background that teen-age fads must be understood. Fads serve two main functions: (1) They have an identification function, symbolically confessing membership in the peer group. (2) They provide security through the facade of "sameness" that, hopefully from the point of view of the teen-ager, makes for undetectability of the individual.

Teen-Age Fads

The *forms* of behavior and appearance that help to provide identification and security for the collectivity remain more or less the same. That means fadist expressions are necessarily limited to a few possible media (clothing, lingo, music, etc.) through which, however, a great variety of styles can be expressed. It must therefore be realized that the seemingly endless varieties of teen-age fads and crazes can be divided into a few relatively simple media of expression.

Before calling attention to the various areas of overt expression, the meaning of *fad* should be clarified. In *A Dictionary of the Social Sciences,* Ray Gold defines fad as:

> markedly novel, trivial, and ephemeral behavior which spreads rapidly through whatever portions of society choose to adopt it. Fad behavior may involve crowd-like imitation directed toward momentary circumvention of folkways and mores; it may also provide substitute ways of expressing normatively thwarted emotions, such as status yearning and sexual drives."[3]

Definitions of fad by other authorities closely concur with the above and emphasize that:

> Fad is a passing fancy or novelty interest. It may relate to slang phrases, types of jokes, modes of conduct, dress and other phenomena. Fads originate generally and spread most rapidly in areas of high stimulation: Hollywood or Broadway. They are most likely to be associated with interest of leisure or play.[4]

---

[3] Ray L. Gold, "Fad," in Julius Gould and William L. Kolb (eds.), *A Dictionary of the Social Sciences* (New York, Free Press, 1964), pp. 256–57.

[4] Henry P. Fairchild, *Dictionary of Sociology and Related Sciences* (New York, Littlefield, Adams & Co., 1965), p. 113.

Fad—a temporary, usually irrational, pursuit, fashion, etc. by numbers of people of some action that excites attention and has prestige.[5] Fads seem to spread primarily among individuals in similar social circumstances.[6]

These definitions agree on several major elements of fads: ephemerality, novelty, triviality (in the sense of being only slightly different from what is permissible in the larger society), creation of a criterion for status, and adherence by people exposed to similar social conditions. These elements can be recognized in teen-age fads and can be paraphrased in the following way: (1) Almost all teen vogues are short-lived, one displacing the next in rapid sequence. It is difficult to determine the average duration of a teen fad; it may range from a few months to several years. (2) For a behavior style to qualify as a fad, it must introduce a relatively *new* way of doing, speaking, grooming, or dressing. It must draw attention and be clearly distinguishable from both the preceding teen-age habit in the given behavior area and the customary folkway in the adult world. (3) The significance of the fad is usually *trivial* compared with the mores of the society. This implies that fads are "odd" and deviant forms of existing folkways, normally within the range of the permissible and not violating any of the serious mores. However, one could certainly find instances where the adult society has reacted with a severity of sanctions toward teen fads that ordinarily is reserved for punishment of infractions of the mores. For example, the vogue of shoulder-length hair for teen-age boys during the late 1960's was judged so negatively by some school administrators, as will be illustrated in detail later, that suspension from school was threatened or actually enforced. (4) Teen-agers use fads as *status measurements*. Fads allow them to achieve prestige in the eyes of their peers by conforming and excelling in observance of the particular vogue. A teen-ager with a Harvard sweat shirt may have slightly greater prestige than a teen-ager with one from a less famous school—regardless of academic significance for the teen-agers involved. Similarly, a boy sporting curls to the shoulder or a "Beatle mop top" draws more awe from his peers—and more ire from his teachers—than one with a conventional haircut in line with adult specifications. (5) Finally, teen fads are meant for *teens only*. This exclusivity is both crescive and deliberate, i.e., fads spring up more or less spontaneously and are imitated by teen-agers without particular scrutiny of their purpose. However, once established, a fad is jealously guarded and deliberately kept from adults. In fact, it has been observed

---

[5] Clarence L. Barnhart (ed.), *The American College Dictionary* (New York, Rondom House, 1962), p. 432.

[6] Leonard Broom and Philip Selznick, *Sociology*, 3rd Ed. (New York, Harper and Row, 1963, p. 253.

that as soon as adults accept and imitate a teen fadist style, teen-agers reject it.

This general background on the nature of fads should be preparation enough to now examine specific areas of the teen-agers' fadist expressions.

Clothing. Clothing is a visual means of communication. Teen-agers are able to categorize people by the clothing they wear and are able to identify in-group members by their appearance. Once clothing has given a teen-ager an idea of the social identity of another person, he is able to pattern his behavior and responses accordingly. Clothing is a subtle and meaningful way of communicating to others the kind of role a person wishes to play in life. If a teen-ager looks like a teen-ager, he is likely to be treated as a teen-ager, just as a schoolteacher who looks like a schoolteacher is likely to be treated as a schoolteacher. It can therefore be concluded that clothing influences a person's social interaction. It has been only within the last two to three decades that social scientists have paid systematic attention to the social-psychological function of clothing and have elucidated the relationship between what a person wears and how people react to him.[7]

Clothing fads serve three additional functions beside the main functions of identification and protective "sameness." First, they serve as a medium or rebellion against the adult world; second, they often afford utilitarian comfort and, third, they allow for aesthetic expression.

In part, the origin of rebellion can be explained by the fact that most teen-agers experience dismay on discovering that their parents and other adults are relatively weak and fallible individuals beset with inconsistencies and a good deal of hypocrisy. They see adults preaching one thing for teen-agers and doing an altogether different thing themselves. The child's dream of the adult's loyalty, honesty, and virtue is shattered when he discovers that promises are frequently broken, as, for example, in divorce, or when he sees his mother say one thing to a neighbor's face and another behind her back, or when smoking and drinking are condemned for children and teen-agers as "bad and unhealthy" while parents go right on indulging in them. The result is that the adult world may take on a "phony" appearance. Not wanting to surrender to this "phoniness and hypocrisy," teen-agers seek to avoid becoming integrated into the adult social structure; many openly reject conventional adult society as "phony" and seek "truth and reality" in their

---

[7] See a report on experiments demonstrating the extent to which types of clothing may affect status ratings in certain social situations: Thomas F. Hoult, "Experimental Measurement of Clothing As A Factor in Some Social Ratings of Selected American Men," *American Sociological Review,*" Vol. 19 (June, 1954), pp. 304–28.

own experience instead. As one facet of the rejection syndrome, the young rebels have a tendency to reject even the conventional garments of the adults and determine their own fashions.

Also, many of the teen fads in clothing reflect nothing more than the desire to be comfortable. The so-called "grannies" were rooted in this need. A "granny" was a ruffled and feminized version of the Hawaiian missionaries' muumuu, a garment that covered the wearer from neck to ankle. Originally, this style was worn on West Coast beaches for protection and comfort after swimming, but gradually it became accepted as street wear. When enough of the garments were worn in residential areas, store managers decided that the fad was worth their investment. "Grannies" sold at $10 to $15 and immediately spread to New York, Chicago, Pittsburgh, and later to virtually all large cities of the United States. By early 1966, "grannies" had become acceptable for dates and general after-school wear in Los Angeles. (It appears that the hippie movement, emerging in the mid-1960's was originally based on just such a rejection. However, what took on form was not a mere fadist mood, but a social movement; it rejected not only conventional clothing, but also middle-class art, philosophy, and values.) In the teen-agers' relation to adults, the "granny" catered not only to their sense of rebellion but also to their desire to set themselves apart from the large society.

Another stream of teen fadist clothing entered the country from the opposite side. It had its starting point with the so-called Mods in England. The Mods, a distinct segment of the English teen world—in a sense, a subculture of the subculture—rejected the conventional English sports jackets, gray flannels, white shirts, and best brown brogues for a wide variety of sartorial expressions. Mod garb for the boys was trim-fitting vests, frilled silk shirts, flower-patterned ties, high-heeled shoes; their female counterparts concurred with long dresses (sometimes similar to the American "grannies," although etiologically unrelated), a great deal of decoration, buttons, bows, lace, and frills. Their mecca was the modernist shops on Carnaby Street in London, where commercial interests, again, reinforced and manipulated the teen-age fad. It spread to the United States in early 1966 when Dayton's Department Store brought the top English designer of Mod clothing, John Stephen, to Minneapolis to open a special shop. The success of the Mod fad in America was considerably more limited than the "granny" fad. There are two possible reasons for its failure to spread through the rest of the land: Mod clothing was too expensive, and it was by far not as comfortable as "grannies," Levis, or sweat shirts.

In 1966, the extremely short skirt, the so-called "miniskirt," emerged as another Carnaby Street creation, utilizing most of the styling elements of the former Mod fashion. The various subforms of the Mod look as well as short hemlines, gradually emerged on the American teen scene and found relatively widespread adherence during the late 1960's.

There were a number of minor and regionally limited American clothing fads during the period of 1965–67. Since youngsters obviously must wear some type of footgear, and since their choice is greatly limited by what is practical, on the market, and within reasonable cost, it might be a mistake to talk of wearing sneakers or loafers as a fad. However, the issue is not so simple. In California in 1966, a preference for battered-looking sneakers evolved—sneakers with raveled edges that would normally result from about six months of wear. Subsequently, they were commercially manufactured that way by B.F. Goodrich and were called "Tradewinds"—or "grubbies" by teen-agers.

It must be cautioned that it would be a mistake to label the persistent wearing of some common garment a fad. If a certain period of duration is exceeded, and certain clothes become customary for one or more generations, they can no longer be defined as fadist. A borderline case between fad and custom is presented by blue jeans, the good name of which was tarnished in the public opinion by association with the leather jacket in the 1950's. However, it seems that blue jeans have been restored to their nondelinquent status as utility wear for boys. Wearables such as blue jeans are not sufficiently novel, ephemeral, and different from the adult custom to warrant the label of fad.

Occasionally, a leading member of some teen-age subgroup asserts his ideas, or the ideas of his group, by adding special adornments to his clothing. Whether a Modish outfit, a "granny," a sweat shirt, or a parka, the identification value of the given garment is enhanced by such buttons as "U.S. Drinking Team," "Make Love, Not War," "Draft Beer, Not Students," "Eros Yes, Morals No."

Music and Dancing. Unlike fads in clothing, music styles usually are of longer duration. Americans have been enthralled by rock 'n' roll music since the early 1950's—longer than any other music fad in recent American history. The music of the Roaring Twenties with its Charleston, Black Bottom, and Shag lasted not longer than 10 years.

However, this does not mean that the rock 'n' roll style has remained unchanged. Starting with 1960, it re-formed itself every two or three years. It was probably this flexibility that made "rock" a viable musical form that kept its basic characteristic of the 1950's. Elvis Presley entered the stage in the mid-1950's and did more than any other performer to introduce rock 'n' roll to American teen-agers. It was an ecstatic and unruly initiation. There were riots in Hartford, Atlanta, San Jose, London, etc.—and Sao Paulo, Brazil, was the site of a riotous storming of the theater. Educators took a dim view of Presley and his fans after they found out from surveys that a majority of Elvis fans had a below C average. A U.S. Senate subcommittee even started investigations of the possible connection between rock 'n' roll and juvenile delinquency. Pablo Casals publicly called rock 'n' roll "poison put to sound," Frank Sinatra condemned it as a "rancid-smelling aphrodisiac," and Samuel Cardinal Stritch compared it to "tribal rhythms."[8] Nevertheless, the fad spread and flourished. The early rock 'n' roll era ended in 1960 when Chubby Checker introduced the twist. For the first time since the decline of the jitterbug the American teen-agers had their own dance again. But about two or three years later the twist became obsolete and taboo for connoisseurs, and such free-style versions as the "Watusi," "hitchhiker," "frug," "jerk," and the "monkey" appeared.

These versions of rock 'n' roll did not remain exclusively American, but spread and become an international fad that captured teen-agers all over the world. Some English musicians, for example, were particularly influenced by American rock 'n' roll and commenced to refertilize the American mainland with their own versions. The British group, the Beatles, came to America in 1964, appeared before almost 70 million onlookers on the Ed Sullivan show, and received one of television's biggest publicity coverages.

Rock 'n' roll did not remain the sole domain of the teen-agers—it captured a large adult following, adults who fervently, and in a sense uninvitedly, imitated the youngsters, forming an adult fan club that was unwanted and embarrassing to the teen-agers. More than 40 percent of the "teen beat" records sold in the United States at one time were bought by persons over 20 years old.[9] As one teen-ager complained: "Nothing is sacred anymore. I mean we no sooner develop a new dance or something and our parents are doing it."[10] Another teen-ager, in an irate letter to the editor of *Teen* Magazine, raged: "The whole world is copying us. . . . We have to babysit while our parents go discothequing. Come on, teens, let's strike back."[11]

Obviously, this type of music was inseparable from dancing. The extremely simple beat seemed monotonous to musicologist and too loud for the sensitive, but had a kinetic effect on dancers that proved compelling to teen-agers and adults alike. As a result, the so-called discotheques, places of sustained rock 'n' roll rhythm and performing go-go girls, multiplied throughout the nation.

The dancing itself resembled a combination of uninhibited pantomime and private choreography, enabling the dancer to be imaginative

---

[8] "The Sound Of The Sixties," *Time* (May 21, 1965), p. 85.
[9] *Ibid.*
[10] "The Sound Of The Sixties," *op. cit.*, p. 84.
[11] *Teen,* Vol. 10 (August, 1966), p. 16.

and creative in steps, gestures, motions, and facial expression. A partner was not really necessary since no bodily coordination between partners, as in the waltz, tango, fox trot, or other conventional dances, was needed. Not even the occasional hand-holding to guide and synchronize each other's movements, as in the jitterbug, was called for. In essence, the partners danced by and for themselves, most of the time paying little attention to each other.

> "It's a kind of fertility rite, designed to combat the sterility of modern life," says a young medical student, asked to account for his generation's dancing style. But this is fertility magic without bodily contact. Cheek-to-cheek dancing would seem out of place, too simple, too sweet, too naive. These people are looking for something else. Asked what that something else is, a student nurse, dancing at one of the lesser spots, says, "It's sort of sexy in a clean way. All those bodies grinding, but never touching." Another girl contributes "I like it when the boys wear real tight pants, and they shake." A third comes out with: "You don't even need a partner. The man doesn't lead, and the girl doesn't have to follow. She can do it without the man. It's equality!"
>
> There have been far-out dances before (remember the lindy hop, the Charleston?), but they did not have the private look of today's exercises.[12]

This style apparently is attractive to most teen-agers because their initial shyness about dancing—sweaty hands, missing a beat, stepping on the partner's toes, etc.—vanishes. In addition, the music customarily is so loud that conversations are an impossibility, thereby removing the often embarrassing situation of not knowing what to say to each other.

Given these factors, inhibitions all but disappear, and highly sensual implications can be observed, the anatomical gyrations of the dancers sometimes frankly suggesting copulatory motions. The judgments and opinions concerning the sexual expressions of some rock 'n' roll dancing have varied widely. Some parents were appalled and condemned all frugging completely; others thought that some of the dances were acceptable. Analytical observers concluded that this type of dancing was "safe sex" for the teen-agers. Harvard psychiatrist Philip Solomon was reported to observe: "These dances are outlets for restlessness, for unexpressed and sublimated sex desires. This is quite healthy."[13] Dr. Lucille H. Blum, a supervisor at the Center for Mental Health in New York, conducted a study via questionnaire and personal interviews that included a sample of teen-agers (median age 18) found dancing at disco-

---

[12] Samuel Grafton, "The Twisted Age," *Look* (Dec. 15, 1964), pp. 37–38.
[13] "The Sound of the Sixties," *op. cit.* p. 88.

theques.[14] The respondents of both sexes indicated that *release* and *abandon* were the major sensations appealing to them in rock 'n' roll dances. Social scientists explained the teen-agers' sensations as gratification obtained through the temporary retreat from environmental tensions and frustrations imposed on them by adults. Dr. Blum reported the statements of some of the dancers:

> The more we frug, the more South Vietnam, lung cancer and getting into your father's college fade into the distance.
>
> I think the society that was partly created for us, but is mainly our fault, is so tense that it is necessary for us to senselessly quiver in a steaming gym on Friday nights.
>
> There is nothing I enjoy more than working up a sweat dancing. It exhausts any built-up strength due to anger or anxiety.[15]

The investigator also found that teen-agers saw adults at a discotheque as trespassers and intruders.

It seems, then, that rock 'n' roll music met a number of the teen-agers' needs—their desire to express themselves bodily without limiting coordination to another moving body, without the need to converse, and without the fear of getting out of step. Moreover, erotic expressions passed with impunity and were rendered relatively inoffensive because of rock 'n' roll dancers' abstention from physical contact.

Explained on the basis of these various functions of rock 'n' roll for modern American teen-agers, its longevity is not surprising.

Hair Styles. The fad that recently netted the teen-agers the most intense adult criticism and enforced opposition was not their clothing, dancing, or music—but the way they groomed their hair. A survey, asking schoolteachers which fad they considered the most disturbing fad among their pupils, disclosed that 88 per cent singled out "long hair for boys."[16] A sizable proportion, 46 per cent, of the pupils themselves found long-haired boys "disturbing," indicating that a particular fad need not be shared or approved by all teen-agers.[17]

It is not ascertainable how and why the fad of long hair for boys developed. Nevertheless, coincidentally or causatively, the problem

---

[14] Lucille H. Blum, "The Discotheque and the Phenomenon of Alone-Togetherness: A Study of the Young Person's Response to the Frug and Comparable Current Dances," mimeographed research report (New York, 1967; awaiting publication in the journal *Adolescence*).

[15] Blum, *op. cit.*, p. 13.

[16] Carolyn L. Schlarbaum, *An Inquiry Into The Opinions Of High School Students And Teachers Concerning Fads*, unpublished research report (Arizona State University, May, 1966).

[17] *Ibid.*

started around the same time, 1964, when the Beatles singing group exhibited their trademark—long hairdos—in the United States. Imitation and proliferation of a number of versions of the hair style became a source of great irritation to American educators. Over the last few years, uncounted reports from all over the United States illustrate the clash of the subcultural practice with the standards of the adult society.

It must be mentioned that the issue of long hair refer almost exclusively to boys. Girls, it seems, enjoy almost unlimited license to fashion their hair in any way they wish, whether short or long, bleached or colored, ribboned or loose. To be sure, feminine hairdos go through fashions too; but since, by societal consensus, *all* of their styles pass as customary and acceptable, deviant or "odd" fads are rarely ascribed to them. The difference between boy and girl hair styles is that the former can be described as fad and the latter as fashion. Fashion, by definition, is a style approved by the larger society and therefore should not be equated with fad.

Here are some illustrations of the nationwide hair style issue, sampling the 1965 to 1966 period. At the Tremper High School in Kenosha, Wisconsin, 175 boys were refused admision because of their long hair. The son of a Rice University professor was suspended from Lamar High School in Houston just five days after the doors opened because he refused to get a "proper" haircut. An explicit stand was displayed by the Dean of Cardinal Hayes High School in the Bronx, he met students returning for the fall semester with a pair of scissors and cut off the locks of two boys. The superintendent of Phoenix Union High School in Phoenix, Arizona, advised a number of youths with long hair not to register for the new semester until they had visited their barber. The headmaster of Atlanta's Lovett School announced that "the Beatle haircut violates what we regard as canons of decency."[18] Federal Judge Richard Duncan of Kansas City ordered a young delinquent to get a haircut because "I refuse to sentence anyone I can't see."[19] It appeared that many teachers harbored similar sentiments and tried to reserve for themselves the right not to teach anyone they could not see.

In some cases the teachers' firm stand on the issue led to exceptional results: a student at Scottsdale High School in Scottsdale, Arizona, was suspended when he tried to run for student government with a hairdo à la Beatle. If the administration's decision was maintained, he planned to finish high school by correspondence courses. The parents of a Union-

---

[18] This sampling was reported by Hal Cooper in an AP report (New York, Dec. 3, 1965).

[19] "The Unkindest Cut For Student Moptops," *Life* (Aug. 24, 1965), p. 4.

ville High School student in Unionville, Pennsylvania, took their son's dismissal to court, arguing in part that as a guitar player in a professional combo group he needed to wear his hair long. The superintendent thereupon adjusted his ruling and let the boy attend high school—but only by phone. The boy subsequently stayed home and attended class by two-way telephone hookup, paid for by the school board.[20] The most extreme outcome of a dispute over hair style occurred in Lancing, England, when a 15-year-old fan of the Rolling Stones, a famous English pop-song group, threw himself to his death under a train after he had been forced to have his long hair cut.[21]

In their own defense, teen-agers point out that long hair has been a symbol of virility ever since Biblical days and confess that they often grow luxuriant tops because their girl friends admire them. Finally, they complain that a more liberal policy on hair styling is necessary to provide them with an opportunity to create more individualistic appearances to compete with girls, who traditionally are allowed more styling alternatives concerning not only hair but also dress, colors, shoes, hats, scarfs, make-up, jewlery, etc. Some frankly rebelling youngsters added to this list that they wear long hair simply because they *want to* and because they want to look *different* from others, especially from adults.

Limited and Minor Fads. The preceding examples of major teen fads by no means add up to a complete list of the fad patterns exhibited by teen-agers during recent years. A number of minor fads were either inconspicuous and did not attract attention, were not appreciably deviant from adult practices and therefore relatively acceptable to the public, or were of merely regional interest. Examples of such minor fads include pierced ears, German war and Nazi medals, and Super Ball.

The wearing of earrings requiring pierced lobes was of sporadic local importance, making its debut in 1965–66. Many parents opposed the fad, arguing that a young teen-age girl should not wear any kind of earrings that permanently scar the ear. However, many parents consented to let the daughter visit a doctor for piercing rather than tempt her to have it done clandestinely by peers and thus risk danger of infection.

A fad that touched many adults as distasteful was the wearing of military and political medals from the German Nazi era. The craze originated in California, where motorcycle gangs exhibited Nazi swastikas and the German Iron Cross. The habit developed into a nationwide fad, and by 1966 it could be found in many cities of the U.S. This spread

---

[20] "Public Schools," *Time* (May 27, 1966), p. 56.

[21] AP Report (Lancing, England, Jan. 19, 1966).

was commercially promoted and exploited by a few manufacturers, one of which in 1966 turned out 24,000 crosses a day.[22]

Super Ball looked like an ordinary handball but had an extremely high bounce quality, returning approximately 90 percent of the height from which it was dropped. This toy ball, more than 6 million of which were manufactured in California by the end of 1965, became the vogue not only with teen-agers but also with adults.[23]

The above examples are sufficient to illustrate the category of limited and minor fads. Obviously, many more examples could be added.

Conclusions. A survey asking teen-agers why they engage in certain fad behavior found the following order of stated reasons: (1) "Everyone else does it." (2) To get attention. (3) For "fun." (4) To be "stylish." (5) To be different from adults. (6) To signify group membership.[24]

What is the meaning of these various reasons supplied by the teen-agers themselves? A social-psychological interpretation would bear in mind the *functions* of fad behavior, i.e., the effects of adherence to fad styles on the individual teen-ager: (1) *An implementation of belonging.* By appearing "like everyone else," by conforming to overt in-group styles, an appearance of uniformity is achieved that forms a tangible medium through which belonging can be reinforced. As a result, the follower of a fad *feels* that he belongs. (2) *A means of self-expression.* To a limited degree, fads afford a means of experimentation in unique-ness. This experimentation must be understood as a collective phenom-enon, i.e., as an effort of teen-agers *in general* to express a style that is uniquely theirs. Their fads are visible and tangible means of showing that they want to be different from adults. The continual fluctuation of teen-age fads can be understood in this light. When adults accept and adopt a teen-age fad, they automatically defeat its function for the teen-agers and most likely induce them to abandon it in favor of a different style. In a sense, teen-agers are kept running from adult imitations. (3) *Rebellion with impunity.* Because of the usually nondelinquent nature of fads and the fact that they are collectively shared, conveying a sense of protection to the individual teen-ager, fads allow for rebellion against the adult world without risk of serious punishment. (4) *A means of communication and identification.* Many fads represent visible (cloth-ing, hairdo) or audible (lingo, music) means of easy identification,

---

[22] Personal communication with Ronnie Jewelry Inc., Providence, R.I. (Surfer crosses were still produced and sold in 1967, although in smaller quantities than in previous years.)

[23] "Fads," *Time* (Oct. 22, 1965), pp. 69–70.

[24] Schlarbaum, *op. cit.*

through which a teen-ager can communicate his membership to certain groups. In a sense, fads are symbolic means of clarifying status for oneself and for others.

Hero Worship

Hero worship is one of man's timeless indulgences. It appears to be such a deep-seated need that if no real heroes are available, supernatural ones tend to be invented. This need is observable in both adults and teen-agers. Depending upon the cultural milieu and ethos, the hero may be a military figure, a political personality, an outstanding athlete, or a popular entertainer. Commensurate with the American ethos that generally stresses civic values more than military values, teen-agers in the United States tend to exhibit special admiration for entertainers, such as singers, actors, and musicians. The worship of these popular heroes proceeds in overt demonstrations. At concerts, cheering crowds manifest their loyalty; in teen-agers' bedrooms, pictures on the wall silently testify admiration; in record stores, sales reveal listeners' adoration; and dress and hairdo styles often imitate those of popular heroes.

The apparent need for teen-age heroes appears to be a compound product of several specific circumstances, some of which are presented in the form of hypotheses:

(1) *Fetishism.* Often, the followers or "worshipers" are visibly less impressed by *what* their idols are saying or singing than by their physical presence and appearance. Young teen-agers are inclined to physically express exuberance and sensual desires and are easily led to scream, touch, and move rhythmically in the presence of their heroes. These expressions of hero worship have frequently been interpreted as sublimation of sexual tension whereby some material aspect of the popular hero, such as his clothing or hair, becomes a fetish. In other words, a fetish is a tangible substitute for the coveted person which can provide a certain degree of erotic gratification. A mild, usually socially acceptable, and widespread fetishistic practice of teen-agers (and adults) is the collecting and/or pinning-up of pictures of their heroes. Sometimes, however, the fetishistic inclination takes more direct forms. A few years ago when Frankie Avalon, a rock 'n' roll ballad singer, performed in New Haven, teen-age girls pulled the shoes off his feet. In Buffalo, a crowd of excited teen-agers trampled him and sprained his back in an effort to touch him and tear off pieces from his clothes.[25]

---

[25] Thomas B. Morgan, "Teen-Age Heroes: Mirror of a Muddled Youth," *Esquire* (March, 1960), pp. 65–73.

On the occasion of their 1966 return to America, the English singing group, the Beatles, were welcomed by frantic sign-carrying ("I love the Beatles") fans and were beleaguered by hundreds of shrieking teen-age girls at their hotels. A teen-ager who asserted that she had a lock from the head of one of the Beatles was literally besieged by other teen-age girls who wanted to touch and kiss it. At numerous performances of the Beatles, their music and lyrics were completely drowned out by the roaring and shrieking teen-age audience, who quite demonstrably were more interested in seeing than in hearing their idols. A conspicuous instance of fetishism occurred in New York where the hotel at which the Beatles stayed decided to cut up the bed sheets on which the English guests had slept into one-inch squares for sale at one dollar apiece. A similar fate awaited the bed sheets at the Astor Tower Hotel in Chicago, which were to be auctioned off to desirous fans.[26]

(2) *Crowd Behavior.* It has been observed that a number of physical expressions of "worshiping," such as screaming, running, jumping, tearing one's own hair, and even "fainting," have a mutually reinforcing effect in a crowd situation. The reinforcement is due to the rewards derived from, first, the prestige assigned to such peer-approved and peer-encouraged actions and, second, the "safe" release of pent-up emotions and tensions, often unabashedly sexual in nature. When idol Frankie Avalon stepped onto the stage at Steel Pier Music Hall in Atlantic City, about 200 teen-age girls in the first six rows and in the side balconies shrieked in the typically violent and mechanical manner usually accompanying such occasions. It was interesting to note that a number of the vociferous teen-agers were not looking at their hero, but at each other, apparently to make sure that they were seen screaming—that is, *belonging.*[27] The report mentioned that the back rows did not scream, but merely applauded conventionally. The inferential explanation of this differential behavior was that the back rows were outside of the bright glow of the footlights and thus outside of the field of observation. "Perhaps, if the management had turned up the house lights, they might have achieved a more perfect pandemonium of a screaming house."[28] Another crowd-inspired behavior style is fainting—or pretending to. During a Milwaukee presentation by Avalon, 21 girls ostentatiously fainted. At another performance on TV, when he sang "Boy without a Girl" the camera showed a number of sobbing teen-agers. *From then on,* this behavior became routine and was imitated wherever he appeared and sang that particular song.[29]

---

[26] UPI Report (Chicago, Aug. 13, 1966).
[27] Morgan, *op. cit.,* p. 65.
[28] *Ibid.*
[29] *Ibid.*

(3) *Identification.* A hero is a ready model to be identified with and imitated. He provides the "worshipers" with an image to which they can aspire. It can be noted that the first-class teen-age hero is a recording star and not a politician, businessman, or intellectual. Compared with the entertainer, even the top athlete is only moderately admired. It has been suggested that the reasons for this preference are the similarity in age and ability of many teen-age entertainers to their followers and the dissimilarity of other outstanding personalities to most crowd-oriented teen-agers. It seems easier for teen-agers to identify with some one who is crowd-oriented like themselves, not outstanding in the truest sense of the word, mediocre, "humble", and nonserious. It must be kept in mind that teen-agers, due to the adolescent experience, have this need for collective protection within which they feel safe from and invisible to adults. They are frightened of exposing themselves individually to evaluation and criticism, and they project this negative feeling onto personalities who are outstanding. Their aversion is aimed at the politician for his *principles,* the businessman for his *enterprise and success,* and the intellectual for devotion to the *hard truths*—all representing values that tend to separate the individual from the crowd, expose him, make him outstanding, possibly unpopular, and therefore insecure. Teen-agers try to escape such exposure due to individuality and instead seek the warmth and the security of the crowd. They prefer virtues of conformity, mediocrity, and sincerity. Through their heroes, songs, and dances they can express themselves without leaving the secure environment of their peer group.

According to the conventional standards of the fine arts, many of the popular writers, singers, and actors can neither write, sing, nor act— but nevertheless show splendid success in their show-business careers. A few years ago the 16-year-old teen-age hero Fabian sang "I'm a Man" and sold 300,000 records. His fans knew that the efforts of several voice teachers had failed completely and that, by traditional standards, Fabian had no singing voice. But this fact was an asset and not a liability. It produced for the teen-age audience an image of "humbleness" and sincerity and provided them with an opportunity to identify because, as Thomas B. Morgan said, "nobody in the audience could sing either. . . . Mediocrity fell in love with its own image."[30] Similarly the English Beatles were admired for their simplicity and sincerity. When asked whether they liked being idolized, they answered their teen-age fans that "we just like the money." Another important element that made the Beatles loved and admired heroes, was the fact that they conveyed a nonserious image. By doing so, they enabled their fans to relax and meet

---

[30] Morgan, *op. cit.,* p. 70.

them on a par. The Beatles admitted publicly that they did not think much of their own music, but that they had "fun" entertaining and getting paid for it.

Another condition that induces identification with many of the teen-age heroes is based upon the subtle rivalry that girls introduce between the idols and their boy friends. Directly or indirectly, boy friends are frequently urged to look and act like the teen-age heroes, and they are rewarded, if they are successful in a certain degree of imitation, with some of the type of admiration that is ordinarily reserved for the popular idols.

(4) *Extending Values.* Heroes represent "significant others" who possess a great potential influence on teen-agers' thinking and value-orientation. However, of all the functions American teen-age heroes perform, extending values is probably the least effective. The need of young teen-agers to express and release emotional dispositions and the use of the hero as a catalyst for that purpose by far supersede the need for more rational formulations and value-orientations during the stressful period of early adolescence.

Nevertheless, one could classify some of the "folk-rock" heroes of the mid-1960's as spokesmen for certain values of adolescents—probably of the *older* and more intellectual adolescents. One of the best known was Bob Dylan, a young poet-songwriter who achieved popularity with such songs as "Tambourine Man," "Substerranean Homesick Blues," and "Like a Rolling Stone." His songs were sharp criticisms of certain social conditions, focusing on civil rights, the threat of nuclear war, and the war in Vietnam. Although his singing made him a millionaire, he maintained an image that teen-agers found acceptable and imitable. To his fans, the scruffy hair, wrinkled shirt, and faded jeans meant that he was one of them.

Another singing hero was Barry McGuire, intensely trying to advance his cause by the song "Eve of Destruction." The topic again was social criticism, warning against the bomb and the United States' involvement in the war in Vietnam. Other "folk-rock" personalities, like the Turtles and the Byrds, followed the lead of Dylan and McGuire and expounded social commentary. However, the "folk-rock" following was not as broad as that of rock 'n' roll performers in general. It included more of the older teen-agers, drawing especially from college students.

(5) *Romanticism.* Romanticism by definition refers to emotions and attitudes that usually are insufficiently based on empirical facts. The appeal of romantic emotions lies in the heroic, remote, mysterious, and idealized. The emotional disposition can be related to a number of areas in life, but is most frequently observed in connection with attitudes toward love relationships. Teen-agers are particularly prone to adhere to

romantic perceptions of the male-female relationship, because they lack the experience of the older generation and are reluctant to accept adult standards, which are normally more realistic. As a result, teen-age heroes can easily capitalize on the romance hunger of their followers, reinforce unrealistic perceptions, and become tangible foci of romantic identifications. A pair of such idols were Sonny and Cher, a young married couple, who sang about love and "belongingness" in the mid-1960's. Their song, "I love Cher and Cher loves me and that is our image" became the shibboleth for teen-age fans and hiked Sonny and Cher's records to best-selling heights, apparently because it reinforced the belief that love conquers everything and makes all efforts unnecessary. Many teen-age heroes depict love as just that kind of magic and thereby touch on a profound need of teen-agers—their need for love, sexual expression, and, in the process, little or no demands on effort and maturity. It is no surprise, therefore, that romantic heroes of "folk-rock," who leave the serious problems of civil rights, the bomb, and war to other singers, enjoy loyal followers who imitate their styles of clothes and hairdos to minute detail—and, most signicantly, internalize their romantic assumptions as presumably valid guidelines for life.

Attitudes and Values

The large majority of the numerous surveys and researches about the values of American youth have a few disturbing shortcomings in common: they lack a precise definition of values, not specifying whether they mean verbal statements concerning important attitudes or behavioral commitments in form of recurrent actions. The former are self-expressions of young people ascertained through polls, questionnaires, and interviews. The Gallup Poll, the University of Michigan Survey Research Center, and the Purdue Opinion Panel are prototypes of the means of collecting such information. Information concerning behavioral commitments is drawn from reliable records and documents, official statistics, and direct observations. Examples would be records listing the teen-agers serving Red Cross, VISTA (Volunteers in Service to America), the Peace Corps, or other organizations with altruistic motives, obviously suggesting a definite value commitment on the part of the participant. Both types of behavior, the verbal and the actional, can be understood as reflecting values, but for the sake of clear cataloging, the former are classified as attitudes and the latter as value commitments.

A problem arises when trying to generalize about the attitudes of American youth. There is really no *one* American youth. So the questions arise: Which American youth? Rural or urban? From which socio-economic stratum? Of what age categories? High school pupils, college students, or drop-outs? Such and other subdivisions complicate any attempt to generalize about what is loosely called American youth. There is no simple solution. At this time it appears that the best procedure is to give some examples from surveys and researchers, pointing out the most salient attitudes that are characteristic of certain types of teen-age respondents.

An additional effort to bring meaningful order into the diversity is the division of attitudes into (1) in-group attitudes and values that spell out the rules and expectations of the interpersonal relations *within* the peer group; and (2) basic attitudes *toward* the out-group, specifically the adult society. The following discussion is thus ordered in three main categories: In-group values, basic attitudes toward the adult society, and value commitments.

(1) *In-group values.* Sociologists have found that any group of individuals who interact over a period of time sooner or later agree on a blueprint for behavior that helps to clarify and expedite recurrent problem-solving, thus developing orderly and predictable behavior patterns. The conscious or unconscious formulation of values is part of this process. Values are emotional commitments to relevant group standards by which experiences and objects are judged and choices are made.

Teen-age groups are no exception to this principle. Although their values are not *entirely* different from those of the adult community, teen-agers have come to observe certain norms and values with a unique accent. It is obviously impossible to present a complete catalog of teen-age values and norms. Therefore, the discussion deals with only a few of the major values, such as those pertaining to friendship and popularity.

Surveys and researchers have repeatedly noted that "popularity" is one of the most emphasized values among today's teen-agers. The dynamics of popularity is a complex matter rarely fully explained or explored. It involves such features as admiration and acceptance by peers, and it can probably be safely assumed that popularity is correlated with the powerful cathexes of prestige and a feeling of belonging. It is therefore no surprise to notice the heavily popularity-oriented responses to a survey questioning the youngsters' views on popularity. A study of high-school students in Hilliard, a suburb of Columbus, Ohio, revealed the immense importance of popularity for the teen-agers. Asked how important it is for a teen-ager to be liked and accepted by other teen-agers, 67% said "of very great importance," 27% "of great importance," 6% "of some importance," and none stated a negative opinion.[31] James S. Coleman in his study *The Adolescent Society* likewise found that there exists a strong desire to be popular. Interestingly enough, the survey revealed that this desire is more intense among girls than boys.[32] Survey data of the Purdue Opinion Poll supported this finding and showed that 60% of the girls answered affirmatively to "want people to like me more," while only 47% of the boys answered in the affirmative. Of the girls, 47% affirmed "wish I were more popular," while only 36% of the boys did.[33] Still another study corroborated this sex-differentiated emphasis and submitted that girls with middle-class background showed a persistent preoccupation with popularity and social success.[34] The most pronounced emphasis on popularity was found among girls of the broad middle class whose fathers occupied managerial, business, and professional positions commonly referred to as upper middle class. These girls daydreamed of popularity and often cited it as a source of worry. Their statements indicated that if they were to change themselves they would like to have more social skill, be more popular, and be accepted by peers. This preoccupation was not exclusively a result of the standards of the high school crowds, but was reinforced by the middle-class parents. On the other hand, lower-class girls and boys regardless of specific family circumstances were markedly less concerned about popularity.

Observation of such remarkable emphasis on popularity among American teen-agers leads the social scientist to ask what the criteria are for being popular. A sample of high school boys and girls at Hilliard revealed that "being courteous, polite, respectful, and friendly to your friends" was considered by far the most important criterion for popularity. This response was followed by "being helpful" and by "being trustworthy and dependable" with almost equal emphasis on both. It was interesting to note that by "being trustworthy and dependable" many of the respondents, especially girls, thought of the quality of being able to "keep a secret" and of "not to talk behind one's back."[35] (See Table 9–1.)

To find out exactly what teen-agers believe makes for unpopular status among themselves, the researcher asked them to give a brief description of what they considered to be an "oddball" or a "square."

[31] Hans Sebald, *The Crisis of Adolescent Discontinuity and the Formation of an Adolescent Subculture in the American Middle Class,* mimeographed research report (Ohio State University, 1960).

[32] Coleman, *op. cit.,* p. 30.

[33] H. H. Remmers and D. H. Radler, *The American Teenager* (New York, The Bobbs-Merrill Co., 1957), p. 85.

[34] Elizabeth Douvan and Joseph Adelson, *The Adolescent Experience,* (New York, John Wiley & Sons, 1966), p. 406.

[35] Sebald, *op. cit.,* p. 31.

TABLE 9–1. Answers and Per Cent Distribution to the Question: What is expected of a teen-ager by his friends in order to be popular with them?

Answers	Per Cent
1. Being courteous, polite, respectful, and friendly to your friends	50
2. Being helpful	28
3. Being trustworthy (especially, "don't talk behind their back") and dependable	27
4. Being an active participant in some activity	20
5. He has to be like them (being different means rejection)	17
6. Doing things to make them like you	14
7. Associate with and be friendly with *all* people	12
8. High morals (especially in regard to opposite sex)	12
9. Talk to them about their problems	12
10. Good and pleasing personality	10
11. Smile at them and be cheerful	8
12. Not being snobbish or "stuck up"	8
13. Good and clean dresser	8
14. Interest in his friends' affairs	7
15. Good looking	2
16. Good grades	2

Source: Hans Sebald, *The Crisis of Adolescent Discontinuity and the Formation of an Adolescent Subculture in the American Middle Class*, mimeographed research report (The Ohio State University, 1960), p. 31.

The factor of unpopularity that was mentioned most frequently among the various descriptions can be summed up as "not joining in on social activities." The second most frequently stated criterion for unpopularity was closely related to the first and was seen in a teen-ager's tendency or habit "not to associate himself with others" and "to keep to himself." The third most frequently mentioned ground for unpopularity referred to appearance and specified that wearing of "wrong clothes" or "being sloppily dressed" makes for an "oddball" or "square."[36] (See Table 9–2.)

Another study of high school students approached the question of popularity by asking what teen-agers consider to be the personal attributes that make a teen-ager qualify for the "leading crowd."[37] James S. Coleman found that in all high schools investigated, girls emphasized "good personality" far more than boys, roughly 40 per cent vs. 20 per cent, though for both groups this quality ranked first. Being good-looking, having good clothes, and having a good reputation ranked next in decreasing order for the girls. For boys, the next criteria, after "good

[36] Sebald, *op cit.*, p. 30.
[37] Coleman, *op. cit.*, pp. 40–42.

TABLE 9–2. Answers and Per Cent Distribution to the Question: What sort
of teen-ager might be considered an "oddball" or a "square?"

Answers	Per Cent
1. Not joining in on social activities	40
2. Not associating himself with others; keeping to himself	25
3. Wearing "unaccepted" clothes (either not keeping up with the fashion or "sloppy")	22
4. Not doing what everybody else is doing	20
5. Getting very good grades and studying hard	18
6. Being boastful	15
7. Being different or thinking differently from the rest	12
8. Acting "silly" most of the time	10
9. One who doesn't get along with others	8
10. Being too modest, shy, or quiet	7
11. Starting troubles	7
12. Use of vulgar language	7
13. One who doesn't have friends	7
14. Smoking or drinking	5

Source: Hans Sebald, *The Crisis of Adolescent Discontinuity and the Formation
of an Adolescent Subculture in the American Middle Class,* mimeographed research
report (The Ohio State University, 1960), p. 30.

personality," consisted of having a good reputation, being athletic, and
being good-looking. In addition, having a car was considered very important. The important difference between the sexes in acceptability into
the leading crowd seemed to be for boys athletic proficiency and possession of a car. It was also found that family background mattered less for
boys and that it was easier for a boy from the "wrong side of the tracks"
to work his way into the leading crowd. It appears, then, that a boy can
achieve the leading crowd, while a girl is more dependent upon what she
is in terms of reputation, family background, neighborhood, etc. This
contrast might be described as based on achieved and ascribed statuses,
respectively.

Values sought in a friend lead to another important area of teen-age
standards. It was found that boys and girls had slightly different expectations, with the former seeking some one who is first "amiable and nice"
and secondly "supporting in trouble," and with the latter seeking a friend
who first of all is "not a gossip" and secondly is "amiable and nice" and
thirdly is "supporting in trouble."[38] Another study discovered that besides desirable personality traits another criterion was considered important in a friend. "Some boys and girls choose or are chosen 'friends'

[38] Douvan and Adelson, *op. cit.,* p. 406.

almost entirely on the basis of status and prestige."[39] However, a modified view is more common, combining the personality prerequisites and
prestige considerations when choosing a friend.

The prestige of a friend, however, can cause complications—especially among girls. There is frequent rivalry among girls for popularity
with boys. A girl-girl friendship has to recognize the problem of differential popularity—i.e., popularity sought among boys and popularity
sought among girls—and make protective adjustments. This process has
disclosed an interesting value-orientation of girls in general. In order to
avoid hostility and excessive envy from her female peer group, the girl
who is popular, or more popular, must learn to accept her good fortune
graciously and modestly. In fact, the adolescent girl ordinarily is far
more concerned about her acceptance by other girls and often uses
her popularity with the boys for its effect on her appraisal by her own
sex peer group.

It would be misleading to assume that teen-agers look exclusively
to their peer group for value orientation. There is no such uniform reference group. In some areas of decision-making they align their values
with peer standards and in other areas with the views and advice of
adults, particularly parents. Information from the Hilliard study (presented in Table 9–3) indicates that adolescents are selective in their
conformity and in certain matters are strongly guided by the opinions
of the peer group and in other matters by their parents or other adults.
In still other matters they listen to both sides, and in some sectors of
life they seem uncertain and lacking in a definite reference group. For
example, in matters of money, choosing courses at school, deciding on
future careers and plans to go to college, they tend to consult their
parents and not their peers. On the other hand, in matters of dating,
clothing, hobbies, attendance of social affairs, choice of magazines, and
joining of clubs, they follow the opinion and advice of their peers.[40]

It must be warned however, that the Hilliard study was conducted
in a more-than-average conservative and nondelinquent community and
that other surveys may possibly present a slightly different picture of
adolescent opinions. Nonetheless, the findings of the Purdue Opinion
Poll, based on a large and presumably representative sample of American
high school youth, also support these data.[41] It is of value to present
both the Hilliard findings and the Purdue Opinion Poll findings because
of an important methodological difference. The Purdue Opinion Polls

---

[39] Caroline M. Tryon, "The Adolescent Peer Culture," in *The 43rd Yearbook of
the National Society for the Study of Education,* Part I, Adolescence (Chicago, The
University of Chicago Press, 1944), p. 230.

[40] Sebald, *op. cit.,* p. 32.

[41] Remmers and Radler, *op. cit.*

TABLE 9–3.   Response Distribution to the Question: If you had to decide between your friends' and your parents' opinion and feeling in the following situations, whose opinion would you consider more important?

Items	Response Distribution in Per Cent*				
	DF	PF	U	PP	DP
1. On what you spend your money	0	6	32	30	32
2. Whom you date	6	27	35	18	13
3. The clubs you join	23	32	22	17	6
4. Advice on your personal problems and troubles	20	14	15	13	38
5. How you dress	12	25	28	25	10
6. Which courses you take in school	1	8	22	27	42
7. Which hobbies you take up	1	16	69	8	6
8. In choosing your future occupation	0	3	33	32	32
9. Which social events you attend	12	33	25	20	10
10. Whether you go to college or not	3	1	33	20	43
11. What books other than those requested by school you read	6	9	65	10	10
12. What magazines you buy	9	23	47	15	6
13. How often you date	10	6	26	28	30
14. Whether you participate in drinking parties	11	0	25	6	58
15. In choosing your future husband or wife	5	3	53	24	15
16. Whether you go steady or not	4	15	40	23	18
17. How intimate you are on a date	5	17	55	13	10
18. To whom you go for information about sex	22	12	18	10	38

* The five possible answers were: DF—Definitely Friends; PF—Probably Friends; U—Undecided; PP—Probably Parents; DP—Definitely Parents.

Source: Hans Sebald, *The Crisis of Adolescent Discontinuity and the Formation of an Adolescent Subculture in the American Middle Class,* mimeographed research report (The Ohio State University, 1960), p. 32.

work with forced-answer questions that sometimes may distort the findings and lead to misinterpretations. The Hilliard study, on the other hand, operated with open-ended questions that allowed the respondent to express what and how he felt, thus presumably yielding more valid information.

Since the two methods produced strikingly similar data, they, in a sense, tested each other's reliability and validity. The nationwide survey produced data that roughly corresponded to the Hilliard findings. Remmers and co-workers found that the typical teen-ager is responsive to the standards of his peers in matters concerning what to wear to a party, what clubs to join, how to act when out with the gang and, above all, how to dress and groom. On the other hand, he tends to consult adults when facing problems and decision-making in areas of political orientation and spending money.[42]

The Purdue Surveys encouraged Remmers and co-workers to make an interesting interpretation: from a great number of the teen-agers' responses a pattern emerged that was classifiable as the "other-directed" syndrome. The pollsters supported their assumptions with examples like the following: 51% of the respondents affirmed that they "try very hard to do anything that will please friends," and 38% thought that "there is nothing worse than being considered an oddball by other people."[43] As the three most common problems, teen-agers mentioned the need to be more liked by people, the need to be more popular, and the need to be sure of themselves. 57% believed in the superiority of religious beliefs over rational approaches to life's problems, and 76% added that they never like to argue about religion.[44] There was a frank disdain for intellectual brilliance; 60% chose to be popular rather than brilliant.[45] According to the researchers, these data illustrate the teen-agers' great desire for popularity and their overriding conformist attitudes.

(2) *Attitudes toward adults.* In spite of sporadic agreement with and dependence on adults, the most typical teen-age attitudes toward them seem to be caution and mistrust. The origin of these negative attitudes is in the adolescent experience that is typical of most American teen-agers. Particularly in the middle class, most children grow up relatively protected until their teens when the exposure to a larger sector of adult life may, in conjunction with other and earlier-mentioned adolescent confusions, bring about serious disturbances and the need to reconsider previous attitudes and beliefs. The teen-ager may find his romantic ideal of marriage endangered by the discovery of marital discord, divorce, and infidelity; he may suffer disappointment when his vision of government as a wise guardian of public order is replaced by the reality of political failures and sometimes questionable maneuvers; he may dislike the impersonality of the public order; and he may be frightened by the demands imposed on him by the social institutions of the adult world. Such revelations are obviously a profoundly disillusioning experience for most adolescents. The majority reaction can be classified as a passive rebellion and an effort to maintain a separate social realm, a subculture. The minority reaction can be seen in the reforma-

---

[42] Remmers and Radler, *op. cit.*
[43] Remmers and Radler, *op. cit.*, pp. 233–36.
[44] Remmers and Radler, *op. cit.*, pp. 170–75.
[45] Remmers and Radler, *op. cit.*, p. 26.

tionist zeal to remake society often characteristic of those young individuals who join formal or informal youth movements and are variously and vaguely called "subversive," "extremists," "leftists," "nonconformists," "hippies," etc. The present discussion is more concerned with the first category of reaction, the typical behavior of the "average" teen-ager who maintains subcultural bonds and passive and somewhat remote relations with the adult society.

The teen-agers' passivity and pessimism concerning the adult world are strikingly reflected in their belief that politicians, statesmen, and military leaders can do little or nothing to promote peace in the world. A nationwide study by the Purdue Opinion Panel found that, of those sampled, only 5%, 5%, and 9% believed in the usefulness of politicians, statesmen, and military leaders, respectively, for establishing and maintaining peace. On the other hand, teen-agers showed a significantly greater degree of trust in religious leaders, and 52% of the respondents thought that such religious could achieve the aforementioned goal.[46]

However, the positive attitude toward religious leaders and religion in general stands relatively isolated among the various teen-age views concerning adult institutions. Generally, discouraged views prevail—such as the belief of more than 50% of the teen-agers that "the large mass of us in the U.S. simply aren't capable of deciding for ourselves what's right and what's wrong."[47] Other attitudes about life in the United States fall in line with this pessimistic perception and form a consistent syndrome. For example, 83% of the teen-agers approve of wiretapping; 60% are for censorship of books, newspapers, and magazines; 26% hold that police should be allowed to search a person and a home without a warrant; about one-third of the respondents thought that free speech should be denied to a person if it seems convenient; 34% held that in some cases the circulation of petitions should be prohibited, and another 32% expressed uncertainty on this point.[48]

In an effort to determine the points of tension and discord between teen-agers and parents, pertinent open-ended questions were submitted to the sample from Hilliard High School. Among the major complaints listed by the respondents were the three issues of dating, spending, and dressing and grooming. It appears that teen-agers demand more freedom in determining their own styles in these sectors. The major complaints included also two nonspecific concerns: the so-called parental "old-fashionedness" and the withholding of responsibilities from teenagers.[49] (See Table 9–4.) It appears that difficulties of intergenerational com-

---

[46] Remmers and Radler, *op. cit.*, p. 174.
[47] Remmers and Radler, *op. cit.*, p. 16.
[48] Remmers and Radler, *op. cit.*, pp. 16–17, 52–53.
[49] Sebald, *op. cit.*, p. 30.

TABLE 9–4.   Answers and Per Cent Distribution to the Question: What do
you think are the major points of conflict and disagreement
between teen-agers and parents?

Answers	Per Cent
1. Teen-age dating (the question of whom, where, how, and how often)	40
2. Parents are old-fashioned and/or don't understand teen-agers	22
3. Parents treat teen-agers as being too young for responsibilities	17
4. Money question: how much and on what teen-agers spend money	15
5. Teen-age clothing and grooming	15
6. Teen-ager's use of car	12
7. Parents don't let their children grow up	12
8. Parents' dislike of teen-age talk, behavior, and interests	10
9. Teen-agers don't try to understand or don't listen to their parents	10
10. Question about school work, grades, and studying	10
11. Parents believe that teen-agers spend too much time outside the family	8
12. Lack of communication	7
13. Questions about work and duties in the home	7
14. Teen-agers' profuse use of the telephone	3
15. Teen-agers not getting enough attention from the parents	2

Source: Hans Sebald, *The Crisis of Adolescent Discontinuity and the Formation
of an Adolescent Subculture in the American Middle Class,* mimeographed research
report (The Ohio State University, 1960), p. 30.

munication are at the root of many of these complaints, which repeatedly
referred to situations in which "parents don't understand what we want,
how we're doing things, and why we are different."

When inquiry focuses on girls only, it seems that it is the question of
clothing that causes the greatest amount of disagreement and conflict
between parents and their daughters. As a study of nearly 2,000 high
school girls indicated, the most important issue for all age-brackets was
clothing, for 62% of the girls under 14 years of age, 48% of the 14- to
16-year-old girls, and 36% of the 17- to 18-year-old girls.[50]

Teen-age attitudes toward material aspects of the adult society show
more attraction than rejection. Generally speaking, the teen-ager wants
neither much more nor much less than his middle-class parents have had.
In 1961, a nationwide Gallup poll sampled over 3,000 boys and girls
between the ages of 14 and 22. The findings revealed that most teen-
agers prefer to settle for moderate success rather than risk failure; hope

---

[50] Douvan and Adelson, *op. cit.,* p. 381.

to marry as early as their living conditions allow; want two or three children; visualize a spouse who is affectionate but not too intellectual, curious, or ambitious; plan on a ranch-type house and a new car; look for a job with a large company; and intend to watch TV each evening.[51]

(3) *Value commitment.* The values and attitudes of American youth as listed and discussed in the preceding passages do not complete the picture of the teen-agers' ambitions and value orientations. In addition to the relatively isolated in-group standards, the slightly rebellious or distrustful attitudes toward the adult world, and the accommodating views concerning the comfort and affluence of the larger society, a sizable proportion of America's teen-age population manifests values that are not only cooperative with adult standards but definitely constructive and creative. These value commitments are obviously not indigenous to the ordinary teen subculture, but rather are expressions of motivation transcending the relatively narrow circle of peers. Justification for a brief discussion of nonsubcultural behavior is twofold: to render a more nearly complete picture of youth values in contemporary America and to provide a contrast to the usually noncreative subcultural behavior of teen-agers.

The American ethos, diffuse and ambiguous as it may seem most of the time, contains recognizable values of cooperation and altruistic service to others, often in contrast to values of competition and individual success-seeking. For reasons that would be worth careful research, many young Americans arrive at the decision to dedicate considerable time and hard work to implementing altruistic values and demonstrate their commitment on the local, national, and international level.

An expression of concern and actual effort for international betterment is the American Peace Corps. More than 100,000 Americans, the majority college-aged youth, had applied for this movement by 1965. Those who were accepted have been volunteering in many parts of the world to bring about more advanced, life-saving, and life-prolonging technological innovations, maintaining at the same time a respectful and sensitive view of the traditional customs and mores of the natives. The success of the Peace Corps, virtually from its inception in 1961, can be attributed to the sincerity and eagerness of American youth who (1) whole-heartedly seize on the opportunity to put into *practice* what theoretically have been American ideals and values of long standing; (2) feel enthusiastic about *being needed* and able to help perform vital tasks; and (3) eagerly accept the opportunity to *learn* more about others and themselves.

---

[51] George Gallup and Evan Hill, "Youth: The Cool Generation," *Saturday Evening Post,* (Dec., 1961), pp. 23–30, 63–80.

Personal expression of young Peace Corps volunteers illustrate these points. An American girl serving in Pakistan had this to say in a letter to a friend back in the States:

> . . . There are 44 lepers, men, women and children, all living together in one old Hindi temple. It is situated about ten miles out of town in a barren, God-forsaken strip of unproductive land. There are no houses for miles and the lepers seem to be a forgotten people. The nuns and missionaries go out regularly with food and bring a little change of scene into their lives. They have a few chickens and a plot of land to farm but it still seems too little and a rather sad and futile existence. It will be the one project we will all be working on together in our free time and everyone is quite enthusiastic about it. Even the fact that we will have to bicycle the ten miles hasn't seemed to dim spirits any. There is so much to do! . . .[52]

A young man teaching mathematics and sciences to underprivileged and ill-prepared boys on the secondary school level in West Africa, living like the natives under harsh and isolated conditions far removed from the affluence and comfort of Western countries, expressed his feelings this way:

> . . . I have always held (somewhat idealistically and academically, to be sure) that there is a certain "oneness" about humanity which no amount of epidermal coloring or cultural uniqueness could hide. The last five months in West Africa have done nothing to alter that view, except insofar as it has strengthened it.
>
> As the Peace Corps idea becomes more real and functional I begin to more and more realize what a rare and wonderful opportunity this whole thing becomes for everyone involved. The need for education here is desperate, and the appreciation we have been getting from people on all levels is no less than astounding. Some are a little hesitant to believe that we would give up the luxuries of America, the good jobs, the money and the conveniences for that which West Africa has to offer, but they are nonetheless glad to have us. . . .[53]

On the national level, definite manifestations of civic concern and political interest have been observable over the past decade. VISTA (Volunteers in Service to America) has attracted thousands of American youngsters. In counties throughout the South, student volunteers assisted in the registration of Negro voters under the direction of such organizations as the Congress for Racial Equality. In Boston, Los Angeles, and other key cities, youthful members of local and state campaigning committees engaged in intensive house-to-house canvassing for selected

---

[52] Joseph F. Kauffman, "Youth and the Peace Corps," in Erik H. Erikson (ed.), *Youth: Change and Challenge* (New York, Basic Books, Inc., 1963), p. 157.

[53] Kauffman, *op. cit.*, p. 158.

candidates. In Washington and a dozen other cities thousands of students picketed against the Cuba quarantine. In the same cities, counter-picket lines of about equal size, also composed of college students, demanded even stronger measures against Cuba. At Harvard, Chicago, Wisconsin, and many other campuses, students worked on the fall mailing of the numerous recently-established student political magazines. "Freedom marches" of all kinds and sizes involved a sizable proportion of student-aged Americans. Many of the traditional service programs of churches have been intensified through the value commitments of American youth in the Catholic Church, the various Protestant denominations, the LDS Church, the service branch of the American Unitarian-Universalist Association, the Quakers, the Brethren Service Commission of the Church of the Brethren, and many others.

These efforts are not isolated phenomena, but elements in a growing pattern of student behavior that has attracted much notice in recent years. College students and an increasing number of high school students seem to become progressively more sensitive to political and humanitarian values and are committing themselves to a large variety of actual work and service projects. Many of the volunteers belong to or work through such organizations as the Candy Stripers, 4-H clubs, CYO, various Boys' Clubs, Boy Scouts, TRI-HI-Y, student governments, different school clubs, NHA, NAACP, LEAP, etc.

It would be impossible to enumerate the multitude of youth service projects that are continuously conducted on the local level throughout the United States. American high school and college youth are lending more than a token hand in many vital and badly needed services. For example, one of the growing service enterprises is Operation Kindness, sponsored by United Community Services, which has 4,300 youth on duty in 106 agencies and institutions in Greater Boston. The unpaid helpers offer a variety of services, from running bingo games to skinning rabbits for medical research at the Peter Bent Brigham Hospital. Operation Kindness has had 2,000 youngsters at work in San Francisco and 3,800 in Philadelphia. Several projects were launched by the youngsters themselves; in the forests of northern Minnesota a group of collegians, representing campuses from Bryn Mawr to Minnesota, are living among the Chippewa Indians, who are 75 per cent unemployed and chronically in conflict with the law.[54] Another example are the so-called Candy Stripers, young hospital volunteers, who lend their help to overworked and understaffed nurses in an estimated one-third of the nation's hospitals. Since its inception in 1942, the idea of the Candy Stripers has captivated some 150,000 teen-age girls, many of them under the age of 16, in all parts

---

[54] "Season For Helping," *Time* (April 30, 1965), p. 49.

of the U.S.[55] To ameliorate the conditions in understaffed mental institutions, volunteer students from Harvard, Radcliffe College, and Brandeis University have been working with chronic psychotics at the Metropolitan State Hospital in Waltham, Massachusetts, on an organized basis for a number of years. Upward of 1,000 students have spent half a day every week during their school year in the institution and have succeeded in improving ward conditions and aiding patients.[56]

The reasons American youth participate in service in the adult world are a complex mixture of motivations. While the desire for service probably is a sincere and prevalent motive, healthy self-seeking, curiosity about travel and other peoples, and patriotic desire to improve the image of the United States are other strong motivational elements.

Every experience has a variety of consequences. Some of the results may coincide with the initial expectations that led to the decision to begin the particular project, i.e., the expectations are borne out and, for example, a certain amount of gratification has been derived from seeing other places and meeting new and interesting people. But there are also the initially unexpected consequences. In the case of the volunteer workers, these latent functions of their overt value commitment can be summed up in the following categories: (1) *Self-testing*. Service work as an integral part of the adult society provides a meaningful status of neophyte in the adult society. It is a means of overcoming self-doubt, uncertainty, and even disillusionment. For teen-agers this experience represents a moratorium before deciding on a career or entering graduate training or starting a job, and is the welcome respite that Erik H. Erikson called a psychosocial moratorium.[57] While serving in a volunteer agency, not only is the delay in vocational decision socially accepted, but there is simultaneously an opportunity to make a prestigious and useful contribution, to assess one's own resources, capabilities, and interests, and thereby apply a valid test to one's identity. (2) *Independence*. Meaningful service is a constructive expression of independence from parents and may be a sound resolution of the adolescent conflict, by working in a position that has the effect on teen-agers of being emancipated from and yet accepted by adults. Peace Corps returnees have revealed in interviews that they appreciated the amount of freedom permitted, the high degree of responsibility given, and the extent to which they could exercise their own initiative. It seems that volunteer service

---

[55] Frank A. Tinker, "The Papago Become Candy Stripers," *Today's Health*, Vol. 4 (October, 1962), p. 36.

[56] Report of the Joint Commission on Mental Illness and Health, *Action for Mental Health*, Science Edition (New York, 1961), pp. 88–89.

[57] Erik H. Erikson, "Ego Identity and Psychosocial Moratorium," in H. L. Witmer and R. Kosinsky (eds.), *New Perspectives for Researh in Juvenile Delinquency* (U.S. Children's Bureau, Publication No. 356, 1956).

carries the unexpected latent function of helping the young individual achieve a social maturity that otherwise would have been delayed or not achieved at all. (3) *Solidification of Values.* Joining volunteer service often is a symptom of the search and experimentation with alternative values. While many other youngsters choose the pursuit of more competitive and material values, those whose attention is focused on the cooperative and humanitarian values of the American ethos are able to undergo a test of their chosen values through service projects. It appears that the outcome of the test usually reinforces these values, and the person engaging in these activities achieves greater certainty and self-assurance. Supporting this assumption is the fact that nearly 10 per cent of those who completed their service with the Peace Corps voluntarily requested permission to prolong their service for an additional period of time.[58]

The Argot of the Subculture

According to linguists, an argot is a "special language" that reflects the idiom of a particular group or social class. It is used by groups of persons who interact over a considerable period of time and share special circumstances. The language of the law is an example of a special language. In the course of their professional activities and associations, lawyers employ a language markedly different from that of ordinary speech. Other examples are the ecclesiastical language and the argots of thieves, the military establishment, miners, medical doctors, etc. All of them use a language of their own, often making it difficult or impossible for outsiders to understand what they say among themselves.

Of course, these sublanguages, or subcultural languages, should not be understood as entirely different or independent from the "standard" language of the society. Rather, they are specialized modifications and adaptations to particular circumstances, using the general language of the adult community as their basis. The sublanguages may differ so much among themselves that most people know only a few well and almost nothing of others. Some are not only unintelligible but also without interest to outsiders.

The common characteristic of special languages is the function of adapting communication to the particular activities, needs, and interests of the group. This implies that the various subsections and subcultures of a society exhibit their own lingo or argot. Medical students have to

---

[58] Joseph G. Colmen, "Volunteerism: A Constructive Outlet for Youthful Energy," *Journal of Marriage and the Family,* Vol. 27 (May, 1965), p. 173.

learn a biological and medical vocabulary; students of this textbook must be familiar with some sociological and psychological terminology. The differences in argot are due to the different needs and interests of the individuals involved, or, as in the case of students, to the different vocational aspirations.

The acquisition of a particular argot usually means more than just learning a new vocabulary and being able to communicate with it. It normally signifies membership in the subculture to which the lingo is indigenous. It promotes group or subcultural cohesiveness and may be used to attract attention and insure privacy through use of esoteric terms. Furthermore, it stands for new knowledge and insights both cognitive and affective. This means that learning a term and acquiring its concept provide both knowledge and understanding about a dimension in the universe and also the capability to "label" certain emotions.

The argot of the teen-agers is such a "special language" and meets many of its definitional criteria. Although it is based on and utilizes the framework of the larger society's language as most argots do, an adult listening to typical teen-agers talk is aware of being a stranger to their ways of thinking and behaving. Iona and Peter Opie, in their study of several thousand English schoolchildren and their lingo *outside of the school,* discovered a lore and terminology of the children's argot that was largely unknown to and certainly unheeded by the adult population.[59] It can safely be assumed that ordinary adults in England as well as in the United States are not familiar with many of the terms and idioms of teen-agers and consequently are not capable of cognizing and reacting in the same way. How, for example, could an uninitiated adult understand and share a teen-ager's state of mind when he hears him say that he is "switched on" or "hip"? The concept evokes a specific comprehension and emotion only on the part of the user of the argot. Usually, the only way to acquire the meaning is to join teen-agers and participate in their activities—provided they accept the adult. Of course, many adults recall their own teen-age days and may be able to roughly equate terms of today's argot with similar terms they used themselves, since many of the experiences, conditions, and circumstances of the adolescent phase have remained the same or very similar throughout recent generations.

The reason why teen-age argots evolve and are tenaciously maintained must be sought in their functions. At least three major functions can be discerned:

(1) Many of the terms of the teen-age argot are shorthand devices, designed to save time when referring to one of the many relatively com-

---

[59] Iona Opie and Peter Opie, *The Lore and Language of School Children,* (Oxford, The Clarendon Press, 1959).

plex processes in which teen-agers are constantly involved. For example, to spell out the fine details and connotations of what is meant when referring to a person or an object as "camp" "cool" would take considerable time and unduly hamper smooth communication. Argot saves time and effort by summing up complex and recurrent phenomena in one word. The word evokes a clear concept for the teen-ager, saves him time and effort, preserves his unique style of in-group communication, and prompts him toward expected subcultural emotions and actions.

(2) Many of the terms and idioms are coined to make possible a more precise reference to certain observations or experiences than the ordinary adult vocabulary would allow. In conjunction with the exposure to his unique adolescent circumstances and conditions, the teen-ager finds that the adult "standard" language does not include a sufficient vocabulary and reservoir of expressions to define and describe many of the ensuing experiences. "For not everything in the world has a name. . . . language singles out for specification only those features which are, in a peculiar sense, common to the social group."[60] The teen-ager meets his need for an adequate and descriptive communication system by modifying the general language and supplementing it with a battery of subcultural words and idioms that, in effect, lead to the establishment of an argot. As a result, the teen-ager uses words which are literally untranslatable into adult language because the empirical referents are unknown in the normal adult environment. In essence, then, having different experiences and perceiving human relationships from a different angle, as teen-agers do, calls for a correspondingly different set of words and idioms.

An example of one of the issues with which teen-agers are presumably more preoccupied than adults is romance. The ubiquitous plots in rock 'n' roll songs, teen-age movies, and TV fare about the trials of love, broken romances, holding hands, going steady, etc., give ample evidence of this preoccupation.

In order to convey the meaning of this relatively unique teen-age emphasis, the youngsters need a language that allows such clear expression. A selection from Jim Wylie's compilation of teen-age vocabulary may illustrate this more clearly:

> Teen lingo creates a whole system of rating or ranking romantic attachments. Girls are judged very harshly. The girl who is pegged as a *scab*, a *shank*, a *bat*, or an *ox* may be shattered forever. But a *fox* is different. Foxes are the good-looking, dyno, out-of-sight

---

[60] G. M. Laguna, *Speech: Its Function and Development* (Yale University Press, 1927), p. 272.

chicks you see mowing suburban lawns on Sunday mornings or smiling out from the cover of *Seventeen*. Getting involved is *getting into something* and, if you're really into something, naturally you T.C.B.—*take care of business*. Although teen marriage is growing it has not yet become a fixed part of American life and pretty soon the time comes to make that move and break it off. For a while after, things seem *played out* and then magically you meet someone new and *rap it all to her*. In a few days you *dig her*, you dig her strong and everything's *very nice, smooth, yes real boss*.

Teen-age language is not only vivid and whimsical; it is clever, highly nuanced, quite sly, and diminutive without the use of the diminutive as a grammatical form. All this requires a certain cuteness of pronunciation and coyness of gesture both personal as well as indicative of the true meaning and stature of a word.[61]

(3) Some words and idioms serve a less instrumental purpose than the above-mentioned two functions of abbreviation and precise reference; they function rather as reinforcers and maintainers of group solidarity. When teen-agers use or hear the term, they are strongly reminded of membership in the subculture.

Although every generation of teen-agers seems to adhere to an argot, its specific content, such as particular words and expressions undergo change from one generation to the next. What was "keen" 20 years ago changed to "tough," "boss" or "dapper," and finally back to "keen"—all referring to roughly the same phenomenon. It is thus with reservation that a specific glossary is presented, since every such attempt will result in a *dated* document. Yet, it is important to give the reader some concrete illustration of the teen-age argot. A limited number of teen-age expressions, in vogue in the second half of the 1960's, is listed below:

cool—a catch-all adjective conveying a meaning of nice and attractive.

play it cool—be calm, don't show emotion; "playing it cool" refers to a type of restrained behavior that tries to hide involvement and the fear of not being able to handle emotions successfully.

bread—money, also called "coins" and "greens."

boss—very nice, acceptable, as "she is a boss dresser."

tough—equivalent of boss.

out-of-it—behind the times, stupid, as a parent may be "out-of-it."

winner—one who is "out-of-it or is unattractive; commonly phrased as "a *real* winner."

stud—one of the boys, in the sense of an acceptable peer.

---

61 Jim Wylie, "What Are They Saying?" *Esquire* (July, 1965), pp. 44–45.

to get wasted—to get drunk.

camp—so completely out of style that it's in style.

bod—body.

hoot—a wild party.

hang—loose, relax, don't get excited.

flick—a movie.

fab—fabulous, great.

hip—in good taste, nearly synonymous with "tough," "boss."

ducking it out—fist-fighting.

switched-on—enthusiastic, interested, agitated as "that music switches me on."

shadow—a close companion.

gig—a Saturday night party.

out-of-sight—exceptionally nice, as "that car is "out-of-sight."

Teen-age argot is divided into sublingos, bearing out the principle that different environments and different needs call for a different vocabulary. It is therefore no surprise to hear the teen-age surfers on the West Coast of the U.S. use a set of words and expressions of their own. The following terminology represents examples of the surfers' argot:

hot dogger—surfer skilled at stunts.

hodad—objectionable, non-surfing hanger-on.

gremmie—young, learning surfer.

surf bunny—a girl who chums with surfers (may or may not surf).

baggies—loose-fitting trunks. (This is good!)

surf's up—fine, big waves.

glassy—smooth-surfaced sea.

bitchin—good, great!

wipe-out—fall off surfboard.

shooting the pier—riding board between pilings of pier.

quasimodo—riding crouched, one arm forward, one back.

hang ten—ten toes hooked over nose of board.

hang five—five toes over nose.

greaser—chap with long, greasy hair, sloppy clothes.

grab your stick—grab your board.

brown-out—riding backward to shore (very difficult).

woody—restored wooden station wagon (highly priced).

soup—foamy part of wave.

head dip—riding front of board, dipping head toward water.

cut back—changing direction.

set—group of waves.

coffin—riding a wave flat on board, arms folded across chest.

spoon—upward slope in board.

bun-hugger—too-tight trunks.[62]

Another sublingo that has more recently emerged among a number of teen-agers is the argot of the psychedelic drug users. This argot is spoken by teen-age and adult users of psychedelic drugs such as LSD, mescaline, psilocybin, STP, DMT, marijuana, etc. A sample of pertinent terms and idioms includes the following:

acid—LSD (lysergic acid diethylamide).

acid head—LSD user.

acid test—take LSD.

trip—a psychedelic experience.

bad trip—an unpleasant LSD experience.

cap—a capsule of LSD.

cubehead—a regular LSD user or a sugar cube soaked in LSD.

drop a cap—swallow a cap of LSD.

flip—become psychotic.

freakout—a bad LSD experience.

guide—a person who does not take LSD while sitting with a user during a session.

travel agent—a person who provides LSD for a "trip."

turn on, tune in, drop out—to alter awareness under LSD influence.

vodka acid—vodka that contains LSD, considered by many users to be an effective preservative for the psychedelic drug.

The question of the origin of certain expression is most difficult to answer. Why do they choose to say "dig" and "neat" and not, for example, "understand' and "nice," or any other word from almost unlimited alternatives? The specific choice may sometimes be a function of codability, i.e., the brevity and phonetic ease of the word, as when teen-agers say "flick" for movie and "bod" for body, in each case preferring a monosyllabic over a dissyllabic term. At other times it may be imitation of a hero or idol who used the term casually or expressly. An illustration, of more local than national significance, was Ghoulardi, a Cleveland TV semi-comedian of the mid-1960s, who invented Knif—fink spelled backward—and began offering Knif buttons. The teen-age TV audience immediately accepted his neologism, spread the vogue, and bought thousands of buttons. In one show, Ghoulardi coined the expression "All the world's a purple Knif." The idiom spread throughout the region and became a popular saying of the teen-agers. Similarly, he named a pet

---

[62] *Look* Magazine (June 30, 1964), p. 55.

crow Oxnard, and subsequently Cleveland's teen-agers called each other Oxnard.[63] However, apart from such specific instances, the question of etiology of argot awaits both more precise theoretical formulation and above all, empirical explorations.

Firmly established, teen-age argot tends to exert great power and influence over adult institutions, the reason being that if adults want to reach and capture the attention and interest of teen-agers, they must literally meet them on their own terms. Over the past decade, it could be observed that various adult agencies have adapted their language to meet the teen-ager more than halfway. This catering to teen-age tastes, values, and practices is noticeable in many institutions of the adult society. It is observable in the demands of students, especially on the high school level, but increasingly also on the college level, that a teacher be not only an intellectual instructor but also an entertainer, preferably on the "buddy" side who "speaks their language" and knows how to "relate to young people." This trend manifests the youngsters' demand that the adult world surrender to their tastes and, above all, not "bother" them with abstractions that they find difficult to apply in *their* world. This rejection of the alien and intruding elements of adults has received a humble and complying hearing on the part of many adult Americans. Instead of coercing teen-agers to live up to adult standards, including the language, they prefer to live "down" (in the chronological and not in the moralistic sense) to teen-age expectations and desires.

Nowhere is this trend and compliance clearer than in the religious institutions where, in order to win young souls, worship, liturgy, and especially prayer are gradually changed to suit teen-age tastes and comprehension. This tendency is most conspicuously exemplified by the adaptations of liturgy to the argot of the teen-agers. A number of clergymen think that the language of the Gospel is puzzling and irrelevant to children from urban areas. The Bible's bucolic imagery, with its reference to sheep, shepherds, fields, sowing and harvesting, etc., is thought to be largely meaningless to them. When a minister told a group of boys in Buffalo about the lilies of the field that neither toil nor spin, he encountered laughter—later he found out that in their argot a "lily" meant a homosexual.[64] The minister subsequently encouraged the boys to rephrase Biblical parables and adapt them to the conditions and the argot of their environment. In this way, the Good Samaritan became the "cool square" who helped a "mugged" victim after a "hood" and a "sneak" (not so "cool" as a "hood") had "passed him by." The Christmas story was modified to show the setting in Buffalo during a convention

---

[63] "What Catches the Teen-Age Mind?," *Time* (Sept. 27, 1963), p. 55.
[64] "The Bible," *Time* (March 5, 1965), p. 44.

when all hotel rooms were taken and the Savior's stable was a hot dog stand in some municipal park. The parable of the lost sheep was re-phrased to be understood as a used-carlot owner who goes looking for the "heap" that someone "snitched." Finally, one boy offered a novel version of the beginning passage of the 23rd Psalm:

The Lord is like my probation officer.
He will help me.
He tries to help me make it every day.
He makes me play it cool.[65]

The significance of argot, for teen-agers as well as for all other sub-groups, must be seen as a concomitant feature of the pluralistic nature of a large and diverse society. Hertzler, the author of *A Sociology of Language,* a most important contribution to the social sciences, em-phasized that there is a "growing tendency toward differentiation and specialization of speech forms and the development of sublanguages within many language communities."[66] This differentiation is a definite trait of the American scene, resulting from yet relatively unexplored factors, such as the increasing specialization of the division of labor, more abrupt distinction between the component positions, the multipli-cation of specific interests, etc. It is a relatively safe hypothesis that the teen-age argot will not only remain but will increase in separateness and distinction from the adult language over the next decade.

The Role of the Automobile

No discussion of life in the American teen-age subculture would be complete without mentioning the role of the automobile. The wide use of motor vehicles is a most conspicuous and typical feature of American life. To illustrate the magnitude of the phenomenon, in 1950 there were approximately 40 million privately owned automobiles registered; nearly ten years later, 70 million; and the predicted figure for 1970 is 90 million.[67]

The American teen-ager has both participated in and been influ-enced by the increasing use of the automobile. In the majority of states, the minimum age for acquiring a driver's license is 16 years. While in

---

[65] Reference 64.

[66] Joyce O. Hertzler, *A Sociology of Language* (New York, Random House, 1965), p. 300.

[67] Ross A. McFarland and Roland C. Moore, "Youth and the Automobile," in Eli Ginzberg (ed.), *Values and Ideals of American Youth* (New York, Columbia University Press, 1961), p. 170.

two states one needs to be only 14 years and in nine states 15, three other states require minimum ages of 17, 18, and 20, respectively.[68] The National Safety Council has estimated that in 1958 there were about six million licensed drivers in the U.S.[69] When these data were related to census figures, it was found that by age 19 four to five boys out of every six and two to three girls out of six were licensed drivers.[70] Another study traced the increase in car ownership through the high school career of boys and found that, taking the average of ten different schools, ownership increased consistently from 5% of freshmen to approximately 50% of senior boys. A more detailed picture concerning car ownership was obtained by comparing the different schools and noting the relationship between type of school (as connoted by the pseudonyms selected) and percentages of ownership: Farmdale, 81%; Marketville, 56%; Elmtown, 42%; Maple Grove, 68%; Green Junction, 64%; Newlawn, 51%; Executive Heights, 42%; Millburg, 37%; Midcity, 46%; St. John's High, 17%.[71] As can be seen, in the rural community of Farmdale nearly twice as many boys owned cars as in Midcity, with small towns like Maple Grove and Green Junction ranking inbetween. The lowest car ownership was observed at a parochial boys' school, St. John's High.

Little factual material is available concerning the amount and the quality of teen-age driving. One source estimated that the total mileage for male youth is several times greater than for female youth and that boys do much more night driving than any other category of drivers.[72] Research in Iowa, operating around the clock, revealed that during daytime hours youth comprised 6% of the drivers on the highway, while from sunset to midnight they increased to 14.8%, and in the hours after midnight to 20.4%. The study also found higher average speeds for young drivers, especially at night time.[73] It is not surprising, therefore, that teen-agers as an age category are more frequently involved in accidents and traffic arrests than any other age group. Two studies in New England states showed that 16-year-old boys had an accident rate of 38.2% and a traffic violation arrest rate of 31.1%. These percentages decreased for subsequent age brackets and by age 20 the rates were

---

[68] New York University Center for Safety Education, *Physical and Mental Requirements for the Driver's License* (New York, 1959).

[69] National Safety Council, *Accident Facts*, 1959 Ed. (Chicago, 1959).

[70] McFarland and Moore, *op. cit.*, p. 172.

[71] Coleman, *op. cit.*, pp. 24–25.

[72] McFarland and Moore, *op. cit.*, p. 172.

[73] A. R. Lauer, "A Sampling Survey of Drivers on the Highways for the 24-Hour Period," in *Driver Characteristics and Accidents*, Highway Research Board Bulletin, No. 73, (Washington, D.C., 1953), pp. 15–25.

9.2% and 21.8%, respectively. A similar age correlation was observable among girls, starting at age 16 with 17.5% for accidents and 4% for arrests, and declining to 2.9% and 2.4%, respectively, at age 20.[74] A University of Michigan study carried out by a team of medical doctors and social scientists found that:

> traffic accidents are the leading cause of death for young men between 16 and 24. Although young male drivers amount to only one-eighth of all registered drivers, they are responsible for a third of all fatal accidents. As a result, they are being killed in epidemic proportions. Last year (1966) the total was 12,200—more than double the number of U.S. servicemen who died in Vietnam. . . .
>
> The researchers found that the young male driver is using the car as an "expressive" instrument to blow off steam after an argument with his family or girl, or to gain relief from problems caused by school grades or draft worries. In finding an outlet for his frustrations and anxieties, he is also unconsciously releasing suicidal and homicidal impulses.[75]

The role of the car can be best understood in terms of its functions for the teen-ager. Besides the manifest function of providing for transportation to school or work, the car usually serves one or several of four additional functions:

(1) Owning or having regular access to a car is *prestigious* in the eyes of peers.[76] The newer or more customized the car, the higher the prestige. A teen-ager may spend all his savings on customizing and maintaining the car according to what his peers consider desirable.

(2) The car is of great *instrumental* importance for dating and related activities. It seems that the ecological conditions of smaller towns, suburbs, and rural areas make a car both more important and more accessible than in larger cities, where public transportation is available and where ecological factors, such as density of population and traffic, limit the use of the automobile.[77] For the teen-age boy, to have a car is not only prestigious but usually imperative when asking a girl for a date, since she may not want to go in a cab or be chauffeured by parents. The car, in most cases, is an indispensable instrument in the American dating syndrome, and a regular pattern can be observed. Usually, the date starts by driving to some public place, such as a movie, and then on to an eating place, such as a malt and hamburger drive-in, "juke-

[74] Connecticut Motor Vehicle Department, "16–20-Year-Old Operators Involved in Accidents and Arrested, July 1955–June 1956," Special Report, (mimeo.) (Hartford, Conn., Aug. 22, 1956).

[75] Reported in "Highways—The Young Killers," *Time* (August 25, 1967), p. 46.

[76] Coleman, *op. cit.*, pp. 41, 43.

[77] Coleman, *op. cit.*, pp. 8, 23f, 129.

joint," drug store, or restaurant. The public aspect of the date is important for several reasons. First, to give the partner a "good time" and supposedly to demonstrate nonexploitative motives; secondly, to earn esteem and prestige in the eyes of the peers by being seen with a date. The next phase of the date is the private and unsupervised conclusion. It has been said that the automobile represents the single most important technological variable in changing courtship patterns.[78] It allows for mobility and privacy, providing American teen-agers with the most frequent setting for sexual experimentation. The modal pattern appears to be that the date normally ends with a period of necking and petting in the car. The Kinsey report discovered that 41 per cent of the respondents mentioned the automobile as the common place for premarital sex relations.[79]

(3) For some boys a car is a *hobby*. In fact, one researcher revealed that the most frequent hobby of high school boys was "working on their cars."[80]

> Many boys enjoy the aspect of engineering and mechanics, spending most of their free time and money on building, modifying, replacing, and adding parts to their automobile and, in pursuit, inadvertently learn the vocation of an auto mechanic. The favorite changes include such things as adding "dual" exhaust; Hollywood mufflers, which give a loud, racing-type exhaust noise; lowering the blocks, resulting in a lower outline; customizing the outside of the car with a custom grill or with added chrome—or, more frequently, stripping the chrome; more elaborate custom work; dual carburetors; or some other engine work.[81]

The boy whose hobby is automechanics frequently is also a so-called "hot-rodder," participating in legal or illegal races. Two psychiatrists conducted a detailed study of this type of teen-age driver and compiled the distinguishing features of 30 subjects.[82] It was found that they were characterized by a stronger than average physique, a background showing evidence of emotional deprivation and an ambivalent relationship with parents, an early development of interest in driving cars, an indifference to reading, an aggressive temperament, and a frequent mood of boredom when away from their hobby. Often, this type of teen-ager

---

[78] Francis E. Merrill, *Courtship and Marriage: A Study in Social Relationships* (New York, William Sloane Associates, Inc., 1949).

[79] Alfred C. Kinsey, *Sexual Behavior in the Human Female* (Philadelphia, W. B. Saunders Co., 1953), Table 78, p. 336.

[80] Coleman, *op. cit.*, p. 12.

[81] Coleman, *op. cit.*, p. 26.

[82] J. C. Neavles and G. Winokur, "The Hot-Rod Driver," *Bulletin of the Menninger Clinic*, Vol. 21, No. 1 (1957), pp. 28–35.

belongs to a specific subculture, the "hot-rodders," and is therefore not entirely typical of the general teen-age subculture.

(4) Finally, driving an automobile can provide a *sense of domination* over something fast and powerful. Since, as a rule, the adolescent experience includes a feeling of restriction and powerlessness, it is conceivable that certain teen-agers take to the car as a substitute outlet for youthful energy and impulses. The car becomes a symbol and an instrument of freedom and escape from adult control and supervision. Psychiatrist J. M. Murray hypothesized that driving a powerful automobile opens up an avenue to express frustration and hostility with a minimum of risk of punishment and often with complete anonymity.[83] Poor or reckless driving habits can often be interpreted as displaced revolt against authority and may take on symptoms such as "cutting in," stealing the right of way, horn blasting, speeding, racing, stopping and starting with screaming tires, and many other forms of obstructionist, show-off, and domineering driving patterns.

No other adult agency is more eager to encourage the kinetic impulses of the teen-agers than the American automobile industry. It has become a lucrative business to cater to the teen-age population, numbering nearly 25 million in the mid-1960s. The car manufacturers are fully aware of the direct and indirect buying power of youth, i.e., their disposable cash and their influence on parents. Detroit has used teen-agers, their ideas and tastes, as style-setters, because they know that if they can sway the teen-agers, they probably will also sway the parents. Car manufacturers have not spared costs to reach the young. For example, Detroit manufacturers distributed to teen-agers a huge number of folders, leaflets, and booklets, containing a variety of information, entertainment, encouragement, and questionnaires. Chrysler Corporation offered a comic book encouraging safe driving, and Lincoln-Mercury came out with a booklet, "How to Earn the Key to Dad's Car," written in the argot of the teen-agers, as, "In certain circles a guy's . . . a swinging cat if he mixes his necking with his driving. . . . But the smart teen knows his score. . . ."[84] Ford, in a more direct attempt to establish rapport with the teen-agers, sent out a folder called "The Fashion Council Forum Page" which, in effect, was a questionnaire inquiring into the tastes and preferences of the teen-agers concerning car body styling. Direct or indirect, through comic books, safe-driving manuals, or blunt questionnaires, the

[83] J. M. Murray, "Emotional Problems In Relation to Driving," in *Action Achievement Report, 8th Annual Massachusetts Governor's Highway Safety Conference* (Boston, May 25, 1954).

[84] Diana Bartley, "Oh Dad, Poor Dad, Junior's Doubled Our Car Payments," *Esquire* (July, 1965), p. 112.

manufacturers have the same goal—to establish rapport with the teen-agers. This process implies a relatively complex exchange of ideas and suggestions, with the manufactuers presenting ideas and gauging opinions, and the youngsters, in turn, reacting with evaluations as well as new suggestions.

It appears that the interplay of the teen-agers' needs and desires for cars and their potential affluence, on one side, and the manufacturers' and dealers' sales technique, on the other side, has resulted in a sizable proportion of American teen-agers driving cars. There is no doubt that the automobile is and definitely will remain an important implement of the teen-agers' lives.

Summary

An adequate catalog and description of all the variables in the life of the American teen-ager would be impossible in one book. This chapter intended to single out only a few basic features, to describe and illustrate them with a number of recent events, and to add a functional inter-pretation. It is the *functional analysis* of major and recurrent themes in the teen subculture that is of foremost importance to students of the social sciences, attempting to give clear answers to the "why?" of certain patterns, to the "what follows if . . .," to the antecedent-consequent rela-tionships. It is therefore from the functional-analytic perspective that the following summary is presented.

(1) Teen-age fads seem to be perennial in as much as they can be observed in all teen-age generations of the modern era. Although peren-nial as a means of vogue expression, the peculiar *content* usually differs from generation to generation. The major fads tend to express themselves in a relatively few everyday living patterns, such as conversation, cloth-ing, music, dance, hair styling, etc. The functions, i.e., the intentional and/or unintentional consequences of teen-age fads amount to: (a) a behavioral commitment furthering the sense of belonging; (b) a means of self-expression and experimentation; (c) rebellion against the adult society with normally little risk of punishment; and (d) a means of communication and identification concerning group membership.

(2) Teen-agers have their heroes and idols and engage in multi-farious patterns of "worshiping" them, including such forms as: (a) fetishism; (b) crowd and mob behavior with reinforcing "contagious" imitation; (c) identification with and imitation of the hero; (d) accept-ing values and attitudes extended by the hero as a "significant other;"

and (e) adhering to and internalizing the hero's generally romantic outlook on life, thereby setting the mood for a high degree of unrealism among teen-agers.

(3) The teen-agers' values and attitudes can be divided into three categories: (a) In-group values. It appears that American youth are greatly preoccupied with the issue of being popular and well-liked by the peers. Teen-agers who tend to manifest the greatest concern with this mattern are upper-middle-class girls. Values sought in a friend differ slightly betwen boys and girls, with the former looking for someone who is amiable, nice, and helpful in trouble, and the latter for someone who is, first of all, not a gossip and then amiable, nice, and helpful in times of trouble. (b) Attitudes toward adults. Although in some decision-making aspects, such as future occupation, how to spend money, and which courses to take at school, teen-agers seek advice from parents and other adults, they generally exhibit a remarkable degree of caution and distrust toward the adult world. Moreover, their opinions regarding what they believe to be proper political behavior show a strong leaning toward conservatism and civil restriction. In line with the conservative tendency are their material expectations, largely coinciding with what is generally defined as middle-class standards. (c) Value commitments. An appreciable number of America's youth are actively busy promoting international betterment through various adult agencies, such as churches, universities, and the Peace Corps. Furthermore, active value commitments that cooperate with adult institutions and reflect adult goals can be observed on the national and local level. Such service commitment helps teen-agers put their ideals into practice, makes them feel socially needed and worthwhile, tests their abilities by providing a social-physchological moratorium during which they may experiment and "find themselves," and provides opportunities to learn cooperative independence from their parents.

(4) Teen-age argot is as puzzling to adults as it is functional for teen-agers. Its functions include the shorthand device or phonetic ease of monosyllabic words, greater relevance to the adolescent experience, and maintenance of group solidarity. The origin of teen-age vocabulary and idioms is extremely difficult to trace and remains mostly obscure and unknown—although the factor of phonetic ease and the imitation of popular heroes often plays an obvious etiological role. A fascinating current development is the adoption of teen-age argot by adult institutions, notably religious institutions.

(5) The automobile probably is the most significant material implement for the American teen-ager. Besides the necessity of having a car

for commuting to school or work, it serves prestige, dating, hobby, and compensatory functions. American automobile manufacturers are aware of the teen-agers' desire to have cars and focus a good part of their sales techniques on America's teen-agers, appealing directly to affluent teen-agers and indirectly, via their influence, to their parents.

part IV

the diversity of adolescent experience

THE TRANSITIONAL PROCESS OF ADOLESCENCE IS NOT A UNIFORM EXPERIENCE for all American teen-agers, but differs significantly according to socio-economic class, racial group, ethnic subcultures, etc. In a sense there is no "all-American" adolescent, since most young individuals can be associated with some distinguishable social, racial, religious, or ethnic background. This, then, challenges the blanket reference to "American" teen-agers and adolescents as made in the preceding parts of this book. The general reference has been made because at least two generalizable elements seem to be involved.

First, the discussion purposely and announcedly focused on the broad American white middle class in which general middle-class values and social processes tend to blur and override specific subcultural values that could arise, for example, from differential religious affiliation or ethnic background. The focus on the middle-class social processes as they affect the adolescent experience appeared justified not only because of the numerical importance that is involved when one deals with the middle-class segment of the United States population, but primarily because the American middle class is in a peculiarly powerful position to influence and "set the tone" for norms, values, and aspirations of the rest of the social strata. These standards come to be viewed as typically American—with the aura of being *correctly* American. The presumably "representational" standards and life view of American people often serve as models and goals for youth in other socioeconomic classes, thus representing a blueprint for behavior that is generalizable *to some degree*. It is true, however, that the reactions to this blueprint and the achievements resulting from the pursuit of its goals differ greatly among the members of distinguishable pluralities.

The second generalizable feature of the discussion in the preceding chapters lies in the core process of adolescent transition, which involves the common problem of making a transition from child to adult status. Certain principles are common to and operative in all modes of adolescent situations, as, for example, the need to ameliorate the unstructured interim situation and find some sort of "bridge" structure that ties the individual over to the social structure of the adult world. In other words, the structural uncertainty may be counted as a common principle, while the different reactions and adjustments may be counted as the result of belonging to such different collectivities as these mentioned above.

The following four chapters are selections that try to exemplify the diversity of the adolescent experience and recognize the existence of different teen-age groups and subcultures. Limitations are again obvious. The great number of slightly or very different modes of adolescent experience defy enumeration. A complete cataloging would have to include the relatively self-contained and isolated teen-age groups of such population segments as immigrant groups, the Italian-American, German-American, Polish-American, Hungarian-American, Armenian-American, Greek-American, and many other so-called "hyphenated" Americans; of racial stocks, such as the American Indian, Japanese, Chinese, and Negro; of religious groups; socioeconomic classes; urban versus rural populations; and possibly even regional populations. From this diversity, only a few examples, hopefully major cases, can be selected for discussion in the following chapters.

negro youth

At the time of the founding of the nation, nearly two Americans in ten were Negroes. This proportion declined gradually until it was one in ten by 1920 and remained unchanged until the 1950's, when it began to increase. Since 1950 the *nonwhite* [1] population has increased at an annual rate of 2.4%, compared with 1.7% for the total United States population. In the mid-1960's, one American in nine was nonwhite; 15% of the children under the age of 14 and 16.4% of the children under one year were nonwhite. Although white and nonwhite birth rates have slightly declined since the 1950's, the ratio of 1.42 nonwhites to 1.0 white has not changed. It has been projected that if the rates of growth between 1950 and 1965 continue, one American in eight will be nonwhite by 1972. [2]

The Negro teen-ager is thus an increasing phenomenon, and the study of the social conditions that affect his adolescent experience is of timely importance. His racial status plus his usually lower socio-economic standing mark his adolescent transition and set it apart from that of other American adolescents, characterizing it with relatively unique problems.

It must be added that any discussion dealing with the United States Negro is an immensely difficult task since nearly every generalization could be countered with evidence of exceptions. It also is an emotional

---

[1] An explanation of the term "nonwhite" in relation to statistics on Negroes is necessary here. Many of the statistics used to describe the Negro situation actually refer to the slightly larger group of nonwhites that, in addition to Negroes, includes such racial groups as Indians, Japanese, and Chinese. The application of the more inclusive reference of nonwhite is dictated by the generality of most statistical data, which often fail to make a more specific breakdown of this group. However, considering that the vast majority of nonwhites are Negro, well over 90%, the statistical descriptions are acceptable as reasonably accurate representations of Negro life.

[2] Daniel P. Moynihan, "Employment, Income, and the Ordeal of the Negro Family," in Talcott Parsons and Kenneth B. Clark (eds.), *The Negro American* (Boston, Houghton Mifflin Co., 1966), pp. 134–59.

issue, and probably any type of interpretation is likely to evoke some sort of emotional reaction among readers. It is with these warnings in mind that some of the major conditions affecting Negro adolescence are presented in the following sections.

The Legacy of Racial Discrimination

Negro teen-agers are part of a racial category that still suffers, although to a diminishing degree, from discrimination, deprivation, and therefore, not surprisingly, from what could be called a collective feeling of inadequacy. Discrimination against Negroes is part of American history. The ancestors of today's Negro teen-agers made their entry onto the American scene as slaves. Over the past generations, new laws have changed the status of the Negro, but a persistent cultural lag hampers the actual implementation of his presumably equal status. This cultural lag is not limited entirely to the white segment of the United States population, but is also a feature of the Negro segment itself, which still feels alienated and distrustful in a white-dominated society that only recently has begun to promise equality and its enforcement.

Contemporary Negro teen-agers are part of the process of reluctant sociocultural change that is gradually reassessing the status of the Negro citizenry. Negro youth try to outlive a legacy of alleged racial inferiority. However, in the process, Negro teen-agers find themselves in ambivalent situations. On the one side, a full and clear identification with a Negro culture is difficult, since American Negro population has grown diffuse and diverse and, moreover, is often integrated into the white community to an extent defying a clear characterization as a "Negro community." Furthermore, identification with Negroes "in general" is usually not ego-strengthening or self-enhancing, since it is reminiscent of the subservient and inferior Negro stereotype. On the other side, identification with and full incorporation into the white community is extremely difficult.

The difficulties in feeling part of the white community and in experiencing self-respect are perpetuated by widespread prejudices and still-existing discrimination. While prejudice is an attitude and not directly tangible, discrimination can frequently be observed in prohibitions and imposed disadvantages. In many parts of the nation, Negro youth are deprived of equal opportunities and access to various facilities as, for example, recreational facilities. As a result, Negro youth is more dependent on streets for recreation and gregarious activities than his white counterpart.

Streets are a true social institutions for many Negro youth. The lack of more private facilities such as tennis courts, swimming pools, bowling alleys, and skating rinks forces Negro teen-agers to gather at street corners, beer joints, soda shops, dance halls, and occasionally at public recreation centers and playgrounds. In many communities Negro young-sters have no place to go other than the street, since more regular and adequate facilities are not available for him. Frederick D. Patterson, in 1951, pointed out that the city of Atlanta provided:

   42 major parks for white Atlantans; 3 for Negroes.
   20 football fields for whites; none for Negroes.
   92 small parkways for whites; none for Negroes.
   16 recreation centers for whites; 3 for Negroes.
   12 swimming pools for whites; 3 for Negroes.
   22 baseball diamonds for whites; 3 for Negroes.
  119 tennis courts for whites; 8 for Negroes.[3]

Most of the facilities reserved for Negroes were substandard and overcrowded, converting them into potential incubators of discontent, tension, and frustration. It appears, then, that the Negro youngster is subject to greater problems of self-respect and identity and shows more negative attitudes toward life than his white counterpart. Thus, it may be expected that the adolescent symptoms of confusion frustration, and anxiety can be observed to a more intense degree among Negro teen-agers.

Deprecatory Self-Perception and Lack of Solidarity

As pointed out above, one of the ominous psychological consequences of the Negro's experience of generations of discrimination and inferior status in a white-dominated society is lack of self-respect. This feeling of personal worthlessness has had disastrous effects on the Negro's ability to achieve a sense of solidarity. It appears that the consistent condi-tioning of the Negro to take and keep an inferior socioeconomic status has had far-reaching impact on his perception of himself. In other words, he has internalized this imposed social inferiority and in many instances has actually come to perceive himself as inferior.

As a consequence, unlike many other suppressed and dominated minorities who managed to preserve a sense of worth and dignity, Amer-

---

[3] Frederick D. Patterson, "Negro Youth on Domocracy's Growing Edge," in Eli Ginzberg (Ed.), *Values and Ideals in American Youth* (New York, Columbia University Press, 1964), p. 215.

ican Negroes may develop the tendency to look at each other as secondary and inferior citizens with whom, if they could manage, they would prefer to have nothing in common. This reluctance to be counted together with persons perceived as equally inferior may be among the reasons why American Negroes have been prevented for so long a time from developing an *esprit de corps,* a sense of solidarity, a united front against oppression.

Obviously, this principle is highly exaggerated and is no longer completely applicable in the light of current Negro movements of the so-called 20th-century Negro Revolution; it is of validity primarily in explaining the long delay in initiating unified action and in explaining the still existent degree of disunity and *anomie* among America's Negro population.

The inclination toward showing mutual contempt and disrespect because of "blackness" is still a significant element in Negro interaction—sometimes observed in the form of humor, at other times as scapegoating or hostility. In the Negro slum culture, several distinctive references are used to refer to one's own and to other's racial origins. One is "black," another is "nigger." "Black" usually carries a negative connotation, while "nigger" can have either a negative or a positive connotation, depending on the context. It is interesting to note that the early understanding of "blackness," including the negative connotation, is not necessarily learned from interaction with whites, but from the Negro community's own perpetuated, to some degree psychologically self-imposed, perception of inferiority. A Negro child internalizes these identity aspects in the context of the family and the Negro neighborhood. In fact, he may grow up and never have heard derogatory or negative labels used by white persons against him or any other Negro. And yet the negative labels persist, prevail, and are carried over from one Negro generation to the next. This endo-transmission of negative self-attitudes is one of the functions of the ghetto as found, for example, in many Northern urban slums. This in-group transmission obscures the prime origin and originator of the negative and deprecatory attitudes—the Caucasian. Only later in life do most Negro children realize that they are actually victims of a near-caste system. This realization comes as a late acquisition in addition to a concept of self and of "blackness" in general that has been acquired through intimate interaction with other Negroes within the ghetto community. If, in addition, the child attends a segregated school where his Negro teachers either overtly or by implication reinforce the Negro community's negative self-perception, the child may be seriously hindered from developing a respectful image of himself and other Negroes.

It is due to such ghetto experience that some Negroes sincerely believe that they are not ready for integration, for being received into the white community. A typical case study revealed how, at the start of their career, a young married couple hoping to move up in the world was quite critical of Negroes: "Our people are not ready for integration in many cases because they really don't know how to act. You figure if our people don't want to be bothered with whites then why the hell should the white man want to be bothered with them."[4] Interestingly, the same couple acquired a radically different view of the issue a few months later after traumatic discovery of discrimination on the part of the white man. Then, rather suddenly, the origin of the inferiority and shortcomings of the Negro community became clear. The same man commented: "Do our color make us look dirty and low down and cheap? Or do you know the real meaning of nigger? Anyone can be a nigger— white, colored, orange, or any other color. It's something that you labeled us with. . . . You give me respect; I'll give you respect."[5] It was, then, not until direct interaction with whites and the experience of an intense personal threat, coupled with exposure to a rebellious ideology, that the Negro interpreted his daily experiences and life conditions and began to place the responsibility for the Negro's situation on the whites.

For those Negroes who spend their lives and pursue their livelihoods within the Negro neighborhood, "black" continues to mean membership in a community of persons who think poorly of each other, who attack and use each other, and who rarely develop a sense of solidarity. "Black comes to stand for a sense of identity as no better than these destructive others. The individual feels that he must embrace an unattractive self in order to function at all."[6]

This should not obscure the fact that many Negro families succeed in avoiding the destructive identity implications of "blackness." They show evidence of family solidarity against the assault of negative connotations from the outside world and make it possible for the children to grow up with an identity that combines Negroness and a perception of personal worth. However, this identity is extremely vulnerable and constantly open to attack by Negro peers who may enviously try to put him in "his place" by reminding him that he is "nothing but a nigger like everybody else" or by whites who may put him down by letting him know directly or by implication that he is "just a nigger."

It is thus obvious that the concept of *identity* plays a central role in forming a person's, or for that matter, a collectivity's, attitudes and

---

[4] Lee Rainwater, "Crucible of Identity: The Negro Lower-Class Family," in Parsons and Clark, *op. cit.*, p. 182.

[5] *Ibid.*

[6] Rainwater, *op. cit.*, p. 193.

behavior patterns. In order to understand the American Negro, social workers, politicians, and authorities dealing with the Negro situation and intending to implement policies or social action programs must be sensitive to the Negro's identity problem. As Robert P. Warren emphasized in *Who Speaks for the Negro?*

> I seize that word *identity*. It is a key word. You hear it over and over again. On this word will focus, around this word will coagulate, a dozen issues, shifting, shading into each other. Alienated from the world to which he is born, and from the country of which he is a citizen, yet surrounded by the successful values of that world, and country, how can the Negro define himself?[7]

Negro socialization results in, at best, a relatively self-accepting youngster, more often an adolescent characterized by ambivalent, conflicting, and negative orientations, and most often an adolescent whose self-perception is not so much conflictful as it is extensively deprecatory. In most cases, growing up in the Negro neighborhood exposes the adolescent to a set of experiences, conceptualized and reflected in self-debasing labels, that conveys to the youth an understanding of himself as a powerless and debased individual who will have to forego many gratifications in life and who often can obtain the few gratifications available to him only through devious means.

It is interesting to note that solidarity and cohesion are absent not only from the Negro community as a whole, but also from smaller social systems, such as neighborhoods, gangs, community organizations, etc. In fact the degree of lack of solidarity often puts a question on whether or not the collectivity can really be called a social "system." More often than not, the collectivity is too fluid, transient, and ephemeral to be defined as an integrated group or social system. For example, it is a common fallacy to assume that, as a rule, the low-prestige Negro youngster is engulfed in organized gang activities. Although this is true in a few extreme urban slum areas,[8] Negro teen-agers are usually not as well-integrated into close-knit groups and gangs as their white counterparts. The reasons for this looseness of affiliation are not entirely clear, but may again be related to the insufficient degree of self-respect and self-confidence. It may also be a partial function of the Negro's *anomic* condition, of his relatively low ability to materially implement his group belonging, and, most significantly, of his matricentric family background. It may be more correct, therefore, to define the typical

---

[7] Robert P. Warren, *Who Speaks for the Negro?* (New York, Random House, 1965), p. 17.

[8] Clifford R. Shaw and Henry D. McKay, *Juvenile Delinquency in Urban Areas* (Chicago, University of Chicago Press, 1942); Frederick M. Thrasher, *The Gang* (Chicago, University of Chicago Press, 1936).

collective formations of lower-class Negro youngsters as *bands* rather than gangs. Most lower-class Negro teen-agers tend to associate in loose and rapidly shifting groups that lack regular and consistent leadership, well-defined criteria for membership, and a clear-cut system of statuses. This lack of peer integration is doubly surprising, if one takes into consideration that the Negro youngster spends most of his free time away from the family and mainly in the street with peers.

Diversity of Negro Youth

In view of this conspicuous lack of solidarity, can one actually speak of a separate subculture for Negro youth? It seems that Negro teen-agers are "a *mélange* of general adolescent patterns and unique ethnic practices."[9] It is probably *because of* the lack of solidarity that Negro teen-agers exhibit unique versions of teen-age behavior. One of the main forces behind these versions is primarily the reaction to *anomie,* the existence in a normless and ambivalent social milieu. Man desires certainty regarding his place, purpose, and goals in life. If these factors are unclear, he tends to grow anxious, dissatisfied, aggressive, or totally apathetic. It seems that a variety of these reactions can be detected in the behavior patterns of modern Negro youth. In other words, there is no uniform expression. Depending on a number of circumstances, the reactions can be divided into several categories.

Lower-class Negro teen-agers, primarily of the urban North, are characterized by aggression on a material, personal, and often delinquent basis. This aggressive behavior can be observed among both ghetto youth and integrated youth, although the two groups may be differently motivated to engage in destructive and delinquent acts. For ghetto youth it is a way of life they have learned by imitation and by acquired self-perception, convincing them that survival depends on being aggressive and, if necessary, deviant. For integrated youth, aggressive and delinquent behavior is more often a function of experiencing "relative deprivation." Negro youth from poor families attending predominantly white schools usually have a difficult time trying to catch up with their better prepared and more adequately family-indoctrinated white counterparts. Their frequent experiences of failure are ultimately interpreted as resulting from rejection and unfair treatment by white people. Their first, and often last, perception of the situation is that

---

[9] Joseph S. Himes, "Negro Teen-Age Culture," in Staten W. Webster (ed.), *Knowing the Disadvantaged* (San Francisco, Chandler Publishing Co., 1966), p. 161.

for some reason white pupils achieve success, such as good grades, money, adequate housing, good clothes, jobs, etc., while the Negro "hasn't got any chance." Such unequal achievements are verifiable facts. They may have come about either through actual discrimination and external barriers to success or through the youth's feeling of inadequacy and the subsequent pernicious effects of the self-fulfilling prophecy.

Regardless of the type of mixture of causation, the Negro child learns early in life that the opportunities and the affluence of middle-class America are not readily available to him. In order to partake of the promises of American affluence, he frequently needs a high school and, more often, college education. But motivation and opportunity for higher education are limited for several reasons. As late as the 1960's, there were still 2½ million Negro children in the South in wholly segregated school systems.[10] In virtually all such systems, the quality of education is below that of the white schools. In the Northern cities, the economic situation of the Negro family and the related value-orientation of the youngster are not conducive to academic learning and training for a middle-class career. First of all, the average Negro child starts out with serious language deficiencies,[11] the significance of which can hardly be overemphasized, since they erect an invisible and yet impenetrable barrier between him and the careers that are ordinarily thought of as white middle-class. He cannot help but realize that he speaks a different language from middle-class individuals. Another factor preventing him from concentration on studies is the poverty of the family, which in most cases requires him to take up a part-time or full-time job while in grade school and frequently causes him to drop out of high school. In addition, there may be lack of privacy at home or a sense of remoteness, almost unreality, in respect to future careers of the middle-class type. The result is a low educational motivation and a high truancy rate.

Middle-class Negro teen-agers, especially those exposed to higher education, engage in more rational and goal-oriented types of aggression within racial and civil-protest movements. This latter version of the Negro youth culture actually is not exclusively Negro, but is joined by a sizable proportion of idealistic and sympathetic white persons who take an active part in protest expressions, such as picketing, freedom marches, sit-ins, etc. In the process of rational and planned reaction against the *anomic* and ambiguous social situation, the Negro youth achieves certainty of outlook, purpose of action, and dedication to a

---

[10] Patterson, *op. cit.*, p. 214.

[11] Otto Klineberg, *Race Differences* (New York, Harper, 1935); Arnold S. Carson and A. I. Rabin, "Verbal Comprehension and Communication in Negro and White Children," *Journal of Educational Psychology*, Vol. 51 (April, 1960), pp. 47–51.

cause, thereby alleviating not only the original ambiguity, but also the traditional inferior status.

Most of these social activists are committed to the peaceful protest movement, staying within the realm of lawful protest, often following the historic example of India's Mahatma Ghandi. During the 1950's and 1960's these protest techniques were promoted by such organizations as the Student Nonviolent Coordinating Committee with the goal of achieving integration and equality. Lewis W. Jones reported a typical statement of an activist Negro youth:

> Well, you see, I'm very confused about my role in life. I have an inferiority complex about being Negro and about being me. I have tried to gain respect by participating in the movement [civil rights, SNCC]. Last year working in SNCC, putting my heart into demonstrations gave me purpose. As a result of my actions (plus others) many places were opened up to Negroes.[12]

There are less peaceful and rational reactions against the traditionally imposed inferior status, irritating *anomie,* and the lack of solidarity and collective identity. A minority of Negro youth can be subdivided into two extremist orientations. On the basis of individual temperament, intellectual—or pseudointellectual—conviction, and mainly differential association, a number of Negro youths are induced to join movements that are "national apartheid" or even "black internationalist" in character.

The *apartheids* are nationalist youth who endorse the Black Muslim ideology and seek to separate themselves from the "white devils." Their need for a clear and strong identity is satisfied by a segregationist cult of blackness. Among them are extremists who believe in aggression and physical violence against the white oppressor.

The "black internationalists" or "black worlders" go a step further than most Black Muslims and extend their revolutionary ideas to the entire world. They visualize a black Utopia where the darker peoples of the world assume leadership and domination of the world and assign to the Caucasians a minority, even subservient, status.

In many instances, the motivation for joining such extremist groups is related to "reaction formation" whereby the deeply felt and experienced inferiority is transformed into an overcompensating complex, now defining the white man as inferior and fit merely to be the slave of the Negro. This switch of polar sentiments and the resultant exaggerated aggression has in recent years been observed among deprived Negroes, organized as the Black Muslim movement in the United States and as

---

[12] Lewis W. Jones, "The New World View of Negro Youth," in Muzafer Sherif and Carolyn Sherif (eds.), *Problems of Youth* (Chicago, Aldine Publishing Co., 1965), p. 81.

the Ras Tafari in the West Indies, who independently arrived at the same conviction of black supremacy and justification of the use of violence.

Regional differences add to the diversity of the Negro youth population. Students of the Negro situation tend to accept five geographic distinctions: (1) Rural South, (2) Urban South, (3) Border Urban, (4) Northern Urban, and (5) Southern Small Town.[13] Although a constant South–North (usually conterminal with rural-urban) migration of Negro youth continues to upset the latest statistics, 1960 figures show that 63% of Negro youth under age 20 lived in the South, with 37% living elsewhere. Of these Southern youth, 30% were "rural nonfarm," 13% "rural farm," and 57% urban.[14] Almost all Northern Negro youth live in urban areas. A specific class of Negro youth consists of those who have had the uprooting experience of migration, usually rural–urban. These marginal youth are characterized by unique and intensified problems of adjustments, so they should not be classified with urban-born and urban-raised youth.

Another important variable of diversity is religion. This factor can be broken down into type of affiliation, degree of commitment, and degree of orthodoxy or otherworldliness. That the religious factor plays a significant role in civic orientation and type of participation in civil rights movements was discovered by a 1967 study that found that secular militancy (not to be equated with mere participation in civil rights activities) and several dimensions of religiosity (such as degree of orthodoxy, frequency of participation at worship services, etc.) were inversely correlated. The inverse pattern can be noticed by comparing the proportions of militant individuals in different categories of religiosity. Per cent militant amounted to 26 per cent for the "very religious," 30 per cent for the "somewhat religious," 45 per cent for the "not very religious," and 70 per cent for the "not at all religious."[15] It was also found that Negroes belonging to sects and religious cults were the least likely to be militant. Negroes belonging to largely white denominations (Episcopal, Presbyterian, United Church of Christ, and Roman Catholic) were most likely to be militant. Members of predominantly Negro denominations(Baptist, Methodist) indicated a moderate, in-between degree of militancy. This pattern remained unchanged even after social class was held constant.

---

[13] Jones, *op cit.*, p. 69.

[14] *Ibid.*

[15] Gary T. Marx, "Religion: Opiate or Inspiration of Civil Rights Militancy Among Negroes?," *American Sociological Review*, Vol. 32 (February, 1967), pp. 67–69.

These divisions among Negro youth show that a general reference to "the Negro youth subculture" is not borne out in reality. Socio-economic differences, family circumstances, educational attainment, religious affiliation, and involvement in oppression-reaction ideologies are some of the major forces that determine the youth's orientation and affiliation. It seems, however, that throughout the variegated expressions of modern Negro youth runs a common strain: the search for identity and self-respect.

Family Life and Lower-Class Affliction

The United States Negro population is disproportionately lower class. For the majority of Negro teen-agers, family life still means lower class life. The two variables, family life and lower-class condition, are intricately intermeshed and, if one intends to make valid generalizations about the vast majority of American Negroes, it would be unrealistic to try to discuss the two separately.

A significant feature of lower-class Negro families is the large number of children. Negro women not only have more children than Caucasian women but have them at a younger age. 1960 statistics show that on the average, 1,000 nonwhite females between the ages of 15 and 19 had 1,247 children, compared with 725 children for their white counterparts. The bulk of this population increase is concentrated in the lower-class stratum. Nonwhite mothers aged 35 to 39 with a family income of over $10,000 had 2.9 children, while those of the same age with less than $2,000 annual income had 5.3 children.[16] An impressive proportion of these children are illegitimate. The findings of a study, Social and Economic Conditions of Negroes, which was ordered in 1966 by President Johnson revealed that the illegitimacy rate among Negroes is 26.3 per cent, compared with 4 per cent for whites.[17]

Another common feature of the lower-class Negro family is the tendency toward matricentrism, in which either the mother or the grand-mother acts as the mainstay of the family unit. Speaking of the Negro population in general, the Negro family is far more likely than the white family to include a working wife: in 1965, 38.4% of Negro families had a wife in the labor force, compared with 28.7% of white families. Also, one of every 4 nonwhite families had a female head, compared to one

---

[16] Moynihan, op. cit., pp. 147–48.

[17] U.S. Bureau of Labor Statistics and Bureau of the Census, Social and Economic Conditions of Negroes (Washington, D.C., November, 1966).

of 11 white families.[18] The practice of females heading the household is particularly prevalent among *poor* urban Negroes. The 1960 United States Census included detailed information on this condition (see Table 10–1) and revealed that 47% of the low-income urban Negro families *with* children had a female head.[19] These figures, however, do not reflect the cumulative incidence of matricentrism, but merely the incidence at a given point in time. In other words, it is safe to hypothesize that because of the high turnover of the legal husband, common-law husband, or visiting man, many more children, perhaps up to two-thirds, in these lower-income urban Negro families will experience family life without a father or an adult male at least once during the first 18 years of their lives. Daniel P. Moynihan says: "It seems very likely that only a minority of Negro women in the urban slum go through their child-rearing years with only one man around the house."[20]

It follows logically that since the slum family tends to be characterized by both father-absence and more children, the mother figure assumes great significance and power for the Negro youth. In fact, the matricentric role of the Negro female with her vitally needed nurturing and leadership functions is suspected of having a belittling effect on the masculinity and self-respect of the Negro male. Researchers have found that the Negro man, being characterized by frequent desertion, separa-

TABLE 10–1. Proportion of Female Heads of Families with Children by Race, Income, and Urban-Rural Residence, 1960.

	Rural	Urban	Total
Negroes:			
under $3,000	18%	47%	36%
$3,000 and over	5	8	7
total	14	23	21
Whites:			
under $3,000	12	38	22
$3,000 and over	2	4	3
total	4	7	6

Source: *United States Census, 1960,* PC (1) D.U.S. Volume, Table 225; State Volume, Table 140.

---

[18] Vera C. Perrella and Elizabeth Waldman in U. S. Bureau of Labor Statistics, Division of Labor Force Studies, *Monthly Labor Review* (March, 1966), p. 258.

[19] *United States Census, 1960,* PC (1) D.U.S. Volume, Table 225; State Volume, Table 140.

[20] Moynihan, *op. cit.,* p. 168.

tion, divorce, and unemployment, is prone to play a secondary and mostly ineffective leadership role. Social workers and sociologists have long observed that masculinity is consistently attacked and demeaned in the Negro slum family. In one case study, teen-age daughters of a husbandless mother who had gone through a number of consorts belittled both their brothers and their different fathers, and even their mother for financially depending on a male. The mother enjoyed recounting her success in having her common-law husband imprisoned for nonsupport:

> but this comes back to haunt her as her daughters accuse her as being no better than they in ability to force support and nurturance from a man. In contrast the girls came off somewhat better than the boys, although they must accept the label of stupid girls because they similarly failed and inconveniently became pregnant in the first place. At least they can and have had children and therefore have some meaningful connection with the ongoing substance of life. There is something important and dramatic in which they participate, while the boys, despite their sexual activities, "can't get no babies."[21]

A disproportionate number of Negro families are on public relief programs. While this appears to be an unavoidable measure for which no workable alternative has yet been found, it is, in a sense, an anti-family practice. Daniel P. Moynihan, director of the Joint Center for Urban Studies at the Massachusetts Institute of Technology, testified before a United States Senate Committee, advancing his opinion that in many instances relief programs give extra impetus to father-absence and family instability. Moynihan believed that many Negro males who cannot find a job decide to leave home to make their families eligible for welfare assistance.[22] In fact, the motivation of many unemployed Negro males to find a job and support their families may be blunted by the knowledge that indigent families will be taken care of.

It can easily be seen that as a result of the easy substitutability of the Negro man in the family, a general downgrading of the male may ensue. It is not uncommon for the boy to see his father treated with indifference or even hostility and contempt by both his own family and the community, including Negroes as well as whites. The lower-class male is therefore not likely to be a respected and desirable masculine model for the boy. Yet identification with an adult male is of great importance for the male child and if imitation and emulation are impaired, role

---

[21] Rainwater, *op. cit.*, p. 191.

[22] Testimony before the U. S. Senate, Dec. 13, 1966, reported by the *New York Times* Service (Dec. 14, 1966).

confusion and related emotional problems may ensue. Some of the prevalent troubles include the Negro boy's inability to handle aggression, make decisions, accept responsibility, and assume leadership. (Maybe this is an additional explanation of the Negro teen-agers' loose, shifting, and unstable peer relations.) Also, a boy growing up in a matricentric environment often is attracted again to a woman who will take over for him, carry out the responsibilities that are his, and, in this way, increase his feelings of inadequacy and inferiority to the point that he becomes a poor model for his own children. This tends to become a cyclic process that, unfortunately, may be perpetuated from generation to generation.

On the other hand, the Negro female may prove to be notably more assertive, reliable, and endowed with leadership qualities. Many Negro females have been conditioned early in their lives to accept and carry out responsibilities, provide badly needed leadership, and make necessary decisions in the absence of the male. In short, they may have to act as both mother and father to their offspring and often to their children's offspring. It is not surprising, therefore, that leadership for improving the Negro's lot is often borne by the Negro woman. This leaves the Negro man with an incapacitating stigma. According to the general cultural norms, he, as the man, is expected to assume leadership and decision-making, while the female is expected to play the more withdrawn and subservient role of traditional femininity. The partial or complete reversal of these roles may have detrimental effects on the psychological as well as social level. "Women whose main interests are those of the men may receive rewards for their endeavors but from the psychological point of view they are in danger of sacrificing their femininity. This, of course, may result in serious psychological disturbances. Men who carry out the female role are ridiculed and suffer the consquences of their role confusion without the admiration of society which the female counterparts sometimes achieve."[23] If this insight is carried over to the Negro's struggle for social equality, a current dilemma becomes more understandable. The patriarchal traditions of American society challenge the Negro male and demand that he behave in certain masculine ways before he qualifies for full equality and positions of power and influence. "In order to attain a position of power, the Negro male must learn to function in the culturally accepted role of the man."[24]

---

[23] Israel Woronoff, "Negro Identification Problems and the Education Process," in Staten W. Webster (ed.), *Understanding the Educational Problems of the Disadvantaged Learner* (San Francisco, Chandler Publishing Co., 1966), p. 294.
[24] *Ibid.*

Needless to say, the impact of such family traits on the Negro youth is profound and can hardly be exaggerated. As mentioned parenthetically above, the influence of matricentrism, plus the consequences of identity problems and the defeatist attitudes of the young Negro male may be a significant part of the explanation for the peculiarly unstable peer relations and relative absence of permanent and cohesive groups among Negro teen-agers. The practice of lower-class Negro boys loosely banding together without achieving firm and lasting leadership, with a good deal of nonspecific frustration and latent aggression, may be primarily a consequence of their family experience.

Other common reactions of Negro youth, particularly boys, to the corollary of racial discrimination, family disruption, and identity uncertainty are often expressed in the form of delinquency, deviant behavior (for example, drug addiction), truancy, dropping out of school, and sexual irresponsibility. A Presidential Commission on Law Enforcement and Administration of Justice published a report in 1967 indicating that the millions of underprivileged nonwhites in the slums of America's cities have crime rates that greatly exceed those of the whites. For example, Negroes have ten times the white arrest rate for murder, almost four times the arrest rate for burglary. Concerning all crimes, Negro teen-agers are arrested about three times as often as white teen-agers, the 1965 ratios being 1,689 and 591 per 100,000 respectively.[25] The Presidential Commission concluded that "if conditions of equal opportunity prevailed, the large differences now found between the Negro and white arrest rates would disappear."[26]

A typical example of an urban 16-year-old Negro boy is Case History #116 in the files of the Phoenix Project in Pupil Motivation, a joint enterprise sponsored by several school districts, Arizona State University, and the Ford Foundation.

> In March of 1965 this pupil was suspended from Phoenix Union High School for the remainder of the school year for disorderly conduct. During the previous academic year he had been suspended on three occasions, for the same reason. The boy has a history of seven contacts with juvenile authorities. He has been picked up for a number of reasons ranging from interrogation to such serious offenses as to assault with a deadly weapon.
>
> Although records indicate average grades in elementary school, in high school his grades had been failures, withdrawals, unsatisfactory grades. School attendance was a source of friction between

---

[25] *The Challenge of Crime,* p. 44.

[26] *The Challenge of Crime,* p. 45.

this pupil and school authorities. The counselor reported that the pupil has a quick temper and is defensive, especially toward people in authority. He comes from a family with a number of social problems. His parents were divorced; his mother had been married three times, and had had several common-law relationships. There are five children. The family receives a welfare grant. A brother had a juvenile record at the age of 9. Both school and juvenile authorities list the pupil's I.Q. at 73. He is considered to be mildly deficient by school personnel. The junior counselor feels this is not accurate and that if the pupil is not of average intelligence, he is probably close to it. Juvenile records list the mother as being mentally retarded. In this multi-problem family there is a major need for professional help from existing community social agencies. The pupil especially needs counseling on a professional level because of this attitude which has him in constant conflict with authority. Both the boy and his mother rejected suggestions for a referral to an appropriate social agency.

This boy has one interest in school and that is to play football. He makes a reasonably good personal appearance and can be fairly easy to talk to if he wishes. He gets along satisfactorily with his peers and seems to have no major difficulty relating to his mother and siblings.

With regular multiple failures and with several demerits and a few suspensions from school, the prognosis for him to complete high school is poor. This pupil's situation is made worse by the fact that his mother openly states that school officials "pick on" the boy and that the major difficulty lies with school personnel and not with her son. With this attitude surrounding him, at least a part of his reaction to school is understandable. This family with many psychological and social problems has rejected efforts to help them. This is what is often referred to as a "hard core" family. So far they have resisted the efforts of every social agency in the community which has come in contact with them.[27]

In sum, then, the majority of the American Negro families differ considerably from the average white family, this difference being a result of the unique combination of racial background, disruptive family life, and persistent socioeconomic depression. The adolescent experience of the Negro youth is affected in highly adverse ways. His racial stigma and his family's inability to compensate with a firm family-supported identity produce a degree of frustration and uncertainty that is rarely found among his white counterparts.

---

[27] Case history #116 from the files of the Phoenix Project in Pupil Motivation.

Negro/White Differentials: Education, Employment, Income, and Health

The nature of the life conditions of the American Negro can obviously be demonstrated only by comparing essential life conditions with those of the white population. It is the resultant differences that are responsible for creating an adolescent experience for the Negro that is modally distinguishable from that of his white counterpart. A range of variegated differentials can be observed. Some of them, including family life and family perception, have already been mentioned in preceding sections. Several additional differences should be discussed that are essential for a fuller understanding the American Negro. No assumption is made that these additional variables will add up to produce a complete picture of the Negro situation. Obviously, in the limited frame of this chapter, only rudimentary references to a few major conditions can be offered.

One of the striking conditions of Negro life is educational substandards. Among the reasons for educational underachievement are segregated schools, where Negro schools are almost invariably below national standards and averages; the poor academic attitudes of Negro youth growing up in the lower-class environment; and the low motivation to acquire higher education in the face of real or imagined limitations concerning success in future professional careers. Reference was made earlier to self-attitudes and motivations that are not conducive to academic success. Here, the point should be made that discrimination practices function as formidable barriers not only to joint but also to *equal* educational experiences.

A nationwide survey during the mid-1960's found that 11% of the Negroes listed education as an area of discrimination, second only to job discrimination.[28] The inferior quality of segregated schools is a common complaint of Negroes. In many Northern urban areas, educational segregation is *de facto* because of residential segregation, while in many parts of the South segregation is still *de jure*. Convincing evidence that educational segregation perpetuates inequality was gathered in many parts of the nation. Comparative data from white, integrated, and *de facto* segregated schools in Chicago illustrate the disadvantages of segregated schooling for the Negro youth.[29] Negro schools, it was found in 1962, were able to appropriate only $269 per pupil, compared with

---

28 William Brink and Louis Harris, "What It's Like to be a Negro," in Edward C. McDonagh and Jon E. Simpson (eds.), *Social Problems: Persistent Challenges* (New York, Holt, Rinehart & Winston, 1965), p. 329.

29 U. S. Commission on Civil Rights Report, *Public Schools, Negro and White* (Washington, D. C., 1962), pp. 241–48.

$342 per pupil in white schools. The annual teachers' salary per pupil amounted to $220 in Negro schools and $256 in white schools. The per cent of uncertified teachers was 49% in Negro schools and 12% in white schools. In addition, the classrooms in the Negro schools were considerably more crowded than those in white schools, averages being 47 and 31 pupils, respectively. Similiary, library resources and other expenditures per pupil were markedly lower for Negro schools. The above-listed expenditures and conditions ranked in between for integrated Chicago schools. (See Table 10-2.)

A similarly unequal situation may be assumed to exist between white and Negro schools in the South. The number of Negro children who are affected by the disadvantages of Southern educational segregation is enormous when one considers that during the 1964–65 school year more than 50% of the biracial Southern school districts still maintained segregated school programs and that only one out of every nine Southern Negro school children attended schools with white Southerners.[30]

A nationwide survey recorded some of the characteristics of such segregated schooling:

> For the nation as a whole white children attend elementary schools with a smaller average number of pupils per room (29) than do any of the minorities (which range from 30 to 33). . . . At high school level the average white has one teacher for every 22 students and the average Negro has one teacher for every 26 students. . . . Negro pupils have fewer of some of the facilities that seem most related to academic achievement: They have less access

TABLE 10–2. Comparison of White, Integrated, and Negro Schools in Chicago, 1962.

Variables of Comparisons	Type of Schools		
	White	Integrated	Negro
Total appropriation per pupil	$342	$320	$269
Annual teachers' salary per pupil	$256	$231	$220
Expenditures per pupil other than teachers' salaries	$86	$90	$49
Per cent uncertified teachers	12 %	23 %	49 %
Number of pupils per classroom	30.95	34.95	46.80
Library resource books per pupil	5.00	3.50	2.50

Adapted from U.S. Commission on Civil Rights Report, *Public Schools, Negro and White* (Washington, D. C., 1962), pp. 241–48.

---

[30] *Southern School News*, Vol. 11, No. 6 (December, 1964), p. 1.

to physics, chemistry, and language laboratories; there are fewer books per pupil in their libraries; their textbooks are less often in sufficient supply. . . . The average Negro pupil attends a school where a greater percentage of the teachers appears to be somewhat less able, as measured by these indicators, than those in the schools attended by average students. . . . At the 12th grade, results of tests in the same verbal and nonverbal skills show that, in every case, the minority scores are farther below the majority than are the 1st graders. . . . A constant difference in standard deviations over the various grades represents an increasing difference in grade level gap. For example, Negroes in the metropolitan Northeast are about 1.1 standard deviation below whites in the same region at grades 6, 9, and 12. But at grade 6 this represents 1.6 years behind, at grade 9, 2.4 years, and at grade 12, 3.3 years. Thus, by this measure, the deficiency in achievement is progressively greater for the minority pupils at progressively higher grade levels. . . . The analysis of school factors suggests that in the long run, integration should be expected to have a positive effect on Negro achievement. An analysis was carried out to seek such effects on achievement which might appear in the short run. This analysis of the test performance of Negro children in integrated schools indicates positive effects of integration.[31]

Segregated schools, then, are shown to be inadequately equipped and to provide poor education. Within segregated educational programs, the concentration of culturally disadvantaged Negro children makes it difficult to provide the intensive program they need if they are to reach an equal footing with their white peers. In racially mixed schools, the Negro children's deficiencies would be ameliorated through association with children more fortunate in background and family stimulation.

In addition to external barriers against educational success, reference should be made once more to the internal barriers—the psychological inhibitions of Negro youth toward education. Indifference or antischool attitudes are reflected in the Negro teen-agers' high dropout rates. Although enrollment in grade school has notably improved—by 1960 virtually all Negro children aged 7 to 13 were in school—Negro high school dropout rates are estimated to be twice as high as those of white teenagers. A survey found that 10% of all Negroes reported that "one or more children in their family had dropped out of high school."[32] Lack of incentive was reported to be a major reason for this high dropout rate. A Mount Vernon, New York, housewife explained her children's

---

[31] James S. Coleman et al., Equality of Educational Opportunity, U. S. Department of Health, Education, and Welfare (Washington, D. C., Government Printing Office, 1966), pp. 9, 12, 21, 29.

[32] Brink and Harris, op. cit., p. 329.

dropping out: "They feel they don't have a chance, so why struggle? I got honors in high school but I can't get a decent job."[33]

This brings the discussion to the issue of Negro employment—or, more ominously, unemployment. The nationwide sample reported by Brink and Harris indicated that 30% of the Negroes felt discriminated against in the area of jobs and employment, making it the area of greatest concern for Negroes. Interestingly enough, there seemed to be greater unhappiness about jobs and wages in the North than in the South. In 1963, over 13% of the Negro population was unemployed, compared to 6% for the total United States population.[34] The concentration of unemployment was in the teen-age bracket where job-seeking nonwhite youth averaged more than double the unemployment rate of white teen-agers. (See Table 10–3.)

Moreover, wages paid were markedly below those of white workers. Although the Negro's wages have risen in absolute terms, they have not increased *proportionately* to white wages for the last two decades. While in 1951, for example, the Negro's average annual income was $2,060, or 62% of the white average of $3,345, by 1962 his wages were $3,023, or only 55% of the white income of $5,462.[35] In a sense, the Negro became

TABLE 10–3.   National Unemployment Rates for Teen-Agers by Race and Sex, for 1965. (in per cent)

Race	Sex	Age Categories			All Teen-Age Categories, 14–19 Both Sexes
		14–15	16–17	18–19	
Nonwhite					
	M	20.3	27.1	20.2	25.3
	F	19.0	37.8	27.8	
White					
	M	7.1	14.7	11.4	12.2
	F	4.4	15.0	13.4	

Adapted from U.S. Dept. of Labor, Bureau of Labor Statistics, *The Negroes in the United States—Their Economic and Social Situation*, Bulletin No. 1511 (June, 1966), pp. 124, 82.

---

[33] Brink and Harris, *op. cit.*

[34] *Ibid.*, p. 328.

[35] Brink and Harris, *op. cit.*

poorer in relation to the white man; the gap between Negro and white income and standard of living widened instead of narrowed.

Well over one-third of Negro teen-agers live in familes that are in great need of extra income, having less than $3,000 annually (as of March, 1965), and would welcome the teen-age child's earnings. Yet in the mid-1960's, 20 to 25% of the Negro boys and 25 to 30% of the Negro girls who had been seeking work were jobless.[36] While unemployment rates for male high school graduates dropped between 1964 and 1965, the rates for dropouts rose substantially. On the positive side, there has been improvement in employment as well as wages for Negro females, including Negro teen-age girls. The female proportion of the nonwhite labor force consistently increased over the last 20 years, from 35.1% in 1950, to 40.2% in 1960, to 41.3% in 1964.[37] It is interesting to note that there are more Negro women college graduates in the United States than Negro male graduates. "Wives of Negro men—whether white or Negro—tend to average more schooling than their husbands, reflecting the generally lower level of schooling of Negro men."[38] It is also interesting to note that the income level of Negro women with one or more years of college has been comparable to that of their white counterparts for many years until the mid-1960's, when they moved *ahead* and achieved a median income of $2,904 as against $2,530 for their white counterparts.[39] (This may, however, be mainly due to a higher proportion of these nonwhite females working full time.) Similiarly, the income of nonwhite women with a high school education improved faster than that of their white counterparts.

Incidentally, this increase in economic power of the young Negro female is likely to substantially reinforce matricentric and matriarchal practices in the Negro family.

However, speaking of the Negro population as a whole and de-emphasizing for a moment the exceptional improvement of educated females, the income gap between whites and nonwhites has broadened. The nonwhite lag in economic development is primarily due to the Negro population's deficient educational achievements. The rate of general economic growth of the United States is outrunning the rate of educational improvement of the Negroes.

---

[36] U. S. Department of Labor, Bureau of Labor Statistics, *The Negroes in the United States, Their Economic and Social Situation*, Bulletin #1511, (Washington, D.C., Government Printing Office, June, 1966).

[37] Moynihan, *op. cit.*, p. 146.

[38] Jessie Bernard, "Note on Educational Homogamy in Negro-White and White-Negro Marriages, 1960," *Journal of Marriage and the Family*, Vol. 28 (August, 1966), p. 276.

[39] Moynihan, *op. cit.*, p. 146.

The greater emphasis placed on educational competence will mean that groups which lose out early in the educational race will be quicky excluded from society as a whole. In the next twenty or thirty years the economic situation of the Negro may become relatively worse, simply because the rate of economic change is such as to outrun the increase in educational opportunities available to him. Apart from a thin stratum who do have better educational opportunities, a large part of the Negro population, more than half, continues to live in the South, many in the agrarian sector. This agrarian population has been relatively excluded from society. In this sense coming into the industrial workforce was a way for the Negro to enter modern society. The fact that a large proportion of the Negro population continues to live in this agrarian situation, many of them functionally illiterate, some of whom will emigrate to the North, means that the position of the Negro will worsen. A disturbing indication today is the dropout rate for Negroes in schools in New York and Detroit. This rate is an indicator of the position of the Negro thirty years from now.[40]

The Negro's inability, at least proportionately, to keep up with the white American in economic improvements has parallel symptoms in other life sectors. Health, for example, is one of the life conditions that shows evidence that the gap between white and Negro development is widening. Nonwhite children and teen-agers up to 17 years of age are more often physically disabled than their white peers. This disability differential holds true regardless of how it is measured, whether in terms of duration of restircted activity, bedriddenness, or days taken off from work.[41] A comparison of life expectancies corroborates this syndrome and indicates that at the peak of working potential at age 30 the nonwhite male has a life expectancy of only 38.5 additional years, compared with that of his white counterpart of 43.7 additional years.[42] Infant mortality again reflects the unequal survival chances for whites and Negroes. Statistics for 1965 show national rates of 21.5 deaths per 1,000 white infants and 40.3 deaths per 1,000 nonwhite infants, or an infant mortality rate that is approximately twice as high for Negroes as for whites.[43]

A 1967 conference of physicians and public health officials on "The Health of the Negro Today and in the Future" at Howard University concluded that the general illness rates and the death rates when contracting diseases, such as tuberculosis, cancer, flu, etc., are considerably

---

[40] Daniel Bell, "The Post-Industrial Society," in Eli Ginzberg (ed.), *Technology and Social Change* (New York, Columbia University Press, 1964), p. 50.

[41] Moynihan, *op. cit.*, p. 146.

[42] Moynihan, *op. cit.*, p. 147.

[43] U. S. Department of Health, Education, and Welfare, *Monthly Vital Statistics,* Vol. 16, No. 1 (April 14, 1967), p. 2.

higher for the Negro than for the white.[44] Negro children visit doctors and dentists far less frequently than do white children; two out of three nonwhite children have never visited a dentist. Ghetto life seems to promote certain diseases and tensions, and it was found that in every age-bracket the incidence rate of hypertension is twice as great in the Negro population as in the white. Nonwhite venereal disease rates exceed the white rates by more than ten times. The experts attending the conference agreed that such symptoms are determined not racially, i.e., biogenetically, but rather by environmental conditions, by the failure of bringing modern medicine to the American poor. The panel of experts agreed that the health gap separating Negroes from whites is growing *wider*.

To sum up, the white population's health continues to improve commensurately with the overall United States economic improvement, while the Negro's health is not affected in an equal manner by the general economic progress of the American society.

Summary

These are thus some of the major life conditions that influence the adolescent experience of the Negro in contemporary America:

(1) He carries with him the legacy of his slave forefathers, confronting numerous obstacles in his spasmodic progress to equality. His self-image is highly influenced by the awareness of his racial background and is beset with deprecatory connotations from which he finds it difficult to escape.

(2) The Negro population as a whole, and the Negro youth in specific, exhibit a singular lack of collective identity and solidarity. This collective passivity can usually be traced to the negative and self-debasing attitudes so often noticeable among Negroes. Such basic psychological preconditions may induce the Negro to project the rejection of himself to the rejection of the collectivity. In the case of most Negro teen-agers, especially lower class, this inability to form cohesive, stable, durable, and goal-oriented groups has frequently been observed. However, the Negro's traditional lack of collective cohesion is increasingly being modified by a sharpening of collective awareness and the growth of an assertive identity.

---

[44] Reported by the Washington Post Service (Washington, D. C., March 13, 1967).

(3) Generalizations about the nature of one or a number of Negro youth subcultures are extremely difficult. Mid-20th-century America has seen a proliferation of Negro movements and orientations. Lower-class youth are characterized by personal, material, and frequently delinquent aggression. This behavior is a product of the unique combination of racial background, lower-class conditions, and ghetto living. A rising Negro middle class furnishes increasing numbers of youth who approach the issue of improving the Negro's lot by more rational and political means. Many educated young Negroes have joined protest movements to achieve integration and equality in peaceful ways. At the same time, such activities alleviate the problem of identity that is central to the modern Negro situation and is at the core of variegated expressions and ideological persuasions of Negro youth. Besides social activist subcultures, there are extremist Negro movements, the "black nationalists" and the "black internationalists," aiming at establishing black supremacy on a national or world basis, respectively.

(4) For most Negroes, family life is lower-class life and combines the insidious factors of lack of self- and other-respect, frequent family disruption, father-absence, illegitimacy, and matricentrism. In the process, masculinity is challenged and demeaned, burdening the young Negro male with extra problems of identity.

(5) The Negro adolescent is expected to make the transition from child to adult under additional conditions of conspicuous disadvantage and adversity. First, he is likely to be undereducated due to actual discrimination, segregated schooling that seldom equals the quality of white or integrated schooling, poor self-attitudes, defeatist perception of the educational institution resulting in the self-fulfilling prophecy, and finally, conditions of lower-class living in a ghetto where privacy, encouragement, and financial means for formal learning are limited. Second, his chances of finding a job are significantly reduced, and even if he finds employment, his wages are considerably below those of the white worker. However, the Negro female shows a trend of her own, more closely approximating and in some cases even exceeding the economic stature of her white counterpart. Third, parallel symptoms have been discovered in the realms of health, infant mortality, and life expectancy, showing evidence of the failure to bring mid-20th-century affluence and equal living standards to the American Negro.

jewish youth

Characterization by Contrast with Negro Youth

It appears strikingly helpful to begin the modal description of Jewish teen-agers by contrasting them to Negro teen-agers. Modern Jewish youth, in more than one way, encounter opposite experiences from the Negro youth. First of all, their parents or grandparents came to the United States as free individuals and were allowed to participate in the general affairs of the country from the very beginning—some degree of anti-Semitism notwithstanding. Another factor that distinguishes Jewish from Negro teen-agers is the salience of their religiocultural background. Even though a Jewish youngster may not believe in the theological doctrines of Judaism, the awareness of an age-old cultural heritage can inspire him with a feeling of belonging that leaves no room for the type of *anomie* experienced by the vast majority of Negro youth. While Jews point with pride to their history of several thousand years and refer to famous names from Moses to Einstein, most Negroes would prefer to forget their short history, which they understandably perceive as a chronicle of humiliation and inferiority. In the case of the Jewish people, pride in a common historical background makes fellow members seem more worthy of assistance and association. As a consequence, Jewish people have been known, envied, and often criticized for their explicit "clannishness." Negroes, on the other side, have exhibited a low degree of unity and mutual appreciation and have only very recently, through protest movements, shown signs of developing some degree of racial and ethnic pride and solidarity. It is a common complaint among Negroes themselves that "Negroes don't stick together" and therefore lose out in the struggle for equality.

The availability as well as the appreciation of education also differ for the two minority groups. Negroes have been one of the least educated population segments in the United States—partially because of discrimination and lack of opportunity and partially because of subcultural norms that held little appreciation for formal education. In contrast, Jews have always exhibited a remarkable emphasis on education—as reflected in statistics showing that 65% of Jewish youth of college age are attending institutions of higher education.[1] This constitutes a percentage roughly twice that of the general American population and several times that of the Negro population.

Another differentiating variable is socioeconomic standing. While the Negro population makes up a substantial portion of America's lower socioeconomic classes, most Jewish families could probably be classified as middle and upper-middle class. Few American Jewish families ever experience the type of crisis that would motivate them to resort to public relief, and the relatively few indigent Jewish families that actually do experience such a crisis are, as a rule, helped by relatives or Jewish welfare agencies. Moreover, their indigency is usually merely situational and not chronic as in the case of many Negro families. Related to socioeconomic class and wealth are, of course, the type of housing and the neighborhood lived in, with Jews and Negroes most likely living at opposite ends of the socioeconomic continuum. Unlike a majority of Negro teen-agers who have to use the streets for recreation and mixing with their peers, Jewish teen-agers normally have access to attractive facilities provided either by their Jewish community, such as the Jewish Community Centers and Hillel Foundations, or by the general public, which very rarely discriminates against Jews.

The Jewish family has traditionally shown a degree of stability and integration that is hardly matched by any other segment of the population and certainly not by the Negro population. Also, Jewish family life is interwoven with ethnic practices, thus giving the children the immense psychological benefit of a number of meaningful rituals and ceremonies that mark religious observances, holidays, family events, and rites of passage.

In sum total, then, Jews are equipped with a center of gravity, their common religiocultural heritage, which is lacking in the Negro population—except in some extremist groups, like the Black Muslims, and in some purposeful protest movements, such as CORE and other determined Negro civil rights organizations.

---

[1] David Boroff, "Jewish Teen-Age Culture," *The Annals of the American Academy of Political and Social Sciences,* Vol. 338 (November, 1961), p. 83.

Diversity within the Jewish Community

It would be misleading to leave the reader with the impression that contemporary American Jews enjoy complete collective cohesion, cultural uniformity, and undiluted ethnic identity. There are several reasons why such overall collective integration is missing from the American scene of the mid-20th century. Two of the main reasons are the internal diversity of the Jewish community and the dynamics of the urban-industrial environment, which has subjected a number of important dimensions of the Jewish community to change. A brief statement concerning the internal diversity follows immediately; a more detailed discussion concerning the changing dimensions of the Jewish community follows in the next section.

To speak of a Jewish teen-age subculture in the singular would be a misconception, since it would indicate the assumption of a uniform and monolithic Jewish culture. There is no such uniformity among the 5½ million American Jews. A more realistic picture of Jewish teen-age life would be conveyed by subdividing the Jewish population into more unique groups based primarily on place of residence, social class, particular theological orientation (Reform, Conservative, Orthodox), time of immigration to the United States, and other important variables. Such diversity, plus a generally diminishing sense of ethnic uniqueness among American Jewry, throws doubt on the justifiability of referring to a general Jewish teen-age subculture.

A more accurate portrayal of the Jewish youth's experience of adolescence should take this diversity into consideration and treat each subgroup's life experiences separately. However, such finely divided discussion is not possible in the brief frame of this chapter and, moreover, is severely limited by lack of reliable research findings covering all these groupings. Focus delimitation is therefore necessary, and primary attention is concentrated on American-born, middle- and upper-middle-class, religiously liberal Jewish youth. The behavior patterns of Jewish youth who are characterized by these criteria tend to resemble those of teen-agers of the Gentile middle and upper-middle class.

In spite of the considerable degree of assimilation into the Gentile society, there is, however, no doubt that a number of unique traits exist among Jewish adolescents that are widespread and typical enough that they can be thought of as being generic to a number of modal expressions.

Jewish Youth's Adjustment to Changing Dimensions of the Jewish Community

Other aspects that modify and limit generalization about a "typical" Jewish youth must take into consideration the sociocultural changes within the Jewish community that apparently continue to diminish the "typicalness" of Jewish youth. A number of forces that have traditionally worked for a sense of Jewish belonging and solidarity, and thus for a collective and personal identity, seem to be waning. Such vanishing or changing forces include ghetto-living, the belief in Judaic theology, anti-Semitism, Zionism, and endogamy.

Yet it should be clearly understood that the effects of these sociocultural changes, largely working toward assimilation of the Jewish minority into the larger Gentile society, have not yet completely erased ethnic uniqueness, but have, in a sense, added a new and unique dimension: the requirement of Jewish youth to adjust to these changes. In other words, the very fact that Jewish youth are exposed to sociocultural change in their community has added identifiable characteristics to their life experiences and has influenced their adolescent process.

The following discussion intends to elaborate on several of the above-mentioned changing dimensions and on how such changes have affected the attitudes, orientations, and opportunities of American Jewish youth.

De-ghettoization. If one views American life as being primarily urban life, then the saying that "Jewish people are like everyone else only more so" appears to have some validity, because the Jewish community in the United States meets all the criteria of general urbanism— "only more so." Urban living patterns were particularly conspicuous in the lives of earlier generations of American Jews, who tended to cluster in inner-city areas, in homogeneous neighborhoods that resembled ghettos. While the mid-20th-century Jewish community is still an urban community, there has been a marked decentralization of Jewish residential areas. The much-written-about population movement to suburbia has also involved a signficant proportion of Jewish people. Fred Massarik studied the ecological patterns of the Jewish population in the United States over the past two to three decades and discovered that most big cities have lost part of their Jewish population to the surrounding suburbs.[2] For example, in the 1920's Buffalo's east side accounted for ap-

---

[2] Fred Massarik, "The Jewish Community," in Edward C. McDonagh and Jon E. Simpson (eds.), *Social Problems: Persistent Challenges* (New York, Holt, Rinehart & Winston, 1965), pp. 14–22.

proximately 70 per cent of the Jewish population of the city. In the 1960's, most of the Jewish population had migrated to various other areas, mostly suburban, and had begun mingling with the rest of the population.[3] Los Angeles' east side Jewish population declined from 35,000 in 1940 to less than 10,000 in 1957, and it migrated to the western part of the city and to various suburbs, notably to the San Fernando Valley. Similar population shifts have been studied in other metropolitan areas, such as Minneapolis and Newark.[4]

The new ecological conditions, where Jews and Gentiles increasingly live next door to each other, have contributed to the blurring of the formerly distinct outlines of the Jewish community in more than merely ecological terms—they have also blurred the psychological outlines. There are no longer as many close Jewish neighbors as there used to be to reinforce each other in respect to the observance of religious and subcultural rituals and holidays; Jewish youngsters mingle increasingly with Gentile neighborhood friends, become members of ethnically mixed peer cliques and gangs, come to divide their loyalty between the home and the peer group, and are tempted to engage in exogamy to a greater extent than their parents. The previously homogeneous association with family, relatives, and Jewish peers in the ghetto-like neighborhood had integrated them into the religious patterns of their religiocultural heritage. Among other things, this provided them with a rite of passage (Bar Mitzvah), which assisted in the transition from child to adult status. Such auxiliary subcultural devices, promoting a sense of identity and easing the adolescent transition, tend to remain unevoked and possibly even disappear in a situation where the members of the subculture live in isolation from each other for more than one or two generations.

Toward secular and liberal religious thought. In respect to the theological specifics of Judaism, more than mere relaxation of religious dicta can be observed—the trend most nearly resembles a forgetting of the religious heritage. A majority of Jewish teen-agers accept their *cultural* Jewishness but see little value in the religious elements. The religious aspects of Judaism appear to be of small significance as an active and compelling force in their lives. Jewish youth involved in a college education are increasingly inclined to perceive a deep and often irreconcilable conflict between science and religion. Nonobservance of and deviance from the religious customs among Jewish people is probably most pronounced among college youth. Observers have found that Jewish college students feel severely challenged by their academic ex-

---

[3] Massarik, *op. cit.*, p. 16.
[4] *Ibid.*

perience and that their childhood notions about religion, especially their credo of a personal God, frequently break down under the influence of courses in philosophy, physical and chemical sciences, psychology, and sociology. For many of them, the divine origin and literal truth of the Scriptures become questionable. The college milieu proves to have a particular shattering and disturbing effect on those students who are well versed in and deeply committed to the doctrines of traditional Judaism. Many of them may have studied the Talmud and Torah (religious writings) or may have attended Yeshiva (Orthodox day school) and acquired a profound conviction about the verity of Judaic teachings. Early in their college career, they perceive fundamental conflicts between what they have learned in the synagogue and the insights of modern science as taught in college. The resultant personal dilemma was succinctly summed up by one student who reasoned: "How can I be a Jew unless I am Orthodox? But since I can no longer be Orthodox, how can I be a Jew?"[5] How can this dilemma be resolved? It seems that most Jewish college students retain the type of religious commitment that, at best, is a *verbal* approval of Judaism and does not entail any pronounced behavioral involvements. They also retain some degree of ethnic loyalty that, however, is more familistic in nature than subcultural.

The extent of alienation from Judaic doctrine on the part of Jewish college students has been revealed by a number of different studies. The National Opinion Research Center at the University of Chicago questioned several thousand 1961 graduates from 135 different colleges and found that 60% of the Jewish students practiced their religion very little or not at all; that only 14% attended religious services with any degree of regularity, that is, at least once a month (contrasted with 88% of Catholic students and 65% of Protestant students); and that a mere 1% of the Jewish students claimed to derive greatest satisfaction from religious beliefs and activities (contrasted with 15% of the Catholic students and 7% of the Protestant students).[6] Alfred Jospe, another observer of Jewish students, presented even more negative findings than the NORC, reporting that although Jewish students professed a high regard for the synagogue (91% agreed that it stands for the best in Jewish life), only 5% testified that they attended services regularly, at least once a month, or that they observed any of the Jewish rituals and

---

[5] Alfred Jospe, "The Sense of Jewish Identity of the Jewish College Student," *The Jewish Digest* (May, 1965), p. 37.

[6] Andrew M. Greeley, *Religion and Career: A Study of College Graduates,* a publication of the National Opinion Research Center (New York, Sheed and Ward, 1963), pp. 152–53.

ceremonies such as the Sabbath, the holidays, Pesah, etc.[7] Even at
Brandeis University, a Jewish-sponsored institution, only about a third
of the students professed "Judaism as a religion," agreeing wholly or substantially with its beliefs and traditions.[8] A study by Joseph Maier and
William Spinrad discovered that only 8% of Jewish teen-agers believed
it important to live in accordance with the teachings of their religion,
while 42% of the Catholic and 15% of the Protestant teen-agers held
this conviction.[9]

The generality and vagueness of Jewish teen-agers' conception of
such fundamental religious principles as, for example, the nature of God,
has been discovered by a survey inquiring into the college students'
choice of definition of what God is or can mean. The responses ranged
from belief in a personal God to the assertion that belief in God is a
superstition. Few Jewish students professed a belief in a personal God.
On the other side, "the largest number of those who indicated any kind
of 'religious' belief, state that they believe in a God about whom they
can say very little except 'that I sometimes sense him as a mighty
spiritual presence permeating all mankind and nature.' "[10] A similar
picture emerged from students' responses to the question: "To whom do
you owe your greatest loyalty—to God, your government, your people,
your family, or none?" The findings showed that 75% of the Catholic
students thought that loyalty to God takes precedence over any other
type of loyalty. Only 10% of the Jewish students indicated such religious
loyalty, while 74% chose their families as the object of greatest loyalty.[11]

These findings invite the conclusion that Judaism for most Jewish
youths is hardly a profound commitment or a deliberate choice of orientation, but rather the passive acceptance of a familiar milieu. A representative Jewish teen-age opinion was voiced by one girl: "I like
the tradition. I like to follow the holidays when they come along. But
you don't have to worship in the traditional way. You can communicate
in your own way. As I see it, there's no real difference between being
Jewish, Catholic, or Protestant."[12]

One can easily see that with these secular attitudes, Bar Mitzvah,
a rite of passage for the Jewish boy, is rapidly vanishing from Jewish
families or is converting into a relatively meaningless ritual that has

---

[7] Jospe, op. cit., p. 36.

[8] Thomas B. Morgan, "The Vanishing American Jew," Look (May 5, 1964), p. 46.

[9] Joseph Maier and William Spinrad, "Comparison of Religious Beliefs and
Practices of Jewish, Catholic and Protestant Students," The Atlanta University Review
of Race and Culture (4th Quarter, 1958).

[10] Jospe, op. cit., p. 35.

[11] Jospe, op. cit., p. 36.

[12] Boroff, op. cit., p. 82.

largely become incongruent with the secular environment to which Jewish teen-agers progressively adapt themselves.

Decline of anti-Semitism. Anti-Semitism, like any strong sentiment, can manifest itself in two forms: *prejudice,* which is a set of attitudes not amenable to the law, and *discrimination,* which is overt action and possibly amenable to the law. Although it is true that American Jews have occasionally been victims of anti-Semitism, its scope and intensity can never be compared with the experiences of Negroes, Mormons, West Coast Orientals, Jehovah's Witnesses, and the American Indians. Moreover, whatever limited anti-Semitism may have existed has markedly decreased over the past decades. In fact, American Jews today enjoy more respect *as Jews* and greater equality as citizens than at any time in American history. This equalization and gradual disappearance of adverse attitudes and practices can be observed in all areas of life. Due to the passing of the Fair Employment Practices laws and the investigations of the Anti-Defamation League, job discrimination against Jews as well as other minority group members declined from being ubiquitous in the 1930's to being rare and virtually nonexistent in the 1960's. This development can also be detected in college admission practices. While the practice of discriminating against Jewish applicants was widespread in the 1920's and '30's and into the early 1940's, when many colleges maintained a quota system which limited the number of Jewish students to a fixed percentage of the student body, today's institutions of higher learning very rarely consider ethnic background as a criterion on which to base the decision for admission. The Anti-Defamation League in cooperation with the American Council on Education has effected a revision of application blanks to eliminate questions regarding the racial or religious background of applicants in more than one thousand schools. The Anti-Defamation League's attack on discrimination in housing included persuasion of owners, actual or threatened exposure of the discriminatory practices in the public press, and the promotion of laws prohibiting differential treatment. The legal implication proved most effective, and in the 1940's the Supreme Court ruled that restrictive leases were not enforceable in the courts of the country. Since then, many city and state ordinances have outlawed housing discrimination of any kind. It must be added that the enforcement of these ordinances and laws did not run into popular opposition. Here was a set of rules for which the general public was ready. It was not another instance of Prohibition, which led to an unsuccessful conclusion.

Jewish teen-agers are aware of the decline of anti-Semitism and freely regard their identity as acceptable to society at large. Most teen-agers think that anti-Semitism, if it exists at all, is mild and usually expressed only in the form of humor, satire, and caricature. It appears that American Jewish teen-agers have, in a sense, even reconciled themselves to the atrocities of the Hitler regime. "One Jewish boy, with the rest of the group assenting, asserted that 'to kill six million Jews you have to be mentally ill.' He then insisted that such people 'need help.'"[13] Such calm and acquiescent evaluation of the massacre of brethren apparently indicates that Jewish teen-agers do not feel persecuted, threatened, or inferior.

The functions of the decline of anti-Semitism include a number of different consequences. The obvious function, intended and strived for, was, of course, the cessation of discriminatory practices and the opening-up of recreational, political, educational, and general social opportunities, which are now virtually unlimited, or at least undifferentiated from the general public. However, a function that was not intended was general decline of *esprit de corps,* the sense of collective belonging, brotherhood, and common destiny nourished by the awareness of a common persecutor from whose enmity and cruelty one can be saved only by strong in-group cohesion, cooperation, and mutual assistance. With the removal of the outside aggressor, a good portion of the above-named in-group senti-ments has also been removed. This, of course, is not to say that all such sentiments and their implementations have disappeared. For example, the Jewish community welfare agencies are still active, effective, and probably will remain that way in the future; the Anti-Defamation League is still carrying on its work; private and official agencies still continue to investigate crimes committed against the Jewish people.

Yet, "being Jewish, for many students, is neither a problem nor a challenge. It's simply a condition of their lives."[14] This means that Jewish background is no longer reason for embarrassment or exultation for a Jewish youth. He has become respectable, and his cause has vanished. His values and norms increasingly align themselves with those of the Gentile environment and become similar, if not identical with the given social setting of the Gentile world. It has been observed that this willing adjustment acquires strong local color. For example, on most campuses Jewish students do not maintain indigenous standards but accept those of the hierarchy of the Anglo-Saxon milieu, which they often mistake for the standards of the macroscopic social situation that they plan to enter upon graduation. A Jewish Harvard student, although regarding his ethnic heritage as fine and respectable and synagogue attendance as commendable, probably is more concerned with projecting

---

[13] Boroff, p. 81.
[14] Jospe, *op. cit.,* p. 34.

a "Harvard personality" than an ethnic model and prefers to look, dress, and talk like the "Harvard man."

Decline of Zionist zeal. For American Jewry, the age-old desire and demand for a Jewish homeland in Palestine long functioned as a symbol of ethnic assertion and in the process, reinforced ethnic solidarity and *esprit de corps.* Old and young Jews the world over found in Zionism a cause worth the investment of time, energy, and finances. Jewish teen-agers could accept it as a unique test of their ethnic identity and vicariously participate in the growth of a young nation. Zionism had the effect of a catalyst, accentuating their feeling of ethnic belonging. However, this was in the 1940's and '50's, before and immediately after the formation of Israel as a Jewish state, when the struggle for its establishment and existence was critical and needed worldwide Jewish support. Today, Israel has entered a formalized and routine phase that is no longer as inspiring as it was in the past. Views and relationships between America's Jews and the "homeland" have become more formal and dispassionate. In fact, the exchange of American and Israeli students has not had the bonding and inspiring effect that was expected. The harsh reality of the kibbutz and the unrealistic attitudes of many affluent American Jews have considerably cooled the enthusiasm of both American and Israeli teen-agers. It appears that young American Jews are becoming increasingly less interested in their Jewish "homeland" and more in comfortable suburbia, exchanging the hard work of the kibbutz for the nearest college campus and enjoying their Gentile neighbor just as much as the *sabra.*

American Jewish youth's disengagement from Zionist passion has manifested itself in several ways. First, the membership of the Inter-collegiate Zionist Federation of America has dropped from 10,000 Jewish students during and after World War II to approximately 2,500 members in the mid-1960's.[15] Another method of measuring Jewish youth's attitudes toward Israel was through surveys. One survey question submitted to Jewish students in the United States was "Assume that you had sufficient funds to visit two foreign countries during your lifetime and could make your decision now, which countries would you choose?" The tabulations found that 69% selected France, with the attractions of Paris constituting their first choice. Twenty-for per cent selected England, and Israel was third choice with only about 20%.[16]

Although the 1967 Israeli-Arab war revitalized some Zionist concern, as an over-all trend Zionism as an instrument against injustice and insecurity has declined. Zionism no longer characterizes Jewish

---

[15] Jospe, *op. cit.,* p. 38.
[16] Jospe, *op. cit.,* p. 39.

collective identity from which Jewish adolescents could derive a sense of cause and solution.

Declining endogamy. The practice of endogamy is another fading Jewish tradition. Intermarriage, or mixed marriage, is defined as the union of a Jew to a Gentile without the explicit promise to raise the children in the Jewish faith. Some observers, including a number of rabbis, are concerned about the great number of young Jewish men and women who are literally threatening the future of Judaism in America through exogamy and their ever-increasing tendency to raise their children outside of the faith. Judaism's strength is perceived as lying in the home, and if the home is not united in the Jewish faith, then Judaism is seen as endangered. Rabbi Max Schenk, president of the New York Board of Rabbis, warned that if the present "alarming" rate of intermarriage is allowed to continue unchecked, "the vitality and the entire future of the Jewish people would be jeopardized."[17] As recently as 1957, the Census Bureau found the intermarriage rate of Jews safely under 10%.[18] But since then the rate has apparently climbed steeply. A number of surveys traced this upward trend. Sociologist Erich Rosenthal gathered data in Washington, D. C., during the late 1950's and found that the rate of intermarriage involving Jews amounted to 13.1%. However, this figure was computed from married couples of all age-brackets. To determine the current trend, the researcher computed the rates for separate generations and found that intermarriage in the older, immigrant generation was as low as 1.4%; for the second generation, the native-born of foreign parentage, 10.2%; and for the third and subsequent generations, 17.9%. In addition, Rosenthal discovered that college-educated Jews showed the highest rate of intermarriage, exceeding the third generation by 100%, with 37%. Furthermore, the study estimated that approximately 70% of the children of mixed marriages were not brought up as Jews.[19]

A different study, focusing on college campuses, supports Rosenthal's findings. For example, it was found that two-thirds of the students at Brandeis University had no objection to marrying a Protestant, and 40% had no objection to marrying a Catholic.[20] Other observations indicate that discrimination because of religious background is fast dis-

---

[17] Quoted by Morgan, *op. cit.*, p. 43.

[18] Bureau of the Census, *Current Population Survey* (March, 1957). (The only Census survey to include a question on religion.)

[19] Erich Rosenthal, "Studies of Jewish Intermarriage in the United States," in *American Jewish Yearbook 1963*, Vol. 64 (Philadelphia, the Jewish Publication Society of America, 1963), pp. 3–53.

[20] Morgan, *op. cit.*, p. 46.

appearing across the country, interdating is increasing, and fraternity memberships are becoming mixed.

However, such institutions as Brandeis University, with an unusually high proportion of intellectual, liberal, and cosmopolitan Jewish students, may not provide a representative picture of Jewish sentiments about intermarriage. One should be prepared to find different opinions at many other schools. For example, Jospe reported that only roughly "10% of the Jewish students who were interviewed say that they are prepared to marry outside their faith (84% say they are opposed to it), while 27% of the Catholic and 45% of the Protestant respondents would."[21] These figures, conveying considerably more conservative attitudes toward intermarriage than is suggested by the Brandeis survey, probably prevail at many campuses where the Jewish segment consists of predominantly upper-middle-class youth who prefer social life to be somewhat more separate and exclusive. As David Boroff pointed out:

> The Hillel director at Wisconsin put it bluntly: "Let's face it. Jewish parents send their daughters here to meet nice, bright Jewish boys." And on a bulletin board at the Hillel house, there was a blunt declaration of its *raison d'être:* "Meet your spouse at the Hillel House."[22]

It is interesting to observe that exogamy is viewed less severely by the Jewish community when it involves a Jewish female, since her children are automatically considered Jews, while the offspring from the union of a Jewish male and a Gentile female are considered Gentile; their inclusion into the Judaic religion usually requires formal conversion procedures.

Stable Dimensions: Familism and Economic Salience

Continuing familism. In general, however, the adverse attitude of Jewish parents toward intermarriage is based less on religious objection than on familistic considerations. Their primary parental concern is more often the marital success of their children, fearing that enduring adjustment would be more difficult and perilous with a mate of a different background and religion. Family orientation is just as noticeable on the part of Jewish youth as it is on the part of their parents. The NORC survey revealed that 71% of the Jewish students stated that they derive

---

[21] Jospe, *op. cit.,* p. 34.
[22] Boroff, *op. cit.,* p. 87.

their greatest satisfaction from family relationships. The figures for Catholic and Protestant students on this question were 59% and 63%, respectively.[23]

Recalling earlier-stated findings reflecting the remarkable religious liberalness of Jewish youths, the most logical explanation for their conservative attitudes toward intermarriage thus appears to be the dimension of familism rather than religiosity.

Several other behavior patterns in Jewish life can probably be better explained by the Jewish emphasis on family orientation and integration than by religious motivation. One trait is the emphasis on premarital chastity. Jewish teen-agers tend to be characterized by a sexual morality that apparently is somewhat more conservative than that of the non-Jewish teen-ager. In Jewish teachings, still influential with and reflected by many Jewish children's behavior, there is a powerful emphasis on premarital chastity, especially for girls. Jewish mothers inculcate in their daughters the admonition that the loss of chastity is catastrophic and that it stands in the way of "self-realization," maturity, and security. Authoritative opinion has it that the resulting sex ethic among Jewish girls condones, in lieu of intercourse, promiscuous petting that preserves technical virginity.[24] Sexual conservatism appears to be but one aspect of an overall syndrome of overprotection of the Jewish girl. It seems that when she is away at school, she is more often financially supported by her parents than is her Gentile friend.

A second family-related characteristic is the low delinquency rate among Jewish teen-agers, a rate consistently lower than that of the Gentile population. Jewish teen-age gang activities are virtually unknown.

Another family-related characteristic is the great value attached to education. The valuation of education is constantly illustrated by sustained family support and encouragement, the high proportion of college attendance by both Jewish boys and girls, and their higher than average academic success. James S. Coleman, in his study of ten high schools, observed that Jewish teen-agers overachieve, relative to Protestants and Catholics, in a number of areas, including social as well as scholastic activities. The Jewish girls overachieve most noticeably as members of the leading crowd (up to 62%; for Jewish boys 56%), as best dressed, and in successful dating.[25]

It is interesting to note that the Jewish teen-agers overachieve at activities wholly consistent with the values of the middle-class Gentile

[23] Greeley, op. cit., p. 153.

[24] Boroff, op. cit., p. 81.

[25] James S. Coleman, The Adolescent Society (New York, Free Press, 1963), pp. 245n, 283.

community—which brings us back to the realization that differences between Jewish and Gentile teen-agers are mainly differences of degree and not differences of kind.

Economic salience. One of the more explicit features of the economic life of the Jewish population is a concentration in certain types of professions and careers. Fred Massarik, in his 1951 Los Angeles study, found that "in general, the greatest portion of the Jewish male labor force is classifiable in the 'manager-proprietor' category (36.8% in Los Angeles, according to the 1951 study)."[26] This "one-third-plus" proportion of the Jewish labor force in the manager-proprietor category appears to hold true for many, if not most, Jewish communities; it is usually followed in size by the professional-technical category, constituting 10 to 20% of the total Jewish labor force, 17.6% in Los Angeles in 1951.[27] A high proportion of the Jewish females were found to work in the clerical and sales branch, slightly more than 50% of them were so classified in the Los Angeles survey.[28]

The conclusion that emerges from these surveys is that the socioeconomic level of the Jewish families is much higher than the average that prevail's in the community at large. (However, the internal diversity of the Jewish population requires qualification of this generalization. It has been found that the Reform group averages an annual income that is higher than that of either the Conservative, Orthodox, or nondefined Jewish groups.[29])

Jewish youth enter thus on an economic scene that promises a more prosperous and successful outcome of economic pursuits than is the case for many of their Gentile friends. These economic achievements are not the result of chance or random incidence. Although the decline of ghetto life affected the economic practices of the Jewish people, leading to more discrete and independent business operation and thus to a reduced role as an integral part of the Jewish community, a certain degree of economic alliance and cooperation still forms a salient feature of Jewish economic life. Being Jewish is more often an asset than a liability, since it ordinarily opens more doors to employment than it shuts. Given the extremely low incidence rate of discriminatory practices against Jewish youth in the United States and given the high proportion of proprietorship and managership within the Jewish population, a Jewish youth seeking a job and trying to embark on a career can freely apply himself to the "external" Gentile business world as well as take advantage of the widespread web of informal social relations and "con-

---

[26] Massarik, *op. cit.*, p. 19.
[27] *Ibid.*
[28] *Ibid.*
[29] *Ibid.*

nections" within the Jewish community. Through family and community connections, the Jewish youth has relatively little difficulty in entering the labor force and finding employment with a Jewish proprietor or manager. The Massarik survey in Los Angeles revealed that among Jewish young people through age 29, 21.6% reported that being Jewish helped them in securing employment, while only 13.5% thought of it as a handicap,[30] the latter being a negative perception that may have been more often the result of rationalization than of actually experienced discrimination.

Summary

Jewish youth contrasts sharply with the Negro youth. His ancestors came to the new continent not as slaves but as free men who participated widely in aspects of local and national life, some degree of anti-Semitism notwithstanding. The religiocultural heritage, though declining in salience, still helps to prevent Jewish youth from feeling the type of *anomie* and worthlessness that is common among the Negro population. The socioeconomic and educational standards of the Jewish people are ordinarily far above those of Negro families.

Generalization as to a uniform Jewish subculture is, however, difficult, since there are a number of distinct subgroups within. Discussion of the diversity as such is evaded, and focus delimitation reserves discussion to middle- and upper-middle-class Jewish youth, mostly of liberal religious orientation, who are characterized by many life conditions and behavior patterns that resemble those of their Gentile friends.

This assimilative process is helped along by a number of changing dimensions in the Jewish community. Over the past two to three decades, ecological shifts have resulted in de-ghettoization of Jewish living habits; religious convictions have partially faded into more secular and cultural values; declining anti-Semitism no longer challenges the Jewish subculture to bring forth united efforts to protect itself; Zionist zeal has changed into relatively dispassionate and usually merely verbal approval of the State of Israel; and endogamy, though still more consistently practiced than among most other religious groups, appears to be gradually losing its stringency.

However, these dynamic processes have still left enough ethnic uniqueness and, in fact, have added unique features through requiring the Jewish youth to adjust to them, so that some degree of generalization

---

[30] Massarik, *op. cit.*, p. 20.

seems justified. Generalizability is particularly supported by an appreciable exhibition of familism among Jewish people and by continuing economic salience and cooperation within the Jewish community.

The conclusion that evolves from this discussion is that, in as far as adolescence refers to status discontinuity, the life conditions of the Jewish adolescent lessen, if anything, the difficulties of the transition to the adult status. The conclusion appears warranted in the light of the closer-knit family and kinship group that is able to provide a number of acceptable adult models; the security of a more stable family life that is not as frequently disrupted by separations, desertions, and divorces as in the Gentile population; some degree of economic "nepotism" and business "connections," which frequently facilitate finding jobs and entering professional careers for the Jewish youth; and a religiocultural tradition that is an ever-present—though increasingly less frequently invoked— source for identity. The Jewish adolescent is thus in a better position than most of his Gentile friends to achieve personal identity and to overcome the intermittent social-structural discontinuity and unclarity of adolescence.

indian youth and
cultural change

Contrary to what is widely believed, the American Indian is not a "vanishing race"—unless ultimately through absorption into the dominant white society, a possibility only in the remote future. Rather, because of both the rapid numerical increase of the Indian population over the last two decades (50% are under age 21),[1] resulting in the pressure and inclination to leave the reservation, and the process of acculturation to the white man's culture, the American Indian is a minority group growing in size and importance. Although many American Indians are leaving their physical and cultural isolation on the reservations and are getting deeply involved in the acculturation process, they remain a distinct minority group, the absorption of which proceeds almost imperceptibly slowly and causes tremendous problems to Indians and whites alike. The basic disturbing and agitating force affecting the American Indian today is *cultural change*. He is abandoning his traditional ways and yet not fully accepting the ways of the dominant culture. *It is in the light of this process of cultural change that the situation of the Indian teen-ager must be viewed.*

It is obviously most difficult to speak of the American Indian in the singular as if he represents a uniform culture, since there are many tribes scattered throughout the entire American continent, which differ markedly in their cultural ways, including language, customs, rituals, beliefs, living habits, etc. However, it is on the strength of the ongoing cultural change that some generalizations can be made. The forces of change exert their impact on all Indians, regardless of whether they are Navahos, Crows, Seminoles, Apache, Sioux, or others, and leave similar residues

---

[1] Francis McKinley, "New Horizons for American Indians," keynote speech at the 18th Annual Convention of the Interstate Indian Council, Santa Fe, New Mexico, Aug. 16–20, 1965; p. 6.

of problems and patterns of reaction. For example, one of the recurrent and typical results is that the Indian teen-ager is thrown into a state of double marginality, suspended between his native culture and the white man's culture and between the status of child and of adult. Needless to say, adolescence for many Indian youngsters is a far more trying and confusing experience than for white teen-agers. If the trials and confusions of this period do not attract as much attention as one might expect, it is because the traditional stoic, calm, and withdrawn behavior patterns of the Indian prevent him from expressing his troubles in overt, especially verbal, ways.

The tribal diversity among American Indians makes it necessary to engage in a relatively abstract discussion that must sacrifice certain differences for the benefit of clearly recognizable *modal characteristics*. The other alternative would be to present an illustrative case study of a particular tribe, which, however, could turn out to be misleading, simplistic, and too ideographic to serve as a valid picture of the overall processes and problems of American Indians. To achieve such a general as well as systematic picture of today's Indian teen-agers, the discussion is divided into three aspects of the subject matter: the traditional psychological features presumably modal among traditional American Indians; the impact of the white man's culture upon these traditional features, modifying and sometimes discontinuing them for the younger generation; and a categorization of several major psychological reactions of Indian youth to the experience of cultural change.

Traditional Psychological Features

Two anthropological researchers at Stanford University, George D. and Louise S. Spindler, concluded on the basis of extensive surveys of ethnographic data, taken from tribes representing all the major Indian cultures in North America with the exception of the Southeastern Woodlands, that a number of psychological characteristics are more widely shared than others and may be regarded as constituting *modal tendencies*.[2] The anthropologists emphasized however, that these tendencies should not be understood as fixed psychological constants that express themselves in identical ways and for identical purposes in different Indian tribes. Rather, these tendencies represent basic themes which allow a variety of versions. It appears that this limited number of psycho-

---

[2] George D. Spindler and Louise S. Spindler, "American Indian Personality Types and their Sociocultural Roots," *Annals of the American Academy of Political and Social Sciences*, Vol. 311 (May, 1957), pp. 147–57.

logical dispositions is still distributed widely enough among adult Indians so that one may, in a very general sense, think of them as characteristic of the personality of the aboriginal American Indian. Included in the portrayal are the following traits: unemotional deportment that kept aggression and interpersonal conflict within the in-group at a minimum; a show of generosity that usually was more prescribed by custom than generated by personal feelings; the almost proverbial Indian stoicism in the face of pain, hunger, hardship, and frustration without complaining or showing discomfort; a high degree of individual autonomy that was correlated with a low degree of dominance-submission arrangements within the sociopolitical structures; a great regard for courage and temerity, especially when it was directed against the out-group; a belief in witchcraft; a disposition to practical jokes that usually was incorporated in tribal customs and rituals, thereby providing a controlled and institutionalized outlet for latent hostility; an inclination to take the present as the only concrete reality and to make decisions only when confronting concrete problems without weighing them in terms of long-range and abstract goals; a basic belief in the powerlessness of the individual confronting the universe, whose powers determine one's fate and from which the individual cannot escape, thereby setting up an attitude of doubt in the ability of personal volition as well as in the wisdom of holding an individual responsible for his action.

The Impact of Cultural Change

Today, these features are undergoing change, and the majority of Indian youth have considerably modified versions of them. The degree of modification or deviation from the aboriginal psychological structure usually depends on the extent of exposure to the outside culture, i.e., there exists a positive correlation between the exposure to the white man's culture and the modification of native ways. Many Indian children and teen-agers receive the white man's education while attending schools taught by white teachers, who almost inevitably serve as models and influential significant others. The Indian youth may be involved in one of three types of schools, the Bureau of Indian Affairs schools, public schools, or mission schools. To illustrate the scope of operation of the different schools, which all together enrolled approximately 142,000 Indian pupils in 1966, the B.I.A. schools included 33%, the public schools 61%, and mission schools 6% of the 142,000 children.[3] School

---

[3] U. S. Department of the Interior, Bureau of Indian Affairs, Division of Education, *Statistics Concerning Indian Education* (Washington, D. C., 1966).

enrollment of Indian youth has steadily increased over the past decades, and in 1966 the Bureau of Indian Affairs reported that approximately 93% of all school-aged Indian youth were in school.[4] The education of the Indian youth under white supervision, notwithstanding the fact that a few adult Indians may have joined the staff, creates a number of complex problems. First of all, the young Indian must usually leave his home if he is to be educated beyond 6th grade. This move throws him into a world totally different from that to which he has been accustomed. His new white peers probably accept him and show their desire to improve his knowledge about the white culture. In the process, they are unaware that their efforts seem paternalistic to the Indian youngster. He cannot help but feel supervised, inferior, and out of place. His reactions to this experience may be multifarious, depending on many variables, most of which cannot be discussed here. The two major reactions, however, consist of a withdrawal from and rejection of the white culture and, usually concomitantly, a feeling of shame and inferiority concerning his native ties. In either case, he cannot avoid continuous cultural conflicts between the traditional Indian ways and the white ways.

This brings us to the conflict between different values. While his tribal experience included the norms of sharing and economic interdependence and cooperation, the white society presents him with norms and values of competition and economic independence. He comes to live between two worlds. On the one hand there is the way of life represented by the culture of the Indians with whom he lived prior to his involvement in the white society. On the other hand, there is the modern American culture with its distinctive patterns and set of values. The more acculturated youths give evidence of severe conflict between modern aspirations and traditional attitudes and behavior patterns. In their passivity, restraint, and expectations of immediate results they are true sons of their Indian heritage. Yet they are no longer content with the simple satisfactions of their fathers. New materialistic goals evolve, the attainment of which can occur only in non-Indian society or on an exceptional reservation that offers advanced economic development.

Those young Indians who have continued their education through high school usually have also received sufficient vocational training to pursue a technical occupation and come to represent the most acculturated group on the reservation. However, the adolescent who is educated, trained to carry out a vocation, and has participated in the technologically advanced life of the white man may often feel limited and restricted in his career on the reservation. His vocational training and aspirations may throw him into an accelerated acculturation process,

---

[4] Reference 3.

since he depends on the white community to materialize his career and to find employment and lucrative business. He may try to join the main stream of American life by moving into a "border" town to set up a more exciting and successful enterprise. But he faces unequal odds. His white competitors have at their disposal more affluence, experience, prestige, and material implementation. Again, just as at the school, he feels patronized, secondary to the white peer, and therefore experiences feelings of inferiority. The only constructive function of this life experience may be that he retains his identity as a member of the Indian minority group—a rather negative manner of preserving identity. And yet, every aspect of public life to which he is exposed exerts pressure on him to adjust to the dominant culture. A near paradox ensues: the young Indian is forced to retain his identity, while at the same time pressured to live like a white man and adjust to the white culture. The difficulties growing out of this paradox leave many Indian teen-agers frustrated and inclined to either react in drastic, sometimes delinquent, styles or to turn to substitute gratifications.

The Indian youth tends to react to these conflicts in various ways. If he finds it impossible to reconcile the two cultures and perceives the patterns as too vastly different, he may either retreat to the minority group, or reject it completely and turn to the majority group—the latter decision being relatively uncommon, since the majority group might not accept him. If he feels rejected by the dominant culture, he occasionally reacts with hostility, becomes vindictive, and develops norms and values defined as delinquent by the dominant culture.

It appears that a common substitute gratification of the Indian youth involves the use of alcohol. Excessive drinking lies at the root of a significant portion of the unusually high crime and delinquency rate of American Indians. "Nationally, the Indian rate for all types of arrests is nearly 3 times that of Negroes and about 8 times that of the whites. . . . Drunkenness alone accounted for 71% of all Indian arrests reported in 1960."[5] Tribal courts regularly report that over half of all juvenile cases can be blamed on alcohol consumption. The hearings before the Senate Subcommittee to Investigate Juvenile Delinquency made special mention of the Indian drinking problem and revealed that in the mid-1950's such tribes as the San Carlos Apaches had to deal with alcohol-related delinquency that comprised 80% of all juvenile cases.[6] The Southern Ute and Mountain Ute reported that 61% of their juvenile cases were caused

[5] Omar Stewart, "Questions Regarding American Indian Criminality," *Human Organization,* Vol. 23 (Spring, 1964), p. 61.

[6] Hearings before the Senate Subcommittee to Investigate Juvenile Delinquency, Committee of the Judiciary, U. S. Senate, 84th Congress, 1st Session, March and April, 1955.

by drinking.[7] Similar reports came from the Navahos, Jicarilla Apaches, and others.[8] In general, these statistics seem to be representative for Indians all over the nation. "Indians have been arrested and convicted for illegal acts while under the influence of liquor at rates several times higher than have individuals of other minority groups. . . . If the reasons for excessive use of alcohol among Indians could be understood, their excessive crime rate would be understood."[9]

The reaction pattern of the Indian teen-ager can perhaps be understood better when one examines several additional items of culture shock. In his encounter with the white culture, he must learn a new concept of time—the white man's concept. The time dimension of Western societies which has traditionally been assumed to be an indisputably unilinear dimension ranging from the past to the future, is not shared by all Indians. For example, the Hopi language, and therefore Hopi thought, does not have tenses. As puzzling as this may appear to a white person, the Hopi do not have a conceptualization of the past, present, or future. There is only the space dimension, in which the Hopi can communicate events, plans, and anticipations just as precisely as the white man in his time dimension. Related to this linguistic peculiarity, the Indians exhibit behavior patterns that, according to "Anglo" standards, appear lethargic, passive, slow, even "lazy." Examination of this type of behavior in the context of the Indian's philosophy and world-view show that he considers life to be subject to supernatural powers over which the individual has no power—so he reasons, why hurry, aspire, plan, and try to determine things when it actually is futile and presumptuous? The Indian teen-ager must drastically revise this passive view and the corresponding behavior patterns if he is to achieve some measure of success and adjustment to the white man's culture. He must learn to plan, carefully budget time and energy, anticipate problems, and have relevant decisions for them in advance—in short, he must learn to think and act in Western abstractions and adjust to the Western type time dimension.

Another difficulty that the Indian youngster is bound to encounter in the white society is the value and stress on individuality. In many tribes, to be conspicuous, to be "different," is frowned upon. The Zuñi Indians of New Mexico serve as an illustration. Even leadership, or aspiration to it, is met with reluctance among them. Quite to the contrary in the white environment, excelling, outdoing, and achievement are valued and encouraged. The Indian pupil attending the white school

---

[7] Reference 6.
[8] *Ibid.*
[9] Stewart, *op. cit.*, p. 66.

finds himself in a strange and embarrassing situation; he is asked to be individualistic, to compete, and to outdo others. His strong inhibitions against "outstanding" and conspicuous behavior may make him feel ill at ease and prompt him to retreat further and remain impassive. Obviously, the customary competitive nature of the white classroom automatically places him in an extremely disadvantageous position. His inhibitions and hesitations slow down his progress and place him behind more competitive peers.

Statistics derived from research on assimilation of the Spokane Indians present a picture of their socioeconomic conditions that may serve as a representative example of what happens when Indians and whites share the same community. Comparison between a random sample of Spokane Indians and whites showed that the Indians had about 84% as much education, 56% as high a level of living, and only 38% as much income as the whites. The data lead to the conclusion that the Indians have not yet acquired the traits that would give them an equal position within the white community.[10] In their background setting, the family and tribe, they learned that the individual does not aspire to be "different." Their early conditioning process deeply ingrained this dictum into their behavior style; anyone who stood out ran the risk of being accused of showing off, and the group would take steps to bring him back in line. The most common social control mechanism was "shaming him out," i.e., ridiculing him, usually by hoots and howls or by teasing. The practice of "shaming out" is apparently a vestige of the aboriginal pattern of imposing discipline and maintaining social order through ridicule by elders or peers.[11]

There is one other aspect of the acculturation process that needs discussion in order to add more insight to the problems of the Indian youth. It has to do with his bilingualism, since he has to learn English in addition to the tribal language with which he grew up. The psychological consequences of bilingualism are not yet fully explored. But it is safe to say that besides the obvious function of communicating in two different ethnic settings, there are overtones of dual thinking, behaving, and belonging. The bilingual teen-ager must always be socioculturally and psychologically oriented to two different worlds. He cannot easily merge the two systems. As a result he has a divided linguistic allegiance and lives a life of divided perceptions where one object or event may have two different interpretations depending on which symbolic framework is applied. The end result of switching back and forth between one

---

[10] Prodipto Roy, "The Measurement of Assimilation: The Spokane Indians," *American Journal of Sociology*, Vol. 67 (March, 1962), p. 551.

[11] Alan Dundes and C. Fayne Porter, "American Indian Student Slang," *American Speech*, Vol. 38 (December, 1963), pp. 273–74.

and the other language and the constant divided perceptions is to create a psychological strain unknown and hardly imaginable to persons who speak only one language or one basic language and one or more "secondary" or academically learned languages. This strain can be so strong that it would not be difficult to measure the neural symptoms that indicate exhaustion, confusion, and inarticulation. A particular element of stress for the bilingual Indian youngster is the fact that he usually has a deep loyalty to the language he learned first, his ancestral language or mother tongue. This *prime conditioning* causes in most bilinguals—in spite of new allegiances, conformities, and commitments—an unconscious resistance to secondary interferences such as the use of other languages. This may show not only in phonetic deficiencies such as accent, but also in complex psychological processes that require logical and abstract formulations in speech or in thought. The Indian youngster normally joins the white society with a strong attachment to the language he learned first. He has a mastery and an ease in speaking it that he is very rarely able to equal later on in any other language. He feels familiar and comfortable with it, and he can express his most private thoughts and feelings and most intricate perceptions with it.[12]

The different facets of the acculturation process, as pointed out in the preceding paragraphs, have considerably altered the traditional psychological portrait of the Indian. Today's Indian teen-agers are characterized by a modified version of the aboriginal personality features. It is safe to assume that nearly all the traditional attitudes are diminishing in importance and adherence. Some traits have undergone greater reduction than others. Among the strongest traits affected by the acculturation process is the belief in witchcraft and supernatural powers that determine one's fate. Through exposure to the white man's education, scientific insight, and rational behavior patterns, the Indian teenager's conviction in tribal beliefs and customs becomes undermined. Just as he realizes the technological superiority, he is inclined to perceive psychological superiority in the white man's system. Nevertheless, the tendency to place power and determination outside of oneself, i.e., to prefer other-determination over self-determination, is still much more prevalent among Indian youth than might be expected after so many years of exposure to and education under the white man. This author has heard young Indians, in the process of completing a college education, express their conviction that certain tribal members have the ability to influence the lives of others by mere mental concentration. In other words, the same principle underlying Voodoo practices or the

---

[12] See a more detailed discussion in Joyce O. Hertzler, *A Sociology of Language* (New York, Random House, 1965), pp. 413*ff*.

tribal oracle of so-called primitive tribes is still operating—call it witch-craft or belief in mystic mental or spiritual powers. Moreover, many Indian youths have merely substituted one system of belief in super-natural forces and determination for another. It is common for Indians to synthesize their ancient supernatural beliefs with the newly imposed creeds of various modern, especially Christian, doctrines; often synthesis is not even necessary since the new belief is equally dependent on out-side supernatural forces. In effect then, many, if not most, Indian youngsters have merely exchanged one belief system for another, both characterized by supernaturalism, both serving the same function, and both convincing the believer of the outside determination of his fate. In fact, the powerlessness that the young Indian experiences when con-fronting the white world, the memory of utter defeat by the white man, and the initially imposed isolation on the reservation represent empirical stimuli that are likely to reinforce an attitude of powerlessness in the philosophical and religious realm. It would be an interesting research topic for the branch of sociology called *sociology of knowledge* to trace the connection between empirically experienced powerlessness and spiritually rationalized powerlessness.

In essence, then, the contemporary Indian teen-ager may not be appreciably different from his forefathers in his outlook on life. This notion was supported by a fascinating study by A. I. Hallowell, who found evidence of the surprising persistence of psychological structures.[13] His research with the Ojibwa Indians included several hundred men, women, and children who varied widely in their degree of acculturation to the white man's way of life. Some of them lived and subsisted almost in the aboriginal mode of life, while some were acculturated to the point of living more or less like other members of the larger society. Hallowell drew up two dimensions, one measuring the apparent degree of accul-turation on the basis of dress, language, religion, housing, etc., the other measuring psychological tendencies and dispositions. His findings were surprising. *He did not find any evidence of parallel psychological shift with increasing acculturation.* What changes he did find, concomitant with acculturation, were not progressive but rather regressive, resulting in disintegration and corrosion of social as well as psychological struc-tures. Corroboration of these findings came from a study by George D. Spindler, who investigated the Menomini Indians, dividing his subjects into four distinct levels of acculturation, from a native-ori-

---

[13] A. I. Hallowell, "Ojibwa Personality and Acculturation," in Sol Tax (ed.), *Proceedings and Selected Papers of the 29th International Congress of Americanists* (Chicago, University of Chicago Press, 1951).

ented base to a thoroughly acculturated white-collar category.[14] With the exception of the highest-level acculturated élite, men who had entered high-prestige positions equivalent to those of white persons in their vicinity, the Indians exhibited a strong stability and retention of traditional personality features, regardless of being native-oriented, in transition, or partially acculturated. These findings should serve as a warning against quickly resorting to the all-too-easy sociological conclusion that a shift in the social structure will immediately effect a corresponding shift in the psychological structure. Just as we talk of a *cultural lag*, we might do well to remember a *psychological lag*. This is not to say that psychological dimensions are static constants, rather that they are slow to change, slow to be reduced or expanded.

There is no doubt that many Indian youngsters learn to become more materialistically oriented, more competitive, and more individualistic. The problem is only that, preserving his minority identity as he does, he finds it difficult to integrate himself in the white community and put these newly acquired traits to good use for himself or others; on the other hand, he finds it equally difficult to feel comfortable and accepted in his native community. This dual social impairment makes for extremely slow change of the psychological structure since it cannot fully use either social system as a base for integration.

A Typology of Reactions

The above characterization of the contemporary Indian teen-ager pictured the most prevalent reaction to the impact of cultural change. The teen-ager reacting in this fashion may be classified as the marginal type. However, the encounter with cultural change can have a number of psychological results. A typology of *reaction types* was suggested by the Spindlers and seems to adequately and exhaustively sum up the possible psychological outcomes.[15] Adapted and modified to fit the Indian adolescent's experience, the paradigm includes five types.

The first, and as we have noted above, most frequently observed, type is the *marginal type*. For purposes of a brief summary, here are his main characteristics. This teen-ager is, in a sense, in a transitory stage, shifting from the Indian to the white style of life, a victim suspended between two different modes of life, with little if any allegiance

[14] George D. Spindler, *Sociocultural and Psychological Processes in Menomini Acculturation*, University of California Publications in Culture and Society, Vol. 5 (Berkeley, Calif., 1955).

[15] Spindler and Spindler, *op. cit.*

to either. Conversely, he often experiences rejection from both sides. His identity as an Indian is at low ebb, the traditional modal personality features are corroded, although whatever is left is definitely Indian and not white. His personality structure has been severely disturbed by the culture shock, the unprepared-for and unsuccessful encounter with the white man's culture, and the impact has left him virtually culturally "paralyzed." The symptoms of the culture shock and of the resulting marginality are numerous and hardly predictable. An Indian youth may exhibit an illogical mixture of hostility and violence and, on the other side, generosity and hospitality. All too frequently, outbursts of irrational behavior are accompanied by drinking—excessive drinking. At least two subtypes can be discerned: the youngster who behaves very aggressively —venting his frustrations and insecurities by irrational and sometimes violent or deviant actions; and the one who is achievement-oriented and attempts by various techniques to obtain white-appreciated statuses, thereby, however, frequently becoming even more frustrated, confused, and marginal. The two poles, the white and the Indian, appear hopelessly equidistant and unattainable to this teen-ager. He knows that the Indian heritage is beyond recall, and he also realizes that the attainment of the white man's style of life is an aim too high and too ambitious to ever materialize for him. And yet, pressures to adjust come from either side, usually incongruous and contradictory to each other. In a sense, the youngster must retain his identity as an Indian and yet learn to live like a second-class white man. The difficulties encountered in this paradoxical and conflicting situation leave the teen-ager without direction, often prodding him on to compensatory and delinquent patterns.

The adolescent period for this type of youth is a most trying experience. He is suspended not only between the Indian and the white world, but also between the world of the child and of the adult, since he no longer has recourse to the meaningful and aiding rituals of passage of his ancestors. As was remarked earlier, the reason why Indian adolescence does not express itself in more overt terms may be ascribed to the retention of stoic manners. It seems that it requires alcohol to loosen his emotions and to relax his psychological controls, as the statistics of the tribal courts reflect the adolescent's problems in the form of an extremely high alcohol-related delinquency rate.

The *native type* refers to a youngster raised almost exclusively as an Indian, with only superficial contacts with whites and their culture, living in and adhering to the traditional world of the Indian, speaking almost exclusively the language of his tribe. Even though the youth may know some English, he cannot be classified as bilingual since the white man's language takes such a secondary place that it hardly affects his thinking and conceptualizing of the world around him. Language barrier is one of the most, if not the most, formidable hinderances to acculturation. The degree of language barrier can be measured by subtracting the teen-ager's English verbal IQ from his native verbal IQ, the difference indicating a crude quotient of the degree of language barrier. In formula form:[16]

$$\begin{array}{c} \text{Native Verbal IQ} \\ - \text{ English Verbal IQ} \\ \hline = \text{Language Barrier} \end{array}$$

If, for example, a young Indian obtains a zero quotient, it would mean that he does not experience any language barrier, that he speaks both languages equally well and is therefore truly bilingual. One would hardly expect a zero or a low language barrier quotient in the case of the native-type teen-ager. Most probably, his proficiency in his mother tongue by far exceeds his English proficiency. Degree of language barrier normally is inversely correlated with acculturation. The native type is thus characterized by a high language barrier and a low degree of acculturation.

The native type represents, as closely as is possible today, the aboriginal personality type of his tribe. The transition from the status of child to the status of adult is guided, guarded, and determined by tribal rules and ceremonies. Helpful orientation is extended through the rites of passage, which clearly indicate to him new responsibilities and new rights. In addition, he is surrounded by visible adult models who are instrumental in introducing him early into the relatively uncomplicated division of labor of the kinship group or native community. One can hardly speak of adolescence in the strict sense of the definition. Since he is not equipped to adequately engage in the competitive and technologically as well as socially complex white society, he is prone to remain in the semi-isolation of his native setting, carry on the ancestral traditions, provide a traditional model for his offspring, and constitute a part of the slim stock of leaders trying to perpetuate his Indian culture.

The *reaffirmative-native type* refers to the teen-ager who spent his childhood in the traditional setting but who during his teens spent some years outside the reservation, usually in boarding schools, becoming closely involved in the white man's socioeconomic system. For one

---

[16] A more elaborate version of this principle can be seen in William R. Holland, "Language Barrier as an Educational Problem of Spanish-Speaking Children," in Staten W. Webster (ed.), *Understanding the Educational Problems of the Disadvantaged Learner* (San Francisco, Chandler Publishing Co., 1966), pp. 338–49.

reason or another, he found the white culture unacceptable or, possibly, was not motivated to adapt to it in the first place. He has returned to the primary-group environment of his family and tribe and prefers the well-defined social structure over the confusing complexity of the white world. He accepts the influence of his elders, who provide direction and meaning and therefore the necessary integrated psychological structure that is so important for mental survival. More than that, he readily and avidly, as far as the impassive and stoic Indian manners allow, reverts back to the tribal customs and ceremonies. This orthodox adherence is a means of overcoming and repressing the doubts that unavoidably arise as a result of experiencing another culture that reflects superiority in more than one way—for example, in health, technology, comfort, etc. The Indian youth attempts to counteract and suppress these doubts that endanger his Indian *gestalt* by eagerly participating in tribal customs. Nevertheless, in many youngsters who have had sufficiently close contact with the dominant culture, a degree of doubt about the adequacy of the Indian ways lingers on. These teen-agers cannot help but be somewhat deficient in their cultural integration into the Indian ways—though by no means to a degree justifying the classification of marginality. Their adolescent period is definitely mollified by their adherence to tribal definitions and rites of passage. Their perception of the statuses of child and adult is unambiguous, although interrupted by a confusing period away at school. But this interruption is better defined as a brush with marginality than as adolescence.

The *deviant type* is not restricted to the delinquent, but focuses primarily on the teen-ager who joins specific religious or ultraethnic subgroups. Such religious groups as the Peyote Cult and the Shaker Church hold a special attraction for the youth in need of a solution to the culture conflict and self-doubt engendered by exposure to situations of culture change. Membership in these esoteric and mystic groups serves several conflict-ameliorating functions. First of all, they provide the opportunity for an emotional outlet, channeling hostility and frustration into acceptable avenues—in other words, sublimating them. It is also a convenient mechanism for reducing inferiority feelings and for building up self-esteem through religious rationalization. In-group standards which may have suffered ambiguity and degradation through the impact of the dominant culture are now revived or revised to lend a new cohesion to the group. In this manner, the Indian youth finds a dignity and a sense of belonging that the ordinary reservation environment cannot give him. The Indian, like any other individual, needs a meaning for life, a rationalization of his frustrations and pains. Given the right psychological constellation and the social opportunity, he can develop it within the framework of special religious structures. The Peyote Cult in specific is apt to substitute, at least temporarily, a fantasy life for the real world, allowing the participant to escape from the indignities and deprivations of his everyday life. This method seems to function as an alternative to outbursts of violence and/or intoxication with alcohol.

How the adolescent's uncertainty concerning child and adult statuses is affected by such activities is hard to say. One is inclined to expect a considerable reduction of ambiguity and uncertainty because of the strong religious attachment, which provides identity in spite of possibly structural vagueness. In some instances, adulthood is a prerequisite for participation in certain religious ceremonies, so that the youngster who is permitted to participate automatically knows that he is now considered an adult.

Finally, the *acculturated type* refers to the teen-ager who, usually as a consequence of his parents' integration in the white community, perhaps because of his father's education and occupation, grows up almost exclusively according to the norms and the values of the white society. Although in essence it is usually the picture of the middle-class standards of living that is envisaged by the acculturated Indians, acculturation may be diverse, proceeding congruously to the structure and class level of the white milieu in which they find themselves. Thus acculturation can occur on the middle-class, labor-class, or upper-class level, or can correspond to any other white subgroup with which the Indian comes in contact.

The psychological constellation of this type shows a marked absence of some of the traditional traits of the aboriginal Indian. Their deportment is more flexible and their emotions are not suppressed by the typical Indian stoicism. Their belief in supernatural powers is adjusted to the "normal" religious versions of the white community, i.e., they are probably members of some "respectable" church or denomination. They do not display the hostility and frustration of their marginal cousins. However, they may show more anxiety instead. This may be due to their concern and lack of complete confidence that they really are acceptable members of the white community.

Actually, this type of teen-ager is assimilated into the white society and participates in the general teen-age subculture in the community of residence. His parents actually may encourage him to observe fads and fashions of his peers, since they are particularly sensitive about their middle-class aspiration and want the child to conform to all aspects of it. The adolescent experience of this type of Indian teen-ager is probably not noticeably different from that of his white peers.

Summary

It is now obvious that generalizations about Indian teen-agers *as a whole* are most difficult, if not unrealistic. The suggested typology is of help in bringing specificity and order into the otherwise too diverse picture. According to the analytical categorizations, most contemporary Indian youth suffer psychological strain under the impact of cultural change. This is particularly true of Indian youth who fall into the category of marginal men. This type, unlike the others, especially the native, deviant, and acculturated types, is faced with a compound marginality that is ambiguous in respect to both ethnic identity and child-adult statuses. The polarity between the white and the Indian culture results in a suspension that is characterized by paradoxical pressures. It is this type of contrapuntal pressure that seems to immobilize the mid-20th-century Indian teen-ager and impede his progress in either direction—the direction of the white as well as of the traditional Indian culture. In other words, the slow change of the psychological structure of the Indian teen-ager is usually due to the circumstance that neither sociocultural system—neither the white nor the Indian culture—is fully meaningful and acceptable to the contemporary Indian youth. As a result, the Indians as a distinct minority group are not, by any means, vanishing or being absorbed; unlike the Jews, for example, they are becoming an increasingly problematic minority group whose problems will continue to vex both the dominant white society and each new generation of Indians.

the lower-class teen-ager

Socioeconomic Differences

The subject matter of social stratification is one of the most controversial areas in sociology. Varying views and theories are offered by students of social structure. Some of the perennial questions concern the dividing lines between the strata; where, why, and how to draw them; the criteria by which to define a social class; and the cultural differences between the strata.

This chapter is not the place to elaborate upon and clarify these issues; instead, care is taken to apply only those assumptions that are widely accepted among sociologists. The most commonly accepted dimensions for measuring socioeconomic status are either objective criteria such as occupation, education, income, type of housing, and neighborhood, or subjective evaluation and classification by members of the community. The most reliable and frequently applied classificatory criterion is the *occupation* of the head of the household. In the case of the lower class, the modal occupation is unskilled labor employed in factories, mills, or as day labor, characterized by frequent unemployment and public relief reliance. Another widely accepted observation refers to certain *cultural* differences between the strata. While not absolutely demarcating one from the other, ethos differences allow generalization of a number of *modal*, that is, most prevalent, features marking the style of life in each stratum. Individuals who find themselves in comparable positions, with similar incomes, education, housing, etc., have, of course, more in common than people from quite different levels of the social structure. This "having-things-in-common" makes, in essence, for a distinct style of life that includes distinct motives, interests, values, aspirations, and perceptions. The commonality is correlated with awareness of belonging to a certain segment of the population and a feeling of "we-ness," which become part of one's social identity. This class awareness of lower-class people, for example, is reflected in such every-day remarks as "they are not our kind of people," "they are ordinary people like us," and "they don't fit in with our bunch."

The children within a given social stratum are raised and indoc-trinated to adhere to the parents' style of life, thus acquiring the class-characteristic behavior and value orientations concerning family rela-tions, sex, work, education, and economic practices. This transmission of a life style is not always consciously carried out by parents, but occurs largely through imitation on the part of children who confront class-differentiated behavior models. The teen-agers of each social class, thus, face different situations, different problems, and select different approaches to solve them. There is a world of difference between a physician's son and an unskilled laborer's son, while there probably is not much difference, if any at all, between the bank teller's boy and the store owner's boy, who both belong to the broad middle class. There is justification, then, for talking separately about middle-class (as has primarily been done so far in this book), lower-class, and upper-class youth.

To illustrate in some depth the influence of the socioeconomic factor on the nature of teen-age life, as was done in preceding chapters with racial and ethnic factors, the lower-class setting was chosen. There are a number of reasons for choosing the lower class over the upper class for this discussion. Youth of the upper class are much more integrated into their families, not as observable as in the middle and lower classes, attend private schools that are far less conducive to creating teen-age subcultures, and, finally, simply cannot be reached as easily for question-ing, interviewing, testing, etc. It is probably more accurate to refer to the upper class as a social stratum that does not exhibit such strong age differentiation as other strata. There is very little evidence that the upper class has a separate teen-age subculture. A characterization of upper-class youth would more or less coincide with that of upper-class people in general.

The picture is quite different in the lower socioeconomic class. Sociologists agree not only on a general adult lower-class ethos, but in addition, on distinct lower-class youth patterns. These patterns include aspects that are related to the situation of the Negro youth, to the delinquent gangs, and to the conditions of the underprivileged. It is true, for example, that recruits for juvenile delinquency come primarily from lower-class youth, but it is obviously not correct to assume that all lower-class youth are delinquents. The reason for the delinquency-proneness, plus other nondelinquent but typically lower-class teen-age behavior patterns, must be sought in the economic, social, and cultural circumstances under which lower-class people live. Certain aspects of lower-class culture, such as basic attitudes, values, and concerns—in short the lower-class ethos—help to explain the behavior of lower-class teen-agers.

The Lower-Class Ethos

The lower-class way of life, like that of any distinct cultural group, is characterized by a number of *core concerns* that command widespread and persistent emotional involvement. These preoccupations have frequently been called "values." However, the term "value" connotes judgmental elements defining "right" and "wrong" and a highly theoretical construct likely to be independent from empirical observation. On the other hand, the use of the term "core concerns" more clearly and unambiguously points to empirically observable behavior patterns. Concerns can also be understood as *dimensions* that range from one extreme to the other, thereby allowing for *degrees* of intensity. For example, the dimension of powerlessness allows measurement of the person who reigns autonomously over his affairs as well as of the person who resigns his fate to presumed or real outside powers. This example shows persons falling at opposite poles of the continuum, while most persons would fall somewhere in between. The empirical operationality, the greater objectivity, and the measurability by degrees are, thus, the main reasons for preferring the term core concerns. Cultural foci in terms of dimensional concerns also facilitate the realization that many of the concerns are typical of the culture or subculture only because of unique emphasis and not because of exclusivity. This implies that many of the lower-class concerns are shared by the middle class; the difference lies only in the degree. Certainly, to refer back to the above example, middle-class individuals experience the feeling of powerlessness and alienation just as lower-class individuals do, only normally to a lesser extent.

With these points of introduction and explanation, a list of major concerns of lower-class people is presented, and their implications for the teen-ager are studied.[1] The order of presentation roughly corresponds to the order of overt attention accorded each, and, in this sense, suggests a weighted ranking of concerns.

---

[1] Credit for developing several of the above and following points and the concept of "focal concern" is given to Walter B. Miller, "Lower-Class Culture as a Generating Milieu of Gang Delinquency," *Journal of Social Issues*, Vol. 14, No. 3 (1958), pp. 5–19.

Trouble. The phrases, "staying out of trouble" and "getting into trouble," are probably nowhere more frequently spoken than among lower-class people, especially the children. These clichés are verbal reminders of their preoccupation with trouble and in degree of preoccupation are equivalent to the middle-class syndrome of "success" and "achievement." However, different valences are attached—"trouble" for the lower class is negative, "success" for the middle class is positive. This in itself, the negative versus positive type of preoccupation, is social-psychologically significant. It suggests a wholly different life atmosphere. For example, a lower-class mother's first impulse when evaluating the suitability of her daughter's boy friend is concern about his trouble potential. "Will he stay out of trouble?" is her first thought. A middle-class, particularly upper-middle-class mother, on the other hand, evaluates the young man primarily in terms of present and/or future "success" potential. "What will he become?" is her most important concern.

Trouble is a catch-all concept applicable to anything that is unpleasant, annoying, or complicating. It is frequently the apt term to refer to brushes with the law, quarrels with the neighbor, and complications with agencies of the middle-class society. For men, trouble often refers to fights connected with drinking. For both men and women it may mean the complicating consequences of sexual involvement, particularly pregnancy out of wedlock. This, of course, is also a source of trouble for the teen-agers and probably ranks second only to trouble with the police. There is reason to believe that the overt compliance with the laws and rules of middle-class society is much less a manifestation of preference and conviction than a desire to "stay out of trouble" and fear of the complicating consequences of unlawful behavior.

Toughness. To be "tough" implies a combination of several qualities. Some of them fall under physical prowess, stressing physical strength, endurance, and athletic skill. The heroes of both the adults and youth of the lower class are the prize fighters, wrestlers, and boxers, and the popular champions of baseball and football. To suggest and simulate an air of prowess, men employ auxiliary devices. Bodily tattoos and certain clothes or the lack thereof, as with men or boys exhibiting their "manly" chests, are intended to underscore the he-man qualities. There is a whole syndrome of psychological tendencies related to the toughness complex. A man must be hard, fearless, and show bravado acts—often in explicit defiance of authority. This is the boy who openly commits punishable acts, knowing that he will be caught and punished, in order to show his fearlessness and toughness. School is considered a "prissy" place, dominated by females and representing "effeminate" values.[2] To be tough often is the reason for individual or street fights; it is a contest to show "who can beat whom." The tough guy regards women as objects of conquest, not allowing himself to exhibit sentimentality or "softness." Urbane or polite forms, the etiquette of the middle class, are "sissy" stuff and not for the tough man. He also shows a sneering disregard for "art." Concerts, ballets, museums, art galleries, etc., are alien phenomena in which only "queers" and upper-class people are interested. The intensity of his preoccupation with masculinity is carried to interesting lengths. For example, he displays an unusual hostility to the homosexual and engages in the near-institutionalized practice of baiting him, often ending in violent physical attacks. The affection he is able to show toward his peers is disguised in almost opposite forms consisting of ostensibly aggressive "kidding," teasing, and playing practical jokes.

The etiology of the cult of toughness or masculinity is not entirely clear. Some of the more direct influences probably stem from the models offered through the mass media, the tough and manly cowboy, detective, or even gangster. A more indirect and complex explanation is frequently offered by clinically inclined psychologists who see in this behavior a reaction formation to the experience of female domination during childhood. It is true that a significant proportion of lower-class males are reared in matricentric households that lack a consistent male figure with whom they could identify and from whom they could learn the essential components of the male role. Since the preadolescent boy may have started to identify with his mother, the only visible model, he later overcompensates and establishes a rigid and intensely negative identification. This reaction formation is defined as a defense mechanism against reverting to the initial identification with the female figure.

Smartness. The quality of being "smart" implies the ability to outfox, outwit, "take," and "con" others, and the concomitant ability not to be "taken" or outwitted oneself. There are two functions of this quality. One is to achieve a goal with a minimum of effort, the utilitarian purpose, and the other is to rise in the eyes of one's peers, the prestige function. To be at the other end of the line would mean to be a "sucker," "easy mark," or a "lush" and invite merciless ridicule. The models of smartness are the card sharks, successful gamblers, and "con" artists, and those who can, if necessary, skillfully mislead cops. Smartness should not for a moment be mistaken for intellectualism, that out-group preoccupation with abstract knowledge, formal learning, and "cultural" things. There is a world of difference between an upper-class parent saying

---

[2] For detailed treatment of this problem, the "female school," see Patricia Sexton, "Schools are Emasculating our Boys," *Saturday Review* (June 19, 1965), p. 57.

"a smart child" and a lower-class parent saying "a smart kid." The former most likely refers to a successful school career and a knowledgeable youngster, and the latter refers to slyness and cleverness in manipulation of others. The regular learning environment for the lower-class youngster is the street corner or other peer hangouts. The favorite techniques of learning and displaying smartness include semiritualized "kidding" and razzing and semiserious mutual invective that tests inventiveness, fast responsiveness, and ingenuity in the application of insulting language. The latter tends to take advantage of the prestigious use of that type of provocative slang that alludes to perverted incestuous sex relations—with the mother as a dominant theme. It is through the contest of verbal and often practical smartness that prestige is allocated and that, in combination with other qualifications such as toughness, leadership roles are achieved.

Excitement. The lower-class person is characterized by deprivations in many areas of life. Among them is the poverty of mental and physical stimuli, lack of *variety* in experiences. If we accept W. I. Thomas's assertion that man has, along with other wishes,[3] a profound longing for new experiences, then the lower class is psychologically severely deprived. Partially through economic limitations and partially through resigned attitudes, he is set in a life style that provides a minimum of flexibility, variety, and novelty of experiences. Besides vicarious supplementation through the mass media, especially TV, he looks for diversion and new experiences in the form of "kicks," "thrills," and delinquent or semidelinquent adventures. However, different segments among the lower-class population rate differently on the excitement dimension. It seems that teen-agers rate significantly higher than adults, who apparently have to a greater degree resigned themselves to the daily monotony of their lives and take to the combination of TV and beer as a simultaneously vicarious and dulling experience. Teen-agers, on the other hand, take to the street corner, to "ridin' around the town" if they have a car, sometimes "raising hell," and getting into trouble "just for the heck of it." Delinquent diversions to break the monotony and to experience the thrill of new adventures take the form of gang fights, riots, and assaults. There is a constant explosive potential for this type of excitement. It is therefore not surprising that the preoccupation with trouble as a portentous and omnipresent threat ranks as a primary concern of lower-class people.

Fate. "Fate" in the lower-class argot means luck or fortune— either good or bad; one is either lucky or unlucky and cannot do much

---

[3] His four "wishes" included the wish for recognition, response, new experience, and security. See W. I. Thomas, *The Unadjusted Girl* (New York, Little, Brown, 1923).

about it. In essence, this set of attitudes is symptomatic of deeply felt *powerlessness*, a feeling that one's life is subject to forces over which one has relatively little control. However, unlike the traditional American Indian who possesses a formal and religious concept of supernatural powers, the lower-class individual looks at fate in terms of informal, nondescript, and areligious "destiny." Comparing this attitude with the previous concern for smartness, one might suspect a break in logic: on the one hand, active smartness and on the other, passive fate. The explanation for this seeming paradox may well lie in a faint rebellion to outwit and, in a sense, adjust destiny to one's life as far as possible.

Fate also serves as a convenient rationalization that the one whom one has outwitted "had it coming anyway," or that "it was meant to happen." By so rationalizing, the smart person feels exonerated of guilt and nondeserving of punishment. Again it is a version of man's age-old magic that ascribes personal failure and moral or legal infractions to outside forces in order to maintain a margin of dignity and self-respect. This makes conditions of misery and deprivation endurable—and, because of the psychological self-condonement, also permanent.

This is the psychological background of the type of behavior that causes middle-class people described as "lazy," unmotivated, unwilling to change, and as reflecting "poor values." It seems to be true that lower-class persons are more concerned with "getting by" than "getting ahead" and in so doing reject the mobility ethic that urges constant striving to higher status and achievements, postponing immediate satisfaction and self-indulgence for long-range goals—in short, they reject the middle-class corollary of worldly asceticism, investment and reinvestment, and deference of gratification.

Anti-intellectualism. Anti-intellectualism, as implied earlier, expresses the lower-class mistrust and aversion for abstract thinking and complex mental constructs. Intellectualism is to be understood as a distinctly different order of mental activity from that defined as smartness, since its emphasis is on formal knowledge, overall perspective on cultural developments, and, above all, *objective* insights into problems, which will lead to mature decisions. In defense of academia it must be said that in spite of—or actually, *because of*—the forced-choice curriculum of college programs, especially the so-called "general education" or "liberal arts" requirements, such general perspective and objectivity can be acquired. A certain degree of knowledge in such fields as art, literature, history, and social sciences, is necessary for a "civilized" outlook on human relations on the personal, communal, national, or international level.

However, in the lower class this type of mental attainment is usually downgraded and equated with effeminacy or "eggheadedness."

Smartness, on the other hand, is highly valued by lower-class youth, because it has little to do with abstraction and systematic and long-range mental exercise. It is more concerned with concrete situations that are present, urgent, and that imply actual sensory and physical involvement. The lower-class adolescent is a pragmatist who shows little interest in exploring the philosophical meaning or the nomothetic quality that could be derived from problem situations. He concentrates rather on *direct* solutions—it is the end result that counts for him. From his point of view, what can be seen, heard, or touched is more likely to be true than are abstract principles. He has a real appreciation for one who can fix things with his hands, who shows motoric skills. This appreciation is typical of deprived individuals whose actual and physical deprivations evoke a primary interest in manipulation of concrete and physical objects. They are not symbolic learners. (To prevent a negative bias, it is necessary to remember that motoric skills are of value and absolute necessity for the survival of society and that the academician who is unable to drive a nail into a board is, in a sense, just as handicapped as the motoric-oriented lower-class person who may be ignorant of the relationship between the so-called "conscience" and cultural environment.) Incidentally, the lower-class person realizes the intellectual's almost proverbial motoric handicap and makes it a major item in his explicit contempt for "eggheads."

The preference for or limitation to concreteness can be seen in many areas of the lower-class person's life. His religious expressions, for example, tend to be much more physical and emotional, such as hand-clapping, singing, even shouting, than those of the middle class, where the sermon is more theological or metaphysical and the congregation quiet and contemplative. Even the symptoms of mental illness reflect the differential in intellectualism. While lower-class patients exhibit disproportionately more conversion hysteria and catatonia, which involve *malfunctions* of the voluntary muscles, middle-class patients, by contrast, exhibit more obsessions and depressions, which are indicative of *inhibitions* of vountary movements and attempts to solve conflicts by complex mental constructs.[4] In the political realm, the relatively uneducated lower-class person lacks perspective, ability to think abstractly, flexibility and therefore does not see the point in long debates and deliberations that involve abstract moral, historical, or legal principles. He desires action and, as a consequence, a government in the form of a strong leader who is a concrete entity and not an abstract set of rules.

---

[4] Daniel R. Miller and Guy E. Swanson, *Inner Conflict and Defense* (New York, Henry Holt, 1960), pp. 310*f*.

Authoritarianism. A person with authoritarian tendencies sees social interaction and social structure in general as a "vertical" arrangement, with superior and inferior individuals, those who command and those who obey. This is significantly different from looking at interpersonal relations as a "horizontal" arrangement in which people are basically equal, although occupying different positions and carrying out different functions. These two world-views can be contrasted as authoritarian and democratic.[5]

Although lower-class people in the United States are obviously a part of the overall democratic system with its social and political ramifications, their perceptions and political attitudes reflect certain authoritarian elements that are not representative of United States democracy. Research with some 600 teen-agers in urban and suburban Ohio areas revealed a signficant inverse correlation between socioeconomic class background and authoritarianism, suggesting that the lower class exhibits a greater amount of authoritarian attitudes than the middle and upper classes.[6] Generally speaking, the lower-class individual holds a number of distinctly illiberal views concerning civil liberties and foreign policies. Although an irregular and infrequent participant in political activities—of the various socioeconomic classes he has the lowest participation in voting—he vociferously expresses criticism and mistrust of the government. However, his attitudes are not logical and consistent. On the one hand, he is distrustful of a strong government and shows intolerant and prejudiced opinions toward it, while on the other hand he craves strong leaders and is intensely intolerant of dissident voices critical of the majority opinion. This polarity and seeming incongruence are typical of the authoritarian personality. Since he sees relationships as made up of either commanding or obeying positions, he is faced with the question of which position *he* is to occupy in a given interpersonal relationship. A clear *either-or answer* is of great importance to the authoritarian person because flexible and vague arrangements, as many equalitarian relationships are, are too frustrating and confusing to him. His need for clear-cut and unambiguous status interaction, although a normal goal and desire for all social beings, is overly intense and exaggerated. In the process of trying to find out which one of the two contrasting positions is the one for him in a given social situation, the authoritarian person tests the firmness and strength of the partner. If the partner "gives in" and shows weakness, he literally is subjugated and placed in the subservient position. If, however, the partner does not "back out," but shows

---

[5] See elaboration in Hans Sebald, "Studying National Character Through Comparative Content Analysis," *Social Forces,* Vol. 40 (May, 1962), pp. 318–22.

[6] Hans Sebald, *Parent-Peer Control and Masculine-Marital Role Perception of Adolescent Boys,* unpublished Ph.D. dissertation (The Ohio State University, 1963).

strength and determination, he is accepted as the "leader," as the ruler. This description is applicable also to the collective level where one party to the interaction process is a social class of the legal authority in general. From the vantage point of lower-class individuals, the middle-class Establishment with its distinct values and standards, as recapitulated by the legal system is perceived as making difficult and unjust demands on the "common man."

The modal outcome of the testing of authority is the compliance of the lower-class person with the authority.[7] He seems to feel more comfortable in the subservient and dependent position—no matter how loudly he may seem to object. His real behavior reflects a desire for security, to mention again one of W. I. Thomas's basic "wishes,"[8] which overrides his desire for economic and social independence. Erich Fromm's key concept of "escape from freedom" is another apt description of this tendency.[9] Dependence, unlike freedom, offers the lower-class person security, protection, and the feeling of being "cared for." Statistics indicate that he has a consistent tendency to enter highly restrictive social milieus that exert stringent controls over his behavior. Institutions such as the armed forces, disciplinary schools, prisons, and various correctional institutions draw a disproportionately high number from the lower class. One might argue that their entry was not by their free volition. However, a twofold counterargument could point out that they do not show the same dismay over spending time in such institutions as middle-class persons, nor does the knowledge or the experience of such confinement seem to deter them for pursuing behavior forms that result in reconfinement, as the high rate of lower-class recidivism shows. An interesting explanation for this recurrent and dependency-resulting behavior focuses on the apparent perception by the lower-class person of the institution as a *nurturing* environment that, in effect, "takes care of him."[10] (However, it should be added that this hypothesis awaits further testing. Moreover, the need for nurturance is certainly not an exclusive cause of institutionalization, as other variables may exert greater force.) It can further be observed that while under the care of the nurturing institution, the lower-class person persistently expresses complaints about the coercive and "unfair" exercise of authority. Upon closer examination, however, it becomes clear that he complies quite willingly with the rules of the institution. His overt resentment usually fulfills a face-saving function by keeping up the veneer of the cultural norm of manliness (it is tough to rebel and to attack), while his behavioral

---

[7] Miller, *op. cit.*, pp. 38–40.

[8] Thomas, *op. cit.*

[9] Erich Fromm, *Escape from Freedom* (New York, Rinehart and Co., 1941).

[10] Miller, *op. cit.*, pp. 12–13.

compliance speaks a different language—the language of security and need for nurturance. After release or escape from the institution and after a period of temporary "freedom," he often will act in such a way as to ensure recommitment.

In sum, then, the lower-class person's authority relationships include three major aspects. First, they are characterized by his perception of the nature of social interaction as a "vertical" arrangement, classifying participants into superior and inferior positions. Secondly, he tends to prefer the subservient, dependent, and more secure position, which provides a milieu of nurturance. Third, he does so in spite of verbal resentment, which merely serves the functions of upholding the subcultural norm of toughness and of testing the firmness of authority.

Lower-Class Youth Facing Middle-Class Demands: Specific Disadvantages

The effect of this specific social-class ethos on the lower-class youngster manifests itself in his everyday life routine, involving school, family, peer relationships, delinquent behavior, street-corner associations, etc. The overall effect is best understood as a complex mixture of experiences that have precipitated into a psychological *Gestalt* with the "core concerns" representing the *Prägnanz* features. Many symptoms evident in the behavior of the teen-agers are direct derivatives of the cultural deprivations of the lower class. A number of such symptoms are discussed.

In the school setting, the "masculine" value of the lower-class youngster leads him to reject the "eager-beaver" and "apple-polishing" style that conforms to the middle-class norms of respecting the teacher, being neat, and accepting the middle-class achievement orientation. Since the teacher is most likely a female, conformity to and compliance with her demands and wishes would be surrender and degradation of masculinity or toughness. This, obviously, pertains primarily to the lower-class *boy*. Statistics reflect a sex-differentiation and show that boys get into trouble more frequently than girls and that delinquency rates are five times higher among boys than girls. For example, 63 per cent of New York's dropouts are boys, and more than twice as many boys as girls under fifteen are first admissions to public mental hospitals.[11]

---

[11] Patricia Sexton, *Education and Income* (New York, The Viking Press, 1961), p. 57.

Full explanation of the disproportionately high delinquency rate among lower-class youth would require more extensive treatment than is possible in this book. Material deprivation, a perception of property, time, and work different from that of the middle class, and the concern with toughness are among the obvious background features that explain their delinquency-proneness. One feature that is not so explicit is the differential report and conviction rate. Lower-class areas are more strictly and tightly patrolled, the youngsters are treated less leniently, and the parents are unable to provide financial cover and protection. An example of this difference was demonstrated a few years ago when upper-class vandalism, resulting in about 200 broken window panes, torn-out telephones, ripped curtains, overturned refrigerators and furniture, ended without legal implications because no charges were pressed and the damages was paid for by affluent parents.[12] Any such act on the part of lower-class youth would almost certainly have resulted in conviction and formal punishment of the vandals.

Another explanation concerns the lower-class youngsters' tendency to congregate at street corners in lieu of better facilities. The street corner gang is not delinquent as such, but it forms a generic type that, to be sure, can easily and quickly be transformed into a delinquent gang. If provoked by outside forces and influences such as hostile gangs, police, encounter with racial, ethnic, or social prejudice, and if a number of lower-class propensities (such as to act tough, prove prowess, show strength, appear smart, and follow an authoritarian leader) are added to the situation, an otherwise harmless street corner gathering can quickly turn into an antisocial and destructive gang.

The proverbial lack of success of lower-class pupils in academic endeavors can hardly be ascribed to lower native IQs of these youth. As Hollingshead stressed in *Elmtown's Youth*, academic failure of the lower class must be explained by both the values of the lower-class child and the bias of the teachers who, deliberately or inadvertently, were more inclined to extend extra help to the higher-class students by talking to them after hours.[13] These findings were supported by a 1961 study by Patricia Sexton, in which the author reported that the failure rate among elementary school children whose families earn $3,000 or less annually was six times higher than among those from families earning $9,000 or more.[14] In addition, it was found that 37 children per 10,000 in the lowest income families could be classified as posing very serious behavior problems while none were classified in this way from

---

[12] "Youth," *Time*, (Sept. 13, 1963), p. 80.

[13] August B. Hollingshead, *Elmtown's Youth* (New York, John Wiley and Sons, 1949).

[14] Sexton, 1961, *op. cit.*

the highest income bracket. The different academic climate is observable not only among pupils *within* schools, but also *among* different schools. Sexton observed significant differences in the socioeconomic background of the student body among her sample of seventeen high schools in one large city. Median income for the families was $5,000–6,000 in the case of five schools, $6,000–7,000 in three schools, $7,000–8,000 in four schools, and over $9,000 in the remaining school. Valid arguments emerged from this study against the assumption that "separate" schools show "equal" standards.[15] Aaron V. Cicourel and John I. Kitsuse emphasize in their research that the academic development and interest of the pupil is significantly influenced by the counselors, who tend to devote more of their time and activities to those students who indicate their intention to go on to college and whose parents support this plan actively and make frequent inquiries at the school concerning their child's progress. These students and their parents belonged almost exclusively to the middle and upper social classes.[16]

Probably the strongest impact of the conditions and concerns of lower-class living can be observed in the anti-intellectualism and anti-abstractionism of the youth. This disadvantage, when challenged by middle-class demands, becomes specifically noticeable in terms of linguistic deficiencies. Regardless of the relatively unmeasurable degree of *native* intelligence, the lower-class youngster is characterized by intellectual retardation in the abstract dimension of verbal functioning. There is an impressive number of corroborating research studies in the professional literature that agree on the paucity of abstract terms and references in the vocabulary of the lower-class youth.[17] As a consequence, lower-class English is inferior to standard English in that it provides an extremely limited perceptual framework permitting only gross intellectual distinctions. On the other hand, standard English with its more refined perceptual framework, as generally used by middle and upper classes, invites much finer distinctions. This notion was forcefully supported by two different studies of Hawaiian English maintaining that a radical simplification of language structure, as in so-called Pidgin

---

[15] Sexton 1961, *op. cit.*

[16] Aaron V. Cicourel and John I. Kitsuse, *The Educational Decision-Makers* (New York, The Bobbs-Merrill Co., 1963).

[17] Three major studies that describe this condition are: David P. Ausubel, "The Effects of Cultural Deprivation on Learning Patterns," in Staten W. Webster (ed.), *Understanding the Educational Problems of the Disadvantaged Learner* (San Francisco, Chandler Publishing Co., 1966), pp. 251–57; Werner Cohn, "On the Language of Lower-Class Children," *School Review*, Vol. 67 (Winter, 1959), pp. 435–40; and Basil Bernstein, "Some Sociological Determinants of Perception, An Inquiry into Sub-Cultural Differences," *British Journal of Sociology*, Vol. 9 (June, 1958), pp. 159–74.

English, makes its nearly impossible to formulate intellectual generalizations.[18] In essence, behavioral scientists studying this linguistic phenomenon seem to agree that in intellectual, analytic, and scientific matters standard English with its elaborate syntax is far superior to lower-class or Pidgin English.

This linquistic deficiency has been found to increase with age, exhibiting a cumulative effect, and thereby demonstrating the effect of continued environmental deprivation.[19] The initial language deficit and the continued environmetal conditioning with low-abstract references make, in the final result, for a nearly irreversible condition. The social class condition concerning the ability to think in abstract terms is already observable in kindergarten. David O. Montague studied the difference that socioeconomic background makes on kindergarteners' arithmetic concepts.[20] Eighty-two pupils from four kindergarten classes were divided into socioeconomic categories and subjected to a number of tests. Significant differences at the .01 level were found between the children coming from low and those coming from high socioeconomic backgrounds. A study with similar hypotheses selected three groups of school children and matched them for age, sex, grade placement, etc., leaving as the experimental variables racial and regional factors, i.e., Negro versus white and southern U.S. versus northern U.S. It was found that the white children were superior to the Negro children and that northern Negro children were superior to southern Negro children, conveying a parallel picture of the educational climate.[21]

The main reasons for the verbal destitution of the lower-class youngsters lie in the deficient models for syntax and vocabulary, the lack of reading at home, and, above all, the lack of *variety* in stimuli. Objects, utensils, toys, pictures, books, and other objects require labeling and can serve as referents for language acquisition.[22] If a child is sub-

---

[18] Bernhard Hormann, "Speech, Prejudice, and the School in Hawaii," in Bernhard Hormann (ed.), *Community Forces in Hawaii* (Honolulu. University of Hawaii, 1956), pp. 232–37; and John E. Reinecke, " 'Pidgin English' in Hawaii: A Local Study in the Sociology of Language," *American Journal of Sociology*, Vol. 53 (March, 1938), pp. 778–89.

[19] Ausubel, *op. cit.*, p. 252.

[20] David O. Montague, "Arithmetic Concepts of Kindergarten Children in Contrasting Socioeconomic Areas," *Elementary School Journal*, Vol. 64 (April, 1964), pp. 393–97.

[21] Arnold S. Carson and A. I. Rabin, "Verbal Comprehension and Communication in Negro and White Children," *Journal of Educational Psychology*, Vol. 51 (April, 1960), pp. 47–51.

[22] The importance of a range of different stimuli for language acquisition was emphasized by at least two studies: Ausubel, *op. cit.*, p. 252; and Montague, *op. cit.*, p. 363.

stantially deprived of the variety of stimuli that he is capable of learning, he invariably falls behind in learning, and the more fortunate peers from the middle and upper social classes will surpass him in intellectual and academic success.

Another area in which abstractness plays a distinguishing role between the social classes is achievement motivation. Achievement motivation can be heavily influenced by either material or symbolic orientation; for example, some individuals find gratification primarily in material attainments, others in symbolic attainment, and still others in a combination of the two. Research has indicated that the lower and the higher social classes generally differ with respect to the values they seek in personal achievement. Middle-class parents, in rearing their children, characteristically assert an *earlier*, a more *regular*, and more *insistent* inculcation concerning the value of individual achievement. In the process, achievement becomes a value for its own sake and often loses its concrete, material, and tangible referent. For example, for the middle-class pupil the mastery of curriculum subjects is highly valued, *regardless* of whether it leads directly to pragmatic applicability and material returns. The mastery is viewed as success in itself and may give the individual both motivation to embark on the achievement process and great satisfaction if he succeeds. This orientation is obviously of considerable abstractness since the attainment may not be equated with material or concrete gains of any kind. The lower-class youngster is not abstractly orientated. Effort for the sake of success as a principle is a rather alien idea to him. He can be motivated more strongly if he envisages a concrete or material reward. Elizabeth Douvan conducted an experiment that tested the above assumptions; specifically, the assertion that a high degree of concreteness is needed to motivate lower-class youngsters, and that, on the other hand, middle-class youngsters would be less likely to change their levels of aspiration with rewards offered.[23] High school students representing both social classes were asked to complete a series of anagrams and motor tests under two different reward conditions. In one, reward was limited to the feeling of having accomplished a norm (abstractness); in the other, a material reward, money (concreteness), for the greatest number of correct answers was added to the feeling of satisfaction. All the students were told they had failed. At that moment, Douvan assumed, failure aroused *achievement want*, a reaction correlated with achievement motivation, and McClelland's Need Achievement Test, a projective TAT test, was administered. Douvan's findings sup-

---

[23] Elizabeth Douvan, "Social Status and Success Strivings," *Journal of Abnormal and Social Psychology*, Vol. 52 (March, 1966), pp. 219–23.

ported the original hypothesis. Both groups responded similarly to the material reward condition, but the strivings of the lower-class subjects dropped sharply when the material reward was absent, while the motivation of middle-class subjects remained at approximately the same level. It may thus be concluded that the achievement motivation of middle-class youth is significantly more generalized, consistent, and abstract-proof.

A number of sociologists have omitted the factor of abstractness from their research design and have focused on motivation and aspiration in general. William H. Sewell and coworkers worked with a sample of more than 4,000 high school seniors in Wisconsin, exploring the relationship between social class background and the students' educational and occupational aspiration level. The results revealed a positive correlation between social class and aspiration for both sexes. The researchers did not deny the importance of other variables but were confident that the social-class status of a youngster's family made an independent contribution to his aspiration level.[24]

However, the relationship between social class and aspirations is often compounded by intervening variables. The Lane County Youth Project, Eugene, Oregon, explored the relationship between social class and academic aspirations and discovered a constellation of variables that, presumably, offers a more sensitive and accurate prediction of a youngster's success level than the simple class-and-aspiration correlation.[25] Although not rendering the latter correlation useless and insignificant, it was found that the teen-ager's categorization as either the college or noncollege type functioned as a more powerful factor than social-class belonging for the prediction of failure. Once a youngster is classified as a college candidate, more attention, counseling, and encouragement are lavished on him, reinforcing his plans and stimulating continuous effort to work toward the academic goal. Correlated features are increased participation in school activities, decline of participation in delinquent activities, and adjustment to the school norms.

Another study, including international samples (United States, England, West Germany, Italy, and Mexico), found that *parental dominance* was just as strong an influence, or even stronger, than social-class background on the youngster's desire to achieve in general and to succeed in

---

[24] William H. Sewell, Archie O. Haller, and Murray A. Straus, "Social Status and Educational and Occupational Aspiration," *American Sociological Review*, Vol. 22 (February, 1957), pp. 67–72.

[25] Kenneth Polk, *Those Who Fail*, Mimeographed Report of the Lane County Youth Project (Eugene, Oregon, February, 1965).

scholastic work in specific.[26] The relationship was found to be inverse, i.e., exaggerated parental dominance was associated with low achievement motivation and poor school progress. Since the effect of social class is not denied by this and other studies, in the case of youngsters who are exposed to the compound effects of lower-class membership and extreme parental dominance, one would expect a double effect and observe extremely low achievement motivation and academic success.

Leonard Reissman, also interested in discovering a refined correlation betwen social class and aspiration level, concurred with the assumption of a *general* correlation between the two variables, but pointed out that even though a person may belong to the middle class, which encourages high achievement, the person may not exhibit high motivational levels if his *reference group* does not stress high achievement.[27] In other words, a person's reference group affects the relationship between social-class background and aspiration level, operating as an *intervening* variable. Although generally a person's reference group tends to be of the same or similar social-class standing as that of his family, it is possible that a person relates to a reference group of different social standing. Robert K. Merton, in his writings on the theory of the reference group has expanded on this premise.[28] As each social class is characterized by certain values and expressions of motivation, the individual who identifies with another class will adopt its characteristics as those of his reference group although it actually is not his membership group. This experience has also been called "anticipatory socialization," and implies the absorption of norms and behavior traits of a higher stratum. However, these are the exceptions and it can safely be generalized that a youngster's socioeconomic background is his foundation for the "building" of aspirational levels.

The deprivations and disadvantages of the lower-class youth are frequently reflected in their lingo. Every mode of speech reflects a concept of behavior, a style of life. In addition to the above-listed major problems of lower-class youth, a number of concerns can be detected in their argot. One of them is their preoccupation with "trouble" and violence, which often manifests itself in individual or gang fights. Social

---

[26] Glen H. Elder, Jr., "Family Structure and Educational Attainment: A Cross-National Analysis," *American Sociological Review*, Vol. 30 (February, 1965), pp. 81–96.

[27] Leonard Reissman, "Levels of Aspiration and Social Class," *American Sociological Review*, Vol. 18 (June, 1953), pp. 233–42.

[28] Robert K. Merton and Alice S. Kitt, "Contributions to the Theory of Reference Group Behavior," in Robert K. Merton and Paul F. Lazarsfeld (eds.), *Continuities in Social Research: Studies in the Scope and Method of "The American Soldier"* (New York, Free Press, 1950), pp. 40–105.

workers literally have to learn the language of the lower-class youth before they can adequately communicate and comprehend that "jacking someone up" or "tightening up his mug" mean beating someone up. A gang fight is often referred to as "duking it out" in an alley or "going down" on a rival gang. Their contempt and aversion for school is another prevalent theme, reflected in the term "warehouse" for a particularly disliked school and "waiting room" for the weekly assembly. It is interesting to note that economic deprivation shows up in the nonexistence of slang words for gadgets they cannot afford or hardly know. A tape recorder, for example, had no equivalent in argot because few lower-class youngsters own one. On the other hand, an old car was called a "short," and "motoring," originally a peculiarly formal British term, was used to refer to driving around town. Sex is another area of concern that is amply covered by lower-class argot; it tends to be freely couched in terms of incestuous, homosexual, and other perverted practices and applied usually in the context of invective and teasing.

The use of lower-class argot in itself is a disadvantage in interaction with the middle-class society. Besides being a limited perceptual tool, it publicly stigmatizes the user as a lower-class individual. His speech, in the absence of other identifiable characteristics, identifies him readily as a member of the lower socioeconomic stratum and may immediately erect an invisible and yet impenetrable barrier between him and the middle-class milieu.

Challenging the Educational Institution

It should be obvious by now that many of the characteristics of the lower-class youth create deep-seated alienation from the middle-class educational institution. School is an alien and frightening territory in which he feels out of place and ill at ease. He is not voluntarily motivated, but compelled by outside forces beyond his control to attend school. His truancy rate is high—the highest among the socioeconomic strata of the society. It is common knowledge that youngsters under compulsion, alienation, or fright are unable to effectively participate in the learning process. For this reason in addition to his nonintellectual home background, the lower-class pupil tends to quickly fall behind his peers from higher and more educationally oriented social classes. His awareness of early academic failures only proves to him that school is not for "his bunch of people." Any remedial effort to correct, or better, to prevent, this fatalistic and alienated attitude must come early, as soon as the youngster enters elementary school. Delayed endeavors have to cope with the accumulated effects of academic defeats and alienating experiences that have taken place since the youngster first started in the middle-class school venture. The challenge to education and teachers is thus to prevent alienation and defeatist attitudes as early as possible and to help establish a sense of meaning, trust, and confidence in the educational process. In order to achieve a sufficient degree of such functional attitudes, educational sociologists have called attention to a number of important prerequisites. These analytic insights have both been suggested as explanations for the persistent failure of the lower-class youth and been used for implementing remedial programs. The following discussion can be understood as serving either function.

As was noted earlier, several studies have focused on the verbal deficiency of the working-class youth, reminding of the programs aiming to help him not to feel personally rejected on account of his deficiency and yet not accepting it as the final version of his linquistic capacity. The serious language deficiency expresses itself in consistent use of substandard English that has been observed among the seriously inadequate students—who, nevertheless, may be endowed with an adequate native intelligence and thus are essentially able to improve on the verbal destitution characterizing them. Their language deficiencies usually include the following points: (1) Impoverished vocabulary consisting primarily of Anglo-Saxon content and stereotypical application; (2) Syntactical mistakes, especially in regard to word inflections; (3) Frequent mispronunciations; (4) Neglect of modifying or describing qualities appropriately; (5) Serious limitations in the use of figurative —abstract—language.

Remedial steps must be taken cautiously. Youngsters are quick to discover the class bias in the middle-class teacher's moralistic deprecation of his language and, as a rule, react with alienation.[29] To prevent this negative reaction, the teacher must be patiently aware of the fact that lower-class argot is the only language that the youngsters are thoroughly familiar with, have communicated with for years to their parents and neighborhod peers, and to which they maintain an emotional attachment. A certain respect must therefore be shown, if the teacher wishes both to achieve the child's confidence and protect his ego. A teacher who publicly degrades the youngster's language undermines his potential affinity for the school, his self-confidence, and his emotional security in general. This does not, of course, mean that standard English

---

[29] See an anthropological treatment of this problem by Norman A. McQuown, "Language-Learning From an Anthropological Point of View," *Elementary School Journal*, Vol. 54 (March, 1954), pp. 402–08.

should not be taught to lower-class children; it only means that attention must be given to a precondition.

To teach lower-class children the alien tongue that we call standard English involves more than technical problems of educational method. The purposes of standard English and formal learning are ordinarily not related to the self-image of the lower-class child; he does not usually think of himself as the kind of person who would speak this stilted-sounding standard language. The problem is probably too large for the school system alone to handle; the whole social structure is involved, particularly our patterns of social mobility and the values of lower-class culture. These considerations, which lie beyond the scope of this article, are mentioned only to indicate the complexity of the problem and the need for skepticism concerning easy solutions.

It should not be difficult for higher-class children to learn to respect and use lower-class speech. For these children know and often use lower-class language. The teacher who has a rational approach to the differences between the two languages, the teacher who is unhampered by moralistic and snobbish attitudes, can help children overcome their ambivalence toward language expression. If he succeeded, the great power of lower-class language to express emotions, a power ordinarily exploited with a clear conscience only by novelists, would become available to all and could extend the range of expressed feelings and perceptions.

The writer does not expect his suggestions to find wide acceptance at this time. We fear lower-class speech and are inclined to give it no quarter. The more precarious our social status in the higher classes—that is, the closer we are to the line that divides the middle from the lower classes or the more recent our ascent from the lower strata—the more insistent we are on the purity of our linguistic credentials. Such insecurity is perhaps especially troublesome to public school teachers, whose separation from the lower classes is often recent and precarious.

Linguistic snobbishness is part of the price we pay educationally for being chained to the demands of our social-class system. But our culture also has a tradition of resisting considerations of social class in dealing with people. Our tradition of emphasizing personal needs of individuals rather than outward social esteem contains the promise of a more rational handling of language problems and a more adequate public school education for all our children.[30]

Eunice S. Newton, director of the Reading Skills Center at Bennett College, submitted seven suggestions useful for teachers faced with the

---

[30] Cohn, *op. cit.*, pp. 438–40.

language problems of lower-class youth.[31] They included the key concepts of respect, exemplification, optimism, models, progress-awareness, practice, and "synonymity"; they can be elaborated in the following way: (1) Derision or deprecation of lower-class language is to be kept from classroom instruction. (2) The teaching method should emphasize specific and concrete references. When figurative or abstract concepts are used, and they certainly should not be avoided, exemplification by concrete phenomena should be added. (3) The teacher must have an optimistic and energetic approach. (4) The students should be provided with a maximum of opportunities to hear correct and creative English. This starts, of course, with the teacher as a consistent model of good English, and continues with supplementation by educational films, plays, recordings, and broadcasts. (5) Students should be provided with some practical means of checking their progress and growth of language proficiency. Evidence of progress can serve as an extraordinary reinforcer of effort and motivation. (Techniques could include comparative before-after recordings, progress charts, and praise by the observant teacher.) (6) Situations should be prepared in which the youngsters can exercise their developing language skills. (Techniques could include discussion groups, short plays, simple orations, composition writing, etc.) (7) Teachers should make frequent use of "synonymity," the habit of restating unfamiliar and abstract terms in a number of different and more familiar ways. A reference to "social consensus," for example, could be paraphrased as the "agreement of the majority of people." [32]

Full awareness of the shortcomings and disadvantages of the culturally deprived children of the working class can lead to further implementation of remedial steps. For example, there is a great need to reorganize and supplement reading materials used in schools, attuning them to the actual experiences and problems of the lower socioeconomic segment of the population. Examination of currently used textbooks reveals that they are concerned predominantly with middle-class philosophy, principles, and living standards, whose empirical referents are largely unknown and alien to the underprivileged youngster; his home, car, clothes, vacations, relatives, friends, etc., simply do not compare with those pictured in the middle-class readers. These books are oriented toward business, industry, politics, and the various occupations from the point of view of the white-collar participant, a vantage point unfamiliar to many working-class youngsters.[33] A reader including features that deal

---

[31] Eunice S. Newton, "Verbal Destitution: The Pivotal Barrier to Learning," *Journal of Negro Education*, Vol. 29 (Fall, 1960), pp. 497–99.

[32] *Ibid.*

[33] Reissman, *op. cit.*

with the positive aspects of the working man's life, his informal ways, cooperative family traditions, and the purpose and meaning of his work contributions, would more than merely capture his interest—they would add to his self-respect and to his self-understanding by stimulating meaningful introspection.

For the child from the working class, action speaks much louder than words. This has two implications. First, he learns more readily when he can manipulate things manually, and, second whatever and however he learns, he asks the question "what can I *do* with it?" He can therefore be more interested in the so-called three R's and the physical sciences than, for example, in art, music, and the social sciences, which strike him as either useless, too abstract, or both. The three R's allow him actual activities; he can read, write, add, subtract, and so forth—all activities involving some degree of motor activity and plausible applicability in everyday life. Beyond such limited school work, the youngster needs special persuasion. A proven technique is to involve youngsters in role-playing. History and memorable events can be impressively taught by having the youngsters play out leading roles of historical figures. Book knowledge would thereby suddenly take on lifelike reality, and the concreteness would make abstractions palatable and gradually comprehensible. Once abstractions are accepted and comprehended in *any* field, a generalizing effect spreads to other fields—if for no other reason than that the fear of intangible reports and abstractions has abated.

Another useful approach may be by means of the new teaching machines developed by B. F. Skinner at Harvard. Learning in many areas could be combined with manual, almost play-like, activities that attract the motoristically-inclined working-class youth.

A much more complicated and pernicious problem emerges from the question of how to deal with the lower-class youth's concern for toughness and masculinity. No doubt, the psychological ramifications of this preoccupation stand in the way of successful learning. However, it appears that no definite answer or remedial program can be suggested that would leave intact the structure of the American school as we know it today. As stated earlier, from the lower-class boy's point of view, school is a "prissy" place run by females, imposing effeminate values, and forcing him into equalitarian association with female classmates. This is not necessarily an unduly subjective perception, if one considers that the vast majority of elementary teachers are women in America (not so in many other countries), and that virtually all public schools are coeducational. There should never be any doubt that the female teacher is an official "socializer" who, by definition, *imposes,* not merely suggests, norms and values—the do's and don't's for the youngsters. For a sizable proportion of lower-class boys this creates a difficult situation, since they are overreacting against females in general in order to preserve an identity that started out ambiguously by having only mother as a model and object of identification. His early experience in a matricentric or matriarchal household develops into a reaction formation that also includes the female teacher as an object of rejection or aggression. The only remedial step that appears feasible is the hiring of more male teachers on the elementary school level to counterbalance the "female school." A number of sociologists and educators have recommended that every effort be made to encourage young men with whom such deprived children can identify to join the teaching profession and accept positions in schools in working-class districts.[34]

The second major problem in connection with the masculinity syndrome deals with the coeducational nature of American schools. It is again the young boy who is the focus of our concern, and certain elements of the reaction directed toward the female teacher also apply to female classmates. Similar antagonism and disassociation, which reinforce a counteridentity vis-a-vis the girl, can be observed. However, the boy–girl relationship in the context of the school contains a number of additional and extremely important elements that are not operant in the boy–teacher relationship. First of all, the boy finds himself thrown in with same-aged females who, for several reasons, are normally ahead of him in maturity. The girl has a facilitated identification process, since, unlike the boy she may keep mother as an uninterrupted model and object of identification; she also matures physically at an earlier age, thus often matching male classmates on the elementary school level in bodily size and strength. In addition, there seems to be a consistent superiority in academic performance on the part of girls in general. Girls, on the average, achieve higher marks.[35] All these factors, the greater psychological stability, the earlier physiological maturing, and the academic superiority, have the effect of placing the boy in an inferior position. This is obviously a great obstacle for the development of a secure self-concept. Early failure in relation to the other sex, especially as measured in terms of academic success, may create a lasting inferiority complex and persistent questions about self-adequacy. Also, a latent distrust and even hostility may be harbored by some boys against the other sex, under whom they experienced defeat in early life. The lasting impression that many girls derive from this interaction process is contempt for the male, who, in their experience, overacted his toughness and at the same time clearly showed inferiority and imma-

[34] Reissman, op. cit.; Sexton (1961), op. cit.

[35] James S. Coleman, The Adolescent Society (New York, Free Press, 1963).

turity in comparison to themselves. In essence, then, the typical American school contributes considerable anxiety to the adolescent experience.[36] If one equates this anxiety with a basic psychological tension, it follows by principle that attempts at tension reduction will be made. It seems that most attempts on the part of the lower-class boy can be classified as either tension avoidance in the form of truancy, early dropping out or attack on the teachers, administrators, and the school system in general as the basic source of tension.

What is the remedial answer to the problems created by coeducation? Is it sex-segregated schools? A grossly simplified answer might be yes. It might solve some of the above-mentioned problems—especially those of the lower-class boy. However, it is certain that a host of other problems would immediately evolve problems perchance more complex and trying than the previous ones. For example, American children would find themselves growing up in a sex-segregated atmosphere necessitating difficult reorientation in the teens when they start dating, courting, and marrying. They would be deprived of the relatively useful knowhow concerning interaction with the opposite sex that today's youngsters have acquired gradually and naturally by the time they reach their teens. The whole question of sex-segregated public schools is too Utopian to receive serious thought by the majority of today's school administrators and, consequently, will remain an unsolved problem on the educational scene. The best that this chapter can do is to point out the difficulties and problems, especially as they affect the lower-class youth, and sharpen thereby the sensitivity and understanding of the teacher.

Finally, there is one more problem that deserves attention. It deals with the overemphasis on *higher* education. Many contemporary politicians and a number of educators tend to generalize the importance and pertinence of higher academic pursuit to the point of recommending it to everyone and establishing it as the norm for every citizen. They try to promote the idea of universal college education as a "right" and as the "normal" experience, thereby automatically undervaluing everyone who is without higher education. Their otherwise admirable democratic fervor overlooks several conditions, making a Procrustean bed of higher education, and underplays the fact that some cannot and some do not want to embark on higher education. Without going into deeper details and ramificatons, and can say that in the first category are those who on the basis of limited native intelligence cannot carry out academic responsibilities; in the second category are those whose background has

---

[36] An application of this thought to the junior high school system is offered by M. Mead, "The Young Adult," in E. Ginsberg (ed.), *Values and Ideals of American Youth* (New York, Columbia University Press, 1961), pp. 37–51.

imbued them with an outlook on life that has no place for an academic career. To pressure either type toward higher education appears functionally inappropriate, since the results may not warrant the effort.

Of particular concern here is the second type, which includes many lower-class youngsters who are manually inclined, desire a technical non-academic occupation, and show a deep disaffection with formal education. By demonstrating academic bias and setting up higher education as the norm for a respectable citizen, educators question the respectability of manual labor. The hypothesis deriving from this argument is that the academic bias can be ego-destroying for the working-class youngster. If the teacher accomplishes control of this bias and reassures the youngster of the respectability and worthwhileness of manual labor—even if it is semiskilled or unskilled—she may spare him feelings of rejection, alienation, and inferiority. As a further result, the lower-class youngster may subsequently perform better in school because he feels accepted. By seeing the world without academic bias and realizing that many youngsters will experience in a manual occupation a satisfactory and meaningful place in life, educators may preclude anxiety and alienation —but *not* necessarily academic excellence.

Adolescence Lower-Class Style: The Peer-Gang Bridge

The lower-class limitations in abstract mental activities are manifest in other than merely verbal behavior. It is, for example, interesting to observe that peer relationships among lower-class youth tend to be much more casual and of the face-to-face type than among middle-class youth. It would be inconceivable to expect lower-class youngsters to form a committee to explore, prepare, or discuss a certain matter and then submit it to another committee for execution. This *is* done in middle-class high schools—but rarely with the participation of lower-class youth, let alone among neighborhood groups or street corner gangs. Lower-class youth prefer to interact *directly* and *concretely* with one another and insofar represent an empirical version of Toennis' famous *Gemeinschaft* concept.[37] On the other side, the middle-class youth operates *somewhat* farther along the continuum toward the *Gesellschaft* pole, which implies more contractual and formalized relationships—in other words, a more

---

[37] Ferdinand Toennis, *Gemeinschaft und Gesellschaft* (1st ed., 1887), translated and edited by C. P. Loomis as *Fundamental Concepts of Sociology* (New York, American Book Co., 1940).

abstract style of interaction. It must be emphasized that the difference is merely a matter of degree and of tendency, since both middle- and lower-class peer group formations fall into the overall category of primary group relationships, virtually synonymous with *Gemeinschaft*.

The most typical collective formation among lower-class youth is the *street corner gang*, thought of as the basic and generic form that may spawn various subforms, among them the delinquent gang. The street corner gang as such is not necessarily delinquent but rather a manifestation of the significance of the street as a social institution providing a medium for congregation and entertainment for the deprived youth. It was mentioned in a previous chapter that this is especially true for the deprived urban Negro youth. However, for deprived white youth the street corner gang takes on a more close-knit and continuous form where leadership is well defined and more consistent over a period of time. This difference is again reflected in the delinquent versions of the street corner gang. Negroes tend to explode in ephemeral and riotous mobs whereas white delinquents show more systematic, planned, and continuous gang activities. In either case, however, a feeling of belonging is engendered through the primary-group affiliation that partially or wholly functions as a substitute for the statuslessness within and alienation from the adult world.

Although the functions of the collective subgroupings in the lower and middle classes are very similar, if not identical (that is, bridging the lack of status between the child and the adult positions) there are several significant differences. First, the material implementations for the lower-class teen-ager are on a more modest level. For example, it is common that none of the gang members owns a car. Second, the scope of intrasubcultural communication is much more limited. Lower-class youth rarely subscribe to the nationwide teen magazines or other extensive networks of information and youth "gossip." Their gang activities are locally confined and exhibit more local color than middle-class teen-age groupings who, in a sense, represent "chapters" of a nationwide subculture. In fact, it seems more appropriate to reserve the concept of "teen-age subculture" to the middle-class teen-age phenomenon and refer to the collective formations of lower-class youth as small and locally confined gangs. Third, as a consequence, lower-class youth do not closely follow teen-age fashions, fads, and hero worship. A seeming anomaly must, however, be mentioned. While middle-class teen-agers are usually the carriers and promoters of youth fads and fashions in the United States, a fair proportion of their argot has traditionally been borrowed from the slang of lower-class youth. Whether the direction of the flow of styles and habits can be generalized to other areas besides the linguistic borrowing is as yet unexplored and awaits systematic research.

Among the number of fascinating hypotheses that could be formed on this question is the idea that standards of material implementation are diffused from the middle-class to the lower-class teen-age subculture. To the extent that these standards are recognized and desired but *unattainable,* frustration and discontent is stimulated among lower-class youth. They realize the relative deprivation, the social and economic inequity between their middle-class peers and themselves, and often derive from such factual observations the impetus and rationalization for delinquent acts.

The status uncertainty that teen-agers experience when they try to relate themselves to the adult world is most likely more complicated and drawn-out for the middle-class youngster. The working-class teen-ager is not as prone to prolong the interim stage by years of higher education, which invariably postpone the individual's full sovereignty. The lower-class youth tends to consider himself an adult as soon as he holds a "steady job," can afford a car, and above all, decides to marry. The time span between child and adult status is thereby shorter and the social-structural involvements are much simpler. For the relatively short interim period, the close-knit peer gang provides an unambiguous and compensating bridge structure.

Summary

Life style and life chances of lower-class youth are significantly affected by a number of relatively unique economic, social, and cultural circumstances. One of the most influential conditions is the lower-class ethos, containing a number of *core concerns* that allow for value orientations and preoccupations that result in unique behavior patterns. Among the core concerns of the lower-class ethos are trouble, a preoccupation with the adversities and complications of life; toughness, a value encouraging fearless, defiant, and bravado acts that usually are meant to uphold an image of masculinity; smartness, the esteemed ability to outfox, "take," and "con" others; excitement, the search for variety of experience and expression to break the monotony of an otherwise deprived life style; fate, a belief in destiny reflecting the feeling of powerlessness; anti-intellectualism, a negative attitude toward abstractness and formal learning; and authoritarianism, the tendency to interpret social interaction in vertical dimensions.

Early acquisition of these core sentiments tends to prepare the youth to become a failure in situations requiring competition with middle-class peers or in general situations that confront him with middle-class demands. For example, the value of being tough and masculine frequently creates friction and disruptive conduct in the school setting. The belief in fate and the related feeling or being powerless in the face of middle-class demands make for poor motivation and defeatist attitudes in school. If the anti-intellectual propensity is added to this syndrome, it is easy to see why youth from the lower socioeconomic stratum are overrepresented among the truants, failures, and dropouts. Of particularly defeat-prone nature are the linguistic deficiencies of lower-class youth. His deficiencies in vocabulary, syntax, and idiom limit his perceptual capability and permit only gross intellectual distinctions and abstractions. This limited ability in abstract reasoning also shows in lower degrees of achievement motivation. While middle-class parents carry out early, regular, and insistent inculcation of the value of individual achievement, lower-class parents are irregular and indifferent in this respect. Although lack of achievement and success orientation is consistently correlated with lower socioeconomic background, researchers have discovered a number of intervening variables that—if operationally applied—are likely to produce a more sensitive and predictable correlation. Examples of such intervening variables include categorizing the pupil as either a college or a noncollege prospect, the degree of parental domination, and the type of reference-group experience.

The educational establishment—middle-class in nature and outlook —is faced with the extremely difficult task of educating the lower-class youngster. A number of educators and behavioral scientists believe that this task can be successfully completed only when teachers become more sensitive toward the linguistic dilemma of the lower-class child, provide more realistic references that include the living conditions of the working man's family, appeal to the practical and motoristically-inclined learning preferences of the lower-class youth, involve the youth with deprived background in various role-playing techniques, and present themselves as identification-objects, implying that male teachers are needed to achieve a situation where the lower-class boy is less inclined to rebel and more able to identify.

Lower-class adolescence is distinguished from middle-class adolescence by more modest material implementation, more limited subcultural expanse and communication, less distinct fashions and fads, and an adolescent time span that usually is shortened by excluding prolonged educational and professional preparation. It appears that the close-knit gang, delinquent or nondelinquent, plays a prominent role in the life of the lower-class youth and functions as an effective bridge between child and adult status that, in a sense, tends to ease the adolescent transition.

special problem areas

part

V

special problem areas

the delinquent adolescent

Definition and Diversity

Any treatment of adolescence that claims to be reasonably complete must include a discussion of juvenile delinquency, since the two phenomena frequently overlap and exhibit significant correlations. Although, of course, not all adolescents are juvenile delinquents, virtually all juvenile delinquents are adolescents, and by definition therefore experience the poorly defined interim between the child and the adult positions. The *semi-anomic* quality of adolescence generates pressures that can lead to delinquency. In addition to the personal confusion of the adolescent, the statusless phase also creates *legal* confusion. There is unclarity as to what constitutes appropriate enforcement and execution of the law. There is often considerable ambiguity as to which agency has jurisdiction for dealing with a law-violating adolescent. Should it be the juvenile or the adult court? Should he, in case of conviction, be placed in a juvenile correctional or adult penal institution? Should the type of offense determine whether he is to stand trial as a child, juvenile, or adult? In short, adolescence has legal as well as psychological implications.

While these questions, which differ considerably from community to community, are by no means satisfactorily resolved, some degree of clarity can be achieved by formulating a general definition of the juvenile delinquent. The term "delinquency" dates back to the time of the ancient Romans, when it was used to refer to failure, neglect of duty, and abandonment of an agreement.[1] Vestiges of this original meaning can still be found today, as in referring to an adult as a "tax delinquent." But the connotation of the term has changed. When preceded by "juvenile," delinquent refers to a minor whom the court has found to have

---

[1] Milton L. Barron, *The Juvenile In Delinquent Society* (New York, Alfred A. Knopf, 1960), p. 11.

violated a federal, state, or local law designed to control both adult and adolescent behavior. There are also complex legal norms defining what is unlawful and improper behavior for *minors only* as a specific segment of the population. Adolescents, then, have to observe two sets of laws, those applying to all, including adults, and those applying exclusively to minors—an augmentation of laws that, obviously, tends to increase the possibility of law violation for youth.

Juvenile laws are often extremely general, even vague, as for example in the state of Illinois, where a delinquent is described as an "incorrigible" growing up in "idleness," "loitering" in the streets at night without a proper excuse, or guilty of "indecent" or "lascivious" conduct. New Mexico, as another example, exceeds Illinois in vagueness by making "habitual" infraction a necessary condition for the definition of delinquency. Its laws refer to "habitual" disobedience, unruliness, truancy, and waywardness, and to "habitually" jeopardizing the health, morals, and welfare of oneself and of others.[2] But exactly how much disobedience amounts to "incorrigibility"? And how often may a youth repeat an act before it is defined "habitual"? Such definitional questions, concerning the degree and the number of infractions, usually find no precise or delimited answer in the legal provisions.

It is virtually impossible to offer a definition of delinquency that is specific and applicable in all states of the United States because levels of tolerance vary from community to community and from agency to agency. The only solution seems to be to resort to a generic concept found in the federal Children's Bureau's statement saying, in essence, that juvenile delinquency constitutes behavior that comes to the attention of law enforcement agencies because it interferes with the rights of others and endangers the welfare of the juvenile, other individuals, or the community in general.[3]

Several more distinctions must be made before the definitional problem can be recognized in full. First, there is the distinction between the "adjudicated" delinquent and the "unofficial" delinquent. The former has officially been arraigned before juvenile authorities or courts, found guilty of certain violations, and channeled into formal corrective measures. The latter has been brought to the attention of the juvenile court, but without a formal court hearing. Unofficial delinquents may also be placed on probation or handled through other corrective measures, which are usually short of institutional confinement. Generally speaking, the policies of the juvenile court in question, as well as resources available

---

[2] Ruth S. Cavan, "The Concepts of Tolerance and Contraculture as Applied to Delinquency," *The Sociological Quarterly,* Vol. 2 (October, 1961), p. 243.

[3] As interpreted by Cavan, *ibid.,* p. 243.

in the community, will determine whether the adolescent is processed as an "official" or "unofficial" delinquent.

A second definitional problem deals with the age of the youthful offender. Very often, the concept of "minor," or in the offending case, "juvenile," is used to connote the status of a youth who is still under his parents' guardianship. Consistent with the tradition of the English common law, there appears to be consensus throughout the United States that the minimum age at which a youth can be considered a juvenile is seven years. Below this age, a child is held incapable of responsibly discerning right from wrong, and therefore, incapable of committing a felony. In practice a child under the age of seven who commits a serious violation is viewed as a dependency or neglect case. On the other hand, the upper age limits defining the juvenile are variable and are complicated by specific stipulations, such as sex differentiation. In a number of states the upper age limit for girls is higher than for boys, despite the fact that the age of consent to marry is usually lower for girls than for boys. In addition, many municipalities maintain modified versions of the state laws that set juvenile definitions which are broader than those of the state courts. More than half of the states set the upper age limit at 18 years; six states—Maine, Massachusetts, Delaware, Kentucky, Louisiana, and Missouri—have set it at 17; and seven states—Vermont, Connecticut, New York, Maryland, North Carolina, Georgia, and Utah—plus Puerto Rico and the Virgin Islands have determined 16 as the age above which a person becomes ineligible for juvenile court consideration.[4]

A third problem impeding a uniform definition stems from the variable *description* of delinquency. Eight states lack clear statutory specifications of what constitutes a juvenile delinquent act. In lieu of statutory references, the judge decides—more or less on the basis of current community norms or his personal evaluation—whether or not the defendant is a juvenile delinquent. On the other hand, in many other jurisdictions specific statutory references are considered, and the defendant is judged delinquent on the basis of violating such specific proscriptions as hitching a ride on the back of a train, bus, or street car; turning on water hydrants; trespassing; soliciting, or selling without a permit; visiting a house of ill repute; wandering in streets at night; sleeping in alleys; patronizing public poolrooms; begging or receiving alms; and so forth.[5]

To compound the problem still further, many behavior forms are classified as normal and permissible for adults but deviant and delin-

---

[4] Sophia M. Robison, *Juvenile Delinquency, Its Nature and Control* (New York, Holt, Rinehart and Winston, 1960), p. 8.

[5] *Ibid.*, pp. 8, 245.

quent for minors. Such behavior as visiting gambling places, associating with "immoral" persons (for example, prostitutes), consuming alcoholic beverages, or smoking cigarettes carries age-differentiated definitions and constitutes delinquent behavior if performed by a person below 18, 17, or 16, depending on the state. Needless to say, these differences between jurisdictions cause great difficulty in compiling reliable statistics on juvenile delinquency for comparative purposes or for showing an overall national profile.

Such confusing statutory specifics, varying community standards, and more understanding attitudes toward youth problems in general have ushered in a flexible rehabilitative orientation and a more relativistic manner of defining juvenile delinquency. The legal definition of juvenile delinquency is shifting to a more eclectic, clinical, and, in terms of statutory codes, less restricted definition. As mentioned earlier, a number of states already have no statutory definition at all, allowing the judge greater freedom and flexibility in forming a nonlegalistic opinion of the overall situation and personality of the youth. Proponents of this policy think that unrestricted definition permits individualized treatment based on need rather than on the nature of the offense, thus giving the juvenile authorities the opportunity to protect and aid minors to a greater extent. Dissenters from this philosophy, however, perceive a number of dangerous possibilities and point out that without the check of precise terms in the law, inadequate parents—who at times are the real "delinquents"—have a free hand in getting their children assigned a juvenile status. A second possible shortcoming of nonstatutory judgment is that it allows for biased treatment of youth of particular ethnic, social class, or racial groups by police and other officials whose subjectivity could conveniently hide under the legal vagueness.

The Question of Collective vs. Individual Delinquency

Juvenile delinquency often has a *collective* connotation and as such may refer to gang, mob, or subcultural forms of delinquent activities. In such instances, the focus is no longer on the individual transgressor, but on the group as a whole—in a sense, applying a philosophy of *social realism* that views the collectivity as an entity endowed with qualities beyond the mere sum of the individual members. Generally speaking, the difference between individual and collective behavior is of relatively little consequence to the legal instance, since Western legal philosophy continues to assign the weight of legal responsibility to the individual actor and not to the collectivity as a whole. However, this difference is of great importance to the social scientist. The origin, method, and result of a delinquent act shows significantly varying patterns depending on individual or collective involvement.

On the collective level, delinquency has been subdivided into several forms, into distinct types of subcultures. Albert K. Cohen and James F. Short, Jr., two criminologists, have suggested a number of positional variables that they hypothesize to be potentially responsible for subcultural delinquency.[6] Such delinquent subcultures include the following types: (1) *The parent male subculture.* This is the small gang or clique, described as "nonutilitarian, malicious, negativistic, versatile, and characterized by shortrun hedonism and group autonomy."[7] It is referred to as "parent" subculture because it is the most common and generic form in the United States. (2) *The conflict-oriented subculture.* This usually is a highly developed form of collective delinquency, exhibited in large gangs, the membership of which may run into the hundreds. They are found to have an elaborate organization that often includes such distinct roles as president, vice-president, war-chief, and armorer. They have a territorial base, a name, a strong sense of corporate identity, and a public personality or "rep" in the gang world. (3) *The drug-addict subculture.* Usually a correlation can be observed between drug addiction and delinquency. In most cases, the addicts were already delinquent before grouping themselves into distinct addict subcultures. Their delinquency is almost always of the nonviolent and income-producing type which is making their drug habit possible, since most addictive drugs are available only in illegal traffic and at great cost. (4) *Semiprofessional theft.* This is a sort of loosely integrated subcultural forerunner of professional adult thiefs who are proficient in skillful and ordinarily nonviolent thievery. In a sense, it is a "stage" in the life history, a specialized delinquency, before ascending to the "élite" thievery of the adult "professionals." (5) *The middle-class delinquent subculture.* With this category, Cohen and Short looked toward the future, anticipating empirical exploration of a not yet very clearly developed phenomenon. The traditional form of middle-class delinquency usually is of the "parent" type, but may evolve into other forms in the future. (6) Finally, the authors ponder the question of *female delinquent subcultures.* They conclude that a girl's association and status are ordinarily involved with and largely dependent on "the status of the males with whom she is identified."[8] However, there are some exceptions

---

[6] Albert K. Cohen and James F. Short, Jr., "Research in Delinquent Subcultures," *Journal of Social Issues,* Vol. 14. No. 3 (1958), pp. 20–37.

[7] *Ibid.*

[8] *Ibid.,* p. 34.

as, for example, where girls organize in gangs for sexual activities, drug addiction, or as counterparts of the male hoodlum gang. Because of sparsity of research in female delinquency, no reliable generalizations can be offered.

Another semicollective type of delinquency that was not mentioned by the authors of the foregoing typology, probably primarily because it is too loosely integrated to be defined as subcultural, could be called *normative delinquency.* "Normative" delinquency refers to the lighter expressions of delinquent patterns that are not deeply-rooted and are often found on school campuses where deviant acts have become the norm for prestige and recognition within the group. These activities are widespread and may include, for example, such habits as window breakage, truancy, drug experimentation, and disruptive behavior in the class room. These behavior patterns are not subcultural in the strict sense of the word, since they are often done by the individual in isolated fashion. They can be called "normative" because they are common offenses, relatively accepted by the peers, and under certain circumstances even expected and respected by peers. "Normative" delinquency allows for considerable individuality, since the act is not always carried out collectively, but usually by one individual at a time. Neverthless, the influence of imitation and peer stimulation is usually so strong that the ensuing behavior *can* sometimes be classified as collective. No doubt, this classification is debatable and should be considered a transitional category between individual and collective behavior.

There are also those youngsters whose motivations as well as acts are highly ideographic and not directly related to collective activities or institutions. These individualistic delinquents may commit offenses that range from minor public disturbances, vagrancy, and theft, to rape and homicide. Examination of the backgrounds of such noncollective delinquents does not necessarily reveal any striking similarities among them in respect to social or psychopathological conditions or to frequency of offense. In fact, an adolescent may be found to have committed a delinquent act out of ignorance or negligence, without malevolence. According to L. M. Hussey's "classic" article, this is quite possible since there are a number of obsolete and technical prescriptions and proscriptions in the legal codes. He conjectures that virtually everyone unknowingly and indeliberately violates enough of these codes to accumulate in just one day a theoretical imprisonment of five years and a fine of nearly $3,000.[9]

---

[9] L. M. Hussey, "Twenty-Four Hours Of A Law-Breaker," *Harper's,* Vol. 160 (March, 1930), pp. 436–39.

Since delinquency takes this variety of forms—subcultural, "normative," and individual—official statistics would do well to differentiate among them and specify the freqency of occurrence of each type. Such differentiation would facilitate sociological research and help social scientists to chart more specific trends and correlations.

Volume, Distribution, and Trends

Whether from official or unofficial sources, prevailing opinion tends to assume that there is an all-time high incidence rate of juvenile delinquency. According to statistics, delinquency appears to be increasing at a faster rate than the adolescent population. While this may be true, social scientists are slow in accepting these figures as a valid picture of the *actual* increase, since there has also been a concomitant increase in new laws and regulations, expansion of law machinery, and improvement of reporting and recording techniques. These innovations may have aided in creating the impression of an all-time high incidence of delinquency.

Over the past decades innumerable new laws have been passed, thus increasing the possibility of violation. A maze of specific legislation, unknown at the beginning of the century, governing the life of contemporary youth, has added laws concerning traffic regulation, compulsory school attendance, child labor regulations, curfews, etc. All these laws impose comprehensive limitations on what a minor may and may not do, while previously control of behavior in these areas, as well as the punishment administered, was considered to be largely the responsibility of parents and guardians. A thorough 1967 investigation of law enforcement and administration of justice in the United States by a presidential commission admitted that:

> Enormous numbers of young people appear to be involved in delinquent acts. Indeed, self-report studies reveal that perhaps 90% of all young people have committed at least one act for which they could have been brought to juvenile court. Many of these offenses are relatively trivial—fighting, truancy, running away from home. Statutes often define delinquency so broadly as to make virtually all youngsters delinquent.[10]

Owing in part to this expansion of legislative enactments and provisions, a corresponding expansion of law enforcement agencies and

---

[10] The President's Commission on Law Enforcement and Administration of Justice, *The Challenge of Crime In A Free Society* (Washington, D.C., Government Printing Office, February, 1967), p. 55.

personnel has followed. In turn, this has led to an increased possibility of delinquency detection and hence to the arrest and prosecution of more violators. In addition, a tendency has evolved to settle minor difficulties through police action and court facilities, while formerly such problems would have been privately settled. Contemporary United States codes and laws specify many forms of conduct as delinquent and punishable that in other countries would merely be regarded as disreputable or in "bad" taste.[11]

Improved techniques of reporting and recording also obscure a valid comparison of today's delinquency incidence with that of previous generations. During previous decades, statistics on crime and delinquency were far less thorough and reliable than today. Moreover there was and still is the confusing question of whether a youngster is a delinquent on the strength of mere detection, on apprehension, or on final adjudication. If these different statuses are not explicitly defined in statistical compilations, comparisons become almost meaningless.

These considerations make researchers sharply aware of the near-insurmountable difficulties in reliably charting trends or making comparisons with bygone or contemporary jurdisdictions. In sum, valid comparisons of law violation over a period of time or across juridical domains require comparable conditions. Such conditions are generally lacking, and where they have been introduced, they often have been in existence too short a time to allow reliable longitudinal comparisons.

The need for a consistent national crime and delinquency census has become obvious. Credit must be given to a number of federal bureaus for attempting to meet this need by systematically gathering nationwide statistics. Three federal agencies report *specific types* of crime and delinquency. The Federal Bureau of Prisons presents statistics on juveniles charged with violations of federal statutes. The data are based on the reports of the arresting agencies, United States probation officers, and marshals and include such information as the minor's age, sex, race, type of offense committed, type of detention, and length of sentence. For those juveniles referred to the Attorney General and held in federal institutions, additional information is available, including IQ, previous delinquent record, degree of education, and religious background.[12] A second source is the Administrative Office of the United States Courts, which obtains figures from courts on juveniles charged

---

[11] See a comparison of American and German crime definition and crime rates in Mabel A. Elliott, "Perspective on the American Crime Problem," *Social Problems,* Vol. 5 (Winter, 1957–58), pp. 184–93. Also see a discussion of international delinquency statistics in Walter A. Lunden, *Statistics On Delinquents and Delinquency* (Springfield, Ill., Charles C Thomas. 1964).

[12] Published in *Federal Prisons.*

with violating federal laws and tried under the Federal Juvenile Delinquency Act. Finally, specific data on delinquency in public and private schools are collected by the U. S. Office of Education.

The two government agencies responsible for preparing the most *comprehensive* picture on delinquency in the United States are the Federal Bureau of Investigation, U. S. Department of Justice, which annually publishes the *Uniform Crime Report,* and the Children's Bureau of the Department of Health, Education, and Welfare, which publishes *Juvenile Court Statistics.* The latter agency has been presenting summary reports from juvenile courts since 1927, during the early years of its operation reporting only official cases and more recently also including unofficial cases. Its information is based on voluntary reports by the various courts, and not until 1956 could the figures submitted be considered representative of the United States as a whole. The more adequate representation was achieved through the technical assistance of the Bureau of the Census, which designed a reliable nationwide sample system. In spite of this improvement, differential administrative customs of courts and probation departments plus several of the pitfalls of cross-juridical data compilation mentioned earlier make it difficult to present a truly representative picture. For example, in some states more than in others, cases are processed by police, sheriffs, or school authorities without recourse to courts.

The agency that seems to present the most complete and reliable picture of United States crime and delinquency is the FBI. Its *Uniform Crime Reports* are a device through which the volume and the trends of delinquency can be determined. But even here caution is recommended. Statistical contributions for the report come from the various states on a voluntary basis and lack completeness. It has been estimated that approximately 85% of the United States population is covered today by the FBI's report. Although carefully adjusted and interpreted, the different data are of course the product of different jurisdictions and therefore retain some degree of incomparability. Furthermore, there are limitations concerning the longitudinal dimension. From the publication's beginning in 1941 to the early 1950's, its information was drawn exclusively from the fingerprint arrest records received by the Identification Division. Starting in 1952, however, the source of data was broadened and included summary reports forwarded to the FBI by police departments throughout the nation. The new method has made available a greater and more detailed volume of information on juvenile delinquency and has made comparisons between the periods prior to and after 1952 extremely difficult. Another change occurred in 1958, when a Consultant Committee on Uniform Crime Reporting initiated further modifications. It was decided to issue annual instead of semiannual publications of the *Uniform Crime Reports* and to adopt a new system for tabulating the Crime Index. This system classified crimes in seven major categories: (1) murder, with differentiation between manslaughter, murder of negligence, and nonnegligent murder; (2) forceable rape, excluding statutory offenses; (3) aggravated assault, excluding simple assault, assault and battery, and fighting; (4) burglary; (5) larceny of $50 or more; (6) robbery; and (7) auto theft.

The mid-1960's findings of the *Uniform Crime Reports* include the year 1965. During that year the population of the country increased by 1.3% according to the U. S. Bureau of the Census. There were 2,780,000 serious crimes during 1965, which amounted to a 6% increase over 1964. A greater percentage of teen-age crimes was recorded in the suburban areas (10,000–50,000 population) than in either the rural or urban areas. The outstanding crimes in suburbs were auto theft, burglary, rape, and aggravated assault, while the most typical crime in cities was robbery.

The arrest trends during the mid-1960's showed the age group under 15 to have the highest rate of increase. These young teen-agers showed a 3.6% increase in the above-mentioned seven categories of the crime index. However, an *extended* list of crimes and delinquencies, comprising 21 categories, showed that teen-agers under 15 had a 5.3% increase in "total" crimes. The age group under 18 showed a .7% increase in the seven-category index and a 3.4% increase in the total

TABLE 14–1. Arrest Trends between 1964 and 1965 by Types of Crime and Age Brackets, in Percentage Increase or Decrease.

Type of Crime		Age	
	Under 15	Under 18	Over 18
1. a. Murder	+20.2%	+ 8.1%	+ 7.4%
b. Manslaughter	+22.2	− 9.6	− 4.3
2. Forceable Rape	+20.9	+13.4	− 0.5
3. Robbery	+ 9.2	+ 5.7	+ 0.8
4. Aggravated Assault	+11.1	+ 7.1	+ 4.9
5. Burglary	+ 7.8	+ 4.4	+ 3.5
6. Larceny	+ 8.1	− 0.1	− 1.3
7. Auto Theft	− 0.6	− 4.6	+ 1.1
Total of Index [a]	+ 3.6	+ 0.7	+ 1.2
Total of all Crimes [b]	+ 5.3	+ 3.4	+ 0.1

[a] Includes a total of the seven crimes of the index of crime.

[b] Includes a total of all crime, which is listed under 21 other headings.

Adapted from Federal Bureau of Investigation, U. S. Department of Justice, *Uniform Crime Reports* 1965, p. 111.

crime report. The seven-category crimes of the age group over 18 rose by 1.2%, while the increase in total crimes amounted to only .1%. Narcotics violations were up 41.5% for the ages under 15, and up 38.1% for the ages under 18. Vandalism increased by 6.3% for the ages under 15, and 5.5% for the ages under 18.[13]

The comparison of urban, suburban, and rural residential areas during 1965 shows an increase in the suburban crime rate that is greater than that of either the city or rural areas. The rate, which is based on the number of offenses per 100,000 population, shows an increase of 3.2% for the urban areas, 7.9% for the suburban, and 1.7% for the rural areas. Narcotics violations were up 39.9% in the city, 69.1% in the suburbs, and decreased 20.3% in the rural areas. Vandalism increased in the urban, suburban, and rural areas by 4.9%, 9.2%, and 8.5%, respectively.[14]

Another way of comparing the extent of teen-age crime in the three residential areas is by percentage of offenders in various age groups. Offenders under 15 years of age made up 23.9% of city crime, 23.8% of suburban crime, and 10.5% of rural crime. The age group under 18

TABLE 14–2.   Trends of Delinquency between 1964 and 1965 By Residential Areas, in Percentage Increase or Decrease, for Ages under 18.

Types of Delinquency	Residential Area		
	Urban	Suburban	Rural
1. a. Murder	+ 7.2%	+16.7%	+47.6%
b. Manslaughter	+ 2.3	−37.0	−34.4
2. Forceable Rape	+12.5	+ 4.2	+22.1
3. Robbery	+ 5.4	+27.0	−15.1
4. Aggravated Assault	+ 6.1	+12.8	+18.8
5. Burglary	+ 5.3	+ 2.1	− 3.9
6. Larceny	− 0.1	+ 4.6	− 6.1
7. Auto Theft	− 4.2	− 3.7	−17.4
Total of Index [a]	+ 0.9	+ 3.1	− 6.8
Total of all Crimes [b]	+ 3.2	+ 7.9	+ 1.7

[a] Includes the seven major categories of crime.

[b] Includes total of all crime, based on a 21-item list.

Adapted from Federal Bureau of Investigation, U.S. Department of Justice, *Uniform Crime Report* 1965, pp. 120, 129, 137.

---

[13] Federal Bureau of Investigation, U.S. Department of Justice, *Uniform Crime Reports* 1965, pp. 1–3, 111.

[14] *Ibid.*, pp. 120, 129, 137.

TABLE 14–3.   Per Cent of Offenders by Age Groups and Residential Areas.

Age	Residential Area			
	Urban	Suburban	Rural	All Areas
Under 15	23.9%	23.8%	10.5%	22.8%
Under 18	49.9	52.8	36.4	48.7
Under 21	63.5	68.0	58.0	63.6
Under 25	74.0	78.4	72.2	73.9

Adapted from Federal Bureau of Investigation, U.S. Department of Justice, *Uniform Crime Reports* 1965, pp. 114, 123, 134, 140.

contributed 49.9% to the urban offenders, 52.8% to the suburban, and 36.4% to the rural criminals.[15]

The offender under 20 years of age tends to repeat more often than the adult criminal. Over a two-year period, the nonrepeaters under 20 amounted to 41.9% while 58.1% were repeaters. Adult statistics show that 52.0% were nonrepeaters, and 48.0% were repeaters.[16]

To demonstrate the trend in delinquency and crime over a longer period of time, comparison is made between 1960 and 1965. The population change from 1960 to 1965 was reported as a gain of 8% for the total United States population. However, for the teen-age segment there was an increase of 17%.[17] The increase in total crime during this period amounted to a surprisingly low 1.8% for age brackets above 18, but amounted to a high of 54.4% for the teen-agers under 18.[18]

In conclusion, during the 1960's the numerical as well as percentage increase of teen-age delinquency appears to have been substantial. Between 1960 and 1965, the per cent of teen-age offenses rose steadily. For example, in 1960, 14.3% of all urban offenders were in their teens.[19] In 1965, 21% of the urban offenders were teen-agers.[20] The 1967 report by a Presidential commission on law enforcement and administration of justice, evaluating reliable statistics including published and unpublished data of the FBI, arrived at the conclusion that "most crimes, wherever they are committed, are committed by boys and young men. . . . Three-quarters of the 1965 arrests for Index crimes, plus petty larceny and

---

[15] Uniform Crime Reports 1965, *op. cit.*, pp. 114, 123, 132, 140.

[16] Uniform Crime Reports 1965, *op. cit.*, p. 31.

[17] Uniform Crime Reports 1965, *op. cit.*, p. 1.

[18] Uniform Crime Reports 1965, *op. cit.*, p. 110.

[19] Federal Bureau of Investigation, U.S. Department of Justice, *Uniform Crime Reports* 1960, p. 93.

[20] *Uniform Crime Reports* 1965, *op. cit.*, p. 123.

TABLE 14–4.   Arrest Trends between 1960 and 1965 by Type of Crime and Age Brackets, in Percentage Increase or Decrease.

Type of Crime	Age	
	Under 18	Over 18
1. a. Murder	+42.5%	+18.6%
b. Manslaughter	− 1.5	+ 4.5
2. Forceable Rape	+34.6	+12.0
3. Robbery	+39.6	+ 6.5
4. Aggravated Assault	+64.2	+23.8
5. Burglary	+26.3	+16.9
6. Larceny	+60.0	+26.7
7. Auto Theft	+43.8	+37.7
Total of Index [a]	+46.9	+23.3
Total of all Crimes [b]	+54.4	+ 1.8

[a] Includes the seven major categories of crimes.

[b] Includes total of all crimes, based on a 21-item list.

Adapted from Federal Bureau of Investigation, U.S. Department of Justice, *Uniform Crime Reports* 1965, p. 110.

negligent manslaughter, were of people less than 25 years old. More 15-year-olds were arrested for those crimes than people of any other age, and 16-year-olds were a close second."[21] The report further disclosed that the 15- to 17-year-old group ranked highest for burglaries, larcenies, and auto thefts. For these three property crimes, 15-year-olds were arrested more than persons of any other age, with 16-year-olds again running a close second. For crimes of violence, the highest ranking age bracket was that of 18 to 20, followed by the 21 to 24 age category.[22] The presidential commission reported rough estimates, based on findings of the United States Children's Bureau and on independent studies, "that one in every nine youths—one in every six male youths—will be referred to juvenile court in connection with a delinquent act (excluding traffic offenses) before his 18th birthday."[23] The general picture of juvenile delinquency in the United States during the mid-1960s is reflected by the *inverse* correlation between arrest rates and age groups. Generally, the higher the age bracket, the lower the arrest rate. "Arrest rates are highest for persons aged 15 through 17, next highest for those 18 through 20, dropping off quite directly with increase in age."[24]

[21] *The Challenge of Crime in a Free Society, op. cit.,* p. 5.

[22] *Ibid.,* p. 44.

[23] *Ibid.,* p. 55.

[24] *Ibid.*

Finally, there is a novel trend in the locality distribution of juvenile delinquency. There was a notable increase in delinquency in the suburban area during the mid-1960s. Teen-agers made up 31.7% of all criminals in the suburban area, compared to 21.1% in the urban and 18.7% in the rural areas.[25]

Causative Theories

A natural question that arises for the public and the behavioral scientist alike is the question of causation of delinquency. History shows that a range of answers has been suggested that have tried to explain delinquency and crime by biogenetic determinants, psychological conditions, social involvement, and physical or ecological environment. Some of these theories are suspected to be fruitless, speculative, nonempirical, and not borne out by reality—as, for example, the biogenetic theory that ascribed causation of delinquency to innate characteristics. Those theories that have been retained by contemporary behavioral scientists and that appear to substantially contribute to the explanation of delinquent and criminal behavior can be summed up under either sociogenic or psychogenic causes, taking social circumstances or personality features, respectively, as their major explanatory foci.

The professional literature reflects considerable ambiguity and controversy as to the compatibility of the psychogenic and sociogenic approaches, and the reader should be alerted to the fact that at times he may encounter the argument that a given approach is able to offer an explanation of crime within a logically closed schema that requires no recourse to other theoretical contributions. At other times, probably more infrequently, the argument is advanced that the two etiological foci should not be understood as incompatible or mutually exclusive, but rather as complementary and supplementary investigations of the origin of law-breaking behavior. The argument cannot be discussed, let alone resolved, in this chapter, and the reader can only be made cognizant of its existence.

This treatment must be further limited, as only the major etiologies dealing with sociogenic aspects will be discussed. Writing and research concerning the sociogenic etiology of crime has been so prolific that no single chapter could possibly do justice to the abundance of thought and empirical findings that have been accumulated in this area. The following discussion can therefore hope to achieve only a cursory sketch of the explanatory attempts in the field of sociological criminology.

---

[25] *Uniform Crime Reports* 1965, *op. cit.*, p. 123.

Probably the most generic theory developed by an American criminologist to explain delinquent and general criminal phenomena has been the "differential association" theory by the late Edwin H. Sutherland, presented in his famous *Principles of Criminology*.[26] Although its usefulness is curtailed by an extremely broad emphasis on the processes of learning in general, it deserves merit for its pioneer work in explaining delinquency as an outcome of social interaction and social learning and not of some type of personal pathology. Sutherland states his theory in terms of nine integral axioms. All of them center around the core proposition that delinquency and criminality can be most effectively explained by the *character of the associations* an individual establishes in his social and personal relationships. The forces most influential in shaping the direction of motives and in patterning attitudes and rationalizations are thought of as growing out of intimate group involvement. A consistent and sufficiently intimate group environment contains all the learning mechanisms that are necessary and basic to any learning process and, depending on the content, may teach delinquent or law-abiding behavior. If the balance of a youth's social exposure is in favor of delinquent teaching, there is a high possibility that he will internalize these teachings and become delinquent. This assumption is diametrically opposed to the purely individualistic points of view of many psychoanalysts and psychiatrists, who tend to regard criminal behavior as an outcome, phase, or symptom of personality malfunctioning.

The "differential association" theory has served as a framework for a number of studies, notably those concerning delinquent contacts outside the family setting, such as involvement with gangs, neighborhood association, cliques, peer groups, etc.

Home life can also be a source of delinquent contact. Within the family two types of learning associations are possible. One is the vertical transmitting of behavior patterns from parents to children, and the other is the horizontal learning process through interaction of sib with sib. The findings of family studies support the theoretical principle of "differential association" by showing that a large proportion of other members of the families of delinquents were also delinquent or criminal. Prominent support came from Sheldon and Eleanor Glueck (1934) who reported that 80% of their delinquent subjects came from homes in which other members were violators of the law.[27]

---

[26] Edwin H. Sutherland, *Principles of Criminology*, 4th ed. (Philadelphia, Lippincott, 1947).

[27] Sheldon Glueck and Eleanor Glueck, *One Thousand Juvenile Delinquents: Their Treatment By Court And Clinic* (Cambridge, Mass., Harvard University Press, 1934).

Other studies have found that the horizontal transmission of delinquent patterns were more influential than vertical transmission. Harry M. Shulman's findings explain the sometimes puzzling situation in which delinquent children grow up under entirely noncriminal parents.[28] The influence of their peers plays an overriding role in directing their motivations and behavior patterns. Peer groups of children and teen-agers can be divided into two main categories: the informal peer groups such as the gang, the clique, and the play group; and the more formally organized groups such as clubs, religious youth groups, and community organizations. The informal-type peer group is frequently outside the direct control of parents and other adults and can exert a counterforce against the nondelinquent home background. If the counterforce is consistent and strong enough, the youth may succumb to it and participate in delinquent activities.

This, of course, does not imply that all peer groups are of the delinquent type. Many of them, if not most, are in conformity with noncriminal home standards. In those cases, however, where the peer group represents a separate and delinquent environment, its influence is extremely powerful and likely to achieve far-reaching conformity to its standards. A youth usually develops greater sensitivity to its sanctions than to those of any other group. His parents, for example, may make decisions concerning the clothes he is to wear, but the peer group's standards are crucial in determining the child's *satisfaction* with the clothes. Similar reactions can be observed in respect to the child's lingo, manners, attitudes toward school, relationships with the other sex, etc.

Another function of the peer group consists of providing a social medium for meeting those basic needs which W. I. Thomas summed up in his "four wishes," security, response, recognition, and new experience.[29] It is especially the need for new experience that frequently plays a prominent role in the etiology of delinquent acts. For boys with access to a range of attractive recreational facilities, this need for new experience can be channeled into athletics; for boys and girls with the proper parental guidance and value orientation it may turn into intellectual explorations; and for the youth without adequate facilities and value-inculcation it may develop into the use of stimulants, habitual gambling, and various predatory exploits. These activities establish a world of adventure and on-going emotional gratification that is hard for the unsympathetic outsider to see and understand.[30]

---

[28] Harry M. Shulman, *Crime And The Community* (Albany, N.Y., The Crime Commission of New York State, 1928).

[29] W. I. Thomas, *The Unadjusted Girl* (New York, Little, Brown & Co., 1923).

[30] See the "Classical" treatment of gangs and gang delinquency in Frederick M. Thrasher, *The Gang* (Chicago, University of Chicago Press, 1936).

The work of Walter C. Reckless and coworkers adds an important corollary to Sutherland's theory of "differential association." Criminologist Reckless has spent many years researching the role of the youth's self-concept as a pivotal phenomenon that can make a youngster move toward either a delinquent or a law-abiding life. This inquiry proved to be of value in explaining the behavior of boys who grow up either in a delinquency-inducing milieu and turn out to be nondelinquent or who grow up in a law-abiding milieu and become delinquent.[31]

A significant improvement in the "differential association" idea was suggested by criminologist Daniel Glaser with the concept of "differential identifications." Association *per se* is a weak explanatory concept that is in need of greater sensitivity and further specificity. A youth, for example, can possibly associate with, or even live with, other delinquent persons and still retain a nondelinquent style of life. What the original version of the "differential association" theory neglects to emphasize is the fact that a certain degree of delinquent *identification* must take place before a youth will become a true delinquent. Notwithstanding the circumstance of association with a delinquent environment, a youth many choose as his object of identification a nondelinquent person or group outside and beyond the delinquent associates and in this way immunize himself against the influence of delinquent peers.[32] The basic idea is that one takes over the behavior of the models with whom one identifies, and that these models do not have to be part of a face-to-face or person-to-person identification process, but can consist of relatively abstract reference groups or reference personalities. For example, a youth could identify with the so-called hippies without having had actual physical contact with such a group.

The explanatory power of the self-concept and of the concept of "differential identification" is so superior to the original version of the "differential association" theory that one could almost call them substitute or alternative approaches to the etiology of criminal behavior instead of mere modifications of the original theory.

A theory that appears to be of explanatory value in relation to the matter of differential opportunities and the genesis of crime and that was mentioned in rudimentary form by the French sociologist Émile

---

[31] Walter C. Reckless, Simon Dinitz, and Barbara Kay, "The Self Component in Potential Delinquency and Potential Non-Delinquency," *American Sociological Review*, Vol. 22 (October, 1957), pp. 566–70.

[32] Daniel Glaser, "Criminality Theories and Behavioral Images," *American Journal of Sociology*, Vol. 61 (March, 1956), pp. 433–44.

Durkheim around the turn of the century[33] was elaborated by a number of American sociologists, among them notably Robert K. Merton.[34] This extremely interesting framework suggests an analytic distinction between cultural goals and the legitimate means by which they can be achieved. The goal, a coveted item or condition, may be clearly described and recognizable and may constitute what people feel is worth striving for. The legitimate means consist of various specified procedures through which individuals seek to obtain the goals without coming into conflict with social or legal norms. However, such legitimate means often may be obscure, vague, or out of reach for certain economic or ethnic segments of the population. Such a societal state of affairs can be called *anomie,* normlessness, which under certain circumstances may prove to be criminogenic. For example, social-structural conditions to which individuals of the lower socioeconomic strata are subject may make difficult the availability of legitimate means for reaching goals that are clearly seen and the achievement of which is socially encouraged. The theory thus allows prediction that population segments suffering from such *anomic* conditions within a society that places emphasis and personal goal attainment without similar emphasis on the legitimate procedures for achieving them will tend to have high rates of criminal and deviant behavior. These forms of "innovating" behavior are designed to achieve the goals by whatever means necessary. Merton argues that crime rates will differ according to the extent of "disjuncture" between the goals that members of the society internalize and their socially structured opportunities for obtaining them. Such a goal/means discrepancy frequently occurs among those individuals in culturally underprivileged positions who lack the necessary education and professional training to successfully partake of the culturally encouraged goals, mostly material in nature, and as a consequence develop high rates of criminal and deviant behavior. Merton's argument does not assert that all persons of lower-class standing will exhibit high crime rates. Disproportionately high crime rates will only emerge when cultural goals are set for them and are internalized by them as significant aims in life, while all along their social position incapacitates them in achieving the aim by legitimate procedures. If, for example, the goals held out to the members of a society differed in accordance with their social-structure abilities, as in a caste society, one would not expect the same criminogenic reaction. It is thus only in *relation to the goal which individuals seek* that the

---

[33] Émile Durkheim, *Suicide: A Study in Sociology,* originally published in Paris, F. Alcan, 1897; Translated by J. A. Spaulding and G. Simpson, (Glencoe, Ill., The Free Press, 1951).

[34] Robert K. Merton, "Social Structure and Anomie, Revisions and Extensions," in *Social Theory and Social Structure* (Glencoe, Ill., The Free Press, 1949).

rate of deviant behavior can be predicted, and not on the basis of mere position in the social strata. In the case of American society, which is not subdivided into caste value systems that would provide differential adjustment to social-structural conditions, one can observe markedly criminogenic reactions because many material goals are internalized by persons of certain socioeconomic and ethnic groups who are not able to find synchronized legitimate access.

An etiological emphasis of a different nature was presented by Albert K. Cohen,[35] who concentrated on the reactions of lower-class youth when confronted by middle-class institutions and values. This confrontation, in Cohen's opinion, represents the key to the explanation of delinquency among working-class youth. Youth of lower socioeconomic strata, because of serious impediments to their social and psychological mobility, face great difficulty in attaining middle-class goals. In reaction to the "culture shock," they tend to resolve their dilemma by gravitating to others in the same frustrating position. The resultant subcultural creation is, in a sense, a form of collective "reaction formation," since it insists on inverting middle-class values. The subcultural values come to constitute an adjustment to their lower-class conditions and provide necessary rationalizations for their antisocial—or at least anti-middle-class—activities. In the process they develop a sense of belonging and security in their subculture. Being more poorly prepared for the competition in the middle-class setting, lower-class youth are prone to be defeated by their middle-class peers in academic, social, and various other achievement areas. The resulting frustration and hostility are concretely reflected in the inverted nature of their subcultural ways. Typical expressions are negative, malicious, and destructive acts. Since there prevails an underlying attitude of defeatism, the delinquent acts are not purposefully aimed at a social goal, but rather are nonutilitarian emotional outlets. Aggression and "toughness" are valued in themselves, and to achieve a reputation for such behavior means high status with the in-group.

Cohen's original etiological contribution, doubtlessly valuable, suffered from analytical limitations. As acknowledged by the author himself, it failed to discern between various separate forms of delinquency and concentrated exclusively on only one type, the destructive gang commonly found in deprived neighborhoods.

In a follow-up treatise, Cohen, with the cooperation of criminologist James F. Short, Jr., tried to remedy this theoretical shortcoming.[36] The

---

[35] Albert K. Cohen, *Delinquent Boys: The Culture of the Gang* (Glencoe, Ill., The Free Press, 1955).

[36] Cohen and Short, *op. cit.*, pp. 20–37.

two students of criminology retrospectively modified the book *Delinquent Boys: The Culture of the Gang* [37] and supplemented it by specifying a number of different delinquent subcultures which, they held, could be verified by empirical research. "Research will undoubtedly reveal that other positional variables such as age, ethnicity, and ecological location and combinations of these variables also correspond to differences in life conditions which give rise to distinctive subcultural variants."[38] The two criminologists suggested a typology of subcultural delinquency, which was discussed in a previous section of this chapter under the heading "The Question of Collective vs. Individual Delinquency."

Another effort to expand the analytic frame was made by Cloward and Ohlin.[39] As in Cohen's original work, they see delinquency as primarily concentrated among lower-class, urban, male adolescents. They also agree with Cohen that delinquency in this population segment is largely a result of the experienced disparity between the middle and lower classes. However, they feel that a youngster's membership in a delinquent subculture is highly influenced by the "differential opportunities" open to him. The two sociologists think that there is more than one delinquent subculture among working-class youth and that a main goal of research should be to detect how selections for delinquency adaptations are made. According to the theory, being typically sociological in emphasis, these selections depend more on characteristics of community organization than on psychological differences among delinquents. In other words, types of delinquency depend on types of illegitimate *opportunities* which, in turn, are primarily dependent on organizational features of the community. Cloward and Ohlin specified three major types of delinquent subcultural adaptations and called them the *criminal-oriented, conflict-oriented,* and *retreatist-oriented.* These types differ from each other in activity patterns as well as in etiological conditions. In terms of behavior, the criminalistic form concentrates on systematic theft as a basic way of life and a major avenue for upward social mobility into the world of organized crime. The conflict form is the result of disorganized communities where traditional agencies and institutions of control have been rendered ineffective due to high rates of population mobility and diversity. The retreatist form provides isolation from conventional values and persons, is focused on "kicks" through drugs, alcohol, and unusual sex experiences; in this form steady work is eschewed in preference to "getting by," and the art of being "cool" is

---

[37] Cohen, *op. cit.*

[38] Cohen and Short, *op. cit.*, p. 24.

[39] Richard A. Cloward and Lloyd E. Ohlin, *Delinquency And Opportunity: A Theory Of Delinquent Gangs* (Glencoe, Ill., The Free Press, 1960).

practiced—in short, this may be a lower-class version of the stereotypical "beat" or hippie personality.

A culturistic etiology of delinquency was advanced by the anthropologist Walter B. Miller.[40] According to Miller a significant part of law-breaking behavior can be explained by a core set of values and problems in lower-class culture, which increases the probability that a youth raised in that cultural milieu will engage in violations of the law. Through many years of observing and analyzing lower-class street corner groups, this anthropologist discovered a number of "focal concerns" of lower-class culture that distinctly set it apart from other positions in the social order. These "focal concerns," which were discussed in Chapter 13, include "trouble," "toughness," "smartness," "excitement," "fate," and "autonomy," and are reiterated here as criminogenic factors. These concerns should not be understood as directly *demanding* violation of the law, but rather as helping to bring about the circumstances that invite criminal behavior. For example, the search for excitement may lead to auto theft, and the stress on toughness may encourage not only verbal insult to start with, but physical violence as a retribution for it.

Virtually all of the above-mentioned etiologies have one assumption in common—the description of the delinquent as a *deviant* whose behavior not only constitutes infraction of legal rules, but also violates the attitudes, norms, and values of the dominant social order. On closer scrutiny, it turns out that in most instances this dominant social order is the value orientation of the middle class. Surprisingly, a recent treatise of delinquency which has gained some sociological prominence takes issue with the assumption that the delinquent and the larger society face each other as antagonists and finds this type of imagery misleading.[41] Sociologists David Matza and Gresham M. Sykes argue that many delinquents are essentially in agreement with society, including the standards that define delinquency as "wrong." Rather than rejecting the conventional ideas of "good behavior," the delinquent tends to accept the dominant norms in *belief*, but renders them ineffective in practice by applying perceptions and attitudes that have the effect of "neutralizing" the legal and social norms that originally were intended as checks and controls on behavior. Various "techniques of neutralization" are on the delinquent market, including such rationalizations and legitimations of law violations as denial of responsibility or the explanation of an injurious act as either rightful revenge or unavoidable defense. Through these techniques, the delinquent succeeds in achieving harmony between his

---

[40] Walter B. Miller, "Lower-Class Culture As A Generating Milieu Of Gang Delinquency," *Journal of Social Issues*, Vol. 14, No. 3 (1958), pp. 5–19.

[41] David Matza and Gresham M. Sykes, "Juvenile Delinquency and Subterranean Values," *American Sociological Review*, Vol. 26 (October, 1961), pp. 712–19.

belief in the dominant social norms and his actual acts, and therefore cannot really be called "antagonistic" toward the larger social order.

This rather novel formulation continues its argument that the delinquent is much more a part of the socially accepted order than is commonly perceived. Matza and Sykes apply the concept of "subterranean values" to point out that the values behind a large portion of juvenile delinquency are far less deviant than are commonly depicted. In fact, they resemble components of the code of the "gentleman of leisure" described so well by Thorstein Veblen, with emphasis on daring and adventure, rejection of disciplined work and labor, a desire for luxury, and prestige through a show of masculinity. It is only the form of expression that differs—the form being labeled "delinquent." In essence, it is not the values that are deviant, but only the forms of expressing them.

Although the authors of this theory admit to significant differences among styles of delinquent behavior, they pursue the idea that some forms of delinquency have a common sociological basis, regardless of social-class belonging. The theory maintains, for example, that all adolescents to some degree engage in a style of life that is characteristic of the typical leisure class. This is so because adolescents are in a transient stage, free from adult responsibilities and the demand for self-support. In this situation, a rejective attitude toward work, an emphasis on personal value rather than acquired skills, and a stress on conspicuous consumption often combine to form the motivation for delinquent acts. "Insofar, then, as these values do lie behind delinquency, we could expect delinquent behavior to be prevalent among all adolescents rather than confined to the lower class."[42] Some types of delinquency can thus be explained by the conversion of leisure values of adolescents into delinquent behavior when such values suffer frustrations. In conclusion, Matza and Sykes emphasize that the explanation of delinquency should be clarified by stressing the delinquent's similarity rather than his dissimilarities to the society of which he is a member.

There is no presumption as to the completeness of the etiological catalog. The scope of presentation of these theories and approaches is limited by the fact that we have only a part of a chapter in which to convey the nature of etiological problems. Sacrifice of a number of limited and specific approaches to explain delinquency must be made— approaches that could also have served to supplement the major theories and could have indicated important research needs.

A final question: what has adolescence, as defined throughout this book, to do with juvenile delinquency? The answer would have to emphasize significant correlations, if not causative relationships, between

---

[42] Matza and Sykes, *op. cit.*, p. 719.

the two phenomena. Adolescence as an etiological assumption is, however, better handled *as a part* of all the above theories and approaches instead of being lifted from the context and used as a separate explanation. *The adolescent condition runs as a consistent and influencing strain through all approaches* and constitutes a modern precondition that has yet to be coped with by theorists and researchers alike. Some of the major elements of adolescence include youth's alienation from the adult world and their status—and consequently identity—confusion, which results in an inclination to rebel, attack, or withdraw. Such sociological and psychological dispositions form latent and ever-ready proneness to delinquent expressions among modern American youth. Specific theories are needed to spell out circumstances under which this proneness will materialize into actual delinquent behavior. Several theories seem to be well equipped to do so, despite their failure, at this time, to *specify* the etiological links between adolescent stress and delinquent consequence.

Approaches to Prevention

The question of prevention is extremely involved and touches on a number of controversial issues. First, what are the goals or objectives of prevention? The answer to this question seems to be relatively simple and clear, and one could say that the goal is the prevention of the *occurrence* and the *recurrence* of delinquent acts. But the answer to the next question is much more uncertain. How should the goal be pursued? Should it be pursued as revenge against the delinquent? Should procedures be aimed toward deterrence, or toward rehabilitation of already delinquent youth? Or should prevention work toward the preclusion of delinquent opportunities and motives? The responses to these questions usually differ greatly, depending on the respondent's philosophy of juvenile delinquency in general and on his social position, especially on his position within the broad action program designed to stem and prevent juvenile delinquency. For example, a social worker may see greater preventive effectiveness in clearing up existing social circumstances that are criminogenic, such as poverty, segregation, ghetto living, educational substandards, etc. A law enforcement officer, however, may be inclined to regard strict laws and their undelayed enforcement as the most effective means of curbing delinquency. Still another person may be more concerned with working directly with delinquent or delinquency-prone youths, assuming that such person-to-person contact and influence constitutes the most effective preventive measure. Finally, a number of individuals tend to view a combination of the above approaches as the most effective means of prevention.

Usually, the policy program suggested rests on the basic philosophy concerning juvenile delinquency to which the given individual subscribes. The reader should be cognizant again that there is a diversity of convictions and premises concerning the departure point of action programs. Two of the major views on juvenile delinquency, and criminal behavior in general, are reflected in the *punitive* and the *rehabilitative* attitudes. Both views, it must be understood, are equally interested in the prevention of the occurrence and recurrence of juvenile delinquency, but advocate different means not only because of their presumably different effectiveness, but also because of different moral premises. Many people believe that punishment is the more effective deterrent as well as the measure that is morally called for. The view has often been challenged by the argument that the rehabilitative and nonpunitive method is not only more effective in the long run but is also morally dictated, since the delinquent youth actually is not delinquent volitionally, but rather is a product of social conditions for which, in a sense, society at large is responsible. Moreover, the last group would contend that punishment frequently will not reform or rehabilitate a delinquent individual but will only reinforce his delinquent tendencies, since some individuals seek to be punished and are thus—through punishment— remotivated to engage in further delinquencies. This contention is hotly disputed by most behavioristically oriented officials and behavior scientists,[43] who prefer to adhere to the basic premise that man is a hedonistic being for whom punishment will deter and leniency will reinforce and perpetuate delinquent behavior.

The present discussion is more interested in reporting prevalent avenues of prevention than in trying to resolve the basic dilemma of conflicting and opposing philosophies on juvenile delinquency. The latter problem, it is feared, will probably remain unsolved for a long time, and its resolution must await help from research that reliably indicates which philosophy and its implementation is more successful in suppressing and preventing juvenile delinquency. The following discussion is therefore limited to a brief overview of existing preventive efforts that attempt to either preclude the development of delinquent behavior or rehabilitate youthful offenders and prevent their recidivism.

The literature describing methods of preventing juvenile delinquency is so comprehensive and diverse that it is impossible to present a complete catalog. The best that can be achieved within a limited

---

[43] See for example, psychiatrist William Glasser, *Realty Therapy* (New York, Harper & Row, 1965).

presentation is the categorization of the various approaches and, accordingly, the selection of a few pertinent illustrations from the array of researches, experiments, community programs, policy enactments, etc. But even a categorization of the preventive measures proves difficult, for the various endeavors are overlapping and interdependent. In spite of these difficulties, three major approaches to delinquency prevention can be discussed in the professional literature: (1) improving environmental conditions; (2) working with delinquent gangs; and (3) treating the individual delinquent. These methods are of course not mutually exclusive and can often be observed in combinations.

Improving environmental conditions. It is an accepted social-psychological dictum that the most influential component of the young person's environment is his family of orientation. The studies of Bradley Buell and coworkers in Minnesota and California demonstrated that the main proportion of America's delinquency is concentrated in less than 5% of the families.[44] An attack on the problems of these "hard core" families may yield salutary results, although so far, few coordinated methods for dealing with this type of family have been developed. It has been suspected that at the bottom of delinquency lies serious parental shortcomings and that an attack on juvenile delinquency should proceed via the reeducation and even punishment of irresponsible parents. A city that took this proposition seriously was San Francisco. In 1943, it initiated a program of instruction classes for parents of delinquents and made attendance compulsory. This program for "delinquent parents," subsequently called the San Francisco Plan, consisted of a series of eight weekly courses designed to inform parents of the city's recreational, public health, and welfare provisions. In addition, lectures were given on basic principles of child development and parent-child relationships. After parents had completed the assigned series of courses, the cases of their delinquent children were reviewed by the juvenile court and final decision made. Care was taken to include only parents who, it was believed, would benefit from the program. A number of parents who were immigrants to the United States were sent, instead, to Americanization classes to help them in their acculturation process.[45]

Several states have gone a step further and passed laws empowering the juvenile court judges to hear, determine, and impose a penalty on the parents of adjudicated delinquents. However, oddly, the efficacy of these punitive measures appears to be low, if not reversed. Judge Paul W. Alexander of Toledo's Domestic Relations and Juvenile Court, con-

---

[44] Bradley Buell, *et. al., Community Planning Through Human Services* (New York, Columbia University Press, 1952).

[45] Barron, *op. cit.,* pp. 325–26.

ducting a seven-year inquiry into 1,028 delinquency cases that involved 500 arrests of the parents, arrived at *no* evidence that punishment of parents had any preventive effect on juvenile delinquency in general. It appeared that holding irresponsible parents responsible for the delinquency of their offspring did not deter other parents from acting irresponsibly and contributing to the delinquency of their children.[46] A similar negative finding was discovered in New York City, where the levying of a fine on parents of truants was found to be ineffective in restoring more regular class attendance. In fact, it was found that after court action the attendance record of truants whose parents were punished improved more slowly than that of children whose parents were not fined. A sizable proportion of the pupils whose parents had been fined had to be repeatedly brought before court during the same school year.[47]

An earlier-timed and less punitive approach to delinquency prevention was worked out by the New York City Department of Public Welfare and the Youth Board.[48] It was a program of "aggressive casework" that tried to persuade resistive families to accept service *before* their children's difficulties became too serious. It was hoped that intervention at an early time in the development of delinquent tendencies would be more effective than later punitive measures. An individual social worker served as a liaison between the delinquency-prone family and the various community resources, instead of the traditional practice of referring the family to a number of different agencies. It was expected that an individualistic treatment would be more effective than diversified referrals. If referrals were indicated, they were processed under the guidance of the social worker in charge of the particular case.

Basing its procedure on the "aggressive casework" program of the New York City Youth Board, a family-centered service plan was introduced in St. Paul, Minnesota in 1954. Six per cent of the city's families, beset with the type of problems that made them delinquency-prone, became the focus of unified efforts to meet their needs. These families had relied on a large share of the community's different welfare services. The mutually isolated, multiple reliance was replaced by a *coordinated* effort of existing health and welfare agencies that eventually led to more efficient procedural practices.[49] Follow-up studies revealed that roughly

---

[46] Barron, *op. cit.*, p. 326.

[47] Herbert A. Landry, *The Prosecution of School Non-Attendants* (New York, State School Board, Division of Administrative Research, 1949).

[48] New York City Youth Board, *Reaching The Unreached* (New York, 1952); also, *How They Were Reached* (New York, 1954).

[49] Charles J. Birt, "Family-Centered Project of St. Paul," *Social Work*, Vol. 1 (October, 1956), pp. 41–47.

two-thirds of the treated families showed moderate to marked improvement in housekeeping and progress toward family unity. It was found that multiproblem families were not such poor treatment risks as had been previously feared. It was also discovered that social workers could openly talk about the delinquency-proneness they saw in the family.[50]

The family-centered approach has become an acknowledged procedure for effectively combating juvenile delinquency. However, the switch from the traditional method of focusing on the individual delinquent to the modern attempt of treating the family as a unit is still provisional and lacks established techniques. Alice Overton, who investigated the results of the St. Paul program, made a number of suggestions: (1) More attention should be paid to the particular style of family interaction *in the home* rather than to the verbal reports made during office interviews. (2) It is important to engage in *joint planning* with the parents, taking into consideration their negative as well as positive reactions to suggestions. (3) The *values and goals* of the individual family must be carefully assessed before introducing official actions. (4) The family's *basic capacity for growth* must be recognized beyond the multiple problems that are apt to obscure potentialities.[51]

Another crucial environmental factor is the availability of recreational facilities. It has traditionally been assumed that delinquency is furthered by leisure-time inactivity. Filling the leisure time of youngsters with creative and socially constructive activities has, therefore, developed into a major goal of a number of delinquency-preventive projects. It is believed that supervised clubs and organized athletic events present sublimation opportunities for children. With this purpose in mind, a number of cities have introduced boys' clubs, offering recreational and athletic opportunities to underprivileged boys. A study of the boys' club in Louisville, Kentucky, showed favorable results.[52] The research method was a comparison of changes in delinquency rates among boys in the area served by the club and boys in two other areas not served by a club, controlling all important variables except the recreational provision. The findings showed that the delinquency rate in the boys' club area dropped much more markedly than in the two control areas. However, the author of the research report admitted that limited statistical techniques were employed which do not allow causative assertions. He

---

[50] Alice Overton, *et. al., Casework Notebook*, 2nd. ed., Family-Centered Project, St. Paul, Minn. (Greater St. Paul Community Chest and Councils, March, 1959).

[51] *Ibid.*

[52] Roscoe C. Brown, Jr., *A Boys' Club and Delinquency, A Study of the Statistical Incidence of Juvenile Delinquency in Three Areas in Louisville, Kentucky* (New York, New York University Center for Community and Field Services, Monograph No. 2, 1956).

recommended a different method for similar studies in the future and advised close observation of 500 matched pairs of boys, from several cities, in which one set of boys belongs to a boys' club and the other does not.

Another comparative study of the effect of recreational facilities was conducted in Chicago.[53] The study included two samples of *delinquent* boys: one that used the recreational facilities, and the other that did not. The findings were inconclusive and indicated small differences. Ten percent of the delinquents who participated in the recreational programs persisted in their delinquent acts, compared to 16% of the continuing delinquents who did not use the recreational facilities.

In spite of this and other [54] findings that do not bear out the expected degree of effectiveness for the boys' club, the power of *collective* involvement can hardly be overemphasized. It must be recalled that the adolescent is in need of a peer status system since he is not yet integrated into the adult status system. This need for a social status is one of the main reasons why he retains membership in the gang. A successful replacement for the gang would again have to be a peer system in which he could attain status and belonging. The idea of the boys' club therefore appears to be reasonable. The problem, nevertheless, is how to attract delinquency-prone youngsters, who usually are intellectually, economically, and racially disadvantaged and are often maladjusted and hostile to the point of refusing to join any club that stands for the middle-class order. For many lower-class youngsters, especially those from the slums, the welfare-inspired boys' club or settlement house is an alien institution unable to attract more than a relatively small proportion of the children and the adolescents of the deprived neighborhoods. Possible ways of accomplishing the shift from membership in the delinquent gang to membership in the nondelinquent club are mentioned in a subsequent discussion on working with gangs.

The role of the church as a preventive agency has gone largely unmentioned—at least in the professional literature. Although it is known that a number of religious denominations sponsor a considerable number of settlement houses and other community facilities in slum areas throughout the United States, few reliable scientific studies of their effectiveness have been published in the journals of the social sciences. One of the few reports is from New Orleans, where the Council of Jewish Women, upon hearing of the high rate of delinquency, decided to establish a place of recreation in the crowded downtown area. An old

---

[53] Ethel Shanas and Catherine Dunning, *Recreation and Delinquency* (Chicago, Chicago Recreation Commission, 1942).

[54] Frederick M. Thrasher, *The Gang* (Chicago, University of Chicago Press, 1936).

warehouse was acquired and converted into "Teen Town," providing recreation for adolescents between 13 and 18. Offering the youngsters a snack bar, a library, art classes, and a band, as well as a share in self-governing by the election of their own Youth Council, it strove to meet the needs of many otherwise underprivileged teen-agers.[55] Similar prevention attempts—however, with a heavy emphasis on proselytizing— have also been made by nondenominational Christian "Teen Challenge" Clubs. A dozen neighborhood centers have been opened in delinquency-prone areas of such cities as Brooklyn, Los Angeles, Detroit, and Phoenix. City governments usually cooperate in securing the necessary buildings for these centers, and the law enforcement agencies frequently refer delinquents to them.

The school, like the family, ranks high in having a formative influence on children and is widely believed to be of potential strength in controlling and preventing juvenile delinquency. It is popularly held that through proper sex education, the school can prevent sex delinquency; through training in self-government, curb antidemocratic behavior; and through longer hours, divert delinquent use of leisure time. More verified by social scientific research is the assumption that teachers can detect early signs of maladjustment in elementary school pupils, signs that may be indicative of subsequent teen delinquency. The classroom is one of the best places to detect intellectual defects and social maladjustment and to observe infractions of rules and regulations. Accordingly, some social scientists have urged that schools should systematically examine first-graders' physical characteristics, aptitudes, disabilities, basic attitudes, etc.[56]

An actual attempt at predelinquent detection in school was carried out in a survey of ten medium-sized cities.[57] With the assistance of the teachers, more than 55,000 children were surveyed. 2.4% of them, mostly 13-year-olds, were identified as predelinquent. The ratio of delinquency-proneness of boys to girls was 4:1, nearly the same as found in juvenile court cases throughout the nation. The primary symptoms of pre-delinquency for boys include rebellion against authority, misconduct, and annoyance of other pupils. Predelinquency of girls, on the other hand, was symptomized primarily by inferiority feelings, preoccupation with sex, and physical overdevelopment.

---

[55] Mildred W. Wells, *Youth and Your Community* (New York, Public Affairs Pamphlet No. 108), pp. 7ff.

[56] Sheldon Glueck and Eleanor Glueck, *Delinquents in the Making* (New York, The Commonwealth Fund, 1952).

[57] Herbert D. Williams, "A Survey of Pre-Delinquent Children in Ten Middle-Western Cities," *Journal of Juvenile Research,* Vol. 17 (July–October, 1933), pp. 163–74.

Similar goals—early identification of delinquency-proneness and forestallment of court referrals—provided the underlying guidelines for a program launched in the schools of Passaic, New Jersey.[58] The Passaic Children's Bureau investigated all children whom teachers, social workers, or others in the community believed to be in need of help. A comprehensive staff, including a psychiatrist, guidance director, social worker, remedial reading instructor, several police officers, counselors, and attendance officers, determined the indicated treatment.

More direct measures to reduce delinquency were initiated in the fall of 1966 in Tucson, Arizona. After the local police chief found that more than 50% of all major crimes were committed by the under-18 age group, he decided to station police officers in six Tucson high schools. Police officers, working from their private offices on the campuses, not only tried to detect predelinquent symptoms and make referrals to the indicated community agency, but were on location to immediately apprehend violators of law and order.[59]

Modern mass media constitute an ever-increasing influence in the lives of the younger generation. It is suspected, for example, that the extensive exposure to TV makes significant impressions on children and teen-agers. The nature and the extent of the impression remain, however, a question to be answered by reliable research. At this time, sociologists and psychologists are still vastly divided in their interpretation of the impact of the mass media. Antedating conclusive research reports, a number of local authorities implemented their concern and decided to censor mass media with the hope of reducing delinquency-inducing models. New Orleans, for example, organized a Mayor's Advisory Committee of seventeen civic leaders to meet weekly for a session of reading comic books and determining their suitability for young readers. Defined as objectionable were such features as: (1) Situations glorifying crime. (2) The portrayal of law enforcement officers as unintelligent or ineffective. (3) Plots that overemphasize crime in relation to morality and justice. (4) Indecent or lascivious acts. (5) Glamorous appraisal of divorce. (6) Exhibit of sadistic torture or extreme cruelty. (7) Scenes advocating prejudice against any race, religion, nationality, or established American institution.[60]

A number of legislators believe that social legislation represents an improvement of environmental conditions for young people. When a

---

[58] Benjamin Fine, *1,000,000 Delinquents* (New York, World Publishing Co., 1955).

[59] A. P. Report (Tucson, Ariz., Aug. 2, 1966).

[60] Barron, *op. cit., p.* 325.

certain degree of legislation is exceeded, however, this becomes a questionable assumption. Laws regulating private as well as public behavior of minors are manifestly intended to prevent delinquency— notwithstanding the fact that a proliferation of such laws may actually *create* delinquent acts by simply increasing violation possibilities. One can, consequently, speak of a disparity between the manifest and the latent functions of social legislation. For the purpose of illustration, the issue of curfew is typical. On the manifest level, it is *intended to reduce* juvenile delinquency by requiring that minors be off the street after dark. It is estimated that more than 3,000 American communities have adopted curfew ordinances for this and other protective reasons. A common curfew regulation demands that persons under the age of eighteen be home after 10:00 P.M. and that parents, in case of violation, be fined. On the latent level, such restrictive ordinances tend to *increase* delinquent behavior, because minors found for one or another reason in the street at night, without otherwise being definable as delinquent, can now be so defined.

Working with delinquent gangs. An approach that aims more at rehabilitating already delinquent youth than at forestalling delinquency *per se* is the work with gangs in some of the larger cities of the United States. A relatively recent technique of working with such groups is the "detached worker" method, where a participant observer actually joins the gang without, at first, trying to change its style of action and interaction. This is an alternative method to the settlement house or the boys' club and aims to reach those juveniles who are too involved in their antisocial gang activities to feel attraction for clubs organized by outsiders. (The modifier "detached" is derived from the fact that the worker is not attached to such centers.) The detached worker seeks out the gang members, avoids moralistic and legalistic judgments, identifies himself with gang members, and assures them that he accepts them as individuals even though he may disapprove of some of their actions. His procedure is generally in agreement with two basic assumptions: (1) The antisocial behavior of delinquent gangs is a reflection of hostility toward adult authority. In most cases, these negative feelings stem from childhood rejection by parents. The aggressive and destructive behavior patterns are therefore, from the gang member's point of view, a justified reaction to the rejective and pain-inflicting adult world. (2) A change in such feelings and negative reactions can only come about through the opportunity of identifying with a new adult model who neither rejects nor inflicts pain on the youngster. Only after the establishment of a meaningful relationship of this type may the adult model gradually go about modifying and redirecting the youngsters' behavior patterns. Such detached-worker approaches were tried out in New York, Chicago, and Boston.[61]

Another method of trying to reach gangs took on the form of the so-called Street Club Projects and was tested in New York, Cleveland, Chicago, and Roxbury, Massachusetts. The key figures of this method are the street workers who are openly associated with a settlement house or community center. Working individually or in small teams, they attempt to make friends with members of neighborhood gangs, assuring them that their primary motive is to invite them to make use of the facilities offered by the community center. In the process, the street worker spends a great deal of time with them, joins them in various activities, and gets to know the personal problems of a number of the boys. Here is a brief description of the type of work in which the street worker is involved. Street worker Kurahara worked with the "Eagles," a New York gang led by a boy called Buzz-saw, and was associated with the Manhattanville Community Center.

> The street worker bides his time and persists in his offers of friendliness. He treats the boys to a cup of coffee, to cigarettes, or to a game of pool. Like buddies in the army, he gets to know each boy as an individual. One boy doesn't go home evenings because ten people occupy three rooms. Harry's mother is often drunk. John is always hungry, and there is never enough food in the house. Jim is a poor reader whose teacher makes fun of him in front of the class. As Kurahara says, one begins to understand the hostility that surrounds these kids and why the gang represents a retreat which offers security, warmth, and sometimes affection. The street worker comes to feel the full effect on the boys of "the long tedious winter nights with nothing to do and nowhere to go to get out of the cold."

> Adults in the area regard the gangs with bitter contempt, commenting, "this used to be a decent neighborhood." The police keep the gang moving. And because he hangs out with the gang, the street worker may be put on the spot if he appears to sanction law-breaking. Sometimes the boys planning a rumble implore the street worker to go away. Usually, however, he stays with them and tries to suggest other ways to settle the dispute. Most of the boys don't really want to fight. However, although few are as violent as Buzz-saw, no one wants to be called "chicken."

> The street worker's first aim is to get close to the leader, who is often a boy with superior ability, but like Buzz-saw, eaten up with resentment which pushes him into indiscriminate hating. As a substitute for the hostile patterns of attack, the street worker suggests

---

[61] Robison, *op. cit.*, pp. 514*ff*.

that it is not "chicken" to settle disputes peaceably or even by a fair fight in a boxing match in the gym.

The program offered these boys when, like Buzz-saw's gang, they eventually move into the community center, is one designed to meet practical as well as leisure-time needs. It may be a brief course in how to prepare for a job, how to fill out applications, or how to make up for deficiencies in their school work.[62]

Generally speaking, the reports from the community centers that adopted the street-worker scheme are optimistic. In the case of the Manhattanville Center, the street workers succeeded in attracting a sizable proportion of the area's delinquency-prone youth, in fact they succeeded in redirecting the entire neighborhood gang's energies. Prior to the application of the street-worker method, the community center was frequently the scence of destruction and vandalism. Through the mediation of such street workers as Kurahara, the boys cooperated in building a lounge in the community center, volunteered in carrying lumber and cement, plastering the walls, building settees, and even painting a mural.[63]

Treating the individual delinquent. The preventive methods focusing directly on the individual consist principally of counseling and child guidance. While the gang workers were primarily concerned with discontinuing delinquent behavior, counselors attempt to *forestall* the development of serious delinquent patterns. Social workers or psychologists base their counseling and guidance work on the hypothesis that delinquency-prone youngsters can be deflected from their problem behavior if they are acquainted with an understanding and accepting adult who is willing to extend friendship and counsel and is able to offer them access to the psychological, social, and economic services of the community.

A noteworthy experiment, trying to test the above hypothesis, was the Cambridge-Somerville Study.[64] Several hundred boys were classified as to their degree of delinquency-proneness, randomly divided into a test group, "T," and a control group, "C," and subjected to observation over a period of several years. Each boy in the "T" group was exposed during this time to careful attention by social workers and counselors. He was helped and encouraged in the adjustment process at school, obtained careful medical attention, organized leisure-time activities, even financial assistance if necessary, and was offered advice on a variety of

---

[62] Robinson, *op, cit.*, p. 511.

[63] *Ibid.*, p. 512.

[64] Edwin Powers and Helen Witmer, *An Experiment in the Prevention of Delinquency; The Cambridge-Somerville Youth Study,* (New York, Columbia University Press, 1951).

personal problems. On the other side, the boys of the control group were not included in these special services. After a period of approximately eight years, the first comparisons were made and, surprisingly, no significant differences between the two groups were found. A subsequent reevaluation of the study, however, revealed some significant relationships—though some contradictory findings that were not expected and did not support the hypothesis still existed. The supporting findings included the observation that boys seen twice a week for at least six months by a counselor had a delinquency rate of 25% compared with 51% for boys seen less frequently. The age factor was found to be significantly related to success in counseling service. Boys who were below ten years of age at the start of the program had a delinquency rate that was less than 30%, in contrast to 66% for those who were older than ten when they started the treatment. The unexpected and contradictory results were explained by certain unforeseen circumstances: (1) The process of the experiment was disturbed by the war (the project started in 1938), which involved changes in personnel and disruption of the emotional tie between the boy and the counselor. (2) Since more than half of the subjects were older than ten years at the outset of the program, basic personality tendencies probably were already formed by previous family interaction which the professional treatment could not erase. (3) Most counselors in the experiment were nonspecialized social workers with relatively little training in psychology. (This circumstance had been introduced deliberately by the initiator of the project to see whether delinquency prevention could be achieved without recourse to professional child guidance and psychotherapeutic techniques.) (4) It also appeared that lack of clarity of the definitions of key concepts, such as "delinquency" and "treatment," made a clear evaluation very difficult, if not impossible.

It must be added, however, that a number of individual case analyses revealed considerable success. Delinquency was markedly reduced under several circumstances: (1) when the emotional problems of the family and the child were not too extreme; (2) when the boy as well as his parents were willing to accept help; and (3) when the counselor's service was consistent and uninterrupted.[65]

The work of child guidance clinics is considerably more specialized than that of general counseling at school or in welfare agencies. The child guidance clinic came into existence with the theory that predelinquent symptoms can be detected during early childhood and that proper treatment can prevent delinquent tendencies from becoming more

---

[65] Lucien Bovet, *Psychiatric Aspects of Juvenile Delinquency* (Geneva, World Health Organization, Monograph Series No. 1, 1951), pp. 46–47.

serious. The treatment takes into consideration the total personality *Gestalt* of the child, rather than merely specific elements. The clientele of the child guidance clinics is sometimes drawn from adjudicated young delinquents referred by the juvenile court for clinical diagnosis and possibly lengthy treatment. Such referrals are often first-offending younger adolescents in whose cases clinical treatment promises to stop further development of antisocial attitudes. These clinics operate under various names and auspices, sometimes called bureaus or institutions for juvenile research, service or guidance centers, etc., and may be sponsored by private organizations, community chest funds, hospitals, or city, county, and state funds.

Although generally there is no rule requiring treatment to follow a rigid step-by-step procedure, the most recommendable manner of attacking the problem includes the following phases: (1) A preliminary interview with the parents is arranged, at which time they present the staff with their understanding of their child's problem. In addition, a number of questions are discussed, including willingness to cooperate, fees, time of visits, and the purpose and procedure of the institution. (2) The child is tested by psychologically trained personnel for IQ and basic attitudes. (3) A pediatrician gives the child a thorough medical examination. (4) The psychiatrist proceeds to see the boy every week. (5) The social worker confers regularly with the parents. (6) Conferences are held between psychiatrist and social worker to cross-check diagnosis, progress, and action plans. (7) If referral was made by school, law enforcement, or other community agency, reports are sent to them about developments. (8) Staff conferences, finally, provide an opportunity for integrating the various findings into a meaningful picture for facilitating final decisions.

This is a description of the ideal and complete procedure. In reality there are numerous shortcomings. One of the foremost is that the majority of the child guidance clinics are understaffed and therefore unable to provide necessary specialized services. Even if there is adequate staffing, patients frequently overcrowd the facilities and thereby create the same effect. Incomplete communication between personnel is another serious drawback that sometimes results in working at cross-purposes. Nevertheless, there is little doubt about the usefulness of the guidance clinic. It proves particularly effective where specialized workers attack the delinquency-generating problems on all fronts, involving parents as well as children in the treatment process.

A theoretical formulation that definitely should constitute an integral part of the clinical approach was offered by Walter C. Reckless, criminologist at Ohio State University. On the basis of his research, he concluded that the most effective bulwark against juvenile delinquency and adult criminality lies in the self-concept that the young adolescent develops. The development of the self-concept can be influenced and guided—a process in which parents, teachers, and social scientists can take a significant part. Reckless and coworkers have already translated their theory into practice. Promising efforts have been made in junior high schools having high delinquency rates in Columbus, Ohio, where a number of self-concept-strengthening innovations were tried out. For example, a special program was reserved for the last hour of each school day in several 6th-grade rooms in which designated boys acted out several modes of behavior—models of health, safety, teamwork, sportsmanship, etc. In addition, boys were taken on tours of such places as the Blind School, Ohio State Electric Laboratory, OSU basketball team, and other stimulating contacts designed to help them acquire appreciation for others and themselves.[66]

A demonstration project combining all approaches. A project that attempted to implement all avenues of prevention was conceived and developed by Mobilization for Youth, Inc., a nonprofit corporation composed of representatives of agencies and institutions on the Lower East Side of New York City and specialists from the School of Social Work of Columbia University.[67] The area of the Lower East Side had been the site of extensive gang violence for more than two decades. Each gang had a high proportion of members who were either school dropouts or truants and had official police records with offenses ranging from disorderly conduct and assault to robbery and burglary. A large proportion of the offenses were directed against law enforcement officers. It was reported that during the first six months of 1961, 1,171 attacks were made on New York policemen trying to make arrests and that the number of policemen injured while performing their duty increased constantly.[68] There were virtually daily reports in the *New York Times* describing such violence. Examples:

> A gang of teen-agers on a pier last evening stole the cap, shoes, and money of a policeman who had jumped into the water to save a man. Before stealing these items the youth had been throwing stones at policemen who were dragging the river off Catherine Slip for the body of a 14-year-old boy. The policemen had chased the youths away, but when the police became preoccupied with saving a middle-aged man who had attempted suicide, the boys returned and

---

[66] "Searching For Juvenile Decency," *Ohio State University Monthly* (February 1964), pp. 10-11.

[67] The local problem as well as the preventive proposals are outlined and discussed in *A Proposal For The Prevention And Control Of Delinquency By Expanding Opportunities,* 2nd. ed. (New York, Mobilization For Youth, Inc., August, 1962).

[68] *Ibid.,* p. 3.

stole the items. The youngsters were not identified and presumably not caught.

A brick hurled at a policeman from a tenement roof killed a bystander on the Lower East Side last night. . . . Two policemen were reported to have responded to a complaint that a man was shooting at children with a rifle. As they subdued a 19-year-old, a hostile crowd milled about, several objects hurtled down from a roof, fatally injuring a 43-year-old man.[69]

Many of the gangs were conterminal with ethnic or racial stocks and engaged in violent street fights with nonmembers, "outsiders," and other gangs. The gangs were a complex assortment of racially and ethnically consistent groups bearing such names as Viscounts, Ballerinos, Persians, Sportsmen, Mayrose, Dragons, Centaurians, Smith-Boys, etc.

All of the above-mentioned types of preventive measures have been initiated: improvements of environmental conditions, working with the gang as a whole, and treatment of individual delinquents. Besides continuous work through the techniques previously described—the street worker, detached worker, community center, boys' club, preadolescent projects, family-centered services, and individual counseling—some entirely new and imaginative methods have been introduced. Among the innovations is the idea of setting up coffee shops for boys and girls age 16 to 21 that compete with existing deviant hangouts. The new facilities and programs are tailored especially to teenagers and convey an agreeable atmosphere that they describe as being "jazzy," "cool," and "concrete." The initiators of the coffee shop project even weigh the ideas of *indigenous* management, drawing managing personnel from the leaders of the juveniles. It becomes necessary to identify those older adolescents who possess constructive, healthy potential as well as respect and influence with their peers. These are the juveniles with real resource capacity who, when employed in managerial positions, can direct the project staff to set up the type of facility that appeals to the adolescent population. In a sense, they become the "advisors" with the flair and the "feel" that the adult staff needs for effective operation.

As a supplement to the actual preventive projects, corresponding research and experimental designs have been outlined by Mobilization for Youth. They are instrumental in assessing the success or failure of the different techniques and approaches.

Mobilization for Youth is a demonstration project on a broad scale. Depending on its outcome, it may well serve as example for the rest of the nation. It is expected that extensive follow-up studies will be published in the near future.

---

[69] Quoted in Reference 67, pp. 2-3.

The question of success of prevention. A natural question that arises at the end of a discussion on prevention is: how *successful* were the measures employed for preventing juvenile delinquency? A clear answer to this question is difficult, since many of the preventive measure described above are either still in progress and have not yet been evaluated, have been evaluated in questionable manners that make valid conclusions and generalizations difficult, or have yielded results that seem to suggest a low success rate.

An example of the type of weak and almost contradictory findings that have frequently come from evaluations of preventive programs can be seen in the Cambridge-Somerville Study mentioned earlier in this section. After several years of carefully controlled differential treatment of school children, it was found, for example, that boys seen twice a week by a counselor had a delinquency rate of 25% compared to 33% for the boys who were seen less than once a month.[70] The small difference of 8% between the two groups is not significant and does not represent an encouraging result of counseling, throwing doubt on the effectiveness of the strategy employed for treating the predelinquent and delinquency-prone youngsters.

Some criminologists feel that the best they can say is that a delinquent has about a 50% chance of being successfully treated under present strategies. Also, the delinquent has about a 50% chance of becoming a nondelinquent if he is *not* treated at all. It must be specified, however, that this type of conclusion is generally based on evaluations of correctional measures that involve adjudicated delinquents and not so much on programs that involve predelinquent or delinquency-prone youths. The study by Walter C. Bailey is a noteworthy illustration of this point.[71] Evaluating 100 reports of empirical evaluations of the outcome of correctional treatment, he found that only approximately one-half of the total sample indicated positive results. The "positive" proportion may be even lower than 50% when one considers the fact that the evaluations were offered by the authors of the research reports themselves and that their conclusions may easily have been influenced by the bias of "wishful thinking." Bailey expressed his suspicion on this matter:

> But, when one recalls that these results, in terms of success or failure of the treatment used, are based upon the conclusions of the authors of the reports, themselves, then the implications of these findings regarding the effectiveness of correctional treatment be-

---

[70] Powers and Witmer, *op. cit.*

[71] Walter Bailey, "Correctional Outcome: An Evaluation of 100 Reports," *The Journal of Crimal Law, Criminology and Police Science,* Vol. 57, No. 2 (June, 1966), pp. 153–60.

come rather discouraging. A critical evaluation of the actual design and the specific research procedures described in each instance would substantially decrease the relative frequency of successful outcomes based upon reliably valid evidence. Therefore, it seems quite clear that, on the basis of this sample of outcome reports with all of its limitations, evidence supporting the efficacy of correctional treatment is slight, inconsistent, and of questionable reliability.[72]

Bailey's conclusion appears warranted in the face of additional evidence of negative or ineffectual outcomes of "preventive treatment." For example, Robert H. Dalton's inquiry into the value of counseling techniques in probation work resulted in a fairly discouraging picture.[73] A literature review by Bernard C. Kirby on the success of treatment programs of delinquents and criminals led him to conclude that "most treatment programs are based on hope and perhaps informed speculation rather than on verified information."[74]

The assessment of past and present policy implementations in the field of prevention thus produces a rather unsuccessful looking picture. However, the outlook does not necessarily need to be discouraging. Several developments are gradually improving preventive strategies. One such development is the increasingly scientific nature of policy implementation on the part of the juvenile authorities. The other is the increasingly sophisticated research conducted in the area of prevention and correction, carefully examining and trying to explain differential outcomes. Finally, valid research findings function as a feedback to experts in the field of administration and treatment of delinquents, such as counselors, social workers, psychiatrists, institutional administrators, etc., who are then able to improve their preventive and rehabilitative techniques.

Summary

Adolescence is a delinquency-prone period in modern man's life cycle. No longer considered a child nor accorded adult status, the adolescent is the victim of vaguely phrased legislation differing among jurisdictions and is largely dependent on individual discretion and bias of the judge and the law enforcement officer and the tolerance level of the given

---

[72] Bailey, *op. cit.*, p. 157.

[73] Robert H. Dalton, "Value And Use Of Counseling Techniques In The Work Of Probation Officers," *Federal Probation*, Vol. 16 (December, 1952), pp. 17–22.

[74] Bernard C. Kirby, "Measuring Effects Of Treatment Of Criminals And Delinquents," *Sociology and Social Research*, Vol. 38 (July–August, 1954), p. 373.

community. Finally, he is the victim of himself—of a transitory phase in his life, beset with identity uncertainty and intense needs for status, security, and new experience.

Delinquent expressions by adolescents can be classified into subcultural, semicollective, and individualistic forms.

Statistics show teen-agers to be the most delinquent group among all age brackets. During the mid-1960's, 15-year-old boys were found to have the highest arrest rates of any age category, with 16-year-olds having the second highest rates. There is also a shift in the locality distribution of juvenile delinquency, with the suburban area having a greater proportion of delinquent adolescents than either the rural or the urban areas. Finally, it must be emphasized that the upsurge in juvenile delinquency is not due merely to the numerical increase of teen-agers, but also to a rate increase. Between 1960 and 1965, the United States teen-age population increased by 17%, but their delinquency increased by 54.4%.[75]

Sociologists have suggested a number of theoretical frameworks designed to help explain delinquent behavior. Of pioneer status is Sutherland's "differential association" theory, stressing that it is the nature of social relationships that induces delinquency or nondelinquency. This broad premise was modified and sensitized by Reckless, who related the concept of self-perception to the genesis of a true delinquent, and also by Glaser, who suggested "differential idenfication" as a more fruitful approach to the explanation of delinquency. These additions gave new dimensions of such importance to the original version of the "differential association" theory that they should probably be considered theories in their own rights. *Anomie,* or the disjuncture between culturally enhanced values and feasible means of attaining them, serves as another etiology of delinquent behavior. Merton's elaboration on this theory attempted to explain a number of "innovating" behavior patterns that frequently can take on criminal forms. Cohen's original work focused on the delinquent reaction of lower-class youth to the unattainable middle-class values. Subsequent expansion, with the cooperation of Short, allowed for a greater variety of categories of subcultural delinquency. An effort to relate differential opportunities to delinquent causation was made by Cloward and Ohlin, who felt that such opportunities depend on organizational features of the community. A culturistic etiology was advanced by Miller, who ascribed criminogenic potential to a number of lower-class "focal concerns." Finally, Matza and Sykes tried to explain a significant portion of juvenile delinquency by the adolescent's life

[75] *Uniform Crime Reports* 1965, *op. cit.,* pp. 1, 110.

experiences, which can be thought of as resembling the proverbial "gentleman-of-leisure" style.

Prevention aims at abolishing or at least reducing the occurrence and recurrence of delinquency. To accomplish this, it focuses on pre-delinquent, delinquency-prone, and actual delinquency-involved youths. Strategies have been initiated to improve environmental conditions and reduce criminogenic factors which may be found in family life, neighborhood, and school, in the lack of recreational facilities, and in the fare of the mass media. Legislation is an important environmental condition of the adolescent, as an excess of laws may result in a greater possibility of committing criminally-defined acts. Preventive work with delinquent subcultures makes use of the "detached worker," the street club with the "street worker," settlement houses, and community centers. Treatment of the individual youth frequently functions as a prophylaxis to prevent delinquency-prone youth from developing into full-fledged delinquents. Social workers, counselors, psychologists, psychiatrists, and educators are actively involved in forestalling the development of serious delinquency. A remarkable demonstration project, Mobilization for Youth, Inc., is trying out a combination of all the above measures on the Lower East Side of New York City.

Careful evaluation of the preventive and rehabilitative work reveals extremely moderate success. In fact, it is suspected that there is only a 50–50 chance that a delinquent will be rehabilitated through official treatment. On the positive side, there is increasing sophistication in the development of preventive strategies and rehabilitative programs.

15

sex, marriage, and teen-agers

No one who intends to achieve a full and realistic understanding of adolescents and their problems can afford to ignore the powerful role that sex plays in their lives. The cultural meaning, the social norms, the teen-ager's needs, and his sexual activities form an interrelated complex that is responsible for a number of typical adolescent experiences, including reactions of guilt, shame, anxiety, joy, and pleasure. Such consequences as premarital pregnancy, marriage, divorce, and venereal disease, while not completely typical of teen-agers, are still increasing fast enough among them to deserve careful attention.

This chapter sketches a picture of the American teenager's involvement in the norms, activities, and consequences of sex and in the process examines various resulting sexual conflicts. No presumption is made of completeness. For example, the discussion focuses primarily on "normal" heterosexual—albeit most likely illicit—activities and leave out the role and the dimension of such practices as homosexuality, autoeroticism, bestiality, fetishism, voyeurism, prostitution, etc., popularly considered "deviant" or "abnormal" activities. These and other sexual problems are certainly matters of grave concern and should be thoroughly studied, but, in the context of this book, must take secondary place to the importance of the heterosexual activities of the majority of male and female adolescents.

Traditional Sex Codes

Codes and customs concerning sexual expressions form a type of blueprint that purports to pattern the sexual activities of the members of society. The relationship between the blueprint and the actual behavior of people may show considerable incongruence. It would be incorrect, however, to consequently dismiss the importance of the blueprint, because the very fact of this incongruence—a result of wide-

392

spread deviation—creates emotional reactions that often are central problems in the lives of adolescents.

In other words, adolescents may *overtly behave* as if there were no specific cultural pronouncements regarding sex and yet covertly react on the emotional level to their deviance from the cultural blueprint. Frequent reactions to deviation are shame, anxiety, and a feeling of worthlessness—in short, problems of self-respect. It is therefore of great importance that the cultural norms purporting to govern sexual activities are understood before investigating the actual sexual patterns. Comparison of the "official" norms and "unofficial" behavior help in the understanding of psychological reactions.

The cultural heritage of American society includes principles of the Judeo–Christian tradition, which for single people dictate ascetic standards and forbid premarital coitus as well as other sexual activities. The only approved sexual activity consists of marital coitus. Although these dogmas are gradually giving way to more secular and sensate-oriented views, hardly any young American can avoid exposure to orthodox views on sex that equate premarital sexual activities with sin and evil. Some teen-agers more than others come under the influence of such religious and moralistic evaluation in the course of their association with parents, relatives, church, and school. Inconsistent with this general negative pronouncement is the tacit agreement on a double standard that has been part of informal religious tradition as well as of folk culture. In effect, it calls for strong condemnation of female sexual transgression, but only mild condemnation, if not tolerance or even encouragement, of male sexual adventure.

The excuse for the male prerogative was based on the assumption that the male has different sexual needs and drives than the female. His sex drive was conceived as more "animalistic" and much stronger than hers and therefore in greater need of fulfillment. For the woman, sex was expected to be of little or no personal interest. Her sexual involvement was mainly seen as an altruistic act satisfying her husband's needs and serving reproductive purposes. A girl's premarital chastity was of immense importance. First, by her chastity she had to live up to the man's image of her as relatively disinterested in sexual matters. The discovery of premarital unchastity would destroy this sexually pure image of the female. Second, in the patriarchal tradition, the women was regarded as unequal to the man and, in a sense, his "property" that no one else should ever "possess." The worth of a woman decreased sharply if virginity was not brought along to the wedding.

The double standard led to an interesting conflict. How could the man, characterized by strong sexual needs and the desire to find a sexually gratifying partner, find full satisfaction with a chaste and sexually disinterested woman? As in numerous aspects of life, man found a suitable rationalization to resolve the conflict and commenced to divide females into "good" and "bad" women. The "good" women were for marriage, i.e., they were premaritally chaste, limited in their sexual interest, and primarily concerned with bearing and rearing children. The "bad" women were not considered suitable marital material but were thought to be available for the man's sexual desires. Reputation and communal judgment were instrumental in drawing a sharp line between the two categories. People did not see the two groupings as overlapping but rather as two different types. This belief had profound psychological effects on both men and women. While a man could find sexual gratification outside, and to some extent inside, the marital bond and still retain self-respect, any personal sexual gratification on the part of the wife resulting from marital, let alone extramarital coitus, would most likely lead to guilt feelings. Any overt indication that she enjoyed sex might arouse the husband's suspicion that she actually was not a "good" woman. Here is the intriguing connection between the blueprint and psychological reaction. It is entirely possible that as a result of cultural indoctrination suggesting the joylessness of sexual activities, she *actually* came to dislike coital activities, thereby verifying and reinforcing the male's belief in the sexual passivity of the female. (Obviously, this is a retrospective inference that is open to questioning.)

This belief was part of the overall patriarchal syndrome introduced into the United States by early Protestantism and, it should be added, maintained by Catholicism as well. In Christianity's view, sex before or outside of matrimony was sinful for both sexes, but far more sinful for the woman. She was constantly reminded to resist evil and the "temptations of the flesh." If a woman was discovered by a Puritan community of New England to have indulged in premarital coitus, a public confession had to be made before the entire congregation.[1] This constituted a much more painful sanction than the secret confessional of the Catholic Church which the Puritans had repudiated.

Although elements of the patriarchal syndrome still persist today, modern trends have largely supplanted them with less dogmatic views permitting, in a more or less tacit concession, some premarital expression for both males and females. The change in basic attitudes has come about over a relatively brief period of time—a period so brief that some social scientists feel justified in calling it the Sexual Revolution.

---

[1] Arthur W. Calhoun, *A Social History of the American Family: Colonial Period*, Vol. 1 (New York, Barnes and Noble, 1960), p. 132.

The Sexual Revolution in the United States

Like all sociocultural phenomena, norms, attitudes, and patterns concerning sex are never static but are dynamic and everchanging elements in the social system. It is therefore seldom possible to specify a period of time as a revolutionary period within which basic changes of social perception have taken place. Yet during the first three decades of the 20th century enough social and technological innovations occurred to change the basic perception of the functions of sex and the role of the woman that the label Sexual Revolution is not out of place. The traditional sex codes as correlated to religious dogma came under severe attack and were undermined by a number of important new developments. At least five major forces of social change can be discerned during that period:

(1) *Female emancipation.* Primarily because of changing economic conditions, the patriarchal family style declined, and a new emphasis on female equality emerged. With the feminist movement of the 1920's and '30's, a number of important social changes concerning the status of the American woman became noticeable. First, with the decline of familistic coercions the female took a greater interest in educational and occupational opportunities away from her family of orientation. She was no longer rigidly controlled by the family and spent a great deal of time in secondary institutions that helped her to unfold talents and trained her for a future career. Second, with increasing social and geographic distance from the parental home, the young woman's decision concerning time of marriage and choice of mate became more an individual than a family enterprise. This change reinforced the female's equal standing and substantiated her freedom in choosing a mate. Third, her sexual equality diminished her dependency on the marital status and on males in general. The male figure was formerly indispensable for her sustenance and shifted with her maturity directly from father to husband. But now the woman was able to remove herself from the influence of the father and yet not enter immediately into a dependency relationship with a husband. This interim provided the woman with a period of freedom and independence heretofore unknown. Fourth, the modern female's perception of the role of sex in her life changed radically. She became enlightened concerning her sexual needs, "rights," and capacities. She expected equal fulfillment and sexual gratification. Fifth, because of her equality in sexual matters, the double standard became increasingly unacceptable to her. She thought of herself as having the same privileges and needs as the male and that therefore the traditional double standard should be abolished, either by

granting her the same sexual liberties or by imposing the same restrictions on the male.

(2) *Medical and technological innovations.* Probably nothing decreased inhibitions and fear of sexual activities for the woman more than the knowledge and the availability of contraceptives. A woman who could successfully rationalize away moral compunctions was virtually free to indulge in sex with impunity. She did not imperil her future by unwanted pregnancy and could enjoy the physical and psychological pleasures of sexual intimacy. This pleasurable aspect was possibly the single most revolutionary feature in the overall Sexual Revolution: the female now openly regarded sex as an enjoyable experience.

(3) *Secularism.* There was a general shift in the perception of marriage and the family as institutions. Formerly, these primary institutions were viewed as sacred, unchangeable, and inviolable arrangements to which man had to adjust rather than adjusting them to suit him. In contrast, the secular philosophy and attitude conceived of such institutions as manmade arrangements that could and should be changed when human needs and comfort call for it. The decline of familism is correlated with the rise of secularism: the focus of concern shifted from the family of orientation to the individual ego. The modern American way of life grants both males and females the right to seek personal pleasure and satisfaction without the impediment of control by the parental family. Another way of characterizing secularism is by calling attention to the modern preference for sensate pleasures over ascetic and orthodox religious principles. Personal need gratification has become a major goal. The relevance of this social change is greatest in regard to the female who, for example, can now easily obtain a divorce if she feels that her personal needs, sexual and otherwise, are not fulfilled in a given marriage.

(4) *The broadening adolescent period.* A by-product of improved medication, sanitation, and nutrition is the earlier onset of puberty.[2] At the same time, a by-product of the progressively more complicated expansion of the division of labor and the social structure in general is the delay in reaching fully acknowledged adult status. The sum effect of the two developments is a longer interim span of adolescence. During these years, the youth is physiologically mature and characterized by fully developed sexual needs. It is somewhat unrealistic to expect that the adolescent can or will practice "deference of gratification" in respect to his sexual tensions and needs until he has completed his schooling,

---

[2] Harley N. Gould and Mary R. Gould, "Age of First Menstruation in Mothers and Daughters," *Journal of the American Medical Association*, Vol. 98 (April, 1932), pp. 1349–352. (See Chapter 5 for fuller discussion and further references.)

which may extend into his early 20's if he decides to go on to college. As long as he is affiliated with an educational institution, it is difficult to accord him full adult status. Not until he has established himself occupationally and can earn his own living has he achieved some of the major criteria of the adult status. In spite of the fact that the period between child and adult statuses has been prolonged, no socially acceptable provisions have been made to allow fulfillment of sexual needs outside of marriage. Premarital chastity, now as before, constitutes a social value. Technically, *any* form of sexual gratification during these adolescent years constitutes a deviation from or a violation of the blueprint. Whatever sexual gratification does take place—autoeroticism, hetero- or homosexuality, or any other form of sexual release—is defined as illicit and punishable. As a result, the majority of adolescents are burdened with frequent strain and conflict. It may be suspected that the rate of illicit heterosexual activities has increased over the last decades as a result of prolonged adolescence and that this prolonged adolescent condition seems to many sympathetic observers to be a mitigating circumstance to the teen-agers' transgressions.

(5) *The titillating mass media.* Another influential force weakening the traditional norms is found in the ubiquitous American mass media. The sexual stimuli presented in the various media are grossly contradictory to the traditional values of chastity and asceticism. Female "sexiness" has become an established value that attracts emulation on the part of the teen-age girl and fervent endeavors of conquest on the part of the teen-age boy. Considering the sexual insecurity that is normally an important part of the adolescent situation, the sex-encouraging influence of movies, TV, advertisements, and a vast range of reading material can hardly be overestimated. Not knowing exactly the part sex is to play in their lives, contemporary youth are susceptible to imitation of the characters presented in the mass media. Modern movie and TV features reflect the contemporary erotic culture and are replete with various sex symbols the imitation of which, without doubt, will encourage and increase premarital sexual activities.

What has been the outcome of the interplay between these new forces and the traditional forces? Professor Winston Ehrmann called it the "great sex dilemma" of the 1930's.[3] Youth was caught between two opposing forces that exerted nearly equal strength and compulsion. However, in the meantime, the two opposing philosophies, including the polar extremes of sacredness versus secularism and chastity versus sex-

---

[3] Winston Ehrmann, "Changing Sexual Mores," in Eli Ginzberg (ed.), *Values and Ideals of American Youth* (New York, Columbia University Press, 1964), pp. 53–70.

uality, have undergone a surprising degree of *rapprochement;* however, this does not mean full agreement. Churches and schools have adopted a more understanding and forgiving stand than might have been suspected 30 years ago, but the "softening" of the traditional standards has not abolished the dilemma. Today's adolescents will find themselves helplessly suspended if they look for *one* right answer, since there are numerous blueprints suggesting resolutions of the sexual dilemma. With the modern emphasis on individuality and personal decision-making, the adolescent is left largely on his own in working out a suitable blueprint and is apt to end up with a set of extremely situational morals.

Isadore Rubin described a number of coexisting value systems that are currently available and seem to present solutions for various temperaments and value subscriptions.[4] He described the major ones as follows: (1) *Traditional repressive asceticism* refers to the orthodox orientation that legitimized sex only in the context of procreation. Many religious dogmas and some contemporary official laws and ordinances are still based on this philosophy. (2) *Enlightened asceticism* is not so much a religious dictum as an advocacy of a disciplined style of life. It recommends chastity more for reasons of self-discipline and as a safeguard against "degeneration" than as divine command. (3) *Humanistic liberalism* disavows rigid precepts, definitely opposes any chastity-by-divine-rule concept, and stresses the importance of the interpersonal relationship. It is in the light of the type of consequences for the partners and the larger environment that premarital sex involvement is to be assessed. A proponent of this blueprint is Professor Lester A. Kirkendall, who recommends that sex acts should be judged by their functions and not by *a priori* metaphysical precepts.[5] (4) *Humanistic radicalism* is in favor of society providing more or less complete sex freedom. However, this freedom can come only after careful preparations. The preconditions of sexual freedom, according to W. R. Stokes,[6] must be created through a "cultural engineering project" that would lead to a reeducation of future generations. (5) *Fun morality* takes the standpoint that sex is a pleasure to which man is normally and naturally entitled. The best known spokesman for this view is Albert Ellis, who bases his argument on clinical observations and maintains that the more complete the

---

[4] Isadore Rubin, "Transition on Sex Values—Implications for the Education of Adolescents," *Journal of Marriage and the Family,* Vol. 27 (May, 1965), pp. 185–89.

[5] Lester A. Kirkendall, *Premarital Intercourse and Interpersonal Relations* (New York, Julian Press, 1961).

[6] Walter R. Stokes, "Guilt and Conflict in Relation to Sex," in Albert Ellis and A. Abarbanel (eds.), *The Encyclopedia of Sexual Behavior* (New York, Hawthorn Books, 1961), pp. 466–71.

sex gratification, the more psychologically healthy the person.[7] Society should revise its sex codes and freely permit premarital intercourse. (6) *Sexual anarchy* as a philosophy and experiment has attracted many persons and has stimulated subcultural formation throughout history, although none of the subcultures could persist. One of the latest and most outspoken advocates was the French jurist Réné Guyon who believed in complete sex freedom with the single limitation that no one may do injury or violence to his fellowman.[8]

These, then, are possible sexual blueprints for youth of today. The realization of some of them, especially the last two categories, would obviously violate contemporary law. But they can nevertheless serve as "reference groups" or sexual ideologies for many individuals.

Educators and counselors are faced with an enormous problem. Which of these blueprints should they advocate in a given case? This raises a complex of ethical, legal, political, and scientific questions. It is difficult to detect a consensus among today's educators and counselors on this question. This impasse was strikingly illustrated at the 1964 conference of the National Association of Women Deans and Counselors, who rallied around the motto "Work Conference on Current Sex Mores," trying to find consensus on what the sex mores should be. As Rubin reported,[9] this conference, like many others before, could not arrive at a consensus on what sex mores should be today.

The scope of the current confusion and vagueness concerning sexual codes is most strikingly exemplified by this failure of experts of guidance, counseling, and policy enactment to reach an agreement. How much less can adolescents themselves be expected to reach a clear understanding of a philosophy of sex? While the "great sexual dilemma" with the corresponding "great debate" continues, adolescents are thrown back on themselves in trying to solve problems for which no clear cultural consensus is available and which will continue to add stress and conflict to their statusless social existence.

Premarital Sexual Behavior

Unlike the statistical information in the area of criminality, information on sexual activities is not available in an annual "Uniform Sex Report." To obtain an approximation of the actual scope and distribution of sexual activities in the United States, a variety of research findings,

---

[7] Albert Ellis, *If This Be Sexual Heresy* (New York, Lyle Stuart, 1963).

[8] Réné Guyon, *The Ethics of Sexual Acts* (New York, Alfred A. Knopf, 1934).

[9] Rubin, *op. cit.*, p. 185.

reflections in the mass media, and the public deportment of the adolescents must be drawn together.

The only comprehensive studies of sexual behavior of the American male and female were done by the late Alfred C. Kinsey and his coworkers.[10] Unfortunately, their monumental research work suffered a number of shortcomings, the most serious one concerning the sampling technique. The sample cannot be classified as random, since it was biased in the direction of urban, middle-class, white, and college-educated persons, and was more or less limited to the Northeastern United States. Moreover, the study was conducted in the 1940's, and the findings are thus considerably dated by now. However, in spite of these drawbacks, most experts in the field of sexology would agree that the Kinsey studies are superior to other studies in the field and definitely preferable to "armchair" speculation. Until an improved study supplies more up-to-date data, the Kinsey studies provide the most comprehensive and objective information on sexual behavior of Americans.

In the course of his survey, Kinsey discovered interesting and quite large differences in amount and type of sexual practices between males and females and among educational levels, age brackets, socioeconomic classes, etc. Some of the findings relevant in discussing teen-agers are presented below.

The chief sexual outlets of boys and girls differ considerably during their teens. Girls have been found to use as a chief outlet autoeroticism and petting, and they remain relatively low in the use of coitus. Boys, on the other hand, include coitus as a chief means of sexual gratification, at the same time also ranking high in masturbatory and petting practices. Kinsey's sample revealed that about one-third of teen-age girls masturbated to orgasm, whereas over 90% of the boys do so.[11] It is interesting to note that lower-class boys practice less masturbation and petting and rely more on coitus than boys from the middle and upper classes, especially those who go to college. Kinsey also found that about one-fifth to one-fourth of the females who were 20 or older at the time of the interview admitted petting to orgasm during their teens, mostly between the ages of 16 and 20. The per cent of nonvirginity for teen-age girls was found to be approximately 20% by the age of 20.[12] The percentages are markedly higher for teen-age boys and show interesting gradations between educational levels. Boys whose education stops before high school show a coitus rate of approximately 80% during their teens. Boys with some high school education show a rate of approxi-

[10] Alfred C. Kinsey, *Sexual Behavior in the Human Male* (1948), and *Sexual Behavior in the Human Female* (Philadelphia, W. B. Saunders Co., 1953).

[11] Kinsey, *op. cit.*, 1953, p. 173.

[12] Kinsey, *op. cit.*, 1953, Chapter Seven.

mately 75%. Boys who go to college show the lowest incidence rate, approximately 50%. It can thus be concluded that the majority of the males have experienced premarital coitus before age 20.[13]

A number of studies on premarital coitus have come up with widely differing percentages. This is not necessarily due to sampling error or widely differing populations, but rather to the different age brackets, which obviously place the subjects at different points in time in the premarital period. A much more consistent incidence rate of premarital coitus has been obtained from samples that investigated married people. The reason for this consistency is obviously the circumstance that the married persons have completed the cycle of premarriage whereas single persons have not. Winston Ehrmann referred to this fact when he surveyed a number of studies and found that six samples of married males indicated a range of premarital coitus incidence between 54% and 98%, whereas twelve samples of unmarried males indicated a range between 32% and 93%. Five samples of married females showed a range between 27% and 50%, whereas eight samples of single females revealed a range between 7% and 26%.[14]

A similar disparity between single teen-age boys and married males was found by Kinsey. While the above-mentioned premarital coitus incidence of *teen-age boys* ranges from 50% to 80%, dependent on the educational level, the range for *married males* in general is from 68% to 98%, again dependent on the educational level. The variable of education functions as an interesting differentiation between the frequencies of premarital coitus for males and females. The correlation between education and male and female frequency shows reverse trends. While the percentages for the male by educational levels are 98% for grade school, 85% for high school, and 68% for college,[15] the percentages for the female are 30% for grade school, 47% for high school, and 60% for college.[16] The interpretation of these data suggests that the positive correlation between the girl's frequency of premarital coitus and her educational level is due to greater age at marriage and an increasingly more secular view of the importance of virginity. The inverse correlation between the boy's frequency of premarital coitus and his educational level may be explained by his relative lack of coital opportunities and the use of other sexual outlets.

The high premarital coitus rate of higher-educated girls is apt to obscure an important factor and may therefore result in a misleading interpretation. While it is true that fewer low-educated females have

---

[13] Kinsey, *op. cit.*, 1948, p. 550.
[14] Ehrmann, *op. cit.*, p. 62.
[15] Kinsey, *op. cit.*, 1953, p. 293.
[16] Kinsey, *op. cit.*, 1953, p. 330.

premarital coitus, those who do have a higher rate of promiscuity, i.e., include a greater number of partners and a higher frequency of the sexual act. Higher-educated girls tend to engage in the premarital act during the two years preceding marriage, with a main portion reserved for the fiancé in the period immediately preceding marriage.[17] Another factor that elucidates the educational difference is the age variable. As a rule, college-educated females have their sexual experiences at an age when most lower-educated girls are already married. Of the girls who experienced premarital coitus, 18% of the grade-school category had premarital coitus by age 15, as compared with only 1% of the college-educated girls. Between the ages of 16 and 20, 38% of the noncollege as compared with 18% of the college-educated girls had experienced premarital coitus. After age 20, the percentages are very nearly the same for the different educational categories.[18]

Another factor that is of importance in understanding the distribution of premarital sexual intercourse is the nature of the social relationship of the partners. The public definition of the situation plays a definite role in the degree and frequency of intimate activities. The nature of the boy-girl association ranges from casual dating, "going steady," being "pinned," to being engaged. Sexual intimacy varies significantly with this order. A study by Robert R. Bell and Leonard Blumberg illustrates this correlation, finding that on an informal dating basis, 46% of the males and 10% of the females had experienced premarital coitus; on the "going steady" basis, 40% and 15%, respectively; and on the level of engagement, 46% and 31%, respectively.[19]

Since the majority of the most comprehensive and reliable studies, notably the Kinsey reports, are markedly dated, the question of the *trends* of sexual behavior over the more recent years becomes of foremost concern. Unfortunately, no such generalizable studies of the magnitude of the Kinsey surveys are available today, and the charting of the trends must necessarily proceed by more general observations and piecemeal research. It is commonly assumed that the trend in premarital sexual activities is characterized by a general increase. The assumption is supported by a study by Lewis M. Terman, who inquired into the premarital sexual experiences of different age groups. The study discovered that for males born before 1890, 51% had had *no* premarital coitus and 5% with "future spouse only." For males born after 1910 only 14% stated that they had not experienced premarital coitus, and 32% admitted premarital coitus with "future spouse only." A similar trend was

[17] Kinsey, *op. cit.*, 1953, p. 286.

[18] Kinsey, *op. cit.*, 1953, p. 285.

[19] Robert R. Bell and Leonard Blumberg, "Courtship Intimacy and Religious Background," *Marriage and Family Living*, Vol. 21 (November, 1959), pp. 358–60.

discovered for the females. Those born before 1890 reported a virginity rate of 86% at the time of marriage, and 9% had had premarital coitus with "future husband only." Of the females born after 1910, only 32% were virgins at the time of marriage, and 45% reported premarital coitus with "future husband only."[20]

One is tempted to extrapolate this trend and expect an even higher premarital coitus incidence today. However, verification of this hypothesis awaits more reliable statistics than are presently available.

It is suspected that the changes in sexual patterns have particularly affected the young female. Although the *traditional* difference of sexual involvement between girls and boys was the girl's inclination to engage in petting-with-affection or coitus-with-love, while the attitude of the male was considerably more exploitative and less emotionally involved, this traditional conservatism of females in general and teen-age girls in specific appears to be on the wane. With the progressive liberalization of the American female and the spreading knowledge and use of birth control devices, the modern teen-age girl seeks more self-gratification and strives to achieve full sexual equality. This current development must be kept in mind when consulting Kinsey's figures, which might appear conservative and modest. Kinsey himself became aware of the trend of the female's increasing sexual liberties when he found that of females born before 1900 only 10% had ever petted to orgasm, whereas of those born in the 1920's almost 30%, thrice the proportion, petted to orgasm in their teens.[21]

That the young female increasingly takes a more active, even aggressive, part in sex play was brought out in the study by Winston Ehrmann in 1959, which questioned the continued existence of the traditional pattern that presupposed the male as the sexual aggressor and initiator. Although the aggressive role may still be slightly dominant with the male, it is no longer as rigidly limited to him as in previous generations. Ehrmann found that only slightly more than half of the interviewed males and females reported that the male *always* initiated sexual activities. Forty-four per cent of both sexes admitted that the female did *on occasion,* and ten per cent of the males and six percent of the females reported that the girl initiated sexual activities *as often as,* or *more often than,* the boy.[22]

It is hard to say whether some of these recent findings are true indications of an actual increase of premarital sexual behavior over the

[20] Lewis M. Terman, *Psychological Factors in Marital Happiness* (New York, McGraw-Hill, 1938), p. 41.

[21] Kinsey, *op. cit.,* 1953, p. 244.

[22] Winston Ehrmann, *Premarital Dating Behavior* (New York, Henry Holt Co., 1959), pp. 63–64.

previous generation, or whether modern youth, unlike their more secretive elders, merely allow themselves a more public expression of sexual deportment. In spite of the difficulty of empirically testing this question, most sociologists agree that premarital sexual activities have increased and intensified over the last two to three decades. They trace the more liberal behavior patterns to at least two major sources. First, the Sexual Revolution added the function of pure pleasure and enjoyment to whatever institutionalized functions sex may already have had; this new function was made feasible through the availability of information and devices to control conception and venereal disease. Second, the technological and medical advances of modern American society have prolonged the span of time during which a young person is no longer a child and not yet an adult and has the full physiological need and capability of engaging in the sex act. American society makes no acceptable provision that will allow release of the natural needs and tensions. It is in the light of these two major explanatory points that most social scientists look at the permarital sexual manifestations of modern time.

Venereal Diseases

One of the detectable consequences of the teen-ager's sexual excursion can be the contraction of VD. Great public concern has been displayed over the last decade about the increasing number of teen-age VD cases. It is true that a large *number* of American teen-agers contract venereal diseases every year, and, in fact, the United States Department of Health, Education, and Welfare announced in 1962 that young persons under 20 are responsibile for one out of every four reported cases of VD. This meant that on a nationwide basis, VD strikes one teen-ager every nine minutes.[23] However, it is quite likely that the *rate* for teen-agers has not greatly increased over previous generations, since the younger age bracket has increased numerically over the past ten years. In fact, the rate of gonorrhea for the age group from 15 to 19 years old has slightly decreased from 408 per 100,000 in 1956 to 386 in 1964. The rate of syphilis for teen-agers, however, has more than doubled within one decade from 10 per 100,000 in 1956 to 23 in 1964. And yet this is a comparatively low increase when contrasted to the rise in the syphilis rate for the older age groups. During the same ten-year period, the rate for the 20–24-year-old bracket increased from 19 to 53, and for the 25–29-

---

[23] U.S. Public Health Service Publication No. 913 (1962).

year-old bracket from 11 to 42.[24] The claim that the incidence of VD among teen-agers is at an all-time high is therefore of dubious veracity and objectivity, since more than 80% of the VD reported concerns older age groups.

An additional characteristic of the teen-age VD incidence rate must be understood. The teen-age VD rate is not evenly distributed throughout the teen population, and the statistics show that VD is highly concentrated in the nonwhite and lower socioeconomic segments of the United States population, While the 1964 syphilis rate for white teen-agers was only four per 100,000, the rate for nonwhites, mostly Negroes, was 152. Similarly, the gonorrhea rate for white teen-agers was 109, while it amounted to 2,300 for nonwhites.[25]

Premarital Pregnancy

Another index that provides some insight into the trends of sexual behavior of teen-agers is their premarital pregnancy rate. (See Table 15–1.) Because females under age 20 are responsible for over 40% of the total illegitimate births in the United States and particularly because their illegitimacy rate has more than doubled between 1940 and 1964,[26] it is commonly believed that more liberal practices and permissive codes have evolved over the past two to three decades. Public concern over this development is continually reflected in such judgments as "those immoral teen-agers" and "they're getting worse every year." Although it may be true that today's sexual expressions suggest greater liberality and less inhibition than during previous generations, the public's persistent preoccupation with teen-agers may be biased and exaggerated.

To view illegitimacy among teen-agers in a fuller and more objective perspective, several qualifications must be stated. The sole reason that illegitimacy among teen-agers amounts to over 40% of all United States illegitimacies, characterizing the teen-age bracket as having the largest number of females with illegitimate children, is that there are *more* teen-agers. Those in the 15 to 19 age bracket in the mid-1960's were born during the baby boom of 1945–1949. There will be rising numbers of teen-agers for several more years to come. This means that even if illegitimacy rates do not change, more illegitimate babies will be

---

24 U.S. Department of Health, Education, and Welfare, *V.D. Fact Sheet—1965,* Tables 7 and 8.

25 *Ibid.*

26 U.S. Department of Health, Education, and Welfare, *Monthly Vital Statistics Report,* Vol. 15, No. 3 (June 14, 1966), pp. 1–2.

TABLE 15-1. Estimated Illegitimacy Rates by Age of Mother, United States, 1940–1964.
(Rates per 1,000 unmarried women in specified age group.)

| Year | Age of Mother | | | | | | | |
	15–44 years	15–19 years	20–24 years	25–29 years	30–34 years	35–39 years	40–44 years
1964	23.4	16.5	40.0	50.1	41.1	15.0	4.0
1963	22.5	15.3	39.9	49.4	33.7	16.1	4.3
1962	21.5	14.9	41.8	46.4	27.0	13.5	3.4
1961	22.6	16.0	41.2	44.8	28.9	15.1	3.8
1960	21.8	15.7	40.3	42.0	27.5	13.9	3.6
1959	22.1	15.7	40.1	47.3	28.6	14.2	3.4
1958	21.0	15.4	37.3	37.8	27.6	13.2	3.2
1957	20.9	15.6	36.5	37.6	26.1	12.7	3.3
1956	20.2	15.7	36.3	36.0	25.3	10.2	2.6
1955	19.3	15.0	33.7	32.1	22.2	10.7	2.7

1954	18.3	14.6	30.0	32.0	19.2	10.3	2.5
1953	17.0	13.8	28.5	27.6	17.9	8.9	2.4
1952	15.6	13.3	25.6	23.1	15.9	8.0	1.8
1951	15.1	13.1	23.2	24.4	14.0	7.8	2.3
1950	14.1	12.6	21.3	19.9	13.3	7.2	2.0
1949	13.3	12.0	21.0	18.0	11.5	6.9	1.9
1948	12.5	11.4	19.8	16.4	10.0	5.8	1.6
1947	12.1	11.0	18.9	15.7	9.2	5.6	1.8
1946	10.9	9.5	17.3	15.6	7.3	4.4	1.8
1945	10.1	9.5	15.3	12.1	7.1	4.1	1.6
1944	9.0	8.8	13.1	10.1	7.0	4.0	1.3
1943	8.3	8.4	11.4	8.8	6.7	3.8	1.3
1942	8.0	8.2	11.0	8.4	6.3	3.8	1.2
1941	7.8	8.0	10.5	7.8	6.0	3.7	1.4
1940	7.1	7.4	9.5	7.2	5.1	3.4	1.2

Source: U.S. Department of Health, Education, and Welfare *Monthly Vital Statistics Report*, Vol. 15, No. 3 (June 14, 1966), p. 2.

born to unmarried girls in their late teens. In 1964, only 1.65% of the 15–19-year-old single girls had illegitimate babies, while, for example, 4% of the 20–24-, and 5% of the 25–29-year-old unmarried females bore illegitimate babies.[27] It may be appropriate to consider the thought that the *general* population, instead of just the younger segment of the population, exhibits greater liberality and permissiveness today, and that the problem may thus be one of the whole population rather than of only the younger portion. This notion can be supported by an examination of Table 15-1, which shows that *all* female age brackets between 15 and 44 have notably increased rates of illegitimacy. Between 1940 and 1964, the illegitimacy rate increased approximately four times for the 20–24 group, seven times for the 25–29 group, eight times for the 30–34 group, four times for the 35–39 group, and three times for the 40–44 group. The increase for the teen-age bracket was only slightly more than double, thereby making it the age group with the lowest rate increase among the various age brackets. The clamor of the public concerning teen-age illegitimacy seems therefore unduly out of proportion.

Another perspective-lending modification is the realization that illegitimacy among the teen-age population is not evenly distributed. In the majority of the reported cases, the girls are Negro, and their general socioeconomic status is low. Illegitimacy among the upper classes is probably lower and less detectable because of their greater recourse to abortion,[28] their more frequent use of the alternative of marrying when faced with pregnancy, and their greater ability to hush up the event and stay out of public statistics. One reason why middle- and upper-class girls are more frequently inclined to decide on marriage as a solution to the problem may be interpreted from the study of Clark E. Vincent, who found that when middle- and upper-class females are faced with premarital pregnancy, it is usually the result of a love relationship, whereas in the case of lower-class females, it is more often the result of a casual affair.[29]

It appears from reliable national statistics that, just as in the case of VD rates, the bulk of premarital pregnancies is limited to specific segments of the teen-age population. In a sense, these serious consequences of sexual activities are more a problem of social class than a problem of youth. Moreover, there is enough evidence to suggest that teen-agers in general are more conservative than the general public

---

[27] Reference 26.

[28] Paul H. Gebhard *et al.*, *Pregnancy, Birth, and Abortion* (New York, Harper & Brothers, 1958), pp. 45, 160.

[29] Clark E. Vincent, "Illegitimacy in the United States," in Evelyn M. and Sylvanus M. Duvall (eds.), *Sexways in Fact and Faith* (New York, Association Press, 1961), p. 143.

would commonly assume. This point is particularly supported by comparing teen-age illegitimacy and VD rates, and their trends over the last decade, with the rates of older age groups.

The question of what to do about the problem of increasing premarital pregnancies is of long standing and serious concern to welfare and juvenile authorities. The attempts to cope with the problem branch into two avenues, the *prophylactic* and the *adjustive*, i.e., efforts to reduce premarital pregnancies in the first place and efforts to help reduce the difficulties and hardships that invariably ensue once an illegitimate birth takes place. The preventive approach is primarily of an educational nature and tries to remind parents of their responsibility for their teenage children and to remind teen-agers themselves of the dangers of premarital sexual intercourse. However, the parents' role in respect to the sex education of their offspring is poorly defined, lacks consensus, and is largely inactive. There is unclarity even in legal instances concerning the rightful extent of parental sex instruction. A 1966 court case in Ohio illustrated this dilemma.[30] After her 13-year-old daughter Mary Ann had given birth to a baby boy, an Ohio mother demanded that she stop seeing boys. At the same time, fearing that the girl might not obey her, the mother advised her to see to it that any future sex partner used a contraceptive. Within 15 months, Mary Ann had her second child—and within a year thereafter, the third child. Juvenile authorities placed the teen-ager in a state school for delinquents, while the mother was arrested on charges of contributing to the delinquency of a minor. A jury found her guilty and gave her a suspended sentence of one year in the workhouse and a $200 fine. The appeal of the sentence created a legal turmoil and brought the jurists face to face with the fact that sex education and the parental role in instructing their children are relatively undefined and obscure issues. The legal impasse was finally resolved by the Court of Appeals, which ruled the mother's action not only her parental right but also her duty. This parental duty was deemed particularly necessary in the light of the school system's gross neglect to offer adequate sex education.

The majority of the few sex education programs that do exist are usually incorporated only marginally into other high school courses, frequently into general biology courses. There are conspicuous regional differences concerning the legality, extent, and quality of such sex education. The large New York City school system, for example, ignores the problem altogether; the Los Angeles system, on the other hand, has a program of elaborate and frank instructions; Washington, D. C. offers probably the nation's most thorough sex education programs—a move

---

[30] "Domestic Relations," *Time* (Jan. 7, 1966), p. 75.

undertaken because it also has the highest VD and premarital pregnancy rates of any United States city; the neighboring state of Virginia lacks any systematic sex education since state law prohibits sex instruction in public schools.[31] In short, there is an obvious lack of consensus concerning the question of sex instruction in the classroom. In some communities, it is shunned as a classroom subject, considered a moral and not an instructional issue. In other places, teachers include sexual information vaguely and evasively in general biology courses; and in still other places, teachers pass the issue on to parents as the presumably proper agents of sex instruction. The end effect of this indecision, circumvention, and neglect is the victimization of the teen-ager who is then left to learn by hearsay, trial-and-error, and sometimes by irreversible experience.

As a result, the social apparatus needed to provide the necessary adjustment in cases of illegitimate birth has grown into a complex and extensive institution, consisting of social welfare agencies, homes for unwed mothers, adoption agencies, etc. It has become customary in American society that an essential part of the solution to the illegitimacy problem is the surrender of the newborn baby to this impersonal apparatus which will then place the child in a presumably adequate foster home. Since illegitimacy, by definition, is outside of the institutionalized norms, the surrendering and adoption process is a delicate and semi-secret procedure involving conflicts, contradictions, and psychological anguish. An authority in the field described it this way:

> There have been—and still are—societies which punish the unmarried mother by forcing her to keep her child, even under distressing and humiliating conditions. Our society, under the guise of a free decision, uses a subtle form of pressure in the opposite direction. The unmarried mother is made to feel that she is totally selfish if she keeps her child. This pressure comes from both family members and professional people. Even if the social worker tries to help the girl to make her own decision, the provisions made for helping unmarried mothers raise their children with dignity are practically nil. Very few day-care services for working mothers exist. Not only are grants for mothers to stay home small, but those who receive them are too often exposed to community scorn. What kind of value system do we transmit to the unmarried mother?
>
> It is a strange contradiction that, while we hope to educate girls for responsibility, we act—not always, but frequently—as if the child they are carrying is a tumor which must be forgotten as soon as it is "removed."

---

[31] "Teaching: The Fourth R," *Time* (Dec. 31, 1965), p. 35.

It is also paradoxical that, while we are trying to educate young people to be truthful, we provide an elaborate network of lies and hiding places during the pregnancy, usually to save the "good reputation" of the family.[32]

Trends in Teen-Age Marriages

The present era, no matter what else it may be characterized by, is certainly characterized by an all-time high popularity of marriage. National statistics reveal that over the past 60 to 70 years the married proportion of the United States population has gradually and consistently increased. In 1900, for example, 59.9% of all males and 58.7% of all females were of married status, as compared with 71.0% and 68.3%, respectively, in 1963.[33] The participation of teen-agers in the marriage vogue has been substantial and was reflected by marked increases over the same period of time. The sharpest increases were reported for white teen-age boys, among whom, between 1910 and 1960, the married proportion increased 6 to 9 times. In the 17-year-old age bracket, for example, the increase was from 0.3% to 1.8%, and in the 16-year-old bracket the increase was from 0.1% to 0.9%. White teen-age girls also increased in married proportions, but not as markedly as their male counterparts. Their rates even decreased slightly in the 17-year-old bracket between 1950 and 1960.[34]

The percentage of married teen-agers has always significantly differed between the white and the nonwhite population. Although the nonwhite teen-age rates have consistently been, and to a great extent still are, higher in most age brackets than the rates of their white peers, the increase has been neither as fast nor as consistent. In fact, slightly lower nonwhite rates can be noted today than in the 1920's and '30's.[35] In 1960, the proportion of married 18-year-olds even fell slightly below the white proportion—a relatively novel phenomenon in comparative vital statistics. The *general* picture and the direction of the trend, however, are hardly affected by the nonwhite decreases, since they represent a minority within the United States population. Because they represent the vast majority, statistics concerning the white population have a considerably greater generalizability to the total United States scene.

---

[32] Gisela Konopka, *The Adolescent Girl in Conflict* (Englewood Cliffs, N.J., Prentice-Hall, 1966), pp. 127–28.

[33] U.S. Bureau of the Census, *Statistical Abstract of the United States Population: 1964* (Washington, D.C., 1964), p. 31. (Based on U.S. population 14 years of age and older.)

[34] *Ibid.*

[35] U.S. Bureau of the Census, *Current Population Reports, Population Characteristics,* 1920 and 1930.

TABLE 15–2. Per Cent of Persons in Teen-Age Brackets who were Married, by Race and Sex, 1910 to 1960.

Age	White						Nonwhite					
	1910	1920	1930	1940	1950	1960	1910	1920	1930	1940	1950	1960
Females												
15	1.1	1.3	1.1	1.0	1.0	2.2	2.1	2.7	2.9	2.6	2.8	2.8
16	3.4	3.8	3.9	3.4	5.6	5.5	6.6	7.8	8.8	7.6	8.1	6.6
17	8.1	9.1	9.1	8.0	12.7	11.7	13.0	17.9	18.7	16.4	17.3	13.3
18	15.9	17.9	17.7	16.2	23.2	23.9	24.4	32.2	32.7	28.9	29.3	23.0
Males												
15	0.1	0.2	0.1	0.1	0.6	0.6	0.1	0.3	0.2	0.3	0.4	0.7
16	0.1	0.3	0.2	0.3	0.6	0.9	0.2	0.6	0.4	0.6	0.4	1.0
17	0.3	0.8	0.6	0.6	1.2	1.8	0.9	1.6	1.4	1.4	1.8	2.0
18	1.2	2.4	1.9	1.9	3.4	5.3	0.3	5.3	4.2	4.2	4.8	5.1

Adapted from U.S. Bureau of the Census, *Current Population Reports, Population Characteristics*, for the respective years.

It is difficult to predict the future development of teen-age marriage trends. Preliminary reports, ahead of the publication of the 10-year-interval complete census, seem to indicate a drop, or at least a leveling-off, of the marriage rates for teen-agers. This new trend may be inferred from the data in Table 15–3.

Reduction in the marriage rates of teen-agers does not appear to be part of a general decline of the popularity of marriage, but rather a new trend characteristic of teen-agers only. The sustained popularity and continued rise of marriage rates for older age brackets is illustrated in Table 15–4, showing that young adults above 20 years of age are entering marital status in increasing numbers and percentages.

Another way of assessing the popularity of marriage among young persons is by looking at the changes in the average age at marriage. National figures show a consistent decrease in the median age over the past generations. (See Table 15–5.) Over a period of 70 years, the age at first marriage decreased for the male by more than three years and for the female by approximately two years.[36]

TABLE 15–3.   Per Cent of Married Teen-Agers for the United States, 1960 and 1965.

Age	Male		Female	
	1960	1965	1960	1965
14–15	0.6	0.6	4.5	3.4
18–19	8.8	7.5	28.1	26.0

Adapted from U.S. Bureau of the Census, *Current Population Reports, Population Characteristics, Series* P-20, No. 144 (Nov. 10, 1965), pp. 10–11.

TABLE 15–4.   Per Cent of Young Adults of Marital Status, for the United States, 1960 and 1965.

Age	Male		Female	
	1960	1965	1960	1965
20–24	44.6	46.3	69.5	65.1
25–29	75.2	81.1	87.4	87.2

Adapted from U.S. Bureau of the Census, *Current Population Reports, Population Characteristics,* Series P-20, No. 144 (Nov. 10, 1965), pp. 10–11.

---

[36] U.S. Bureau of the Census, *Current Population Reports, Population Characteristics, Series* P-20, No. 144 (Nov. 10, 1965), p. 3.

Again, however, a change of trend appears to be imminent. Between 1950 and 1960, a leveling-off process took place, with the ages at first marriage for both males and females remaining almost stable from 1950 to 1960. Starting with 1960, a slight rise in the average age was reported. The latest statistics would give the male and the female a higher average for the 1960–1965 period than for the 1950–1960 period.[37] (See Table 15–6.)

The foregoing data and statistics are helpful in gaining a realistic perspective on youthful marriage in the United States. It can be said, in sum, that the marriage rate of the United States population in general is at an all-time high. The part of teen-agers in this "marriage boom" is revealed by marked increases in the teen-age marriage rates over the

TABLE 15–5. Median Age at First Marriage, by Sex, for the United States, 1890–1960.

Year	Male	Female
1960	22.8	20.3
1950	22.8	20.3
1940	24.3	21.5
1930	24.3	21.3
1920	24.6	21.2
1910	25.1	21.6
1900	25.9	21.9
1890	26.1	22.0

Adapted from U.S. Bureau of the Census, *Current Population Reports, Population Characteristics,* Series P-20, No. 144 (Nov. 10, 1965), p. 3.

TABLE 15–6. Median Age at First Marriage, by Sex, for the United States, 1960–1965.

Year	Male	Female
1965	22.8	20.6
1964	23.1	20.5
1963	22.8	20.5
1962	22.7	20.3
1961	22.8	20.3

Adapted from U.S. Bureau of the Census, *Current Population Report, Population Characteristics,* Series P-20, No. 144 (Nov. 10, 1965), p. 3.

----

[37] Reference 36.

past 60 years, which reached an all-time high in 1950, leveled off at that time, and seem to be slightly decreasing at the present time. Verification, however, of this apparent novel trend must await future census publications. In spite of the possible minor decrease, the popularity of marriage among teen-agers remains extremely high, and the per cent of teen-agers getting married will definitely remain greater than that of past generations.

Reasons for Younger Age at Marriage

What are the various conditions that can be listed in an effort to explain the upsurge of marriage rates among mid-20th-century youth? The following list draws from the recurrent and presumably explanatory themes found in the professional literature. This list does not pretend to be complete or to suggest a certain order of importance of reasons. It also should be understood that these reasons are interrelated, overlap with one another, and differ in the degree to which they can be empirically verified.

(1) *Economic feasibility*. A factor that seems to be significantly correlated with age at marriage is the economic situation. The improved economic conditions since the turn of the century are correlated with a gradual decline of the median age. It has become increasingly possible for younger couples to gather the material implementations necessary for marriage and family maintenance. The current prosperity plus the security of constant employment and income, not only for the young man but also for the young wife, the prospect of parental support if hardship should arise, the occupational fringe benefits including medical plans and other safeguards against health hazards, and the extensive public relief and support programs available in times of unemployment or disability all act to reduce the economic and material barriers to early marriage.

(2) *Glorified image of marriage*. The mass media, particularly motion pictures and television, to which teen-agers are extensively exposed, tend to present a glorified image of married life. Marriage is pictured as a "happy" and problemless institution. Entering it bears the promise of automatic termination of loneliness, personality problems, sexual frustrations, etc. It is assumed to be the answer to the excessive contemporary craving for romance and glamour. In its final effect, marriage is depicted as a panacea for all troubles. It is interesting to observe that many modern movies end with the hero and the heroine happily "finding each other," "settling down," and getting married. At

that moment the story's plot is exhausted, and its problems, dangers, and risks come to an end—in a sense suggesting that all troubles have now been abolished. Rarely, if at all, does the typical teen-age movie *start* with married life, realistically showing its problems and risks. The glorifying misrepresentation cannot fail to make marriage extremely enticing to the teen-ager who, normally, is beset with the often agonizing task of trying to learn how to cope with himself and the world around him. Thus, he is only too eager to accept a suggestion that pretends to be an escape from his problems.

(3) *Anti-deference of gratification.* Our age is unabashedly an era of hedonism that puts a premium on the achievement of personal happiness, success, and "self-realization." Deference of gratification is no longer a value or a virtue but, instead, a nuisance. In the light of this hedonistic ethos, marriage is viewed as a rightly deserved gratification and an institution whose soothing services may be invoked without delay when frustration is felt. Such frustrations may involve the desire for companionship, the need for security, and the craving for sexual gratification. In the unswerving "pursuit of happiness," marriage and a young family are not seen as limitations or liabilities, but as opportunities for immediate satisfaction.

(4) *The draft problem.* The constant impending threat of being drafted into the armed services frequently acts as another inducement for young men to marry early. This trend was presumably observed at the time of the Korean War and has more recently reappeared during the military operations in Southeast Asia. Several types of marriage motivation have grown out of the awareness of possible induction into the services. First, many young men wish to enjoy married life *now*, rather than waiting a number of years until reentering civilian status. Second, they dislike the idea of going away for years without having someone to whom they "belong," someone who will wait for them and allow them to have roots in normal civilian life. Finally, for a number of young men there is a strong motivation to use marital status as a means for deferment or exemption from overseas military duty.

(5) *Escapism.* A young marriage may often be an escape from an unhappy home or from the drudgery of school work. Intergenerational conflict and habitual tensions in interpersonal relations in the home play a prominent role in this explanation. Many frustrated young people try to escape from parental control, thinking that once they are married their tensions and conflicts will vanish.

(6) *Earlier sexual maturation.* The progressively earlier onset of puberty for girls and boys and the correspondingly earlier development of sexual needs are powerful inducers to precocious sexual experimenta-

tion, dating, courtship, and marriage. As has been pointed out in a previous chapter, today's teen-agers develop physiologically approximately two years earlier than previous generations of teen-agers.

(7) *Deferment of parenthood.* Given knowledge of and access to means of birth control, the fear that marriage may immediately lead to children and the responsibilities of parenthod has been removed. Rather than assuming such burdens, a large proportion of young married couples are now free to enjoy their conjugal companionship and the sexual gratification that is part of it. With this serious parental function postponed, a certain number of teen-agers, who otherwise might feel reluctant to marry early, feel that they have a chance to enjoy the "fun" part of marriage.

(8) *Desire for adult status.* Some social scientists suspect that teen-agers look upon marriage as some kind of initiation rite into adulthood, since traditionally marriage has been, and largely is, considered an institution for adults only. The pressures of adolescence, especially the experience of the unstructured and statusless aspects of that period, and the absence of other effective rites of passage, may induce teen-agers to decide on marriage as a definite method of establishing themselves as adults. In a sense, there is a magical hope that the ritual will turn them into mature, reasonable, and autonomous adults.

(9) *The bandwagon effect.* Marriage has become "the thing to do." Not only have younger marriages become quite acceptable to the majority of the population (at some colleges one-fourth to one-third of the undergraduates are married),[38] but young people are often directly or indirectly encouraged by their married peers. The marriage of a friend or acquaintance encourages and contributes to another, and soon the feeling spreads that "everybody is doing it."

(10) *The twosome nature of social life in the United States.* Not only is there a casual bandwagon effect and a general acceptance of younger marriages, but there are subtle *pressures* working to make married life appear more comfortable and practical. Social life in the United States is a twosome experience. Generally speaking, such affairs as parties, dances, dining, and movies are considered twosome experiences. A young woman is expected to have an escort, a young man is

---

[38] In 1964, the U. S. Bureau of the Census presented figures that showed that 942,000 out of the 4,644,000 students enrolled in college were married. This means that on a nationwide basis roughly 1/5 of all college students were married. U. S. Bureau of the Census, *Current Population Reports, Population Characteristics,* Series P-20, No. 148 (Feb. 8, 1966), p. 13. However, the proportion of married students seems to be somewhat higher on state-supported campuses as illustrated, for example, by Arizona State University where approximately 6,000 out of nearly 21,000 students were married in 1967.

expected to bring along a date, partner, or girl friend. If an individual engages in such social affairs in stag fashion more frequently than is customary, he or she may be looked upon as odd. College men are frequently heard complaining about the trouble they have in "lining up" a date for the weekend or for a special event. They complain that they spend "hours" on the phone trying to get a girl to go out with them. The married status may look particularly enticing at such worrisome times, conveying a vision of "instant date," of saving time, and of freedom from embarrassment. Sometimes, no doubt, these worries are warranted because participation in a social event actually may be contingent upon bringing a date or a partner. The proportion of social events requiring such twosome participation and the general cultural desirability of doing so are probably greater and more intense in the United States than in most other countries.

(11) *Stimulation of sexual appetites.* Again the mass media must be held responsible for titillating and enticing the teen-ager's sexual fantasies. The emphasis on sex appeal and the intense physical expression of love makes it difficult for teen-agers to handle sexual arousals. This results in the unwillingness to defer sexual gratification until after marriage and in the increasing premarital pregnancy rate which, in many cases, leads to "forced" marriages. Welfare workers in the metropolitan area of Phoenix, Arizona, have related to this author that a pregnant high school girl, trying to explain the background of her predicament, referred to the ubiquitous sex enticement, saying that "wherever you look and wherever you go, there's something about sex. It makes you look foolish not to find out about it yourself." Another girl in similar difficulties put it this way: "We were 'going steady' and were together just all the time. There are not really many places to go to around here—the drive-in movies and the downtown movies. That's about all. After you have seen all the movies, you just park the car, and if you are in love, you know—that's it."

(12) *The insecurity of our time.* Finally, the general insecurity of our time is often thought of as encouraging young marriages. Many young people feel powerless and think that they cannot do anything about the H-bomb or the threats of war and the draft. In addition, as described in an earlier chapter, the general American culture is too vague and lacking in the compelling ideation needed to alleviate fears and anxieties. It appears, therefore, that the anxieties concerning possible impending national or international disasters generate in youth a need to develop deep attachments with someone in order to achieve security. For many teen-agers, especially for those most insecure and most in need of escaping from problems, the only substantial security

imaginable is a relationship that will provide unquestionable loyalty, affection, and warmth. Marriage, they trust, is the type of relationship that will give then these qualities.

The Problem of Teen-Age Divorce

Although marriage is usually not considered a social problem *per se*, it may be classified as one when teen-agers are involved because of the unusually high proportion of teen-age marriages ending in divorce, annulment, or separation. The divorce rate (normally including the annulments) is three to four times higher among couples who were married when the wife, husband, or both were teen-agers than among couples who were married when both spouses were over 20. An impressive number of studies have focused on this problem and found, virtually without exception, that there exists a significant correlation between teen-age marriage and marital failure. Reliable examples of such sociological research include the study by Thomas P. Monahan revealing a consistent correlation and showing that the older the age at marriage, the lower the divorce rate.[39] Hugh Carter and Alexander Plateris found that in the divorces occurring in 1960, 16% of the males and 45% of the females had married before reaching the age of 20, while in the marriages contracted in that year only 13% of the males and 37% of the females were under 20.[40] The Family Court Center in Toledo, Ohio, found in the course of a five-year period that over two-thirds of the divorce cases heard involved couples in which the bride had been under 21 at marriage.[41] An Indiana study working with a sample of divorced and a sample of happily married couples disclosed that a significantly higher proportion of the divorced women had married before the age of 18 and the men before the age of 21. On the average, the divorced women had married two years younger and the divorced men one year younger than the happily married women and men.[42] Census data authoritatively corroborate these findings. In a survey by the Bureau of the Census, women were asked about their age at first marriage and how many times

---

[39] Thomas P. Monahan, "Does Age at Marriage Matter in Divorce?" *Social Forces*, Vol. 32–33 (October, 1953–May, 1955), pp. 81–87.

[40] Hugh Carter and Alexander Paternis, "Trends in Divorce and Family Disruption," in U.S. Department of Health, Education, and Welfare, *Indicators* (August, 1963).

[41] Family Court Center, *Annual Report* (Toledo, Ohio, 1953).

[42] Harvey J. Locke, *Predicting Adustment in Marriage: A Comparison of a Divorced and Happily Married Group,* (New York, Holt, Rinehart, and Winston, 1951), pp, 101–02.

they had been married. It was discovered that women who had been married once had a median age of 21.1 years at first marriage, compared with 19.9 years for those who had been married more than once. The Census report indicated that this age difference had been a consistent pattern for more than three decades, implying that persons remarrying had been married the first time at an age approximately two years younger than those married only once.[43]

In addition to the age-at-marriage factor, the incidence of marital failure is of course affected by additional circumstances. For example, it was found that nonwhite divorce and separation rates generally exceeded those of whites, being twice as large in most age brackets. This suggests not only a racial but also a social-class differential. However, even when a number of factors associated with social status were controlled, marriages contracted at younger ages still showed a significantly higher divorce and separation rate than those contracted after 20.[44] In an Iowa study, Burchinal and coworkers discovered that marital failure rates varied among the three stauts levels used. However, marriages involving brides 19 or younger had higher failure rates in *all* status categories than marriages involving brides who were 20 or older.[45]

What can be said in terms of explanation for the high rates of marital failure among teen-age marriages? In the first place, as a basic explanatory premise, one might suspect unrealistic and immature motivations for getting married. In fact, it probably would be fruitful to reexamine the list of reasons for younger age at marriage that was presented in the preceding section of this chapter. However, since the fallacy in most of the motivations is obvious, only a few specific aspects shall be reconsidered.

Although the general economic situation has improved to a point allowing many teen-agers to marry, a substantial number of them still accept parental subsidy after they are married. Rather than being an asset, this practice can easily turn into a marital liability. One of the perils of the subsidy situation is that it opens the door for the giver to make suggestions. If parental suggestions are not accepted by the young couple, the parents may feel that the children are ungrateful in accepting financial aid but not advice. The young couple may grow restless with feelings of guilt and/or resentment. This may introduce dis-

---

[43] U.S. Bureau of the Census, *Current Population Reports, Population Characteristics, Series P-20*, No. 67 (May 2, 1956), p. 3.

[44] Lee G. Burchinal, "Trends and Prospects for Young Marriages in the United States," *Journal of Marriage and the Family*, Vol. 27 (May, 1965).

[45] Lee G. Burchinal and Loren E. Chancellor, "Survival Rates among Religiously Homogamous and Interreligious Marriages," *Social Forces*, Vol. 41 (May, 1963), pp. 353–62.

content, conflict, and stress into an otherwise wholesome young marriage. Even if the young couple can manage to be financially independent, however, and may appear to have an adequate income, there still remains the question of wise and consensual budgeting.[48] It seems that many teen-age married couples have great difficulties in learning to handle financial matters and, as is commonly known, financial problems constitute the grounds for a sizable proportion of divorces.

Probably one of the most acute forms of marital disintegration lies in unreal premarital visions of marital bliss—especially as shown in the fare of the mass media. The daily reality of married life simply cannot live up to the glorified image presented by the mass media. After a relatively brief duration of time early in the marriage, the young spouses frequently become deeply disillusioned with what appears to them to be an unsuccessful marriage. Wendell Johnson called this process the IFD disease, i.e., *Idealization*, making impossible, unrealistic, and ideal demands on life, which leads to *Frustration*, because real life does not bear out the expectations, which in turn leads to *Demoralization* (or Disintegration, or Despair).[47] The degree of demoralization usually is most severe for the teen-ager who has used marriage as an escape from home or school. The young escapist soon discovers that a marital relationship, especially in its initial stage, is not at all free of problems. To his surprise, the ego-sensitive escapist may find that the new human relationship is not unlike the one he tried to escape and that the necessary adjustments are just as difficult as in the previous environment. The outcome of this disillusionment often brings back the old insecurity. It is then that the teen-agers realize, frequently too late to help save the faltering marriage, that Insecurity A plus Insecurity B does not make Security C, but rather Insecurity AB.

Young people who were victims of the bandwagon effect may frequently discover that they were blindly following the wrong drummer and that their decision to marry was not only fallacious in respect to the timing and choosing of the particular partner, but fallacious in the most basic sense, i.e., in the assumption that they were marital material in the first place. The popular and wide-spread assumption that everyone has the proper aptitudes and proficiencies to engage in a marital relationship is extremely dangerous and completely ignores the fact that some persons would be much better off not married at all. Perhaps these individuals would recognize this and see themselves in a more realistic

---

[46] Robert O. Herrmann, "Expectations and Attitudes as a Source of Financial Problems in Teen-Age Marriages," *Journal of Marriage and the Family*, Vol. 27 (February, 1965), pp. 89–90.

[47] Wendell Johnson, *People in Quandaries* (New York, Harper & Bros., 1964), pp. 14, 18, 488.

way, were it not for sometimes subtle, and at other times not so subtle, social pressures that urge him to follow suit and get married.

Adulthood in a complex urban-industrial society cannot be acquired by some semimagic rite of passage, be it the driver's license, Bar Mitzvah, or marriage. There is no short cut to learning the adult role and the mature performance of adult responsibilities. In as complex a society as ours, this process demands long years of education, training, and plain experience. The adolescent who intends to achieve adult status by precocious marriage is therefore nothing more than an "underqualified adult." This semiadult individual may not be able to carry out the demands directed at him without surrendering. This surrender may be in the form of divorce or separation.

A characteristic that has repeatedly been found to have some degree of correlation with divorce is premarital pregnancy. Harold T. Christensen and coworkers, for example, concluded from their research that premarital pregnancy is followed by a *substantially* higher than average rate of divorce.[48] Their samples included populations from Utah, Indiana, and Denmark. They found that couples who were married when the bride was pregnant showed a disproportionately high rate of marital failure, and that the folklore of the cementing effect of the child is largely a myth. In Denmark, 20.9% of all sample couples experienced divorce; but 29.9% of the couples that had their first child within the first 9 months of marriage ended in divorce; and 31.3% of the couples that had their child within the first six months of marriage ended in divorce. In Indiana, the average divorce rate was 8.8%, but it was 14.5% for the birth-within-the-first-nine-months category, and 16.9% for the birth-within-six-months category. In Utah, the rates were 4.9%, 13.1%, and 17.2%, respectively.[49]

The primary reason that young marriages starting out with a premartial pregnancy do not survive is probably the fact that such marriages were partially or wholly involuntary on the part of one or both partners. Among several concurring studies, Lee G. Burchinal's study in Iowa found that if both spouses were high school students, 87% of the marriages were forced by pregnancy.[50] As a consequence, the teenagers may have been neither willing nor prepared for the marital relationship, let alone for parenthood.

---

[48] Harold T. Christensen and Hanna H. Meissner, "Studies in Child-Spacing: III —Premarital Pregnancy as a Factor in Divorce," *American Sociological Review,* Vol. 18 (December, 1953), pp. 641–44.

[49] *Ibid.*

[50] Lee G. Burchinal, "Research on Young Marriages: Implications for Family Life Education," *The Family Life Coordinator,* Vol. 9 (September–December, 1960), pp. 6–24.

The divorce-proneness of teen-age marriages has also been noticed in other countries. Official statistics from England indicate that, whatever the duration of the marriage, the divorce rate was consistently much higher for the teen-age brides than for those over 20, especially if marriage was postponed until after the age of 25.[51] The same nation-wide English figures also show that one child does little to stabilize a marriage of teen-agers, because it frequently takes place only to legitimate the baby.

The frequency of premarital pregnancy is, in turn, correlated with other factors that necessitate expansion of the explanatory statement. It has been found, for example, that the incidence of premarital pregnancy is influenced by the type of parent–child relationship or the general style of interpersonal relations prevailing in the teen-ager's family of orientation. It has been repeatedly hypothesized that a tense and conflict-ridden home background induces teen-agers, especially teen-age girls, to use marriage as a means for escape. This escape is often preceded by sexual involvement, possibly again consisting of an attempt to escape from a home environment that lacks in sufficient warmth and security. Also, such sexual involvement and subsequent marriage can often be interpreted as an act of rebellion against parents and authority or as a symptom of confusion or lack of values. Two family sociologists stated their hypothesis by suggesting that "more of those who marry early do so to escape unhappy home surroundings or to defy parental dominance than is true of those who marry later."[52] Tests of this hypothesis have yielded supporting data. One research discovered that "girls who marry early have less satisfactory relationships with their parental families."[53] The findings of another study revealed significant correlation between early marriage and premarital pregnancy and a relatively unhappy home background.[54] Additional research found evidence that married teen-age girls suffer "ego deficiencies" to a markedly greater extent than single girls of the same age.[55] It has also been found that married teen-age girls were emotionally less stable and balanced than single girls of the same age, as measured by the Emotionality Scale of

---

[51] "Divorce," *The Economist*, Vol. 202 (March 3, 1962), p. 794.

[52] Judson T. Landis and Mary G. Landis, *Building A Successful Marriage* (Englewood Cliffs, N.J., Prentice-Hall, 1963), p. 129.

[53] J. Joel Moss and Ruby Gingles, "The Relationship of Personality to the Incidence of Early Marriage," *Marriage and Family Living*, Vol. 21 (November, 1959), p. 377.

[54] Samuel H. Lowrie, "Early Marriage: Premarital Pregnancy and Associated Factors," *Journal of Marriage and the Family*, Vol. 27 (February, 1965), p. 53.

[55] Floyd M. Martinson, "Ego Deficiency as a Factor in Marriage," *American Sociological Review*, Vol. 20 (April, 1955), pp. 161–64.

the Minnesota Personality Scale.[56] <u>On the basis of these examples of</u>
<u>research evidence, it is thus possible to interpret the existing correlation</u>
<u>of such variables as "ego deficiency," emotional immaturity, and unhappy</u>
<u>home background with premarital pregnancy and early marriage not</u>
<u>merely as an association, but as evidence of a casual relationship.</u> The
evidence, therefore, seems to support the above hypothesis. Needless to
say, the young people entering marriage with such escapist motivations
have a difficult time, since they choose marriage unrealistically as a
presumed panacea capable of magically solving tensions and problems.
In reality, this type of teen-ager usually finds that he is not equipped
with the necessary problem-solving ability and experience needed to
make a successful marriage.

In sum, then, it can be seen that the relationship between early
marriage and divorce is not simple. There are a number of compounding
<u>factors that add to the failure-proneness of teen-age marriages. Some of</u>
<u>the factors that are known or suspected are immature expectations,</u>
<u>dependency on parental subsidies, temptation to use marriage as a</u>
<u>premature and ineffectual "rite of passage" to adulthood, premarital</u>
<u>pregnancy, forced marriage, lower socioeconomic background, and inter-</u>
<u>personal disturbances and conflicts in the family of orientation.</u>

A natural question that follows from this discussion is: what can be
done about these problems? A full treatment of this question would
obviously extend beyond the framework of this chapter and lead to
biased and strongly value-oriented suggestions. Nevertheless, let it be
at least mentioned that the preventive and remedial suggestions range
from radical advocation of some type of "trial marriage" that presumably
would give the couple opportunity to thoroughly test compatibility and
marital proficiency before the final legal contract, to emphasis on formal
marriage preparation and family life education through the service of
an accredited institution, to the suggestion that new legal provisions be
drawn up that restrict marriage to well-qualified applicants and, in
addition, make an older age at marriage mandatory. Although specula-
tions on such innovations and Utopias have their rightful place, in this
chapter greater concern is with empirical data and scientific predictions
which, incidentally, are usually the most effective starting point for
"social engineering." A simple and yet most insightful instrument for
forecasting marital competence and satisfaction has been suggested by
Lee G. Burchinal.[57] This device might be called a measurement helpful
in detecting danger points and potential marriage-destroying circum-

---

[56] J. Joel Moss and Ruby Gingles, "A Preliminary Report of a Longitudinal
Study of Early Marriages in Nebraska," paper read at the Midwestern Sociological
Society Convention in Minneapolis (April 27, 1958).

[57] Burchinal, op. cit., 1965, p. 251.

stances. Burchinal included thirteen basic issues in his list that presumably are related to the general outcomes of young marriages. (See Table 15–7.) In the case of some problem areas, research has borne out the significance of these factors on the question of marital success; in other cases, inferences from general knowledge of correlated features of marital competence are applied. The author suggested that they be used tentatively and, if possible, that they be verified by research. The prediction of marital success is divided into three categories: poor, intermediate, and best. A given couple can use the "test" in self-assessment and check off the various conditions applying to them. An accumulation of "poor" conditions would obviously throw doubt on the survival of the marriage or future marriage, while an accumulation of "best" conditions would represent an encouraging and favorable forecast for the couple's marriage. A serious-minded couple could use this brief social-psychological analysis as the basis for more involved and thorough steps including, if deemed necessary, professional counseling.

Summary

The traditional cultural dicta concerning sexual standards have undergone noticeable modifications over the past few generations. These changes came about rapidly enough and were sufficiently radical that the term Sexual Revolution is applicable to the shifts in attitudes and practices during the first third of the century. The driving forces involved in the process of this social change included emancipation of the female, medical and technological innovations, growing secularism, the broadening adolescent period, and the sensual nature of the influential mass media. The previously rigid and absolutistic blueprint for behavior in sexual matters underwent extensive disintegration and was replaced by relativistic and secular alternatives. The change from the monolithic sexual code to pluralistic sexual codes entailed not only greater individual freedom and liberalism, but also conflict, confusion, and the challenge for the adolescent to choose his sexual philosophy. The modern scene offers a range of possible blueprints for sexual behavior, from traditional repressive asceticism to fun morality and sexual anarchy.

As far as can be ascertained by research findings, general public deportment, and soundings of the mass media, the sexual expressions and practices of contemporary youth are more intensive and extensive than those of preceding generations. The traditional prerogative of the male to be the aggressor has been qualified by increasing female initia-

TABLE 15–7. Hypothesized Relationships between Selected Characteristics and Outcomes of Young Marriages*
Forecast of Marital Competence and Satisfaction

Characteristic	Poorest	Intermediate	Best
Ages at Marriage	Both 17 or younger	Female 17, male 20 or older	Female at least 18, male 20 or older
Educational attainment	Both school dropouts	Female dropout, male high school graduate	Both high school graduates, male, at least, with some post-high school education
Pregnancy	Premarital pregnancy	No premarital pregnancy, pregnancy immediately following marriage	Pregnancy delayed until at least one year following marriage
Acquaintance before marriage	Less than six months, no engagement period, formal or informal	One year, at least, with at least six months engagement or understanding to marry	Several years, with at least six months engagement or understanding to marry
Previous dating patterns	Limited number of dating partners, went steady immediately, or short period between first date and first date with fiancé	Some dating experience before first dating fiancé	Numerous different dates, played the field, some previous experience with going steady
Personality dynamics	Generally poor interpersonal skills, lacking maturity, limited interests, poor personal and social adjustment	Mixed	Generally competent in interpersonal relations, flexible, mature, maintaining healthy and pleasurable relations with others

Motivation for marrying	Drift into marriage, because of pregnancy, seemed like the thing to do, just wanted to, or other impulsive reasons with no strong emphasis on marital and parental roles	Mixed, marriage as preferred to career, though had previous post-high-school educational aspirations and for females perhaps tentative plans to work, etc.	No post-high-school educational aspirations and, for females; marriage, family, and homemaking preferred as career over working, living independently; positive emphasis upon role as wife and mother
Status of families of orientation	Both lower	Mixed, lower, and middle or high	Both middle or high
Parental attitudes before marriage	Strongly opposed	Mildly opposed or resigned acceptance	Supportive once the decision was clear
Wedding	Elopement and civil ceremony		Conventional, hometown, and church-sanctioned
Economic basis	Virtually completely dependent upon relatives	Low dependence upon relatives, mostly independent income, even if near hardship level	At least assured income above self-perceived hardship level
Residence	Always lived with in-laws or other relatives	Doubled up with relatives some of the time, independent other periods of time	Always maintained own independent place of residence
Post-marriage parental views	Rejecting or punitive, assistance provided as a method of controlling the marriage	Cool	Psychologically supportive, since-rely want to help the young couple, assistance provided with no strings attached

* Reprinted with the permission of the author and the publisher from Lee G. Burchinal, "Trends and Prospects for Young Marriages in the U.S.," *Journal of Marriage and the Family*, Vol. 27 (May, 1965), p. 251.

tive. The age-old double standard is similarly on the wane. With more and more economic independence and educational equality, females also assume their equal share in matters of sexual gratification and amorous liberties.

Venereal disease and premarital pregnancy are among the detectable and detrimental consequences of the teen-agers' sexual activities. The rates of syphilis as well as premarital pregnancy have markedly increased for teen-agers over the past decades. And yet the publicity given this development seems out of proportion when one considers that of *all* age groups teen-agers show the *smallest* increases.

Programs intended to *prevent* these increasing problems are either nonexistent or nonconsensual at this time; they differ greatly by locale and are often limited by moralistic and legalistic considerations. In some places and regions, educational programs are incorporated in public schools, while in others they are strictly prohibited. After the *fait accompli*, the problem must be dealt with by *adjustive* measures. One semisecret way out of the predicament of premarital pregnancy is adoption—an increasing practice that has stimulated the growth and institutionalization of an involved social apparatus.

The popularity of marriage has grown to phenomenal heights in mid-century America, with the participation of teen-agers as avid as it is problematic. Reasons for the increase in teen-age marriages include economic feasibility, glorified image of marriage, unwillingness to defer sexual gratification, the draft problem, escapism from problems at home or in school, earlier maturation and development of sexual tensions, ability to defer parenthood, desire for adult status, the bandwagon effect, the couple-contingent nature of social life, and the insecurities of our time. There is a difference between the white and nonwhite marriage rates, with the marriage rates of nonwhite teen-agers traditionally exceeding those of white teen-agers. This differential appears to be narrowing, with the white rates increasing faster than those for nonwhites. Another significant trend is the leveling-off of the present marriage rates, with possibly even a decrease in teen-age marriages in the near future. It seems that in addition to the factors believed to encourage young marriages, a number of new factors are currently evolving that may offset the others and prompt youths to postpone marriage until their early twenties. Emphasis on school and post-high-school attendance; the growing attraction of job and career possibilities for young unmarried women; rising levels of material as well as interpersonal expectations from marriages; the intensified efforts of counseling, guidance and family life education programs; and increasing knowledge and use of contraceptive means and subsequent reduction of "forced" marriages are among the main reasons that contribute to the currently greater reluctance for marriage at younger ages, to the decrease in impulsive young marriages, and, consequently, to the possible overall reduction of teen-age marriages.

Marriages contracted by teen-agers may rightly be classified as social problems because their divorce and separation rates are disproportionately high, by far exceeding the rates of couples getting married at an older age. Researchers have found an almost perfect inverse correlation between age at marriage and rate of marital failure. There are many complex reasons for this correlation. Most explanations can be based on the utterly unrealistic expectations and immature motivations that prompted marriage. Particularly salient background features prevalent in many cases of disintegration of teen-age marriages include the problems of parental subsidies, misrepresentations of the marital relationship by the mass media, especially the movie industry, disillusionment of escapists facing interpersonal problems in marriage that are similar to those they tried to get away from, victimization by the bandwagon effect, assumption that marriage works as a rite of passage to adult status without first having mastered adult responsibilities, and, finally, premarital pregnancy that leads to marriage without being fully willing or prepared for it.

Effective programs to prevent immature teen-age marriages and to avert the worst consequences when they do take place must be based on objective research findings. An example of forecasting the outcome of the teen-age marriage was presented in the form of a list of crucial conditions, which indicate a range from "poor" to "best" marital propsects.

16

a modern educational problem: the dropout

Educational Trends in the United States

One of the most revered values in American life is formal education. The American ethos upholds the "right" of every citizen to have an education—elementary, secondary, and higher—as being as basic and undisputable as the so-called "pursuit of happiness." It has even been suggested that for increasing numbers of American students educational endeavor beyond high school has become ritualistic, pursued with no more motivation or fervor than compliance with the "thing to do."

"Education for all" has not *always* been the conviction of the American public. Until late in the last century, public education was primarily an elementary school affair. Preparation for higher education was accomplished in private secondary schools and a few public schools. For example, in 1870, American teen-agers could choose from among only 800 public high schools.[1] Those who attended institutions of secondary education, usually had college in mind. Although in 1900 only 11 per cent of the high-school-aged youth were in school, two-thirds of the graduates did go on to college—a proportion that has never been equalled since then.[2] The appraisal of a high school education in the United States was influenced by the European tradition that considered secondary education in the French *lycée*, the English grammar school, or the German *Gymnasium* as the proper experience for the "educated class." The children of farmers and workers were usually not thought of as being members of this class. The pattern for the farm boy was to

---

[1] James S. Coleman, *Adolescents and the Schools* (New York, Basic Books, 1965), p. 5.
[2] *Ibid.*

leave school before or directly after the eighth grade to work within the agricultural family unit. Similarly, workers' sons left school at the same time to assume apprenticeship for a trade.

The current popular adoration of secondary and higher education is thus a relatively novel phenomenon. However, it would be a misconception to interpret this recent development as the exclusive result of adherence to a value *in abstracto*. There are a number of pragmatic reasons for this fervent valuation. One reason simply involves the fruits of education and vocational training, which have increased the amenities and comforts in life. Another reason, currently most pressing, is the need to keep teen-agers out of the labor force. This necessity has developed gradually with increasing industrialization, automation, anti-child-labor legislation, and the rural-urban migration. Modern industry has done away with the apprenticeship period and thereby put teen-agers on a potential par with adults in terms of full-time employment and productivity. However, at the same time, automation has arrested the increase of blue-collar jobs while expanding the number of white-collar positions that require high school training—clerks, accountants, salesmen, office workers, etc. In effect, the division of labor no longer needs—or even allows—the labor of children. Barred from the labor force as well as from free-roaming idleness, America's teen-agers were "institutionalized" and delivered into the care of high schools. The institution of secondary education not only kept them out of the way, but even succeeded in preparing some of them for the new white-collar jobs. High school education ceased to be a voluntary matter for the few who sought preparation for higher education and became an involuntary mandate for all. Statistics illustrate the trend: in 1900, 11% of the high-school-aged youngsters attended school; in 1920, 32%; in 1930, 51%; in 1940, 73%; and in the late 1960's the percentage has risen to over 90%.[3]

This shift in educational emphasis implies a modification in the function of the high school. No longer were high school graduates destined only for college, but instead primarily for business and industry. Concomitant with the growth of the proportion of teen-agers attending high school there was a decline in the proportion of graduates enrolling in college. The college-entering proportion dropped from two-thirds in 1900 to about half in 1920 and finally to about one-third in 1940,[4] indicating that the majority of teen-agers preferred to go directly into jobs after graduation. This preference stimulated significant changes in the curricula of secondary schools. Now the preparation was more for the immediate vocational field than for extended higher education. This

---

[3] Coleman, *op. cit.*, p. 7.
[4] *Ibid.*

new emphasis gave rise, indeed often priority, to such short-range and "practical" goals as typing, bookkeeping, industrial arts, shop, and mechanics.

This change in the function of the high school, coupled with the coercive nature of attendance, has produced an essentially new atmosphere in the secondary school system. Academic preparation is no longer the prime objective; rather, general "life preparation" has moved into the foreground. An NEA committee attested to the new orientation in 1918 by issuing seven basic principles of secondary education: health, command of fundamental mental processes, mature home-membership, vocational preparation, civic education, constructive use of leisure time, and ethical character.[5] The pursuit of these principles clearly constitutes more than merely academic endeavor, but rather a general program for "life adjustment." The responsibilities of high school teachers now included not only transmission of knowledge, but character formation, the instillment of motivation, and the counseling of personal problems. In essence then, by taking over character-forming functions from the family, secondary education became more a place of general socialization than of information service. Furthermore, this socialization experience was not optional; teen-agers had to submit to it, and teachers were burdened with the extra task of convincing them that school was worthwhile.

However, this is not the end of the story of modern education in the United States. Industrialization and automation have progressed to the point where youth's labor is undesired not only after the eighth grade, but even after high school. Thus, college education is now developing into another means of preventing youth from swamping the labor market, while at the same time trying to prepare them for the ever-increasing number of white-collar and other more sophisticated positions. As a consequence, the steady decline of the proportion of high school graduates enrolling in college from 1900 to the 1940's has been arrested and is being reversed. The latest trend indicates that an increasing proportion of high school graduates are becoming interested in college. There is every reason to assume that college attendance will continue to increase, resembling the growth rate of high schools since the turn of the century. Since 1950, there has been a 10% average annual increase in students entering college for the first time to work toward a degree. As enrollment in institutions of higher learning increases, certain problems formerly confined to secondary education will likewise develop on the college level. We will—and to a large extent already do—

---

[5] Coleman, *op. cit.*, p. 8.

talk about the "problem" of the college dropout. But a discussion of this emerging problem would exceed the framework of this chapter. Thus, reference to the dropout problem means the high school dropout.

The Extent of the Dropout Problem

The term "dropout" is applied to everyone who leaves high school without a diploma. Today, the act of dropping out of school is usually interpreted as an indication of a youngster's unwillingness or inability to learn. The reason authorities and the general public consider the act of dropping out with as much dismay as they currently do emerges from the foregoing discussion: outside of high school there is no appropriate place for the high-school-aged youngster. As someone crudely and yet fittingly put it: "Quitting school prematurely messes up the social structure." Failure to provide an alternative status to that of a high school student is as much a function of the general cultural value orientation of the society as of modern economic conditions that pattern social structure.

Some of the statistics documenting the scope of the problem are misleading. It is true that the number of dropouts has increased over the past decades. The *rate* of dropouts, however, has not increased, and has, in fact, decreased. This seeming contradiction is easily explicable when one recalls that the teen-age population has increased as a consequence of the baby boom of the late 1940's. If there are *more* dropouts today than previously, it is because there are many more teen-agers to start with. It has been estimated, for example, that the number of dropouts during the decade 1960–70 will amount to approximately 7½ million teen-agers—a figure unprecedented during any previous decade.[6] On the other hand, the dropout rate at the mid-1960's was around 30%, which constitutes a notable decrease from the rate of more than 50% in 1949.[7] The public concern about the dropout problem is thus due to the increase in the sheer number of dropouts.

The high school enrollment after January, 1965, is expected to increase at the rate of 3% per year until 1980. The Bureau of the Census reported an enrollment of 10.1 million high school students in 1960. By 1970, the Bureau predicts a high school enrollment of 15.1 million

---

[6] U. S. Senate, 89th Congress, 2nd Session, *Profile on Youth—1966*, Senate Document No. 124, Part I (Washington, D. C., Government Printing Office, August, 1966), pp. 2, 30.

[7] Daniel Schreiber, *Guidance and the School Dropout* (Washington, D. C., National Education Association of the United States, 1964), p. 2.

students.[8] 26 million students will pass through high school during the 1960–70 period. Most experts estimate that there will be a minimum of 7½ million high school dropouts during this period, with 2½ million of them having acquired less than an eighth-grade education.[9] James S. Coleman has offered a carefully computed estimate of 7.3 million dropouts for that period, based on the assumption that the change in the rate of dropouts that took place between 1960 and 1962 (a decrease from 31.5% to 30.3%) has set a reliable trend.[10]

The dropout incidence is not evenly distributed throughout the high school population, but differs from community to community. The dropout rate of roughly 30% during the mid-1960's has been derived from such widely varying settings as rural, urban, and suburban communities. The highest dropout rate may be expected in those urban high schools that draw their students from neighborhoods composed of predominantly lower socioeconomic classes and minority groups. The prevailing value orientation as well as the trying economic conditions among slum or semislum dwellers are not conducive to a high valuation of education among their children. Youngsters from such neighborhoods are known for their chronic truancy and tendency to drop out of school as soon as they reach age 16. More often than not, hardly any serious official effort is made through counseling or tutoring to persuade them to remain in school until graduation, because they usually have established a record of being problematic, if not delinquent, and are considered a "bad influence" on their peers, who otherwise might successfully complete secondary education. A social worker's report concerning a typical case from a lower-class neighborhood in the metropolitan area of Phoenix runs as follows:

> Jim, 16 years, was next to the oldest in a family of six children. He hardly remembered his father who left when he was about seven years old. His parents never obtained a legal divorce; yet another man moved in and lives with them. A baby, a half-sister to Jim, resulted from this living arrangement. During the interval between his father's departure and the new man's arrival on the scene, Jim's mother tried to make a living by doing various odd day jobs. On occasions, she would take Jim or his elder brother along to cleaning jobs and ask them to help. More often, she would ask

---

[8] Donald J. Bogue, "Population Growth in the United States," in Philip M. Hauser (Ed.), *The Population Dilemma* (Englewood Cliffs, N.J., Prentice-Hall, 1964), p. 78.

[9] J. R. Ingraham, "Education and Unemployment," *American Vocational Journal,* Vol. 37 (May, 1962), p. 10.

[10] Coleman, *op. cit.,* pp. 54, 64.

Jim to stay home and babysit for the younger siblings. Due to these conditions and a general indifference toward school, Jim became a chronic truant and had some trouble with the juvenile authorities. He neglected his school work to the point of not being able to advance at the end of his first year in high school. The moment he turned 16 years old, he quit school. School officials made attempts to talk to him and his mother; but to no avail. Jim indicated indifference toward school and stated that he was "glad it was all over." Mother insisted that she needed the boy to help make a living for the family and that he had a job lined up. Although it was discovered that Jim had no job whatsoever and hardly tried to find one despite his mother's pleas, he was not willing to return to school. The latest observations indicate that Jim has associated himself with members of a neighborhood gang known for their involvement with narcotics.[11]

The rural environment also presents a temptation to leave high school prematurely. The youngster may prefer, or actually be asked by his parents, to join the family's common agricultural enterprise. Unlike the urban slum setting, a job is waiting for him, and success in the agricultural vocation does not, in his and his parents' opinion, depend on schooling beyond the eighth grade. Although most farm families see to it that the children fulfill their legal requirement and stay in school up to 16 years of age, they may consent to, or even suggest, withdrawal after that age. The farm people's rejection of schooling beyond the three basic "R's" was strikingly illustrated by the Amish refusal to send their children to high school. As reported in an earlier chapter (see Chapter 5), the rural Amish did not see any point in prolonged secondary education since their life's work, farming, did not require abstract learning. Furthermore, the high school might plant "wordly" thoughts in the minds of their offspring. Official coercion had to be applied to force the Amish to send their teen-agers to high school.

Probably the lowest incidence rate of premature termination of the high school career is found in the middle-class suburban community. The value orientation as well as long-range professional plans keep the youngsters in high school until graduation. For a sizable proportion of the youth of suburbia, high school is a preparation for college. In fact, a number of upper- and middle-class youngsters prefer to attend a special prep school rather than the general high school in their own community.

In summary, then, the *number* of dropouts has increased, the *rate* of dropouts has steadily decreased, and the national average is a com-

---

[11] Personal communication with social workers in the metropolitan area of Phoenix, Arizona (1967).

posite figure that includes widely differing high school populations. Urban high schools contribute most extensively to the national dropout average, followed by rural, with suburban schools having the lowest rate.

Who are the Dropouts?

In the attempt to isolate the major characteristics of dropouts, a number of important factors in the lives of teen-agers are investigated and divided for easier discussion into separate sections. These factors are socioeconomic conditions, family interaction, peer association, and school life. In addition, numerous idiosyncratic personal problems play an important role in the decision of the adolescent to remain in school or to drop out. The various conditions overlap, and characteristics of dropouts found in one sector are most probably correlated with characteristics in other sectors, thus forming an overall syndrome for the dropout rather than isolated and discrete features.

Socioeconomic status. The preceding section already touched on some of the social conditions that are associated with dropouts. One of those mentioned was social class, a forceful influence deserving further thought. Dropouts coming from lower socioeconomic strata constitute a significantly higher proportion of the total dropouts than those from middle and upper classes—the respective percentages being 63%, 24%, 13%.[12] Sociological research, as early as August B. Hollingshead's study of high school youth in *Elmtown's Youth*,[13] has consistently indicated a significant correlation between socioeconomic background and school adjustment, academic achievement, college orientation, and the dropout rate. For example, Hollingshead found that, regardless of intelligence, one-third of the lower-class pupils as opposed to only 5% of the combined middle- and lower-class pupils received failing grades.[14] Another researcher, Jackson Toby, found that the social class position of the teen-ager's family is of great influence in patterning the youth's basic orientation to education and that the middle-class student has definite advantages over his lower-class peers in academic competition:

(1) His parents are probably better educated and are therefore more capable of helping him with his school work if this should be

---

[12] Alvin L. Bertrand, "School Attendance and Attainment: Functions and Dysfunctions of School and Family Social Systems," *Social Forces,* Vol. 40 (March, 1962), p. 231.

[13] August B. Hollingshead, *Elmtown's Youth* (New York, John Wiley & Sons, 1949).

[14] *Ibid.,* p. 173.

necessary; (2) his parents are more eager to make his school work seem meaningful to him by indicating, implicitly or explicitly, the occupational applications of long division or history; (3) the verbal skills which he acquires as part of child training on the middle-class status level prepare him for the type of training that goes on in school and give him an initial (and cumulating) advantage over the lower-class child in the classroom situation; and (4) the coordinated pressure of parents, friends, and neighbors reinforce his motivation for scholastic success and increase the probability of good school adjustment.[15]

In recent research, sociologist Irving Krauss was able to confirm the plausible hypothesis that significantly more middle-class teen-agers view high school as a preparation for college than do lower-class teen-agers. The proportions are 64% and 41%, respectively.[16]

The definition of social class is usually based on a number of criteria. One of the most important criteria is occupation—in the case of the adolescent, the occupation of his father. If this factor is singled out and correlated with the dropout rate, the influence of social class on school attendance can be reliably demonstrated. A Louisiana study discovered that 77% of farm youth remaining in high school had fathers who were operators or part-time operators of farms and that 23% had fathers who were laborers.[17] *These proportions were significantly changed among the drop-outs.* 48% of the dropouts among rural youth had fathers who operated or owned a farm, while 52% had fathers who were laborers. Among the in-school teen-agers with nonfarm backgrounds, 30% had fathers who were businessmen or professionals, and 70% had fathers who were wage laborers. 100% of the dropouts with nonfarm backgrounds had fathers who were wage laborers; there were no dropouts whose fathers were professionals or businessmen. This negative correlation between social class and dropout rate has also been confirmed by the application of the Minnesota Multiphasic Personality Inventory (MMPI), which is considered an effective measurement of personal and social characteristics. Sociologists Starke R. Hathaway and Elio D. Monachesi applied a carefully constructed research design that used more than 15,000 Minnesota high school students in a follow-up study spanning several high school generations.[18] The findings revealed

---

[15] Jackson Toby, "Orientation to Education as a Factor in the School Maladjustment of Lower-Class Children," *Social Forces,* Vol. 35 (March, 1957), p. 266.

[16] Irving Krauss, "Sources of Educational Aspirations Among Working-Class Youth," *American Sociological Review,* Vol. 29 (December, 1964), p. 868.

[17] Bertrand, *op. cit.,* p. 231.

[18] Starke R. Hathaway and Elio D. Monachesi, *Adolescent Personality and Behavior* (Minneapolis, The University of Minnesota Press, 1963).

that among day-laborer families 38% of the boys and 32% of the girls dropped out of school, while among professional families only 5% of the boys and 5% of the girls left school prematurely.[19] The results of the research involving the MMPI corroborated the Louisiana findings and also revealed differential dropout rates between the children of farmers (owners and operators) and those of farm laborers.[20]

Family interaction. Innumerable research findings agree that the *quality of interaction* in the adolescent's family of orientation has the greatest influence on his school behavior. One study focused on a number of dimensions of interpersonal behavior that are operative in such primary groups as the family.[21] Family sociologist Lucius F. Cervantes selected, among other things, the dimensions of interpersonal understanding and acceptance, depth of communication, joint leisure activities, and happiness, measuring these qualities against dropouts and graduates. In all cases, the dropouts ranked signficantly lower than their graduating peers. For example, 84% of the dropouts, but only 18% of the graduates, manifested "very little" or "little" intrafamily understanding and acceptance. 81% of the dropouts were characterized by "very infrequent" or "infrequent" communication within the home, while only 20% of the graduates fell into these categories. On the joint leisure scale 79% of the dropouts and 25% of the graduates fell into the "very infrequent" and "infrequent" categories. 60% of the dropouts reported their home as being "very unhappy" or "unhappy," while 64% of the graduates reported

TABLE 16–1. Dropout Rate of High School Students by Socioeconomic Background and Sex.

Socioeconomic Category	Girls Per Cent	Boys Per Cent
Day Laborer	32	38
Semiskilled	18	19
Farmer	11	21
Clerical	12	13
Professional or Semiprofessional	5	5

Adapted from Starke R. Hathaway and Elio D. Monachesi, *Adolescent Personality and Behavior* (Minneapolis, The University of Minnesota Press, 1963), pp. 177–78.

[19] *Ibid.*, pp. 93–94, 177, 178.

[20] *Ibid.*

[21] Lucius F. Cervantes, "Family Background, Primary Relations, and the High School Drop-Out," *Journal of Marriage and the Family,* Vol. 27 (May, 1965), pp. 218–23.

it as "very happy" or "happy" and only 22% as "very unhappy" or "unhappy." Another important variable in small group interaction is the degree of consensus among members concerning behavior expectations. It should not be taken for granted that in such a small and intimate group as the family a common agreement has necessarily been reached concerning standards and norms in specific situations. It is more realistic to view consensus as a *variable* rather than a constant. One study has shown that the degree of intrafamily consensus is significantly related to the school success of the sons. Boys who were well-adjusted in school came from families with high consensus, boys consistently underachieving in school came from families with lower consensus, and boys known for problematic aggressiveness came from homes with the least family consensus.[22]

The extent of the parents' education is frequently reflected in their offsprings' school accomplishment. The earlier-mentioned Louisiana study discovered an *inverse* correlation between years of schooling of the parents and the dropout rate of their children.[23] Thus, the higher the education of the parents, the lower the dropout rate of the children. (See Table 16–2.) These findings are supported by numerous other studies, among them one in Maryland showing that 70% of the mothers

TABLE 16–2.   School Attendance Related to Education of Parents.

Education of Parents	In-School Youth Per Cent	Dropouts Per Cent
Father		
0–8 grades	55	76
9–12 grades	38	24
College experience	7	0
Mother		
0–8 grades	34	69
9–12 grades	53	31
College experience	13	0

Adapted from Alvin L. Bertrand, "School Attendance and Attainment: Functions and Dysfunctions of School and Family Social Systems," *Social Forces*, Vol. 40 (March, 1962), p. 231.

---

[22] Barbara G. Myerhoff and William R. Larson, "Primary and Formal Aspects of Family Organization: Group Consensus, Problem Perception, and Adolescent School Success," *Journal of Marriage and the Family*, Vol. 27 (May, 1965), pp. 213–217.

[23] Bertrand, *op. cit.*, p. 231.

and 80% of the fathers of the dropouts had never finished high school.[24] Furthermore, among these parents, 25% of the mothers and 30% of the fathers had never completed the sixth grade.

The opinion of the parents concerning the importance of a high school education is also relevant. Asked whether the lack of high school education is a disadvantage, more than 90% of the parents of in-school youth thought that it was a "great" disadvantage, while only 60% of the parents of dropouts thought so.[25]

A definite relationship between family size and achievement motivation, and thus attendance, was discovered.[26] The children of larger families consistently exhibited lower achievement motivation than children of smaller families. This finding might have been expected since large families are typical of lower classes, and studies have shown that they have a low valuation of educational achievement. But it is interesting to note that even *within* the same social stratum large families tend to produce lower achievement motivation in their children.

Finally, the broken home is a characteristic strongly associated with dropping out of school. Children whose parents are divorced or separated are likely to drop out at roughly twice the rate of their peers from intact families. These dropouts amount to more than one-third of all the teen-agers from broken families.[27]

Peer association. Some social scientists believe that the peer group has such a strong influence on the teen-ager that in many situations it can override the advice of parents and teachers.[28] Sometimes, the pressure of the peer group and the contagion of collective behavior are strong enough to introduce a teen-ager to delinquent activities. However, most of the findings supporting these hypotheses came from studies and surveys dealing with either high school students or delinquent gangs. What about the dropouts? To what degree is he enmeshed in peer relations?

There is reason to believe that if a dropout is deeply involved in peer activities, they are most probably delinquent activities. The bulk of dropouts are lower-class youths who probably have severed most

---

[24] Percy Williams, "School Drop-Outs," *NEA Journal,* Vol. 52 (February, 1963), pp. 10–12.

[25] Bertrand, *op. cit.,* p. 231.

[26] Bernard C. Rosen, "Family Structure and Achievement Motivation," *American Sociological Review,* Vol. 26 (August, 1961), pp. 574–85.

[27] Hathaway and Monachesi, *op. cit.,* pp. 93, 94, 181.

[28] See examples: James S. Coleman, *The Adolescent Society* (New York, Free Press, 1963); Hans Sebald, *The Crisis of Adolescent Discontinuity and the Formation of an Adolescent Subculture in the American Middle Class,* mimeographed research report (The Ohio State University, 1960).

ties with formal adult institutions. Unless this youngster has a job or is seriously seeking one, he is almost totally absorbed in adolescent activities revolving around the gang and heterosexual pursuits. What the high school and the clique are to the in-school youth, the gang is to the jobless male dropout, i.e., a bridge device to span the gap between childhood and adulthood. The gang commands the dropout's loyalty and he, in return, obtains security, belonging, and exciting adventures. Most middle- and upper-class youth do not form gangs, since they have adequate transitional institutions, such as advanced education and family–social-class sponsorship in jobs. On the other hand, even before they drop out, lower-class youngsters tend not to become members of cliques. The nature of cliques and gangs is class-selective in a differential mode. The study of *Elmtown's Youth* revealed that 90% of the students limited their association to student cliques, while the remaining 10% were lower-class and had gang associations.[29]

The delinquency-proneness of the dropout is supported by several studies. Convincing support came from the Minnesota study that employed the MMPI to assess the dropout's characteristics.[30] The findings revealed considerable overlap between the students who drop out and those who were delinquent. In fact, 39% of the boys and 31% of the girls who dropped out had a delinquency rating. It is interesting to note that the delinquency rate for the male dropout was only 1.62 times the base rate for all males, but for the female dropout it was 2.98 times the base rate for all females. This indicates that dropping out and delinquency are more closely related for girls than for boys. It was also noticed that delinquent teen-agers tend to drop out most frequently during the early years of high school, suggesting that their causes for dropping out reach peak intensity in the eighth grade or earlier.[31] Thus, remedial measures should be initiated at early school levels.

Further support for the assumption that a significant correlation exists between dropping out and delinquency comes from a study of working-class youth in six metropolitan areas.[32] This study attempted to clarify the question of whether the youth culture in the United States is independent of or dependent on parental control, i.e., whether youth choose parent or age-mate influences. An important conclusion arose from this investigation: there exists a decided cleavage between responses given by the dropouts and by the matched high school grad-

[29] Hollingshead, *op. cit.*, p. 210.
[30] Hathaway and Monachesi, *op. cit.*
[31] *Ibid.*, p. 95.
[32] Lucius F. Cervantes, *American Youth Culture: Independent or Dependent?*, a mimeographed paper read at the Annual Convention of the American Sociological Association (Chicago, 1965).

uates. The dropouts operate within an independent adolescent subculture. This is reflected in their responses to questionnaires concerning
intergenerational mutual understanding and in their attitudes toward
their parents' disapproval of their choice of friends. On the other hand,
the graduates' attitudes and value orientations indicate that their subculture is characterized by harmony with parental values, by a considerable degree of acceptance of parental guidance, and by integration into
adult society. (Part of the findings can be seen in Table 16-3.)

These findings challenge the assumption of those social scientists
who maintain that a strikingly independent *general* youth subculture
does in fact exist. Examples of this assumption were discussed in chapter
eight, when reference was made to such sociologists as Talcott Parsons
who described the youth culture as being independent of and antagonistic to adult expectations and as commanding compulsive conformity
within its ranks.[33] James S. Coleman based his inquiry on large-scale
research and likewise arrived at the conclusion that the American teen-
ager "is cut off from the rest of society, forced inward toward his own
age group . . . and maintains only a few threads of connection with the
outside adult society."[34] This type of conclusion does not differentiate
between in-school and dropout youth—in fact, it emphasizes that school
youth are put into age-segregated enclaves that foster subcultural
expression.

TABLE 16–3. Teen-Agers' Reactions to Parental Opposition to Their
Friends.[a]

	Dropouts		Graduates	
	%	N	%	N
Ignore parents; retain friend	53.3	80	7.3	11
Retain friend secretly	4.7	7	2.0	3
Evaluate objections; act as see fit	19.3	29	17.3	26
Gradually reject friend	12.0	18	30.0	45
Reject friend, internalization of parental values	10.7	16	43.3	65
Total	100	150	100	150

[a] The hypothesis that dropouts more characteristically reject parental authority
is sustained at the .001 level of statistical significance.

Source: Lucius F. Cervantes, *American Youth Culture: Independent or
Dependent?* mimeographed paper read at the Annual Convention of the American
Sociological Association (Chicago, 1965), p. 9.

---

[33] Talcott Parsons, *Essays in Sociological Theory* (New York, Free Press, 1949),
p. 324.

[34] Coleman, *op. cit.*, 1963, p. 3.

The answer to the question of whether an independent or a dependent teen-age subculture exists remains controversial and awaits conclusive testing. One may, however, be certain at this time that in the case of dropouts an independent subculture does exists, that they are involved in delinquent activities to a larger extent than their in-school peers, and that they are cut off from adult institutions and reject parental advice.

School life. Probably the most outstanding element in the dropout's attitudes toward school life is his *lack of interest* in the kind for work that school requires. Of the dropouts in the Minnesota study one boy out of three and one girl out of five cited disinterest as their reason for dropping out.[35] It is true that both the delinquent and the dropout are unhappy with school activities and discipline, but they often have different motivations. The dropout's dissatisfaction stems not so much from the appeal of alternative activities but rather from a basic rejection of school activities. The delinquent, on the other hand, may be in conflict with school discipline because he prefers what he thinks are more adventurous and exciting activities. This distinction is obviously only applicable when the dropout is nondelinquent.

As was noted earlier, this negative and indifferent attitude is reflected in the academic performance of the dropout. It has been found that the usual grade distribution of *all* youth in school runs as follows: 45% have B's or above, 51% have C's, and 8% have D's or lower. The distribution among drop-outs deviates significantly: 15% have B's or above, 46% have C's, and 39% have D's or lower.[36] A similar reflection of disinterest is found in the frequency with which dropouts have to repeat grades. The same study found that 83% of the in-school youths did not have to repeat any grades, while 16% had to repeat two or more grades. In contrast, among the dropouts only 35% did not have to repeat any grades, while 39% had to repeat one grade, and 26% had to repeat two or more grades.[37] Another study, sponsored by the National Child Labor Committee and including 1,000 dropouts in five midwestern communities, revealed that 52% had repeated at least one grade.[38] The repetition usually occurred on the elementary level, with the first, third, and fourth grades being the most commonly repeated years. Another upsurge of repetition reappeared later, in the ninth grade in junior high school and the tenth grade in high school.[39]

---

[35] Hathaway and Monachesi, *op. cit.*, p. 94.

[36] Bertrand, *op. cit.*, p. 231.

[37] *Ibid.*

[38] Charles M. Allen, *Combatting the Drop-Out Problem* (Chicago Science Research Associates, 1956).

[39] *Ibid.*, p. 8.

Low marks, repetition of grades, and dropping out of school are not necessarily an indication of low intelligence. This issue is further complicated by the fact that there are no reliable measures of *native* intelligence. The ordinary IQ tests rely on culturally learned knowledge, especially verbal knowledge, that potential dropouts rarely have developed to a sufficient degree. Therefore, the findings of the Minnesota study—disclosing that among teen-agers with below-average IQ scores, 29% of the boys and 21% of the girls drop out, while among those with above-average scores, only 6 to 7% drop out[40]—is not particularly revealing and is not to be equated with the teen-agers' native ability to learn. Some authors insist that the records of IQ scores show that the average dropout is by no means uneducable.[41] Although, on the average, he tends to score lower than his in-school peers, a nationwide study by the United States Department of Labor discovered that 70% of the dropouts in the sample had IQ scores above 90. In fact, a 6-year study in the state of New York disclosed that 13% of the dropouts had IQ scores above 110.[42] In a Maryland study, almost 50% of the dropouts had average or above-average intelligence.[43] Thus, the decisive factor in dropping out is primarily the basic attitude and not the ability of the adolescent.

Idiosyncratic, personal problems. The preceding statement concerning the role of intelligence is a generalization frequently modified by exceptions. There is no doubt that for a number of teen-agers intelligence is a limiting factor that not only will, but even *should*, lead to withdrawal from regular high school. The failure of such intellectually handicapped students to withdraw from school might result in a reduction of the general learning level of the rest of the students.

Other limiting factors are physical and mental health. A teen-ager who, because of prolonged or repeated injury or illness, has fallen seriously behind his high school peers in academic learning and whose parents are not determined that he catch up, may decide to terminate his humiliating and frustrating situation by dropping out of school. Problems of mental and emotional health are considerably more difficult to recognize and are frequently symptomized by rebelliousness, unwillingness to learn, serious adjustment problems, and a variety of neurotic expressions, including anxiety, depression, agitation, inability to concentrate, withdrawal from social contacts, and inability to communicate. Often there is confusion in distinguishing between emotionally troubled

---

[40] Hathaway and Monachesi, *op. cit.*, p. 93.

[41] Daniel Schreiber, "School Drop-Out," *NEA Journal*, Vol. 51 (May, 1962), p. 51.

[42] *Ibid.*

[43] Williams, *op. cit.*, p. 11.

students and delinquent students; the two types of expression are not necessarily identical and one does not automatically lead to the other. In fact, the earlier-mentioned MMPI study discovered that neurotic, socially introverted, and schizoid adolescents are more likely to drop out of school than to become delinquent.[44]

Of the many forms that adolescent rebellion can take, underachievement is probably the most subtle. It is rarely recognized for what it is either by the student himself or by parents and teachers. Thus, consistent underachievement of an otherwise bright youngster may seem inexplicable. By the time the rebellious undercurrent is recognized, it may be too late for treatment or effective salvage of a career. "What is so commonly termed laziness, lack of will power, or poor attitude is at heart often a sullen resentfulness expressed by a stubborn refusal to do anything demanded by authority."[45] Psychiatrist Graham B. Blaine thinks that schools and parents unintentionally reinforce unconscious feelings of resentment by taking overly punitive attitudes toward students performing dissatisfactorily in their school work. Ultimately, such students may be driven to the point of dropping out of school.

It should not come as a surprise to parents and educators that some adolescents are profoundly influenced by the material affluence of American society and very early develop a desire to acquire material conveniences instead of a secondary education for which they may see no direct application to their lives. They can see, however, in such products as the car a direct application to their lives. Many teen-agers cannot resist the lure of the illusory independence that they associate with a second-hand automobile. Some high school principals list as the number one dropout cause the desire to have an automobile. Youngsters have been known to drop out of school in order to maintain a car. They prefer to work, save money, and then buy a car. Or sometimes parents buy a car for a teen-ager and then expect him to keep the car operating. After the youngster has the car, he begins to realize the expense of maintaining it and, rather than giving it up, he chooses to give up school and education.

Although the dropout population is divided almost equally between the sexes—boys making up only slightly more than half, or 53%[46]—some of the reasons for dropping out differ radically between them. Boys who drop out frequently list military service or a job as reasons; a survey showed that one in four had dropped out for military service, one in

---

[44] Hathaway and Monachesi, *op. cit.*, p. 93.

[45] Graham B. Blaine, *Youth and the Hazards of Affluence* (New York, Harper & Row, 1966), p. 30.

[46] Schreiber, *op. cit.*, 1964, p. 4.

seven to work.[47] Few boys quit school because of marriage. On the other hand, the majority of the female dropouts, 53%, were the result of marriage or illegitimate pregnancy.[48] It has been estimated that *not* including the girls who drop out because of illegitimate pregnancy, 175,000 girls leave school annually to marry.[49] As many as 5% of *all* high school girls drop out because of pregnancy in any given year.[50]

Characteristics listed as personal and idiosyncratic are generalizable to small segments of the dropout population. A complete cataloging of all *possible* personal reasons for dropping out of school is, of course, unachievable in this chapter. Another reminder: most reasons and motivations for dropping out are interrelated. For example, the pregnancy rate of high school girls is cross-correlated with social-class background; the adolescent's indifference to education is significantly influenced by educational achievement of the parents; residence in slum neighborhood is correlated with delinquency, etc. It follows logically that those adolescents characterized by more than one or two of the typical dropout characteristics are all the more prone to become dropout candidates.

What After School?

When the dropout leaves school, he finds himself dealing with a labor market in which he has little bargaining power. One of the first realizations he will confront is that unemployment of youth is a social problem in the United States. During the early 1960's, the unemployment rate for youth between 16 and 20 years of age was 16.8%, as compared to an overall unemployment rate of 7.7%.[51] He will also come to realize that dropouts contribute disproportionately to the ranks of unemployed youth because they are undereducated and generally fall into the lower-status and unskilled-worker categories. These categories are characterized by an unemployment rate twice as high as the rates of all other job categories.

As a dropout, he will usually begin, and in most instances stay, at the bottom of the job pile. He will face recurrent periods of joblessness during every decline of business, decline of the labor demand, or general

---

[47] Hathaway and Monachesi, *op. cit.*, p. 94.

[48] *Ibid.*

[49] Schreiber, *op. cit.*, 1962, p. 52.

[50] Lucius F. Cervantes, *The Dropout* (Ann Arbor, The University of Michigan Press, 1965), p. 153.

[51] Arthur J. Goldberg, Secretary of Labor, reported in the *New York Times* (June 5, 1961).

economic depression. As a consequence, he loses jobs frequently and tends to become a member of the "hard core" of the unemployed and of those "last to be hired and first to be fired." It has been found that at least two-thirds of the unemployed have less than a high school education. During the early 1960's, the average rate of unemployment among high school graduates 16 to 21 years of age was 13%; for dropouts of the same age bracket, the rate fluctuated between 20% and 30%. In fact, it was found that among youth living in urban slums the unemployment rate rose as high as 70%.[52] These estimates are supported by the United States Department of Labor, which announced that the percentage of unemployment among persons with less than a high school education is approximately double that of high school graduates and triple that of persons with some college education.[53]

The difficulty that the dropout has in finding a job is not necessarily due to psychological rejection or being branded a "failure" by society, but rather is a result of certain conditions that exist in the modern labor market. Dropouts will find it increasingly more difficult to obtain jobs because the types of positions they can ably fill are becoming more and more obsolete. It has been estimated that only 5% of the available jobs will be of the unskilled variety by 1970 and that, starting with 1965, there will be three unskilled workers for every two available unskilled job positions.[54]

Those of the dropouts who hold jobs derive an income considerably lower than that of high school graduates. By the time a person reaches his peak earning power in life, the high school graduate is making approximately 20% more than the person who dropped out of school prematurely. Statistics supplied by the U.S. Bureau of the Census indicate that during the mid-1960's, the median income of persons 25 years and over with only eight years of elementary school fell into the $5,000–6,000 annual income bracket; those with one to three years of high school fell into the $6,000–7,000 bracket, those with four years of high school fell into the $7,000–8,000 bracket, and those with four or more years of college fell into the $10,000–15,000 bracket.[55]

If current trends continue, the lot of the dropout will become more dismal in the future. The President's Commitee on Youth Unemployment investigated this problem and related questions and presented a number

---

[52] Daniel Schreiber, "Drop-Out and Delinquent: Promising Practices Learned from a Year of Study," *Phi Delta Kappa,* Vol. 154 (February, 1963), pp. 215–21.

[53] U.S. Department of Labor, *Manpower, Challenge of the Sixties* (Washington, D. C., Government Printing Office, 1960), p. 17.

[54] *Ibid.*

[55] U.S. Bureau of the Census, *Current Population Reports: Consumer Income,* Series P-60, No. 47 (Sept. 24, 1965), pp. 27–28.

of estimates and predictions.[56] During the 1960's, 26 million boys and girls will leave school and seek jobs, a figure representing a 40% increase over the 1950's. By the late 1960's, 3 million youth will be added to the labor force each year. Of the 26 million youth who will enter the labor force between 1960 and 1970, roughly 12 million will have completed high school, 6½ million will have some college, and 7½ million will not have completed high school. If the mid-1960's rate of youth unemployment persists, while the teen-age population increases, by 1970 the number of unemployed youths will be close to 1½ million. *Predictably, a high proportion of these jobless adolescents will be dropouts.* Hardest hit will be youth from the urban slum and rural areas. Youngsters from slum neighborhoods, who are predominantly members of minorty groups, such as Negroes and Puerto Ricans, will have an unemployment rate double or triple that of their white age-mates. Only about one in ten boys who lived on farms during the 1960's can expect to make an adequate living in agriculture. While the teen-age proportion of the labor force is growing rapidly, job opportunities for unskilled workers will either remain the same or even decrease, and for farm workers they will drop at least 20%. Yet in the past, these jobs constituted important sources of beginning occupations for teen-agers coming out of school. By contrast, there will be a 40% increase in job positions for professionals and skilled workers and a 20% increase for sales workers, managers, and proprietors.

All things considered, the future of the dropout is not very encouraging. In order to find a satisfactory job—or any job at all—more education and longer training are required. On the average, the professional or technical workers of today have more than four years of college; clerical workers have training and education in excess of their high school diploma. These academic requirements and specialized training programs will increase in importance in the future. Automation, mechanization, and other scientific advances are responsible for the decreasing number of unskilled jobs. The school dropout of the future may well become a dropout from the usable labor force.

Preventive and Remedial Attempts

The basic difference between the preventive and remedial approaches is the timing of relevant actions and programs. Preventive actions are intended to bear upon the *potential* dropout, to change some of his

---

[56] President's Committee on Youth Unemployment, *The Challenge of Jobless Youth* (Washington, D. C., April 24, 1963), pp. 2–3.

behavior patterns and to reorient his attitudes concerning education. In essence, the goal of the preventive approach is to keep the youngster in school until graduation. Remedial efforts deal with the problems of the adolescent after he *actually* has dropped out of school. Here the attempt is made to alleviate the worst consequences of the premature termination of secondary education.

Prevention. Authorities and educators cannot resort to legal authority to force the teen-ager to stay in school after he has reached age 16. The actions of concerned adults are limited to "friendly persuasion" or to making school life more attractive and meaningful to the potential drop-out—thereby hopefully cutting down the dropout rate. The question that arises naturally from this situation is: what can be done to improve the *holding power* of school?

In many school districts, administrators and educators have taken a second look at their school curricula, wondering—with self-conscious candor—whether the subjects themselves, as well as the methods of presenting them to the students, can be blamed for the continuing dropout incidence. There are voices who claim that a sizable proportion of a high school education is not "usable" after graduation. These opinions, offered primarily by the students, indicate the intensely pragmatic philosophy of Amercian teen-agers. They tend to equate schooling with the barter value in the market place: "Will it get me a good job?" Such pragmatic thinking tends to confuse education with training and defines school as a place of preparation for a technical skill. Many schools have responded to this student demand by reexamining their curricula and providing students with more practical and directly utilitarian pursuits, such as sewing, drafting, mechanics, typing, bookkeeping, etc. It is true that such concrete subjects elicit a more favorable response on the part of teen-agers in general and lower-class youth in particular than do abstract subjects dealing with literature, history, social sciences, philosophy, etc.—the applicability and usability of which after graduation cannot be visualized easily. (Although this is not the place to delve into details or to take sides, it should at least be mentioned that a lively controversy involving different philosophies of education has ensued, which has attempted to come to terms with the question of the purpose of secondary education in a dynamic urban-industrial society.) Sociological research has repeatedly indicated that children from lower socioeconomic classes can be more easily interested in concrete subjects, which not only carry the promise of security of future jobs but for which they also have a greater proficiency than for abstract learning.[57] Lower-

---

[57] David P. Ausubel, "The Effects of Cultural Deprivation on Learning Patterns," in Staten W. Webster (ed.), *Understanding the Educational Problems of the Disadvantaged Learner* (San Francisco, Chandler Publishing Co., 1966), pp. 251–57;

class children, a perennial source of dropouts, are notoriously poor learners in abstract subjects and would probably find a modified curriculum that includes job-preparatory courses more attractive and meaningful.

Some social scientists believe that another possible way to increase the holding power of school lies in changing the *structure* of secondary education, thus allowing the adolescent greater freedom to choose his training and giving him the option to move from one school to another rather than compelling him to go every day to a school he did not choose, to a teacher he does not like, or to do things he considers meaningless or childish. James S. Coleman thinks that the federal government's aid to education should be employed to establish free supplementary schools of various kinds, offering subjects and specializations which could not be incorporated into the regular high school. "Such schools could be attended part of the day on a voluntary basis through a released-time arrangement with the city's public schools."[58] By having more responsibility placed on himself for completing his education and being given flexible alternatives that allow him to go about it in the way he feels is the most suitable and successful, the adolescent may develop stronger motivations to achieve his educational goals. However, whether a structural innovation of this sort would be an effective prevention against dropping out for the child who *starts* with already low motivations and substandard goals remains a question to be tested.

A virtual campaign on a nationwide basis has developed during the past years, using the mass media to plead with potential dropouts to stay in school and to appeal to parents to sustain their children's educational interests and endeavors. The campaign is complete with posters, and advertisements on TV, radio, and in the daily press.

Legal initiative was recommended as another means to act on a national basis. Consideration was given to the possibility of increasing the age of compulsory school attendance to perhaps 18 years of age. This proposal came under severe criticism, and opponents pointed out that it is already extremely difficult under present regulations to enforce compulsory attendance to age 16. If potential dropouts were coerced to stay in school for another two years, the problems of rebellion and delinquent activities would increase sharply. These extra two years would probably not add to the education of the hard core of the dropout-prone youth, but might disturb the learning process of the rest of the student body. In effect, not much more would be gained from such legal coercion than

Werner Cohn, "On the Language of Lower-Class Children," *School Review*, Vol. 67 (Winter, 1959), pp. 435–40, Basil Bernstein, "Some Sociological Determinants of Perception, An Inquiry into Sub-Cultural Differences," *British Journal of Sociology*, Vol. 9 (June, 1958), pp. 159–74.

[58] Coleman, *op. cit.*, 1965, p. 65.

making school the custodian of reluctant youth and delaying their entry into the labor force by one or two years. Chances are the potential dropout would not be any better suited to join the labor force than those who presently leave school at 16.

Many educators feel that the vital feature of the holding power of school lies in giving more personal attention to the individual student. Counseling, guidance, and advisement personnel should be increased and their scope of work expanded to include more students while still focusing on individual cases. It should be expanded to give ample opportunity to any student seeking help or advice, and it should be focused specifically on those students coming from underprivileged homes and exhibiting the characteristics typically found in dropouts. Several implications arise from this policy. These implications have resulted in at least two programs designed to aid the dropout-prone youth. First, potential dropouts must be identified before special attention can be given to them. Prevention by *early detection* of potential dropouts has become a keynote in many school systems. Home background, attitudes, and academic capability are carefully examined to determine what type of help, advice, or tutoring is necessary for a given youngster.

A typical early detection check list, as used by many schools, would include such evaluative items as the following (characteristics indicative of dropout-proneness are added in parentheses): physical size (smaller or larger than his age group); health (frequently ill, easily fatigued); participation in out-of-school activities (none); participation in school activities (none); grade retardation (one year or more retarded); father's occupation (unskilled or semiskilled); educational achievement of the parents (grade 7 or below); number of children in family (five or more); school-to-school transfers (pattern of "jumping" from school to school); attendance (chronic absenteeism; 20 days or more per year); learning rate (below 90 IQ); ability to read (two years or more below grade level); school marks (predominantly below "C"); reactions to school control (resents controls); acceptance by pupils (not liked); parental attitude concerning the value of high school graduation (negative, vascillating); pupil's interest in school work (indifferent or adverse); and general adjustment (poor).

All of these items have been found to be significantly correlated with an adolescent's decision to drop out of school. Consistently negative responses to them indicate vulnerability to dropping out and form an interrelated syndrome. The early recognition of the extent and intensity of the syndrome can be the guide to corrective and preventive work with the child.

The success of early detection programs was demonstrated by New York's Higher Horizon Program.[59] This program began in the late 1950's as an experimental guidance project involving a single junior high school in a low socioeconomic neighborhood. Currently, there are close to 100 schools with thousands of students participating in the program. Generally, the program starts in the third grade and extends through junior high school. Students are given intelligence tests and arithmetic and reading ability tests at the beginning of the school year. At least one full-time guidance counsellor is employed at each school. The program does not stop with classroom instruction, but includes a number of cultural experiences, such as visits to libraries, museums, theaters, concerts, etc. While such experiences may be routine from any middle-class teenagers, children from poor homes are rarely exposed to them, and the program has attempted to fill this void. Also, the parents of youngsters participating in the Higher Horizon Program receive attention through guidance, newsletters, and workshops. Checkups revealed that participating youth gained an average of 13 IQ points over a period of three years. (The average gain for girls was 11 points, for boys 17 points.) A test group of 81 pupils showed the following gains over a period of three years. More than one-fourth, 21 pupils, showed gains of more than 21 points; thirteen students gained between 21 and 30 points; six students gained between 31 and 50 points; and two students gained between 51 and 60 points. At the beginning of the test period, only 26% scored in the IQ category of 110 and above as compared with 58% three years later. This increase was of particular interest because students from a low socioeconomic background usually show a decrease in their age-appropriate IQ scores as they grow older. In general, it was found that approximately 40% more students are finishing high school now than before the inauguration of the Higher Horizon Program.

The second implication of this policy resulted in the establishment of Project Head Start. This provides pre-elementary school instruction in the form of semiplay and semiteaching programs for children from underprivileged homes. As has been pointed out earlier, these children already lag noticeably behind their middle-class age-mates on their first day in elementary school. Their comprehension of abstractions and their proficiency in learning to read and write are on the average markedly lower than those of children whose parents set a more abstract and learned tone at home. The effect of giving these underprivileged children a head start over their more advanced peers is greater academic and intellectual equality when they start competing in the first grade. This results in reduced academic failure and its accompanying feelings of

[59] Schreiber, *op. cit.*, 1963.

frustration, disappointment, and loss of motivation in lower-class children. Thus, by means of selective pre-elementary schooling, an attempt is being made to reduce the dropout incidence during high school.

Remedial efforts. What can be done to avert hardship and serious problems once a teen-ager has dropped out?

The immediate reaction to the dropout problem is frequently the attempt to persuade the youngster to return to regular high school or to make up secondary education through night courses, adult education programs, correspondence courses, etc. A return to regular high-school life, even if the dropout were willing, is often not advisable because of the lapse of time and the consequent age difference. However, some cases are exceptional. For example, high-school girls who get pregnant are invited back to school as soon as their condition allows. Even during pregnancy, some schools set up special classes that enable expectant mothers—wed or unwed—to continue their education without interruption. Some high schools in the city of Phoenix made arrangements whereby the pregnant girl is withdrawn from regular classes before her condition becomes apparent to the rest of the student body and is placed in separate, accredited classes so that she can pursue her educational career without interruption.

Alternative ways of completing secondary education are limited, take longer, and are availabe in only a few localities. Sometimes a dropout may complete the requirements for high school diploma while in the armed forces. A comprehensive standard examination at the conclusion of adequate preparation in the various subjects may belatedly furnish him with a high school degree. Another institution enabling delayed completion of high school was established by the Encyclopaedia Britannica Company in Chicago, offering evening high school primarily for dropouts and applying advanced techniques of teaching. Generally speaking, the results showed excellent performance by the once rebellious adolescents.

Regardless of these attempts, the principal solution of the dropout problem lies in the absorption of the dropout into the labor force. Thus, remedial action calls for expansion of job possibilities for these out-of-school adolescents. This is a complex and trying enterprise, since the dropout's lack of marketable skills, his underdeveloped academic ability, and social immaturity narrow his placement possibilities. However, there are a number of possible methods that could reduce the oversupply of untrained dropouts.

First, existing job opportunities for which dropouts qualify must be made known to them. New channels of publicizing such positions have to be initiated. The typical dropout from the lower class lacks occupational contacts and role models within his immediate environment. In contrast, the middle-class teen-ager's father knows a manager, or other high-placed worker, who can give him advance information about job openings. Considering that only a small fraction of jobs are obtained through such formal channels as employment agencies and newspaper ads, it becomes clear that the lower-class lack of occupational "connections" is a formidable barrier to employment. Role models, which are the natural bridge to adult careers, are largely absent in the lives of youth from deprived inner-city areas. The importance of role models and direct contacts has been noted:

> How a young man goes about entering his chosen occupation is determined by the adequacy of his information about that occupation, by the extent to which he has been able to observe others entering and working in that occupation. Whether or not he seeks the best training for it, under appropriate auspices, depends partly upon the quality of his contact with people in that occupation. Whether or not he applies for jobs in the proper places, at the proper time, and in the proper manner, also is in part the result of how much opportunity he has had to observe others going through the same process, and of the adequacy of the understanding of the occupational mores which he has acquired through family activities, discussion and contacts.[60]

A second remedial program consists of selectively stimulating the rate of new job creation, thus increasing the demand in those sectors of the labor market where there is oversupply. This approach is obviously severely limited by the natural growth of the modern economy, which simply does not call for as many unskilled workers as are available.

A third possible remedial approach would involve expanding the existing job-training programs and moving the dropouts from areas of heavy oversupply of labor to areas with moderate supply, thus giving the youngster greater assurance of lasting employment and, while the period of training lasts, keeping him out of the saturated labor force at least part of the time. Programs such as the Job Corps and the Urban Youth Service Corps, developed in New York City, are promising beginnings. These living-training-working arrangements have a number of useful functions: (1) they prepare the dropout for jobs he could otherwise never obtain; (2) they enable completion of interrupted education and open up opportunities for further, higher education; (3) they teach the adolescent how to carry out work responsibly, developing in him the ability to enter a successful career in the labor force; and (4) they relieve the labor market of the oversupply of unskilled youth. Through

---

[60] Donald E. Super, *The Psychology of Careers* (New York, Harper & Bros., 1957), p. 244.

such working-training programs, situations such as can be encountered in New York City could be corrected—where only five qualified persons are available for every seven skilled openings, with particularly serious shortages in the fields of auto mechanics, nursing, and stenography. At the same time, there is 75% unemployment among youth in the slum areas.[61] New York City is not an isolated case. Almost all larger American cities exhibit this type of incongruity. Selective training of dropouts and careful placement of them in the labor force would reduce unemployment and hardship among underprivileged adolescents as well as improve the overall economic structure by more adequately balancing supply and demand of labor.

Summary

High school education has become not only a "basic right" but also a basic expectation. This tendency reflects not merely an abstract value of the American society, but also the necessity of keeping the nation's youth from entering the labor force at an age when they are unprepared for the ever-increasing white-collar and technical positions. It is primarily these economic factors that have changed the phenomenon of dropping out from a private decision to a public problem.

It is true that the nation's dropouts have increased over the past decades and are expected to amount to more than 7 million individuals between 1960 and 1970. But the numerical increase is primarily a function of the increased number of teen-agers in the population. The actual per cent of dropouts per given age group has decreased.

The incidence of dropping out varies significantly with a number of major variables. Socioeconomic status of the student's family is one of the most important influences and has been found to be inversely correlated with dropping out, i.e., the lower the social class the higher the dropout rate. The quality of interaction within the family group is another significant influence on the youth's school behavior. Such interpersonal aspects as understanding and acceptance, communication, joint leisure activities, adjustment, and consensus differ greatly between dropouts and graduates. The families of dropouts score markedly lower in these dimensions than those of graduates. The extent of the parents' education and their opinion regarding the value of education are reflected in

---

[61] A Proposal for the Prevention and Control of Delinquency by Expanding Opportunities, 2nd ed. (New York, Mobilization for Youth, Inc., August, 1962), pp. 95–96.

their offspring's school accomplishment. The higher their education and the greater their valuation of education, the lower the dropout rate of their children. A comparison of family size and school attendance revealed that children from large families consistently exhibit lower achievement motivation than children from smaller families. Children from broken homes have twice the dropout rate of children from stable homes. The delinquency rate among dropouts is considerably higher than among graduates. Although there are roughly as many boys as there are girls who drop out, they often do so for different reasons. Some boys quit school to join the armed forces or to get married and/or to get a job; a significant number of girls quit school because they get married and/or are pregnant.

The situation in which the dropout finds himself after he leaves school is rather severe. He discovers that he has low bargaining power for jobs, is not advancing in his career, has a low income, and is frequently unemployed. Endeavors to keep youth in school until graduation include efforts to increase the holding power of the school by adjusting the curriculum to the more practical interests of the teen-agers, reconstructing educational procedures, establishing an "early detection" system, rechanneling financial aid, and establishing a more effective and comprehensive counseling and guidance service. Some success has been achieved by special pre- or extra-school preparation of culturally underprivileged children. Project Head Start and New York's Higher Horizon program are examples of such successful innovations.

Efforts to improve the life conditions of youth who have already dropped out are few and not yet well developed. Potential remedial approaches include the following: (1) The possibility could be explored as to whether the young individual is willing to complete his education by correspondence, extension, or other special arrangements. (2) Employment opportunities for dropouts could be more carefully examined. (3) The visibility of existing job opportunities could be improved. (4) The employability of the dropout could be improved by specially designed work-and-study projects.

17

drinking and the use of drugs

The Nature and Effects of the Chemicals

What exactly is the nature of those chemical substances that are craved by some, abhorred by many, and stealthily experimented with by adolescents? One would expect that the answer is commonly understood and does not need reiteration; after all, alcohol and the various illicit drugs have been known for many generations, and problems incurred through their use are by no means a novelty. And yet, still today, so many misconceptions surround the subject of drugs that, as a first step, some myths should be exposed before viewing the problem in detail.

There are a number of known drugs that are habit-forming or addictive. The use of and dependence on these chemicals are considered dangerous or undesirable in American society and, consequently, their distribution is limited or altogether prohibited. In addition, there are a number of other drugs that are neither habit-forming nor addictive nor physiologically detrimental but which are nevertheless prohibited because their effects are regarded as perilous to the mental welfare of the user and the safety of his fellow man. It is impossible to deal in one chapter with each individual drug and the teen-agers' involvement with it. To make a discussion in a brief frame possible, the chemicals are divided into three categories: alcohol, opiates, and hallucinogenic drugs. Categorization of the substances in this manner is warranted because each type is characterized not only by its particular physiological effect but also by its social-psychological meaning and legal implications.

Alcohol. A frequent misconception about alcohol is that it acts as a stimulant. Actually, it is a protoplasmic poison with a depressant effect on the nervous system. Taken in sufficient quantity, it can render a person unconscious by functioning as a general anesthetic. In fact, before other methods were developed, alcohol was sometimes used medically as an anesthetic. But as such it has one major drawback: the dose that renders a man unconscious is also very close to the lethal amount. The widespread misconception that alcohol is a stimulant probably arose because it affects the nervous system selectively. When sufficient alcohol has passed from the blood into the brain, its first effect is a reduction of nervous activity in that area of the cerebral cortex that is responsible for censoring and restricting thinking. It is this effect to which many people allude when they, half seriously, assert that "the superego is that part of man's personality which is soluble in alcohol." Having depressed the critical thinking process, a more uninhibited expression of biological and sensate needs and drives can take place. It is this phase of alcoholic influence that often is misunderstood and taken as the result of some stimulating action. Subsequent phases of alcoholic intoxication, however, will also depress other areas of the cerebral cortex and thus lead to a more general, including libidinal, depression. When the concentration of alcohol in the blood reaches about .1%, the depressant effect spreads to those nervous centers in the brain that regulate motor movements. The person experiences difficulty in walking, general motor coordination, and talking—taking on the typical "heavy tongue" slur of intoxicated individuals. At a concentration of about .2% of alcohol in the blood, emotional uncoordination will result; at .3%, the sensory perceptions become impaired; at .4% to .5%, the person becomes comatose; and at .6% to .7%, the drinker may die from paralysis of the centers controlling breathing and heart beat.

The question whether alcohol is habit-forming or addiction-producing is not quite free of controversy. It seems that habituation depends on the personality of the individual consumer. For normal persons, it is not a habit-forming drug. Furthermore, it normally has no accumulative effect on the body that would warrant classifying it as an addictive and dependency-forming substance. But for persons with a psychological predisposition, such as acute escapist desires, it can be habit-forming, and ultimately such persons can develop extreme dependence with symptoms of addiction. The Expert Committee on Alcohol of the World Health Organization classifies alcohol as intermediate between habit-forming and addiction-producing, occasionally leading to compulsive craving and crippling dependence, and therefore being a potential peril to personal and social well-being.[1]

Opiates. The group of drugs loosely called opiates are pain-killing and euphoria-inducing chemicals derived from or equivalent to opium. The best known are morphine and heroin; others are codeine, meperi-

---

[1] World Health Organization, Technical Report Series No. 84, Expert Committee on Alcohol, *First Report* (March, 1954), pp. 10–11.

dine (Demerol), and methadone (Amidone, Dolophine). The term narcotics is often used synonymously with opiates.

A popular misconception concerning the nature of opiates is that the
drug's effects make a person dangerous and violent. The truth again is
that opiates are depressants and lower the user's level of nervous and
bodily activities. Opiate effects include analgesia (relief of pain), seda-
tion (freedom from anxiety, reduction of motor activity, muscular relaxation), hypnosis (drowsiness), and euphoria (a sense of well-being and
contentment).[2] The relationship between narcotic addiction and criminality, as far as there is a correlation, is *indirect*. There is nothing in the
drugs themselves that would incite a person to commit criminal offenses.
On the contrary, the physiological effect would only reduce antisocial
sentiments and violent impulses. Even sexual desires markedly diminish,
rendering invalid another popular myth that associates sex orgies and
"sex fiendishness" with narcotic addiction. When addicts commit criminal
offenses, it is usually in order to obtain the means of continuing the use
of the drug.

There is no doubt about the addictive nature of opiates. Addiction
implies physical dependence—a type of dependence that has nothing to
do with mere habit or with the satisfaction of some vague emotional
craving. The morphine or heroin addict's organism depends on a regular
supply of the chemical just as a normal organism depends on the regular
supply of important vitamins. And just as a normal man reacts adversely
and becomes ill if his supply of vitamins stops, the addict reacts adversely and becomes ill if his supply of heroin or morphine stops. It is
usually this violent and painful reaction that drives the addict to seek
the next dose. Addiction, then, is a physicochemical reality in which a
drug, circulated in specific concentrations in the organism for a sufficient
length of time, actually changes the body chemistry to the degree that
functioning without it is difficult. The term "addiction" should thus
be limited to drugs that produce physiological dependence, as in
the case of heroin or barbiturates. In the case of marijuana, mescaline,
LSD, etc., the term "addiction" is probably misleading. There are significant differences between drugs that are addictive and drugs that are
merely habit-forming—the former having a physiological plus an emotional effect, and the latter primarily an emotional effect only.

Hallucinogens. The group of drugs commonly referred to as hallucinogens includes (1) LSD, short for lysergic acid diethylamide; (2)
mescaline, an extract from the tops of the peyote cactus; (3) psilocybin,
first found in the so-called sacred mushrooms of southern Mexico; and

---

[2] David P. Ausubel, *Drug Addiction: Physiological, Psychological, and Sociological Aspects* (New York, Random House, 1958), p. 18.

(4) marijuana, the best known and most widely distributed of all of them. These drugs have a hallucinatory or at least perception-altering effect and influence the user's perception of the world within and without. The result can be either acutely insightful and realistic, penetrating mental defense mechanisms, overcoming culturally learned stereotypes, rigid linguistic categories, inhibitions, "blind spots," etc., or fantastically distorted and extremely nonrealistic. The former type of perception can be of great value in therapy and self-development, the latter type may be classified as a temporary psychotic episode endangering the safety of the user and others around him. The danger usually arises not from violent behavior but rather from misperceived identity or circumstances. For example, a few years ago, a student under the influence of LSD walked into rush-hour traffic believing he was God and that nothing could harm him.

Other possible effects of these drugs include synesthesia, a cross-over from one sense to another, so that subjects "hear" colors, "smell" sounds, or "see" ideas and thoughts. Sometimes there is also a sharp improvement in recall, and subjects become able to accurately remember minute details of past events. Often there is a merging of thought and emotion, producing a sense of mental unity and existential integration. Extreme changes of perception can reach dimensions that justify classification as changes of personality. Instances of this nature include dissociation, detachment, impulsivity, and, most important of all, mood intensification. Also, intensification of outside stimuli is common. Colors are perceived as being extraordinarily vivid, bright, and gay—a traffic light may be seen as an object of surpassing beauty. Listening to music may become a tremendous esthetic experience, with the listener becoming aware of the finest nuances. *The mood of the individual is decisive*—in a depressed state, a Beethoven symphony may arouse suicidal grief, in another state of mind, rhapsodic joy.

The perception-altering potency varies greatly with the different hallucinogens. LSD is so powerful that a dose of between 20 to 100 micrograms (an amount hardly visible to the bare eye) is sufficient to provide a "trip." The next powerful drug is psilocybin, followed by mescaline, and, finally, marijuana.

Psychedelic drugs are not addictive. Under certain personality conditions, they may however be habit-forming. The more powerful drugs of this group, e.g., LSD, STP, can cause the so-called "flashbacks," i.e., periodic recurrence of the drug-induced perception without retaking the chemical. The above-mentioned drugs represent only a few of the presently best known examples of the psychedelic (hallucinogenic) group.

Scope, Distribution, and Trends

The scope of the adolescents' involvement with these chemicals includes a quantitative as well as qualitative aspect, i.e., *how many* of them use the various drugs and *to what degree*. Information answering these two questions is difficult to obtain and, at best, consists only of rough estimates.

Alcohol. Alcohol is the most widely used of the chemicals under discussion. It is estimated that approximately 70 million individuals in the United States drink alcoholic beverages of some type and that this figure will climb to 100 million by 1970 if present trends continue.[3] Approximately five million drinkers are currently classified as alcoholics.[4] There is obviously a marked difference between the social drinker and the alcoholic—the difference measureable by degree of dependence on alcohol. An alcoholic is so dependent on alcohol and drinks with such regularity that he is considered chronically ill—psychologically, somatically, or psychosomatically. An extension of his problems includes the inability to adequately carry out his social and economic responsibilities. Only an insignificant proportion of the alcoholics are teen-agers. Surveys have indicated that the median age for alcoholics is the mid-forties.[5] Yet teen-age consumption of alcohol is widespread and is sometimes a prelude to alcoholism in later life. A number of studies have tried to assess the dimensions of drinking among high school youth. A recent study in a middle-sized midwestern city found that only 8% of the teen-agers were complete abstainers and that 92% had drunk or tasted alcohol at some time. Among these teen-agers, about 68% had had a drink or taste of alcohol only on a single occasion, 23% were occasional drinkers, and about 1% were frequent or "heavy" drinkers.[6] Another study was made in Nassau County, New York, among 1,000 high school students. Approximately 14% reported complete abstention, and among the users, 43% reported occasional or frequent drinking. The percentage of teen-age consumption was found to increase with age but to reach a

---

[3] Barry A. Kinsey, *The Female Alcoholic, A Social Psychological Study* (Springfield, Ill., Charles C. Thomas, 1966), p. 3.

[4] Mark Keller, "The Definition of Alcoholism and the Estimation of its Prevalence," in D. I. Pittman and C. R. Snyder (eds.), *Society, Culture, and Drinking Patterns* (New York, John Wiley & Sons, 1962), chapter 1, pp. 310–29.

[5] "Kansas State Commission on Alcoholism Activities in 1953–54," *Quarterly Journal of Studies on Alcohol,* Vol. 16 (March, 1955).

[6] George L. Maddox and Bevode C. McCall, *Drinking Among Teen-agers* (New Brunswick, N.J., Rutgers Center for Alcohol Studies, 1964), pp. 26–27.

plateau in the late teens, generally between 19 and 20. Similar findings were obtained on the college level. A 1951 survey included 17,000 students in 27 colleges. The proportion of alcohol users differed among the various institutions and ranged from 65% to 92% for men and from 39% to 89% for coeds.[8] The proportion of *frequent* drinking on the college level was markedly higher than on the high school level. The importance of the age factor was clearly demonstrated by a Wisconsin study showing a *direct* correlation between alcohol consumption and age. It was found that 51% of the 14-year-old youth, 59% of the 15-years-olds, 65% of the 16-year-olds, 71% of the 17-year-olds, and 78% of the 18-year-olds drank "sometimes."[9] A survey of the Purdue Opinion Poll, sampling 3,000 high school pupils in all parts of the country, found a corresponding shift of opinion. The proportion of those who said they disapprove of drinking decreased steadily from 65% in the ninth grade to 48% in the twelfth grade.[10]

Religious affiliation is another factor that influences drinking patterns. A study done on the college level found that consumption of alcoholic beverages was most common among Jewish students, with 94% of the men and 84% of the women reporting use of alcohol. For Catholics the distribution was 90% for men and 78% for women. Protestants reported 77% for men and 60% for women. Mormon students reported the lowest rates, 54% for men and 23% for women.[11] The same tendency was brought out by the Purdue Opinion Poll, finding that 65% of the Protestants, 45% of the Catholics, but only 34% of the Jewish high school students disapproved of drinking. Accordingly, 28% of the Protestants, 52% of the Catholics, and 52% of the Jewish students admitted to drinking "sometimes."[12] These differences seem to bear evidence that culture plays an important role in shaping attitudes and behavior. As is commonly known, the various religious groups hold widely divergent views on the question of drinking. The Jewish religion does not oppose drinking and frequently includes wine in its religious rituals and family festivities. (Consumption of alcoholic beverages in connection

---

[7] Hofstra Research Bureau, Psychological Division, *Use of Alcoholic Beverages by High School Students in Nassau County Related to Parental Permissiveness* (New York, Sheppard Foundation, 1954).

[8] Robert Strauss and Sheldon D. Bacon, *Drinking in College* (New Haven, Yale University Press, 1953).

[9] John L. Miller, *Attitudes of High School Students Toward Alcoholic Beverages*, mimeographed (University of Wisconsin, Bureau of Economics, Sociology, and Anthropology, 1956).

[10] *Purdue Opinion Poll for Young People*, Vol. 8 (Lafayette, Ind., Purdue University, January, 1949), pp. 17–18.

[11] Strauss and Bacon, *op. cit.*, p. 51.

[12] *Purdue Opinion Poll for Young People*, *op. cit.*

with religious rituals was not counted as "drinking" in the surveys.)
Neither is there an official injunction against drinking among Catholics.
In contrast, many Protestant denominations and sects oppose and
condemn the use of alcohol.

The question of what teen-agers drink and how much of each type
was explored by a 1964 study. A breakdown of drinking preferences
among users of alcoholic beverages indicated that for boys, beer is the
most frequently used alcoholic beverage, with more than 50% reporting
drinking one or more bottles in an average week. Approximately-one
fourth of the girls reported drinking one or more bottles of beer during
an average week. The difference in drinking habits between the sexes
diminishes radically in the case of wine, whisky and mixed drinks. In
fact, if we ignore the "no answer" category, proportionately more girls
than boys drink mixed drinks.[13] (See Table 17-1 for details.)

The problems accruing from the behavior of teen-agers under the
influence of alcohol are mostly unrecorded. Harmful and even fatal
results from drinking span a range from fights and quarrels, sexual
offenses, and unwanted pregnancies to disastrous accidents. For some of
these consequences there is no reliable official record. But for accidents
found to happen "under the influence," the reports of the National Safety
Council allow some estimates. It appears that in one-fourth of all fatal
accidents, a driver or a pedestrian had been drinking. The figures of
the annual Uniform Crime Reports reveal that more than one million
arrests are made for drunkenness each year. However, it must be emphasized that teen-agers constitute a small minority in these statistics. Between 1% and 6% of the teen-agers who report established patterns of
drinking report that they have experienced serious resultant personal or
social complications. Some authors have developed a scale of social complication comprising four basic items: (1) failure to meet social responsibilities; (2) destruction of friendships; (3) accident or injury; (4) official
punishment or discipline. A study of college students found that 66%
of the male users and 85% of the female users had never experienced
any type of complication as a result of their drinking. Among the 34%
of the men who admitted to some complications, 6% were involved in
accidents, injuries, or formal punishment. Among the 15% of the coeds
who had experienced some complications, approximately 1% were involved in consequences of such seriousness.[14]

One warning must be added. The above statistics may slightly
underestimate the drinking problem in the *general* teen-age population,
because the figures were obtained from either high school or college

[13] Maddox and McCall, *op. cit.*, p. 28.
[14] Strauss and Bacon, *op. cit.*

students. It is possible that the type of adolescent who is most likely to get into trouble as a result of his drinking is more likely to drop out of school and is consequently not included in these surveys, thus giving the findings a slightly biased slant.

TABLE 17–1. Self-Estimates of Consumption of Various Alcoholic Beverages in an Average Week among Users,[1] by Sex, in Per Cent.

Average weekly consumption	Drinkers	
	Boys	Girls
Beer		
Rarely or never use	44	73
Between 1 and 3 bottles	22	15
Between 3 and 6 bottles	19	8
More than 6 bottles	13	2
No answer [2]	2	2
Totals	100	100
Wine		
Rarely or never use	60	61
Between 1 and 3 wine glasses	18	25
Between 3 and 6 wine glasses	5	0
More than 6 wine glasses	3	4
No answer [2]	14	10
Totals	100	100
Whisky		
Rarely or never use	64	69
Between 1 and 3 shot glasses	16	17
Between 3 and 6 shot glasses	5	4
More than 6 glasses	6	2
No answer [2]	9	8
Totals	100	100
Mixed Drinks		
Rarely or never use	63	69
Between 1 and 3 mixed drinks	9	19
Between 3 and 6 mixed drinks	4	2
More than 6 mixed drinks	3	2
No answer [2]	21	8
Totals	100	100

[1] Users are defined as teen-agers who are not abstainers, including occasional as well as frequent drinkers.

Adapted from George L. Maddox and Bevode C. McCall, *Drinking among Teen-Agers* (New Brunswick, N.J., Rutgers Center of Alcohol Studies, 1964), p. 28.

Opiates. No one knows the *total* number of narcotic addicts in the United States. The *known* addicts represent only a fraction of the total number of addicted individuals and are included in official statistics of the federal government. Nongovernmental estimates put the number of addicts at about three times the official or known figure. A number of years ago, the actual number of addicts in the United States was estimated to be 150,000.[15] However, nongovernmental estimates vary considerably among the observers, thus the official statistics are deemed more reliable for the purpose of this discussion.

By the mid-1960's, the number of *known* drug addicts in the United States was reported to be between 50,000 and 60,000. Of these addicts, a relatively small proportion, 3% to 4%, were under the age of 21. Narcotic addiction, primarily referring to dependence on *heroin*, is therefore more an adult than an adolescent problem. As an illustration, the figures released by the Federal Bureau of Narcotics, at the end of 1965, showed that out of a total of 57,199 active addicts in the United States, only 1,973, or 3.4% were under the age of 21. There were only 138 known addicts 17 years or younger, constituting .2% of the total addicts. 1,835 older adolescents, 18 to 20 years of age, amounted to 3.2% of the total addicts.[16]

TABLE 17–2.   Known Narcotic Addicts Under 21 Years of Age in the United States, as of December 31, 1965.

Age		Number	Per Cent
15		5	0.2
16		27	1.4
17		106	5.4
18		265	13.4
19		577	29.2
20		993	50.4
	Total	1,973	100

Adapted from U.S. Treasury Department, Bureau of Narcotics, "Traffic in Opium and Other Dangerous Drugs," for the year ending Dec. 31, 1965 (Washington, D. C., Government Printing Office), p. 45.

[15] Joint Committee of the American Bar Association and the American Medical Association on Narcotic Drugs, *Drug Addiction: Crime or Disease?* (Bloomington, Ind., Indiana University Press, 1961), p. 28.

[16] U. S. Treasury Department, Bureau of Narcotics, *Traffic in Opium And Other Dangerous Drugs,* for the year ending Dec. 31, 1965, (Washington, D. C., Government Printing Office), p. 45.

The 21-and-younger age group showed an interesting ethnic and racial composition. Negro youth contributed 24.4%, Puerto Ricans 21.2%, Mexican-Americans 5.0% and all other whites 49.3%.[17] As is readily visible, the Puerto Rican and the Negro minority groups are vastly over-represented. It must be clear that the above figures refer to known addicts who have established a chronic dependence on opiates and not to one-time or occasional users, or to persons arrested for possession of drugs.

It is difficult to chart the trend of youthful drug addiction. There was a total of 3,178 persons under the age of 21 admitted to the two United States Public Health Service Hospitals in Lexington, Kentucky, and Fort Worth, Texas, in the period between 1935 and 1960. While up to 1948 the yearly teen-age admissions did not exceed 50, such admissions have annually exceeded 100 since 1949. Peak years were 1950 and 1951 with more than 400 and 300, respectively.[18] However, since young people as a population segment have numerically increased over the past decades, a corresponding numerical increase in drug addiction does not necessarily mean an actual spread of the problem. Moreover, refined detection, more accurate recording methods, and a greater readiness to hospitalize victims may create the impression that we are dealing with a problem of greater magnitude than previously. The stastistics of hospitalization and, especially, of police arrest for narcotic violations should be viewed with these circumstances in mind. Another factor thwarting attempts to reliably chart the trends of juvenile addiction is the *legal* confusion concerning classification of drugs. When social and biological scientists refer to "narcotics," they mean addictive opium derivatives. However, the police records and legal statistics include the use of possession of marijuana, cocaine, and other drugs under "narcotic" offenses. Actually, these drugs are not opiates, and their effects are not comparable to those of opiates. Official statistics reporting "drastic" increases in juvenile "narcotic" offenses are therefore not comparable with previous records.

LSD. Hallucinogenic drugs, although by no means new in knowledge and use, are a relatively new concern of the authorities and are currently attracting fervent interest by users and anti-users alike. In a sense, these drugs, with the exception of marijuana, caught Americans by surprise. The American society was neither socially nor juridically prepared to cope with the increase in the use of mescaline, psilocybin, and *especially* LSD. As a consequence, no official record can reveal the scope and distri-

---

[17] *Traffic in Opium And Other Dangerous Drugs,* op. cit., pp. 40–41, 45.

[18] David W. Maurer and Victor H. Vogel, *Narcotics and Narcotic Addiction* (Springfield, Ill., Charles C. Thomas, 1962), p. 263.

bution of their use. If any estimates are to be made at all, they must necessarily rely more on reports of the general mass media and the tentative hypotheses of social scientists than on precise data from official or professional sources.

Among hallucinogenic drugs, LSD is one of the most powerful and consequential. (Another extremely powerful hallucinogenic drug which allegedly surpasses LSD in intensity is the so-called STP, spelled out by hippies as serenity, tranquility, peace; known to Dow Chemical Company as 4-methyl-2,5-dimethoxyalphamethylpenethylamine. Little was known about this drug by 1968, and its use or abuse was not widespread.) It is LSD that causes authorities most concern and that seems to be responsible for increasing numbers of problematic consequences. The following discussion focuses, therefore, primarily on LSD.

There is consensus among observers that the problem is located on and around college and university campuses. There are at least two suspected reasons for this type of concentration. First, the type of person inclined to use and experiment with hallucinogenic drugs is different from the person tending to use opiates or alcohol. Taking hallucinogenic drugs is not so much an escapist habit as it is an act of curiosity and experimentation. College students, relatively more curious and enterprising than the general population and more ready to experiment with anything that provides psychedelic (consciousness-expanding) experience, are attracted by these new and strange catalysts. Students, by definition interested in new knowledge and mental processes, can therefore be expected to show a particular interest in psychedelic drugs. Second, knowledge about the drugs as well as the substances themselves are more readily available in the academic environment. In fact, given lysergic acid to start with, LSD is relatively easy to prepare by a student majoring in chemistry. It is suspected that, as a result, college students have greater access to the drug than anybody else. One common form of black-market distribution of LSD has been through impregnated sugar cubes, costing from $2.50 to $5.00 for 100 micrograms, enough for an eight- or ten-hour "trip." Another technique is to mix LSD with water, soak the solution up in handkerchief, let it dry, and, finally, cut it up in small pieces to be chewed. The possession and distribution of LSD is hard to track down because the compound is odorless, colorless, and tasteless, and so potent that a gram, equal to at least 10,000 "trips," could be hidden in one cigarette.

In the mid-1960's, illegal LSD was manufactured primarily by amateurs. However, the potential profit involved may tempt organized crime to enter the manufacturing and distributing activities. The current extent of amateur-type and campus-related activities with hallucinogenic drugs was illustrated by a report from Arizona State University.[19] In the fall of 1966, police officers raided a residence in the campus neighborhood and arrested a young couple for possession of twelve pounds of marijuana, a bottle of LSD, some amounts of peyote, various types of stimulant pills, two sacks of dried hallucinogenic mushrooms, and other herbs and chemicals.

Another way of discovering the scope of use and the type of person involved is to examine the people who come to public attention because of unforeseen and disastrous effects of the drug. Current knowledge of how many and what groups of individuals are using hallucinogens is derived less from sociological research than from reports of health centers, hospitals, and mortuaries. Dr. Henry B. Bruyn, director of the Student Health Service of the University of California at Berkeley, estimated that about 25% of the student body at Berkeley have smoked, or are smoking, marijuana.[20] This estimate was arrived at by an "educated guess" based on a great deal of contact with students in and out of the Health Service, talks or "bull sessions" with student groups, etc. An increasing source of detectability is hospitalization of patients with post-LSD symptoms. The Neuropsychiatric Institute at the University of California, Los Angeles, reported that between 1965 and 1966 the incidence of LSD cases increased to 12% of all cases seen by the psychiatric emergency service.[21] The Los Angeles study reported no decreases in the rate of such LSD patients after the new Federal Drug Abuse Control Amendment went into effect on February 1, 1966. The report also mentioned similar increases in post-LSD patients during 1966 at other nearby psychiatric facilities, such as the Los Angeles County General Hospital and the Los Angeles Central Receiving Hospital. Among the cases described was that of the boy who tried to commit suicide because he perceived his body melting away. He had taken one dose of LSD and remained suicidal for more than two weeks. Other patients required long-term treatment and were sent to state hospitals. Another source of information on the extent of the use of the hallucinogenic drugs are the fatal outcomes. For example, in August of 1966, a 20-year-old Berkeley youth attending a "trip" party fell to his death from a third-story window. He jumped out of the window not because of suicidal intentions, but, it was concluded, because he thought he could fly.[22]

---

[19] *State Press* (Arizona State University, Sept. 22, 1966), p. 1.

[20] News conference at the Annual Meeting of the American College Health Association (Washington, D. C., March, 1967), plus personal communication.

[21] J. Thomas Ungerleider, *et al.*, "The Dangers of LSD," *Journal of the American Medical Association*, Vol. 197 (Aug. 8, 1966), pp. 389–92.

[22] UPI Report (Berkely, Calif., Aug. 1, 1966).

Of great concern to parents and the authorities is the fact that LSD has spread to high schools and prep schools. Numerous reports document that by 1968 this pattern had reached nation-wide dimension. One report referred to Sherman Oaks, California, where a 17-year-old reported the operation of a sales ring at his school that was pushing LSD at a penny a microgram.[23] More than 2,500 high school students in the upper-middle class in the school district of Great Neck, New York, long considered a "model" community, were the subjects of a carefully designed research.[24] School officials discovered a surprisingly high drug involvement, and the survey results were published in the *Guide Post,* the school's newspaper. Nine per cent of the students were found to have tried illicit drugs, most often marijuana. Two hundred seven had smoked marijuana and many said they "definitely would use it again." Fifty-five had used LSD or other strong hallucinogenic drugs. Such drugs were easily available. For example, 23% of the students had seen peers use marijuana, 21% had had the opportunity to buy marijuana, and 8% had had the opportunity to buy other psychedelic drugs, including LSD. Most surprising, only two-thirds of the students felt that marijuana should be illegal, and 25% felt that it should be legal. Another report made headlines in Phoenix, Arizona, anouncing that a shocking number of high school students had been discovered using LSD or marijuana.[25] At least 70 teen-age users had been detained by police or referred to juvenile authorities. What called the attention of the authorities to the teen-age users was the perilous post-LSD symptoms in the case of several of the youngsters. Nightmarish perceptions led several of the youthful users to the brink of suicide. One boy had to be forcibly stopped from throwing himself in front of a moving truck on one of the major streets in the city. A girl fired a bullet into her own shoulder when she attempted to commit suicide.

From these reports, unfortunately not yet officially systematized, the conclusion emerges that teen-agers use hallucinogenic drugs far more extensively than they use opiates, that their use of hallucinogenic drugs is second in extent to alcohol, and that the psychedelic drug problem is observable on most, if not all, large campuses of the United States. It is difficult at this time to forecast a trend, because stringent legal measures to dam the current increase will most likely be established in the future. Until then, a rapid increase of problems resulting from the use of the various psychedelic drugs can be expected.

---

[23] "Psychiatry," *Time* (March 11, 1966), pp. 44–46.

[24] *Guide Post,* Vol. 37 (Great Neck, N. Y., Feb. 15, 1967), pp. 1ff.

[25] "Phoenix Teen-Agers Using Drugs," *Arizona Republic* (Nov. 5, 1966), p. 1.

Characteristics of Adolescent Drinkers and Drug Users

Alcohol. The American adolescent grows up in a society where a large proportion of the adult population uses alcoholic beverages freely and publicly. The customs of the United States allow and often encourage drinking, and the child grows up associating it with conviviality, the celebration of social events, and, presumably, "having a good time." Alcohol is customarily thought of as capable of doing something *for* the user, not *to* him. Sooner or later most adolescents encounter situations in which they are tempted to experiment with alcoholic beverages, either because they are curious, because their parents include them in their drinking habits, because they wish to imitate adult behavior patterns, or because they find it a means of expressing their rebellion against being classified as less than adult.

Because of the adult connotation of drinking, older teen-agers, further along in assuming the adult role, show considerably more involvement in drinking. Boys are particularly vulnerable to the cultural image. They are prone to imitate drinking customs because drinking has a masculine connotation and gives the user prestige in the eyes of his peers. In all known studies, consistent differences were found between boys and girls in their attitudes and actions concerning alcohol. A type of cultural double standard seems to apply to drinking, according to which boys not only drink more, but are often *expected* to drink more.

Socioeconomic status plays a significant role in respect to time of onset and degree of alcoholic involvement. The life experiences of lower-class youth usually tend to encourage an earlier claim to adult status than those of the middle-class youth.

In addition to age, sex, and social class, several studies found that poor school attitudes and a high dropout rate are variables significantly correlated with drinking. August B. Hollingshead, in his study, *Elmtown's Youth,* noted that the use of alcoholic beverages is much more common among drop-outs than among those who remain in school.[26] A similar conclusion was drawn from a more recent study which sampled approximately 2,000 eleventh- and twelfth-grade students in three public high schools in a middle-sized midwestern city.[27] Data from the Lane County Youth Project in Oregon indicated that several dimensions

---

[26] August B. Hollingshead, *Elmtown's Youth* (New York, John Wiley & Sons, 1949), pp. 408*ff.*

[27] Maddox and McCall, *op. cit.,* p. 100.

of alienation from school were significantly associated with drinking patterns of high school youth. Comparison of *academic success,* objectively indicated by grades, with drinking habits showed that youths with modal grades of "D" or "F" were more likely to drink than those with modal grades of "A," "B," or "C."[28] (See Table 17–3.)

Since it is customary that the school concerns itself not only with the academic aspect of student life, but with the informal social life as well, a second measurement of alienation from school is the youth's *participation* in extracurricular activities. Although not as strong as in the case of academic marks, participation in organized school activities does show some relationship to drinking. The correlation tends to be inverse, i.e., the less participation in school activities the greater the indulgence in drinking.[29] (See table 17–4.)

A third dimension of alienation deals with the youth's *evaluation* of the school. Students who think that "school is dull and boring" are more involved in drinking than their peers who disagree with this opinion.[30] (See table 17–5.)

On the basis of evidence from these three dimensions plus other findings, the director of the Youth Project concluded that drinking youth are basically alienated and constitute a subculture.[31] Further interpretation of the findings led the researcher to associate the teen-agers' drinking involvement with *rebelliousness.*[32] For youth, school is an adult-con-

TABLE 17–3.   Incidence of Drinking Among Adolescent Males According to Modal Grade Point Earned (in per cent).

| | Modal Grade | | | | |
	A	B	C	D	E
Nondrinkers	76	67	49	39	43
Occasional Drinkers	17	7	37	40	24
Regular Drinkers	4	3	9	12	19
Unknown	3	3	5	9	14
Total	100	100	100	100	100
N =	(70)	(231)	(343)	(137)	(21)

Kenneth Polk, *Drinking and the Adolescent Culture,* a mimeographed research report (Eugene, Oregon, Lane County Youth Project, December, 1964).

[28] Kenneth Polk, *Drinking and the Adolescent Culture,* mimeographed research report (Eugene, Ore., Lane County Youth Project, December, 1964), p. 11.

[29] *Ibid.,* p. 12.

[30] *Ibid.,* p. 14.

[31] *Ibid.,* p. 26.

[32] *Ibid.,* p. 8.

TABLE 17–4. Incidence of Drinking Among Adolescent Males According to Participation in a Club or Other Organized Activity (in per cent).

	Participants In One or More Organizations	Nonparticipants
Nondrinkers	61	49
Occasional Drinkers	32	33
Regular Drinkers	4	10
Unknown	3	8
Total	100	100
N=	(380)	(408)

Kenneth Polk, *Drinking and the Adolescent Culture,* mimeographed research report (Eugene, Oregon, Lane County Youth Project, December, 1964).

TABLE 17–5. Incidence of Drinking Among Adolescent Males According to Agreement with the Statement: "School is dull and boring." (in per cent)

	Agree Strongly Or Somewhat	Slightly Agree Or Disagree	Disagree Strongly or Somewhat
Nondrinkers	39	52	61
Occasional Drinkers	38	37	29
Regular Drinkers	17	6	5
Unknown	6	5	5
Total	100	100	100
N=	(142)	(201)	(451)

Kenneth Polk, *Drinking and the Adolescent Culture,* mimeographed research report (Eugene, Oregon, Lane County Youth Project, December, 1964).

trolled institution, and rebelliousness against adults in general is expressed as rebelliousness against school in specific. This rebelliousness, according to many observers, does not express itself on the individual level, but becomes a collective expression in the form of peer involvement. The Lane County Youth Project measured the extent of peer contacts and found that the more extensive such contacts were, the more likely the young person was to drink.[33] (See table 17-6.)

---

[33] Reference 28.

TABLE 17–6. Incidence of Drinking Among Adolescent Males According to
the Amount of Time per Week Spent with Friends (in
per cent).

	No Nights Per Week	1 or 2 Nights Per Week	3 or More Nights Per Week
Nondrinkers	73	57	35
Occasional Drinkers	21	32	41
Regular Drinkers	3	6	16
Unknown	3	5	9
Total	100	100	100
N=	(132)	(480)	(168)

Kenneth Polk, *Drinking and the Adolescent Culture,* mimeographed research
report (Eugene, Oregon, Lane County Youth Project, December, 1964).

This and other findings were taken by the researcher as indication
that a peer culture with collective habits did in fact exist.[34] Since school
is only one manifestation of the adult culture, the youth's alienation
would be expected to show when they were confronted by other adult
agencies or agents as well. Parents are certainly among the adult agents
whom teen-agers invariably have to confront. Consistent with the anti-
adult hypothesis, it was expected that youth strongly oriented toward the
peer subculture would exhibit greater "social distance" from their parents
than youth integrated to a lesser extent in their peer group. This issue
was tested in two ways. First, nearly 800 subjects were asked to state
whether they would join a club in opposition to parental wishes. Second,
they were asked whether their parents knew of their whereabouts and
activities. The responses to both items were then compared to the respondents' drinking habits. Both tests supported the hypothesis that degree of parent-alienation is directly correlated to degree of drinking
involvement.[35] (See tables 17–7 and 17–8.)

The question concerning the relationship between youthful drinking
and delinquency has rarely been satisfactorily answered. A main difficulty involved is the failure to state the question in a clear manner. If
delinquency is understood as an individual act violating legal rules, then
most underage drinking would automatically be defined as delinquency.
But if the question aims at knowing whether drinking is associated with
other acts of delinquency, then the answer depends on *what type* of
delinquency. A recent monograph, summarizing delinquency research
in the United States, noted that drinking is not a typically central activity

[34] Kenneth Polk, *op. cit.*, p. 26.
[35] *Ibid.*, pp. 18–19.

TABLE 17-7. Incidence of Drinking Among Adolescent Males According to Responses to the Hypothetical Question: "Let's Say You had Always Wanted to Belong to a Particular Club in School, and then Finally You were Asked to Join. But then You Found out that your Parents Didn't Approve of The Group. Do You Think You would. . .?" (in per cent)

	Definitely Join Anyway	Probably Join	Probably Not Join	Definitely Not Join
Nondrinkers	30	42	63	70
Occasional Drinkers	47	41	28	21
Regular Drinkers	15	10	5	5
Unknown	8	7	4	4
Total	100	100	100	100
N =	(64)	(220)	(389)	(101)

Kenneth Polk, *Drinking and the Adolescent Culture,* mimeographed research report (Eugene, Oregon, Lane County Youth Project, December, 1964).

TABLE 17-8. Incidence of Drinking Among Adolescent Males According to Their Agreement with the Statement: "My Parents Always Know Where I am and What I am Doing." (in per cent)

	Agree Strongly Or Somewhat	Slightly Agree Or Disagree	Disagree Strongly or Somewhat
Nondrinkers	65	54	36
Occasional Drinkers	29	36	41
Regular Drinkers	5	7	17
Unknown	1	3	6
Total	100	100	100
N =	(385)	(219)	(176)

Kenneth Polk, *Drinking and the Adolescent Culture,* mimeographed research report (Eugene, Oregon, Lane County Youth Project, December, 1964).

or focus of the delinquent *gang*. Delinquent gangs usually do not make the regular and heavy use of alcohol a condition for group acceptance. On the contrary, it appears that inebriation and the dulling effect of alcohol are considered undesirable and dysfunctional to the welfare of such groups and therefore discouraged.[36] On the other side, research has

---

[36] Richard A. Cloward and Lloyd E. Ohlin, *Delinquency and Opportunity: A Theory of Delinquent Gangs* (Glencoe, Ill., The Free Press, 1960), chapter 15.

indicated that drinking and delinquency are positively correlated. The conclusion that appears logical is that alcohol-associated delinquency is usually not the type that is gang-related. Exactly what type of delinquency is correlated with drinking has not yet been clearly stated. The Lane County Youth Project does present correlations on drinking and delinquency but describes the latter simply in terms of "appearance of youth in police or juvenile court records for any offense other than a traffic violation."[37] The research continues then to report significant parallels between drinking and two types of problem behavior, one type constituting official delinquency as described above and the other, behavioral problems as perceived by teachers. Teen-agers in either problem category show a considerably higher use of alcoholic beverages than "normal" youth. The subjects were, in addition, divided into dropouts and in-school youth. It is interesting to note that the teen-agers with the highest rate of regular or occasional drinking were the in-school problem students with 73%, followed by the dropout delinquents with 67%, the in-school delinquents with 61%, the dropout nondelinquents with 53%, and, finally, the "normal" in-school youth with 36%.[38] (See table 17-9.)

It must be understood that the type of "drinking" that was the subject matter of the above studies is rarely a problem in itself. It is *asso-*

TABLE 17–9.   Incidence of Drinking Among Adolescent Males Comparing "Normal" Youth and "Problem" Youth, Including Delinquents, Dropouts, and Youth Seen by Their Teachers as "Behavioral Problems." (in per cent)

	Dropouts [1]		In-School Youth		
				Nominated	
		Non-		Behavioral	"Normal"
	Delinquent	delinquent	Delinquent	Problems	Youth
Nondrinkers	33	47	29	21	59
Occasional Drinkers	63	38	39	46	31
Regular Drinkers	4	15	22	27	5
Unknown	0	0	10	6	5
Total	100	100	100	100	100
N=	(27)	(26)	(93)	(33)	(665)

[1] Data were gathered from interviews conducted with a group of 53 male youth who had withdrawn from high school prior to graduation.

Kenneth Polk, *Drinking and the Adolescent Culture,* mimeographed research report (Eugene, Oregon, Lane County Youth Project, December, 1964).

---

[37] Kenneth Polk, *op. cit.,* p. 22.
[38] *Ibid.*

ciated with certain problems, thereby becoming characteristic of certain teen-agers, but is rarely a problem that can be called an *alcoholic* problem. In other words, the question of alcoholism is a different issue and is the exception rather than the rule among teen-agers. And yet some teen-agers, a small minority of those who drink, do so as a *prelude* to serious alcoholism. Preliminary detection of such youths might be based on a number of the above-reported correlations. But deep-seated and less explicit psychological complexes may play a decisive role. How can teen-agers with this type of psychological burden be identified? Most experts believe that pre-alcoholics are characterized by elements of basic personality imbalance. In the case of the adolescent the numerous anxieties associated with the ordinary problems of moving toward adult status constitute a basic invitation to escapist bevhaior. If this situation is complicated by the unavailability of legitimate social resources for the development and maintenance of a conception of self that is satisfactory to him and others, he may attempt to deal with this inadequacy by joining juvenile gangs or organized crime, becoming identified with deviant groups, or engaging in such escapist behavior as the use of narcotics or alcohol. In other words, such basic needs as a sense of security, belonging, and identity, if not met in a normal setting and in a legal manner, may lead to substitute or escapist actions. A Wayne University study selected for thorough examination of personal and social characteristics a number of boys under 18 years of age who had had a police record of drunkenness. These apparent candidates for alcoholism differed from other boys in that they (1) had poorer school relations and more antagonistic attitudes toward their teachers and classmates; (2) received more failing grades; (3) came from broken homes; (4) exhibited either indifferent or hostile attitudes toward their homes; (5) failed to attend church; (6) did not use public recreational facilities; and (7) had parents who were described by investigating police officers as indifferent or antagonistic.[39]

In summary, before one can start listing characteristics of teen-age "drinkers," it is necessary to specify the *degree* of the teen-ager's involvement with alcohol, since certain social and personal characteristics are covariant with the degree of drinking. The involvement with alcohol can be visualized as a matter of degree, varying on a continuum from (1) relatively harmless, occasional drinking, consisting of nothing more than a mere imitation of a permissible adult custom; to (2) peer-associated drinking that has overtones of rebelliousness against and alienation from adult institutions; to (3) heavy "escapist" drinking symp-

---

[39] William W. Wattenberg and John B. Moir, *Teen-Age Drinkers*, multilithed (Social Science Research Center, Wayne University, 1955).

tomatic of serious personality problems. Harmless and occasoinal drinking is primarily correlated with sex and age, implying that modest consumption of alcohol by boys and older teen-agers tends to be culturally condoned. The more rebellious and delinquency-prone drinkers are characterized by rejective and hostile attitudes toward adult institutions, showing especially in poor school performance and greater social distance from parents. The heavy teen-age drinkers, possibly at the beginning of careers as alcoholics, are characterized by a psychological imbalance prompting them to seek escape through the medium of alcohol. This last group represents, fortunately, a small minority of the adolescent users of alcohol.

Opiates. Since opiates differ qualitatively from alcohol and other drugs, what type of teen-ager would use them and take the chance of becoming addicted?

In a few instances, teen-agers have to use narcotic drugs continually during an extended illness of to relieve painful injuries. They are classified as "accidental" or "medical" addicts. These youngsters are otherwise —psychologically—healthy and normal, and reasonably satisfied with themselves and adjusted to their social environment. Taking drugs is for them not so much a "kick" or "thrill" as a feeling of relaxation and release from pain. Only a small per cent of the known addicts suffers from this type of medical addiction. A study including 1,000 addicts at the federal hospital in Lexington, Kentucky, discovered that only 5% of them had become addicted through medical treatment.[40]

A typical illustration of medical addiction is Charles, a 19-year-old college student who woke up one morning suffering pain so excruciating and paralyzing that he was unable to move. Later in the hospital, doctors continued to give him increased doses of morphine to relieve the pain caused by kidney stones. When Charles was finally released from the hospital, his kidneys cured and functioning painlessly, he found that he could not stop taking morphine without becoming sick from *withdrawal symptoms*. Not wanting to continue the use of the drug illegally, Charles submitted to legal treatment immediately and was successfully cured. Since he had no special emotional problems, he was not motivated to continue using the drug voluntarily.

A much larger proportion of teen-age addicts form a dangerous and expensive drug dependence because of feelings of insecurity, inadequacy, and anxiety. This type of teen-ager appears unable to feel happy and relaxed, no matter how hard he tries, and usually deserves the definition of neurotic. He feels that he is faced with problems and conflicts that he

---

[40] Victor H. Vogel and Virginia E. Vogel, *Facts About Narcotics* (Chicago, Science Research Associates, Inc., 1951), p. 20.

cannot solve. From an outside observer's point of view, the problems may appear simple and exaggerated, not warranting the anxiety displayed; but for the neurotic teen-ager they loom threateningly, producing a feeling of powerlessness and anxiety.

Among the multitude of potential escape avenues—alcohol, criminality, constructive sublimations, etc.—he somehow happens onto narcotics. The medical officer in charge of the Public Health Service Hospital in Lexington reports some typical explanations given by such neurotic drug addicts:

> After my folks got divorced I just didn't care any more, and heroin made me forget my troubles.
>
> I was sick and missed a lot of work—drugs made me feel better.
>
> My girl quit me and I started running with a gang of addicts to get even with her.
>
> I had a chip on my shoulder after my dad died because he was the only friend I had. I was trying to get even with someone—the world, I guess.
>
> When my husband left me I worried a lot. Then I started taking drugs. They relaxed me and I didn't care any more, but I'm worse off now than I was before.[41]

Another addiction-prone type of teen-ager is the psychopathic adolescent. His emotions are deficient in those qualities that make man a social, sympathetic, and compassionate human being. He is extremely antisocial, egotistic, lacking in respect for the welfare of others, and rejecting the norms and values of the group. Once a psychopath sets himself a goal, he will pursue it without regard to the welfare of others, elbowing his way through life completely indifferent to the distress he causes. Because the psychopath symptomatizes his condition in social relations, experts have come to interchangeably call him *sociopath*.[42] In contrast to the deficiencies in emotional ability, the cognitive ability of the psychopath is not impaired. While he seems unable to learn proper social sentiments, he is quite adroit in controlling his actions and impulses to avoid suspicion, detection, and punishment. In other words, he knows right from wrong perfectly well, but does not have the *emotional* motivation to differentiate between them in his own actions. An adolescent with this type of personality uses opiates for the pleasure or "thrill" they give him and tends to use them as long as he can do so with impunity and without regard for the consequences his actions may have on others.

---

[41] Vogel and Vogel, *op. cit.*, p. 23.

[42] Hervey Checkley, *The Mask of Sanity* (St. Louis, The C. V. Mosby Co., 1964), pp. 8–9.

A case study describes how Robert, a young boy diagnosed as psychopathic, arrived at the use of heroin:

> From the time he was 8 until the age of 11 he lived with an unreasonably strict, unmarried aunt. His mother was ill and couldn't take care of him. During this time he was very cruel to younger children and to pets. He was also suspected of starting several fires in the neighborhood. At 14, he quit school in spite of the efforts of his parents and the school authorities to get him to remain. He spent his time with older boys and men who stole tools from construction jobs. At 15, he was sent to reform school where he caused a great deal of trouble. At 16, he ran away and joined a cheap carnival where he helped operate a crooked gambling wheel. At 17, he started using heroin because his friends recommended it for a "thrill" and at 18, he was finally arrested for peddling drugs. His only reason for using heroin was, "I like it and it's nobody's business if I use drugs."[43]

A third possible explanation concerning the origin of teen-age addiction deals with collective inducement, the encouragement and pressure exerted by the peer group. Involvement with an adolescent subculture that has established the use of certain drugs as the norm of the in-group can sometimes influence a teen-ager who is relatively normal and nondelinquent. This teen-ager has neither desire nor need for the drugs, but becomes the victim of his association with a group of young addicts who persuade him to try them. A large portion of the teen-age addicts at Lexington have been found to be "victims by persuasion." These essentially normal and nondelinquent boys and girls go along with the gang to be acceptable to the members. Some explain their experience in this way:

> I got curious from being around others who were using it so I started.
>
> I was getting along all right without any drugs but they said I was "chicken" if I didn't try 'em.
>
> They had sort of a club in my school and you couldn't belong if you didn't smoke marihuana, and pretty soon we were all using heroin instead of marihuana.
>
> For a long time heroin only made me sick but I kept using it so I could go with the gang.[44]

The majority of these teen-agers had no delinquency record prior to their addiction. After the addiction was established, however, their dependence on the drug led them to commit crimes in order to continue its use.

---

43 Vogel and Vogel, *op. cit.*, p. 25.
44 *Ibid.*, p. 21.

Not all peer-related drug addiction evolves as a consequence of "friendly persuasion." A significant proportion of teen-age addicts have joined deviant gangs because of their personality problems and the profound gratification derived from the combination of the reinforcing group environment and the drug-induced euphoria. At one and the same time, they thereby acquire status in an in-group and find a medium, usually heroin, through which to alleviate their anxieties. Understandably, these are the most difficult cases to detect and cure. Their group environment provides shelter, refuge, and reinforcement, and their personality problems oppose discontinuation of the drug. Sooner or later, the deviant gang environment becomes the terminal environment for the neurotic teen-ager using drugs—that is, terminal *prior* only to the hospital or the prison.

In addition to the psychological traits mentioned above, recent sociological studies have revealed that youthful drug addicts are characterized by a consistent pattern of background features. The ecological distribution of drug additcion probably is the most conspicuous feature among the findings. Studies in New York, Chicago, Detroit, and other large cities have shown a persistent and clear relationship between dilapidated and overcrowded living conditions and drug addiction. The inhabitants of these slum areas are persons of lower socioeconomic and minority-group status and are characterized by high rates of other types of social pathology, such as delinquency, dropping out of school, truancy, unemployment, family disintegration, poverty, etc.[45] It is also in this sort of neighborhood that addiction has reached collective dimension in terms of subcultures or delinquent gangs. For example, a number of the gangs on the Lower East Side of New York City, that were known to use addictive drugs, mostly heroin and cocaine, included the Ballerinos, Smith Boys, Centaurians, Eastmen, Persians, and Viscounts.[46] The addiction-proneness in these neighborhoods was traced not only to purely socioeconomic factors, but to a peculiar cultural climate. An attitude survey indicated that high-use neighborhoods were characterized by a pervasive outlook on life that can be described as pessimistic antisocial hedonism.[47]

It is obvious by now that there is ro single "type" among addicts. Typification is complicated since the types may range from the "accidental" to the neurotic, psychopathic, or subcultural addict. The son of a rich businessman contracting addiction to morphine in the hospital

[45] Isidor Chein *et al.*, *The Road to H: Narcotics, Delinquency, and Social Policy* (New York, Basic Books, 1964), p. 78.

[46] *A Proposal for the Prevention and Control of Delinquency by Expanding Opportunities* (New York, Mobilization for Youth, Inc., 1962), p. 8.

[47] Chein *et al., op. cit.*, p. 92.

is a quite different type, sociologically and psychologically, from the poverty-stricken minority group member enmeshed in a delinquent and heroin-addict subculture. Nevertheless, some degree of generalization adolescents in certain socioeconomic environments run a relatively greater risk of encountering and using narcotics than do those in other social settings. In addition, there appears to be further selectivity in these high-risk categories, insofar as it is the more troubled, neurotic, and psychopathic youth who takes up drugs.

Hallucinogens. It is extremely difficult to answer the question of what type of youngster would use hallucinogenic drugs. The difficulty is compounded by the fact that this category includes a number of drugs differing in potency, that the various subtypes attract a variety of users, and that the depth of involvement varies greatly among them. It is safe to make the nondescript generalization that, just as in the case of alcohol and other drugs, hallucinogens attract the troubled, maladjusted, and unstable. However, more than alcohol or any other drug, psychedelic drug are of particular attraction to the curious and intellectual. Another peculiarity associated with the use of hallucinogens is a higher degree of group-relatedness and peer involvement than in the case of other drugs.

To provide the discussion with logical order, it appears reasonable to divide the vast range of users of hallucinogens into three main categories: the *fun users,* the *troubled users,* and the *intellectual users.* Although these classes overlap, the seriousness of involvement and the type of psychedelic drug used tend to differ markedly among them.

The *fun users* are ordinarily not pathological or chronically delinquent. Most probably, they are relatively normal teen-agers whose acquaintance with the drug consists of a single experiment or some occasional episodes. They do it for entertainment, enjoying the "play" of perceptions under the influence of the hallucinogen. Their "play" and experimentation are motivated by a more or less innocuous curiosity to "see what happens," or, more frequently, by inducement and invitation on the part of peers. In fact, surveys have discovered that many one-time or occasional users are merely complying with group pressure. These conformist users have no real need themselves to use and to continue using the drug. A Massachusetts high school sophomore who extricated herself from a group of marijuana users reported: "I tried marijuana because of curiosity. I was friendly with a whole group of kids who were considered hippies. However, after a few weeks I realized these people were either mixed up or were hoping they were."[48] She eventually quit the group with plans to never use drugs again. This statement is typical

---

[48] Alice Lake, "Drugs: A Student Report," *Seventeen* (September, 1966), p. 254.

of numerous reports of teen-agers who became involved with "pot" or LSD, virtually involuntarily. Once enmeshed in a group of marijuana users, a compelling image of the user is projected; it is "cool" or "boss" to use the drug, and well-known beat authors or songsters are held up as models worth emulation. An 18-year-old freshman in New York who once had been swept along by this cultist type of subculture believes that not even stable teen-agers are immune from the drug habit and relates that "at the beginning drugs seem very romantic. You see pretty girls taking drugs. You see people who look like Bob Dylan taking drugs, and you think you can be like them."[49]

Acceptance into this type of deviant peer group is based on joining the drug habit. The process of becoming initiated into the subculture of the marijuana users was investigated by sociologist Howard S. Becker.[50] His study emphasizes that the power of symbols plays a significant role in helping the beginner learn the habit, recognize the effects of the drugs, and perceive them as pleasurable. It takes *others* to convey to the novice how he should interpret the sensations resultant from smoking "pot." Without this "coaching-in-perception," the beginner may not only fail to detect the symptoms of marijuana but even fail to find them pleasurable. His initiated friends tell him about the quality of feeling "high" and that it is a "great" feeling.

> The novice, then, eager to have this feeling, picks up from other users some concrete referents of the term "high" and applies these notions to his own experience. The new concepts make it possible for him to locate these symptoms among his own sensations and to point out to himself a "something different" in his experience that he connects with drug use. It is only when he can do this that he is high.[51]

The above descriptions and reports bring out one important fact, experimentation with hallucinogenic drugs is usually a group phenomenon. This is particularly true in the case of marijuana.

The collectivizing tendency of marijuana has become noticeable on high school and college campuses. In the mid-sixties, there were numerous arrests and raids on the big campuses of the nation. For example, in 1966, nineteen students were arrested for drug violation at the Ohio State University. A few weeks later, a score of Pennsylvania State University students, one aged 17, were arrested for using marijuana. Similar disturbances and raids took place at Brandeis, Brown, Cornell, the Univer-

---

[49] Reference 48.

[50] Howard S. Becker, "Becoming A Marihuana User," *American Journal of Sociology,* Vol. 59 (November, 1953), pp. 235–42.

[51] *Ibid.,* p. 238.

sity of California, the University of Miami College in New York, and others.[52] Besides these official violators, caught in the statistics of the police, a majority of cases go either undetected or unpublicized. In 1967, it was estimated that marijuana had found its way to every major college campus and large high school in the country.

Psychedelic drugs tend to be of greater interest to middle-class teenagers who are relatively more curious and desirous to experiment than to lower-class adolescents who might prefer such escapist drugs as alcohol and opiates, which provide them with instant amnesia concerning the surrounding squalor and poverty. This hypothesis is supported by the earlier-mentioned inquiry into drug habits of high school students in the upper-middle socioeconomic community of Great Neck, N.Y.[53] The 1967 study revealed a surprisingly deep drug involvement among youth with affluent and prestigious family backgrounds, shattering illusions that the public as well as social scientists may have had about a presumed upper-middle-class "immunity" against extensive youthful drug violations. Additional supporting data came from a 1966 survey of *Seventeen* Magazine, sampling more than 1,000 subscribing girls.[54] The readership of this magazine is recruited primarily from the middle- and upper- socioeconomic classes. A surprisingly high rate of drug experimentation was discovered among these girls. About 6% of the subjects had used drugs for other than medicinal purposes at least once. Half of these "experimenters" had used marijuana, 75% of them between the ages of 15 and 17, 18% at 14 or younger, the rest at age 18 and older. 30% of these girls were still using drugs at the time of the survey. This means approximately 1 in every 60 girls in the sample was taking illicit drugs.[55] Comparable estimates for boys, who have been found to compare with females in a 4 to 1 ratio in drinking and most illicit drugs uses, would amount to 1 in every 15. One may expect that again at least half of these boys experimented with marijuana, implying that 1 in every 30 boys has experimented with it at least once. It must be remembered that these estimates concern middle and upper social classes and that the proportion of teen-age drug users in the lower classes remains a matter of conjecture.

The *troubled users* usually form the core of the deviant subculture. They engage in sustained use of the hallucinogenic drugs because of personality problems. They are usually the "elders" of the group who introduce nonusers, often relatively normal youth, to their ranks, and they

---

[52] Lake, *op. cit.*, p. 253.
[53] *Guide Post, op. cit.*
[54] Lake, *op. cit.*
[55] *Ibid.*, p. 170.

frequently fall into the category of alienated youngsters popularly called *hippies*. Their alienation from society is symbolized not only by indulgence in prohibited drugs but also by exhibition of nonconformist clothes and hair styles. Many of them tend to couch their personality problems in rationalizations that make the adult society their favorite scapegoat. These deviant and thoroughly maladjusted adolescents manifest their dissatisfaction and hostility in a rebelliousness that sometimes makes use of prohibited drugs. Their affinity for drugs is therefore not so much a result of curiosity about bizarre effects of hallucinogens as rebelliousness and a desire to have status and security in a close-knit in-group. In some cases, their alienation is so deep that they feel absolutely powerless to do something about the course of current events in the world, and they develop a fatalistic attitude. A college student described several alienated friends who used marijuana and peyote regularly. "With them it's not just a healthy rebellion but a basic malaise. They don't do it for kicks. These kids don't think there are any thrills left. It's more than boredom. It's partly a feeling of helplessness, that everything is wrong with their world and that there's nothing they can do about it."[56]

Often these alienated youngsters exhibit astonishing sophistication and know-how in intellectualizing their condition, in the process often siding with political or philosophical views opposed to and extremely unpopular with current middle-class standards.

The troubled users are the perpetuators of the argot of the drug world. In the mid-1960's, a marijuana cigarette was a "joint;" a "nickel bag" was five dollars worth of loose marijuana tobacco; an "acid-head" took a "trip," but a "pot-head" was likely to "turn on." This argot, more than any other indication, suggested the existence of a deviant subculture.

There is reason to believe that troubled marijuana users are ready candidates for more serious types of drugs. Many boys and girls who have become habituated to marijuana or any other hallucinogenic drug try opiates—and some "get hooked" and change from habituation to addiction. Usually it starts out with someone in the group suggesting that it is "cool" or "in" to try heroin, and he dares others to try it. He assures them that the sensation is much better than the mild effects of marijuana. The dynamics of small group interaction again play a vital role in winning adherents to the new drug.

While official statistics on the problem of troubled users are nonexistent, Dr. Gerald L. Klerman of the Yale University Medical School estimated that at least 10% of the students at such large urban univer-

---

[56] Lake, *op. cit.*, p. 252.

sities as Harvard, Berkeley, Stanford, etc., are *chronic* users.[57] Whether chronicness can be equated with troubledness is of course a question that remains to be verified by empirical research.

The *intellectual users* of hallucinogens are probably in the minority. These teen-agers take a serious and studious interest in psychedelic drugs, attempting to find out whether these chemicals can heighten creativity and deepen insights into one's own personality and into the world without. Intellectual users are more likely to experiment with potent LSD, mescaline, or psilocybin than with marijuana.

This type of user has most probably heard about the psychedelic possibilities of LSD through academic communication. He may have followed the public debates—or polemics—of Drs. Timothy Leary and Richard Alpert, erstwhile Harvard psychologists, and become impressed with their theory that psychedelic drugs are instrumental in expanding human consciousness to a degree that makes fuller use of man's brain potential. Their argument, basically neurological, is that the over ten billion cells in the human brain are vastly underused and that psychedelic drugs like LSD have the power to revolutionize man's mental capacity.[58]

The intellectual user may also be interested in the application drugs are currently finding in religious research. Psychiatrist Walter Pahnke, who holds a Harvard theology degree, and his associate William Richards, who has a degree in the psychology of religion, contend that through the use of high-powered psychedelic drugs, such as psilocybin, mescaline, and LSD, it is now possible to induce a state of mind resembling or duplicating mystical consciousness. Experiments under strict laboratory controls have been conducted with a group of divinity students at Boston University, demonstrating that "instant mysticism" is possible.[59] A similar source of incitement for the imagination of some religious teenagers may be the peyote cult of the semi-Christian Native American Church, drawing its membership from the Navaho Indians, who use mescaline-containing peyote cacti at their religious meetings.

The intellectual user tends to be the older adolescent or young adult, most likely enrolled in an institution of higher education, less dependent upon subcultural learning and pressure, and more likely to be undetected

---

[57] Gerald L. Klerman, M. D., Yale University Medical School, personal correspondence (November, 1966).

[58] Timothy Leary, Richard Alpert, and Ralph Metzner, "Rationale of the Mexican Psychedelic Training Center," in Richard Blum (ed.), *Utopiates* (New York, Atherton Press, 1965), pp. 178–86.

[59] Walter N. Pahnke and William A. Richards, "Implications of LSD and Experimental Mysticism," *Journal of Religion and Health,* Vol. 5 (July, 1966), pp. 175–208.

in his experimentations. In the absence of any statistics, it can only be conjectured that they are the small minority among the users of hallucinogens.

Questions of Law, Prevention, and Cure

Society has a definite stake in the productivity and efficiency of its members and goes to great lengths to preserve and maintain these qualities. Most, if not all, of the chemicals under discussion are considered to detract from and reduce man's ability to carry out his social obligations and make creative contributions. In an effort to stem and control detrimental consequences arising from the use of these drugs, laws have been established. These regulations aim to prevent excessive and inappropriate use of the drugs. They spell out under what conditions, if any, these drugs may be taken. The conditions usually include such factors as age of user, quantity allowed to be taken at one time, and time and place in which it may be used.

Alcohol. In the case of alcohol, the American society maintains relatively relaxed and permissive regulations. All adults are generally permitted to drink. There are some rules, either by law or etiquette, that prohibt drinking in certain public places, such as parks, fairs, streets, and campuses. But in other places, such as bars, restaurants, and homes, drinking is allowed, although often restricted to certain hours. These curfews must be observed under penalty of law. In the home, providing neighbors are not disturbed, drinking is virtually unrestricted. However, excessive drinking is penalized; a person found intoxicated in a public place is subject to arrest. The age at which society declares a person eligible for drinking differs among the states, but generally it is either 18 or 21. Underage drinking is considered delinquency.

Teen-agers are aware of these restrictions and know that an identification card is needed to purchase alcoholic beverages legally and that being caught drinking or possessing alcohol may mean reprimand for themselves and for their parents. However, awareness does not seem to serve as a powerful deterrent, but merely as an invitation to caution. Studies have shown that teen-agers desirous of drinking can secure alcoholic beverages relatively easily at home, at the grocery store, via a friend of legal age, or by means of a forged or borrowed ID card. It has also been observed that the self-image of drinking teen-agers is free from such connotations as "law-breaker" or "delinquent" and that they tend to judge drinking more in situational than moralistic terms. This is not surprising, considering the extensive as well as intensive use of the mass media for advertising alcoholic beverages and the general permissiveness concerning adult drinking, which demonstrates that alcohol consumption is both accepted and customary.

Opiates. American narcotic laws, in effect, define adult addicts as criminals and teen-age addicts as delinquents. This stringent view is primarily the result of the Harrison Act passed by Congress in 1914 and various supplementary statutes added since then. Unauthorized use, possession, sale, or transfer of drugs is severely punished. Heroin, for example, is altogether barred from the United States and may be neither produced nor possessed. Politicians and legislators have been particularly concerned about the involvement of minors in the use and traffic of illicit drugs and have promoted formidable measures to protect youth from addictive drugs. Congressional investigation in the mid-1950's led to the enactment of the Narcotics Control Act of 1956, which established mandatory sentences of high minimum for narcotic offenders, even permitting the death penalty for those selling narcotics to persons under 18. An example of the severity of punishment was demonstrated by Justice Aaron F. Goldstein of the New York State Supreme Court, who in 1964 sentenced a 21-year-old man to serve a minimum of 63 years in prison for peddling heroin to high school pupils. He was quoted as saying: "My only regret is that the state legislature has so far failed to prescribe the death penalty for this dastardly crime, which is worse than murder."[60]

Many observers, among them jurists and social scientists, have objected to such harsh legislation on the grounds that it insufficiently differentiates between addict and nonaddict peddlers, that it unreasonably intimidates and restricts physicians in treating addicts, and that it drives addicts underground, possibly into dealings with organized crime. Such legislation promotes the possibility that a youngster who gets involved with drugs will, as a consequence, acquire a self-perception of delinquent and later on join the ranks of a criminal subculture. Moreover, cut off from legal supplies of narcotics, the teen-age addict naturally seeks illicit drug sources. The demand stimulates the formation and operation of an extensive black market. The prospects of huge profits attract organized crime and make the risk involved in the manufacture and distribution of illicit drugs worthwhile. According to some estimates, the retail value of the opium-derived heroin may exceed more than 1,000 times the orginal price of the opium. For example, 10 kilograms of opium worth $350 at the source abroad sells, in the form of 5% heroin, for $410,000 at New York City price.[61] Since black market prices are exorbitant, they usually exceed the financial resources of the youthful

---

[60] AP Report (Sept. 30, 1964).
[61] Richard L. Williams, *The Drug Takers* (New York, Time Inc., 1965), p. 42.

addict and prompt him to try to obtain the means by delinquent behavior, such as stealing, robbing, burglarizing, prostituting, etc.

In spite of the severity of the laws, the prevention of addiction has not been very successful. Government estimates have placed the number of addicts in the vicinity of 55,000, but almost all nongovernmental experts agree that this figure greatly understates the real extent of the problem. Many expert observers feel that American laws have not been at all successful in eliminating addiction, but have instead compounded and complicated the problem by stimulating additional acts of delinquency, deepening the addicts' immersion in addict subcultures, and encouraging the formation of huge underground drug operations.

A dysfunction of stringent antinarcotic laws that is of particular interest to sociologists is the breeding of specialized subcultures. It is usually through subcultures that teen-agers are induced to take drugs, become addicted, and join the deviant group. Such subcultures carry out two main functions, the "circulatory" and the "survival" functions. The former refers to the system of roles and interrelationships through which addicts secure illicit drugs. With few exceptions, such as the physician-addict relationship of the well-to-do and influential addict, whose "legitimate" source is a pharmacist or doctor, all addicts are forced to enter the complex network of the underground in order to have access to drugs. The "survival" function includes such features as rationalizations and ideologies that justify the addiction, defensive communication (including argot), warning systems, ritualistic and cyclic patterns, the attractive personal relationships, and the recruiting process.

It is the recruiting process that is of great relevance to the discussion on teen-agers. The addict members of the subculture, equally or even more completely than the nonaddict peddlers, are responsible for introducing teen-agers to drug-taking. In essence, then, some observers feel that inadequate narcotic legislation, based more on emotional overbearance than social-scientific insight, breeds subcultures which recruit teen-agers and thereby perpetuate the drug problem in America.

Hallucinogens. As was mentioned earlier, the popular discovery—or, better, rediscovery—of hallucinogenic drugs is currently causing a considerable stir among social scientists, medical experts, legislators, and politicians. Actually, the knowledge about and the use of hallucinogenic drugs is nothing new and has been widespread throughout the ages—mostly with impunity and legal tolerance. Marijuana, for example, has been known in various forms throughout many parts of the world. As a derivative of the hemp plant, it is known as *hashish, bhang, charas,* etc. It is estimated that in the 1930's roughly 200 million people throughout

the world were users of one or another form of marijuana.[62] Mescaline
has been ingested in the context of the peyote cult, using the small
peyote cactus of the Rio Grande Valley. Mushrooms containing psilocybin have been eaten in religious rituals by natives of southern Mexico.
Generally speaking, the use of these drugs appears to have had no
harmful effect on cultural standards or social well-being among the
respective peoples.

What is it then that explains the extraordinary reaction to these
drugs in contemporary American society? At least four major conditions
may help to explain the social sensitivity against popular use of hallucinogens. (1) It is not limited, as in the cases of the "sacred mushrooms"
and the peyote cult among the Native American Church, to religious
rituals where the effects are institutionalized and, thus, socially controlled. (2) Unlike other cultures in past years, these drugs are no longer
limited to adults, but have reached youth who, it is assumed, respond
with a lesser degree of social responsibility to the drug's effects. (3) New,
extremely powerful hallucinogens have been discovered, LSD and the
so-called STP, the effects of which surpass any heretofore known hallucinogenic chemicals. (4) In general, customs—by definition characterized
by irrational elements—simply do not favor the use of such perception-
altering drugs in the United States.

In spite of these clearly antagonistic social forces, the American
society was not prepared to cope with the recent upsurge in the use
of hallucinogenic drugs. No decisive federal legislation, except in the
case of the mildest of the hallucinogenic drugs, marijuana, had been in
existence. In a sense, this situation represented a striking instance of
cultural lag. Predictably, this lag was made up in time by pertinent
legislation. In 1968, stricter federal laws were passed. Before 1968, in the
absence of sufficient federal legislation, about half of the states had
enacted laws against possession of LSD. New York in 1965, and California and Nevada in 1966, were among the first states to add prohibitory
statutes concerning LSD to their criminal codes. A number of other
states followed suit. However, as late as 1967, there was reluctance on
the part of the Food and Drug Administration to recommend a decisive
prohibition in regard to LSD. The FDA's official stand was indicated in
1966 by Commissioner James L. Goddard in his testimony before a
Senate subcommittee. He explained that the FDA's reluctance was
prompted by practical circumstances and warned that if a strict law
were passed, roughly 10% of the college students would have to be
placed in the category of criminals and would be driven underground,

---

[62] Lawrence Kolb, *Drug Addiction* (Springfield, Ill., Charles C Thomas, 1962),
p. 156.

thus making it difficult to find and treat those suffering from dangerous psychotic effects; and the pursuit of legitimate research with LSD would be greatly hindered.[63]

Instead of enacting official laws, Commissioner Goddard was in favor of applying more informal methods to stop the increased use of LSD. He sent a letter to deans of men and women, campus housing administrators, and heads of science departments at more than 2,000 colleges and universities, urging them to help combat the "insidious and dangerous" experimentations on the part of students. He admitted his deep concern with a "most hazardous situation," emphasizing that "unless strong concerted action is taken, an untold number of our students may suffer permanent mental and physical injury."[64]

Irrational elements in law and custom. From the above discussion one can see that during the mid-1960's the most powerful of the hallu-cinogens, LSD, was relatively unchecked by law and was easily accessi-ble to teen-agers. Strangely enough, marijuana, the mildest among the hallucinogenic chemicals, was and is thoroughly covered by law, and teen-agers using it are defined as "narcotic" offenders. Another character-istic of United States drug legislation is its permissive code in regard to alcohol and nicotine. Yet experts insist that the degree of danger and the lethal effects arising from the use of alcohol and tobacco are as high as or even markedly higher than in the case of marijuana. The extent to which public emotions about certain drugs can influence legal procedures was shown in the criticism leveled against the report of scientists in New York City when a committee, including a pharmacologist, a sociologist, a psychologist, and psychiatrists, made a comprehensive study of the effects of marijuana. Their report was severely attacked because it showed little evidence that juvenile delinquency, school problems, and crime were marijuana-induced. The role of marijuana as such an inducer had been played up in previous fare of the mass media.[65] Law enactment as well as law enforcement hardly so much as bothered to consider these findings in subsequent decisions and procedures; rather, they favored public emotions and myths.

An explanation for such apparent illogic in the legal code can be found in the principle that assumes that the emergence of most of our laws is a *crescive* process. Laws spring from the customs and ethics of the community and are therefore rarely the product of logical and scientific deliberations. This principle has been brought to the front in recent arguments over the question of LEMAR, "Legalize Marihuana."

[63] Warren R. Young and Joseph R. Hixson, *LSD on Campus* (New York, Dell Publishing Co., 1966), pp. 150–51.

[64] *Ibid.,* p. 17.

[65] Kolb, *op. cit.*

Young people supporting the LEMAR movement agree that it is an irrational inconsistency to allow the use of other dangerous drugs, notably alcohol, but stringently forbid the use of marijuana. A knowledgeable observer of this issue pointed out that more than five million Americans defined as alcoholics and additional millions of Americans under the influence of alcohol are responsible for a large proportion of the nation's marriage and family disintegration (drunkenness ranks high as a reason for divorce), disastrous accidents, homicidal violence, property damage, and other harmful behavior. The damage done under the influence of alcohol has been estimated to amount to $500,000,000 annually in the United States.[66] Yet use of alcohol remains relatively unrestricted. On the other side, the degree of toxicity or social harmfulness associated with marijuana is minor, if existent at all. Nevertheless, marijuana was banned in 1937, the prohibition was absolute, no exceptions are tolerated, and the teen-age user is branded a criminal or delinquent offender. Joel Fort thinks that this peculiar situation is the result of the irrational power structure of American society and an indication of the formidable might of lobbying that assures alcohol the status of a legal product.[67]

Consequences of this legal situation may include striking incongruities. For example, an adult who offers a youngsters a drink, thereby indirectly causing him to subsequently have a fatal automobile accident, may get away with a warning or a light fine. In contrast, an adult introducing a youngster to marijuana with no subsequent ill effects may be sent to a penal institution for many years or even the rest of his life.

Surveys indicate that a large number of teen-agers are aware of the legal irrationality and favor legalization of marijuana. They believe that it is a safe drug, free of harmful side effects, giving only pleasure. Typical responses of teen-agers defending their use of marijuana were: "Why do people social drink? I blow pot at parties not to rebel or to be different but because I enjoy it and don't feel that it is wrong." Or: "Under pot everything is very nice. Liquor gets you violent, but with pot you have a constant smile on your face."[68]

Confusing legal terminology. Such slogans as *Teen Dope Ring Exposed* or *Marijuana-Addicted Kids Nabbed* are well-known headlines of the daily press. In actuality the so-called "teen dope ring" turns out to consist of nothing but a few high school students who were found smoking "joints," i.e., marijuana cigarettes. The teen-agers became delinquents and narcotic offenders at the moment the police officers apprehended them. From a medical point of view, the reference "narcotic" is

---

[66] Joel Fort, "Social and Legal Responses to Pleasure-Giving Drugs," in Richard Blum (Ed.), *Utopiates* (New York, Atherton Press, 1965), pp. 205–23.

[67] *Ibid.*

[68] Lake, *op. cit.*, p. 249.

reserved to addictive opiates. Unfortunately the mixture of popular and legal phraseology has a tendency to expand this definition and label the use of any forbidden drug a narcotic offense. This confusion is carried over into legal and official statistics, thus making comparison between the extent of the use of opiates and that of marijuana and other drugs very difficult. This confusion also impairs reliable charting of trends, since the classification of narcotic offense, previously restricted to opiates, now includes the use of other types of drugs as well. In effect, this lack of specification renders police statistics nearly invalid and useless and makes interpretation impossible.

Such ill-advised references to teen-agers experimenting with marijuana as "dope addicts" and "narcotic offenders" has not only a confusing effect, but also a profound impact on the self-image of the teen-agers. By popular and legal assessment, they are "criminals" or at least "delinquents." Given the youths' knowledge of the potential destruction residing in a bottle of liquor and the relatively harmless effects of marijuana, they are prone to rebel against such labels, perceiving them as unwarranted discrimination, and they tend to develop a contempt for existing laws.

Beyond legislation: social and personal conditions. The persistence of the drug problem over the past decades suggests that laws alone do not represent an effective preventive reaction to the problem. Drinking and the use of illicit drugs usually are symptoms of deep-seated adverse conditions of personal or social nature. Trying to eliminate symptoms by punishing them is rarely effective; at best, only temporary and situational delay of the same or substitute symptom is effected. A lasting elimination of symptoms can only be achieved by elimination or thorough alteration of underlying causes.

Obviously, deep-reaching programs capable of changing such basic conditions are hardly in existence at this time. Discussing them is a Utopian exercise, a statement of ideal conditions which either will never come or will come only in the far future.

The idea of raising a generation of teen-agers who will not use illicit drugs is closely connected with the question of what makes them use the drugs originally. These generic conditions that a basic preventive attempt will have to take into consideration can be divided into personal, family, and general social problems. The main category among the personal problems is made up of teen-agers with excessive anxieties and frustrations. In their case, preventive efforts call for medical and psychological help. Their problems are emotional in nature, and mere legislation and law enforcement are likely to worsen their attitudes by adding punishment and rejection to hurt, thus driving them farther away from feeling understood and accepted. The causes for pathological personal reactions frequently spring from the teen-ager's family. In an era when the only permitted amateur is the parent, unskilled and irresponsible child-raising is a pernicious source of crippled personalities. Failure to equip the youngster with a viable identity and personal security almost invariably results in deviant or escapist activities that make the use of illicit drugs attractive and desirable. On the broader social level, as long as there are feelings of extreme relative deprivation among individuals of lower socioeconomic strata, there will be substitute and escapist behavior. As long as society fails to present acceptable incentives for creative and rewarding social contributions, rebellious and alienated substitutions may include illicit drugs. It is important, however, that these incentives and goals which society presents to young people *can* be materialized for the families of lower-class youth. If there are attractive goals without tangible and legally usable ways to achieve them, teen-agers face a type of *anomie* that is not only alienating but infuriating since they actually see the goals materialize for their peers with more influential and well-to-do parents.

In essence, then, effective prevention can occur only when policy implementation is preceded by a three-pronged gauging of the problem. For youngsters who have become addicted or drink excessively because of certain personality problems, some kind of direct therapy and counseling are indicated. Where family life is the source of the problem, some official measures should be taken to improve the quality of inter-parent and parent-child relations. Various socioeconomic ills that breed addict subcultures can only be attacked by broad federal and local-based social reforms.

After the fait accompli. In the face of the law's impotency to deter adolescents from using illicit drugs or engaging in excessive drinking, and in the absence of effective programs to eliminate underlying basic personal and social conditions that result in motivation to use illicit drugs, the only thing left to do after habituation or addiction has been established is to undergo the *cure*.

In the case of opiates, addicted teen-agers are placed into the many of the known Public Health Service hospitals at Lexington Kentucky, or Fort Worth, Texas. The comprehensive treatment in these institutions includes gradual withdrawal from the drugs, vocational and recreational activities, and limited psychotherapy. Besides the two federal hospitals, it is possible to obtain treatment in a few private or community hospitals and occasionally even on the basis of outpatient treatment. These types of medical treatment usually bypass police procedures and are probably initiated by responsible and well-to-do parents.

The extent of permanent cure from addiction through such formal institutions is not encouraging. It has been estimated that the failure of permanent cure at the federal hospitals in Lexington and Fort Worth has amounted to 75% of the dischargees. An even greater failure rate was discovered by a followup study by the Columbia University School of Public Health, finding that 91% of a group of 147 adolescents discharged from Riverside Hospital in New York returned to regular daily use of drug.[69] Such persistence in using drug suggests that environmental conditions underlie the addiction problem and that upon release from the hospital the teen-ager will relapse into his previous way of life. This relapse seems particularly frequent in the cases of teen-agers who had to submit to involuntary treatment and who tend to resume taking drugs because of rebellion and hostility against authorities.

An additional and more recent treatment possibility for adolescents opened up with the development of the Synanon Houses. In these centers, former addicts work with and live with current ones, helping them to withdraw from drugs and attempting gradually to win them over to antidrug attitudes and positive social values. This program is based on strong self-motivation and voluntary participation in group discussions and other sociological techniques. Although there are no definite statistics from the Synanon Foundation, the relapse rate is expected to be extremely low—primarily because treatment starts on a voluntary basis in the first place and, secondarily, because many patients become permanent members of the setup, thus substituting dependence on Synanon for dependence on drugs. This outcome characterizes Synanon more as a protective community than as a therapeutic program aimed at eventual reintegration of the patient into the outside world.

Unlike the case of narcotic addiction, the cure of alcoholism is less institutionalized, with hardly any compulsory measure in the statutes that could be used to coerce the alcoholic to submit to treatment. From some vantage points, this is a plausible laxity: after all, if mandatory cure were introduced, roughly six million Americans would crowd institutions. The lack of legal initiative also reflects, of course, the greater degree of customary acceptability of the alcoholic condition.

Teen-agers who are heavy drinkers, to a point approaching or achieving alcoholism, come to the attention of the authorities usually through only one symptom—drunkenness. In the state of intoxication, they are treated as delinquents and not as patients. As a delinquent the teen-ager or his parents may be reprimanded or lightly punished, but he is not retained for treatment. Unless parents, friends, or teachers take the initiative, the youngster may never be treated as a patient. Moreover, hardly any coercion can be applied. If treatment should materialize, the

---

[69] Alfred M. Freedman, "Treatment of Drug Addiction in a Community General Hospital," *Comprehensive Psychiatry*, Vol. 4 (June, 1963), p. 199.

cooperation of the teen-ager is required. If such cooperation is obtained, arrangement can be made to enter upon one or a mixture of several methods of treatment. The teen-ager may submit to medical treatment and take "Antibooze," any of a number of chemicals that will trigger a violent nausea at the moment alcohol is swallowed. However, unless the adolescent has enough self-motivation and willpower to overcome his compulsive drinking, antialcoholic medication will break down in the long run. It is more common to approach the problem by psychotherapy, to help the teen-ager understand the personality problem that underlies his compulsion to drink and to strengthen an identity strong enough to oppose alcoholic tendencies. However, in order for this method to be successful, long and extremely expensive treatment is called for.

A method, not only less expensive and of shorter duration but of even greater effectiveness, has been developed by sociologically oriented experts. Group therapy uses the power of group reinforcement to reorient the drinking adolescent. Again, however, this method depends on self-interest and the good will of the participant. This method will not appeal to the adolescent who is deeply antisocial and unwilling to change. Alcoholics Anonymous, in some respects a counterpart of the Synanon Foundation, has incorporated the basic elements of group therapy and the idea of fellowship. Again, this organization can be of help only to those who know about it, have the right connections, and, above all, have the will to change. Many adolescents, embarking on the career of alcoholism, have not yet realized that they are toying with a serious and possibly lifelong affliction. For many of them, heavy drinking and drunkenness is a form of rebellion that fulfills a need at that time. The need is pathological, a perilous substitution for mature and realistic need fulfillment. Unless definite efforts are made to correct this personality dysfunction, drinking will become a habitual and ultimately an addictive malady.

In the absence of basic preventive programs changing the life conditions of escapist-prone youths and in the absence of legal measures forcing alcoholic and pre-alcoholic adolescents to submit to treatment, alcoholism will most likely remain what it is now: America's largest and most widespread personal problem.

Summary

Of the chemicals that have been discussed, alcohol is the most widely used, with approximately 6 million alcoholics and 70 million additional users in the United States. The customary acceptance of alcoholic beverages is reflected in teen-agers' habits. Studies have shown that only a small minority of teen-agers abstain from alcohol and that this minority grows consistently smaller with progressing age. Factors significantly associated with teen-agers' atitudes toward, and actual use of, alcohol include sex, socioeconomic status, religious affiliation, peer involvement, school experiences, delinquency, and relationships with the parents. Drinking, being a "masculine" expression in the American culture, obviously is a habit more characteristic of boys than girls. Lower-class youngsters, assuming adult roles earlier in life than their middle- and upper-class counterparts, start drinking at an earlier age. The vast majority of Jewish and Catholic youth have relaxed and permissive attitudes toward drinking; Protestant youth show more hesitation; and the majority of the Mormon teen-agers abstain from alcohol. Incidence of drinking is directly correlated with the amount of time spent with peers. Academic performance is inversely correlated with drinking, i.e., drinking teen-agers earn more "D's" and "E's" than their nondrinking peers. Other aspects of school life, such as participation in extracurricular activities and the perception of education as being worthwhile, are similiarly related and form an overall syndrome of alienation. Youngsters classified as delinquent or problematic exhibit a higher rate of alcohol consumption than "normal" youth. However, there is lack of clarity as to what type of delinquency is alcohol-related. In any case, it does not seem to be the typical gang delinquency. Teen-agers who drink also show a greater degree of alienation from their parents.

Only 3% to 4% of the known narcotic addicts are persons under 21 years of age. However, it is suspected that these official statistics underestimate the narcotic problem among teen-agers. The majority of teenage addicts are members of subcultures that offer protection against detection; many more teen-agers experiment only occasionally and do not come to the attention of the authorities. Members of the lower socioeconomic class and of minority groups, such as Negro or Puerto Rican, are overrepresented among teen-age addicts.

The problem of hallucinogens appears to be concentrated on the academic campuses of the nation. One of the most powerful of the psychedelic drugs, LSD, has become of foremost concern to the authorities. No official statistics concerning the use of this drug are available, and estimates have been based largely on the unforeseen and often tragic effects of the drug. Teen-agers taking psychedelic drugs can be subdivided into fun users, troubled users, and intellectual users. The most precarious type is the troubled user, since he is a likely candidate for opiate experimentation—and addiction.

Current legislation is exceedingly lenient concerning alcohol consumption, extremely stringent concerning opiates, and markedly confused and unprepared concerning hallucinogens. Critics accuse the current narcotic laws of being illogical and unscientific, merely compounding the problem, unreasonably intimidating physicians in treating addicts, and driving users of illicit drugs underground to form deviant subcultures and to deal with organized crime. Particularly confusing is the legal terminology that defines use of any prohibited drug as a "narcotic" offense, thereby equating, for example, the use of marijuana with the use heroin. Many teen-agers object to this lack of discrimination and support the LEMAR movement. One of their most powerful arguments condemns the legal leniency concerning alcohol, holding it responsible for allowing and virtually inviting immense destruction and human tragedy.

Critics have argued that, rather than ineffectively legislating against use of certain drugs, the basic underlying personal, family, and social conditions that stimulate use of illicit drugs should be remedied. However, in the absence of such deep-reaching programs, the only remaining alternative is cure or rehabilitation once addiction or habituation has been established. In the case of narcotic addiction, a teen-ager is ordered to a medical center for treatment. Since hallucinogenic drugs do not cause addiction, cure or help becomes necessary only in instances of unforeseen post-LSD episodes. Alcohol-dependence does not incur mandatory cure, and a teen-ager may or may not consent to treatment. As a result, a teen-ager who exhibits clear signs of pre-alcoholism is likely to embark virtually unhindered on the career of an alcoholic.

summary, conclusions, and outlook

adolescence in perspective

Overview

The phenomenon of modern adolescence should not be viewed as a stage that has always existed in the life cycle of man, as a part of the social dynamics of *all* societies, or as an inevitable natural component of man's life experience. The adolescent or teen-ager as we know him today is a modern *invention*, a product of urban-industrial life, which includes a number of adolescence-generating features. As Albert K. Cohen reminiscingly observed, " a few years ago it occurred to me that when I was a teen-ager, in the early depression days, there were no teen-agers! The teen-ager has sneaked up on us in our own lifetime, and yet it seems to us that he has always been with us."[1]

The assumption that adolescence is a timeless and universal part of social life is a fallacy that, in a sense, is quite understandable in the light of current manifestations of teen-age activities that appear to be a natural component of the social order. Adolescence has affected the vast majority of contemporary teen-agers to such an extent that the terms teen-ager and adolescent are almost interchangeable. Adolescence as a social malaise shows itself in ubiquitous symptoms observable in individual problems as well as collective disturbances. It would indeed be an atypical newspaper anywhere in the United States that failed to report daily occurrences reflecting the adolescent phenomenon in some form— sometimes in the form of individual or collective delinquency, sometimes in the form of tolerated and even admired and imitated subcultural activities, and sometimes in the form of serious problems of identity.

The adolescent problem is obviously not limited to the United States, but has become an everyday problem in many other societies which have a number of social, technological, and cultural characteristics in common

---

[1] Albert K. Cohen, "Foreword," in F. Musgrove, *Youth and the Social Order* (Bloomington, Ind., Indiana University Press, 1965), p. ix.

with American society. Rather than pursuing the dubious assumption that the teen-age subculture in the United States represents the decisive and causative factor for the emergence of adolescence in other countries, it appears more realistic to explain the currently almost worldwide evolvement of adolescence by a number of innate conditions of urban-industrial life.

These adolescence-inducing conditions of the urban-industrial setting can be roughly divided into two categories, the social-structural factors and the cultural factors. The most decisive structural condition necessary for the development of adolescence lies in the nature of the division of labor existing in the particular society. This division is of course greatly influenced by the type of technology and economic system prevailing at the time. Within this division of labor, the prime condition for adolescence consists of *the discontinuity of socialization between the status of the child and the status of the adult*. This discontinuity stretches over a period of several years, a period of time that in fact is becoming progressively longer and that is beset with a corollary of status uncertainty and problems of identity. The youth no longer occupies the relatively well-defined and clearly circumscribed "generalist" status of the child and has not yet achieved adult status. To acquire a more stable and consistent personal identity, the youth must await occupancy of a "specialist" status in the adult division of labor. It is through the incumbency of a specific and clearly defined position, facilitating clear and meaningful relationships with others and enabling the young adult to see himself in the perspective of consistent and permanent status relationships, that the adolescent's anguished question of "Who am I?" is gradually answered and replaced by a more stable and lasting self-perception.

The reliance on a specific position within the social structure for deriving a personal identity is a relatively recent innovation of modern society and has increased correlatively with the decrease of cultural control. This means, in a historical perspective, that as the persuasiveness of the cultural ethos decreased and became too nonspecific to be of sufficient salience for life-orientation, the importance of the vocational or professional position for meaning and behavioral orientation increased. In short, identity-genesis and identity-reinforcement shifted from the general cultural ethos to the vastly more specific and discrete social position. This shift constitutes an attempt on the part of modern man to reanchor his identity and can be understood as a natural reaction to unstructuredness and uncertainty. Man has an apparent need for clearly defined norms and expectations that enable him to engage in meaningful and predictable, in fact viable, behavior.

It can readily be seen that a life situation offering noncompelling cultural guidelines and highly diversified and discrete adult positions imposes unusually trying circumstances on the youth. At a time when he is confronted with basic questions of identity and is least certain of himself, he is expected to make up his mind and decide on his future career. This choice is made difficult by the largely invisible work arrangements of the parents, especially the father, which is a circumstance that impairs imitation and gradual learning of adult responsibilities. A teenager finding himself in such a situation must often rely on trial-and-error experimentation in order to find a satisfactory position. Predictably, a frequent outcome of this predicament is dissatisfaction and disappointment with a vocational choice that turns out to be not what the youth had expected. Often he can change the unsatisfactory position only by incurring hardship, since he may have made marital and family commitments in the meantime. Indifference toward and dissatisfaction with the career and a correlated impact on his self-perception may be the chronic outcome of this predicament.

There are a number of additional factors arising from the combined impact of social-structural discontinuity and cultural nonspecificity that exert an adolescence-generating influence on the teen-ager's life. Several of these important antecedent features should be briefly reviewed.

(1) A social organizational feature deserving particular attention is the modern family. The family, which normally provides the early primary group environment of the young, has undergone significant structural change over the past generations. Among the changes pertinent for the discussion of the adolescent phenomenon was the shift from the consanguine to the nuclear family—a shift that created a drastic reduction of concrete adult models and concrete "significant others" for the youth. It also brought along a reduction of familial peers such as cousins and other blood-related playmates. Lack of clan association naturally leads to association with nonfamilial peers whose background experiences and attitudes frequently differ greatly and who, over a period of time, tend to evolve into an influential collectivity that forms some type of corporate identity standing discrete from, if not in opposition to, the family system. The habit of associating with nonfamilial peers is thus one initial factor among several important factors that encourages modern youth to form and maintain independent subcultures.

The facts that the parents' job and adult responsibilities have largely been moved away from the home setting and that the training and education for a life career consequently take place outside the home lead to the phenomenon of *in loco parentis*. The teen-ager or young adult who is removed from his family for career training and education falls under the authority of a formal institution. This institution assumes *in loco parentis* authority that accords the youth neither child nor adult status and thereby accentuates the typical adolescent symptoms of status uncertainty.

A number of sociologists have hypothesized that the contemporary vagueness in cultural precepts and the modern emphasis on individual freedom have burdened marriage and the family with a heretofore unknown intensity of personality functions whereby the parties to the conjugal unit seek personal satisfaction and security in the primary group affiliation of marriage or family. However, an interesting conflict tends to ensue: gratification from the marital and familial affiliation is often curtailed by such modern counterforces as individualism and secularism, which tend to neutralize the beneficial effects of familism. The effects of individualistic and secular philosophy are also observable in the abrogation of the placement function of the family. The adolescent is now largely on his own in determining and working out his future career and social standing. There is even suspicion that the primariness of group interaction of the modern family has shifted slightly toward secondariness.

The combined effect that these changes in family structure and function have on the adolescent is the teen-ager's tendency to become involved in peer subcultures, to make family-independent career decisions, and to become engaged in nonfamilial career preparation—all circumstances and tendencies that place the youth in subcultural environments and make his transition into adulthood more difficult.

(2) Scientific and technological progress has a constant modifying impact on the social dynamics of modern society. It is an obvious truism that the greater the amount of technological innovation the greater the modifying effects on social life. This principle significantly affects the relationship between generations since rapid technological and social changes constantly alter life conditions and render the life adjustments of one generation at least partially invalid and inadequate for the next generation. One could thus derive an axiom and say that the faster the rate of sociocultural change the greater the degree of intergenerational conflict. This conflict is reflected in several ways. Probably the most basic problem can be seen in the differences between the norms and values held by the older and the younger generations. Most sociologists agree on the existence of some type of cultural inertia that is particularly noticeable among parents and other members of the older generation who have acquired their values, formed a workable normative *Gestalt*, and with age find it progressively more difficult to alter their *Weltanschauung*. They are thus subject to cultural lag, which manifests itself not only in misunderstandings but in disapproval and often in outright rejection of the younger generation's style of life. Of course, the reaction also works the other way around, and youth are quick to judge elders

and their ways as obsolete and old-fashioned. Besides suffering from a general cultural lag, parents also tend to suffer from a number of specific knowledge lags since it is virtually impossible for them to keep up with the latest information and insights provided by the fast moving science and technology of the American society. Children and adolescents, whose full-time job is to keep up with latest knowledge and insights and who are placed for this purpose under the intellectual guardianship of a number of experts, are as a result better informed in many aspects of life than their parents. Because of the fast accumulation and obsolescence of knowledge, the role of teaching technical and purely intellectual aspects in the family setting is now almost reversed. It is the teen-ager who is in a position to give information to his elders about the world of science, technology, and the arts.

The cultural lag and the various knowledge lags are not the only negative experiences of the majority of modern parents. Social scientists, educators, and political figures have repeatedly voiced their doubts concerning the pedagogic qualifications of a sizeable proportion of American parents and have even ascribed part of the responsibility for the development of the typical teen-age behavior to amateur parenthood and dysfunctional familial folkways and mores. If one adds to this negative and almost parent-deprecatory syndrome the fact that because of the current population explosion, parenthood is no longer an asset but almost a liability to society, then one may justifiably expect extraordinary reactions on the part of American parents. The reactions have taken on a variety of forms, with one major reaction couched in an apologetic *mea culpa*. Parents, in the true tradition of American democracy, have resorted to communication, information, and equality as a means for *rapprochement* between the generations. An overly idealistic approach of this type is obviously doomed to fail since it neglects to realistically assess the nature of the socialization process, which is not conducive to a true equalitarian relationship between the socializer and the socializee. Another reaction on the part of parents and of adults in general is one of reassertion of traditional authority. This reaction came with the awareness that teen-agers, in spite of their superior and up-to-date technological knowledge, are wanting in superior insights into life problems—the mature solutions of which require more than classroom learning and technical knowledge.

A significant part of the intergenerational frictions of our age is a clash of subtle psychological dispositions that has been called the "clash of inferiority complexes."[2] On one side, parents are constantly exposed to

---

[2] Clifford Kirkpatrick, *The Family as Process and Institution* (New York, The Ronald Press, 1963), pp. 266–67.

the American "youth cult" that cannot fail but create a feeling of inferiority in the face of declining strength, prowess, and youthful appearance. On the other side, youth cannot help but feel inferior in the face of many formal and informal restrictions that limit their activities and privileges. The interplay between the two "complexes" results in a cumulative and mutually reinforcing cycle that is apt to perpetuate reciprocal resentment.

(3) Although Momism is, strictly speaking, a psychological problem, it has reached an incidence rate in the American society during the mid-20th century that may qualify it as a sociological problem. The sociological implications lie in the circumstance that the incidence rate of Momism is associated with regular patterns in the social structure. First, cases of Momism occur more frequently in the American middle class than in other social strata. Second, it is more likely to appear in families where the mother is college-educated, leans toward "scientific" child-rearing, and has made motherhood a substitute career for a desired career away from home. A deep-seated feeling of relative deprivation may thus become a consistent psychological undercurrent in all of her home activities. Third, the development of Momism is greatly facilitated, if not made possible, by father-absence. The situation is usually not one of total father-absence, but rather of partial father-absence, in which father's middle-class occupation requires him to spend a significant portion of his leisure time away from home. The relevance of Momism to the adolescent problem lies in its adolescence-prolonging effect—an effect that handicaps the youth emotionally to the degree that he becomes unable to make independent decisions and to maturely carry out adult responsibilities, thus remaining an adolescent beyond the normal age range.

(4) Among the various conditions that the urban-industrial setting presents to the teen-ager, one can immediately recognize a major antecedent of adolescence: the social-structural discontinuity between the statuses of the child and the adult. This discontinuity is maintained and the transition between the statuses thereby made more difficult because of a multispecific division of labor. The nature of this division causes a certain degree of social alienation, thus breaking down communication; establishes separate realms for work and for home life, thus precluding informal and gradual introduction into adult responsibilities; causes longer and nonfamilial periods of education and training, thus delaying the assumption of adult status; stimulates social mobility, thus allowing generational discontinuity of life patterns; and finally necessitates widespread socialization by secondary institutions, thus often delaying if not impairing the ability to function as a mature adult.

The technologically and medically advanced urban-industrial environment affords better nutrition and medication for the young, thereby lowering the age of onset of puberty without concomitantly lowering the age at which adult status is accorded. As a result, the interim period between childhood and adulthood is becoming progressively longer.

Finally, modern life conditions make an appreciable share of affluence available to the teen-age segment of the population. Teen-agers not only have access to a surprisingly great amount of freely disposable cash, but they have been found to have far-reaching influence over the purchasing patterns of the adult population. In responding to the economic power of American youth, business, industry, and a good number of adult institutions have begun catering to the tastes and styles of teen-agers, trying to establish brand loyalties, to predict and manipulate collective whims, and to set up teen-age "advisory boards" as sounding boards for marketing assessment. Teen-age affluence also has a collectivizing function whereby material implementations, access to mass communication media, and participation in various fads and crazes facilitate and stimulate the growth of teen subcultures. As a result, a sizable proportion of teen-age spending is not random but is used to enhance prestige among peers and to reinforce subcultural styles.

(5) It has been emphasized that the American culture lacks a compelling ideation able to provide meaning, determination, and a "cause" for the young members of the society, and that it thereby contributes the sustaining cause to the evolvement of an unstructured and confusing interim phase between the child and the adult status. However, this emphasis should not be understood as a denial of the existence of all or any cultural values. The American culture *does* suggest a number of strong values, but not in the form of an integrated ethos that is as totalitarian, action-oriented, and "cause"-suggestive as the types of ethos that have been experienced by teen-agers in a few other countries or at different historical periods. The very nature of the American ethos stresses individuality and democracy and thereby places the burden of deciding on a "cause," on life meaning, and on goal aspirations in the hands of the individual rather than in the action programs of a nationwide *Hitler-Jugend, Komsomol,* or "Red Guard." A noncompelling and individualistic ideation of the type such as the modern American ethos taxes the imagination and creativity of youth to a far greater extent than that of the totalitarian regime that presents to its youth ready-made action programs and ready-made identities. However, the price paid for this freedom of self-exploration and individual identity determination is a longer and more confused search—in short, a prolonged adolescent period.

In addition to the noncompelling nature of the American ethos, a number of the values that are extended by the American culture are beset with negative and ambivalent elements. For example, the cultural view of pubescence, a biological process common to all adolescents, is largely evasive, semitaboo, and often negative. Another cultural dilemma can be found in the disjuncture between biological maturity and social maturity, requiring the teen-ager to resign himself to a semistatus that does not fully recognize his matured biological needs and does not make any legal provisions for expressing them premaritally. The implication here is that because of the progressively lower age at puberty, the nondescript adolescent period between pubescence and the accordance of adulthood again is caused to become progressively longer.

The American culture does not offer a definite rite of passage in the form of a public ceremony proclaiming the transition into adulthood. There are a number of legal abrogations up to the age of 21, after which the young adult normally is legally endowed with full adult privileges. But the problem is that prior to the "voting age" there is a confusing mixture of rights and obligations that consists, in largely unknown and fluctuating proportions, of adult, child, and "in-between" norms and expectations. It is thus difficult to speak of a public rite of passage at 21 years of age or at any other age since there is no consistent and pivotal ritual that would proclaim the total assumption of a new role.

Other elements of confusion in the American culture are two types of value schisms that burden the youth with the unusually intricate task of trying to determine which norms and expectations apply to him in what situation and at what time. One of the schisms can be called the "all-American" dichotomy of values. It has been asserted that the American culture is diverse and inconsistent enough to offer for each value an opposing one. This may be true to some degree, especially as it involves the polar values of competition vs. cooperation, work vs. leisure, piousness vs. freethinking, individualism vs. conformity, sexuality vs. chastity. The second type of schism includes the child-adult polarities and consists of such opposite pairs as responsibility vs. nonresponsibility, sex vs. sexlessness, and dominance vs. submission.

The American culture is also characterized by a number of "blank" sectors, anomic elements that fail to designate and specify the norms and means for achieving culturally suggested goals. Thus a lower-class teen-ager, for example, may be exposed to cultural values enhancing material success and achievement, but may fail to recognize feasible approaches or legitimate norms for attaining the goal. Teen-age reaction to his unstructured condition is a gravitating toward each other into a subcultural environment that has clearer norms, values, and demands which the adolescent finds easier to comply with.

(6) There is reason to believe that the conception of the process of personality development as suggested by such early sociologically-

oriented social psychologists as George H. Mead,[3] Charles H. Cooley,[4] and James M. Baldwin [5] is a conception more fitting the social setting of the 19th century than that of the 20th century. These early writers took as their point of departure for the explanation of the development of the personality and the "self" the small and relatively well-integrated community with a style of social interaction consisting primarily of face-to-face interaction and allowing an identification process involving primarily concrete personal models. The modern scene calls for considerable modification and expansion of this simple premise, and social scientists have recommended that a number of new circumstances be taken into consideration. First, the reference groups available to the child and teen-ager growing up in the modern setting have increased in number as well as abstractness, implying that the idea of the reference group has become sufficiently abstract to include not only membership groups and clearly visualized nonmembership groups, but also anticipatory reference groups without concrete group form as well as mental reference constructs not confined to any one clearly known grouping. Moreover, a person's reference groups are affected by the social dynamics of modern society and are subject to frequent changes, shifts, and conflicting orientations. On the level of person-to-person interaction, the concept of "significant other" has also undergone diversity and abstractness. It is no longer the simple identification process with a given adult model, traditionally the parent, that is instrumental for a modern youth to derive an idea of what he himself wants to be. Multitudes of significant others have invaded the home by way of the mass media, especially television. In lieu of formerly consistent and concrete "reference persons" the modern urban youth is bombarded with multiple models who are more suggestive of situational behavior and methods of problem-solving than of permanent and consistent value premises that can be used in assessing a range of different situations. The characters and plots reflected by the mass media are not the only forces to promote situationality of behavior and to obstruct the learning of value-derived behavior, i.e., behavior derived from internalized basic premises. Situationality of action and attitude is also promoted by the increasing vagueness and loss of distinct contours of a number of social roles. The diminishing clarity of blueprints for behavior for such general roles as, for example, the

---

[3] George H. Mead, *Mind, Self and Society* (Chicago, University of Chicago Press, 1934).

[4] Charles H. Cooley, *Human Nature and the Social Order* (New York, Scribner's, 1902).

[5] James M. Baldwin, *Mental Development in Child and Race* (New York, The Macmillan Co., 1906), and *Social and Ethical Interpretations in Mental Development* (New York, The Macmillan Co., 1897).

female and the male roles has been noted by many social scientists and has been held in part, responsible for, aggravating the adolescent process.

The style of modern personality development has been aptly portrayed by Erving Goffman in his work *The Presentation of Self in Everyday Life*,[6] in which he couches the description of social interaction in the language of the theater, pointing out that contemporary urban-industrial man has to present himself as varying *personae* on an array of different "stages"—a social-psychological condition that raises serious questions concerning the "real character" behind the "situational character." Modern urban adolescents are thus faced with a novel style of socialization, a style that is vastly more complex, impersonal, and abstract than that of teen-agers of previous generations. It is therefore no surprise that many social scientists conceptualize the number-one psychiatric problem of our time as the problem of identity.

Under the foregoing six points, an attempt was made to sum up the major antecedent conditions of adolescence and to explain why the second half of the 20th century is characterized by acute adolescent problems. These antecedent points are negative because they are selected to explain something that is largely considered negative itself, namely adolescence. Thus, it is not a subjective bias of some sort but rather an attempt to selectively scan the causative features, the dysfunctional conditions, that produce adolescence.

Continuation of the sociological analysis of adolescence leads logically to the next point: the *consequences* of adolescence. The major sociological consequence of adolescent discontinuity expresses itself in collective forms and presents us with a relatively novel social problem in the history of mankind. From whatever knowledge we have, it seems safe to conclude that there has never before been as massive a recession of the young from the adult society into their own subsociety, which is not only different but even opposed to adult standards. Manifestations of their subcultural life are manifold and can be observed in distinct and recurrent fads, styles, crazes, hero worship, attitudes, values, argot, and various material implementations. Many of these subcultural expressions have been insufficiently researched, and the only sources of information are often popular media through which teen-agers express themselves directly, such as songs, dances, fashion, teen magazines, etc.

The American society has a vastly heterogeneous population, and the various racial, ethnic, socioeconomic, and religious, segments confront their youth with different life conditions. Accordingly, the adolescent experience is varied and rarely manifests itself in identical ways in the

---

[6] Erving Goffman, *The Presentation of Self in Everyday Life* (Garden City, N.Y., Doubleday & Co., 1959).

different segments. It is impossible to present in one book a complete catalog that would do justice to the diversity of the adolescent experience. Instead of attempting to exhaust the diversity, only a few illustrations are mentioned. For example, the Negro adolescent's life is highly influenced by his racial background, which burdens him with a legacy of discrimination, prejudice, and the internalized forms of these factors. This means that he has derived a deprecatory self-perception and has internalized it as part of his identity. It may be this factor of low self-esteem that has prevented the Negro from developing collective solidarity until only very recently. Lower-class family life, ghetto living, and marked disadvantages in education, employment, income, and health are other factors which complicate the Negro youth's transition from childhood to adulthood. On the other side, Jewish youth are considerably more integrated into the larger society and, in fact, have access to educational and economic opportunities that the majority of Negroes dare not even dream of. The major predicament of American Indian youth is the experience of culture shock and his marginality between two incompatible cultures. Lower-class youth are highly influenced by a lower-class ethos that automatically sets them in opposition to and often in actual conflict with the standards of the middle class and the law. However, a strong peer loyalty and a simplified social-structural involvement form a bridge structure that has some ameliorating effect during the adolescent transition.

Finally, a sociological analysis of adolescence must at least mention some of the prevalent and recurrent problems that are associated with, if not causally related to, adolescence. Juvenile delinquency, a much-discussed topic, is still poorly defined and diversely explained and has stimulated opposing thoughts on prevention and rehabilitation. At the present time, in the face of a rising incidence rate of delinquency, known techniques of prevention and rehabilitation have proven to have a mere 50–50 chance of helping the youthful offender stay out of trouble.[7] Premarital sexual activities, premarital pregnancies, venereal diseases, marriage, and divorce among teen-agers appear to have increased over the past generation and constitute formidable social problems for which, again, preventive and rehabilitative measures are either lacking or ineffective. The dropout problem is no longer a pedagogic problem but has become an economic liability, since modern labor market conditions cannot absorb unskilled laborers at the rate in which they continue to enter the labor market. Drinking and the use of drugs among teen-agers has

---

[7] Walter Bailey, "Correctional Outcome: An Evaluation of 100 Reports," *The Journal of Criminal Law, Criminology and Police Science,* Vol. 57 (June, 1966), pp. 153–60.

become the focus of great concern and interest of legislators, law enforcement agencies, educators, and many social scientists. This concern was
particularly aroused by the mid-1960's upsurge in teen-age use of psychedelic drugs, especially the powerful LSD, which was used not only
by numbers of college students but also by high school pupils.

These points, then, briefly sum up the sociological analysis of the
adolescent phenomenon, making use of a simple structural-functional
framework that allows the presentation of a range of antecedents, the
major consequences, the diversity of the adolescent experience, and a
number of illustrations concerning related problem areas.

Research Needs

Sociological research in the area of adolescence and teen-age behavior
reflects markedly uneven tendencies, with evidence of great interest and
thorough coverage in some sectors and of no or little interest and coverage in other sectors. Although there may be perfectly good reasons for
this unevenness, such as selectivity based on interest, available funds,
feasibility of research, etc., it is nevertheless regrettable that a subject
as important as the youth of the nation is not examined in a more systematic manner. The issue of teen-age marriages, for example, has received extensive attention, and sociologists have published prolifically
on this topic describing when, where, whom, and why teen-agers marry.
(See for example the May, 1965, issue of the *Journal for Marriage and
the Family,* where no fewer than six different research reports deal with
the problem of teen-age marriage.) On the other side, questions
inquiring into the methods of advertisements and attempts at opinion
formation particularly aimed at children and teen-agers and how such
attempts influence and pattern the youngsters' perception and purchasing
habits have been greatly neglected as a research area for sociologists.
(Economists and experts in business administration appear to be similarly guilty of this neglect. Surveys of professional journals in these fields
proved relatively futile in yielding pertinent research findings.) In view
of the increasing affluence of young Americans this question would
obviously prove to be of more than academic value.

There are a number of other research gaps, and the need to fill them
through reliable sociological investigations should be pointed out.

A conspicuous sparsity of precise knowledge exists in the area
broadly defined as collective behavior. Study in this area calls for
scrutiny of such phenomena as the development and fluctuations of teen-
age fads, crazes, and hero worship. It is interesting to note, for example,

that such a fervent, widespread, and controversial activity as teen-age dancing has not yet been systematically studied by sociologists. At the time this book was written, there was not one reliable sociological research published concerning teen-age dancing which attempted to present an attitudinal as well as behavioral distribution and attempted to answer such questions as who dances, how often, with whom, where, why, and how. Dr. Lucille H. Blum, supervisor of the Mental Health Center in New York City, made an effort toward needed study when she interviewed teen-agers found dancing in discotheques; but her sample was too small and her objective too limited to qualify as sociological research.[8] Another limited, yet more sociological, study was under way in 1967, conducted in the metropolitan area of Phoenix, Arizona, to test correlations between dance preferences and background information of teen-agers who frequent public dance halls.[9]

Another area that calls for systematic research concerns the relationship between the various mass media and teen-agers. For example, what is the social corollary of teen-agers who expose themselves to certain selected types of fare of the mass media? How does it affect them? And how do teen-age styles and tastes affect the producers of mass media fare? It must be said that although some of these questions have been researched,[10] more up-to-date investigation is needed, especially concern-•ng the influence of teen-age tastes on the media's productions. One mass medium that for some reason has been largely omitted by sociological research is the teen magazine. Not until systematic content analyses have been applied and tested is there any way of knowing whether sociologists have missed a source of insight into teen-age behavior.

One area of teen-age behavior that is in definite need of systematic research and thorough updating of information concerns sexual activities. The only study from which comprehensive information about the sexual practices of teen-agers could be derived was the Kinsey reports of the 1940's, which are obviously considerably dated.[11] The professional as

---

[8] Lucille H. Blum, *The Discotheque and the Phenomenon of Alone-Togetherness: A Study of the Young Person's Response to the Frug and Comparable Current Dances* (New York, mimeographed unpublished research report, 1967).

[9] Gilbert Rudolph and Hans Sebald, *Teen-Agers at Public Dance-Halls* (Arizona State University, Department of Sociology, unpublished research paper, 1967).

[10] See for example Wilbur Schramm, *Process and Effects of Mass Communication* (Urbana, Ill., University of Illinois Press, 1954); and B. Berelson, "Communications and Public Opinion," in Wilbur Schramm (ed.), *Communications in Modern Society* (Urbana, Ill., University of Illinois Press, 1948), pp. 168–85.

[11] Alfred C. Kinsey *et al.*, *Sexual Behavior in the Human Male* (Philadelphia, W. B. Saunders Co., 1948); and *Sexual Behavior in the Human Female* (Philadelphia, W. B. Saunders Co., 1953).

well as the popular literature is replete with "guesses" and hypotheses, and many reluctant estimates are "suggested" with the assurance that "nobody knows for sure. . . ."

The question of subcultural formation has received some attention by sociologists. However, little systematic information is presented as to how the more generic assumption that humans who face confusion and uncertainty tend to gravitate toward age-mates experiencing similar predicaments applies to the teen-age scene. Exactly what takes place at the dawn of subcultural formation when teen-agers engage in so-called "exploratory gestures?" Also, exactly what are the mechanisms operative in the process whereby younger teen-agers learn subcultural norms and values from their older peers? In other words, what exactly are the channels and processes of subcultural transmission?

Among the unanswered questions concerning teen-age affluence are questions not so much of *what* they buy—there are exhaustive itemized lists on teen consumptions—but of *why* and *how* they acquire certain items. Answers to the "why" might provide a link to the understanding of subcultural reinforcement and the nature of peer standards. Answers to the "how" would fill in information on how much and by what means teen-agers acquire financial power.

The issue of intergenerational conflict is presented more on the basis of hypothesis, inference, and nonsystematic content analysis than on the basis of reliable studies. There is enough *general* evidence to safely allow the assumption that intergenerational conflict does in fact exist, but *specific* correlations, social variables, and accentuating circumstances are relatively unknown.

How does a "generalist" teen-ager decide on a "specialist" future career? Sociologists of occupational careers are in the process of clarifying this question, and more precise answers should be forthcoming soon. However, the corollary questions surrounding this general question are multitudinous, and some special aspects such as the question of how the transition to the "specialist" status is affected by *in loco parentis* authority of the educational and training institutions should be investigated in detail.

An interesting problem that has consistently been analyzed in a biased and one-sided manner concerns the relationship between social-class background and academic success, with intelligence as the intervening variable. Sociologist Bruce K. Eckland pointed out that while research has paid ample attention to the circumstances which mask and obscure the lower-class child's intelligence, it has largely neglected the fact that upper-class upbringing often masks and obscures the child's low intelligence.[12] Inquiry might reveal that in certain social situations the adolescent's display of socially approved manners and conformity to etiquette and "good" style tends to be defined as intelligent behavior.

A question that has seldom been asked concerns the type of social institutions that administer the *coup de grace* to the adolescent period and the manner in which they effect the transition to the adult status. Emergence from adolescence entails a completely different style of living and a radical shift of values, and questions should be asked about *which* institutions are particularly helpful during this final orientation. In this connection, the adult-initiating and adult-reinforcing roles of such institutions as the military, the labor force, marriage, civic clubs, political parties, and community organizations should be examined. It could be easily hypothesized that the degree of involvement in these institutions is directly correlated with changes in self-perception. But such correlations should be checked against a number of intervening variables such as time of entry into institution, personal motivation, type of program offered to novice, institutional responsibilities assumed by novice, etc. Research findings that would elucidate the effects of institutional efforts to change the identity of the novice would obviously be of functionality to such organizations and institutions. This knowledge could be used for desirable restructuring of programs and activities to increase their effectiveness in helping the older adolescent make the final transition into adulthood and bolster up his incipient identity as an adult.

The problem of identity is intricately connected to virtually all of the above issues and forms a complex system of intermeshed dimensions. At least two somewhat more specifically directed questions should be posed. One question deals with those youths who experience generational mobility by entering a career, or the preparatory phase for such a career, that brings along discontinuities of life patterns and life adjustments familiar to them through their upbringing in the family of orientation. Since personal identity is closely dependent on social regularities and the accomplishment of consistent social adjustments, the research question posed aims at finding out under which social conditions is the transient adolescent's experience of alienation, *anomie*, and maladjustment minimized or maximized. This is an extremely timely research objective, considering that the majority of teen-agers, especially boys, take up jobs or careers that are dissimilar to those of their parents. The other question involving the problem of identity aims at discovering information that would elucidate the role of the family of orientation as a value-

---

[12] Bruce K. Eckland, "Genetics and Sociology: A Reconstruction," *American Sociological Review*, Vol. 32, (April, 1967), pp. 173–94.

instilling agency in the face of the weak and nondescript cultural premises on which the modern youth finds it increasingly difficult to rely for a holistic *Weltanschauung*. Under what familial, peer, school, or religious circumstances does family influence balance cultural *anomie*? Under what family conditions does either peer or parental identification prevail? Which familial conditions prepare the minds of the young for the ready indoctrination of mass media characters, and under what circumstances do the young develop immunity to imitation and internalization of mass media models? Such questions and many other related ones concerning the process of identity development are in most timely need of answers—a challenge which sociologists and social psychologists have only partly met.

Finally, there are numerous unanswered questions concerning the diversity of experience and of expression of adolescence. While some minority groups, such as American Negroes and the American lower class, are relatively well researched, other groupings, such as the Mexican-American of the United States Southwest, have been grossly neglected by systematic sociological research. Also, more sociological and especially more social-psychological research should be completed concerning the situation of the American Indian youth undergoing cultural shock on, around, and away from his reservation.

These research suggestions do not pretend to be exhaustive and to cover all areas of needed research. Rather, they are rough pointers to give the reader a general idea of the state of sociological research in the broad area of teen-age behavior, to alert beginning sociology students to research possibilities, and to stimulate further thinking about and more precise formulations of research propositions.

Outlook

The adolescent, like numerous other characteristics of the modern era, will in all probability remain a permanent component of the social dynamics of urban-industrial society. It is safe to predict that adolescence will for many coming generations remain the poorly structured and ill-defined interim phase that it is today. It is possible, however, that in the far future some type of institutionalization of the teen-age status will gradually be extended by the adult society and thereby provide a clearer, less ambiguous, and more consensual social position for youth. In the meantime, society at large will continue to be puzzled and sociologists fascinated by the daily expression of adolescent confusion and uncertainty. Since there is absolutely no reason to assume that urbanism and industrialism will decline in the future, and since the major casual factors of adolescence are embedded in urban-industrial conditions, there is no prospect that the teen-age scene will undergo appreciable change during the 20th century.

As long as society maintains an overall structural arrangement that produces a relatively unstructured interim between the child and the adult status, a fissure will run through the society separating the adolescents from their seniors. The ensuing recession of the young into their own peer groups has resulted in an adolescent subculture that has grown powerful not only within its youthful following but also within numerous sectors of the adult world. One interesting feature that will undoubtedly persist in the future is the tendency of a considerable proportion of the adult population not only to acquiesce in the face of growing teen-age influence but even to make gestures of joining and imitating adolescents. Teen-agers are linked to the adult world by various institutions such as family, church, education, etc. But in the past few years teen-agers have come to exert an ever-increasing degree of influence over the operation of these institutions, and specific teen subinstitutions have evolved within or alongside the parental institutions. This trend has been exemplified by the tendency to inaugurate specific forms of "youth worship" reflecting teen-age lingo and behavior, by the tendency to encourage youth governments in schools, by the tendency to allow children a voice on the family "council." The trend of giving youth a voice in the operation of previously adult institutions will continue, gain strength, and spread to still other adult realms.

Teen-age fads and styles will continue to perpetuate the new endeavor on the part of business and industry to establish brand loyalties and to predict the collective moods of the teen-agers. There will be an ever-increasing youth-orientation in nearly all aspects of business and the economic order, but particularly in advertisement, the movie industry, clothing industry, car manufacture, TV productions, and the marketing techniques of cosmetics. Predictably, an abundant economy is bound to stimulate artificial want. There are already signs indicating that adolescents have started to compensate for psychological insecurity by material possessions and implementations. Material implementations create status. They enhance personal significance and build social power within one's peer group. With continuing adolescent unstructuredness, one can expect an ever-increasing inclination on the part of teen-agers to compensate by possession. There is reason to believe that such compensation will become increasingly possible since the teen-agers' share of the affluence is increasing and not decreasing. Estimates of the National Education Association set the annual teen-age spending on "goods and services designed to satisfy their special needs and whims" (not including basic necessities for life) at $21 billion by 1970.[13] This is nearly twice the amount spent by teen-agers in 1963. To lend these figures perspective—on the basis of National Education Association figures, $21 billion would buy approximately 4000 jet airliners or surmount the total book budgets of all the libraries in the United States and Canada for roughly the next 200 years. (This projection is obviously limited to the assumption that no national or international disturbance of any magnitude will deflect either the course of the general economic development of the United States or the course of more specific teen-age events as they currently evolve.)

The numerical power of the teen-age population will continue, and the United States population will retain a large proportion of teen-agers. A look at the projected population statistics assures us that there will not be any noteworthy change in the proportion of the youthful segment of the United States population and that teen-agers will remain the large segment they presently represent. Figures of the Bureau of the Census predict that betwen 1965 and 1985 the population proportion of the 5–13-year-olds will remain relatively stable and change from 18.4% to 18.3%, that of the 14–17-year-olds will change from 7.2% to 6.9%, and that of the 18–24-year-olds from 10.3% to 11.1%.[14]

As mentioned earlier, the diversity of adult reactions to the recession of youth and to the teen-agers' actual or imagined imposition of their tastes and values on adult institutions included strong opposition and the parental attempt to reestablish the traditional respect and authority of the elders. Intergenerational conflict will thus persist and, if anything, change to more intense forms. The clash of inferiority complexes will not abate—especially not while the typical American "youth cult" continues to create subtle feelings of inadequacy and inferiority among the parental generation.

There are current massive efforts on the part of the federal government and a number of other agencies to improve the living conditions of various deprived minority groups and to bring their living standards to a par with the average American middle class. Such programs as Head Start, the Job Corps, the Neighborhood Youth Corps, and other projects

---

[13] National Education Association, Department of Home Economics, Youth and Money (Washington, D. C., 1964), pp. 4–5.

[14] U.S. Department of Commerce, Bureau of the Census, *Current Population Reports*, P-25, No. 286 (July, 1964), pp. 46–50.

sponsored by such agencies as the Office of Economic Opportunity are bound to eventually have some leveling effect on the youths from various population segments—the effect being mainly one of upgrading the socioeconomic conditions of underprivileged youth. As a result of these nationwide efforts, one may expect that the diversity of the adolescent experience among the different subsegments of the U.S. population will gradually diminish, lose some distinct expressions, and slowly gravitate toward what is today the middle-class style of adolescence. The qualification "slowly" cannot be overemphasized and applies especially to the Negro adolescent. In fact, as has been mentioned earlier, expert opinion predicts a widening gap between Negro and white socioeconomic achievements and improvements. (See discussion and references in Chapter 10.) Nevertheless, gauging the development beyond the immediate and near future, it can be assumed that the political credo and the philosophical dicta on which the United States was founded will gradually exert a leveling effect on the diversity of the life experiences (especially as they depend on socioeconomic conditions) of every new generation.

In the area of special problems, one of the most exasperating teen-age problems will remain the spreading experimentation with psychedelic drugs, especially LSD. In fact, the use of these drugs spread with such rapidity and to such an extent that the Federal Food and Drug Administration decided to advise against strict legislation concerning the use of LSD, since such action would jeopardize the very foundations of the collegiate establishment by facing it with the task of arresting a sizable proportion of college students.[15] Experimentation with psychedelic drugs will continue to spread to younger age brackets, and the habit will involve more and more high school pupils. The exact magnitude to which the drug problem will swell and the nature of the solution which will be offered for its control are impossible to predict at this time.

Another problem that will undoubtedly grow in prominence is the sexual expression of teen-agers. However, any forecast in this area is necessarily a speculation. One is tempted, nevertheless, to conclude that biologically mature adolescents—mature for an ever-longer period of time before being accorded adulthood—who learn increasingly more about contraceptive devices and who know how to avail themselves of such conveniences will be inclined to engage in a greater amount of heterosexual experimentation and gratification than was true of previous generations who were less informed, had less access to convenient bio-

---

[15] Warren R. Young and Joseph R. Nixon, *LSD On Campus* (New York, Dell Publishing Co., 1966), pp. 150–51.

chemical contraceptives, and as a result were possibly more inhibited in respect to premarital coitus.

Juvenile delinquency will continue to increase, probably not only in absolute numbers but also in terms of rates. It is extremely difficult to say whether this increase will be entirely due to "real" increases, i.e., due to an actual increase over delinquent acts committed per teen-age capita during previous generations, or if it will be partially due only to increased legislation making offenses more likely. One aspect of juvenile delinquency that will probably undergo marked change deals with the way juvenile courts and judges have been proceeding with youth offenders. Based on the Supreme Court's 1967 rule in the review of the famous *Gault vs. Arizona* case, more formal court proceeding and fewer informal decisions based on the judge's discretion will have to be adopted throughout the nation.

The adolescent in the school environment will continue to represent a challenge to the educational institution. The lure of affluence via a job, the general aversion to deference of gratification, and the desire for early marriage are formidable forces against which the best qualified educators are sometimes helpless. Recently a tendency has developed that most probably will become more accentuated in the near future—the tendency to make high school curricula more "functional," pragmatic, and suited to the practical preferences of teen-agers. Such "practical" preferences and needs will continue to be implemented by more emphasis on technical skill preparation, such as auto mechanics, electronics, welding, cabinetmaking, work with electrical appliances, etc. Such changes toward greater "functionality" are usually expected to prove effective in combating the drop-out rate. While it is probably true that the drop-out rate will decline further, it may not be due so much to the increased attractiveness of the school, but rather to the increasing unattractiveness of the labor market with a progressively lower absorption rate of unskilled labor.

One of the most discussed topics in sociology is the family institution and the question of its future fate. It may be recalled that a main controversy in family sociology pivots around the question of whether the number of functions performed by the family will decline further, or whether marriage and the family have reached a plateau, have become stable again, and perform a more specialized function of personality security and identity formation. This author's forecast on so formidable and emotion-laden an issue falls in line with the latter assumption and endorses the view that the family has arrived at a specialized functionality that will be subject to little if any change over the near future. Adolescents, their relationships to their families, and whatever familial problems they have today will remain more or less the same for generations to come.

Adolescence: An Option Toward Identity Growth

Many of the aspects that were discussed in the outlook on the future state of affairs of adolescents may appear negative and pessimistic. However, let it be said that the time of adolescence encompasses more than the problem of adolescent discontinuity. It also includes elements of meaningful preparation for adulthood, the joys and delights found in peer friendships, play, and adventure, and the stimulating exploration of a "new world." For most teen-agers, it is a time of relative freedom from the stringent demands of adult life and form the responsibility of providing for one's own livelihood, a time of romantic anticipations, of bubbling curiosity, of fascination in discovering new dimensons, of sexual exploration and exuberance.

It can be seen, then, that the adolescent period has many perspectives. It is true that status discontinuity represents a basic underlying condition that is reflected in many if not most activities of the teen-ager; it is also true that this discontinuity represents a major dimension in the lives of modern teen-agers, but it is not the only dimension that is characteristic of this period.

To those who worry excessively about modern adolescence, nostalgically reciting past and presumably adolescence-free days and wishing they could replace adolescents with a "cause"-oriented national youth, let them be reminded of the perennial folly of the sorcerer's apprentice who conjured up a phenomenon that he could not call back. Psychiatrist Irene M. Josselyn, who has spent nearly a lifetime of dedication in helping young people, has set the question of American adolescence in what this author believes is a most valid and insightful perspective:

> It is easy to cite cultures in which certain adolescent problems are not found. Without doubt, for example, a dictatorship that does not permit any selectiveness in identity minimizes the struggle of the adolescent; a primitive society that predefines adult roles also removes the responsibility from the adolescent to find his own unique self. A democracy in which each person has a right to his own identity as long as that identity does not jeopardize that of others undoubtedly places the greatest burden upon the adolescent and the greatest burden upon those who live with him. Our national history, however, is the story of the growth of a nation which realized its individual self-identity in late adolescence and created leaders in adult life who chose the methods of evolution rather than those of revolution. Many of the troubled adolescents of yesterday have become the progressive thinkers of today because they were

allowed time to be adolescents and were permitted to become adults with an individual self-identity.[16]

This insight puts into clear perspective what probably is the most significant dimension of adolescence and lends a fitting note on which to end the sociological analysis of the adolescent experience. Imposed alternatives for the process of adolescence would mean a regression to some form of mental servitude that is secure—but secure to soon.

---

[16] Irene M. Josselyn, M.D., "The Older Adolescent," in Eli Ginzberg, (ed.), *Values and Ideals of American Youth* (New York, Columbia University Press, 1964), pp. 34–35.

AUTHOR INDEX

SUBJECT INDEX

Achievement orientation, 326-327, 334-336, 443-450

Adolescence
  adult reaction to, 17-20, 61-69, 112-116, 517, 518
  and culture, 8, 20, 130-161
  and family life, 29-51
  and rural-urban migration, 18-20
  and social structure, 8, 20, 95-98
  as identity growth, 521-522
  causes of, 8, 15, 16ff., 29, 34, 502-510
  definition, 9-14
  diverse experiences of, 29, 263-264, 265ff.
  historical evolvement, 14-20
  social differentiation, 263-264, 320ff.

Adults as models, 33, 69

Affluence, teen-age
  consumption patterns, 111-116
  England, 5
  future of, 517-518
  influencing collective identity, 110-111, 118, 507
  state of research, 514
  types of income, 116-117

Alienation, social, 97-98

Allowance, 116

Amish youth, 100-101

Anomie, 98, 127, 156-160, 161, 268, 368-369, 515-516

Apache, 131, 309, 310

Apprenticeship, 37, 96

Armed forces, 91-92

Attitudes, teen-age
  toward adults, 241-244
  toward religion, 241, 242

Australian aborigines, 139

Australian adolescents, 7

Authoritarianism, 155-156, 328-330

Automobile
  and dropout, 445
  arrests and accidents, 256-257
  functions, 118, 257-260
  legal aspects, 255-256
  teenage ownership, 113, 255-256
  teen-age style-setting, 115

Bali, 154

Bar Mitzvah, 139-140

Blousons, noirs, 7

Bodgies, 7

Boys' clubs, 377-378

Cambridge-Somerville Study, 383-384, 388

Canadian (Montreal) adolescents, 200-201

Candy Stripers, 246-247

Cheyenne, 151-152

Child
  bilingual, 311, 315-316
  care, 105-110
  counseling, 383-384
  emotionally disturbed, 165-166
  guidance clinic, 384-385
  isolate, 164
  welfare, 106, 165

Child-rearing
  father-role minimized, 92
  neurotic results, 73, 78, 84-92

2-18	2, 3, 4
2-25	,,
3-4	no class
3-11	5, 6
3-18	Test
4-1	7
4-8	,,
4-15	8, 9
4-22	10, 11, 13, 16
4-29	,,
5-6	15
5-13	
5-20	Final